رياض الصالحين

RIYADH-US-SALEHEEN

ARABIC-ENGLISH

Vol. I

Compiled By

IMAM ABU ZAKARIYA YAHYA BIN SHARAF AN-NAWAWI

Translated By

S. M. MADNI ABBASI

KITAB BHAVAN
New Delhi-110002

KITAB BHAVAN
Publishers, Distributors, Exporters & Importers
1784, Kalan Mahal, Darya Ganj,
New Delhi - 1100 02 (India)

Phones : (91-11) 23277392/93, 23274686, 32906494
Fax : (91-11) 23263383

Website : www.kitabbavan.net
: www.kitabbavan.com

Email : nasri@vsnl.com
: nusrat@bol.net.in

1st Published in India : 1984
11th Edition : 2014

ISBN : 81-7151-242-9 (Set)
ISBN : 81-7151-243-7 (Vol. I)

Book Code No. : (set) 0003

Printed & Published in India by :
Nusrat Ali Nasri for KITAB BHAVAN
1784, Kalan Mahal, Darya Ganj,
New Delhi - 1100 02 [India]

RIADH-US-SALEHEEN VOL. I

CONTENTS

Preface		ix
A Short Biographical Account of Hazrat Imam Nawawi		xvi
Chapter 1	Sincerity, Selflessness and Intention behind All Actions and Matters -- Open or Secret	1
Chapter 2	Penitence	10
Chapter 3	Resignation	28
Chapter 4	On Truthfulness	46
Chapter 5	On Divine Contemplation or Meditation	50
Chapter 6	On Piety	57
Chapter 7	On Belief and Trust in Allah	59
Chapter 8	On Perserverance in Religion	67
Chapter 9	On Contemplation over the Creation of the Universe and the Things therein	69
Chapter 10	To surpass in Virtuous Deeds and Incentive for the Same	70
Chapter 11	On Self Denial	73
Chapter 12	On Doing virtuous Deeds Increasingly towards the Closing years of One's Life and Urging Others for the Same	82
Chapter 13	On Different Ways Doing Good	85
Chapter 14	Following a Middle Course in Prayer	95
Chapter 15	To Be Steady and Regular in Virtuous Deeds	105
Chapter 16	Injunctions for Regular Observation of the Holy Prophet's (S.A.W.) Practice and Its Conditions	106
Chapter 17	Significance of Obedience of the Commands of Allah and the One Who Invited to it, or Ordained for Good and Forbade from Evil	114
Chapter 18	Innovation in Religion and Heresy Prohibited	116
Chapter 19	Inventing New Ways of Virtue and Vice	118
Chapter 20	Recommending for Good, Inducement for Doing Good and Tempting Towards Vice	120
Chapter 21	Cooperation in Good and Virtuous Deeds	123
Chapter 22	Tendering Good Advice	125

Chapter 23	Enjoining Virtue and Forbidding Evil	126
Chapter 24	Divine Wrath on a Person Who Verbally Enjoins Virtue and Prohibits vice but Acts Contrarily	134
Chapter 25	Return of Deposits to Owners	135
Chapter 26	Prohibition of Cruelty and Injustice and Their Eradication	142
Chapter 27	Respecting the Dignity of Muslims, Their Rights and Compassion for Them	152
Chapter 28	Covering Shortcomings of Muslims	159
Chapter 29	Helping the Needy Muslims	160
Chapter 30	Recommendation	162
Chapter 31	Reforming and Reconciling People	163
Chapter 32	Superiority of the Poor and Weak among Muslims	166
Chapter 33	Kind Treatment of Orphans, Girls, the Weak, the Poor and Lowly and Mercy and Affection upon Them, Generosity and Soft-Treatment	172
Chapter 34	Kind Treatment of Women	177
Chapter 35	A Husband's Rights on His Wife	181
Chapter 36	Spending for the Members of the Family	184
Chapter 37	Spending the Most Cherished and the Best Thing for the Sake of Allah	187
Chapter 38	Obligation of a Person to Enjoin the Obedience of Allah on His Family Members, Grown up, the Children and All the Subordinates and to Forbid the Disobedience and to Chastise and Check from Its contraventions	189
Chapter 39	Rights of the Neighbour and Good Treatment of Him	191
Chapter 40	Benevolence Towards Parents and Good Treatment of the Relatives	194
Chapter 41	Prohibition of Disobedience of Parents and Repudiation of Ties of Blood Relation	205
Chapter 42	Virtue of Doing Good to Friends of Parents and Relations and Wives and Others Who are Entitled to Respect	208
Chapter 43	Honouring the Members of the Family of the Holy Prophet (S.A.W.) and Their Virtues	211
Chapter 44	Honouring the Ulama, the Pious and the Learned Persons, to Prefer Them on Others and to Express Their Dignity	214
Chapter 45	Visiting Holy and Virtuous Persons and Keeping Company with Them; Soliciting Their Favour and Visiting Sacred Places	219

Chapter 46	Virtues, Importance and Etiquette of Sincere Love for the Sake of Allah	227
Chapter 47	Signs of Allah's Love for His Servants and the Efforts for its Adoption and Struggle for its Achievements	231
Chapter 48	Caution Against Persecution of the Virtuous, Aged and Poor and Needy Persons	233
Chapter 49	Assessing People as Regards their Apparent Conduct and Entrusting Their Hidden Secrets to Allah	234
Chapter 50	Fear (of Allah)	239
Chapter 51	Cherishing Hope and Expecting Good from Allah	247
Chapter 52	Virtues of Maintaining Good Opinion and High Hope from Allah	264
Chapter 53	Combining Hope and Fear	266
Chapter 54	The Excellence of Being Moved due to Fear of Allah and Love of Him	268
Chapter 55	The Excellence of Indifference to the World and the Contentment on the Small Portion and Virtues of Poverty	272
Chapter 56	The Excellence of Hunger and Leading of Life of Abstinence, Subsisting on Meagre Food and Clothing and Abstaining from Luxuries of Life and Sex	286
Chapter 57	Contentment, Chastity and Moderation in Earning and Spending and Ugliness of Asking Without Need	307
Chapter 58	Acceptance of a Thing which is Bestowed without Asking for it	314
Chapter 59.	Earning by own Efforts and Refraining from Asking and Taking Lead in Giving	314
Chapter 60	Generosity and Spending in a Good Cause with Trust in Allah	316
Chapter 61	On Prohibition of Miserliness and Naggardliness	323
Chapter 62	On Self Sacrifice and Service	324
Chapter 63	Striving for the Matters Relating to Hereafter and Longing for Blessed and Virtuous Things	327
Chapter 64	The Excellance of the Thankful Rich Person and Acquisition of Legitimate Wealth and to Spend It Appropriately	328
Chapter 65	Remembering the Death and Lesser of Aspirations	331
Chapter 66	Preference to Visit Graves for Males and What the Visitor Should Say	335

Chapter 67	Abhorrance of Praying for Death on Account of Some Impending Calamity, and Justification for Longing for Death for Apprehending Some Mischief in Religion	337
Chapter 68	On Piety and Discarding the Doubtful	338
Chapter 69	Preference for Seclusion During the Corrupt Period, Fearing Trial for His Religion or Involvement in Unlawful or Doubtful Acts	342
Chapter 70	Merits of Associating with People and Participation in Their Gathering and to Be Present in Their Good Deeds and Partaking in Their Sessions for Religious Discourse, Visiting Sick Persons, Presence in Funeral Prayers, Satisfying the Needs of the Needy, to Guide Their Ignorants, and Having Sense of Obligations and Responsibilities; to Do What Is Ordered and Abstaining from What Is Forbidden, and to Keep One's Body and Soul Clean from Impurities (Vices) and to Put up Patiently with Hardships	344
Chapter 71	Curteous Treatment and Humility towards Believers	344
Chapter 72	Arrogance and Self-Esteem Not Permitted	348
Chapter 73	On Good Manners	351
Chapter 74	Affability, Tolerance and Patience	354
Chapter 75.	To Forgive and Ignore the Vulgars	357
Chapter 76	Enduring Hurt and Annoyance	360
Chapter 77	Resentment on Violation of the Rules of Shariah and Supporting and Helping the Religion of Allah (Islam)	360
Chapter 78	On Duty of Public Officials to Deal the People with Kindness, Sincerity and Affection And Prohibition of Deceiving and Oppressing them, Not Keeping in View Their Welfare, and Being Careless Towards Them and Their Needs	363
Chapter 79	On a Just Ruler	365
Chapter 80	Necessity of Obedience to Persons in Authority in Sinless Acts and Prohibition of Obedience in Sinless Acts	367
Chapter 81	Prohibition of Asking for the Post of Authority and Leadership If Appointed to Such a Post, Should Relinquish It When Not Necessary	371
Chapter 82	Sultans, Qazis and Administrators Are Exhorted to Appoint Good Advisers, and	373

	Prohibited to Associate with Bad Companions	
Chapter 83	One Who Asks for a Judicial or Executive Post or Longs for One Should Not Be Appointed as Such	374
	BOOK OF MANNERS	375
Chapter 84	On Modesty, Its virtues and How to Develop It.	375
Chapter 85	On Keeping a Secret	376
Chapter 86	On Fulfilment of Pledge and Promise ...	380
Chapter 87	Perseverance and Safeguarding a Good Practice	381
Chapter 88	Soft Speaking and Cheerful Face While Meeting Somebody	382
Chapter 89	Preference of Clarity of Discussion, Its Elucidation to the Addressee and Its Repetition If He Does Not Follow without It.	383
Chapter 90	On Listening with Attention and Drawing the Attention of the Listeners	383
Chapter 91	On Moderation in Preaching	384
Chapter 92	On Dignity and Poise	386
Chapter 93	On Maintenance of Dignity and Poise in Prayers and in Achievement of Knowledge and Learning	387
Chapter 94	Honouring the Guest	388
Chapter 95	Virtue of Communicating and Congratulating on Good News	389
Chapter 96	Saying Farewell, Tendering Parting Advice and Good Wishes and Prayers to a Companion and Asking for Prayers from Him ..	396
Chapter 97	Seeking Divine Consultation and Guidance	399
Chapter 98	Virtues of Going to Eidgah, Visiting a Patient Pilgrimage for Hajj, Journey for Jihad, Funeral Prayers etc., Going by One Route and Return by Another for Getting Most of the Opportunities for Worship	400
	BOOK OF EATING MANNERS	401
Chapter 99	Prefering the Use of Right Hand for Performance of All Good Acts	401
Chapter 100	To Start Eating with the Name of Allah And to End with the Praising And Thanking Allah	405

Chapter 101	Not to Find Fault with Food and to Appreciate It.	408
Chapter 102	What a Fasting Person Should Do When Invited to Eat	408
Chapter 103	When an Invited Person Is Accompanied by an Uninvited Person	409
Chapter 104	On Eating What is in Front of you and to Teach a Person, Who Does Not Know the Manners of Eating	409
Chapter 105	On Prohibition of Eating Two Dates or Other Fruits in One Morsel Without the Permission of the Companions	410
Chapter 106	What to Do and What to Say When a Person Eats But is No Satisfied	410
Chapter 107	Directing to Eat from the Side of the Vessel and Prohibition of Eating from Its Middle	411
Chapter 108	Repugnance of Eating While Resting on a Pillow or Reclining	412
Chapter 109	Eating with Three Fingers and Virtues of Licking the Fingers and Abhorrance of Wiping Them before Licking. Excellence of Licking the Cup, and Picking up the Morsel That Has Fallen and Eating It. Permission to Wipe the Fingers with Knees or Sole etc., After Licking Them	412
Chapter 110	Sufficiency of Food	414
Chapter 111	Etiquette of Drinking Water and Merits of Taking Three Breaths Outside the Vessel, and Abhorrance of Breathing inside the Vessel. The Person First Drinking should Pass on the Vessel to Persons Sitting on His Right	415
Chapter 112	Prohibiton of Drinking Direct from a Water Skin.	416
Chapter 113	Prohibition of Blowing on Drinking Water	417
Chapter 114	Permission for Drinking Water While Standing but It Is Better to Drink Water While Sitting	417
Chapter 115	One Who Serves Drink, Should Be the Last Person to Drink	419
Chapter 116	Preference to Drink from Any Clean Vessel Except of Gold and Silver. Prohibition of the Use of Silver and Gold Vessels for Drinking, Eating and Toilet, and Permission for Drinking Water through Mouth Directly from Canal etc.	419

BOOK OF DRESS 422

Chapter 117	Etiquette of Dressing, Preference of Wearing White Clothes, and Permission for the Use of Red, Green, Yellow and Black Colour Clothes of Cotton, Woollen and other Varieties Except Silk	422
Chapter 118	Prefering for Wearing a Shirt or Tunic ...	425
Chapter 119	The Length of Shirt and Sleeves, Size of Loin Cloth and the Turban. Prohibition of Letting Loose Any of These Garments Exhibitng Arrogance, and Disliking for Repugnance of Letting Loose (These Garments) Unintentionally	426
Chapter 120	On Discarding Decent Clothing Out of Humility	433
Chapter 121	Virtues of Moderation in Dressing and Avoidance of Such Garments Without Necessity of Religious Justification........	433
Chapter 122	On Prohibition of Wearing Silk by Men and Sitting on It and Permission to Females to Wear Silk	433
Chapter 123	Permission to Wear Silk in Case of Scabies	435
Chapter 124	Prohibition of Sitting and Riding on Skin of Leopard	435
Chapter 125	What to Say (Supplicate) When Wearing a New Dress or New Pair of Shoes	436
Chapter 126	Virtues of Beginning with the Right Side When Putting on Dress	436
Chapter 127	Etiquettes of Sitting, Reclining, Sleeping and Dreaming	437
Chapter 128	Justification for Lying Down Flat on the Back; and When There Is No Risk of Exposure of Any Private Parts of the Body It Is Permissible to Put One Foot on the Other, and Sitting With Legs Put Across and Putting Rest Band Round Waist and Legs	439
Chapter 129	Etiquette of Sitting in Company	440
Chapter 130	Dreams and Relevant Things	445

BOOK OF SALUTATION 448

Chapter 131	Virtues of Salutation and the Direction to Give Currency to It	448
Chapter 132	On the Manner of Greeting	450
Chapter 133	On the Etiquette of Greeting	453

Chapter 134	Virtues of Repetition of Greeting When Two Persons Meet Each Other Again and Again	453
Chapter 135	Virtues of Greeting When Entering into the House	454
Chapter 136	On Greeting the Children	455
Chapter 137	On a Husband Greeting His Wife and a Woman Greeting Her Such Relations Whom She Cannot Marry; And Greeting Stranger Women, Provided There Is No Apprehension of Some Mischief	455
Chapter 138	Prohibition of Taking a Lead in Saluting Non-Muslims And How to Respond to Their Greeting; Permission of Greeting a Mixed Gathering of MUSLIMS and NON-MUSLIMS	456
Chapter 139	Justification of Greeting When Arriving and Departing from a meeting or Leaving a Friend or Companion	457
Chapter 140	Etiquette of Asking Permission to Enter	457
Chapter 141	It Is Sunnah When One Who Seeks Permission to Enter Is Asked as to Who He Is, He Should Tell His Name and Not I and So	459
Chapter 142	Justification of Replying to Saying of Al Hamdo lil-lah by one Who Sneezes and Repugnance on Replying When He Does Not Say so and What to Do When Sneezing and Yawning	460
Chapter 143	Preference for Hand-Shake and Pleasant Appearance of Face When Meeting with Some Ones and Kissing the Hand of a Pious man, and Kissing One's Son to Express Love, and of Embracing a Man Returning from Journey and Disliking of Bowing Head Before Him	462

PREFACE

The majesty and importance of the sayings or traditions of the Prophet of Islam, Muhammad (S.A.W.), leaving aside their general moral value, can be fully appreciated only when one becomes aware that the whole religious, moral, social and political framework of nearly one-third of the humanity rests on the divine book, the Holy Quran, and Sayings and Acts or *Sunnah*,of the Holy Prophet (S.A.W.).

The way of living of the Holy Prophet (S.A.W.) and his sayings are a commentary on the Holy Quran and they supplement it. The importance of the Holy Prophet's (S.A.W.) sayings and actions and their difference from those of other religious leaders, is that when the quotations of these leaders may become the object of veneration or admiration, only in the absence of any sanction to enforce them, the sayings (traditions) and the way of living *(Sunnah)*of the Prophet of Islam (S.A.W.) have already acquired the force of law. A believer may question the authenticity of a particular saying or Sunnah, but when once its genuineness is established, it is as binding upon him as any verse of the Holy Quran.

The Holy Quran together with the traditions and the Sunnah of the Holy Prophet (S.A.W.) are the source of the Sharia or the Islamic Jurisprudence. The Holy Quran is the divine word of Allah revealed to the Holy Prophet (S.A.W.). It is for the Muslims of every school the unquestionable main source and final authority for all laws — religious, civil or criminal.

Our Holy Prophet Muhammad (S.A.W.), is the last Messenger of Allah, and his message is the last divine message from the Almighty Allah to his servants. There will be no more prophets after the Holy Prophet of Islam (S.A.W.). As such Allah not only revealed His last Communication to him, He also made him a perfect specimen of a human being, and commissioned him as His last messenger, warner and guide for the humanity. The Holy Prophet (S.A.W.) combined all that was the best in morals and manners, and he was the very embodiment of all that was preached and enjoined in the Holy Quran, which says:

> "Certainly there is for you in the Messenger of Allah an excellent examplar." (33:21)

The Holy Prophet of Islam (S.A.W.)was a perfect model to be copied and followed; in other words,he was the Quran personified. Every aspect, every one of his actions, his behaviour in home-life and outside, is recorded and preserved in its minutest details, to serve as a guide and example for the mankind.

The great Indian leader Mr. M.K. Gandhi in his foreword to Sir Abdullah Al-Mamun Al-Suhrawardy's *"The Sayings of Muhammad"*, says: "They (the sayings) are among the treasures of mankind, not merely Muslims." Count Leo Tolstoy, the famous Russian writer and thinker, had come to appraise and appreciate the august personality of the Holy Prophet (S.A.W.) through this book containing the sayings of the Holy Prophet (S.A.W), which he always carried with him. A copy of this book was found in the large over-coat in which he had wrapped himself before setting out on that last walk of his to die in the fields he used to till.

The Holy Quran, no doubt, is the chief source of the Islamic Law. However, any point not covered explicitly by the Quran, is solved by a reference to the Holy Prophet's (S.A.W.) words or actions, or words and actions of his companions, approved by him. The Holy Prophet's (S.A.W.) actions and words were attentively heard and observed by his family members and companions, who preserved every word and action of his in their hearts and passed them intact to the next generations. They rightly believed that evey word that came out of his mouth, or action, was inspired by Allah.. This belief is corroborated by the Holy Quran:

"He was taught by One Mighty in Power."

(53:2—5)

and

> "Verily those who swear fealty unto thee (Muhammad) only swear fealty unto Allah: the hand of Allah is over their hands."
>
> (48:10)

In view of the importance of the sermons and sayings of the Holy Prophet (S.A.W.) for our guidance, it is necessary that a Muslim should supplement his knowledge of the Holy Quran by the sayings of the Holy Prophet (S.A.W.).

It is also a fact that while the Holy Quran is the Word of Allah, the Hadis and Sunnah are not. They are delivered in the language of the Holy Prophet (S.A.W.). The language of the two differ and those acquainted with the Arabic language can differentiate between them from their diction. The Holy Quran is undoubtedly a master-piece — matchless and inimitable. No human being can imitate it or produce even a single line like it. This is a standing challenge, but unanswered since the last 1400 years. The Holy Quran is a living miracle and a proof of the truth and veracity of the Holy Prophet (S.A.W.) and Islam. Nevertheless, the language of the traditions, though not upto the standard of the language of the Holy Quran, surpasses any other wordly writing in composition and eloquence. They are classed as superb and excellent piece of Arabic literature.

After the Holy Book these *Ahadis* (traditions) and Sunnah of the Holy Prophet (S.A.W.) have played very important role in the making and development of the Law of Islamic Sharia. These are regarded as the basic principles of Muslim faith. They contain exhaustive material and guidance on all aspects of a Muslim's life. Therefore without some knowledge of the traditions and Sunnah, it would be difficult for a Muslim to know the proper approach to the problems of life, and know his rights and duties in his day to day life.

These traditions and Sunnah contain matters covering all departments of human life, and they are, in fact, the Treasure Chest of good manners and excellent morals aimed at improving spiritual and material life of a person. To follow the footsteps of the Holy Prophet (S.A.W.) should, therefore, be the aim of a Muslim to achieve success and salvation in this world and in the Hereafter. In a verse Allah has directed us:

> "Say, if you love Allah, then walk in my footsteps and Allah will love you." (3:31)

Now something about the collection and preservation of these traditions and Sunnah. In pre-Islamic Arabian society there were hardly three dozen persons who could read and write. This was a time when making of books in a systematic manner or any publishing industry was unknown. The Hungarian writer Ignaz Goldziher says that "The Arabs did not like reading and writing, and entirely depended for reproduction mostly on their remarkable memory." Professor Nicholson in his "A Literary History of the Arabs", says: "Writing was sparingly used by the Arabs, and pre-Islamic poetry which had attained a high level of excellence was preserved only by oral tradition." This situation helped rise a class of professionals who made their power of memory a lucrative business. One of such professionals, Hammad, claimed and proved, that he could recite for each letter of the alphabet one hundred long poems rhyming in that letter. He further claimed that he knew by heart 27,000 poems. Another person, Abu Zam Zam, once recited poems of one hundred poets bearing the name of 'Umar'. Yet another professional reciter (Rawi) claimed that he could recite poems continuously for one month without resorting to any repetition. It will be interesting to quote a recent example. Hasan-al-Banna, the famous Egyptian genius and savant, was once called upon to recite a few couplets from a particular Divan, and in reply he read out, extempore, one thousand couplets from that Divan, and said that he could quote more. Similarly he remembered by heart the names of 3,00,000 members of the Ikhwan-ul-Muslemoon.

In the beginning, the traditions of the Holy Prophet (S.A.W.) and his Sunnah, were memorised by his family members and companions, who were very close to him and enjoyed the privilege of being constantly in his company. These persons were, therefore, in a better position to hear and watch the activities of the august personality.

These collectors and reporters of the traditions and Sunnah were extremely pious persons, possessing excellent and inimitable moral character. These honest and God-fearing persons used to either write down or commit to their memories these traditions and Sunnah of the Holy Prophet (S.A.W.). Since the circulation of Hadis and Sunnah increased, they were being recited, by those who knew and remembered them, at different public places, mosques and gatherings. Although bulk of these traditions had been recorded, a considerable number of traditions were preserved in the hearts of the close associates of the Holy Prophet (S.A.W.).

After some time as a result of political rivalries between the followers of Hazrat Ali nd Amir Mu'awiya, each group started producing sayings, commands and directions of the Holy Prophet (S.A.W.) in defence of their view-point. At this time hypocrites and enemies of Islam, started forging fake traditions and false anecdotes about the life and mission of the Holy Prophet (S.A.W.). They mingled a lot of spurious traditions with true ones. To check this racket Muslim scholars and theologians felt the necessity of devising some system to control spread of fake traditions and to sort out genuine traditions from the false ones.

In the year 101 A.H. Hazrat Umar bin Abdul Aziz, a pious and virtuous Caliph, appointed some learned Ulama (theologians) to sort out the genuine traditions. These learned Ulama laid down rules to find out the sources of the traditions and the biographical data of the narrators with special attention to their religious views. Their efforts resulted in the creation and development of critical sciences like 'Ilm-ul-Hadis', 'Ilm-ur-Rijal' and 'Ilm-ul-Asma'. Accordingly each and every tradition was subjected to the severest scanning and scrutiny as regards its language, style, form, redaction and vocabulary Then the idea or the subject matter of the tradition was minutely examined as regards its coherence with the Holy Quran and other traditions and its relevance with other established historical facts. The content or subject matter was also tested for its judiciousness and rationality. Last of all every chain of reporters (Isnad) was subjected to the most exacting tests of historicity and verification, in accordance with the principles laid down in "Ilm-ur-Rijal", or the critical examination of the minutest details of the personal life of thousands of the companions of the Holy Prophet (S.A.W.) and contemporaries. This is the modus operandi of enquiry, evolved by the Muslim scholars, more than one thousand years ago, to assess the authenticity or otherwise of a historical fact. At this time the western nations were ignorant of these sophisticated branches of the art and science. This Islamic criticism or enquiry was objective and scientific textual research of a type which is unique and unparalleled and which the world has never seen nor probably will see.

As a result of the research and labour of these learned theologians (Ulama) many standard books dealing with the lives of the narrators, specially their character and behaviour in their day to day life and their reputation for honesty, were written and published. In this exercise the style of narration of the narrators and the subject matter was thoroughly probed. Some of the notable traditionists or compilers who systematically worked on these lines were Ibn-i-Shihab Az-Zuhri and Abu Bakr ibn Hazm. An idea about the care and labour involved in the collection and sifting of traditions can be had from these instances.

Hazrat Aiyub Ansari travelled from Madina to Egypt to collect one Hadis (tradition); similarly Hazrat Jabir bin Abdullah spent one month on his journey to obtain one Hadis from Hazrat Abdullah bin Anas. Another collector of these traditions learnt that a certain person knew one Hadis. Accordingly he journeyed long to meet the said person. On reaching his destination he made enquiries about the said person. Somebody pointed this person who was then trying to catch hold of his horse which had strayed by showing an empty bucket as if it had some food for the horse The collector, seeing this person, thus decoying an animal, thought that such a person is not reliable enough, and therefore his version of a Hadis cannot be accepted, and he returned home without talking to the said person.

In the second century of the Hijri era and thereafter, a large number of scholars of traditions have worked on this subject and have left valuable record of their marvellous research and codification of traditions; among these luminaries were Hazrat Abu Juraij in Mecca, Imam Malik in Madina, Imam Sufyan Sauri in Kufa, Imam Hammad bin Salma in Basra, Imam Abdullah bin Mubarak in Khurasan, Imam Auzaee in Syria and Imam Abu Hanifa in Iraq. Imam Abu Hanifa is the founder of the Hanafi School, Imam Malik is the founder of Maliki School, Imam Shafi'i is the founder of Shafi'i School and Imam Ahmad bin Hanbal founded the Hanbali School of Islamic Law.

The work done so far on the compilation and codification of traditions was not very comprehensive. As for instance Imam Malik's Muwa-tta contained only 1700 sayings of the Holy Prophet (S.A.W.) dealing with only few topics like prayer fasting, Zakat, pilgrimage etc. Therefore it was felt necessary to make such compilations more comprehensive and representative by including all the subjects and widen its scope to embrace the whole of the Muslim world. Accordingly with this end in view work on larger scale involving minute critical research of the traditions was taken up by eminent scholars like Imam Muslim (d. 181 A.H.) and Imam Bukhari (d. 256 A.H.).

The chief characteristic of this work was to attach to each tradition a chain of its reporters or authorities, tracing upto the original narrator. Besides this, very thorough and detailed investigation was carried out about the moral character, truthfulness, religious views and power of memory of a reporter. Imam Bukhari paid much attention to the careful examination of each tradition and sorting out the most authentic ones out of the thousands of traditions then in circulation. Out of a lot of 6,00,000 traditions placed before him, he selected only 7,275 and included them in his book *'Sahih-al-Bukhari'*, which is a master-work of research scholarship and hard labour. Similarly Imam Muslim picked up only 9,200 traditions out of 3,00,000. The collections of Imams Bukhari and Muslim are very much respected by the Muslims who regard them only next to the Holy Quran.

Afterwards, these two books were supplemented by four more compilations known as the "Four Sunans" of Imam Abu Daud

(d. 275 A.H.), Imam Tirmizi (d. 279 A.H.) Imam Ibn-i-Majah (d. 295 A.H.) and Imam Nasai (d. 303 A.H.). Besides these, there is the most important compilation of Imam Ahmad bin Hanbal (d. 241 A.H.).

These collections of sayings and anecdotes of the Holy Prophet (S.A.W.) apart from their religious and moral values, are the most authentic and day to day record of the events and happenings of the early days of Islam They are very useful for writing books on history, biography etc. The Hungarian scholar Ignaz Goldziher in volume II of his book *'Muslim. Studies'*, says that these traditions throw much light on the development and spread of Islam during its early stages and on the political, social and sectional movements during this period.

The collection of Hadis is so large and voluminous that it is not possible for every man to read them, understand them and remember to act upon them Therefore it was necessary to compile a condensed volume containing important and selected traditions for those who may not have enough time to read the bulky volumes. Such a book is one titled as "*Riadh-us-Saleheen*" or the "Garden of the Virtuous Persons", in two parts by the great saintly scholar and traditionist, Hazrat Imam Mohiuddin Abu Zakariya Yahya bin Sharaf An-Nawawi of Nawa in Syria, who lived from 631 A.H. (1233 A,D.) to 676 A.H.(1278 A.D.).

Imam Nawawi has taken pains to select about 1900 traditions from Muslim and Bukhari and one or two other standard books on Hadis, like "Muwatta' of Imam Malik. He has arranged these traditions under different topics. The learned author has supplemented these traditions with appropriate verses from the Holy Quran. He has given these verses in the beginning of the chapter containing traditions on a particular topic. This creates an awful respect in the minds of the readers, and confirms the point that the traditions are the annotations of and adjunct to the Holy Quran. In the original Arabic text, some items coming under more than one chapter, have been repeated. In the present translation, however, such duplicate items have been omitted.

The present work is a literal translation of the first part of the Arabic text, and care has been taken to adhere to the original text as far as possible.

The personality of Imam Nawawi doesn't need any introduction, as he is already well-known in the Islamic world. Suffice it to say that he is one of the greatest theologian, traditionist, savant, saint and self-denying person, who had forsaken the world and worldly comforts, and throughout led a retired life, devoted to the service of Muslims and Islam. In his devotion to religion and praying, piety and self-denial, he is perhaps one of those who are unparalleled.

Imam Nawawi is the author of a large numebr of books, particularly on traditions and their commentaries. But his *'Riadh-us-Saleheen'* is one of the most important, very useful and popular book. For the last hundreds of years it has been serving as guide and a compendium of useful information to Muslim Ulama and theologians, and of great help to them in preaching Islam and its practice.

Since the original work is in Arabic, it is not possible for a large number of non-Arabic knowing Muslims to derive any benefit from it. Although a number of translations of such useful books are now available in other languages like Urdu, Turkish and Persian, yet there are not many in English and other languages spoken in the West. Hence this English translation of '*Riadh-us-Saleheen*' is presented to the English-knowing people particularly Muslims. This book will also be of great help to the new Muslim generation and the new brethren in Islam, living in Europe, America and other parts of the globe, to enable them to mould their life in accordance with the Islamic code of ethics. It should be borne in mind that true Islamic education alerts the mind to the meaning and value of life and enlivens it and guides in all its pursuits. Islam is a religion which is complete in all respects and the last word from Allah, the Almighty. It is a coherent and systematic human philosophy, a natural way of life and a practical creed.

The Muslims, living in non-Muslim countries have to face a number of problems; they not only live in an alien environment but are surrounded by un-Islamic and strange customs and practices. Life in these countries is no doubt exciting and interesting, but this is all a mirage, ultimately it leads to frustration, despondency and ruin. In such a situation, it is very difficult for a Muslim to maintain his Islamic identity, if they are not properly equipped and instructed in Islamic manners and way of life.

It is hoped that this book will enable these Muslims to preserve their Muslim character, no matter what others around them may be doing.

S.M. MADNI ABBASI

January 5, 1983.

A short Biographical Account of Imam Nawawi

Imam Mohiuddin Abu Zakaria bin Sharaf An-Nawawi, is known as Imam Nawawi in short. His surname (Laqab) is Mohiuddin, his Kunniyat (a name derived from a person's father, mother or son) is Abu Zakaria (i.e. father of Zakaria). He is also called as Hazami, after his ancestor Hazam An-Nawawi.

Imam Nawawi was born in the first month (Moharram) of 631 A.H. (corresponding to 1233 A.D.), in a saintly family of Nawa, a village near Damascus. The Imam spent his adolescence and attained maturity in this village where he memorised the Holy Quran.

Ustad Marakashi, a saintly person of Nawa, says: 'I saw Sheikh Nawawi at Nawa when he was a youth aged 10 years. Other boys of his age used to force him to play with them, but the Sheikh would not like to play with them, and would remain busy in his studies. If his colleagues insisted on his joining them in their games, the Sheikh would (in disgust) start weeping.' Ustad Marakashi further says: 'I started loving (Imam) Nawawi immensely from that moment.

Imam Nawawi's father wanted that his son should join him in his business, but on account of his lofty anddsaintly temperament, the latter did not like this. The nature had ordained him for a noble mission. He therefore, showed no inclination for business. During this time, he completed his reading of the Holy Quran, and thus he acquitted himself well with the first step of his learning.

Imam Nawawi's father had by now realised the heavenly intellectual gifts of his son.. Keeping in view his quest for learning, the father resolved to arrange for a proper and befitting education for his son. Therefore, he took him to Damascus, which city was then a cradle of learning. In Damascus Imam Nawawi started his studied under renowned teacher, Kamal bin Ahmad.

Imam Nawawi says: "When I attained the age of 19 years, my father took me to Damascus, where I joined Madrasa Rawaha. I studied in this institution for two years. During my stay in Madrasa Rawaha, I lived on the food supplied by the Madrasa. However, in 4½ months I was able to commit to memory in full, the book entitled "*Tambih*', Afterwards I learnt by heart some parts of the book "*Mohazzab*", but major part of my time was spent in the study of commentaries and correction of books. When my teacher, Ustad Ishaq Maghribi (R.A.) saw my interest and progress in my studies, he started loving me immensely and envinced greater concern for my education. In 650 A.H. I performed Hajj along with my father and stayed in the city of Madina for 1½ months."

His Preoccupation with His Studies

Ata-ud-din bin Atar says that Sheikh Nawawi told him (Ata-ud-din) that the (Sheikh Nawawi) used to study about 12 subjects daily from his teachers; some of the subjects were "Sahih Muslim" (a book of traditions), Syntax and Etymology, Logic and Principle of Fiqh or Islamic Jurisprudence etc. Imam Nawawi further says: "Almighty Allah blessed my time and memory and enabled me to complete my studies." The Imam also reveals the fact that: "Once I thought that I should study medicine, and for this purpose I even purchased a book on the subject. But soon after this I started feeling sullenness and inactivity, as if my heart has plunged into darkness; so much so that I even lost (interest) and control on my favourite subjects This state continued for some time, when all of a sudden it dawned upon me that my studies of medicine were of no use to me. I, therefore, at once sold the book on medicine and removed all literature on this subject from my house. This gave me relief and enlightened my heart.

His Teachers and Guides

Imam Nawawi studied Hadis from the celebrated Mohaddisin (traditionists) of his time, and was taught Islamic Jurisprudence and its principles and Logic by great scholars. The number of his teachers is very large. Some of these were:

1. Abu Ibrahim Ishaq bin Ahmad al-Maghribi,
2. Abu Muhammad Abdur Rahman bin Nooh Almaqdisi.
3. Abu Hafs Umar bin Asa'ad Ar-Rabia,
4. Abul Hasan Arbali,
5. Abu Ishaq Ibrahim Muradi,
6. Abul Baqa Khalid bin Yusuf Nablusi,
7. Zia bin Tasam Hanafi,
8. Abul Abbas Ahmad Misri,
9. Abu Abdullah Jiyani,
10. Abul Fath Umar bin Bandar,
11. Abu Ishaq Wasti,
12. Abu Abbas Maghribi,
13. Abu Muhammad Tanukhi,
14. Abu Muhammad Abdur Rahman Ambari,
15. Abul Farj Maqdisi,
16. Abu Muhammad Ansari,

etc. etc.

These are the most leanred and celebrated teachers of this age, under whom Imam Nawawi quenched his thirst for learning.

His Students

Like his teachers, the number of Imam Nawawi's students is large

Some of his pupils were:

(1). Alauddin bin Athar (2) Abul Abbas Ahmad bin Ibrahim (3) Abul Abbas Jafri (4) Abul Abbas Ahmad bin Farj (5) Rashid Ismail bin Moallim Hanafi (6) Abu Abdullah Hambli (7) Abul Abbas Wasti (8) Jamaluddin Sulaiman bin Omar Al-Dara'ee (9) Abul Farj Maqdisi (10) Badr Muhammad bin Ibrahim (11) Shams Muhammad bin Abi Bakr (12) Shihab Muhammad bin Abdul Khaliq (13) Sharaf Hibbullah (14) Abul Hajaj Mazni, etc. etc.

His Piety

Imam Nawawi was not only an accomplished scholar, savant and litterateur par excellence, he was a highly pious person, very much devoted to praying and a devout Darwesh. He always strictly followed the Sunnat or the traditions and practices of the Holy Prophet (S.A.W.) He always ate rough and simple food and refused invitations to sumptuous dinners and feasts, and wore coarse cloth dress. In this way he lived his entire life.

The learned persons, elite of the society and the common man of the period greatly respected the Imam on account of his piety, learning and excellent character. They always looked for an opportunity to present something to him, but he never accepted anything by way of gift or present from anybody, as he led a life of total retirement from the world, and spurned all pomp and show and worldly riches. The Imam never accepted any monetary allowance, benefit or favour from the Government of the day. It is said that only once the Imam accepted as a gift a small water-carrier *(Lota)* from a poor man, and on the insistence of a religously learned person (Alim-e-Deen) he ate a simple and coarse food sent by him at his (Imam's) house. Except these two instances, Imam Nawawi never accepted anything from anybody nor he ate any food presented by any person. Likewise he never ate any fruit, simply because the gardens of Damascus from where the fruits came, were either trust properties or some illegitimate and unlawful practices were involved in their production.

The Imam spent most of his time either in the spread and expansion of religious knowledge or in prayers and penance. He used to take very little rest, and would take only one meal and drink water only once a day.

His Works

The learned Imam lived for only 46 years but even during this short period he had written a large number of books on various subjects, each of which is a master-work and treasure full of permanent knowledge and information.

Some of the works of the Imam are enumerated below:

1 **"Commentary on Sahih Bukhari"**. About this book Imam Nawawi

says: 'In this Commentary I have presented nice and valuable knowledge."

"Al-Minhaj Fi Sharah Muslim bin Al-Hajjaj." About this commentary the Imam says: "Had I not anticipated weakness of endurance and paucity of readers (book lovers), I would have been a bit more exhaustive and would have expanded the work to more than 100 volumes, but (for this reason) I have followed a medium course." At present this commentary is available in only two volumes. Sheikh Shamsuddin Muhammad bin Yusuf Qunvi Hanafi (died 788 A.H.) has abridged this work.

3. **"Riadh-us-Saleheen".** An English translation of this work is presented herewith. It is a collection of nearly 2000 selected but authentic traditions supported by relevant Quranic verses, arranged subjectwise.
4. **"Kitab-ur-Rauza"**, which is an abridgement of 'Sharah Kabir Rafie.'
5. **Commentary on "Mohazzab"**
6. **"Tahzib-ul-Asma-was-Sifat"**
7. **"Kitab-ul-Azhar"**
8. **"Arba'een**
9. **"Taqreeb"**
10. **"Irshad fee Uloomul Hadees"**
11. **"Kitab-ul-Mubahamat"**
12. **"Ezah"**
13. **"Batian"**
14. **"Manasik"**
15. **"Sharah Sahih Bukhari", (Naqis)**
16. **"Sharah Sunan Abi Daud" (Naqis)**
17. **"Tabaqat Fuqha-ash-Shafia"**
18. **"Risala Istahbab-al-Qiam-ul-Ahl-ul-Fazal"**
19. **"Risala fee Qiamayul Ghanaim"**
20. **"Fatawa"**
21. **"Jama-us-Sunnat"**
22. **"Khulasatul Ahkaam"**
23. **"Manaqib-ush-Shafie"**
24. **"Bustan-ul-Arifeen"**
25. **"Mukhtasir Usud-ul-Ghaba"**

and others.

His Death

In 676 A.H. Imam Nawawi returned all the books taken by him on loan, to their respective owners; he visited the graves of his teachers and elders and prayed for them. On this occasion he was so much moved that he became tearful. Thereafter bidding goodbye to his friends and admirers he turned towards his home town Nawawi. A group of his acquaintances accompanied him beyond Damascus to bid him farewell.

They asked him: "When shall we meet again"? The Imam said: "After two hundred years." Those present on the occasion understood that by this the Imam meant the Day of Judgement.

After this the Imam went to Bait-ul-Maqdis (Jerusalem), where he visited the tomb of the Prophet Abraham (Hazrat Ibrahim, A.S.) and then returned to his home town Nawa. Soon after his arrival at this place, he fell ill and expired on the night of Wednesday the 14th of the month of Rajab, 676 A.H. in the life time of his father.

When the news of the death of Imam Nawawi reached Damascus, the city and its neighbouring areas were plunged into grief and the Muslims were overwhelmed with sorrow. The Qazi-ul-Quzat, (the Chief Justice) of Damascus, Izzuddin Muhammad bin Sa'igh, visited the Imam's grave in Nawa, along with a deputation of the dignitaries, and prayed for him. A number of poets composed elegies eulogising the Imam and lamenting his demise. Sheikh Wali-ud-Din bin Khateeb (R.A.), the compiler of Mishkat has dedicated his book "Akmal fee Asma-ur-Rijal", to Imam Nawawi.

ABBREVIATIONS USED

1.	S.A.W.	Sal-lal-laho ‘Alaihi wa Sal-lam (Peace be upon him)
2.	R.A.A.	Radi Allaho ‘Anhu — or ‘Anha — or ‘Anhum (Allah was pleased with him — or with her — or with them).
3.	R.A.	Rạhmaṭ-Allah-e-‘Alaih (Allah’s mercy be upon him).

بسم الله الرحمن الرحيم

CHAPTER I

Sincerity, Selflessness and Intention behind all Actions and Matters — Open or Secret

قَالَ اللهُ تَعَالَى : وَمَا أُمِرُوا إِلاَّ لِيَعْبُدُوا اللهَ مُخْلِصِينَ لَهُ الدِّينَ
حُنَفَاءَ وَيُقِيمُوا الصَّلاَةَ ، وَيُؤْتُوا الزَّكَاةَ ، وَذَلِكَ دِينُ الْقَيِّمَةِ
[البينة : ٥] وَقَالَ تَعَالَى : لَنْ يَنَالَ اللهَ لُحُومُهَا وَلا دِمَاؤُهَا وَلَكِنْ يَنَالُهُ
التَّقْوَى مِنْكُمْ [الحج : ٣٧] وَقَالَ تَعَالَى : قُلْ إِنْ تُخْفُوا مَا فِي
صُدُورِكُمْ أَوْ تُبْدُوهُ يَعْلَمْهُ اللهُ [آل عمران : ٢٩] .

Allah, the Exalted, said:

1. And they are ordained naught else than to serve Allah, keeping religion pure for him, as man by nature upright and to establish worship and to pay the poor-due. That is true religion. (98:5)
2. Their flesh and their blood reach not Allah, but the devotion from you reacheth Him (22:37)
3. Say (O Muhammad): Whether ye hide that which is in your breasts or reveal it, Allah knoweth it. (3:30).

١٠ — وَعَنْ أَمِيرِ الْمُؤْمِنِينَ أَبِي حَفْصٍ عُمَرَ بْنِ الْخَطَّابِ بْنِ نُفَيْلِ
بْنِ عَبْدِ الْعُزَّى بْنِ رِيَاحِ بْنِ عَبْدِ اللهِ بْنِ قُرْطِ بْنِ رَزَاحِ بْنِ عَدِيِّ
ابْنِ كَعْبِ بْنِ لُؤَيِّ بْنِ غَالِبٍ الْقُرَشِيِّ الْعَدَوِيِّ .رضي الله عنه ، قَالَ :
سَمِعْتُ رَسُولَ اللهِ صلى الله عليه وسلم يَقُولُ : « إِنَّمَا الأَعْمَالُ بِالنِّيَّاتِ ،
وَإِنَّمَا لِكُلِّ امْرِئٍ مَا نَوَى فَمَنْ كَانَتْ هِجْرَتُهُ إِلَى اللهِ وَرَسُولِهِ
فَهِجْرَتُهُ إِلَى اللهِ وَرَسُولِهِ ، وَمَنْ كَانَتْ هِجْرَتُهُ لِدُنْيَا يُصِيبُهَا ، أَوِ
امْرَأَةٍ يَنْكِحُهَا فَهِجْرَتُهُ إِلَى مَا هَاجَرَ إِلَيْهِ » مُتَّفَقٌ عَلَى صِحَّتِهِ

رواه إماما المحدثين : أبو عبد الله محمد بن إسماعيل بن إبراهيم
ابن المغيرة ابن بردزبه الجعفي البخاري ، وأبو الحسين مسلم بن
الحجاج بن مسلم القشيري النيسابوري رضي الله عنهما في صحيحيهما
اللذين هما أصح الكتب المصنفة .

1. Hazrat Umar bin Khattab (R.A.A.) has related: ‘I heard the Holy Prophet (S.A.W.) as having said: that intention determines the worth of a person’s actions and he will attain what he intends. If by immigration his aim is to please Allah and His Messenger (S.A.W.) then his migration is for this purpose; and if he migrates seeking the attainment of some worldly object, or for the sake of marrying a woman and as such his migration will be reckoned for that particular object.

(*Bukhari and Muslim*).

Imam Nawawi says that Imam Abu Abdullah Muhammad Bukhari and Imam Abu Husain Muslim (R.A.) have quoted this tradition in their respective books, which are the most authentic books on this subject.

٢ ـ وعن أم المؤمنين أم عبد الله عائشة رضي الله عنها قالت: قال
رسول الله صلى الله عليه وسلم : «يغزو جيش الكعبة فإذا كانوا ببيداء من
الأرض يخسف بأولهم وآخرهم» . قالت: قلت: يارسول الله ، كيف
يخسف بأولهم وآخرهم وفيهم أسواقهم ومن ليس منهم !؟
قال : «يخسف بأولهم وآخرهم ، ثم يبعثون على نياتهم»
متفق عليه هذا لفظ البخاري .

2. Hazrat Ayeshah (R.A.A.) has related that the Holy Prophet (S.A.W.) said: A *Lashkar* (Army) will advance towards the K‘aba and when it reaches the plain of Bedai Medina, the entire *Lashkar* will be devoured by the earth. Whereupon she said: Messenger of Allah (S.A.W.), why those who were unwillingly accompanying the *Lashkar*, and those who did not belong to the Lashkar, should suffer?’ The Holy Prophet (S.A.W.) replied, ‘the whole army will be swallowed up by the earth, but on the Day of Judgement they will be raised according to their motives.’ (*Muslim and Bukhari* but the wording is of *Bukhari*).

٣ ـ وعن عائشة رضي الله عنها قالت قال النبي صلى الله عليه وسلم :
«لا هجرة بعد الفتح ، ولكن جهاد ونية ، وإذا استنفرتم
فانفروا» متفق عليه

3. Hazrat Ayesha (R.A.A.) has related that the Holy Prophet (S.A.W.) said: 'Since Mecca had fallen migration by Muslim, is no longer necessary; but jihad (Striving and fighting) in the cause of Allah and a longing for it remains incumbent whenever you are called upon to do so (by the Imam), you should respond' (*Bukhari and Muslim*).

٤ ـ وَعَنْ أَبِي عَبْدِ اللهِ جَابِرِ بْنِ عَبْدِ اللهِ الأَنْصَارِيِّ رَضِيَ اللهُ عَنْهُمَا قَالَ : كُنَّا مَعَ النَّبِيِّ صلى الله عليه وسلم فِي غَزَاةٍ فَقَالَ : « إِنَّ بِالْمَدِينَةِ لَرِجَالاً مَاسِرْتُمْ مَسِيراً ، وَلا قَطَعْتُمْ وَادِياً إِلاَّ كَانُوا مَعَكُمْ حَبَسَهُمُ الْمَرَضُ » وَفِي رِوَايَةٍ : « إِلاَّ شَرَكُوكُمْ فِي الأَجْرِ » رَوَاهُ مُسْلِمٌ

ورواهُ الْبُخَارِيُّ عَنْ أَنَسٍ رَضِيَ اللهُ عَنْهُ قَالَ : رَجَعْنَا مِنْ غَزْوَةِ تَبُوكَ مَعَ النَّبِيِّ صلى الله عليه وسلم فَقَالَ : « إِنَّ أَقْوَاماً خَلْفَنَا بِالْمَدِينَةِ مَاسَلَكْنَا شِعْباً وَلا وَادِياً إِلاَّ وَهُمْ مَعَنَا ، حَبَسَهُمُ الْعُذْرُ »

4. Hazrat Jabir bin Abdullah (A.A.) has related: 'Once we were with the Holy Prophet (S.A.W.) in a *jihad*, when he said: "There are some people still in Madina who are with you in spirit wherever you march and whatever valley you traverse. It is only their indisposition that has kept them from being with you in person". According to another version. He (S.A.W.) said: "They are your partners in recompense". (*Muslim*).

Imam Bukhari has attributed this to Hazrat Anas that "we were returning from the campaign of Tabuk with the Holy Prophet (S.A.W.) when he said: "There are people left behind in Madina who neither accompanied us, nor crossed any vale but never-the-less they are with us in spirit. They simply could not join us on account of their excusses."

٥ ـ وَعَنْ أَبِي يَزِيدَ مَعْنِ بْنِ يَزِيدَ بْنِ الأَخْنَسِ رضي الله عَنْهُمْ ، وَهُوَ وَأَبُوهُ وَجَدُّهُ صَحَابِيُّونَ ، قَالَ : كَانَ أَبِي يَزِيدُ أَخْرَجَ دَنَانِيرَ يَتَصَدَّقُ بِهَا فَوَضَعَهَا عِنْدَ رَجُلٍ فِي الْمَسْجِدِ فَجِئْتُ فَأَخَذْتُهَا فَأَتَيْتُهُ بِهَا ، فَقَالَ : وَاللهِ مَا إِيَّاكَ أَرَدْتُ ، فَخَاصَمْتُهُ إِلَى رسول اللهِ صلى الله عليه وسلَّمَ فَقَالَ : « لَكَ مَانَوَيْتَ يَايَزِيدُ ، وَلَكَ مَا أَخَذْتَ يَامَعْنُ » رواه البخاريُّ

5. Hazrat Ma'an bin Yazid, Ibn Akhnas (R.A.A.) grand-son, father and grand-father respectively are the Companions of the Holy Prophet (S.A.W.). Hazrat Ma'an says: "My father set aside some dinars for charity and gave them to a person in the mosque. I went to that person and took back the money from him and brought the same to my father, who said: 'I did not want to give these dinars to you.' So we went to the Holy Prophet (S.A.W.) and submitted the matter to him (S.A.W.). He (S.A.W.) said to my father: 'Yazid you have earned due reward for your intentions;" and to me he (S.A.W.) said: 'Ma'an, you are entitled to what you have taken.' (*Bukhari*).

٦ – وعن أبي إسحاق سعد بن أبي وقاص مالك بن أهيب بن
عبد مناف بن زهرة بن كلاب بن مرة بن كعب بن لؤي القرشي
الزهري رضي الله عنه ، أحد العشرة المشهود لهم بالجنة ، رضي الله
عنهم ، قال : « جاءني رسول الله صلى الله عليه وسلم يعودني عام حجة
الوداع من وجع اشتد بي فقلت : يارسول الله إني قد بلغ بي من
الوجع ما ترى ، وأنا ذو مال ولا يرثني إلا ابنة لي ، أفأتصدق بثلثي
مالي ؟ قال : لا قلت : فالشطر يارسول الله ؟ فقال : لا ، قلت :
فالثلث يارسول الله ؟ قال الثلث والثلث كثير – أو كبير – إنك أن تذر
ورثتك أغنياء خير من أن تذرهم عالة يتكففون الناس ، وإنك
لن تنفق نفقة تبتغي بها وجه الله إلا أجرت عليها حتى ما تجعل
في في امرأتك قال : فقلت : يارسول الله أخلف بعد أصحابي ؟
قال : إنك لن تخلف فتعمل عملا تبتغي به وجه الله إلا ازددت
به درجة ورفعة ، ولعلك أن تخلف حتى ينتفع بك أقوام ويضر
بك آخرون . اللهم أمض لأصحابي هجرتهم ، ولا تردهم على
أعقابهم ، لكن البائس سعد بن خولة » يرثي له رسول الله صلى الله
عليه وسلم أن مات بمكة . متفق عليه

6. Hazrat Sa'ad Ibn Abi Waqqas (R.A.A.) (one of the ten who had been given the advance glad tidings of admission into Paradise) has said, "Once I was lying seriously ill and the Holy Prophet (S.A.W.) came to see me. This happened in the year when the Holy Prophet

(S.A.W.) performed the Farewell Pilgrimage. I said to him; 'Messenger of Allah, you see my condition. I have considerable money and property and my sole heir is my daughter. Can I, then, give away two third of my assets in charity?' He said: 'No'. I then submitted, 'One-half, O Messenger of Allah?' (S.A.W.). Again he said: 'No'. I again submitted, "well then one-third, O Messenger of Allah'? On which he said: 'One-third is sufficient, and one-third is more than enough. It is better to leave your children better off than in penury, forced to beg for their sustenance. Whatever you spend for the sake of Allah, even for a morsel of food that you put in the mouth of your wife, Allah will reward you. Then I said: "Messenger of Allah (S.A.W.), I will be left behind when my colleagues depart." He said: "You will certainly not be left behind. Whatever you do seeking the pleasure of Allah, will raise your position in the society. I am sanguine that you will live long enough for the good of Muslims and for punishing non-believers. Then he prayed to Allah. 'O Allah, Make the emigration of my Companions complete and successful, and they may not retract. But the one to be pitied was Sa'ad Ibn Khaulah who was left behind and died in Mecca, and the Messenger of Allah (S.A.W.) invoked mercy and compassion of Allah for him. *(Bukhari and Muslim)*.

٧ – وَعَنْ أَبِي هُرَيْرَةَ عَبْدِ الرَّحْمن بْنِ صخرٍ رضِي الله عَنْهُ قَالَ: قَالَ رسولُ الله صلى الله عليه وسلم : « إنَّ اللهَ لا يَنْظُرُ إلَى أجْسَامِكُمْ ، وَلَا إلَى صُوَرِكُمْ ، وَلَكِنْ يَنْظُرُ إلى قُلُوبِكُمْ وأعْمالِكُمْ » رواه مسلم

7. **Hazrat Abu Hurairah** (R.A.A.) has related that the Holy Prophet (S.A.W.) said: 'Allah does not go after your bodies and appearances, but He scans your hearts.' *(Muslim)*.

٨ – وَعَنْ أبي مُوسَى عَبْدِ اللهِ بْنِ قَيْسٍ الأَشْعَرِيِّ رضِي الله عنه قَالَ: سُئِلَ رسول الله صلى الله عليه وسلم عَنِ الرَّجُلِ يُقَاتِلُ شَجَاعَةً ، ويُقَاتِلُ حَمِيَّةً وَيُقَاتِلُ رِيَاءً ، أَيُّ ذلِكَ فِي سَبِيلِ اللهِ ؟ فَقَالَ رسول اللهِ صلى الله عليه وسلم : « مَنْ قَاتَلَ لِتَكُونَ كَلِمَةُ اللهِ هِيَ الْعُلْيَا فَهُوَ فِي سَبِيلِ اللهِ » مُتَّفَقٌ عَلَيْه

8. **Hazrat Abu Musa Ash'ari** (R.A.A.) has said: "The Holy Prophet (S.A.W.) was asked: "which of the three persons carries on *jihad* for the sake of Allah, one who fights to show his chivalry, or one who fights for the sake of self-respect and honour, or one who fights ostentatiously?" He (S.A.W.) replied: 'One who fights to uphold the message of Allah, is the person who carries on *Jihad* in the cause of Allah."

(Bukhari and Muslim).

٩ ــ وَعَنْ أَبِي بَكْرَةَ نُفَيْعِ بْنِ الْحَارِثِ الثَّقَفِيِّ رَضِيَ اللهُ عنه أنَّ النَّبِيَّ صلى الله عليه وسلم قال : « إِذَا الْتَقَى الْمُسْلِمَانِ بِسَيْفَيْهِمَا فَالْقَاتِلُ وَالْمَقْتُولُ فِي النَّارِ » قُلْتُ : يارَسُولَ اللهِ ، هَذَا الْقَاتِلُ فَمَا بَالُ الْمَقْتُولِ ؟ قَالَ : « إِنَّهُ كَانَ حَرِيصاً عَلَى قَتْلِ صَاحِبِهِ » متفقٌ عليه

9. **Hazrat Abu Bakarah Saqfi** (R.A.A.) tells that the Holy Prophet (S.A.W.) has said: "When two Muslims fight with each other with swords in hands and one is killed, both are destined for Hell." I said, 'Messenger of Allah (S.A.W.), as to the one who kills the other is understandable; but why the other who is killed should go to Hell?" He (S.A.W.) answered "The other was also eager to kill his opponent." (*Bukhari and Muslim*).

Note: The idea behind this tradition is that when two Muslims get incited simply on account of personal grudge and animosity and are fighting with each other, this act of theirs is so heinous that both of them have been condemned to Hell.

١٠ ــ وَعَنْ أَبِي هُرَيْرَةَ رَضِيَ اللهُ عنه قال : قال رسول الله صلى الله عليه وسلم : « صَلاَةُ الرَّجُلِ فِي جَمَاعَةٍ تَزِيدُ عَلَى صَلاَتِهِ فِي سُوقِهِ وَبَيْتِهِ بِضْعاً وَعِشْرِينَ دَرَجَةً وَذَلِكَ أَنَّ أَحَدَهُمْ إِذَا تَوَضَّأَ فَأَحْسَنَ الْوُضُوءَ . ثُمَّ أَتَى الْمَسْجِدَ لا يُرِيدُ إِلاَّ الصَّلاَةَ ، لا يَنْهَزُهُ إِلاَّ الصَّلاَةُ . لَمْ يَخْطُ خُطْوَةً إِلاَّ رُفِعَ لَهُ بِهَا دَرَجَةٌ . وَحُطَّ عَنْهُ بِهَا خَطِيئَةٌ حَتَّى يَدْخُلَ الْمَسْجِدَ . فَإِذَا دَخَلَ الْمَسْجِدَ كَانَ فِي الصَّلاَةِ مَا كَانَتِ الصَّلاَةُ هِيَ تَحْبِسُهُ ، وَالْمَلاَئِكَةُ يُصَلُّونَ عَلَى أَحَدِكُمْ مَادَامَ فِي مَجْلِسِهِ الَّذِي صَلَّى فِيهِ يَقُولُونَ : اللَّهُمَّ ارْحَمْهُ ، اللَّهُمَّ اغْفِرْ لَهُ ، اللَّهُمَّ تُبْ عَلَيْهِ . مَالَمْ يُؤْذِ فِيهِ ، مَا لَمْ يُحْدِثْ فِيهِ » متفقٌ عليه ، وَهَذَا لَفْظُ مُسْلِمٍ.

10. **Hazrat Abu Huraira** (R.A.A.) has reported that the Holy Prophet (S.A.W.) said: "Prayer in congregation (in a mosque) is more than twenty-five times greater in merit than prayer at home or in the shop etc." Therefore, when a person makes his ablutions carefully and proceeds to the mosque with the sole purpose of joining in the service, his status rises in grade at every step, and one of his sins is wiped out. From the moment he enters the mosque he is accounted as a participant in the prayer while waiting for the prayer to begin, and, so long as he causes no inconvenience to anyone and is in a state of purity, the angels

continue to pray for his salvation, and they say 'O Allah, have mercy upon him; Allah, forgive him,; Allah, be compasionate for him''
(*Bukhari and Muslim*).

١١ – وَعَنْ أَبِي الْعَبَّاس عَبْدِ اللهِ بْنِ عَبَّاس بْنِ عَبْدِ الْمُطَّلِبِ رَضِي
اللهعنهما ، عَنْ رسول الله ، صلى الله عليه وسلم ، فِيمَا يَرْوِي عَنْ رَبِّهِ ، تَبَارَكَ وَتَعَالَى
قال : « إِنَّ اللهَ كَتَبَ الْحَسَنَاتِ وَالسَّيِّئَاتِ ثُمَّ بَيَّنَ ذَلِكَ : فَمَنْ هَمَّ بِحَسَنَةٍ
فَلَمْ يَعْمَلْهَا كَتَبَهَا اللهُ تَبَارَكَ وَتَعَالَى عِنْدَهُ حَسَنَةً كَامِلَةً ، وَإِنْ
هَمَّ بِهَا فَعَمِلَهَا كَتَبَهَا اللهُ عَشْرَ حَسَنَاتٍ إِلَى سَبْعِمَائَةِ ضِعْفٍ إِلَى
أَضْعَافٍ كَثِيرَةٍ ، وَإِنْ هَمَّ بِسَيِّئَةٍ فَلَمْ يَعْمَلْهَا كَتَبَهَا اللهُ عِنْدَهُ حَسَنَةً
كَامِلَةً ، وَإِنْ هَمَّ بِهَا فَعَمِلَهَا كَتَبَهَا اللهُ سَيِّئَةً وَاحِدَةً » متفقٌ عليه

11. Hazrat Abdullah Ibn Abbas (R.A.A.) has narrated that the Holy Prophet (S.A.W.) repeated Allah's affirmation that He has defined good and evil and has expounded their gradation. Therefore, one who makes up his mind to do a good deed, is rewarded by Allah for one full measure of it, and if he then proceeds to carry it out Allah rewards him from ten to seven hundred times and even many times more. He, who is inclined towards an evil deed, but does not carry it out, is rewarded by Allah for one full measure of good deed. Should he carry it out, he is debited only by one evil deed. (*Bukhari and Muslim*).

Note: Such traditions which the Holy Prophet (S.A.W.) relates on divine authority by stating that "Allah the Almighty says so and so' are called Qudsi or holy and undisturbed by the narrators of traditions.

١٢ – وعن أَبِي عَبْدِ الرَّحْمَنِ عَبْدِ اللهِ بْنِ عُمَرَ بْنِ الْخَطَّابِ ، رضي
الله عنهما قال : سَمِعْتُ رسول الله صلى الله عليه وسلم يَقُولُ : « انْطَلَقَ ثَلاثَةُ
نَفَرٍ مِمَّنْ كَانَ قَبْلَكُمْ حَتَّى آوَاهُمُ الْمَبِيتُ إِلَى غَارٍ فَدَخَلُوهُ .
فَانْحَدَرَتْ صَخْرَةٌ مِنَ الْجَبَلِ فَسَدَّتْ عَلَيْهِمُ الْغَارَ ؛ فَقَالُوا : إِنَّهُ
لاَيُنْجِيكُمْ مِنْ هَذِهِ الصَّخْرَةِ إِلاَّ أَنْ تَدْعُوا اللهَ بِصَالِحِ أَعْمَالِكُمْ .
قال رجلٌ مِنْهُمْ : اللَّهُمَّ كَانَ لِي أَبَوَانِ شَيْخَانِ كَبِيرَانِ ، وَكُنْتُ
لاَ أَغْبِقُ قَبْلَهُمَا أَهْلاً وَلا مالاً . فَنَأَى بِي طَلَبُ الشَّجَرِ يَوْماً فَلَمْ
أُرِحْ عَلَيْهِمَا حَتَّى نَامَا فَحَلَبْتُ لَهُمَا غَبُوقَهُمَا فَوَجَدْتُهُمَا نَائِمَيْنِ .

فَكَرِهْتُ أَنْ أُوقِظَهُمَا وَأَنْ أَغْبِقَ قَبْلَهُمَا أَهْلاً أَوْ مَالاً . فَلَبِثْتُ – وَالْقَدَحُ عَلَى يَدِي – أَنْتَظِرُ اسْتِيقَاظَهُمَا حَتَّى بَرَقَ الْفَجْرُ وَالصِّبْيَةُ يَتَضَاغَوْنَ عِنْدَ قَدَمِي – فَاسْتَيْقَظَا فَشَرِبَا غَبُوقَهُمَا . اللَّهُمَّ إِنْ كُنْتُ فَعَلْتُ ذَلِكَ ابْتِغَاءَ وَجْهِكَ فَفَرِّجْ عَنَّا مَانَحْنُ فِيهِ مِنْ هَذِهِ الصَّخْرَةِ ، فَانْفَرَجَتْ شَيْئاً لا يَسْتَطِيعُونَ الْخُرُوجَ مِنْهُ . قَالَ الآخر : اللَّهُمَّ إِنَّهُ كَانَتْ لِي ابْنَةُ عَمٍّ كَانَتْ أَحَبَّ النَّاسِ إِلَيَّ » وفي رواية : « كُنْتُ أُحِبُّهَا كَأَشَدِّ مَا يُحِبُّ الرِّجَالُ النِّسَاءَ ، فَأَرَدْتُهَا عَلَى نَفْسِهَا فَامْتَنَعَتْ مِنِّي حَتَّى أَلَمَّتْ بِهَا سَنَةٌ مِنَ السِّنِينَ فَجَاءَتْنِي فَأَعْطَيْتُهَا عِشْرِينَ وَمِائَةَ دِينَارٍ عَلَى أَنْ تُخَلِّيَ بَيْنِي وَبَيْنَ نَفْسِهَا فَفَعَلَتْ ، حَتَّى إِذَا قَدَرْتُ عَلَيْهَا » وفي رواية : « فَلَمَّا قَعَدْتُ بَيْنَ رِجْلَيْهَا ، قَالَتْ : اتَّقِ اللهَ وَلا تَفُضَّ الْخَاتَمَ إِلاَّ بِحَقِّهِ ، فَانْصَرَفْتُ عَنْهَا وَهِيَ أَحَبُّ النَّاسِ إِلَيَّ وَتَرَكْتُ الذَّهَبَ الَّذِي أَعْطَيْتُهَا ، اللَّهُمَّ إِنْ كُنْتُ فَعَلْتُ ذَلِكَ ابْتِغَاءَ وَجْهِكَ فَافْرُجْ عَنَّا مَانَحْنُ فِيهِ ، فَانْفَرَجَتِ الصَّخْرَةُ غَيْرَ أَنَّهُمْ لا يَسْتَطِيعُونَ الْخُرُوجَ مِنْهَا . وَقَالَ الثَّالِثُ : اللَّهُمَّ اسْتَأْجَرْتُ أُجَرَاءَ وَأَعْطَيْتُهُمْ أَجْرَهُمْ غَيْرَ رَجُلٍ وَاحِدٍ تَرَكَ الَّذِي لَهُ وَذَهَبَ ، فَثَمَّرْتُ أَجْرَهُ حَتَّى كَثُرَتْ مِنْهُ الأَمْوَالُ ، فَجَاءَنِي بَعْدَ حِينٍ فَقَالَ : يَاعَبْدَ اللهِ أَدِّ إِلَيَّ أَجْرِي ، فَقُلْتُ : كُلُّ مَاتَرَى مِنْ أَجْرِكَ : مِنَ الإِبِلِ وَالْبَقَرِ وَالْغَنَمِ وَالرَّقِيقِ . فَقَالَ : يا عَبْدَ اللهِ لا تَسْتَهْزِئْ بِي ! فَقُلْتُ : لا أَسْتَهْزِئُ بِكَ ، فَأَخَذَهُ كُلَّهُ فَاسْتَاقَهُ فَلَمْ يَتْرُكْ مِنْهُ شَيْئاً ، اللَّهُمَّ إِنْ كُنْتُ فَعَلْتُ ذَلِكَ ابْتِغَاءَ وَجْهِكَ فَافْرُجْ عَنَّا مَا نَحْنُ فِيهِ ، فَانْفَرَجَتِ الصَّخْرَةُ فَخَرَجُوا يَمْشُونَ » متفقٌ عَلَيْهِ

12. Hazrat Abdullah Ibn Umar (R.A.A.) has related that he heard the Holy Prophet (S.A.W.) recount the following: "Three persons of a people before you, were on a journey when they were overtaken by a storm and therefore they took shelter in a cave. A rock slipped down from the mountain and blocked the exit from cave. One of them said: The only way for deliverance left is to beseech Allah in the name of some virtuous deed. Thereupon one of them supplicated, O Lord, my parents were very old, I used to offer them their nightly drink of milk before my children and the other members of the family. One day I went astray far away in search of green trees and could return only after my parents had gone to sleep. When I had milked the animals and brought their nightly drink to them, they were fast asleep, but I did not like to disturb them, nor would give any part of the milk to my children and other members of the family till after my parents had had their drink. Thus, with the vessel in hand, I awaited their awakening till the flush of dawn, while the children cried out of hunger at my feet. When they woke up, they had their drink. O Lord, if I did this thing seeking only Thy pleasure, then do Thou relieve us of the distress wrought upon us by this rock. Thereupon, the rock moved a little but not enough to let them pass out. Then the second man supplicated: O Lord, I had a cousin whom I loved more passionately than any man loves a woman. I tried to seduce her but she would have none of me, till in a season of great hardship due to famine, she approached me (for help) and I gave her one hundred and twenty dinars on condition that she would have sexual intercourse with me. She agreed, and when we got together and I was just going to have intercourse with her, she pleaded: 'Fear God, and do not break the seal unlawfully'; whereupon I moved away from her, despite the fact that I desired her most passionately; and I let her keep the money I had given her. O Lord, if I did this thing seeking only Thy pleasure, do Thou move the distress in which we find ourselves.' Again, the rock moved a little but not enough to let them pass out. Then the third supplicated: "O Lord, I hired some labourers and paid them their dues, but one of them left leaving behind what was due to him. I invested it in business and the business prospered greatly.' After a time the labourer came back and said: 'O servant of God, hand over to me my wages. I said to him: All that you see is yours; camels, cattle, goats and slaves.' He said: 'Don't play joke with me, O servant of Allah' I assured him: 'I am not joking'. So he took all of it sparing nothing. Lord, if I did this seeking only Thy pleasure, do thou relieve us of our distress.' The rock then moved away, and all the three came out of the cave safe and sound." (*Bukhari and Muslim*).

Note: This tradition has a number of advantages. Among these, one is to seek Allah's mercy and help during trials and tribulations and to make one's good and pious deeds as an agency for securing the same; another point worth notice is the high merit of service of the parents. The importance and virtues of chastity, fulfilment of pledge, return of trust and fair consideration in dealings are also among good deeds of great merit according to this tradition: And sincerity and honesty of purpose are no doubt the title of this chapter. In short, according to Islam incentive for all good work should only be the compliance of Allah's orders and His pleasure, and no worldly gains, nor hypocracy, ostentation, publicity or demand of any monetary gain.

* * * * * * * * * * *

CHAPTER 2

Penitence

قال الله تعالى : وتُوبُوا إلَى الله جَميعاً أيُّهَ المُؤْمِنُونَ لَعَلَّكُمْ تُفْلِحُونَ

[النور : ٣١] وقال تعالى : اسْتَغْفِرُوا رَبَّكُمْ ثُمَّ تُوبُوا إلَيْهِ [هود : ٣]

وقال تعالى : يَـأَيُّهَا الَّذين آمَنُوا تُوبُوا إلَى الله تَوْبَةً نَصُوحاً [التحريم : ٨]

Allah, the Exalted, has said:

4. **"And turn unto Allah together, O believers, in order that ye may succeed." (24:31).**
5. **'And (bidding you): Ask pardon of your Lord and turn to him repentant." (11:3).**
6. **"O ye who believe: Turn unto Allah in sincere repentence." (66:8).**

١٣ – وعَنْ أبي هُرَيْرَةَ رضي الله عنه قال : سَمِعْتُ رسول الله صلى الله عليه وسلم يَقُولُ : « والله إنّي لأَسْتَغْفِرُ الله وأتُوبُ إلَيْهِ في اليَوْمِ أكْثَر مِنْ سَبْعِين مرَّةً » رواه البخاري

13. Hazrat Abu Hurairah (R.A.A.) relates that he heard the Holy Prophet (S.A.W.) say: "Allah is my witness, that I seek His forgiveness and turn to Him more than seventy times a day." (*Bukhari*).

١٤ – وعَنَ الأَغَرِّ بْن يَسَار المُزَنِيِّ رضي الله عنه قال : قال رسول الله صلى الله عليه وسلم : « يا أيُّها النَّاسُ تُوبُوا إلى اللهِ واسْتَغْفِرُوهُ فإنّي أتُوبُ في اليَوْمِ مائةَ مَرَّةٍ » رواه مسلم

14. Aghirr bin Yasar Muzani relates that the Holy Prophet (S.A.W.) has advised his followers: 'Turn to Allah, ye people, offer repentance and seek His forgiveness. I myself offer my reprentance to Allah a hundred times a day." (*Muslim*).

١٥ – وعَنْ أبي حَمْزَةَ أنَسِ بن مَالِكٍ الأَنْصَارِيِّ خَادِمِ رسول الله صلى الله عليه وسلم، رضي الله عنه قال : قال رسول الله صلى الله عليه وسلم : « لَلَّه أفْرَحُ بِتَوْبَةِ عَبْدِهِ مِنْ أحَدِكُمْ سَقَطَ عَلَى بَعِيرِهِ وقد أضَلَّهُ في أرضٍ

فَلاةٍ » متفقٌ عليه .

وفي رواية لمُسْلِمٍ : « للهُ أَشَدُّ فَرَحاً بِتَوْبَةِ عَبْدِهِ حِينَ يَتُوبُ إِلَيْهِ مِنْ أَحَدِكُمْ كان على رَاحِلَتِهِ بِأَرْضِ فَلاةٍ ، فَانفَلَتَتْ مِنْهُ وعَلَيْهَا طَعَامُهُ وشَرَابُهُ فأَيِسَ مِنهَا ، فَأَتَى شَجَرَةً فَاضْطَجَعَ في ظِلِّهَا ، وقد أَيِسَ مِنْ رَاحِلَتِهِ ، فَبَيْنَمَا هُوَ كَذلكَ إِذْ هُوَ بِها قَائِمَةً عِنْدَهُ ، فَأَخَذَ بِخِطَامِهَا ثُمَّ قَالَ مِنْ شِدَّةِ الفَرَحِ : اللَّهُمَّ أَنْتَ عَبْدِي وأنا رَبُّكَ أَخْطَأَ مِنْ شِدَّةِ الفَرَحِ »

15. Hazrat Anas bin Malik (R.A.A.), an attendant of the Holy Prophet (S.A.W.) reports that the Holy Prophet (S.A.W.) has said: "Allah is more pleased with the repentance of His servant than would be one of you who were to lose his camel in a barren desert and then find it suddenly." (*Bukhari and Muslim*).

The version in *Muslim* adds: Allah is more pleased with the repentance of His servant than would be one of you who were to lose his riding camel, which carries his food and drink, in barren desert, and losing all hopes of finding it, he were to lie down in the shade of a tree, and then should suddenly find it standing near him and seizing its nose string, in his extreme happiness, should blurt out: O Allah, 'Allah', Thou art my servant and I am Thy Lord.' He commits this slip of tongue due to immense happiness and expresses his penitence and seeks Allah's forgiveness. On his penitence Allah is much more pleased.

١٦ – وعَنْ أَبي مُوسى عَبْدِ اللهِ بنِ قَيْسٍ الأَشْعَرِيِّ رضي الله عنه عن النَّبيِّ صلى الله عليه وسلم قال : « إن الله تعالى يَبْسُطُ يَدَهُ باللَّيْلِ ليَتُوبَ مُسِيءُ النَّهَارِ ، ويَبْسُطُ يَدَهُ بالنَّهَارِ ليَتُوبَ مُسِيءُ اللَّيْلِ حَتَّى تَطْلُعَ الشَّمْسُ مِنْ مَغْرِبِها » رواه مسلم

16. Hazrat Abu Musa Ash'ari (R.A.A.) relates that the Holy Prophet (S.A.W.) has said: "Allah will continue to hold out his hand at night so that he who has sinned during the day might repent, and to hold out his hand during the day so that one who has sinned at night might repent, and Allahwill continue to do so till the sun rises from the West i.e. till the Day of Resurrection." (*Muslim*).

١٧ – وعَنْ أَبي هُرَيْرَةَ رضي الله عنه قال : قال رسول الله صلى الله عليه وسلم : « مَنْ تَابَ قَبْلَ أَنْ تَطْلُعَ الشَّمْسُ مِنْ مَغْرِبِها تَابَ اللهُ عَلَيْهِ » رواه مسلم

17. Hazrat Abu Hurairah (R.A.A.) relates that the Holy Prophet (S.A.W.) has declared that: Allah will continue to accept the repentance of His creatures till the sun rises from West (Day of Judgment) (*Muslim*).

١٨ — وعَنْ أبي عَبْدِ الرَّحمن عَبْدِ الله بن عُمَرَ بن الخطَّاب رضي الله عنهما عن النَّبيِّ صلى الله عليه وسلم قال : « إنَّ اللهَ عزَّ وَجلَّ يَقْبَلُ تَوْبَةَ العَبْدِ مَالَمْ يُغَرْغِرْ » رواه الترمذي وقال : حديثٌ حسنٌ .

18. Hazrat Abdullah Ibn Umar (R.A.A.) relates that the Holy Prophet (S.A.W.) has said: "Allah, the Lord of honour and glory, will accept the repentance of His servant till his death-rattle begins."

(*Tirmizi*).

Note: This tradition is classed as Hasan, i.e. of a high degree of authenticity.

١٩ — وعَنْ زرِّ بن حُبَيْشٍ قالَ : أتَيْتُ صَفْوانَ بْنَ عَسَّالٍ رضي الله عَنْهُ أسألُهُ عَنِ المَسْحِ عَلَى الخُفَّيْنِ فقالَ : ما جاءَ بِكَ يازِرُّ ؟ فَقُلْتُ : ابْتغاءُ العِلْمِ ، فقالَ : إنَّ المَلائكةَ تَضَعُ أجْنِحتَها لِطالِبِ العِلْمِ رِضاءً بما يَطْلُبُ ، فَقُلْتُ : إنَّه قد حَكَّ في صَدْري المَسْحُ عَلَى الخُفَّيْنِ بَعْدَ الغائِطِ والبَوْلِ ، وكُنْتَ امْرءاً مِنْ أصْحابِ النَّبيِّ صلى الله عليه وسلم ، فَجِئْتُ أسألُكَ : هَلْ سَمِعْتَهُ يَذْكُرُ في ذلِكَ شَيْئاً ؟ قالَ : نَعَمْ ، كانَ يأمُرنا إذا كُنَّا سَفْراً — أوْ مُسافِرينَ — أنْ لا نَنْزِعَ خِفافَنا ثَلاثَةَ أيَّامٍ ولَيالِيهنَّ إلاَّ مِنْ جَنابَةٍ ، لَكِنْ مِنْ غائطٍ وبَوْلٍ ونَوْمٍ . فَقُلْتُ : هَلْ سَمِعْتَهُ يَذْكُرُ في الهَوَى شَيْئاً ؟ قالَ : نَعَمْ كُنَّا مَعَ رسول اللهِ صلى الله عليهِ وسلم في سَفَرٍ ، فَبَيْنَا نَحْنُ عِنْدَهُ إذْ نادَاهُ أعْرابي بصَوْتٍ لَهُ جَهْوَرِيٍّ : يامُحَمَّدُ ، فأجابَهُ رسولُ اللهِ صلى الله عليه وسلم نَحْواً مِنْ صَوْتِه : « هاؤُمُ » فَقُلْتُ لَهُ : وَيْحَكَ اغْضُضْ مِنْ صَوْتِكَ فإنَّكَ عِنْدَ النَّبيِّ صلى الله عليه وسلم ، وقَدْ نُهيتَ عَنْ هذا ! فقالَ : واللهِ لا أغْضُضُ . قالَ الأعْرابيُّ : المَرْءُ يُحِبُّ القَوْمَ ولَمَّا يَلْحَقْ بِهِمْ ؟ قالَ النَّبيُّ صلى الله عليه وسلم : « المَرْءُ مَعَ مَنْ أحَبَّ يَوْمَ القِيامَةِ » فَما

زَالَ يُحَدِّثُنَا حَتَّى ذَكَرَ بَاباً مِنَ الْمَغْرِبِ مَسِيرَةُ عَرْضِهِ أَوْ يَسِيرُ الرَّاكِبُ فِي عَرْضِهِ أَرْبَعِينَ أَوْ سَبْعِينَ عَاماً . قَالَ سُفْيَانُ أَحَدُ الرُّوَاةِ . قِبَلَ الشَّامِ خَلَقَهُ اللهُ تَعَالَى يَوْمَ خَلَقَ السَّمَاوَاتِ وَالأَرْضَ مَفْتُوحاً لِلتَّوْبَةِ لا يُغْلَقُ حَتَّى تَطْلُعَ الشَّمْسُ مِنْهُ » رواه الترمذي وغيره وقال: حديث حسن صحيح .

19. Hazrat Zirr Ibn Hubaish (R.A.A.) relates: 'I went to Hazrat Safwan Ibn Assal (R.A.A.) to inquire about the wiping out with the hands over the leather socks in the course of ablutions. He asked me: 'Zirr, what brings you here.' I replied, 'acquisition of knowledge.' He said: "Angels spread their wings out of pleasure for one who seeks knowledge at what he seeks. I told him that some doubt has arisen in my mind concerning the wiping out the hands over leather socks in the course of ablutions after one has been to the privy or the urinal. Now, you are one of the Companions of the Holy Prophet (S.A.W.) and I have come to ask you. Did you hear him say anything on this subject?" He answered, 'Yes, he directed us that while on a journey, we need not take off our leather socks for washing the feet in the course of ablutions consecutively for three days and nights, except after consorting with your wives. In other cases, e.g. sleep, answering the calls of nature etc. mere possing of the hands over leather socks or shoes would suffice during that period." I then asked him, "Did you hear him say anything concerning love and affection.' He replied. 'We were with the Holy Prophet (S.A.W.) in the course of a journey when a rustic Arab called out to him in a loud and rough tone, "O Muhammad:" the Holy Prophet (S.A.W.) answered him almost in the same tone, "Well, I am here." I said to the Arab, "Woe be to thee; don't talk loudly in his (S.A.W.) presence. Thus has Allah directed us." Replying to me he said: "I will not soften my tone, and then adressing the Holy Prophet (S.A.W.) again he said, 'What about a man who loves a people but has not yet been admitted to the same." The Holy Prophet (S.A.W.) answered, 'On the Day of Judgment a person will be in the company of those he loves.' He then resuming his talk with us referred to a gateway somewhere in the West, both the ends of the width of which could be covered by a rider in forty or seventy years. (Hazrat) Sufyan, who is one of the narrators of this Hadis, adds: This gateway is towards the direction of Syria. Allah has created this gateway alongwith the universe and the heavens. It is open for repentance and will not be closed till the Sun rises from the West.

This Hadis is classed as Hasan. (*Tirmizi and others*).

٢٠ ـ وَعَنْ أَبِي سَعِيدٍ سَعْدِ بْنِ مَالِكِ بْنِ سِنَانٍ الْخُدْرِيِّ رضي الله عنه أن نَبِيَّ الله صلى الله عليه وسلم قال : « كَانَ فِيمَنْ كَانَ قَبْلَكُمْ رَجُلٌ

قَتَلَ تِسْعَةً وَتِسْعِينَ نَفْساً ، فَسَأَلَ عَنْ أَعْلَمِ أَهْلِ الأَرْضِ ، فَدُلَّ عَلَى رَاهِبٍ ، فَأَتَاهُ فقال : إِنَّهُ قَتَلَ تِسْعَةً وتِسْعِينَ نَفْساً ، فَهَلْ لَهُ مِنْ تَوْبَةٍ ؟ فقالَ : لا ، فَقَتَلَهُ فَكَمَّلَ بِهِ مِائَةً ، ثُمَّ سَأَلَ عَنْ أَعْلَمِ أَهْلِ الأَرْضِ ، فَدُلَّ عَلَى رَجُلٍ عَالِمٍ فقالَ : إِنَّهُ قَتَلَ مِائَةَ نَفْسٍ فَهَلْ لَهُ مِنْ تَوْبَةٍ ؟ فقالَ : نَعَمْ ، وَمَنْ يَحُولُ بَيْنَهُ وَبَيْنَ التَّوْبَةِ ؟ انْطَلِقْ إِلَى أَرْضِ كَذَا وكَذَا ، فَإِنَّ بِهَا أُنَاساً يَعْبُدُونَ اللهَ تعالى فَاعْبُدِ اللهَ مَعَهُمْ ، وَلا تَرْجِعْ إِلَى أَرْضِكَ فَإِنَّهَا أَرْضُ سُوءٍ ، فانْطَلَقَ حَتَّى إِذَا نَصَفَ الطَّرِيقَ أَتَاهُ المَوْتُ ، فَاخْتَصَمَتْ فيه مَلائِكَةُ الرَّحْمَةِ ومَلائِكَةُ العَذَابِ . فقالَتْ مَلائِكَةُ الرَّحْمَةِ : جَاءَ تَائِباً مُقْبِلاً بِقَلْبِهِ إِلَى اللهِ تعالى ، وقالَتْ مَلائِكَةُ العَذَابِ : إِنَّهُ لَمْ يَعْمَلْ خَيْراً قَطُّ ، فَأَتَاهُمْ مَلَكٌ في صُورَةِ آدَمِيٍّ فَجَعَلُوهُ بَيْنَهُمْ ـ أَيْ حَكَماً ـ فقالَ : قِيسُوا مَا بَيْنَ الأَرْضَيْنِ فَإِلَى أَيَّتِهِمَا كَانَ أَدْنَى فَهُوَ لَهُ ، فَقَاسُوا فَوَجَدُوهُ أَدْنَى إِلَى الأَرْضِ الَّتِي أَرَادَ ، فَقَبَضَتْهُ مَلائِكَةُ الرَّحْمَةِ ، متفقٌ عليه

وفي روايةٍ في الصحيح : « فَكَانَ إِلَى القَرْيَةِ الصَّالِحَةِ أَقْرَبَ بِشِبْرٍ ، فَجُعِلَ مِنْ أَهْلِهَا » وفي رِوايةٍ في الصحيح : « فَأَوْحَى اللهُ تَعَالَى إِلَى هَذِهِ أَنْ تَبَاعَدِي ، وإِلَى هَذِهِ أَنْ تَقَرَّبِي ، وقالَ : قِيسُوا مَا بَيْنَهُمَا ، فَوَجَدُوهُ إِلَى هَذِهِ أَقْرَبَ بِشِبْرٍ فَغُفِرَ لَهُ » . وفي روايةٍ : « فَنَأَى بِصَدْرِهِ نَحْوَهَا » .

20. Hazrat Abu Sa'eed Khudri (R.A.A.) relates that the Holy Prophet (S.A.W.) said: 'A person from amongst a nation of the past, having slain ninety-nine persons, inquired as to who was the most learned person in the world. He was directed to a monk (who had given up the world). He (The self-confessing assassin) went to the hermit and said: 'I have killed ninety-nine persons. Is there any chance of repentance left for me?" The hermit answered: "No". The man killed the hermit also and completed his century of victims. The killer asked again, 'Who is the most learned person in this world?' He was directed to a learned man. Accordingly he went to him and said. 'I have killed one hundred persons. Is there any hope of repentance left for me?' The learned man said, "Yes, nothing can stand between you and repentance: Proceed to such and such land. In this land are (pious) people who worship God. Join them in the worship of God and do not return to your home country because it is an evil place. The man started for this land. He had covered only half the distance when he met with his death. A dispute arose between the angel of mercy and the angel of torment as to who should take charge of his soul. The former pleaded that since he had come as a penitent turning towards God, and the latter contended that the deceased had never done a good deed. Then there arrived an angel disguised as a human and the contending angels agreed that he should be the arbiter between them. He directed them to measure the distance between the two lands. To whichever he is nearer, to that one he belongs. So they carried out the measurement and found the land of pious persons to be closer. The angel of mercy thus took charge of him. *(Bukhari and Muslim)*.

One version says that he was found to be closer to the land of the pious persons by the width of a hand and was thus accounted as one of them. Another version is that God directed the space on one side to expand and the space on the other to shrink, and then said; "Now carry out the measurement." It was found that he was nearer to his goal by the width of a hand and was forgiven. It is also related that he came closer by crawling.

٢١ – وعَنْ عَبْدِ اللهِ بنِ كَعْبِ بنِ مَالكٍ ، وكَانَ قائِد كَعْبٍ رضي الله عنه مِن بَنيهِ حِينَ عَمِيَ قَالَ : سَمِعْتُ كَعْبَ بنَ مَالكٍ رضي الله عنه يُحَدِّثُ بحَديثِهِ حِين تَخَلَّفَ عن رسول الله صلى الله عليه وسلم في غَزْوَةِ تَبُوكَ . قَالَ كَعْبٌ : لَمْ أتَخَلَّفَ عَنْ رسول الله ، صلى الله عليه وسلم ، في غَزْوَة غَزَاهَا قَطُّ إلاَّ في غَزْوَةِ تَبُوكَ ، غَيْرَ أنّي قَدْ تَخَلَّفْتُ في غَزْوَةِ بَدْرٍ ، ولَمْ يُعَاتَبْ أحَد تَخَلَّفَ عَنْهُ ، إنَّمَا خَرَجَ رسول الله صلى الله عليه وسلم والمُسْلِمُونَ يُرِيدُونَ عير قُرَيْش حتَّى جَمَعَ اللهُ تعَالَى بَيْنَهُمْ وبَيْنَ عَدُوِّهِمْ عَلَى غَيْرِ ميعَادٍ . ولَقَدْ شَهِدْتُ مَعَ رسولِ اللهِ صلى الله عليه وسلم لَيْلَةَ العَقَبَةِ حِينَ تَوَاثَقْنَا عَلَى الإسْلامِ ، ومَا أُحِبُّ أنَّ لِي بِهَا مَشْهَدَ بَدْرٍ ، وإنْ كانَتْ بَدْرٌ أذْكَرَ في النَّاسِ مِنْهَا .

وكَانَ مِن خَبَرِي حِينَ تَخَلَّفْتُ عَنْ رسولِ الله ، صلى الله عليه وسلم ، في غَزْوَةِ تَبُوكَ أنّي لَمْ أكُنْ قَطُّ أقْوَى وَلا أيْسَرَ مِنّي حِينَ تَخَلَّفْتُ عَنْهُ في تِلْكَ الغَزْوَةِ ، وَاللهِ مَا جَمَعْتُ قَبْلَهَا رَاحِلَتَيْنِ قَطُّ حتَّى

جَمَعْتُهُمَا في تِلْكَ الْغَزْوَةِ ، وَلَمْ يَكُنْ رسول الله صلى الله عليه وسلم يُرِيدُ غَزْوَةً إلاَّ وَرَّى بِغَيْرِهَا حَتَّى كَانَتْ تِلْكَ الْغَزْوَةُ ، فَغَزَاهَا رسول الله صلى الله عليه وسلم في حَرٍّ شَدِيدٍ . وَاسْتَقْبَلَ سَفَراً بَعِيداً وَمَفَازاً وَاسْتَقْبَلَ عَدَداً كَثِيراً . فَجَلَّى لِلْمُسْلِمِينَ أَمْرَهُمْ لِيَتَأَهَّبُوا أُهْبَةَ غَزْوِهِمْ فَأَخْبَرَهُمْ بِوَجْهِهِمِ الَّذي يُرِيدُ ، وَالْمُسْلِمُونَ مَعَ رسولِ الله كَثِيرٌ وَلا يَجْمَعُهُمْ كِتَابُ حَافِظٍ « يُرِيدُ بِذَلِكَ الدِّيوَانَ » قالَ كَعْبٌ : فَقَلَّ رَجُلٌ يُرِيدُ أَنْ يَتَغَيَّبَ إلاَّ ظَنَّ أَنَّ ذَلِكَ سَيَخْفَى بِهِ مَالَمْ يَنْزِلْ فيهِ وَحْيٌ مِنَ اللهِ ، وَغَزَا رسول الله صلى الله عليه وسلم تِلْكَ الْغَزْوَةَ حِينَ طَابَتِ الثِّمَارُ وَالظِّلالُ فَأَنَا إِلَيْهَا أَصْعَرُ فَتَجَهَّزَ رسول الله صلى الله عليه وسلم وَالْمُسْلِمُونَ مَعَهُ ، وَطَفِقْتُ اغْدُو لِكَيْ اتَجَهَّزَ مَعَهُ ، فَأَرْجِعُ وَلَمْ أَقْضِ شَيْئاً ، وَأَقُولُ في نَفْسي : أَنَا قَادِرٌ عَلَى ذَلِكَ إِذَا أَرَدْتُ ، فَلَمْ يَزَلْ يَتَمَادَى بي حَتَّى اسْتَمَرَّ بالنَّاسِ الْجِدُّ ، فَأَصْبَحَ رسول الله صلى الله عليه وسلم غَادِياً وَالْمُسْلِمُونَ مَعَهُ ، وَلَمْ أَقْضِ مِنْ جِهَازِي شَيْئاً . ثُمَّ غَدَوْتُ فَرَجَعْتُ وَلَمْ أَقْضِ شَيْئاً ، فَلَمْ يَزَلْ يَتَمَادَى بي حَتَّى أَسْرَعُوا وَتَفَارَطَ الْغَزْوُ . فَهَمَمْتُ أَنْ أَرْتَحِلَ فَأُدْرِكَهُمْ . فَيَالَيْتَني فَعَلْتُ ، ثُمَّ لَمْ يُقَدَّرْ ذَلِكَ لي . فَطَفِقْتُ إِذَا خَرَجْتُ في النَّاسِ بَعْدَ خُرُوجِ رسول الله صلى الله عليه وسلم يَحْزُنُني أَنِّي لا أَرَى لِي أُسْوَةً . إِلاَّ رَجُلاً مَغْمُوصاً عَلَيْهِ في النِّفَاقِ . أَوْ رَجُلاً مِمَّنْ عَذَرَ اللهُ تعالَى مِنَ الضُّعَفَاءِ ، وَلَمْ يَذْكُرْني رسول الله صلى الله عليه وسلم حَتَّى بَلَغَ تَبُوكَ ، فقالَ وَهُوَ جَالِسٌ في الْقَوْمِ بِتَبُوكَ : ما فَعَلَ كَعْبُ بْنُ مَالِكٍ ؟ فقالَ رَجُلٌ مِنْ بَنِي سَلِمَةَ : يا رسول الله حَبَسَهُ بُرْدَاهُ . وَالنَّظَرُ في عِطْفَيْهِ . فقالَ لَهُ مُعَاذُ بْنُ جَبَلٍ رضي الله عنه : بِئْسَ ما قُلْتَ ! وَاللهِ يا رسول الله ما عَلِمْنَا عَلَيْهِ إِلاَّ خَيْراً ، فَسَكَتَ رسولُ الله صلى الله عليه وسلم . فَبَيْنَا هُوَ عَلَى ذَلِكَ رَأى رَجُلاً مُبْيِضاً يَزُولُ بِهِ السَّرَابُ ، فقالَ رسولُ الله صلى

الله عليه وسلم : كُنْ أبَا خَيْثَمَةَ ، فَإذَا هُوَ أبُو خَيْثَمَةَ الأنْصَارِيُّ وَهُوَ الَّذي تَصَدَّقَ بِصَاعِ التَّمْرِ حِينَ لَمَزَهُ المُنَافِقُونَ قَالَ كَعْبٌ : فَلَمَّا بَلَغَنِي أنَّ رسول الله صلى الله عليه وسلم قَدْ تَوَجَّهَ قَافِلاً مِنْ تَبُوكَ حَضَرَنِي بَثِّي ، فَطَفِقْتُ أتَذَكَّرُ الكَذِبَ وَأقُولُ : بِمَ أخْرُجُ مِنْ سَخَطِهِ غَداً وَأسْتَعِينُ عَلَى ذلكَ بِكُلِّ ذِي رَأْيٍ مِنْ أهْلِي ، فَلَمَّا قِيلَ : إنَّ رسول الله صلى الله عليه وسلم قَدْ أظَلَّ قَادِماً زَاحَ عَنِّي البَاطِلُ حَتَّى عَرَفْتُ أنِّي لم أنجُ مِنْهُ بِشَيْءٍ أبَداً ، فَأجْمَعْتُ صِدْقَهُ ، وَأصْبَحَ رسول الله صلى الله عليه وسلم قَادِماً ، وكَانَ إذا قَدِمَ مِنْ سَفَرٍ بَدَأَ بالمَسْجِدِ فَرَكَعَ فِيهِ رَكْعَتَيْنِ ثُمَّ جَلَسَ لِلنَّاسِ ، فَلَمَّا فَعَلَ ذلكَ جَاءَهُ المُخَلَّفُونَ يَعْتَذِرُونَ إلَيْهِ وَيَحْلِفُونَ لَهُ ، وَكَانُوا بِضْعاً وَثَمَانِينَ رَجُلاً فَقَبِلَ مِنْهُمْ عَلانِيَتَهُمْ وَبَايَعَهُمْ وَاسْتَغْفَرَ لَهُمْ وَوَكَلَ سَرَائِرَهُمْ إلَى الله تَعَالَى حَتَّى جِئْتُ . فَلَمَّا سَلَّمْتُ تَبَسَّمَ تَبَسُّمَ المُغْضَبِ ثُمَّ قَالَ : تَعَالَ ، فَجِئْتُ أمْشِي حَتَّى جَلَسْتُ بَيْنَ يَدَيْهِ ، فقالَ لِي : مَا خَلَّفَكَ ؟ ألَمْ تَكُنْ قَدِ ابْتَعْتَ ظَهْرَكَ ! قَالَ قُلْتُ : يَارسولَ الله إنِّي والله لَوْ جَلَسْتُ عِنْدَ غَيْرِكَ مِنْ أهْلِ الدُّنْيَا لَرَأيْتُ أنِّي سَأخْرُجُ مِنْ سَخَطِهِ بِعُذْرٍ ، لَقَدْ أُعْطِيتُ جَدَلاً ، وَلَكِنَّنِي وَالله لَقَدْ عَلِمْتُ لَئِنْ حَدَّثْتُكَ اليَوْمَ حَدِيثَ كَذِبٍ تَرْضَى بِهِ عَنِّي لَيُوشِكَنَّ الله يُسْخِطُكَ عَلَيَّ، وَإنْ حَدَّثْتُكَ حَدِيثَ صِدْقٍ تَجِدُ عَلَيَّ فِيهِ إنِّي لأرْجُو فِيهِ عُقْبَى الله عَزَّ وَجَلَّ ، وَالله مَا كَانَ لِي مِنْ عُذْرٍ ، وَالله مَا كُنْتُ قَطُّ أقْوَى ولا أيْسَرَ مِنِّي حِينَ تَخَلَّفْتُ عَنْكَ .

قالَ : فقالَ رسول الله صلى الله عليه وسلمَ : « أمَّا هَذَا فَقَدْ صَدَقَ ، فَقُمْ حَتَّى يَقْضِيَ اللهُ فِيكَ » وَسَارَ رِجَالٌ مِنْ بَنِي سَلِمة فاتَّبَعُونِي ، فَقَالُوا لِي : وَالله مَا عَلِمْنَاكَ أذْنَبْتَ ذَنْباً قَبْلَ هَذَا ، لَقَدْ عَجَزْتَ فِي أنْ لاتَكُونَ اعْتَذَرْتَ إلَى رسول الله صلى الله عليه وسلم بِمَا اعْتَذَرَ إليهِ المُخَلَّفُونَ

فَقَدْ كَانَ كَافِيَكَ ذَنْبَكَ اسْتِغْفَارُ رسول الله صلى الله عليه وسلم لَكَ . قَالَ : فوالله ما زَالُوا يُؤَنِّبُونَنِي حَتَّى أَرَدْتُ أَنْ أَرْجِعَ إِلَى رسول الله صلى الله عليه وسلم فأُكَذِّبَ نَفْسِي ، ثُمَّ قُلْتُ لَهُمْ : هَلْ لَقِيَ هَذَا مَعِيَ مِنْ أَحَدٍ ؟قَالُوا : نَعَمْ لَقِيَهُ مَعَكَ رَجُلانِ قَالا مِثْلَ مَا قُلْتَ ، وَقِيلَ لَهُمَا مِثْلُ مَا قِيلَ لَكَ ، قَالَ قُلْتُ : مَنْ هُمَا ؟ قَالُوا : مُرَارَةُ بْنُ الرَّبِيعِ الْعَمْرِيُّ،وهِلال بْن أُمَيَّةَ الْوَاقِفِيُّ ؟ قالَ : فَذَكَرُوا لِي رَجُلَيْنِ صَالِحَيْنِ قَدْ شَهِدَا بَدْراً فِيهِمَا أُسْوَةٌ . قالَ : فَمَضَيْتُ حِينَ ذَكَرُوهُمَا لِي.وَنَهَى رسول الله صلى الله عليه وسلم عَنْ كَلامِنَا أَيُّهَا الثَّلاثَةُ مِنْ بَيْنِ مَنْ تَخَلَّفَ عَنْهُ ، قالَ : فاجْتَنَبَنَا النَّاسُ — أَوْ قالَ : تَغَيَّرُوا لَنَا — حَتَّى تَنَكَّرَتْ لِي فِي نَفْسِي الأَرْضُ ، فَمَا هِيَ بالأَرْضِ الَّتِي أَعْرِفُ ، فَلَبِثْنَا عَلَى ذلكَ خَمْسِينَ لَيْلَةً . فَأَمَّا صَاحِبَايَ فَاسْتَكَانَا وَقَعَدَا فِي بُيُوتِهِمَا يَبْكِيَانِ ، وَأَمَّا أَنَا فَكُنْتُ أَشَبَّ الْقَوْمِ وَأَجْلَدَهُمْ ، فَكُنْتُ أَخْرُجُ فَأَشْهَدُ الصَّلاةَ مَعَ الْمُسْلِمِينَ ، وَأَطُوفُ فِي الأَسْوَاقِ وَلا يُكَلِّمُنِي أَحَدٌ ، وَآتِي رسول الله صلى الله عليه وسلم فَأُسَلِّمُ عَلَيْهِ ، وَهُوَ فِي مَجْلِسِهِ بَعْدَ الصَّلاةِ ، فَأَقُولُ فِي نَفْسِي : هَلْ حَرَّكَ شَفَتَيْهِ بِرَدِّ السَّلامِ أَمْ لا ؟ ثُمَّ أُصَلِّي قَرِيباً مِنْهُ وَأُسَارِقُهُ النَّظَرَ ، فَإِذَا أَقْبَلْتُ عَلَى صَلاتِي نَظَرَ إِلَيَّ ، وَإِذَا الْتَفَتُّ نَحْوَهُ أَعْرَضَ عَنِّي ، حَتَّى إِذَا طَالَ ذلكَ عَلَيَّ مِنْ جَفْوَةِ الْمُسْلِمِينَ مَشَيْتُ حَتَّى تَسَوَّرْتُ جِدَارَ حَائِطِ أَبِي قَتَادَةَ وَهُوَ ابْنُ عَمِّي وَأَحَبُّ النَّاسِ إِلَيَّ ، فَسَلَّمْتُ عَلَيْهِ فَوَاللهِ مَا رَدَّ عَلَيَّ السَّلامَ ، فَقُلْتُ لَه : يَا أَبَا قَتَادَةَ أَنْشُدُكَ بِاللهِ هَلْ تَعْلَمُنِي أُحِبُّ اللهَ وَرَسُولَه صلى الله عليه وسلم؟فَسَكَتَ ، فَعُدْتُ فَنَاشَدْتُهُ فَسَكَتَ ، فَعُدْتُ فَنَاشَدْتُه فَقَالَ : اللهُ وَرَسُولُهُ أَعْلَمُ . فَفَاضَتْ عَيْنَايَ ، وَتَوَلَّيْتُ حَتَّى تَسَوَّرْتُ الْجِدَارَ ، فَبَيْنَا أَنَا أَمْشِي فِي سُوقِ الْمَدِينَةِ إِذَا نَبَطِي مِنْ نَبَطِ أَهْلِ الشَّامِ مِمَّنْ قَدِمَ بِالطَّعَامِ يَبِيعُهُ بِالْمَدِينَةِ يَقُولُ : مَنْ يَدُلُّ عَلَى كَعْبِ بْنِ مَالِكٍ ؟ فَطَفِقَ النَّاسَ يُشِيرُونَ لَه إِلَيَّ حَتَّى جَاءَنِي فَدَفَعَ

إليَّ كتاباً من ملك غسان ، وكنت كاتباً . فقرأته فإذا فيه : أما بعد فإنه قد بلغنا أن صاحبك قد جفاك ، ولم يجعلك الله بدار هوان ولا مضيعة ، فالحق بنا نواسك فقلت حين قرأتها : وهذه أيضاً من البلاء فتيممت بها التنور فسجرتها ، حتى إذا مضت أربعون من الخمسين واستلبث الوحي إذا رسول رسول الله صلى الله عليه وسلم يأتيني ، فقال : إن رسول الله صلى الله عليه وسلم يأمرك أن تعتزل امرأتك ، فقلت: أطلقها ، أم ماذا أفعل؟ قال : لا بل اعتزلها فلا تقربنها ، وأرسل إلى صاحبي بمثل ذلك . فقلت لامرأتي: الحقي بأهلك فكوني عندهم حتى يقضي الله في هذا الأمر ، فجاءت امرأة هلال بن أمية رسول الله صلى الله عليه وسلم فقالت له : يارسول الله إن هلال بن أمية شيخ ضائع ليس له خادم ، فهل تكره أن أخدمه؟ قال : لا ، ولكن لا يقربنك . فقالت : إنه والله ما به من حركة إلى شيء ، ووالله مازال يبكي منذ كان من أمره ما كان إلى يومه هذا . فقال لي بعض أهلي : لو استأذنت رسول الله صلى الله عليه وسلم في امرأتك ، فقد أذن لامرأة هلال بن أمية أن تخدمه ؟ فقلت : لا أستأذن فيها رسول الله صلى الله عليه وسلم ، وما يدريني ماذا يقول رسول الله صلى الله عليه وسلم إذا استأذنته فيها وأنا رجل شاب ! فلبثت بذلك عشر ليال ، فكمل لنا خمسون ليلة من حين نهى عن كلامنا .

ثم صليت صلاة الفجر صباح خمسين ليلة على ظهر بيت من بيوتنا ، فبينا أنا جالس على الحال التي ذكر الله تعالى منا ، قد ضاقت علي نفسي وضاقت علي الأرض بما رحبت ، سمعت صوت صارخ أوفى على سلع يقول بأعلى صوته : يا كعب بن مالك أبشر ، فخررت ساجداً ، وعرفت أنه قد جاء فرج . فآذن رسول الله

صلى الله عليه وسلم النَّاسَ بِتَوْبَةِ الله عزَّ وَجَلَّ عَلَيْنَا حِينَ صَلَّى صَلاةَ الْفَجْرِ فَذَهَبَ النَّاسُ يُبَشِّرُونَنَا ، فَذَهَبَ قِبَلَ صَاحِبَيَّ مُبَشِّرُونَ ، وَرَكَضَ رَجُلٌ إِلَيَّ فَرَساً وَسَعَى سَاعٍ مِنْ أَسْلَمَ قِبَلِي وَأَوْفَى عَلَى الْجَبَلِ ، وَكَانَ الصَّوْتُ أَسْرَعَ مِنَ الْفَرَسِ ، فَلَمَّا جَاءَنِي الَّذِي سَمِعْتُ صَوْتَهُ يُبَشِّرُنِي نَزَعْتُ لَهُ ثَوْبَيَّ فَكَسَوْتُهُمَا إِيَّاهُ ببشارته ، وَالله مَا أَمْلِكُ غَيْرَهُمَا يَوْمَئِذٍ ، وَاسْتَعَرْتُ ثَوْبَيْنِ فَلَبِسْتُهُمَا وَانْطَلَقْتُ أَتَأَمَّمُ رسول الله صلى الله عليه وسلم يَتَلَقَّانِي النَّاسُ فَوْجاً فَوْجاً يُهَنِّئُونَنِي بِالتَّوْبَةِ وَيَقُولُونَ لِي : لِتَهْنِكَ تَوْبَةُ الله عَلَيْكَ ، حَتَّى دَخَلْتُ الْمَسْجِدَ فَإِذَا رسول الله صلى الله عليه وسلم جَالِسٌ حَوْلَهُ النَّاسُ ، فَقَامَ طَلْحَةُ بْنُ عُبَيْدِ الله رضي الله عنه يُهَرْوِلُ حَتَّى صَافَحَنِي وَهَنَّأَنِي ، والله مَا قَامَ رَجُلٌ مِنَ الْمُهَاجِرِينَ غَيْرُهُ ، فَكَانَ كَعْبٌ لا يَنْسَاهَا لِطَلْحَةَ . قَالَ كَعْبٌ : فَلَمَّا سَلَّمْتُ عَلَى رسول الله صلى الله عليه وسلم قال وَهُوَ يَبْرُقُ وَجْهُهُ مِنَ السُّرُورِ : أَبْشِرْ بِخَيْرِ يَوْمٍ مَرَّ عَلَيْكَ مُذْ وَلَدَتْكَ أُمُّكَ ، فَقُلْتُ : أَمِنْ عِنْدِكَ يارسول الله أَمْ مِنْ عِنْدِ الله ؟ قَالَ : لا بَلْ مِنْ عِنْدِ الله عَزَّوَجَلَّ ، وَكَانَ رسول الله صلى الله عليه وسلم إِذَا سُرَّ اسْتَنَارَ وَجْهُهُ حَتَّى كَأَنَّ وَجْهَهُ قِطْعَةُ قَمَرٍ ، وَكُنَّا نَعْرِفُ ذَلِكَ مِنْهُ ، فَلَمَّا جَلَسْتُ بَيْنَ يَدَيْهِ قُلْتُ : يا رسولَ الله إِنَّ مِنْ تَوْبَتِي أَنْ أَنْخَلِعَ مِنْ مَالِي صَدَقَةً إِلَى الله وَإِلَى رَسُولِهِ . فَقَالَ رسول الله صلى الله عليه وسلم : أَمْسِكْ عَلَيْكَ بَعْضَ مَالِكَ فَهُوَ خَيْرٌ لَكَ . فقلتُ : إِنِّي أُمْسِكُ سَهْمِي الَّذِي بِخَيْبَرَ . وَقُلْتُ : يَارَسُولَ الله إِنَّ الله تَعَالَى إِنَّمَا أَنْجَانِي بِالصِّدْقِ ، وَإِنَّ مِنْ تَوْبَتِي أَنْ لا أُحَدِّثَ إِلاَّ صِدْقاً مَا بَقِيتُ ، فَوَالله مَا عَلِمْتُ أَحَداً مِنَ الْمُسْلِمِينَ أَبْلاه الله تعالى فِي صِدْقِ الْحَدِيثِ مُنْذُ ذَكَرْتُ ذَلِكَ لِرَسُولِ الله صلى الله عليه وسلم أَحْسَنَ مِمَّا أَبْلانِي الله تعالى . وَالله مَا تَعَمَّدْتُ كِذْبَةً مُنْذُ قلتُ ذَلِكَ لِرسول الله صلى الله عليه وسلم إِلَى يَوْمِي هَذَا ، وَإِنِّي لأَرْجُو أَنْ يَحْفَظَنِي الله تعالى

فيمَا بقِيَ ، قال : فأنزَلَ الله تعالى : لَقَدْ تابَ اللهُ علَى النَّبيِّ وَالمُهَاجِرِينَ وَالأَنصَارِ الَّذينَ اتَّبعُوهُ في ساعةِ العُسْرَةِ حتَّى بلَغَ : إنَّهُ بِهِمْ رَءُوفٌ رَحِيمٌ . وعلَى الثَّلاثةِ الَّذينَ خُلِّفُوا حتَّى إذا ضاقتْ علَيْهِمُ الأَرضُ بِمَا رَحُبَتْ حتَّى بلَغَ : اتَّقُوا اللهَ وكُونُوا معَ الصَّادِقِينَ [التوبة: ١١٧ ، ١١٩] قالَ كَعْبٌ : واللهِ ما أنعَمَ اللهُ علَيَّ مِن نِعمةٍ قطُّ بعْدَ إذْ هداني اللهُ للإسْلام أعْظَمَ في نفْسي مِنْ صِدْقِي رسولَ الله صلى الله عليه وسلم أنْ لا أكُونَ كَذَبْتُهُ ، فأَهْلِكَ كما هلكَ الَّذينَ كَذَبُوا ؛ إنَّ الله تعالى قال للَّذينَ كَذَبُوا حينَ أنزَلَ الوَحْيَ شرَّ ما قالَ لأحَدٍ ، فقالَ الله تعالى : سَيَحْلِفُونَ باللهِ لَكُمْ إذَا انْقَلَبْتُمْ إلَيْهِمْ لِتُعْرِضُوا عَنْهُمْ فأعْرِضُوا عَنْهُمْ إنَّهُمْ رِجْسٌ ومأْوَاهُمْ جَهَنَّمُ جزَاءً بِمَا كانُوا يَكْسِبُونَ . يَحْلِفُونَ لَكُمْ لِتَرْضَوْا عنهُمْ فإنْ تَرْضَوْا عَنْهُمْ فإنَّ اللهَ لا يَرْضَى عَنِ القَوْمِ الفَاسقِينَ [التوبة : ٩٥ ، ٩٦] .

قالَ كَعْبٌ : كُنَّا خُلِّفْنَا أيُّهَا الثَّلاثةُ عَنْ أمْرِ أولئكَ الَّذينَ قَبِلَ منْهُمْ رسُولُ الله صلى الله عليه وسلم حِينَ حلَفُوا لَهُ ، فبَايَعَهُمْ واستغفرَ لهم ، وأرجأَ رسولُ الله صلى الله عليه وسلم أمْرَنا حتَّى قضَى الله تعالَى فيه بذلِكَ ؛ قال الله تعالى : (وَعلَى الثَّلاثَةِ الَّذينَ خُلِّفُوا) ولَيْسَ الَّذي ذكَرَ مِمَّا خُلِّفْنَا تخلُّفَنا عن الغَزْوِ ، وإنَّمَا هوَ تَخْليفُهُ إيَّانا وإرْجاؤُهُ أمْرَنا عمَّنْ حلَفَ له واعتَذَرَ إليهِ فقَبِلَ مِنهُ . متفقٌ عليه . وفي روايةٍ « أنَّ النَّبيَّ صلى الله عليه وسلم خرَجَ في غزْوةِ تبُوكَ يوْمَ الخميسِ ، وكانَ يُحِبُّ أنْ يخرُجَ يوْمَ الخميسِ » وفي رواية : « وكانَ لا يقْدَمُ مِن سفَرٍ إلاَّ نهاراً في الضُّحَى فإذَا قَدِمَ بدَأَ بالمسْجِدِ فصلَّى فيهِ ركْعتَيْنِ ثُمَّ جلَسَ فيهِ »

21. Hazrat Abdullah bin Ka'ab (R.A.A.) who had become his father's guide when the latter had become blind, recounts that he heard from his father, Hazrat Ka'ab Ibn Malik, a full account of the incident of his father's remaining behind the Holy Prophet (S.A.W.) when he proceeded on the campaign of Tabuk. Hazrat Ka'ab said: "I had accompanied the Holy Prophet (S.A.W.) in every campaign except that of Tabuk. I also could not join the Holy Prophet (S.A.W.) in the battle of Badr, and in that case there was no question of any penalty, for the Holy Prophet (S.A.W.) and the Muslims had in view only the reconnoitering of the Quraish caravan with no intention to fight. But nevertheless Allah brought about a clash between them and their enemies unexpectedly. I was present with the Holy Prophet (S.A.W.). But I do not want to compare my presence at Aqabah with my presence at Badr for all the fame of Badr, although at Aqabah we undertook solemnly to remain stead-fast in Islam. As regards my failure to accompany the Holy Prophet (S.A.W.) in the campaign of Tabuk I may elucidate my points. I was in very good health and had considerable money at the time of this campaign than at any other time. At this time I had two riding camels, and never before did I have two. Whenever the Holy Prophet (S.A.W.) decided on a campaign, he would not disclose this fact till the last moment. On this occasion firstly the season was mercilessly hot, the journey was long and tedious through deserts and inhospitable tracts without greenery or water and the number of the enemy was large. The Holy Prophet (S.A.W.) therefore had clearly warned the Muslims of the perils and risks in the campaign and asked them to make full preparations. The number of those ready to accompany the Holy Prophet (S.A.W.) on this mission was also large. No register would have been sufficient for writing down the names of all the Mujahids accompanying the Holy Prophet (S.A.W.). Most of those who did not want to go on jihad thought that their absence will go unnoticed unless their defection was disclosed through Divine revelation. Also the fruit on the trees had ripened and their shade had become thicker, and this fact also worked in my mind.

The Holy Prophet (S.A.W.) and his followers who had volunteered to accompany him busied themselves with the preparations for the venture. I used to go out in the morning with intentions to do something in connection with my preparation along with them, but would return without settling anything, saying to myself: 'There is enough time. I can get ready whenever I wish.' This went on and the Mulsims completed their preparations. At last the day came when the Holy Prophet (S.A.W.) started with his followers for the front, but I had not yet done anything for my departure. and the Muslims were already on the march. I thought I would go forth alone and overtake them. I wish I could have done so, but it was not destined to be so. Now when I went about in the town, it pained me much to see that among those who had been left behind like me, were either suspected hypocrites or were exempted from war service due to old age or some infirmity by Allah. I did not see any other person like me. The Holy Prophet (S.A.W.) made no mention of me till after he had arrived at Tabuk. There, while sitting among the people, one day he inquired. "What had happened to Ka'ab?" A man from the Bani Salimah tribe said: "O! Holy Prophet (S.A.W.) he (Ka'ab) did not come with us on account of his two robes and his pride for finery." On this Hazrat Mu'az Ibn Jabal rebuked the accuser by stating that he was unfair to Ka'ab. "O Prophet of Allah, we do not see anything wrong in Ka'ab." The Holy Prophet (S.A.W.) said nothing. At this time he (S.A.W.) observed someone at a distance in the desert clad in white and exclaimed: May it be Abu Khaisamah: and indeed he proved to be. He was the one who was taken as a beggar by the hypocrites, when he contributed a small quantity of dates. When I learnt that the Holy Prophet (S.A.W.) was returning home from Tabuk, I felt much anguish and started inventing false excuses in my mind which might help to save myself from his chastisement. I also consulted some members of my family with sound judgment. When I heard that the Holy Prophet's (S.A.W.) arrival was imminent I realized that no false excuse would help me, and I therefore decided to speak truth. He (S.A.W.) arrived the next morning. It was his (S.A.W) practice that when he returned from a journey he (S.A.W.) would go first to the mosque and offer two raka'ts of optional prayer, and then would meet the people. He (S.A.W.) did the same on this occasion too, and those who had stayed back from the campaign, came forward and began to put forward their excuses on oath. Such persons were a little over eighty. The Holy Prophet (S.A.W.) accepted their excuses re-newed their oaths, prayed for them for their forgiveness and committed to Allah whatever they had in their minds. When my turn came and I saluted him, he smiled; but anger was visible from his smile. He (S.A.W.) said: "Come forward." So, I stepped forward and sat down before him (S.A.W.). He (S.A.W.) asked: "What kept you back?" Had you not purchased your mount?" I replied, "O Messenger of Allah (S.A.W.), were I confronted by someone other than your august self, i.e. any other man of the world, I could manage to escape his displeasure by some equivocation but I know that if I were to concoct before you (S.A.W.) a false story today, which might even convince you (S.A.W.) but certainly Allah will soon arouse your (S.A.W.) anger against me over something else. On the other hand, if I tell you (S.A.W.) the truth and you get angry with me, I might still hope for mercy from Almighty Allah. By Allah I have no excuse. I was never so healthy and stronger and more moneyed than when I kept back myself from accompanying you (S.A.W.). The Holy Prophet (S.A.W.) said: 'This man has told the truth. Now withdraw, till Allah decides your case.' Some men of Bani Salimah followed me out of the mosque and remarked: 'We did not know that you have committed a fault before this; then why you failed to put an excuse before the Holy Prophet (S.A.W.) like others who had held back from the campaign? Your crime would have been forgiven through the prayer of the Holy Prophets (S.A.W.).' They kept on reproaching me so vehemently that I felt inclined to go back to the Holy Prophet (S.A.W.) and contradict my statement. Then I asked them "Is there any other case similar to mine?" They said. "The cases of **Murararah bin Rabi'a 'Amiri and Hilal bin Umayyah Waqifi.**" Among these were two persons who were virtuous and had not only taken part in the battle of Badr, but also possessed many good qualities, and as such I felt strengthened in my original thinking.

Thereafter the Holy Prophet (S.A.W.) asked the Muslims not to talk with three of us. People used to avoid us, and became strangers for us. I thought as if I was in an alien country. This state of affairs lasted for fifty days. My other two companions were so much overtaken by shame and misery that they retired from the world and shut themselves in their homes. But I being the youngest and the strongest of the three used to go out and join the Muslims in prayer and walked in the streets but nobody would talk to me. I used to present myself before the Holy Prophet (S.A.W.) when he sat in the mosque after prayer, and I would salute him, and was inquisitive to know whether he had moved his lips acknowledging my salutation or not. Moreover I used to stand in prayer near the Holy Prophet (S.A.W.) when I noted that he (S.A.W.) would look towards me when I was busy in my prayer and would look elsewhere when I looked towards him (S.A.W.) I was much tortured and in anguish on account of the stern attitude of the Muslims towards me. In this state, one day I went and climbed over the boundary wall of the garden of my cousin, and fast friend, Abu Qatadah, and saluted him, but he did not reply. I said to him: "Abu Qatadah, I ask you in the name of Allah! You must be aware that I love Allah and His Prophet (S.A.W.). But he kept quiet. I repeated my request. Still there was no reply from Qatadah. I repeated my request thrice," when he said: "Allah and His Prophet (S.A.W.) know better." On hearing this I could not hold my tears," and returned back home.

One day I was loitering in a market of Madina when I saw a peasant from Syria, who was selling food grains asking the people: Could some of you tell me the address of Ka'ab bin Malik? Somebody pointed towards me. The peasant came to me and gave a letter from the King of Ghassan. As I was literate enough I read it. Its contents were 'We have learnt that the person with whom you have associated (i.e. the Holy Prophet S.A.W.) is treating you unjustly. God has not made you to be disgraced and ill-treated. Come over to us and we shall make every effort to please you.' After reading this letter I said to myself: 'This too is a trial for me,' and I threw the letter into the oven.

When forty days out of 50 had passed away and no divine orders about us were revealed, a bearer of the Holy Prophet (S.A.W.) came to me and said: 'The Holy Prophet (S.A.W.) directs you not to cohabit with your wife.' I enquired: 'Should I divorce her or what should I do?' He said: 'No,only abstain from associating with her.' The Holy Prophet (S.A.W.) had issued similar orders to my two companions as well. As such I asked my wife to go to her parents and stay with them till Allah determines this matter.' Another person condemned like me, Hilal bin Umayyah's wife went to the Holy Prophet (S.A.W.) and prayed 'Messenger of Allah (S.A.W.) Hilal bin Umayyah is old and is unable to look after himself, nor has he an attendant. Would it therefore, displease you if I continue to serve him?' He (S.A.W.) said: 'Provided he does not cohabit with you.' She said: '(He being old) has no desire for sex. Ever since this incident, he is continuously weeping.' Some of my people suggested to me that I also seek the permission of the Holy Prophet (S.A.W.) so that my wife may also look after me as the wife of Hilal bin Umayyah does. 'I shall not bother the Holy Prophet (S.A.W.) for such permission because I did not know what he would say moreover I was young (unlike Hilal).'

Ten more days and nights passed like this since my social boycott and on the fifty-first morning, after the dawn prayer, I was sitting in my house in a depressed mood and the world in spite of its extent, as Allah the Almighty has described, seemed narrowing and small to me, I suddenly heard some one shout at the top of his voice from the crest of Mount Sala' 'O Ka'ab bin Malik be happy there is good news for you'. Immediately after hearing this I fell into prostration (to express my thanks) and realized that some means for my consolation have been found out. It seems that the Holy Prophet (S.A.W.) had informed the audience at the time of the dawn prayer that Allah, the Exalted has graciously accepted our repentance and as such several people had set out to break the happy news to all of us. Some went to my other two companions. One rushed on horse towards my house. A member of the tribe of Aslam climbed up the hill (and loudly announced the news) and his voice was heard by me before the arrival of the horseman. When the person, whose voice I had heard, arrived to congratulate me I presented both the pieces of my garments to him. By Allah on that day I had no extra dress to wear, and therefore had to borrow a pair, and started to pay my respects before the Holy Prophet (S.A.W.). On my way to the Holy Prophet's house I came across groups and crowds of people who congratulated me, on the acceptance of my repentance by Allah. Ultimately when I reached the mosque I found the Holy Prophet (S.A.W.) sitting there surrounded by his followers. Of them, only (Hazrat) Talaha Ibn Ubaidullah stood and rushed towards me, and shaking my hand, congratulated me. He was the only gentleman out of the Emigrants who received me so warmly and I have never forgotten this gesture of his.

Hazrat Ka'ab continuing his statement says: 'When I saluted the Holy Prophet (S.A.W.), his face was shining with joy' and he said: 'Be pleased with the best day of all the days that have passed since your birth.' I submitted: 'Messenger of Allah (S.A.W.) is this (favour) from your august self or from Allah?' He answered: 'Of course it is from Allah.' It was his practice that his happiness would be evident from his face which used to shine like a piece of moon, and thus we could guess that he (S.A.W.) was happy. After this I submitted to him: 'Messenger of Allah (S.A.W.), as a *coup de grace* to my repentance, I want to present my entire property to Allah and His Messenger (S.A.W.) to be spent in charity. He said: 'It would be better for you to continue retaining a part of your property. On this I said that I would hold back my share of property which is in Khaibar. I then further submitted: 'Messenger of Allah (S.A.W.).

Allah the Exalted, has granted me deliverance only on account of truth and therefore in order to finalise my repentance I resolve that for the rest of my life I shall speak nothing but truth. Since when I declared this before the Holy Prophet (S.A.W.), Allah, the Exalted, has not tried anyone so severely in the matter of telling the truth as He has tried me. To this day, since my declaration, I have never had any temptation to tell a lie, and I hope that Allah will continue to protect me against it during the rest of my life.

Allah, the Exalted revealed:

'Allah hath turned in mercy to the Prophet (S.A.W.) and to the Muhajirin and the Ansar who followed him in the hour of hardship. After the hearts of a party of them had almost swerved aside, then turned He unto them in mercy 'Lo' He is full of Pity, Merciful for them.

And to the three also (did He turn in mercy who were left behind, when the earth, vast as it is, was straitened for them, and their own souls were straitened for them till they bethought them that there is no refuge from Allah save toward Him. Then turned He unto them in mercy that they (too) might turn (repentant unto Him). Lo! Allah! He is the Relenting, the Merciful.

O ye who believe! Be careful of your duty to Allah, and be with the truthful. (9:117–119).

Hazrat Ka'ab continuing said that ever since Allah had bestowed the blessing of Islam upon him, the greatest boon was his telling the truth before the Holy Prophet (S.A.W.), and not lying to him and ruining himself as were ruined those who did tell lies to him. In His revelation Allah has severely condemned those who indulge in speaking lies. Allah says in the Holy Quran:

"They will swear by Allah unto you (that we were compelled to do so) when ye return unto them, that ye may let them be. Let them be, for Lo! they are unclean, and their abode is hell as the reward for what they used to earn. They swear unto you, that ye may accept them. Though ye accept them, Allah verily accepteth not wrong doing folk." (9:95–96).

Hazrat Ka'ab says that the cases of three of us except those who had made excuses on oath before the Holy Prophet (S.A.W.), were left hanging and which he (S.A.W.) had admitted and received their pledges and prayed for their salvation. But the Holy Prophet (S.A.W.) had kept our cases pending till Allah Almighty decided it Himself. When Allah the Exalted says.

"And to the three also 'did He turn in mercy who were left behind' (9:118).

It does not mean that we lagged behind from jihad but it means that Allah deferred our cases till after the disposal of the cases of those persons who pleaded on oath before the Holy Prophet (S.A.W.) and he accepted their excuses. Another version says that the Holy Prophet

(S.A.W.) left for Tabuk campaign on Thursday, and he liked to go on journey on Thursday. Yet another tradition says he used to return from a journey, in day light before noon. Immediately on arrival he would go to the mosque and offer two *Rakats* of *Nafil* (optional) prayers and then would sit down there. (*Bukhari and Muslim*)

٢٢ – وَعَنْ أبي نُجَيْدٍ – بضمّ النّون وفتح الجيم – عِمْرَانَ بْنِ الحُصَيْنِ الخُزَاعِيِّ رضي الله عنهما أنَّ امْرَأةً مِنْ جُهَيْنَةَ أتَتْ رسول الله صلى الله عليه وسلم وَهِيَ حُبْلَى مِنَ الزِّنَا ، فقالَتْ : يا رسول الله أصَبْتُ حَدّاً فَأقِمْهُ عَلَيَّ ، فَدَعَا نَبِيُّ الله صلى الله عليه وسلم وَلِيَّهَا فقالَ : أحْسِنْ إلَيْهَا ، فإذَا وَضَعَتْ فَأْتِنِي ، فَفَعَلَ فَأمَرَ بِهَا نَبِيُّ الله صلى الله عليه وسلم ، فَشُدَّتْ عَلَيْهَا ثِيَابُهَا ، ثُمَّ أمَرَ بِهَا فَرُجِمَتْ ، ثُمَّ صَلَّى عَلَيْهَا . فقالَ لَهُ عُمَرُ : تُصَلِّي عَلَيْهَا يا رسول الله وقَدْ زَنَتْ ؟ قالَ : لَقَدْ تَابَتْ تَوْبَةً لَوْ قُسِمَتْ بَيْنَ سَبْعِينَ مِنْ أهْلِ المدينةِ لَوَسِعَتْهُمْ ، وَهَلْ وَجَدْتَ أفضَلَ مِنْ أنْ جَادَتْ بِنَفْسِهَا لِلهِ عزَّ وجل ؟ ! » رواه مسلم

22. Hazrat Imran bin Husain, reports that a woman belonging to the Juhainah tribe, became pregnant as a result of adultery. She came to the Holy Prophet (S.A.W.) and admitted her guilt and requested for being punished in accordance with the Quranic injunction. The Holy Prophet (S.A.W.) sent for her guardian and asked him to treat her well and to bring her back to him after delivery. The guardian did carry out the orders and brought her back to Holy Prophet (S.A.W.) who adjudicated and asked for her execution as the Holy Quran says. For this purpose, her clothes were tied round her body and she was stoned to death. Thereafter, the Holy Prophet (S.A.W.) led her funeral prayers. Hazrat Umar Farooq then remarked: "O Prophet of Allah! She is an adulterous and you are leading her funeral prayers." The Holy Prophet (S.A.W.) said: "Yes, she had repented in such a way that if this repentance is distributed among 70 persons of Madina then it would have covered them all. There can not be a better and higher degree of repentance than this, in which case she chose to speak the truth at the cost of her life simply for the sake of Allah's pleasure. (*Muslim*).

٢٣ – وَعَنِ ابْنِ عَبَّاسٍ رضي الله عَنهما أن رسول الله صلى الله عليه وسلم قال : « لَوْ أنَّ لابْنِ آدَمَ وَادِياً مِنْ ذَهَبٍ أحَبَّ أنْ يَكُونَ لَهُ وَادِيَانِ ، وَلَنْ يَمْلأَ فَاهُ إلاَّ التُّرَابُ ، وَيَتُوبُ اللهُ عَلَى مَنْ تَابَ » متفقٌ عليه

23. Hazrat Ibn-i-Abbas and Hazrat Anas-Ibn Malik reported that the Holy Prophet (S.A.W.) has said that if the son of Adam had in his possession a vale filled with gold, he would not remain content with it and would aspire for two more such vales. His mouth (greediness) can only be filled (satisfied) with the dust of grave (i.e. when he dies). Allah the merciful accepts repentance from every body who offers repentance to Him. *(Agreed upon)*

٢٤ ـ وَعَنْ أَبي هُرَيْرَةَ رضي الله عنه أن رسول الله صلى الله عليه وسلم قال: « يَضْحَكُ اللهُ سُبْحَانَهُ وَتَعَالَى إِلَى رَجُلَيْنِ يَقْتُلُ أَحَدُهُمَا الآخَرَ يَدْخُلانِ الْجَنَّةَ . يُقَاتِلُ هَذَا في سَبِيلِ اللهِ فَيُقْتَلُ ، ثُمَّ يَتُوبُ اللهُ عَلَى الْقَاتِلِ فَيُسْلِمُ فَيُسْتَشْهَدُ » متفقٌ عليه

24. Hazrat Abu Hurairah relates that the Holy Prophet (S.A.W.) has said that Allah the Most High will be very happy with two types of persons, one of whom kills the other and both of them will go to heaven (after their death) one of them having been already slain in the cause of Allah, is in heaven. Thereafter Allah, will have mercy for the assassin, who will embrace Islam, and will fight for the sake of Allah and will be slain (and enter paradise). *(Bukhari and Muslim)*.

* * * * * * * * * * *

CHAPTER 3

Resignation

قال الله تعالى : يَا أَيُّهَا الَّذِينَ آمَنُوا اصْبِرُوا وَصَابِرُوا [آل عمران : ٢٠٠] وقال تعالى وَلَنَبْلُوَنَّكُمْ بِشَيْءٍ مِنَ الْخَوْفِ وَالْجُوعِ وَنَقْصٍ مِنَ الأَمْوَالِ وَالأَنْفُسِ وَالثَّمَرَاتِ وَبَشِّرِ الصَّابِرِينَ [البقرة : ١٥٥] وقال تعالى : إِنَّمَا يُوَفَّى الصَّابِرُونَ أَجْرَهُمْ بِغَيْرِ حِسَابٍ [الزمر : ١٠] وقال تعالى : وَلَمَنْ صَبَرَ وَغَفَرَ إِنَّ ذَلِكَ لَمِنْ عَزْمِ الأُمُورِ [الشورى: ٤٣]

وقال تعالى : اسْتَعِينُوا بالصَّبْرِ وَالصَّلاةِ إِنَّ اللهَ مَعَ الصَّابِرِينَ [البقرة : ١٥٣]

وقال تعالى : وَلَنَبْلُوَنَّكُمْ حَتَّى نَعْلَمَ الْمُجَاهِدِينَ مِنْكُمْ وَالصَّابِرِينَ [محمد : ٣١] وَالآياتُ في الأَمْرِ بالصَّبْرِ وَبَيَانِ فَضْلِه كَثِيرَةٌ مَعْرُوفَةٌ

Allah the exalted says:

7. O ye who believe! Endure, out-do all others in endurance, be ready, and observe your duty to Allah, in order that ye may succeed. (3:200).
8. And surely we shall try you with something of fear and hunger, and loss of wealth and lives and crops; but give glad tidings to the steadfast. (2:155).
9. Verily the steadfast will be paid their wages without stint. (39:10).
10. And verily whoso is patient and forgiveth lo! that, verily, is (of) the steadfast heart of things. (42:43).
11. O ye who believe! Seek help in steadfastness and prayer. Lo! Allah is with the steadfast. (2:153).
12. And verily we shall try you till we know those of you who strive hard (for the cause of Allah) and the steadfast, and till we test your record. (47:31).

There are many verses praising resignation and calling upon the Muslims to have recourse to the same.

٢٥ – وَعَنْ أَبي مَالِكٍ الحَارِثِ بنِ عَاصِمٍ الأَشْعَرِيِّ رضي الله عنه قَالَ: قَالَ رسول الله صلى الله عليه وسلم: «الطُّهُورُ شَطْرُ الإيمَانِ، وَالحَمْدُ للهِ تَمْلأُ المِيزَانَ، وَسُبْحَانَ اللهِ وَالحَمْدُ للهِ تَمْلآنِ – أَوْ تَمْلأُ – مَا بَيْنَ السَّمٰوَاتِ وَالأَرْضِ، وَالصَّلاةُ نُورٌ، وَالصَّدَقَةُ بُرْهَانٌ، وَالصَّبْرُ ضِيَاءٌ، وَالقُرْآنُ حُجَّةٌ لَكَ أَوْ عَلَيْكَ. كُلُّ النَّاسِ يَغْدُو، فَبَائِعٌ نَفْسَهُ فَمُعْتِقُهَا، أَوْ مُوبِقُهَا» رواه مسلم

25. Hazrat Abu Malik Ash'ari says that the Holy Prophet (S.A.W.) has said that cleanliness is equal to half the faith and to say '*Alhamdo Lillah*' meaning all the praise is for Allah helps the scale of actions to outweigh; the utterance of '*Subhan Allah*' (Holy is Allah) and '*Alhamdo Lillah*' (All the praise is for Allah) are good enough to fill the space between the heavens and the earth (with blessings). The *Salat* is light, alms giving is proof (of one's faith), and to be steadfast is as good as light, and the Holy Quran is a plea in your favour or against you (as the case may be). Everyone begins his morning ready to bargain with his soul as a stake and frees it or loses it (*Muslim*).

Note: With the dawn of the day a person embarks upon his day's works and if he keeps his eyes on the Day of Judgement in his actions, then he frees himself from the torture of that Day; and if he prefers his wordly affairs (gains) over those of the Hereafter, then he is surely the loser.

٢٦ ـ وَعَنْ أَبِي سَعِيد سَعْد بْنِ مَالِكِ بْنِ سِنَانٍ الْخُدْرِي رضي الله عنهما : أَنَّ نَاساً مِنَ الأَنْصَارِ سَأَلُوا رسول الله صلى الله عليه وسلم فَأَعْطَاهُمْ . ثُمَّ سَأَلُوهُ فَأَعْطَاهُمْ . حَتَّى نَفِدَ مَاعِنْدَه . فَقَالَ لَهُمْ حِينَ أَنْفَقَ كُلَّ شَيْءٍ بِيَدِهِ : « مَا يَكُنْ عِنْدِي مِن خَيْرٍ فَلَنْ أَدَّخِرَهُ عَنْكُمْ ، وَمَنْ يَسْتَعْفِفْ يُعِفَّهُ الله ، وَمَنْ يَسْتَغْنِ يُغْنِهِ الله . وَمَنْ يَتَصَبَّرْ يُصَبِّرْهُ الله . وَمَا أُعْطِيَ أَحَدٌ عَطَاءً خَيْراً وَأَوْسَعَ مِنَ الصَّبْرِ » متفقٌ عليه

26. Hazrat Abu Sa'eed Khudri (R.A.A.) relates that some people from among the Ansar requested the Holy Prophet (S.A.W.) to give them something, and he gave them; they asked again and he gave them till he exhausted all that he had. Then he said to them; 'Whenever there is anything with me, I do not hesitate to give you. Remember: One who desires chastity, Allah makes him chaste; One who wants contentment, Allah makes him contented; and the person who aspires for steadfastness, Allah bestows steadfastness upon him. No one has been awarded a bounty better than patience and submission, (*Bukhari and Muslim*)

٢٧ ـ وَعَنْ أَبِي يَحْيَى صُهَيْبِ بْنِ سِنَانٍ رضي الله عنه قال : قال رسول الله صلى الله عليه وسلم : « عَجَباً لِأَمْرِ الْمُؤْمِنِ إِنَّ أَمْرَهُ كُلَّهُ لَهُ خَيْرٌ ، وَلَيْسَ ذَلِكَ لِأَحَدٍ إِلَّا لِلْمُؤْمِنِ : إِنْ أَصَابَتْهُ سَرَّاءُ شَكَرَ فَكَانَ خَيْراً لَهُ ، وَإِنْ أَصَابَتْهُ ضَرَّاءُ صَبَرَ فَكَانَ خَيْراً لَه » رواه مسلم

27. Hazrat Suhaib bin Sinan (R.A.A.) relates that the Holy Prophet (S.A.W.) said: 'The case of a believer is wonderful; there is good for him in everything, and this characteristic is exclusively for him alone. If he experiences something pleasant, he is grateful to Allah and that is good for him; and if he comes across some adversity, he is patient and submissive and that too is good for him'. (*Muslim*).

٢٨ ـ وَعَنْ أَنَسٍ رضي الله عنه قال : لَمَّا ثَقُلَ النَّبِيُّ صلى الله عليه وسلم جَعَلَ يَتَغَشَّاهُ الْكَرْبُ . فَقَالَتْ فَاطِمَةُ رضي الله عنها : وَاكَرْبَ أَبَتَاه . فَقَالَ : « لَيْسَ عَلَى أَبِيكِ كَرْبٌ بَعْدَ الْيَوْمِ » فَلَمَّا مَاتَ قَالَتْ : يَاأَبَتَاه أَجَابَ رَبّاً دَعَاه ، يَا أَبَتَاه جَنَّةُ الْفِرْدَوْسِ مَأْوَاه ، يَا أَبَتَاه إِلَى جِبْرِيلَ نَنْعَاه ؛ فَلَمَّا دُفِنَ قَالَتْ فَاطِمَةُ رضي الله عنها : أَطَابَتْ أَنْفُسُكُمْ أَنْ تَحْثُوا عَلَى رسول الله صلى الله عليه وسلم التُّرَابَ ؟ رواه البخاري

28. Hazrat Anas (R.A.A.) says that when the illness of the Holy Prophet (S.A.W.) became so grave as to make him unconscious, Hazrat Fatimah (R.A.A.) exclaimed: 'Ah, the suffering of my dear father': and the august father reassured her; 'There is no more suffering for thy father after today.' When he passed away she said: 'Ah, my father! he has responded to the call of his Lord; Ah, my father! heaven has become his abode; Ah, my father! We inform Angel Gabriel of your demise.' When he was laid to rest she said: 'How you could stand the agony of burying the Messenger of Allah?' (*Bukhari*).

٢٩ – وَعَنْ أَبِي زَيْدٍ أُسَامَةَ بْنِ زَيْدِ بْنِ حَارِثَةَ مَوْلَى رسول الله صلى الله عليه وسلم وَحِبِّهِ وَابْنِ حِبِّهِ ، رضي الله عنهما ، قال : أَرْسَلَتْ بِنْتُ النَّبِيِّ صلى الله عليه وسلم: إنَّ ابْنِي قَدِ احْتُضِرَ فَاشْهَدْنَا ، فَأَرْسَلَ يُقْرِئُ السَّلَامَ وَيَقُولُ : « إنَّ لِلهِ مَا أَخَذَ ، وَلَهُ مَا أَعْطَى ، وَكُلُّ شَيْءٍ عِنْدَهُ بِأَجَلٍ مُسَمًّى ، فَلْتَصْبِرْ وَلْتَحْتَسِبْ » فَأَرْسَلَتْ إلَيْهِ تُقْسِمُ عَلَيْهِ لَيَأْتِيَنَّهَا . فَقَامَ وَمَعَهُ سَعْدُ بْنُ عُبَادَةَ ، وَمُعَاذُ بْنُ جَبَلٍ ، وَأُبَيُّ ابْنُ كَعْبٍ ، وَزَيْدُ بْنُ ثَابِتٍ ، وَرِجَالٌ رضي الله عنهم ، فَرُفِعَ إلَى رسول الله صلى الله عليه وسلم الصَّبِيُّ ، فَأَقْعَدَهُ فِي حِجْرِهِ وَنَفْسُهُ تَقَعْقَعُ ، فَفَاضَتْ عَيْنَاهُ ، فَقَالَ سَعْدٌ : يا رسول الله مَا هَذَا؟ فَقَالَ : « هَذِهِ رَحْمَةٌ جَعَلَهَا اللهُ تَعَالَى فِي قُلُوبِ عِبَادِهِ » وفي روايةٍ : « فِي قُلُوبِ مَنْ شَاءَ مِنْ عِبَادِهِ وَإِنَّمَا يَرْحَمُ اللهُ مِنْ عِبَادِهِ الرُّحَمَاءَ » متفقٌ عليه

29. Hazrat Usamah bin Zaid (R.A.A.) a freed slave and trusted companion of the Holy Prophet (S.A.W.) relates that a daughter of the Holy Prophet (S.A.W.) sent for him as her son was on the verge of death. He sent his salutation to her with the Message: 'To Allah belongs that which He bestowed and to Him belongs that which He takes. Everything has its period fixed by Him. Let her be resigned (with the will of Allah), and hope for His grace and recompense? She repeated her request begging him in the name of Allah to see her. He stood up and started to her house accompanied by Hazrat S'ad bin 'Ubadah (R.A.A.), Hazrat Zaid bin Sabit (R.A.A.) and others. When he reached there, the child was presented to him (S.A.W.) and he (S.A.W.) took it in his lap. Seeing the agony of the child his eyes started shedding tears, whereupon Hazrat Sa'ad (R.A.A.) said: 'O Messenger of Allah, what is this?' He (S.A.W.) replied: 'This is compassion which Allah has placed in the hearts of His servants (and according to another version in the hearts of such of His servants as He has willed) and Allah has compassion on such of His servants as are compassionate.' (*Bukhari and Muslim*)

٣٠ ــ وَعَنْ صُهَيْبٍ رضي الله عنه أن رسول الله صلى الله عليه وسلم قال : « كَانَ مَلِكٌ فِيمَنْ كَانَ قَبْلَكُمْ ، وَكَانَ لَهُ سَاحِرٌ . فَلَمَّا كَبِرَ قَالَ لِلْمَلِكِ : إِنِّي قَدْ كَبِرْتُ فَابْعَثْ إِلَيَّ غُلَاماً أُعَلِّمْهُ السِّحْرَ ؛ فَبَعَثَ إِلَيْهِ غُلَاماً يُعَلِّمُهُ ، وَكَانَ فِي طَرِيقِهِ إِذَا سَلَكَ رَاهِبٌ ، فَقَعَدَ إِلَيْهِ وَسَمِعَ كَلَامَهُ فَأَعْجَبَهُ ، وَكَانَ إِذَا أَتَى السَّاحِرَ مَرَّ بِالرَّاهِبِ وَقَعَدَ إِلَيْهِ ، فَإِذَا أَتَى السَّاحِرَ ضَرَبَهُ ، فَشَكَا ذَلِكَ إِلَى الرَّاهِبِ فَقَالَ : إِذَا خَشِيتَ السَّاحِرَ فَقُلْ : حَبَسَنِي أَهْلِي ، وَإِذَا خَشِيتَ أَهْلَكَ فَقُلْ : حَبَسَنِي السَّاحِرُ .

فَبَيْنَمَا هُوَ عَلَى ذَلِكَ إِذْ أَتَى عَلَى دَابَّةٍ عَظِيمَةٍ قَدْ حَبَسَتِ النَّاسَ فَقَالَ : الْيَوْمَ أَعْلَمُ آلسَّاحِرُ أَفْضَلُ أَمِ الرَّاهِبُ أَفْضَلُ ؟ فَأَخَذَ حَجَراً فَقَالَ : اللَّهُمَّ إِنْ كَانَ أَمْرُ الرَّاهِبِ أَحَبَّ إِلَيْكَ مِنْ أَمْرِ السَّاحِرِ فَاقْتُلْ هَذِهِ الدَّابَّةَ حَتَّى يَمْضِيَ النَّاسُ ، فَرَمَاهَا فَقَتَلَهَا وَمَضَى النَّاسُ ، فَأَتَى الرَّاهِبَ فَأَخْبَرَهُ . فَقَالَ لَهُ الرَّاهِبُ : أَيْ بُنَيَّ أَنْتَ الْيَوْمَ أَفْضَلُ مِنِّي ، قَدْ بَلَغَ مِنْ أَمْرِكَ مَا أَرَى ، وَإِنَّكَ سَتُبْتَلَى ، فَإِنِ ابْتُلِيتَ فَلَا تَدُلَّ عَلَيَّ ، وَكَانَ الْغُلَامُ يُبْرِئُ الْأَكْمَهَ وَالْأَبْرَصَ ، وَيُدَاوِي النَّاسَ مِنْ سَائِرِ الْأَدْوَاءِ . فَسَمِعَ جَلِيسٌ لِلْمَلِكِ كَانَ قَدْ عَمِيَ ، فَأَتَاهُ بِهَدَايَا كَثِيرَةٍ فَقَالَ : مَا هَهُنَا لَكَ أَجْمَعُ إِنْ أَنْتَ شَفَيْتَنِي ، فَقَالَ : إِنِّي لَا أَشْفِي أَحَداً ، إِنَّمَا يَشْفِي اللهُ تَعَالَى ، فَإِنْ آمَنْتَ بِاللهِ تَعَالَى دَعَوْتُ اللهَ فَشَفَاكَ ، فَآمَنَ بِاللهِ تَعَالَى فَشَفَاهُ اللهُ تَعَالَى ، فَأَتَى الْمَلِكَ فَجَلَسَ إِلَيْهِ كَمَا كَانَ يَجْلِسُ فَقَالَ لَهُ الْمَلِكُ : مَنْ رَدَّ عَلَيْكَ بَصَرَكَ ؟ قَالَ : رَبِّي . قَالَ : وَلَكَ رَبٌّ غَيْرِي ؟! قَالَ : رَبِّي وَرَبُّكَ اللهُ ، فَأَخَذَهُ فَلَمْ يَزَلْ يُعَذِّبُهُ حَتَّى دَلَّ عَلَى الْغُلَامِ ، فَجِيءَ بِالْغُلَامِ فَقَالَ لَهُ الْمَلِكُ : أَيْ بُنَيَّ قَدْ بَلَغَ مِنْ سِحْرِكَ مَا تُبْرِئُ الْأَكْمَهَ وَالْأَبْرَصَ وَتَفْعَلُ وَتَفْعَلُ فَقَالَ : إِنِّي لَا أَشْفِي أَحَداً ، إِنَّمَا يَشْفِي اللهُ تَعَالَى ، فَأَخَذَهُ فَلَمْ يَزَلْ

يُعَذِّبُهُ حَتَّى دَلَّ عَلَى الرَّاهِبِ ؛ فَجِيءَ بِالرَّاهِبِ فَقِيلَ لَهُ : ارْجِعْ عَنْ دِينِكَ ، فَأَبَى ، فَدَعَا بِالمِنْشَارِ فَوَضَعَ المِنْشَارَ فِي مَفْرِقِ رَأْسِهِ ، فَشَقَّهُ حَتَّى وَقَعَ شِقَّاهُ ، ثُمَّ جِيءَ بِجَلِيسِ المَلِكِ فَقِيلَ لَهُ : ارْجِعْ عَنْ دِينِكَ فَأَبَى ، فَوُضِعَ المِنْشَارُ فِي مَفْرِقِ رَأْسِهِ ، فَشَقَّهُ بِهِ حَتَّى وَقَعَ شِقَّاهُ ، ثُمَّ جِيءَ بِالغُلَامِ فَقِيلَ لَهُ : ارْجِعْ عَنْ دِينِكَ فَأَبَى ، فَدَفَعَهُ إِلَى نَفَرٍ مِنْ أَصْحَابِهِ فَقَالَ : اذْهَبُوا بِهِ إِلَى جَبَلِ كَذَا وَكَذَا فَاصْعَدُوا بِهِ الجَبَلَ ، فَإِذَا بَلَغْتُمْ ذِرْوَتَهُ فَإِنْ رَجَعَ عَنْ دِينِهِ وَإِلَّا فَاطْرَحُوهُ ، فَذَهَبُوا بِهِ فَصَعِدُوا بِهِ الجَبَلَ فَقَالَ : اللَّهُمَّ اكْفِنِيهِمْ بِمَا شِئْتَ ، فَرَجَفَ بِهِمُ الجَبَلُ فَسَقَطُوا ، وَجَاءَ يَمْشِي إِلَى المَلِكِ ، فَقَالَ لَهُ المَلِكُ : مَا فَعَلَ بِأَصْحَابِكَ ؟ فَقَالَ : كَفَانِيهِمُ اللهُ تعالى ، فَدَفَعَهُ إِلَى نَفَرٍ مِنْ أَصْحَابِهِ فَقَالَ : اذْهَبُوا بِهِ فَاحْمِلُوهُ فِي قُرْقُورٍ وَتَوَسَّطُوا بِهِ البَحْرَ ، فَإِنْ رَجَعَ عَنْ دِينِهِ وَإِلَّا فَاقْذِفُوهُ ، فَذَهَبُوا بِهِ فَقَالَ : اللَّهُمَّ اكْفِنِيهِمْ بِمَا شِئْتَ ، فَانْكَفَأَتْ بِهِمُ السَّفِينَةُ فَغَرِقُوا ، وَجَاءَ يَمْشِي إِلَى المَلِكِ . فَقَالَ لَهُ المَلِكُ : مَا فَعَلَ بِأَصْحَابِكَ ؟ فَقَالَ : كَفَانِيهِمُ اللهُ تعالى . فَقَالَ لِلْمَلِكِ إِنَّكَ لَسْتَ بِقَاتِلِي حَتَّى تَفْعَلَ مَا آمُرُكَ بِهِ . قَالَ : مَا هُوَ ؟ قَالَ : تَجْمَعُ النَّاسَ فِي صَعِيدٍ وَاحِدٍ ، وَتَصْلُبُنِي عَلَى جِذْعٍ ، ثُمَّ خُذْ سَهْمًا مِنْ كِنَانَتِي ، ثُمَّ ضَعِ السَّهْمَ فِي كَبِدِ القَوْسِ ثُمَّ قُلْ : بِسْمِ اللهِ رَبِّ الغُلَامِ ، ثُمَّ ارْمِنِي ، فَإِنَّكَ إِذَا فَعَلْتَ ذَلِكَ قَتَلْتَنِي . فَجَمَعَ النَّاسَ فِي صَعِيدٍ وَاحِدٍ ، وَصَلَبَهُ عَلَى جِذْعٍ ، ثُمَّ أَخَذَ سَهْمًا مِنْ كِنَانَتِهِ ، ثُمَّ وَضَعَ السَّهْمَ فِي كَبِدِ القَوْسِ ، ثُمَّ قَالَ : بِسْمِ اللهِ رَبِّ الغُلَامِ ، ثُمَّ رَمَاهُ فَوَقَعَ السَّهْمُ فِي صُدْغِهِ ، فَوَضَعَ يَدَهُ فِي صُدْغِهِ فَمَاتَ . فَقَالَ النَّاسُ : آمَنَّا بِرَبِّ الغُلَامِ ، فَأُتِيَ المَلِكُ فَقِيلَ لَهُ : أَرَأَيْتَ مَا كُنْتَ تَحْذَرُ قَدْ وَاللهِ نَزَلَ بِكَ حَذَرُكَ . قَدْ آمَنَ النَّاسُ . فَأَمَرَ بِالأُخْدُودِ بِأَفْوَاهِ السِّكَكِ فَخُدَّتْ وَأُضْرِمَ فِيهَا النِّيرَانُ وَقَالَ : مَنْ لَمْ يَرْجِعْ عَنْ دِينِهِ فَأَقْحِمُوهُ فِيهَا أَوْ قِيلَ لَهُ : اقْتَحِمْ ، فَفَعَلُوا حَتَّى جَاءَتِ امْرَأَةٌ وَمَعَهَا صَبِيٌّ لَهَا ،

فَتَقَاعَسَتْ أَنْ تَقَعَ فِيهَا ، فَقَالَ لَهَا الْغُلَامُ : يَا أُمَّاهْ اصْبِرِي فَإِنَّكِ عَلَى الْحَقِّ ، رواه مسلم

30. Hazrat Suhaib Roomi (R.A.A.) relates that the Holy Prophet (S.A.W.) said: 'Among the ancient peoples there was a king who had a magician (in his service). When the latter grew old, he said to the king. 'Since I am getting old, please depute a young man whom I could teach magic.' Accordingly the king sent to him a young man to be taught the art of magic. In the young man's way to the magician, lived a monk with whom the boy used to sit and listened to his talk. He was so pleased with the discourse of the monk that every time he went to the magician, he would sit with the monk on the way. This would make him late. The magician would therefore, beat him, and the young man complained to the monk of this. He told him: 'When you are afraid of the magician say to him 'My people detained me; and when you apprehend some questioning from the people of your house, say to them: 'I am late on account of the monk.' This stratagem continued for some time. Once the young man saw that a huge beast had blocked the passage of the people, the young man said to himself. 'Now I can ascertain whether the magician is better or the monk.' So he took up a stone and said: 'Allah!. If the conduct of the monk is more to Thy liking than the practice of the magician, then do Thou bring about the death of this beast, so that the people can pass;' and he then hit the beast with the stone and killed it, thus enabling the people to pass; The young-man told the monk of this, who said to him: 'Son, today you have taken a lead over me and I think that now you have arrived at a stage when you might be harmed. Should that happen, do not disclose my whereabouts.'

The young-man started curing people suffering from blindness from birth, leprosy and other diseases. This news reached a royal courtier who had become blind. He went to the young-man with many presents and said; "All this will be yours if you will cure me.' The young-man said to him: 'I do not cure anyone. It is Allah who alone grants cure. If you will declare your faith in Allah, I will pray for you and He will grant you health.' As such he declared his faith in Allah who restored his sight. He thereafter went to the royal court and sat there as usual. The king asked him 'who has restored thy sight?' The man answered: 'My Allah'. The king inquired; 'Have you a God beside me?' He replied: 'Allah is your sustainer as well as my sustainer'. The king ordered the courtier to be arrested and tortured till he disclosed the name of the young-man who was brought before the monarch who said to him: 'Son, have you become so adept in magic that you can cure people suffering from blindness, leprosy and other ailments?' The boy said: 'I do not cure anyone. It is Allah who heals.' Then he was also arrested and tortured till he let the king know the name and address of the monk who was likewise summoned and directed to repudiate his faith, but he refused. The king sent for a saw which was placed in the middle of the monk's head and he was cut down in two: Thereafter the King's courtier was sent for and asked to renounce his faith. He also declined and consequently was cut down. Then the young man was brought forward and asked to renounce his cult, but he also declined to do so. The king entrusting the young man to his men asked them: 'Take him to such and such mountain and when you reach the top, and if he still refuses to renounce his faith, throw him down from the top.' They took him to the top of the mountain. There he supplicated: 'Allah! Help me free from these in whatever manner You deem fit'. Accordingly an earth-quake shook the mountain, and the king's men fell down. The young-man came back to the king who asked: 'What has happened to your companions?' He answered: 'Allah has saved me from them.' He was then handed over to another group of men who were asked to take him in a small boat to the sea and in case of persistence in refusing to abandon his faith, to hurl him into the sea. As such they took him alongwith them, and then he prayed: 'Allah! Deliver me from these persons in whatever manner You may like!' The boat sank with its load and the king's men were drowned, and the young man again walked back to the king who asked him 'What have thy companions done?' He answered: 'Allah has rescured me from them' and added: 'You will not be able to kill me unless you do what I tell you.' The king inquired: 'What is that?' The young man answered "Assemble the people in an open space and hang me from the trunk of a palm-tree." Then take an arrow from my quiver and placing it in the middle of a bow say: In the name of Allah, the Lord of this young man; and shoot the arrow at me. If you do this you will be able to kill me.' The king proceeded accordingly. The people were made to assemble in an open space, the young-man was hanged from the trunk of a palm-tree, the king took an arrow from his quiver and placing it in the middle of a bow said: 'In the name of Allah, the Lord of this young-man;" and shot it. The arrow struck the young-man in the temple who raised his hand to his temple and died.

Seeing this the people said: 'We declare our faith in the Lord of this young-man.' The king was informed: 'Look! what you have apprehended has happened; the people have declared their faith in the Lord of this young man.' The king ordered trenches to be excavated on both sides of the roads; when they were ready fire was lighted in them. Then it was announced that any person refusing to forsake his faith, would be thrown in the fire-lit trenches, or asked to jump in. This went on. A woman came forward accompanied by a boy but hesitated to be thrown in the fire whereupon the boy encouraging her said. "Mother! Be steady; you are on the right path. (*Muslim*).

٣١ — وَعَنْ أَنَسٍ رضي الله عنه قال : مَرَّ النَّبِيُّ صلى الله عليه وسلم بامْرَأَةٍ تَبْكِي عِنْدَ قَبْرٍ فَقَالَ : « اتَّقِي اللهَ وَاصْبِرِي » فَقَالَتْ : إِلَيْكَ عَنِّي ؛

فَإِنَّكَ لَمْ تُصَبْ بِمُصِيبَتِي! وَلَمْ تَعْرِفْهُ ، فَقِيلَ لَهَا : إِنَّهُ النَّبِيُّ صلى الله عليه وسلم ، فَأَتَتْ بَابَ النَّبِيِّ صلى الله عليه وسلم ، فَلَمْ تَجِدْ عِنْدَهُ بَوَّابِينَ، فقالت : لَمْ أَعْرِفْكَ ، فقالَ : « إِنَّمَا الصَّبْرُ عِنْدَ الصَّدْمَةِ الأُولَى » متفق عليه

وفي رواية لمُسْلِمٍ : « تَبْكِي عَلَى صَبِيٍّ لَهَا » .

31. Hazrat Anas bin Malik (R.A.A.) relates that the Holy Prophet (S.A.W.) once happened to pass by a woman who had lost her son and was crying over his grave. He said to her: 'Fear Allah and be steadfast.' The woman not knowing who he was retorted: 'Leave me alone; you have not suffered as I have.' Soon after someone told her that he was the Holy Prophet (S.A.W.). She proceeded to the house of the Holy Prophet (S.A.W.) and not finding any servant at the door, went in and said to him 'I had not recognised you.' He (S.A.W.) said: 'Steadfastness means to be resigned (to the will of Allah) at the time of the first shock of grief.' (*Bukhari and Muslim*).

٣٢ – وَعَنْ أَبِي هُرَيْرَةَ رَضِيَ الله عنه أَنَّ رسول الله صلى الله عليه وسلم قالَ : « يَقُولُ اللهُ تعالى : مَا لِعَبْدِي المُؤْمِنِ عِنْدِي جَزَاءٌ إِذَا قَبَضْتُ صَفِيَّهُ مِنْ أَهْلِ الدُّنْيَا ثُمَّ احْتَسَبَهُ إِلاَّ الجَنَّةَ » رواه البخاري

32. Hazrat Abu Hurairah (R..A.A.) relates that the Holy Prophet (S.A.W.) said: Allah, the Glorious, says: 'I have no better reward, other than Paradise, for a believing servant of mine who is patient and resigned, when I take away one of his beloved one among the most cherished things of the world'. (*Bukhari*).

٣٣ – وَعَنْ عَائِشَةَ رَضِيَ الله عنها أَنَّهَا سَأَلَتْ رسول الله صلى الله عليه وسلم عَنِ الطَّاعُونِ ، فَأَخْبَرَهَا أَنَّهُ كَانَ عَذَاباً يَبْعَثُهُ اللهُ تعالى عَلَى من يَشَاءُ ، فَجَعَلَهُ اللهُ تعالى رَحْمَةً لِلْمُؤْمِنِينَ ، فَلَيْسَ مِنْ عَبْدٍ يَقَعُ فِي الطَّاعُونِ فَيَمْكُثُ فِي بَلَدِهِ صَابِراً مُحْتَسِباً يَعْلَمُ أَنَّهُ لا يُصِيبُهُ إِلاَّ مَا كَتَبَ اللهُ لَهُ إِلاَّ كَانَ لَهُ مِثْلُ أَجْرِ الشَّهِيدِ » رواه البخاري

33. Hazrat Ayesha (R.A.A.) relates that once she asked the Holy Prophet (S.A.W.) as to what the plague was. The Holy Prophet (S.A.W.) told her that 'the plague is a divine punishment with which Allah punishes those He determines; but that He has made it a thing full of blessings for the Muslims. If a servant of Allah is afflicted with this epidemic and continues to stay in his town with patience, hoping for due recompense from Allah, realising that only that will happen to him which Allah has already determined for him, he will surely have a reward equal to that of a martyr.' (*Bukhari*)

٣٤ – وَعَنْ أَنَسٍ رضي الله عنه قال : سَمِعْتُ رسولَ الله صلى الله عليه وسلم يَقُولُ : « إنَّ اللهَ عزَّ وجلَّ قَالَ : إذَا ابْتَلَيْتُ عَبدِي بحَبِيبَتَيهِ فَصَبَرَ عَوَّضْتُهُ مِنهُمَا الجَنَّةَ » يُرِيدُ عَيْنَيْهِ ، رواه البخاري

34. Hazrat Anas bin Malik (R.A.A.) relates that he heard the Holy Prophet (S.A.W.) saying that Allah, the Exalted, says: 'When I afflict a servant of mine in respect of two of his most useful and precious organs (meaning his eyes) and he proves resigned to the affliction, I bestow Paradise on him in their stead'. (*Bukhari*).

٣٥ – وَعَنْ عَطَاء بْن أَبِي رَبَاحٍ قالَ : قالَ لِي ابْنُ عَبَّاسٍ رضي الله عنهما : أَلا أريكَ امرَأَةً مِنْ أَهْلِ الجَنَّةِ ؟ فَقُلْتُ : بَلَى ، قالَ : هَذِهِ المرْأَةُ السَّوْدَاءُ أَتَتِ النبيَّ صلى الله عليه وسلم فقَالَتْ : إنِّي أُصْرَعُ ، وَإنِّي أَتَكَشَّفُ ، فَادْعُ الله تعالى لِي قَالَ : « إنْ شِئْتِ صَبَرْتِ وَلَكِ الجَنَّةُ ، وَإنْ شِئْتِ دَعَوْتُ الله تعالى أنْ يُعَافِيَكِ » فَقَالَتْ : أَصْبِرُ ، فَقَالَتْ : إنِّي أَتَكَشَّفُ ، فَادْعُ اللهَ أَنْ لا أَتَكَشَّفَ ، فَدَعَا لَهَا . متفقٌ عليه

35. Hazrat Ata bin Abi Rabah (R.A.A.) relates that Hazrat Ibn Abbas (R.A.A.) said to him: 'May I show you a woman who is one of the dwellers of Paradise?' He said: 'Of course'. Hazrat Ibn Abbas then pointed to an ebony coloured woman and said: 'This woman came to the Holy Prophet (S.A.W.) and said: 'Messenger of Allah, I suffer from epilepsy and when I am under a fit my body gets exposed. Please pray to Allah for me.' He (S.A.W.) said: 'If you choose to be patient while suffering under this ailment, you will get paradise, or if you like I shall pray that Allah may cure you.' She said: 'I shall bear it with patience, but please pray that my body may not get exposed while I am under attack.' He (S.A.W.) prayed as desired by her. (*Bukhari and Muslim*).

٣٦ – وَعَنْ أَبِي عَبْدِ الرَّحْمنِ عَبْدِ الله بْن مَسْعُودٍ رضي الله عنه قال : كَأَنِّي أَنْظُرُ إلَى رسول الله صلى الله عليه وسلم يَحْكِي نَبِياً مِنَ الأَنْبِيَاء ، صَلَوَاتُ اللهِ وَسَلامُهُ عَلَيْهِمْ ، ضَرَبَهُ قَوْمُهُ فَأَدْمَوْهُ وَهُوَ يَمْسَحُ الدَّمَ عَنْ وَجْهِهِ ، يَقُولُ : « اللَّهُمَّ اغْفِرْ لِقَوْمِي فَإنَّهُمْ لا يَعْلَمُونَ » متفقٌ عليه

36. Hazrat Abdullah bin Mas'ud (R.A.A.) relates that he recollects as if he is looking at the Holy Prophet (S.A.W.) when he narrated an incident from the life of a prophet who was beaten and injured so severely by his people that he was bleeding profusely and he had to wipe away the blood from his face, while supplicating thus: 'Allah', forgive my people for they know not.' *(Bukhari and Muslim)*.

٣٧ – وَعَنْ أَبِي سَعِيدٍ وأَبِي هُرَيْرَةَ رضي الله عنهما عن النَّبيِّ صلى الله عليه وسلم قَالَ : « مَا يُصِيبُ المُسْلِمَ مِنْ نَصَب وَلا وَصَبٍ وَلا هَمٍّ وَلا حزَنٍ وَلا أذىً وَلا غَمٍّ ، حتَّى الشَّوْكَةُ يُشَاكُهَا إلاَّ كَفَّرَ اللهُ بِهَا مِنْ خَطَايَاهُ » متفقٌ عليه

37. Hazrat Abu Sa'eed (R.A.A.) and **Hazrat Abu Hurairah** (R.A.A.) related that the Holy Prophet (S.A.W.) said, 'For any trouble, illness, worry, grief, hurt or sorrow which afflicts a Muslim, even the pricking of a thorn, Allah removes in its stead some of his (minor) sins."

(Bukhari and Muslim).

٣٨ – وَعَنِ ابْنِ مَسْعُودٍ رضي الله عنه قال : دَخَلْتُ عَلَى النبي صلى الله عليه وسلم وَهُوَ يُوعَكُ فَقُلْتُ : يَارَسُولُ الله إنَّكَ تُوعَكُ وَعْكاً شَدِيداً قال : « أجَلْ إنِّي أوعَكُ كَمَا يُوعَكُ رَجُلانِ مِنْكُمْ » قُلْتُ : ذلكَ أنَّ لَكَ أجْرَيْنِ ؟ قال : « أجَلْ ذلكَ كَذلكَ مَا مِنْ مُسْلِمٍ يُصِيبُهُ أذىً ، شَوْكَةٌ فَمَا فَوْقَهَا إلاَّ كَفَّرَ اللهُ بِهَا سَيِّئَاتِهِ ، وَحُطَّتْ عَنْهُ ذُنُوبُهُ كَمَا تَحُطُّ الشَّجَرَةُ وَرَقَهَا » متفقٌ عليه

38. Hazrat Abdullah Ibn Mas'ud (R.A.A.) relates: 'I visited the Holy Prophet (S.A.W.) when he had fever.' I said to him: 'Messenger of Allah! You have very high fever.' He said: 'Indeed, the intensity of my fever is equivalent to two persons.' I said: 'That is because you have twice the recompense.' He (S.A.W.) said: 'That is so.' He further added: 'When a Muslim gets hurt with any harmful thing e.g. the prick of a thorn, or even more than this, Allah wipes out in its stead some of his (minor) sins which (sins) fall away from him as leaves shed from a tree. *(Bukhari and Muslim)*.

٣٩ – وَعَنْ أَبِي هُرَيْرَةَ رضي الله عنه قال : قال رسول الله صلى الله عليه وسلم « مَنْ يُرِدِ اللهُ بِهِ خَيْراً يَصِبْ مِنْهُ » : رواه البخاري

39. Hazrat Abu Hurairah (R.A.A.) relates that the Holy Prophet (S.A.W.) said: 'When Allah wants to favour somebody He tries him by putting him under some hardship'. *(Bukhari)*.

٤٠ — وَعَن أنَس رضي الله عنه قال : قال رسولُ الله صلى الله عليه وسلم :
« لا يَتَمَنَّيَنَّ أحَدُكُم المَوْتَ لِضُرٍّ أصابَهُ ، فإنْ كانَ لا بُدَّ فاعِلاً
فَلْيَقُل : اللَّهُمَّ أحْيِني ما كانَتِ الحَيَاةُ خَيْراً لي وَتَوَفَّني إذا كانَت
الوَفَاةُ خَيْراً لي » متفقٌ عليه

40. Hazrat Anas bin Malik says that the Holy Prophet (S.A.W.) said: 'No one should wish for death because of any misfortune that befalls him. If anybody should be so much hard up with life he should say: 'Allah, keep me alive so long as life is good for me, and I may die when death is better for me.' (*Bukhari and Muslim*).

٤١ — وَعَنْ أبي عبدِ الله خَبَّابِ بْنِ الأرَتِّ رضي الله عنه قال : شَكَوْنَا
إلَى رسول الله صلى الله عليه وسلم وَهُوَ مُتَوَسِّدٌ بُرْدَةً لَهُ في ظِلِّ الكَعْبَةِ ،
فَقُلْنَا : ألا تَسْتَنْصِرُ لَنَا ألا تَدْعُو لَنَا ؟ فَقَالَ : قَدْ كَانَ مَنْ قَبْلَكُم
يُؤْخَذُ الرَّجُلُ فَيُحْفَرُ لَهُ في الأرْضِ فَيُجْعَلُ فيهَا ، ثُمَّ يُؤْتَى بالمِنْشَارِ
فَيُوضَعُ عَلَى رَأْسِهِ فَيُجْعَلُ نِصْفَيْن ، وَيُمْشَطُ بِأمْشَاطِ الحَدِيدِ مَا دُونَ
لَحْمِهِ وَعَظْمِهِ ، مَا يَصُدُّهُ ذلكَ عَنْ دِينِهِ ، وَالله لَيُتِمَّنَّ اللهُ هَذَا الأمْرَ
حَتَّى يَسِيرَ الرَّاكِبُ مِنْ صَنْعَاءَ إلَى حَضْرَمَوْتَ لا يَخَافُ إلاَّ اللهَ وَالذِّئْبَ
عَلَى غَنَمِهِ ، وَلَكِنَّكُمْ تَسْتَعْجِلُونَ » رواه البخاري
وفي رواية : « وَهُوَ مُتَوَسِّدٌ بُرْدَةً وَقَدْ لَقِينَا مِنَ المُشْرِكِينَ شِدَّةً ».

41.Hazrat Khabbab bin Arat (R.A.A.) relates: 'We complained to the Holy Prophet (S.A.W.) of our increasing persecution by non-believers of Mecca. He was then reclining in the shade of the Ka'aba, having made a pillow of his sheet. We requested: 'Why do you not pray for heavenly help for us? Why do you not request for Allah's help for us?' He answered: 'From among those who have gone before you, a man would be caught and held in a pit dug for him in the earth and he would then be sawn in two with a saw placed over his head, or his flesh would be combed away from his bones with iron combs, but none of this would wean him awy from his faith. Allah will surely help Islam complete its mission, till a rider will proceed from San'aa to Hadharmaut, fearing nothing save Allah and the danger of the wolf concerning his sheep. But you appear to be in too much of a hurry.' (*Bukhari*).

٤٢ — وعن ابن مَسْعُودٍ رضي الله عنه قال : لَمَّا كَانَ يَوْمُ حُنَيْنٍ آثَرَ
رسول الله صلى الله عليه وسلم نَاساً في القِسْمَةِ : فَأعْطَى الأقْرَعَ بْنَ حَابِسٍ

مائَةً مِنَ الإبِلِ ، وَأَعْطَى عُيَيْنَةَ بْنَ حِصْنٍ مِثْلَ ذلِكَ ، وَأَعْطَى نَاساً مِنْ أَشْرَافِ الْعَرَبِ وَآثَرَهُمْ يَوْمَئِذٍ فِي الْقِسْمَةِ . فَقَالَ رَجُلٌ : وَاللهِ إِنَّ هٰذِهِ قِسْمَةٌ مَا عُدِلَ فِيهَا ، وَمَا أُرِيدَ فِيهَا وَجْهُ اللهِ . فَقُلْتُ : وَاللهِ لأُخْبِرَنَّ رَسُولَ اللهِ صلى الله عليه وسلم ، فأتيته فأخبرته بما قال ؛ فتغير وَجْهُهُ حَتَّى كَانَ كَالصِّرْفِ . ثُمَّ قال : « فَمَنْ يَعْدِلُ إِذَا لَمْ يَعْدِلِ اللهُ وَرَسُولُهُ ؟ ثُمَّ قال : يَرْحَمُ اللهُ مُوسَى قَدْ أُوذِيَ بِأَكْثَرَ مِنْ هٰذَا فَصَبَرَ » . فَقُلْتُ : لا جَرَمَ لا أَرْفَعُ إِلَيْهِ بَعْدَهَا حَدِيثاً . متفقٌ عليه

42. Hazrat Abdullah Ibn Mas'ud (R.A.A.) relates: 'In the course of fighting at Hunain, the Holy Prophet (S.A.W.) in order to win the hearts of some new converts to Islam favoured some people in the distribution of spoils. He gave Aqr'a ibn Habis and Uyainah Ibn Hisan a hundred camels each and showed favour also to some of the respectable Arab Leaders. A man objected to this and said: 'This is not a fair distribution aimed at winning the pleasure of Allah. (Hearing this) I resolved to apprise the Holy Prophet (S.A.W.) of this, and accordingly I went to him and informed about this (gossip). On hearing this the face of the Holy Prophet (S.A.W.) grew red and he said: 'Who will then do justice if Allah and His messenger do not:' and he further added: 'May Allah have mercy on Moses (Peace be upon him), he was troubled more than this, but he was patient.' Hearing this I said to myself: 'I shall never tell anything of this nature to him again'. (*Bukhari and Muslim*).

٤٣ – وَعَنْ أَنَسٍ رَضِيَ الله عنه قال : قال رسول الله صلى الله عليه وسلم : « إِذَا أَرَادَ اللهُ بِعَبْدِهِ خَيْراً عَجَّلَ لَهُ الْعُقُوبَةَ فِي الدُّنْيَا ؛ وَإِذَا أَرَادَ اللهُ بِعَبْدِهِ الشَّرَّ أَمْسَكَ عَنْهُ بِذَنْبِهِ حَتَّى يُوَافِيَ بِهِ يَوْمَ الْقِيَامَةِ » .

وَقَالَ النَّبِيُّ صلى الله عليه وسلم : « إِنَّ عِظَمَ الْجَزَاءِ مَعَ عِظَمِ الْبَلاءِ ، وَإِنَّ اللهَ تعالى إِذَا أَحَبَّ قَوْماً ابْتَلاهُمْ ، فَمَنْ رَضِيَ فَلَهُ الرِّضَا ، وَمَنْ سَخِطَ فَلَهُ السُّخْطُ » رواه الترمذي وَقَالَ : حَدِيثٌ حَسَنٌ .

43. Hazrat Anas bin Malik (R.A.A.) relates that the Holy Prophet (S.A.W.) said: 'When Allah wants to favour a servant of His, He involves him in some misfortune in this world earlier. And when He decrees evil for him, He gives him plenty of rope in this world, but would take him to task on the Day of Judgment.' He also said: 'Only hard work brings high reward and when Allah, the Exalted, likes a people, He puts it under trials. Therefore one who accepts and passes this trial, gets Allah's pleasure, and for him who eludes this trial will get His wrath. (*Tirmizi*).

٤٤ - وَعَنْ أَنَسٍ رضي الله عنه قال : كَانَ ابْنٌ لأَبي طَلْحَةَ رضي الله عنه يَشْتَكِي ، فَخَرَجَ أَبُو طَلْحَةَ ، فَقُبِضَ الصَّبيُّ ، فَلَمَّا رَجَعَ أبو طَلْحَةَ قال : مَا فَعَلَ ابْنِي ؟ قَالَتْ أُمُّ سُلَيْم وَهِيَ أُمُّ الصَّبيِّ : هُوَ أَسْكَنُ مَا كَانَ ، فَقَرَّبَتْ إلَيْهِ الْعَشَاءَ فَتَعَشَّى ، ثُمَّ أَصَابَ مِنْهَا ، فَلَمَّا فَرَغَ قَالَتْ: وَارُوا الصَّبيَّ ، فَلَمَّا أَصْبَحَ أَبُو طَلْحَةَ أَتَى رسولَ الله صلى الله عليه وسلم فأَخْبَرَهُ ، فَقَالَ : « أَعَرَّسْتُمُ اللَّيْلَةَ ؟ » قال : نَعَمْ ، قال : « اللَّهُمَّ بَارِكْ لَهُمَا » ؛ فَوَلَدَتْ غُلاماً ، فَقَالَ لِي أَبُو طَلْحَةَ : احْمِلْهُ حَتَّى تَأْتِيَ بهِ النبي صلى الله عليه وسلم ، وَبَعَثَ مَعَهُ بِتَمَرَاتٍ ، فَقَالَ : « أَمَعَهُ شَيْءٌ ؟ » قال : نَعَمْ ، تَمَرَاتٌ ، فَأَخَذَهَا النَّبيُّ صلى الله عليه وسلم فَمَضَغَهَا ، ثُمَّ أَخَذَهَا مِنْ فِيهِ فَجَعَلَهَا في فِي الصَّبيِّ . ثُمَّ حَنَّكَهُ وَسَمَّاهُ عَبْدَ الله . متفقٌ عليه .

وفي روايةٍ لِلْبُخَارِيِّ : قال ابْنُ عُيَيْنَةَ : فَقَالَ رَجُلٌ مِنَ الأَنْصَارِ : فَرَأَيْتُ تِسْعَةَ أَوْلاد كُلُّهُمْ قَدْ قَرَؤُوا الْقُرْآنَ ، يَعْنِي مِنْ أَوْلادِ عَبْدِ الله الْمَوْلُودِ .

وفي روايةٍ لمسلِم : مَاتَ ابْنٌ لأَبي طَلْحَةَ مِنْ أُمِّ سُلَيْمٍ ، فَقَالَتْ لأَهْلِهَا : لاتُحَدِّثُوا أَبَا طَلْحَةَ بابنِهِ حَتَّى أَكُونَ أَنَا أُحَدِّثُهُ ، فَجَاء فَقَرَّبَتْ إلَيْهِ عَشاءً فَأَكَلَ وَشَرِبَ ، ثُمَّ تَصَنَّعَتْ لَهُ أَحْسَنَ مَا كَانَتْ تَصَنَّعُ قَبْلَ ذلِكَ ، فَوَقَعَ بهَا ، فَلَمَّا أَنْ رَأَتْ أَنَّهُ قَدْ شَبِعَ وَأَصَابَ مِنْهَا قَالَتْ: يَا أَبَا طَلْحَةَ ، أَرَأَيْتَ لَوْ أَنَّ قَوْماً أَعَارُوا عَارِيَتَهُمْ أَهْلَ بَيْتٍ فَطَلَبُوا عَارِيَتَهُمْ ، أَلَهُمْ أَنْ يَمْنَعُوهُمْ ؟ قَالَ : لا ، فَقَالَتْ : فَاحْتَسِبْ ابْنَكَ . قالَ : فَغَضِبَ ، ثُمَّ قال : تَرَكْتِني حَتَّى إذَا تَلَطَّخْتُ ثُمَّ أَخْبَرْتِنِي بِابْنِي ؛ فَانْطَلَقَ حَتَّى أَتَى رسول الله صلى الله عليه وسلم فَأَخْبَرَهُ بِمَا كَانَ ، فَقَالَ رسولُ الله صلى الله عليه وسلم : « بَارَكَ اللهُ في لَيْلَتِكُمَا » قال : فَحَمَلَتْ ، قال : وَكَانَ رسول الله صلى الله عليه وسلم في سَفَرٍ وَهِيَ مَعَهُ ، وكَانَ رسولُ الله صلى الله عليه وسلم إذَا أَتَى الْمَدِينَةَ مِنْ سَفَرٍ لا يَطْرُقُهَا طُرُوقاً فَدَنَوْا مِنَ الْمَدِينَةِ ، فَضَرَبَهَا الْمَخَاضُ ،

فَاحْتَبَسَ عَلَيْهَا أَبُو طَلْحَةَ ، وَانْطَلَقَ رسولُ الله صلى الله عليه وسلم
قَالَ : يَقُولُ أَبُو طَلْحَةَ : إِنَّكَ لَتَعْلَمُ يَارَبِّ أَنَّهُ يُعْجِبُنِي أَنْ أَخْرُجَ
مَعَ رسول الله صلى الله عليه وسلم إِذَا خَرَجَ ، وَأَدْخُلَ مَعَهُ إِذَا دَخَلَ ، وَقَدِ
احْتَبَسْتُ بِمَا تَرَى ، تَقُولُ أُمُّ سُلَيْمٍ : يَا أَبَا طَلْحَةَ مَا أَجِدُ الَّذِي
كُنْتُ أَجِدُ، انْطَلِقْ ، فَانْطَلَقْنَا، وَضَرَبَهَا الْمَخَاضُ حِينَ قَدِمَا فَوَلَدَتْ
غُلاماً . فَقَالَتْ لِي أُمِّي : يَا أَنَسُ لا يُرْضِعُهُ أَحَدٌ حَتَّى تَغْدُوَ بِهِ عَلَى
رَسُولِ الله صلى الله عليه وسلم ، فَلَمَّا أَصْبَحَ احْتَمَلْتُهُ فَانْطَلَقْتُ بِهِ إِلَى
رسول الله صلى الله عليه وسلم . وَذَكَرَ تَمَامَ الْحَدِيثِ

44. **Hazrat Anas bin Malik (R.A.A.)** relates: '(Hazrat) Abu Talaha had a son who was sick. Hazrat Abu Talaha had to go out and the boy expired during his absence. When he came back he enquired from his wife: 'How is the boy?' Um Sulaim, the mother of the boy, replied: 'Better than before.' Then she placed his evening meal before him. After he had taken his meal he slept with her. At last she broke the said news to him: "Arrange for the burrial of the boy.' In the morning Abu Talaha went to the Holy Prophet (S.A.W.) and apprised him of the event. He (S.A.W.) enquired: 'Were you together last night?' Abu Talaha replied in the affirmative on which the Holy Propht (S.A.W.) supplicated: 'Allah: bless them both.' Thereafter she gave birth to a boy. Hazrat Abu Talaha asked Hazrat Anas to take the newly born baby to the Holy Prophet (S.A.W.) He took some dates also with him. The Holy Prophet (S.A.W.) enquired; 'Is there anything with him?' Hazrat Abu Talaha said: 'Yes, some dates.' The Holy Prophet (S.A.W.) took a date and having chewed it, put it in the mouth of the baby and while blessing named it Abdullah. (*Bukhari and Muslim*).

Another version of *Bukhari* adds: Ibn Uyainah relates that a man from the Ansar told him that he saw nine sons of this Abdullah, every one of whom had read the Quran. In this connection Muslim's account says: When Abu Talaha's son from Umm Sulaim died, she said to other members of the family: 'Do not tell Abu Talaha about (the death of) the boy: I shall myself tell him. When he came, she put the evening meal before him which he ate. Then she dressed up herself well as she used to do, and then they were together. Thereafter she said to him: 'Abu Talaha, tell me if someone lends something to another and there-after takes it back, would the borrower be in the right to hold back the borrowed article?' He answered: 'No'. On which she said: 'Then hope for the reward from Allah in respect of that which has befallen your son. Hazrat Abu Talaha was upset and said: 'You kept me in dark about my son's condition till after we had been together.' So he left her and went to the Holy Prophet (S.A.W.) and told him what had happened. He said; 'May Allah bless your night.' Then she got conceived. Thereafter the Holy Prophet (S.A.W.) was on a journey and Hazrat Abu Talaha and his wife were with him. It was Holy Prophet's (S.A.W.) practice that when he returned from a journey, he would not enter Madina by night. When they approached Madina, her labour pains started. So Hazrat Abu Talaha stayed with her and the Holy Prophet (S.A.W.) went ahead. Then Hazrat Abu Talaha prayed: 'Allah! Thou knowest, that how much I am desirous that I should have the privilege of accompanying the Holy Prophet (S.A.W.) when he goes out and that I should return with him when he returns, and now I am detained here on account of the 'situation', Thou seest'. On this Umm Sulaim said: 'Abu Talaha, I no longer feel pain. Let us proceed. So they proceeded and she gave birth to a boy on reaching Madina. Hazrat Anas continued, 'My mother said to me: 'Anas, no one should suckle the baby till after we have taken it to the Holy Prophet (S.A.W.) tomorrow.' Next morning I took the baby to the Holy Prophet (S.A.W.) The rest of the story is the same as already stated above.

٤٥ – وَعَنْ أَبِي هُرَيْرَةَ رَضِيَ اللهُ عنه أن رسول الله صلى الله عليه وسلم قال : « لَيْسَ الشَّدِيدُ بِالصُّرَعَةِ ، إِنَّمَا الشَّدِيدُ الَّذِي يَمْلِكُ نَفْسَهُ عِنْدَ الْغَضَبِ » متفقٌ عليه

45. **Hazrat Abu Hurairah** (R.A.A.) relates that the Holy Prophet (S.A.W.) said: 'The strong one is not he who knocks out his adversary; the strong one is he who keeps control over his temper.

(*Bukhari and Muslim*).

٤٦ – وَعَنْ سُلَيْمَانَ بْنِ صُرَدٍ رَضِيَ اللهُ عنه قال : كُنْتُ جَالِساً مَعَ النَّبِيِّ صلى الله عليه وسلم ، وَرَجُلَانِ يَسْتَبَّانِ ، وَأَحَدُهُمَا قَدِ احْمَرَّ وَجْهُهُ . وانْتَفَخَتْ أَوْدَاجُهُ . فقال رسولُ الله صلى الله عليه وسلم : « إِنِّي لَأَعْلَمُ كَلِمَةً لَوْ قَالَهَا لَذَهَبَ عَنْهُ مَا يَجِدُ ، لَوْ قَالَ : أَعُوذُ بِاللهِ مِنَ الشَّيْطَانِ الرَّجِيمِ ذَهَبَ مِنْهُ مَا يَجِدُ . فَقَالُوا لَهُ : إِنَّ النَّبِيَّ صلى الله عليه وسلم قَالَ : تَعَوَّذْ بِاللهِ مِنَ الشَّيْطَانِ الرَّجِيمِ » متفق عليه

46. **Hazrat Sulaiman bin Surad** relates that he was sitting with the Holy Prophet (S.A.W.) when two persons fell out and exchanged hot words; the face of one of them became red and the veins of his neck got swollen. The Holy Prophet (S.A.W.) said: 'If he could repeat a phrase (prayer) I know, he would get rid of the condition in which

he is. The phrase is: *A'oozo billahe minash shaitanir Rajeem* (I seek refuge with Allah against satan, the rejected one.). So they communicated this prayer to the said person. (*Bukhari and Muslim*).

٤٧ — وَعَنْ مُعَاذ بْنِ أَنَسٍ رَضِيَ اللهُ عنه أَنَّ النَّبِيَّ صلى الله عليه وسلم قالَ : « مَنْ كَظَمَ غَيْظاً ، وَهُوَ قَادِرٌ عَلَى أَنْ يُنْفِذَهُ ، دَعَاهُ اللهُ سُبْحَانَهُ وتَعَالَى عَلَى رُؤُوسِ الْخَلائِقِ يَوْمَ الْقِيَامَةِ حَتَّى يُخَيِّرَهُ مِنَ الْحُورِ الْعِينِ مَاشَاءَ » رواهُ أَبُو دَاوُدَ ، وَالتِّرْمِذِيُّ وقال : حديثٌ حسنٌ .

47. Hazrat Mu'az bin Anas (R.A.A.) relates that the Holy Prophet (S.A.W.) said: 'One who in spite of having the capacity to avenge (a wrong) controls his anger, will be singled out and called by Allah, the Holy, the Exalted, over and above the multitude on the Day of Judgment, and given to choose a black-eyed houri.' (*Abu Daud and Tirmizi*).

٤٨ — وَعَنْ أَبِي هُرَيْرَةَ رَضِيَ اللهُ عنه ، أَنَّ رَجُلاً قَالَ لِلنَّبِيِّ صلى الله عليه وسلم : أَوْصِنِي ، قَالَ : « لاتَغْضَبْ » فَرَدَّدَ مِرَاراً ، قَالَ : « لاتَغْضَبْ » رواه البخاري .

48. Hazrat Abu Hurairah (R.A.A.) relates that a man requested the Holy Prophet (S.A.W.) to advise him. He (S.A.W.) said: 'Do not be over powered by anger.' The man repeated his request several times. Every time the Holy Prophet (S.A.W.) said: 'Do not be over powered by anger.' (*Bukhari*).

٤٩ — وَعَنْ أَبِي هُرَيْرَةَ رَضِيَ اللهُ عنه قال : قال رسول الله صلى الله عليه وسلم : « مَايَزَالُ الْبَلاءُ بِالْمُؤْمِنِ وَالْمُؤْمِنَةِ فِي نَفْسِهِ وَوَلَدِهِ وَمَالِهِ حَتَّى يَلْقَى اللهَ تعالى وَمَا عَلَيْهِ خَطِيئَةٌ » رواه التِّرْمِذِيُّ وقال : حديثٌ حسنٌ صحيحٌ

49. Hazrat Abu Hurairah (R.A.A.) relates that the Holy Prophet (S.A.W.) said: 'A Muslim male or female, remains subject to trials (in this world) in respect of self, children and property till he or she faces Allah, the Exalted, (on the Day of Judgment) in a state in which all his or her sins have been remitted .' (*Tirmizi*).

٥٠ — وَعَنْ ابْنِ عَبَّاسٍ رَضِيَ اللهُ عنهما قال : قَدِمَ عُيَيْنَةُ بْنُ حِصْنٍ فَنَزَلَ عَلَى ابْنِ أَخِيهِ الْحُرِّ بْنِ قَيْسٍ ، وكَانَ مِنَ النَّفَرِ الَّذِينَ يُدْنِيهِمْ عُمَرُ رَضِيَ اللهُ عنه ، وكَانَ الْقُرَّاءُ أَصْحَابَ مَجْلِسِ عُمَرَ رَضِيَ اللهُ عنه وَمُشَاوَرَتِهِ كُهُولاً كَانُوا أَوْ شُبَّاناً ، فَقَالَ عُيَيْنَةُ لابْنِ أَخِيهِ : يَاابْنَ

أخي لَكَ وَجهٌ عِندَ هَذا الأَميرِ فَاستَأذِنْ لي عَلَيهِ ، فاستَأذَنَ فَأذِنَ لَهُ عُمَرُ . فَلَمّا دَخَلَ قالَ : هِيْ يَاابنَ الخَطّابِ، فَوَاللهِ مَا تُعطِينا الجَزْلَ وَلا تَحكُمُ فِينا بالعَدْلِ ، فَغَضِبَ عُمَرُ رضي الله عنه حَتَّى هَمَّ أنْ يُوقِعَ به، فَقَالَ لَهُ الحُرُّ : يَا أَميرَ المُؤْمِنِينَ إنَّ اللهَ تعالى قَالَ لِنَبِيِّهِ صلى الله عليه وسلم : خُذِ العَفْوَ وَأْمُرْ بِالعُرْفِ وَأَعرِضْ عَنِ الجَاهِلِينَ [الأعراف : ١٩٨] وَإنَّ هَذا مِنَ الجَاهِلِينَ ، وَاللهِ مَا جَاوَزَهَا عُمَرُ حِينَ تَلاهَا ، وكَانَ وَقّافاً عِندَ كِتَابِ اللهِ تعالى . رواه البخاري

50. Hazrat ibn Abbas (R.A.A.) relates '(Hazrat) Yuainah ibn Hisn came to Madina and stayed with his nephew, Hazrat Hurr Ibn Qais, who was one of those who were very close to Hazrat Umar and was privileged to join his councils. Hazrat Uyainah said to Hazrat Hurr: 'my dear nephew, you enjoy the confidence of the Amir-ul-Momineen, will you obtain permission for me to see him:! Accordingly Hazrat Hurr asked for the requisite permission which Hazrat Umar granted. When Hazrat Uyainah came before Hazrat Umar, he addressed him thus: 'Son of Khattab' you do not grant us much nor do you deal fairly with us.' Hazrat Umar was annoyed and would have struck him when Hazrat Hurr said: 'Amir-ul-Momineen Allah said to His Prophet (S.A.W.): Keep to forgiveness (O Muhammad) and enjoin kindness and turn away from the ignorant.' (7:199). This one (Hazrat Uyainah) is one of the ignorants.' When Hazrat Hurr recited this Hazrat Umar calmed down and did not move from his seat. He always strictly followed the Book of Allah. (*Bukhari*).

٥١ — وَعَنِ ابنِ مَسعُودٍ رضي الله عنه أنَّ رسول الله صلى الله عليه وسلم قال : « إنَّهَا سَتَكُونُ بَعدِي أَثَرَةٌ وَأُمُورٌ تُنكِرُونَهَا ! قَالُوا : يَارَسُولَ الله فَمَا تَأْمُرُنَا ؟ قال : تُؤَدُّونَ الحَقَّ الَّذي عَلَيكُمْ ، وَتَسأَلُونَ اللهَ الذي لَكُمْ » متفقٌ عليه

51. Hazrat Ibn Mas'ud relates that the Holy Prophet (S.A.W.) said: 'After me there will be discrimination and you will observe things, that you will disapprove.' A companion asked: 'Messenger of Allah, (S.A.W.) what do you command us to do in such a situation? He said: 'Discharge your duties and supplicate Allah for His bounties.' (*Bukhari and Muslim*).

٥٢ — وَعَنْ أَبي يَحيَى أُسَيدِ بنِ حُضَيرٍ رضي الله عنه أنَّ رَجُلاً مِنَ الأَنصَارِ قال : يا رسولَ الله أَلا تَستَعمِلُني كَمَا استَعمَلتَ فُلاناً فَقَالَ :

« إِنَّكُمْ سَتَلْقَوْنَ بَعْدِي أَثَرَةً ، فَاصْبِرُوا حَتَّى تَلْقَوْنِي عَلَى الْحَوْضِ »
متفقٌ عليه

52. Hazrat Usayd bin Huzair (R.A.A.) relates that an Ansari Muslim requested the Holy Prophet (S.A.W.) why do you not appoint me as an executive as you have appointed so and so?' He (S.A.W.) replied: 'You will see discrimination after I am gone but be patient till you meet me on the banks of *Kausar* fountain in Paradise.'

(*Bukhari and Muslim*).

٥٣ ـ وَعَنْ أَبِي إِبْرَاهِيمَ عَبْدِ اللهِ بْنِ أَبِي أَوْفَى رضي الله عنهما أَنَّ رسول الله صلى الله عليه وسلم فِي بَعْضِ أَيَّامِهِ الَّتِي لَقِيَ فِيهَا الْعَدُوَّ ، انْتَظَرَ حَتَّى إِذَا مَالَتِ الشَّمْسُ قَامَ فِيهِمْ فَقَالَ : «يَا أَيُّهَا النَّاسُ لا تَتَمَنَّوْا لِقَاءَ الْعَدُوِّ ، وَاسْأَلُوا اللهَ الْعَافِيَةَ ، فَإِذَا لَقِيتُمُوهُمْ فَاصْبِرُوا ، وَاعْلَمُوا أَنَّ الْجَنَّةَ تَحْتَ ظِلَالِ السُّيُوفِ» ثُمَّ قال النَّبِيُّ صلى الله عليه وسلم: «اللَّهُمَّ مُنْزِلَ الْكِتَابِ وَمُجْرِيَ السَّحَابِ ، وَهَازِمَ الْأَحْزَابِ ، اهْزِمْهُمْ وَانْصُرْنَا عَلَيْهِمْ » متفقٌ عليه وَبِاللهِ التَّوْفِيقُ .

53. Hazrat Abdullah Ibn Abi Aufa (R.A.A.) relates that the Holy Prophet (S.A.W.) was once on a campaign and while waiting for the sun to set, he stood up and addressed his companions: 'Do not provoke fighting and supplicate Allah for protection and security. But when you are confronted with the enemy, be steadfast and remember that Paradise is under the shadow of the swords.' Then he supplicated: 'O Allah, Revealer of the Book, Driver of the Clouds, Vanquisher of Hosts, Vanquish them and helps us overcome them'. (*Bukhari and Muslim*).

* * * * * * * * * *

CHAPTER 4

On Truthfulness

قال الله تعالى : يَا أَيُّهَا الَّذِينَ آمَنُوا اتَّقُوا اللهَ وَكُونُوا مَعَ الصَّادِقِينَ [التوبة : ١١٩] وقال تعالى : وَالصَّادِقِينَ وَالصَّادِقَاتِ [الأحزاب : ٣٥] وقال تعالى : فَلَوْ صَدَقُوا اللهَ لَكَانَ خَيْرًا لَهُمْ [محمد : ٢١] .

Allah, the Exalted, has said:

13. O ye who believe! Be careful of your duty to Allah, and be with the truthful (9:119).

14. Lo! Men who surrender unto Allah, and women who surrender (33:35).

15. Obedience and a civil word. Then, when the matter is determined, if they are loyal to Allah it will be well of them (47:21).

٥٤ ـ فَالأَوَّلُ عَنِ ابْنِ مَسْعُودٍ رضي الله عنه عن النَّبِيِّ صلى الله عليه وسلم قال : « إِنَّ الصِّدْقَ يَهْدِي إِلَى الْبِرِّ وَإِنَّ الْبِرَّ يَهْدِي إِلَى الْجَنَّةِ ، وَإِنَّ الرَّجُلَ لَيَصْدُقُ حَتَّى يُكْتَبَ عِنْدَ اللهِ صِدِّيقاً ، وَإِنَّ الْكَذِبَ يَهْدِي إِلَى الْفُجُورِ ، وَإِنَّ الْفُجُورَ يَهْدِي إِلَى النَّارِ . وَإِنَّ الرَّجُلَ لَيَكْذِبُ حَتَّى يُكْتَبَ عِنْدَ اللهِ كَذَّاباً » متفقٌ عليه

54. Hazrat Abdullah Ibn Mas'ud (R.A.A.) relates that the Holy Prophet (S.A.W.) said: 'A true action leads to the path of virtue and good deeds, and virtue paves the way of a person to Paradise, and the said person continues to speak the truth till in the sight of Allah he is named Siddiq or Truthful. Lying leads to vice, and vice leads to indecent acts and if a person goes on lying till in the sight of Allah he is named a liar. *(Bukhari and Muslim)*.

٥٥ ـ الثَّانِي : عَنْ أَبِي مُحَمَّدٍ الْحَسَنِ بْنِ عَلِيِّ بْنِ أَبِي طَالِبٍ ، رضي الله عنهما . قال : حَفِظْتُ مِنْ رسول الله ، صلى الله عليه وسلم : « دَعْ مَا يَرِيبُكَ إِلَى مَا لا يَرِيبُكَ : فَإِنَّ الصِّدْقَ طُمَأْنِينَةٌ ، وَالْكَذِبَ رِيبَةٌ » رواه التِرْمذي وقال : حديثٌ صحيحٌ .

55. Hazrat Hasan bin Ali (R.A.A.) relates that he learnt the following from the Holy Prophet (S.A.W.): 'Leave alone that which involves thee in doubt, and adhere to that which is free from doubt, for truth is comforting and falsehood is disturbing.' *(Tirmizi)*.

٥٦ ـ الثَّالِثُ : عَنْ أَبِي سُفْيَانَ صَخْرِ بْنِ حَرْبٍ . رضي الله عنه . في حديثه الطَّوِيلِ فِي قِصَّةِ هِرَقْلَ . قالَ هِرَقْلُ : فَمَاذَا يَأْمُرُكُمْ ـ يَعْنِي النَّبِيَّ صلى الله عليه وسلم ـ قالَ أَبُو سُفْيَانَ : قُلْتُ : يقولُ : « اعْبُدُوا اللهَ وَحْدَهُ لا تُشْرِكُوا بِهِ شَيْئاً ، وَاتْرُكُوا مَا يَقُولُ آبَاؤُكُمْ ، وَيَأْمُرُنَا بِالصَّلاةِ ، وَالصِّدْقِ ، وَالْعَفَافِ . وَالصِّلَةِ » متفقٌ عليه

56. Hazrat Abu Sufyan (R.A.A.) relates as part of his statement about Hiraclius that the latter asked him what does he (i.e. the Holy Prophet S.A.W.) teach you, and Abu Sufyan said: 'He tells us: 'Worship Allah alone and do not associate anything with Him, and discard all that your ancestors said; and he commands us to observe prayer, to tell the truth, to be chaste and to strengthen the ties of kinship by helping those who are related to you. (*Bukhari and Muslim*).

٥٧ ـ الرَّابِعُ : عَنْ أَبي ثَابِتٍ . وَقِيلَ : أَبي سَعِيدٍ . وَقِيلَ : أَبي الوَلِيدِ . سَهْلِ بنِ حُنَيْفٍ ، وَهُوَ بَدْرِيٌّ ، رضي الله عنه . أن النبي صلى الله عليه وسلم . قال : « مَنْ سَأَلَ اللهَ ، تعالى ، الشَّهَادَةَ بِصِدْقٍ بَلَّغَهُ اللهُ مَنَازِلَ الشُّهَدَاءِ . وَإِنْ مَاتَ عَلَى فِرَاشِهِ » رواه مسلم

57. **Hazrat Sahl bin Hunaif** (R.A.A.) relates that the Holy Prophet (S.A.W.) said: 'One who supplicates to Allah sincerely for martyrdom is raised by Him to the status of a martyr although he dies in his bed. (*Muslim*).

٥٨ ـ الخامِسُ : عَنْ أَبي هُرَيْرَةَ ، رضي الله عنه ، قال : قال رسول الله صلى الله عليه وسلم : « غَزَا نَبِيٌّ مِنَ الأَنْبِيَاءِ صَلَوَاتُ اللهِ وَسَلامُهُ عَلَيْهِمْ فَقَالَ لِقَوْمِهِ : لا يَتْبَعَنِّي رَجُلٌ مَلَكَ بُضْعَ امْرَأَةٍ . وَهُوَ يُرِيدُ أَنْ يَبْنِيَ بِهَا وَلَمَّا يَبْنِ بِهَا . وَلا أَحَدٌ بَنَى بُيُوتاً لَمْ يَرْفَعْ سُقُوفَهَا . وَلا أَحَدٌ اشْتَرَى غَنَماً أَوْ خَلِفَاتٍ وَهُوَ يَنْتَظِرُ أَوْلادَهَا . فَغَزَا فَدَنَا مِنَ القَرْيَةِ صَلاةَ العَصْرِ أَوْ قَرِيباً مِنْ ذلكَ ، فَقَالَ لِلشَّمْسِ : إِنَّكِ مَأْمُورَةٌ وَأَنَا مَأْمُورٌ . اللَّهُمَّ احْبِسْهَا عَلَيْنَا . فَحُبِسَتْ حَتَّى فَتَحَ اللهُ عَلَيْهِ ، فَجَمَعَ الغَنَائِمَ . فَجَاءَتْ ـ يَعْنِي النَّارَ ـ لِتَأْكُلَهَا فَلَمْ تَطْعَمْهَا ، فَقَالَ : إِنَّ فِيكُمْ غُلُولاً ، فَلْيُبَايِعْنِي مِنْ كُلِّ قَبِيلَةٍ رَجُلٌ ، فَلَزِقَتْ يَدُ رَجُلٍ بِيَدِهِ فَقَالَ : فِيكُمُ الغُلُولُ ، فَلْيُبَايِعْنِي قَبِيلَتُكَ ، فَلَزِقَتْ يَدُ رَجُلَيْنِ أَوْ ثَلاثَةٍ بِيَدِهِ فَقَالَ : فِيكُمُ الغُلُولُ . فَجَاؤُوا بِرَأْسٍ مِثْلِ رَأْسِ بَقَرَةٍ مِنَ الذَّهَبِ ، فَوَضَعَهَا فَجَاءَتِ النَّارُ فَأَكَلَتْهَا ، فَلَمْ تَحِلَّ الغَنَائِمُ لأَحَدٍ قَبْلَنَا ، ثُمَّ أَحَلَّ اللهُ لَنَا الغَنَائِمَ لَمَّا رَأَى ضَعْفَنَا وَعَجْزَنَا فَأَحَلَّهَا لَنَا » متفقٌ عليه

58. **Hazrat Abu Hurairah** (R.A.A.) relates that the Holy Prophet (S.A.W.) said: 'One of the earlier prophets while going on *Jihad* (a religious war in the cause of Allah) announced among his people that a person who had married a woman whom he has not yet brought to his house but intends to do so or one who has built the walls of a house

but has not yet put a roof on them, or one who has purchased pregnant goats or she camels and is awaiting the birth of their kids should accompany him. After this he started for the town, which was his objective. He reached there a little before sunset and said to the sun 'Thou art bound by the command of Allah and I am also commissioned to wage war. He then prayed: Allah! hold the sun back for us; and it was held back till Allah gave him the victory. Thereafter the spoils were collected to be burnt as an offering, but the fire would not consume them. Then he announced: 'Someone among you has embezzled a portion of the spoils, so now let one man from each tribe renew the covenant at my hands.' In this process the hand of one man got stuck with the hand of the prophet and he declared. 'Some one of your tribe has been guilty of embezzlement; 'So now let each man of your tribe renew the covenant at my hands.' In this process, the hands of two or three persons got stuck with the hand of the prophet and he said tht one of them had been guilty of embezzlement . Upon this they produced a cow head of gold which was placed among the spoils and the fire consumed them. The Holy Prophet added: 'Spoils of war were not lawful for anyone before us. Allah made them lawful for us in view of our weakness and lack of means.' (*Bukhari and Muslim*).

٥٩ ـ السادِسُ : عن أبي خالدٍ حكيمِ بن حزامٍ . رضي الله عنه ، قال : قال رسول الله صلى الله عليه وسلم : « البَيِّعَانِ بالخِيَارِ ما لم يَتَفَرَّقا ، فإن صَدَقا وبيَّنا بُورِكَ لَهُما في بيعهِمَا ، وإن كَتَمَا وكَذَبَا مُحِقَتْ بركَةُ بَيْعِهِما متفقٌ عليه

59. Hazrat Hakeem bin Hizam (R.A.A.) relates that the Holy Prophet (S.A.W.) said: 'A sale agreement is revocable till the buyer and seller part company. If they tell the truth and disclose everything relevant to the transaction, it becomes full of blessings for both of them; but if they speak falsely and conceal that which should be disclosed, the blessing of the transaction is wiped out.'

(*Bukhari and Muslim*).

Note: Truthfulness generally means to speak truth, but in Islam the word has a wider connotation, and accordingly it includes sincerity of action also. The basis of correctness of every word and action of a person, is that his heart and tongue should be in harmony with each other, and this is called truth.

Imam Ghazali has enumerated six types of truth (1) Truth in speech (2) Truth in intention and motive (3) Truth in determination or resolve (4) Truth in carrying out determination (5) Truth in action and (6) Truth in matters of faith and religion.

It will be seen that truth is the basis of many virtues. A person who is not truthful, will have all sorts of vices in his heart;

and one who is truthful will be able to achieve each and every virtue easily. A person who is well versed in these virtues can be called a perfectly truthful person.

* * * * * * * * * *

CHAPTER 5

On Divine Contemplation or Meditation

قال الله تعالى : الَّذِي يَرَاكَ حِينَ تَقُومُ وَتَقَلُّبَكَ فِي السَّاجِدِينَ
[الشعراء : ٢١٩] وقال تعالى : وَهُوَ مَعَكُمْ أَيْنَمَا كُنْتُمْ [الحديد : ٤]
وقال تعالى : إِنَّ اللهَ لاَ يَخْفَى عَلَيْهِ شَيْءٌ فِي الأَرْضِ وَلاَ فِي السَّمَاءِ [آل
عمران : ٣] وقال تعالى : إِنَّ رَبَّكَ لَبِالْمِرْصَادِ [الفجر : ١٤] وقال تعالى:
يَعْلَمُ خَائِنَةَ الأَعْيُنِ وَمَا تُخْفِي الصُّدُورُ [غافر : ١٩] والآياتُ في
الْبَابِ كَثِيرَةٌ مَعْلُومَةٌ

Allah, the Exalted, has said:

16. Who seeth thee when thou standest up (to pray). And seeth thine abasement among those who fall prostrate (in worship) (26:218—219).
17. And He is with you wheresoever ye may be (57:4).
18. Lo! Nothing in the earth or in the heavens is hidden from Allah (3:5).
19. Lo! thy Lord is ever watchful. (89:14).
20. He knoweth the traitor of the eyes, and that which the bosoms hide (40:19).

٦٠ ـ وَأَمَّا الأَحاديثُ ، فَالأَوَّلُ : عَنْ عُمَرَ بن الخطابِ ، رضي الله عنه ،
قال : «بَيْنَمَا نَحْنُ جُلُوسٌ عِنْدَ رسولِ الله، صلى الله عليه وسلم ، ذَاتَ
يَوْمٍ إِذْ طَلَعَ عَلَيْنَا رَجُلٌ شَدِيدُ بَيَاضِ الثِّيَابِ ، شَدِيدُ سَوَادِ الشَّعْرِ ،
لا يُرَى عَلَيْهِ أَثَرُ السَّفَرِ ، وَلا يَعْرِفُهُ مِنَّا أَحَدٌ ، حَتَّى جَلَسَ إِلَى النَّبِيِّ ،
صلى الله عليه وسلم ، فَأَسْنَدَ رُكْبَتَيْهِ إِلَى رُكْبَتَيْهِ ، وَوَضَعَ كَفَّيْهِ عَلَى
فَخِذَيْهِ وقالَ : يَا مُحَمَّدُ أَخْبِرْنِي عَنِ الإِسْلامِ ، فقالَ رسولَ الله صلى الله
عليه وسلم : الإِسْلامُ أَنْ تَشْهَدَ أَنْ لا إِلَهَ إِلاَّ اللهُ ، وَأَنَّ مُحَمَّداً رسولُ اللهِ
وَتُقِيمَ الصَّلاةَ ، وَتُؤْتِيَ الزَّكاةَ ، وَتَصُومَ رَمَضَانَ ، وَتَحُجَّ الْبَيْتَ إِنِ

استطعت إليه سبيلا . قال : صدقت . فعجبنا له يسأله ويصدقه
قال : فأخبرني عن الإيمان . قال : أن تؤمن بالله ، وملائكته ، وكتبه ،
ورسله ، واليوم الآخر ، وتؤمن بالقدر خيره وشره . قال : صدقت .
قال : فأخبرني عن الإحسان . قال : أن تعبد الله كأنك تراه ، فإن
لم تكن تراه فإنه يراك . قال : فأخبرني عن الساعة . قال : ما المسؤول
عنها بأعلم من السائل . قال : فأخبرني عن أماراتها . قال : أن تلد
الأمة ربتها ، وأن ترى الحفاة العراة العالة رعاء الشاء يتطاولون
في البنيان . ثم انطلق ، فلبثت مليا ، ثم قال : ياعمر أتدري من
السائل ؟ قلت : الله ورسوله أعلم . قال : فإنه جبريل أتاكم يعلمكم
أمر دينكم » رواه مسلم

60. Hazrat Umar bin Khattab (R.A.A.) relates: 'Once while we were sitting with the Holy Prophet (S.A.W.), all of a sudden a man appeared whose clothes were very neat, whose hair was very black, who bore no mark of travel and who was not known to any of us. He sat down by the side of the Holy Prophet (S.A.W.) with his knees touching those of the Holy Prophet (S.A.W.). Placing his hands on his thigh he said: 'Muhammad (S.A.W.): Enlighten me about the reality of Islam. The Holy Prophet (S.A.W.) said 'Islam is that you should bear witness that there is no God save Allah alone, and that Muhammad (S.A.W.) is His Messenger, and that you should observe Prayer, pay the *Zakat* (poor due), observe the fast during Ramazan, and perform the pilgrimage to the House of Allah if you have the means. The man said: 'That is right.' We were surprised that he makes enquiries (as if he knows nothing) and also confirms the correctness of the answer. He then said: 'Tell me about Faith.' The Holy Prophet (S.A.W.) said: 'That you should believe in Allah, His Angels, His Books, His Prophets-the Day of Judgment and that you should believe that He determines the fate. The man said: 'That is right. Now tell me about the due performance of obligations.' The Holy Prophet (S.A.W.) said: That you should worship Allah as if you are seeing Him, and if you are not seeing him but bear in mind that He is watching you.' The man said: 'Now tell me about the Day of Judgment.' The Holy Prophet (S.A.W.) said: 'I know only as much as you know.' The man then said: 'Well, let me know some of the signs of the Day of Judgment. The Holy Prophet (S.A.W.) replied: 'That the maid servant should give birth to her master and that bare-footed, bare bodied, money-less goatherds should be seen living with arrogance in great mansions. Then the man departed, and I stayed there for a while. The Holy Prophet (S.A.W.) said to me. 'Umar, do you know who the questioner was.' I said: 'Allah and His Messenger (S.A.W.) know better.' He then said: 'It was Gabriel who came to instruct and teach you the principles of your religion.' (*Muslim*).

Note: According to Imam Nawavi the handmaid giving birth to her master means that the number of handmaids in the 'Harams of Sultans will be much increased: they may give birth to their master's children including their daughters who may be called in tradition as of noble descent; or children may rebel against their parents and such children may consider their mothers as handmaid.

٦١ — الثَّاني : عَنْ أَبي ذَرٍّ جُنْدُبِ بْنِ جُنَادَةَ ، وَأَبي عَبْدِ الرَّحْمنِ مُعَاذِ بْنِ جَبَلٍ ، رضي الله عنهما ، عَنْ رسول الله ، صلى الله عليه وسلم ، قال : « اتَّقِ اللهَ حَيْثُمَا كُنْتَ وَأَتْبِعِ السَّيِّئَةَ الْحَسَنَةَ تَمْحُهَا ، وَخَالِقِ النَّاسَ بِخُلُقٍ حَسَنٍ » رواهُ التِّرْمِذِيُّ وقال : حديثٌ حسنٌ .

61. Hazrat Abu Zarr (R.A.A.) and Hazrat Mua'z bin Jabal (R.A.A.) relate that the Holy Prophet (S.A.W.) said: 'Fear Allah, wherever you may be; do a virtuous act after an evil act as former will undo the latter, and behave well with the people. (*Tirmizi*).

٦٢ — الثَّالثُ : عَنِ ابْنِ عَبَّاسٍ ، رضي الله عنهما ، قال : « كُنْتُ خَلْفَ النَّبِيِّ ، صلى الله عليه وسلم ، يَوْماً فَقَالَ : « يَا غُلامُ إِنِّي أُعَلِّمُكَ كَلِمَاتٍ : « احْفَظِ اللهَ يَحْفَظْكَ ، احْفَظِ اللهَ تَجِدْهُ تُجَاهَكَ إِذَا سَأَلْتَ فَاسْأَلِ اللهَ ، وَإِذَا اسْتَعَنْتَ فَاسْتَعِنْ بِاللهِ ، وَاعْلَمْ : أَنَّ الأُمَّةَ لَوِ اجْتَمَعَتْ عَلَى أَنْ يَنْفَعُوكَ بِشَيْءٍ ، لَمْ يَنْفَعُوكَ إِلاَّ بِشَيْءٍ قَدْ كَتَبَهُ اللهُ لَكَ ، وَإِنِ اجْتَمَعُوا عَلَى أَنْ يَضُرُّوكَ بِشَيْءٍ ؛ لَمْ يَضُرُّوكَ إِلاَّ بِشَيْءٍ قَدْ كَتَبَهُ اللهُ عَلَيْكَ ؛ رُفِعَتِ الأَقْلامُ ، وَجَفَّتِ الصُّحُفُ رواهُ التِّرْمِذِيُّ وقَالَ : حديثٌ حسنٌ صحيحٌ .

وفي روايةِ غيرِ التِّرْمِذِيِّ : « احْفَظِ اللهَ تَجِدْهُ أَمَامَكَ ، تَعَرَّفْ إِلى اللهِ في الرَّخَاءِ يَعْرِفْكَ في الشِّدَّةِ ، وَاعْلَمْ أَنَّ مَا أَخْطَأَكَ لَمْ يَكُنْ لِيُصِيبَكَ ، وَمَا أَصَابَكَ لَمْ يَكُنْ لِيُخْطِئَكَ ، وَاعْلَمْ أَنَّ النَّصْرَ مَعَ الصَّبْرِ ، وَأَنَّ الْفَرَجَ مَعَ الْكَرْبِ ، وَأَنَّ مَعَ الْعُسْرِ يُسْراً »

62. Hazrat Ibn Abbas (R.A.A.) relates: 'Once I was riding (on an animal) behind the Holy Prophet (S.A.W.) when he said: 'Boy, I would like to teach you something. Be careful and follow Allah's commands perseveringly. Allah will protect you. You should safeguard His rights, and you will always find Him with you; if you need something, ask Allah, and when you need help, solicit Allah alone for the same. Bear it in mind that if all the people combine together to grant you some benefit, they would not be able to do so except that which Allah has determined for you and that if all of them were combined together to do you harm, they would not be able to do so except that which Allah has determined for you. The pens have been set aside and the writings of the book of fate have become dry (*Tirmizi*).

Other books on tradition add: safeguard the commandments of Allah, you will find Him before you; remember Him when in easy circumstances, He will remember you in adversity. Remember that which has led you to commit wrongs will not lead you aright, and that which has guided you to good will not show you the correct path, and that which has helped you to do good, will not mislead you. Bear in mind that (Allah's) help comes only with steadfastness and prosperity comes after agony and sorrow; and every ordeal is followed by easy circumstances.

٦٣ ـ الرَّابِعُ : عَنْ أَنَسٍ رضي الله عنه قالَ : « إِنَّكُمْ لَتَعْمَلُونَ أَعْمَالاً هِيَ أَدَقُّ فِي أَعْيُنِكُمْ مِنَ الشَّعْرِ ، كُنَّا نَعُدُّهَا عَلَى عَهْدِ رسول الله صلى الله عليه وسلم مِنَ الْمُوبِقَاتِ » رواه البخاري . وقال : « الْمُوبِقَاتُ » الْمُهْلِكَاتُ .

63. Hazrat Anas (R.A.A.) had said 'You (very often) commit acts which you consider as less important than a hair (lesser evil), whereas during the days of the Holy Prophet (S.A.W.) we used to consider them as fatal (serious evil or great sin). (*Bukhari*).

٦٤ ـ الْخَامِسُ : عَنْ أَبِي هُرَيْرَةَ ، رضي الله عنه ، عن النبي صلى الله عليه وسلم ، قال : « إِنَّ الله تَعَالَى يَغَارُ ، وَغَيْرَةُ اللهِ ، تَعَالَى ، أَنْ يَأْتِيَ الْمَرْءُ مَا حَرَّمَ اللهُ عَلَيْهِ » مُتَّفَقٌ عَلَيْهِ

64. Hazrat Abu Hurairah (R.A.A.) relates what the Holy Prophet (S.A.W.) said: 'Allah is self-respecting and His self-respect is roused by a person indulging in acts which He has forbidden.

(*Bukhari and Muslim*).

٦٥ ـ السَّادِسُ : عَنْ أَبِي هُرَيْرَةَ رضي الله عنه أَنَّهُ سَمِعَ النَّبِيَّ صلى الله

عليه وسلم يقولُ : « إنَّ ثلاثةً مِنْ بَنِي إسرائيلَ : أبرَصَ ، وأقرعَ . وأعمَى ، أرادَ اللهُ أنْ يبتليَهمْ فبعثَ إليهمْ ملَكاً ، فأتَى الأبرَصَ فقالَ : أيُّ شيءٍ أحبُّ إليكَ ؟ قالَ : لونٌ حسنٌ ، وجلدٌ حسَنٌ . ويذهبُ عنّي الّذي قدْ قذرَنِي النّاسُ ؛ فمسحَهُ فذهبَ عنهُ قذرُهُ وأعطِيَ لوناً حسَناً . قالَ : فأيُّ المالِ أحبُّ إليكَ ؟ قالَ : الإبلُ – أوْ قالَ البقرُ – شكَّ الرّاوِي – فأعطِيَ ناقةً عُشَراءَ ، فقالَ : باركَ اللهُ لكَ فيها .

فأتَى الأقرعَ فقالَ : أيُّ شيءٍ أحبُّ إليكَ ؟ قال : شعرٌ حسَنٌ ، ويذهبُ عنّي هذَا الذي قذرَنِي النّاسُ ، فمسحَهُ فذهبَ عنهُ ، وأعطِيَ شعراً حسَناً . قال : فأيُّ المالِ أحبُّ إليكَ ؟ قالَ : البقرُ ، فأعطِيَ بقرةً حاملاً ، وقالَ : باركَ اللهُ لكَ فيها .

فأتَى الأعمَى فقالَ : أيُّ شيءٍ أحبُّ إليكَ ؟ قال : أنْ يردَّ اللهُ إليَّ بصرِي فأبصرَ النّاسَ ، فمسحَهُ فردَّ اللهُ إليهِ بصرَهُ . قال : فأيُّ المالِ أحبُّ إليكَ ؟ قال : الغنَمُ ، فأعطِيَ شاةً والِداً . فأنتجَ هذانِ وولّدَ هذَا ، فكانَ لهذَا وادٍ مِنَ الإبلِ ، ولهذَا وادٍ مِنَ البقرِ ، ولهذَا وادٍ مِنَ الغنَمِ .

ثُمَّ إنّهُ أتَى الأبرَصَ في صورتِهِ وهيئتِهِ ، فقالَ : رجُلٌ مسكِينٌ قدِ انقطعَتْ بيَ الحبالُ في سفرِي ، فلا بلاغَ لِيَ اليومَ إلاَّ باللهِ ثُمَّ بكَ ، أسألُكَ بالّذي أعطاكَ اللّونَ الحسَنَ ، والجلدَ الحسَنَ ، والمالَ ، بعيراً أتبلّغُ بهِ في سفرِي ، فقالَ : الحقُوقُ كثيرةٌ . فقالَ : كأنّي أعرِفُكَ ، ألمْ تكنْ أبرَصَ يقذَرُكَ النّاسُ فقيراً ، فأعطاكَ اللهُ !؟ فقالَ : إنّما ورِثتُ هذَا المالَ كابِراً عنْ كابرٍ ، فقالَ : إنْ كُنتَ كاذباً فصيّرَكَ اللهُ إلى ما كُنتَ

وأتَى الأقرعَ في صورتِهِ وهيئتِهِ ، فقالَ لهُ مثلَ ما قالَ لهذَا ،

وَرَدَّ عَلَيْهِ مِثْلَ مَارَدَّ هَذَا ، فقالَ : إنْ كُنْتَ كَاذِباً فَصَيَّرَكَ اللهُ إِلَى مَا كُنْتَ .

وَأَتَى الأَعْمَى فِي صُورَتِهِ وَهَيْئَتِهِ ، فقالَ : رَجُلٌ مِسْكِينٌ وابْنُ سَبِيلٍ انقَطَعَتْ بِيَ الحِبَالُ فِي سَفَرِي ، فَلا بَلاغَ لِيَ اليَوْمَ إلاّ باللهِ ثُمَّ بِكَ ، أَسْأَلُكَ بِالَّذِي رَدَّ عَلَيْكَ بَصَرَكَ شَاةً أَتَبَلَّغُ بِهَا فِي سَفَرِي ؟ فقالَ : قَدْ كُنْتُ أَعْمَى فَرَدَّ اللهُ إِلَيَّ بَصَرِي ، فَخُذْ مَا شِئْتَ وَدَعْ مَا شِئْتَ ، فَوَاللهِ مَا أَجْهَدُكَ اليَوْمَ بِشَيْءٍ أَخَذْتَهُ لِلهِ عَزَّ وجلَّ . فقالَ : أَمْسِكْ مَالَكَ فَإِنَّمَا ابْتُلِيتُمْ ، فَقَدْ رَضِيَ اللهُ عنكَ ، وَسَخِطَ عَلَى صَاحِبَيْكَ » متفقٌ عليه

65. **Hazrat Abu Hurairah** (R.A.A.) relates that he heard the Holy Prophet (S.A.W.) say that 'Allah in order to test three persons from amongst the Bani Israel — one of whom was a leper, the other was bald-headed and the third a blind person, — sent an angel to them in the form of a human being. The angel came to the leper and asked him; 'What is that thing you like best?' He said: 'A fine colour and neat skin and cure from this disease on account of which people hate me.' The angel ran his hand over his body and his disease vanished, and his body got fine colour. Then the angel further asked him as to what property he would like the best?' The man said: Camels or cows. (The narrator is doubtful). The man was accordingly given a she-camel ten months pregnant; and the angel said: May Allah bless it for thee. Then the angel went to the bald-headed man and asked him as to what was that thing which he liked the best. The man replied: Beautiful hair and cure of the ailment, due to which people hate me. The angel ran through his hand (over his head) and his disease was cured and he was granted beautiful hair. Then the angel asked him 'What property would you like best.' The man said: 'Cow'. Hence he was given a cow carrying a calf; and the angel then said: 'May Allah bless it for thee.' Then the angel came to the man who was blind, and asked him: 'What is that thing which you would like best?' He said: 'That Allah may restore his sight so that he may see the people around him. The angel ran his hand over the blind man's eyes and Allah restored his sight. Then the angel asked him: 'What property would you like best?' The man said: 'Goats.' He was given a she-goat which was pregnant and carrying a kid. These animals in due course gave birth to their kids multiplying very soon so that one had a valley full of camels, the other, a velley full of cows and bulls and the third, a valley full of goats.

After sometime, the angel visited the laper in his original form and said to him: I am a poor and needy person, having spent all the means of sustenance in the course of my journey, and I have now nothing left for the completion of my journey except, Allah. I beg you, in the name of Allah who has given you a decent colour and a neat skin and much wealth, to furnish me with a camel to enable me complete my journey. The man expressed his inability to oblige the angel and said: 'I have many obligations to fulfil'. The angel said: ' It appears as if I have seen you before. Are you not a leper, who was shunned by people and was poor, whom Allah enriched? The man said: 'I have inherited this property from my ancestors.' The angel said: 'If you are speaking a lie, may Allah return you to the condition in which you were.' Then he came to the bald-headed person in his original form, and repeated his request to him, and got a reply similar to the one he had received from the leper. To this one also he said: If you are speaking a lie may Allah return you to the condition in which you were.'

Then the angel visited the blind man in his old appearance and said to him: I am a poor traveller. My assets have been spent and I am unable to reach my destination except with the help of Allah. I beg you in the name of Allah Who has given back your sight, to give me a goat that might prove of help to me in reaching my destination. The man said: 'Indeed I was blind and Allah restored my eye-sight. You may take what you will, and leave what you like. By Allah, I shall not refuse you anything you may wish to take in the name of Allah, the Lord of honour and glory. The angel said. 'Keep all you have. All three of you were being tried. Allah is, indeed, pleased with you and is angry with your companions. (*Bukhari and Muslim*).

٦٦ ـ السَّابِعُ : عَنْ أَبِي يَعْلَى شَدَّادِ بْنِ أَوْسٍ رضي الله عنه عن النبي صلى الله عليه وسلم قال : « الْكَيِّسُ مَنْ دَانَ نَفْسَهُ ، وَعَمِلَ لِمَا بَعْدَ الْمَوْتِ ، وَالْعَاجِزُ مَنْ أَتْبَعَ نَفْسَهُ هَوَاهَا ، وَتَمَنَّى عَلَى اللهِ » .

رواه التِّرْمِذِيُّ وقال : حديثٌ حَسَنٌ .

66. Hazrat Abu y'ala bin Shaddad bin Aus (R.A.A.) quotes the Holy Prophet (S.A.W.) as having said: A wise person is one who keeps a watch over his bodily desires and passions, and checks himself from that which is harmful and strives for that which will benefit him after death; and a foolish person is one who subordinates himself to his cravings and desires and expects from Allah the fulfilment of his futile desires (*Tirmizi*).

٦٧ ـ الثَّامِنُ : عَنْ أَبِي هُرَيْرَةَ رَضِيَ الله عنه قال : قال رسول الله صلى الله عليه وسلم : « مِنْ حُسْنِ إِسْلامِ الْمَرْءِ تَرْكُهُ مَالا يَعْنِيهِ » حديثٌ حسن رواه التِّرْمذيُّ وَغَيْرُهُ

67. Hazrat Abu Hurairah (R.A.A.) relates that the Holy Prophet (S.A.W.) said: 'It is part of the excellance of a person's Islam that he should discard that is of no benefit to him either in this world or the Hereafter.' (*Tirmizi*)

٦٨ ـ التَّاسِعُ : عَنْ عُمَرَ رضي الله عنه عَنِ النَّبِيِّ صلى الله عليه وسلم قال : « لا يُسْأَلُ الرَّجُلُ فيمَ ضَرَبَ امْرَأَتَهُ » رواه أبو داود وغيره .

68. Hazrat Umar (R.A.A.) relates that the Holy Prophet (S.A.W.) said that a person will not be questioned about the beating of his wife (for reform) (*Abu Daud and others*).

CHAPTER 6

On Piety

قال الله تعالى : يَاأَيُّهَا الَّذِينَ آمَنُوا اتَّقُوا اللهَ حَقَّ تُقَاتِهِ [آل عمران : ١٠٢] وقال تعالى : فَاتَّقُوا اللهَ مَا اسْتَطَعْتُمْ [التغابن : ١٦] وهذه الآية مبينة للمراد من الأولى . وقال الله تعالى : يَاأَيُّهَا الَّذِينَ آمَنُوا اتَّقُوا اللهَ وَقُولُوا قَوْلاً سَدِيداً - [الأحزاب : ٧٠] وَالآيَاتُ في الأَمْرِ بالتَّقْوَى كَثِيرَةٌ مَعْلُومَةٌ ، وقال تعالى : وَمَنْ يَتَّقِ اللهَ يَجْعَلْ لَهُ مَخْرَجاً وَيَرْزُقْهُ مِنْ حَيْثُ لا يَحْتَسِبُ [الطلاق : ٢ ، ٣] وقال تعالى : إِنْ تَتَّقُوا اللهَ يَجْعَلْ لَكُمْ فُرْقَاناً وَيُكَفِّرْ عَنْكُمْ سَيِّئَاتِكُمْ وَيَغْفِرْ لَكُمْ وَاللهُ ذُو الْفَضْلِ الْعَظِيمِ [الأنفال : ٢٩] والآيَاتُ في البَابِ كَثِيرَةٌ مَعْلُومَةٌ

Allah, the Exalted, has said:

21. Ye who believe! Observe your duty to Allah with right observance, (3:102)
22. So keep your duty to Allah as best you can (64:16)
23. O ye who believe! Guard your duty to Allah, and speak words straight to the point. (33:70)
24. And will provide for him from (a quarter) whence he hath no expectation. (65:3)
25. O ye who believe! If ye keep your duty to Allah, He will give you discrimination (between right and wrong) and will rid you of your evil thoughts and deeds, and will forgive you. Allah is of infinite bounty (8:29)

٦٩ ـ وَأَمَّا الأَحَادِيثُ فَالأَوَّلُ : عَنْ أَبِي هُرَيْرَةَ رضي الله عنه قال :
قِيلَ :يا رسولَ اللهِ مَنْ أَكْرَمُ النَّاسِ ؟ قال : « أَتْقَاهُمْ » . فقَالُوا : لَيْسَ
عَنْ هَذَا نَسْأَلُكَ ، قَالَ : « فَيُوسُفُ نَبِيُّ اللهِ بْنُ نَبِيِّ اللهِ بْنِ نَبِيِّ اللهِ بْنِ
خَلِيلِ اللهِ » قَالُوا : لَيْسَ عَنْ هَذَا نَسْأَلُكَ ، قال : « فَعَنْ مَعَادِنِ الْعَرَبِ
تَسْأَلُونِي ؟ خِيَارُهُمْ فِي الْجَاهِلِيَّةِ خِيَارُهُمْ فِي الإِسْلَامِ إِذَا فَقُهُوا »
متفقٌ عليه

69. Hazrat Abu Hurairah (R.A.A.) relates: The Holy Prophet (S.A.W.) was asked: 'who is the most honoured and respected person among the people? He said: One who fears Allah the most. The companions said: 'We don't mean this.' He said: 'Then, he can be Prophet Joseph the son of a prophet of Allah (Jacob), grand son of another prophet of Allah (Isaac), great grand son of another prophet Abraham, the Friend of Allah. They said: 'This too is not what we mean.' The Holy Prophet (S.A.W.) said: Then do you ask me about some Arab families. Then remember those who were worthy of honour before Islam, are worthy of honour in Islam also, provided they are fully instructed in it. (*Bukhari and Muslim*).

٧٠ ـ الثَّانِي : عَنْ أَبِي سَعِيدٍ الْخُدْرِيِّ رضي الله عنه عن النبي صلى الله
عليه وسلم قال : « إِنَّ الدُّنْيَا حُلْوَةٌ خَضِرَةٌ ، وَإِنَّ اللهَ مُسْتَخْلِفُكُمْ فِيهَا
فَيَنْظُرَ كَيْفَ تَعْمَلُونَ ، فَاتَّقُوا الدُّنْيَا وَاتَّقُوا النِّسَاءَ ؛ فَإِنَّ أَوَّلَ فِتْنَةِ
بَنِي إِسْرَائِيلَ كَانَتْ فِي النِّسَاءِ » رواه مسلم

70. Hazrat Abu Sa'id Khudri relates that the Holy Prophet (S.A.W.) said: 'The world is green and fertile. Allah has made you His deputy and representative on earth, so that He might watch you as to how you behave in this world. So beware of the attractions of the world and the mischief resulting from your relationship with women. Bani Israel had their first mischief on account of women. (*Muslim*).

٧١ ـ الثَّالِثُ : عَنْ ابْنِ مَسْعُودٍ رضي الله عنه أَنَّ النَّبِيَّ صلى الله عليه
وسلم كَانَ يَقُولُ : « اللَّهُمَّ إِنِّي أَسْأَلُكَ الْهُدَى وَالتُّقَى وَالْعَفَافَ وَالْغِنَى »
رواه مسلم

71, **Hazrat Abdullah Ibn Mas'ud** (R.A.A.) relates that the Holy Prophet (S.A.W.) used to pray to Allah that: 'I solicit guidance, piety, chastity and abundance from Thee.' (*Muslim*)

٧٢ ــ الرَّابِعُ : عَنْ أَبِي طَرِيفٍ عَدِيِّ بْنِ حَاتِمٍ الطَّائِيِّ رضي الله عنه قال : سَمِعْتُ رسول الله صلى الله عليه وسلم يَقُولُ : «مَنْ حَلَفَ عَلَى يَمِينٍ ثُمَّ رَأَى أَتْقَى لِلَّهِ مِنْهَا فَلْيَأْتِ التَّقْوَى» رواه مسلم

72. Hazrat Adi Ibn Hatim (R.A.A.) states that I heard the Holy Prophet (S.A.W.) say: 'If a person undertakes to do a thing and then discovers something else which may be better than the first, he should do the better one.' (*Muslim*)

٧٣ ــ الْخَامِسُ : عَنْ أَبِي أُمَامَةَ صُدَيِّ بْنِ عَجْلانَ الْبَاهِلِيِّ رضي الله عنه قال : سَمِعْتُ رسول الله صلى الله عليه وسلم يَخْطُبُ فِي حَجَّةِ الْوَدَاعِ فَقَالَ : «اتَّقُوا اللهَ ، وَصَلُّوا خَمْسَكُمْ ، وَصُومُوا شَهْرَكُمْ ، وَأَدُّوا زَكَاةَ أَمْوَالِكُمْ ، وَأَطِيعُوا أُمَرَاءَكُمْ ، تَدْخُلُوا جَنَّةَ رَبِّكُمْ» رواه التِّرْمِذِيُّ ، في آخر كتاب الصَّلاةِ وَقال : حديثٌ حسنٌ صحيح

73. Hazrat Abu Umamah Bahili (R.A.A.) relates that he heard the address of the Holy Prophet (S..A.W.) on the occasion of the last Pilgrimage in the course of which he said: 'Maintain an awful respect for Allah, observe the five time prayers daily, keep the Ramazan fast; pay the *Zakat* (poor due) and obey those in authority among you (except when they order you to commit sin); you will then enter the Paradise of your Sustainer.' (*Tirmizi*)

Note: Literal meaning of *Taqwa* (Piety) is to abstain and refrain from committing a wrong. But according to the Hadis and the Quran, it means the state of mind in which the omnipotency and ever presence, and watchfulness of Allah is created and it develops the distinction of good and bad, and this feeling leads a person towards virtue and checks him from vice.

* * * * * * * * * * *

CHAPTER 7

On Belief and Trust in Allah

قال الله تعالى : وَلَمَّا رَأَى الْمُؤْمِنُونَ الأَحْزَابَ قَالُوا : هَذَا مَا وَعَدَنَا اللهُ وَرَسُولُهُ ، وَصَدَقَ اللهُ وَرَسُولُه ، وَمَا زَادَهُمْ إِلاَّ إِيمَاناً وَتَسْلِيماً [الأحزاب : ٢٢] وقال تعالى : الَّذِينَ قَالَ لَهُمُ النَّاسُ إِنَّ النَّاسَ قَدْ جَمَعُوا لَكُمْ فَاخْشَوْهُمْ فَزَادَهُمْ إِيمَاناً وَقَالُوا : حَسْبُنَا اللهُ وَنِعْمَ الْوَكِيل

فَانْقَلَبُوا بِنِعْمَةٍ مِنَ اللهِ وَفَضْلٍ لَمْ يَمْسَسْهُمْ سُوءٌ وَاتَّبَعُوا رِضْوَانَ اللهِ ، وَاللهُ ذو فَضْلٍ عَظِيمٍ [آل عمران : ١٧٣ ، ١٧٤] ، وقال تعالى : وَتَوَكَّلْ عَلَى الْحَيِّ الَّذي لا يَمُوت [الفرقان : ٥٨] . وقال تعالى : وَعَلَى اللهِ فَلْيَتَوَكَّلِ الْمُؤْمِنُونَ [إبراهيم : ١١] . وقال تعالى : فَإِذَا عَزَمْتَ فَتَوَكَّلْ عَلَى الله [آل عمران : ١٥٩] . وَالآيَاتُ في الأَمْرِ بالتَّوَكُّلِ كَثِيرَةٌ مَعْلُومَةٌ . وقال تعالى : وَمَنْ يَتَوَكَّلْ عَلَى اللهِ فَهُوَ حَسْبُهُ [الطلاق:٣] أي : كَافِيهِ : وَقال تعالى : إِنَّمَا الْمُؤْمِنُونَ الَّذِينَ إِذَا ذُكِرَ اللهُ وَجِلَتْ قُلُوبُهُمْ وَإِذَا تُلِيَتْ عَلَيْهِمْ آيَاتُه زَادَتْهُمْ إِيمَاناً وَعَلَى رَبِّهِمْ يَتَوَكَّلُونَ [الأنفال : ٢] وَالآيَاتُ في فَضْلِ التَّوَكُّلِ كَثِيرَةٌ مَعْرُوفَةٌ

Allah, the Exalted, has said:

26. And when the true believers saw the clans they said: This is that which Allah and His messenger promised us.
Allah and His Messenger are true. It did but confirm them in their faith and resignation. (33:22)

27. Those unto whom men said: Lo! the People have gathered against you, therefore fear them. (The threat of danger) but increased the faith of them and they cried: Allah is sufficient for us! Most Excellent is He in whom we trust! So they returned with grace and favour from Allah, and no harm touched them. They followed the good pleasure of Allah, and Allah is of infinite bounty, (3:173—174)

28. And trust thou in the Living One Who dieth not, (25:58)

29. In Allah let believers put their trust (14:11)

30. And when thou art resolved, then put thy trust in Allah. Lo! Allah loveth those who put their trust (in Him). (3:159)

31. And whosoever putteth his trust in Allah, He will suffice him. (65:3)

32. They only are the (true) believers whose hearts feel fear when Allah is mentioned, and when the revelations of Allah are recited unto them they increase their faith, and who trust in their Lord (8:2)

٧٤ ــ فَالأَوَّلُ : عَنِ ابْنِ عَبَّاسٍ رضي الله عنهما قال : قال رسولُ الله صلى الله عليه وعلى آله وسلم : « عُرِضَتْ عَلَيَّ الأُمَمُ ، فَرَأَيْتُ النَّبِيَّ وَمَعَهُ الرُّهَيْطُ ، وَالنَّبِيَّ وَمَعَهُ الرَّجُلُ وَالرَّجُلانِ ، وَالنَّبِيَّ وَلَيْسَ مَعَهُ أَحَدٌ

إِذْ رُفِعَ لِي سَوَادٌ عَظِيمٌ فَظَنَنْتُ أَنَّهُمْ أُمَّتِي ، فَقِيلَ لِي : هَـٰذَا مُوسَى وَقَوْمُهُ وَلَـٰكِنِ انْظُرْ إِلَى الأُفُقِ ، فَنَظَرْتُ فَإِذَا سَوَادٌ عَظِيمٌ ، فَقِيلَ لِي : انْظُرْ إِلَى الأُفُقِ الآخَرِ ، فَإِذَا سَوَادٌ عَظِيمٌ ، فَقِيلَ لِي : هَذِهِ أُمَّتُكَ ، وَمَعَهُمْ سَبْعُونَ أَلْفاً يَدْخُلُونَ الْجَنَّةَ بِغَيْرِ حِسَابٍ وَلا عَذَابٍ » ثُمَّ نَهَضَ فَدَخَلَ مَنْزِلَهُ ، فَخَاضَ النَّاسُ فِي أُولَـٰئِكَ الَّذِينَ يَدْخُلُونَ الْجَنَّةَ بِغَيْرِ حِسَابٍ وَلا عَذَابٍ ، فَقَالَ بَعْضُهُمْ : فَلَعَلَّهُمْ الَّذِينَ صَحِبُوا رسولَ الله صلى الله عليه وسلم ، وَقَالَ بَعْضُهُمْ : فَلَعَلَّهُمُ الَّذِينَ وُلِدُوا فِي الإِسْلامِ ، فَلَمْ يُشْرِكُوا بالله شيئاً ـ وَذَكَرُوا أَشْيَاءَ ـ فَخَرَجَ عَلَيْهِمْ رسول الله صلى الله عليه وسلم فَقَالَ : « مَا الَّذِي تَخُوضُونَ فِيهِ ؟ » فَأَخْبَرُوهُ فَقَالَ : « هُمُ الَّذِينَ لايَرْقُونَ ، ولايَسْتَرْقُونَ ولايَتَطَيَّرُونَ ، وَعَلَى رَبِّهِمْ يَتَوَكَّلُونَ » فَقَامَ عُكَّاشَةُ بْنُ مُحْصِنٍ فَقَالَ : ادْعُ اللهَ أَنْ يَجْعَلَنِي مِنْهُمْ ، فَقَالَ : « أَنْتَ مِنْهُمْ » ثُمَّ قَامَ رَجُلٌ آخَرُ فَقَالَ : ادْعُ اللهَ أَنْ يَجْعَلَنِي مِنْهُمْ فقال : « سَبَقَكَ بِهَا عُكَّاشَةُ » متفقٌ عليه

74. **Hazrat Ibn Abbas** (R.A.A.) relates that the Holy Prophet (S.A.W.) said: 'I was shown (in dream or inspiration) many nations. I saw a prophet with a small party, some prophets had only one or two followers with them, and some had none. Then suddenly I saw a huge crowd and I thought that they might be my people, but I was informed: These are Prophet Moses and his follwers', but look towards the horizon. I looked and saw a huge crowd. Then I was asked to look to the other side of the horizon, and there too I saw a great multitude. I was informed: These are your followers, and among them, there are seventy thousand who shall enter Paradise without any accounting or suffering. Then the Holy Prophet (S.A.W.) stood up and went into his chamber and his companions began speculating about those who would enter Paradise without any accounting or suffering: Some said: that they might be those who have the honour of having been associated with the Holy Prophet (S.A.W.) some others guessed that: It may be that they are the persons who have been born Muslims and have never associated anyone with Allah; and so forth. On hearing this the Holy Prophet (S.A.W.) came out of his room and asked: What are you discussing, the gathering apprised him accordingly. He said: They are those who do not make charms or amulets nor use them, and do not believe in omens, but trust in their Lord. On this a companion Hazrat Ukasha bin Muhsin (R.A.A.) stood up and requested to supplicate

Allah that he may be made one of them. The Holy Prophet (S.A.W.) said: 'You are one of them.' Then another companion stood up and asked for the same. The Holy Prophet (S.A.W.) answered: 'Ukasha has taken a lead over yo (*Bukhari and Muslim*).

٧٥ ــ الثَّانِي : عن ابْنِ عَبَّاسٍ رضي الله عَنهما أيضاً أنَّ رسول الله صلى الله عليه وسلم كَانَ يَقُولُ : « اللَّهُمَّ لَكَ أَسْلَمْتُ وَبِكَ آمَنْتُ ، وَعَلَيْكَ تَوَكَّلْتُ ، وَإِلَيْكَ أَنَبْتُ ، وَبِكَ خَاصَمْتُ . اللَّهُمَّ أعُوذُ بِعِزَّتِكَ ؛ لا إِلَهَ إِلاَّ أَنْتَ أَنْ تُضِلَّنِي ، أَنْتَ الحَيُّ الَّذي لاتَمُوتُ ، وَالْجِنُّ وَالإِنْسُ يَمُوتُونَ » متفقٌ عليه . وهَذَا لَفظُ مُسْلِمٍ وَاخْتَصَرَهُ البُخَارِيُّ .

75. Hazrat Ibn Abbas (R.A.A.) relates that the Holy Prophet (S.A.W.) used to supplicate: Allah, to Thee I have submitted, in Thee do I believe and in Thee I put my trust, to Thee do I turn and to Thee do I submit my case for judgment. Allah! I seek refuge with Thee in the name of Thy honour; there is no one worthy of worship save thee, that Thou safeguard me against going astray. Thou art the Ever-Living, whereas men and genie, will all die. (*Bukhari and Muslim*).

٧٦ ــ الثَّالِثُ : عَن ابْنِ عَبَّاسٍ رضي الله عنهما أيضاً قال : « حَسْبُنَا اللهُ وَنِعْمَ الوَكِيلُ ، قَالَهَا إِبْرَاهِيمُ صلى الله عليه وسلم حِينَ أُلْقِيَ فِي النَّارِ ، وَقالهَا مُحَمَّدٌ صلى الله عليه وسلم حِينَ قَالُوا : إِنَّ النَّاسَ قَدْ جَمَعُوا لَكُمْ فَاخْشَوْهُمْ فَزَادَهُمْ إِيمَاناً وَقَالُوا : حَسْبُنَا اللهُ وَنِعْمَ الوَكِيلُ » رواه البخاري

وفي روايةٍ له عن ابْنِ عَبَّاسٍ رضي الله عنهما قال : « كَانَ آخِرَ قَوْلِ إِبْرَاهِيمَ صلى الله عليه وسلم حِينَ أُلْقِيَ في النَّارِ : حَسْبِيَ اللهُ وَنِعْمَ الوَكِيلُ » .

76. Hazrat Ibn Abbas (R.A.A.) relates that when Abraham was thrown into the fire, his words were, 'Sufficient for me is Allah and an excellent Guardian is He.' So did the Holy Prophet (S.A.W.) when he was told that people have mustered against him, and as such he should fear them, this only added to his faith in Allah, as well as, of the Muslims; and he and the Muslims said: 'Sufficient for us is Allah and an excellent Guardian is He' (*Bukhari*)

٧٧ ــ الرَّابِعُ : عَنْ أَبِي هُرَيْرَةَ رضي الله عنه عن النبي صلى الله عليه وسلم قال : « يَدْخُلُ الجَنَّةَ أَقْوَامٌ أَفْئِدَتُهُمْ مِثْلُ أَفْئِدَةِ الطَّيْرِ » رواه مسلم

77. **Hazrat Abu Hurairah (R.A.A.)** relates that the Holy Prophet (S.A.W.) said: 'Many people will enter Paradise whose hearts will be like the hearts of birds, that is their hearts will be soft like those of the birds, or they will be contented or their hearts will be soft due to the fear of Allah (*Muslim*).

٧٨ ـ الْخَامِسُ : عَنْ جَابِرٍ رضي الله عنه أَنَّهُ غَزَا مَعَ النَّبِيِّ صلى الله عليه وسلم قِبَلَ نَجْد ، فَلَمَّا قَفَلَ رسول الله صلى الله عليه وسلم قَفَلَ مَعَهُمْ ، فَأَدْرَكَتْهُمُ الْقَائِلَةُ فِي وَادٍ كَثِيرِ الْعِضَاهِ ، فَنَزَلَ رسولُ اللهِ صلى الله عليه وسلم ، وَتَفَرَّقَ النَّاسُ يَسْتَظِلُّونَ بالشَّجَرِ ، وَنَزَلَ رسولُ الله صلى الله عليه وسلم تَحْتَ سَمُرَةٍ ، فَعَلَّقَ بِهَا سَيْفَهُ ، ونِمْنَا نَوْمَةً ، فَإِذَا رسولُ الله صلى الله عليه وسلم يَدْعُونَا ، وَإِذَا عِنْدَهُ أَعْرَابِيٌّ فَقَالَ : « إِنَّ هَذَا اخْتَرَطَ عَلَيَّ سَيْفِي وَأَنَا نَائِمٌ ، فَاسْتَيْقَظْتُ وَهُوَ فِي يَدِهِ صَلْتاً ، قَالَ : مَنْ يَمْنَعُكَ مِنِّي ؟ قُلْتُ : اللهُ ـ ثَلاثاً » وَلَمْ يُعَاقِبْهُ وَجَلَسَ . متفقٌ عليه

وفي روايةٍ : قَالَ جَابِرٌ : كُنَّا مَعَ رسول اللهِ صلى الله عليه وسلم بِذَاتِ الرِّقَاعِ ، فَإِذَا أَتَيْنَا عَلَى شَجَرَةٍ ظَلِيلَةٍ تَرَكْنَاهَا لرسول الله صلى الله عليه وسلم ، فَجَاءَ رَجُلٌ مِنَ الْمُشْرِكِينَ ، وَسَيْفُ رسول الله صلى الله عليه وسلم مُعَلَّقٌ بالشَّجَرَةِ ، فَاخْتَرَطَهُ فَقَالَ : تَخَافُنِي ؟ قَالَ : « لا » قَالَ : فَمَنْ يَمْنَعُكَ مِنِّي ؟ قالَ : « اللهُ » .

وَفِي روايةِ أَبِي بكرٍ الإسماعيلي في صحيحِهِ : قال : مَنْ يَمْنَعُكَ مِنِّي ؟ قَالَ : « اللهُ » قال : فَسَقَطَ السَّيْفُ مِنْ يَدِهِ ، فَأَخَذَ رسولُ الله صلى الله عليه وسلم السَّيْفَ فَقَالَ : « مَنْ يَمْنَعُكَ مِنِّي ؟ » فَقَالَ : كُنْ خَيْرَ آخِذٍ ، فَقَالَ : « تَشْهَدُ أَنْ لا إِلَهَ إِلاَّ اللهُ ، وَأَنِّي رسولُ الله ؟ » قال : لا ، وَلَكِنِّي أُعَاهِدُكَ أَنْ لا أُقَاتِلَكَ ، وَلا أَكُونَ مَعَ قَوْمٍ يُقَاتِلُونَكَ ، فَخَلَّى سَبِيلَهُ ، فَأَتَى أَصْحَابَهُ فَقَالَ : جِئْتُكُمْ مِنْ عِنْدِ خَيْرِ النَّاسِ

78. **Hazrat Jabir (R.A.A.)** related that he accompanied the Holy Prophet (S.A.W.) in a campaign of *Jihad* towards Nejd and at the end of the battle, returned with him. At mid day the party reached a valley full of thorny trees, where the Holy Prophet (S.A.W.) staged a halt and his companions scattered in search of shade. He hung up his sword from the branch of a tree and lay down in its shade. We also took a siesta and suddenly we heard the Holy Prophet (S.A.W.) calling us. We hastened to him and saw that a desert Arab was sitting near him. The Holy Prophet (S.A.W.) said to us: 'This man drew my sword against me while I was asleep. I woke up and saw that he had the naked sword in his hand, and said to me: 'Who can now save you from me?' I told him: 'Allah will save me' and repeated this sentence thrice. The Holy Prophet (S.A.W.) sat up and did not punish this man.

(*Bukhari and Muslim*).

Another version according to Hazrat Jabir (R.A.A.): 'We were with the Holy Prophet (S.A.W.) in the campaign of Zạt-ir-Rique. We came to a shady tree and left it for him (the Holy Prophet) to rest. A pagan came and seeing the sword of the Holy Prophet (S.A.W.) which was hanging from the tree, drew it, and said to him "Are you not afraid of me?" He answered: 'No', Then the man asked: 'Who is there to save you from me?' The Prophet (S.A.W.) answered: 'Allah'. Abu Bakr Ismaili has added in his book that 'thereupon the sword fell from the Man's hand' and the Holy Prophet (S.A.W.) having secured it asked him: 'Who will now save you from me?' The man said: 'Be a good captor.' The Holy Prophet (S.A.W.) asked him 'Will you affirm that there is no god save Allah, and that I am His Messenger?' The man refused and said: 'But I promise you that I will not fight against you, nor will I join those who do so.' The Holy Prophet (S.A.W.) let him go free. He went back to this people and told them 'I have come back to you from one who is the best of mankind.'

٧٩ ـ السَّادِسُ : عَنْ عُمَرَ رضي الله عنه قال : سَمِعْتُ رسولَ الله صلى الله عليه وسلم يَقُولُ : « لَوْ أَنَّكُمْ تَتَوَكَّلُونَ عَلَى اللهِ حَقَّ تَوَكُّلِهِ لَرَزَقَكُمْ كَمَا يَرْزُقُ الطَّيْرَ ، تَغْدُو خِمَاصاً وَتَرُوحُ بِطَاناً» رواه الترمذي ، وقال : حديثٌ حسنٌ

79. Hazrat Umar Bin Khattab (R.A.A.) relates that he heard the Holy Prophet (S.A.W.) say: 'If you put your faith completely in Allah, He will arrange for your sustenance in the same way as He provides for the birds. They go out in the morning with their stomachs empty and return filled in the evening.'

(*Tirmizi*).

٨٠ ـ السَّابِعُ : عَنْ أَبِي عِمَارَةَ الْبَرَاءِ بْنِ عَازِبٍ رضي الله عنهما قال : قال رسول الله صلى الله عليه وسلم : « يَا فُلَانُ إِذَا أَوَيْتَ إِلَى فِرَاشِكَ فَقُلْ: اللَّهُمَّ أَسْلَمْتُ نَفْسِي إِلَيْكَ ، وَوَجَّهْتُ وَجْهِي إِلَيْكَ : وَفَوَّضْتُ

أمري إليكَ ، وألجأتُ ظهري إليكَ ، رغبةً ورهبةً إليكَ ، لا ملجأ ولا منجى منكَ إلاَّ إليكَ ، آمنتُ بكتابكَ الذي أنزلتَ ، ونبيكَ الذي أرسلتَ ، فإنكَ إنْ متَّ من ليلتكَ متَّ على الفطرةِ وإنْ أصبحتَ أصبتَ خيراً » متفقٌ عليه

وفي روايةٍ في الصحيحين عن البراء قال : قال لي رسول الله صلى الله عليه وسلم : « إذا أتيتَ مضجعكَ فتوضأْ وضوءكَ للصلاةِ ، ثمَّ اضطجعْ على شقكَ الأيمنِ وقلْ : وذكرَ نحوهُ ، ثمَّ قالَ : واجعلهنَّ آخرَ ما تقولُ »

80. Hazrat Bra'a Ibn A'zib relates: The Holy Prophet (S.A.W.) advised me: 'When you go to sleep at night you should pray: 'Allah, I submit myself to Thee, and concentrate my mind on Thee, and commit my affairs to Thy care, and make Thee my support out of love and fear of Thee. There is no escape from Thee, nor security against Thee save in Thyself. I believe in the Book that Thou hast sent down and in the Prophet Thou hadst raised .' Then if you die that night you will die in purity and if you survive you will come across more good.

(*Bukhari and Muslim*)

Another version says: The Holy Prophet (S.A.W.) said to me: 'When you are ready for bed wash (perform ablution) as you would do for *salat*, then lie down on your right side and supplicate (as above) and let these be your last words (before sleeping).

٨١ — الثامنُ : عنْ أبي بكرٍ الصدِّيق رضي الله عنه عبدِ اللهِ بنِ عثمان بن عامرِ بن عُمَرَ بن كعب بن سعدِ بن تيْم بن مُرَّةَ بنِ كعبِ بن لؤيِّ بن غالبٍ القرشيُّ التيميُّ رضي الله عنه — وهوَ وأبوهُ وأمُّهُ صحابةٌ ، رضي الله عنهم — قال : نظرتُ إلى أقدام المشركينَ ونحنُ في الغارِ وهمْ على رؤوسنا فقلتُ : يا رسول الله لوْ أنَّ أحدهمْ نظرَ تحتَ قدميهِ لأبصرَنا . فقالَ : « ما ظنُّكَ يا أبا بكرٍ باثنينِ الله ثالثهما » متفقٌ عليه

81. Hazrat Abu Bakr Siddique (R.A.A.) Bin Abdullah Bin Usman Bin Hamir Bin Umar Bin Ka'ab Bin Saad Bin Taim Bin Marrah Bin K'ab Bin Luwai Bin Ghalib al Quraishie Taimie who alongwith his father and mother are all companions,relates: When the Holy Prophet (S.A.W.) and I were hiding in the Cave Saur and were being tracked by the

Meccans, I saw their feet above us outside the cave and I said: 'Messenger of Allah, if one of them were to look down below his feet he would see us.' He said: 'Abu Bakr! What would you think of two with whom Allah is the third?' (*Bukhari and Muslim*).

٨٢ — التَّاسِعُ : عَنْ أُمِّ الْمُؤْمِنِينَ أُمِّ سَلَمَةَ ،وَاسْمُهَا هِنْدُ بِنْتُ أَبي أُمَيَّةَ حُذَيْفَةَ الْمَخْزُومِيَّةُ ، رضي الله عنها أن النبي صلى الله عليه وسلم كانَ إذَا خرَجَ مِنْ بَيْتِهِ قالَ : « بسْمِ اللهِ ، تَوَكَّلْتُ عَلَى اللهِ ، اللَّهُمَّ إنِّي أعُوذُ بِكَ أنْ أَضِلَّ . أوْ أُضَلَّ ، أَوْ أَزِلَّ أَوْ أُزَلَّ ، أَوْ أَظْلِمَ أَوْ أُظْلَمَ ، أَوْ أجْهَلَ أَوْ يُجْهَلَ عَلَيَّ » حديثٌ صَحيحٌ رواه أبو داود ، والتِّرْمذيُّ وَغَيْرُهُمَا بِأسانيد صَحيحةٍ . قالَ التِّرْمذي : حَديثٌ حسنٌ صحيحٌ ، وهذا لفظ أبي داود .

82. Hazrat Umm Salamah (R.A.A.) (Mother of the Faithful) relates that when the Holy Prophet (S.A.W.) used to go out of the house he prayed thus: 'I go out in the name of Allah, with my trust in Him. Allah, I solicit Thy protection against committing wrong or being led astray, or against any misstep or being caused to err or against exceeding my limits or being trespassed against, or against misbehaving towards someone or anyone should misbehave with me'.

(*Abu Daud and Tirmizi*).

٨٣ — الْعَاشِرُ : عَنْ أنس رضي الله عنه قال : قال رسول الله صلى الله عليه وسلم : « مَنْ قَالَ — يَعْنِي إذَا خرَجَ مِنْ بَيْتِهِ — : بِسْمِ اللهِ تَوَكَّلْتُ عَلَى اللهِ ، وَلا حَوْلَ وَلا قُوَّةَ إلاَّ باللهِ ، يقالُ لَهُ : هُدِيتَ وَكُفِيتَ وَوُقِيتَ ، وَتَنَحَّى عَنْهُ الشَّيْطَانُ » . رواه أبو داود والترمذي، والنسائي وغيرهم . وقال الترمذي : حديثٌ حسنٌ ، زاد أَبُو داود : « فيقول : — يَعْنِي الشَّيْطَانَ — لِشَيْطَانٍ آخرَ: كَيْفَ لَكَ بِرَجُلٍ قَدْ هُدِيَ وَكُفِيَ وَوُقِيَ» ؟

83. Hazrat Anas Bin Malik (R.A.A.) relates that the Holy Prophet (S.A.W.) said: ''He, who on coming out of his house prays: 'I go out (of my house) in the name of Allah, with my trust in Him: it is only Allah ''Who grants me power to be saved from committing sin or grants power to do good'', then this man is shown the right path and is protected, and the Satan withdraws from him.

(*Abu Daud, Tirmizi and Nisai*).

Abu Daud Adds; 'One Satan says to another 'How can you subdue a person who is guided, is covered and is saved?'.

٨٤ — وَعَنْ أَنَسٍ رضي الله عنه قال : كَانَ أَخَوَانِ عَلَى عَهْدِ

نبي صلى الله عليه وسلم ، وكَانَ أَحَدُهُمَا يا تِي النبيَّ صلى الله عليه وسلم ، وَالآخَرُ يَحْتَرِفُ . فَشَكَا الْمُحْتَرِفُ أَخَاهُ للنبي صلى الله عليه وسلم فقال : لَعَلَّكَ تُرْزَقُ بِه » رواه التِّرْمذي بإسناد صحيح على شرطِ مسلم

84. Hazrat Anas Bin Malik (R.A.A.) relates that during the days of the Holy Prophet (S.A.W.) there were two brothers, one of whom used to serve the Holy Prophet (S.A.W.) and the other used to look after his business. One day the latter complained to the Holy Prophet (S.A.W.) that his other brother does nothing (to earn a living). The Holy Prophet (S.A.W.) replied: 'It is just possible that you are being helped to earn your living on account of him.' (*Tirmizi*)

Note: *Tawakkul* literally means to confide or trust some body. According to the terminology of Holy Quran and Hadis, it means implicit faith and trust in Allah. But there is a distinction as to in what matters to confide in divine will. The deceptive *Sufis* and *Faqirs* (Mendicants) have described inactivity and disregard to the principle of cause and effect, as *Tawakkul*. In fact it is necessary to undertake a task or errand with full planning and determined efforts, and trust that if this work is good for us, Allah will certainly help us. And this is *Tawakkul*.

* * * * * * * * * * *

CHAPTER 8

On Perseverance in Religion

قال الله تعالى : فاسْتَقِمْ كَمَا أُمِرْتَ [هود : ١١٢] وقالَ تعالى :
إنَّ الَّذينَ قالُوا رَبُّنَا اللهُ ثُمَّ اسْتَقَامُوا تَتَنَزَّلُ عَلَيْهِمُ المَلائِكَةُ أَن لا تَخَافُوا ولا تَحزَنُوا وَأَبْشِرُوا بالْجنَّةِ الَّتِي كُنْتُمْ تُوعَدُونَ ، نَحنُ أَوْلِياؤُكُمْ في الحَياة الدُّنْيا وَفي الآخرَةِ ولَكُمْ فيهَا مَا تَشْتَهي أَنْفُسُكُمْ وَلَكُمْ فيها ما تَدَّعُون [فصلت : ٣٠ ، ٣٢]
وقال تعالى : إنَّ الَّذينَ قالُوا رَبُّنَا اللهُ ثُمَّ اسْتَقَامُوا فَلا خَوْفٌ عَلَيْهِمْ. ولا هُمْ يَحْزَنُونَ أُولَئكَ أَصْحَابُ الجنَّةِ خَالدينَ فيهَا جزَاءً بِمَا كَانُوا يَعْمَلُونَ [الأحقاف : ١٣ ، ١٤] .

Allah, the Most High, has said:

33. So tread thou the straight path as thou art commanded.(11:112)
34. Lo! Those who say: Our Lord is Allah; and afterwards are upright, the angels descend upon them saying: Fear not, nor grieve, but hear good tidings of the paradise which ye are promised. We are your protecting friends in the life of the world and in the Hereafter. There ye will have (all) for which ye pray, (41:30--31).
35. Lo! Those who say: Our Lord is Allah, and thereafter walk aright, there shall no fear come upon them neither shall they grieve. Such are rightful owners of the Gardens immortal therein, as a reward for what they used to do. (46:13—14)

٨٥ – وَعَنْ أبي عَمْرٍو ، وقيل : أبي عَمْرَةَ سُفْيَانَ بنِ عبدِ الله رضي الله عنه قال : قُلْتُ : يَارسول اللهِ قُلْ لِي في الإسْلامِ قَوْلاً لا أسْأل عَنْه أحَداً غَيْرَكَ . قال : « قُلْ : آمَنْتُ باللهِ : ثُمَّ اسْتَقِمْ » رواه مسلم

85. Hazrat Sufyan Ibn Abdullah (R.A.A.) says: I requested the Messenger of Allah (S.A.W.): Give me some such comprehensive guidance about Islam, after which I may not have to ask anyone else. He (S.A.W.) said: 'Affirm: I believe that Allah is my only Sustainer and then be steadfast. (*Muslim*)

٨٦ – وَعَنْ أبي هُرَيْرَةَ رضي الله عنه : قال : قال رسول الله صلى الله عليه وسلم « قَارِبُوا وَسَدِّدُوا ، واعْلَمُوا أنَّه لَنْ يَنْجُوَ أحَدٌ مِنْكُمْ بعَمَلِه ، قَالُوا : وَلا أنْتَ يَا رَسُولَ الله ؟ قال : « وَلا أنَا إلاَّ أنْ يَتَغَمَّدَنِي الله بِرَحْمَةٍ مِنْه وَفَضْلٍ » رواه مسلم

86. Hazrat Abu Hurairah (R.A.A.) tells that the Holy Prophet (S.A.W.) declared: Follow the principles of Islam strictly and be firm: and remember that no one can achieve redemption, through his action. Someone asked 'Not even you O Prophet of Allah?' He said: 'Nor I, except that Allah should cover me with his mercy and grace? (*Muslim*).

Note: According to *Ulema* (Muslim theologians) perseverance means to make the obedience of Allah obligatory and to lead a life of servility to Him.

* * * * * * * * * *

CHAPTER 9

On Contemplation over the Creation of the Universe and the Things therein.

قال الله تعالى : إِنَّمَا أَعِظُكُمْ بِوَاحِدَةٍ أَنْ تَقُومُوا لِلَّهِ مَثْنَى وَفُرَادَى ثُمَّ تَتَفَكَّرُوا [سبأ : ٤٦] . وقال تعالى : إِنَّ فِي خَلْقِ السَّمَوَاتِ وَالأَرْضِ وَاخْتِلَافِ اللَّيْلِ وَالنَّهَارِ لَآيَاتٍ لِأُولِي الأَلْبَابِ . الَّذِينَ يَذْكُرُونَ اللَّهَ قِيَاماً وَقُعُوداً وَعَلَى جُنُوبِهِمْ وَيَتَفَكَّرُونَ فِي خَلْقِ السَّمَوَاتِ وَالأَرْضِ رَبَّنَا مَا خَلَقْتَ هَذَا بَاطِلاً سُبْحَانَكَ الآيات[آل عمران: ١٩٠، ١٩١] . وقال تعالى : أَفَلَا يَنْظُرُونَ إِلَى الإِبِلِ كَيْفَ خُلِقَتْ وَإِلَى السَّمَاءِ كَيْفَ رُفِعَتْ وَإِلَى الجِبَالِ كَيْفَ نُصِبَتْ وَإِلَى الأَرْضِ كَيْفَ سُطِحَتْ فَذَكِّرْ إِنَّمَا أَنْتَ مُذَكِّرٌ [الغاشية : ١٧ ، ٢١] . وقال تعالى : أَفَلَمْ يَسِيرُوا فِي الأَرْضِ فَيَنْظُرُوا الآية [القتال : ١٠] . والآيات في الباب كثيرةٌ .

وَمِنَ الأَحَادِيثِ الحَدِيثُ السَّابِقُ : « الكَيِّسُ مَنْ دَانَ نَفْسَهُ » .

Allah, the Exalted has said:

36. Say (Unto them, O Muhammad): I exhort you unto one thing only that ye awake, for Allah's sake, by twos and singly and then reflect: (34:46)
37. Lo! in the creation of the heavens and the earth and in the difference of night and day are tokens (of His Sovereignty) for men of understanding. Such as remember Allah, standing, sitting, and reclining, and consider the creation of the heavens and the earth (and say) our Lord! Thou created not this in vain. Glory be to Thee! Preserve us from the doom of fire. (3:190—191).
38. Will they not regard the camels, how they are created? and the heaven, how it is raised? And the hills how they are set up? And the earth, how it is spread? Remind them, for thou art but a remembrancer. (88:17—21)
39. Have they not travelled in the land to see the nature of the consequence for those who were before them? (47:10)

* * * * * * * * * * *

CHAPTER 10

To Surpass in Virtuous Deeds and Incentive for the Same

قال الله تعالى : ﴿ فَاسْتَبِقُوا الْخَيْرَاتِ ﴾ [البقرة : ١٤٨] . وقال تعالى : ﴿ وَسَارِعُوا إِلَى مَغْفِرَةٍ مِّن رَّبِّكُمْ وَجَنَّةٍ عَرْضُهَا السَّمَوَاتُ وَالأَرْضُ أُعِدَّتْ لِلْمُتَّقِينَ ﴾ [آل عمران : ١٣٣]

Allah, the Glorified has said:

40. So vie with one another in good works (2:148)
41. And vie one with another for forgiveness from your Lord, and for a Paradise as wide as are the heavens and the earth, prepared for those who ward off (evil) (3:133)

٨٧ ــ فَالأَوَّل : عَنْ أَبِي هُرَيْرَةَ رضي الله عنه أن رسول الله صلى الله عليه وسلم قال : « بَادِرُوا بِالأَعْمَالِ الصَّالِحَةِ ، فِتَناً كَقِطَعِ اللَّيْلِ الْمُظْلِمِ يُصْبِحُ الرَّجُلُ مُؤْمِناً وَيُمْسِي كَافِراً . وَيُمْسِي مُؤْمِناً وَيُصْبِحُ كَافِراً ، يَبِيعُ دِينَهُ بِعَرَضٍ مِنَ الدُّنْيَا » رواه مسلم

87. Hazrat Abu Hurairah (R.A.A.) deposes that the Holy Prophet (S.A.W.) said: Lose no time to do good work for soon there will be series of mischiefs like some parts of a dark night. A person will get up in the morning a believing Muslim, and will turn a renegade in the evening, or go to bed believing and get up in the morning disbelieving. He will be ready to sell his faith for a secular gain. (*Muslim*).

٨٨ ــ الثَّانِي : عَنْ أَبِي سِرْوَعَةَ ــ بكسرِ السينِ المهملةِ وفتحها ــ عُقْبَةَ بْنِ الْحَارِثِ رضي الله عنه قال : صَلَّيْتُ وَرَاءَ النَّبِيِّ صلى الله عليه وسلم بِالْمَدِينَةِ الْعَصْرَ ، فَسَلَّمَ ثُمَّ قَامَ مُسْرِعاً فَتَخَطَّى رِقَابَ النَّاسِ إِلَى بَعْضِ حُجَرِ نِسَائِهِ ، فَفَزِعَ النَّاسُ مِنْ سُرْعَتِهِ ، فَخَرَجَ عَلَيْهِمْ ، فَرَأَى أَنَّهُمْ قَدْ عَجِبُوا مِنْ سُرْعَتِهِ ، فَقَالَ : « ذَكَرْتُ شَيْئاً مِنْ تِبْرٍ عِنْدَنَا ، فَكَرِهْتُ أَنْ يَحْبِسَنِي ، فَأَمَرْتُ بِقِسْمَتِهِ » رواه البخاري .

وفي رواية له : « كُنْتُ خَلَّفْتُ فِي الْبَيْتِ تِبْراً مِنَ الصَّدَقَةِ ؛ فَكَرِهْتُ أَنْ أُبَيِّتَهُ » . « التِّبْرُ » قطعُ ذَهَبٍ أَوْ فِضَّةٍ .

88. Hazrat Utbah Ibn Haris (R.A.A.) tells: 'I joined the Afternoon Prayer led by the Holy Prophet (S.A.W.) in Madina. The moment he finished the prayer he stood up and stepping across the line of the worshippers hastened to one of his chambers. People in the gathering were surprised by such haste. When he came back, explaining his action he said: 'I recalled that there was left with me a piece of silver (or gold) and this disturbed me. I have now arranged for its distribution.

(*Bukhari*).

Another version says: There was left with me a piece of silver (or gold) which was meant for charity. I was disturbed that it should remain with me overnight.

٨٩ ـ الثَّالث : عَنْ جَابِرٍ رضي الله عنه قال : قال رجلٌ للنبيِّ صلى الله عليه وسلم يَوْمَ أُحُد : أَرَأَيْتَ إنْ قُتِلْتُ فَأَيْنَ أنا ؟ قَالَ : « في الْجَنَّةِ » فَأَلْقَى تَمرَاتٍ كُنَّ في يَدِهِ . ثمَّ قَاتَلَ حَتَّى قتلَ . متفقٌ عليه

89. Hazrat Jabir (R.A.A.) relates that one man requested the Holy Prophet (S.A.W.) on the day of the battle of Uhud: 'Tell me, where shall I be if I am killed in battle just now.' He answered: 'In Heaven.' The man threw away the few dates he had in his hand, plunged into the battle and fought on till he was martyred. *(Agreed Upon).*

٩٠ ـ الرَّابع : عن أبي هريرة رضي الله عنه قال : جَاءَ رجلٌ إلى النَّبيِّ صلى الله عليه وسلم ، فقال يا رسول الله : أيُّ الصَّدَقَةِ أعْظَمُ أجْراً ؟ قَالَ : « أنْ تَصَدَّقَ وَأَنْتَ صَحِيحٌ شَحِيحٌ تَخْشَى الْفَقْرَ ، وَتَأْمُلُ الْغِنَى ، وَلا تُمْهِلْ حَتَّى إذَا بَلَغَت الْحُلْقُومَ . قُلْتَ : لِفُلانٍ كَذَا وَلِفُلان كَذَا ، وَقَدْ كَانَ لِفُلان » متفقٌ عليه

90. Hazrat Abu Hurairah (R.A.A.) relates that a man came and requested the Holy Prophet (S.A.W.): which act of alms giving is most virtuous?' He (S.A.W.) answered: 'That which you give away while you are in good health, and have keen desire to amass wealth, and afraid of adversity and longing for money. Do not delay spending in charity till you are in the throes of death and then say: 'To So and So this, and to So and So that, for by then they already belong to So and So.' (*Bukhari and Muslim*)

٩١ ـ الخامس : عن أنس رضي الله عنه ، أنَّ رسول الله صلى الله عليه وسلم أخَذَ سَيْفاً يوْمَ أُحُدٍ فَقَالَ : « مَنْ يَأْخُذُ مِنِّي هَذَا ؟ فَبَسَطُوا أَيْدِيَهُمْ ، كُلُّ إنْسَانٍ مِنهُمْ يَقُول : أَنَا أَنَا . قَالَ : « فَمَنْ يَأْخُذُهُ بِحَقِّهِ ؟ » فَأَحْجَمَ الْقَوْمُ ، فَقَالَ أَبُو دجَانَةَ رضي الله عنه : أَنَا آخُذُهُ بِحَقِّهِ ، فَأَخَذَهُ فَفَلَقَ بِهِ هَامَ الْمُشْرِكِينَ . رواه مسلم

91. **Hazrat Anas** (R.A.A.) relates that the Holy Prophet (S.A.W.) took up a sword on the day of the battle of Uhud and said: 'Who will take this sword from me?.' Everyone stretched forth his hand saying: 'I, I'. The Holy Prophet (S.A.W.) said 'Who will discharge its full responsibility?' The audience hesitated. But Hazrat Abu Dujanah (R.A.A.) the companion said: 'I take it with its responsibility' and with it he slew a number of idol worshippers. (*Muslim*)

٩٢ ــ السَّادس : عن الزُّبَيْرِ بنِ عديّ قال : أتَيْنَا أنَسَ بنَ مَالكٍ رضي الله عنه فَشَكَوْنَا إليْهِ مَا نَلْقَى منَ الحَجَّاجِ . فَقَالَ : « اصْبروا فإنَّه لا يَأْتي زَمَانٌ إلاَّ والَّذي بَعْدَه شَرٌّ منه حتَّى تَلْقَوْا ربَّكُم » سَمِعْتُه منْ نَبيِّكُمْ صلى الله عليه وسلم . رواه البخاري

92. **Hazrat Zubair Ibn Adiyy** (R.A.A.) tells: We approached (Hazrat) Anas Ibn Malik (R.A.A.) and complained to him about the ill treatment and torture caused to us by Hajjaj Bin Yusuf (a cruel Governor during Umayyad reign). He advised us to be patient and said: Each period is followed by a worse time. I have heard this from the Holy Prophet (S.A.W.). (*Bukhari*).

٩٣ ــ السَّابع : عن أبي هريرة رضي الله عنه أن رسول الله صلى الله عليه وسلم قال : « بادِروا بالأعْمَالِ سَبْعاً ، هَلْ تَنْتَظرونَ إلاَّ فَقْراً مُنْسياً ، أوْ غنىً مُطْغياً ، أوْ مَرَضاً مُفْسداً ، أوْ هَرَماً مُفْنداً أوْ مَوْتاً مُجْهزاً أوِ الدَّجَّالَ فَشَرٌّ غائبٍ يُنْتَظَر ، أوِ السَّاعَةَ فالسَّاعَةُ أدْهَى وأمَرُّ ! » رواه التِّرمذي وقال : حديثٌ حسنٌ .

93. **Hazrat Abu Hurairah** (R.A.A.) states that the Holy Prophet (S.A.W.) said: 'Lose no time to do good work before you are caught up by one of the seven calamities. Then by way of warning he recounted, a starvation which may impair your wisdom, or a prosperity which may mislead you, or an ailment which may damage your health, or an old age which may harm your senses, or a sudden death or the appearance of Dajjal (Antichrist). All these are bad events which may be awaited; or the Doomsday, but this day is indeed very hard and bitter. (*Tirmizi*)

٩٤ ــ الثامن : عنه أن رسولَ الله صلى الله عليه وسلم قال يومَ خَيْبَر : « لأعْطِينَّ هَذه الرَّايَةَ رَجُلاً يُحبُّ اللهَ وَرَسُولَه ، يفْتَح الله عَلَى يَدَيْه » قال عُمَر رضي الله عنه : مَا أحْبَبْتُ الإمَارَةَ إلاَّ يَوْمَئذٍ ، فتَساوَرْتُ لَهَا رَجَاءَ أنْ أُدْعَى لَهَا ، فَدَعَا رسول الله صلى الله عليه وسلم عليَّ بن أبي

طالب ، رضي الله عنه ، فأعطاه إياها ، وقال : « امش ولا تلتفت حتى
يفتح الله عليك » فسار علي شيئاً، ثم وقف ولم يلتفت، فصرخ :
يا رسول الله ، على ماذا أقاتل الناس ؟ قال : « قاتلهم حتى يشهدوا
أن لا إله إلا الله ، وأن محمداً رسول الله ، فإذا فعلوا ذلك فقد
منعوا منك دماءهم وأموالهم إلا بحقها ، وحسابهم على الله »
رواه مسلم

94. It is reported by Hazrat Abu Hurairah (R.A.A.) that on the eve of the battle of Khaibar, the Holy Prophet (S.A.W.) said: 'I shall offer this standard to one who loves Allah and His Messenger, may Allah grant (us) victory through him.' Hazrat Umar (R.A.A.) relates: 'I had never desired a command, but that day I hoped that I might be given this chance. However, the Holy Prophet (S.A.W.) called (Hazrat) Ali Bin Abi Talib (R.A.A.) and handed the standard to him and said: 'Go ahead and pay no heed to anything else till Allah bestows victory through you.' Hazrat Ali (R.A.A.) on hearing this, proceeded a little and then halted and without turning, asked in a loud voice: 'Messenger of Allah, (S.A.W.) for what shall I fight with them'. He answered: 'Fight on till they affirm that there is none worthy of worship save Allah, and that Muhammad is His Messenger. 'If they do that, their lives and their properties should remain safe, (of course) subject to the obligations under Islamic law and they will be accountable to Allah.' (*Muslim*).

* * * * * * * * * * *

CHAPTER 11

On Self-denial

قال الله تعالى : وَالَّذِينَ جَاهَدُوا فِينَا لَنَهْدِيَنَّهُمْ سُبُلَنَا وَإِنَّ اللَّهَ
لَمَعَ الْمُحْسِنِينَ [العنكبوت : ٦٩] . وقال تعالى : وَاعْبُدْ رَبَّكَ حَتَّى
يَأْتِيَكَ الْيَقِينُ [الحجر: ٩٩] . وقال تعالى : وَاذْكُرِ اسْمَ رَبِّكَ
وَتَبَتَّلْ إِلَيْهِ تَبْتِيلاً [المزمل: ٨] : أي انقطع إليه . وقال تعالى : فَمَنْ
يَعْمَلْ مِثْقَالَ ذَرَّةٍ خَيْراً يَرَه [الزلزلة : ٧] . وقال تعالى : وَمَا
تُقَدِّمُوا لأَنْفُسِكُمْ مِنْ خَيْرٍ تَجِدُوهُ عِنْدَ اللَّهِ هُوَ خَيْراً وَأَعْظَمَ
أَجْراً [المزمل : ٢٠]. وقال تعالى : وَمَا تُنْفِقُوا مِنْ خَيْرٍ فَإِنَّ اللَّهَ بِهِ

عَلِيمٌ [البقرة : ٢٧٣] والآيات في الباب كثيرةٌ معلومة

Allah, the Almighty, has said:

42. As for those who strive in Us, We surely guide them to our paths, and Lo!. Allah is with the good. (29:69)
43. And serve thy Lord till the inevitable (i.e. death) cometh unto thee. (15:99)
44. So remember the name of thy Lord and devote thyself with a complete devotion. (73:8)
45. And whoso doeth good an atom's weight will see it then. (99:9)
46. Whatsoever good ye send before you for your sake, ye will surely find it with Allah, better and greater in the recompense. (73:20)
47. And whatsoever good thing ye spend, Lo! Allah knoweth it. (2:273)

٩٥ ـ فالأول : عن أبي هريرة رضي الله عنه . قال : قال رسول الله صلى الله عليه وسلم : « إنَّ الله تعالى قال : مَنْ عادَى لي وَلِيّاً فَقَدْ آذَنْتُهُ بالحَرْب . وَما تَقَرَّبَ إليَّ عَبْدِي بِشَيْءٍ أَحَبَّ إليَّ مِمَّا افْتَرَضْتُ عَلَيْهِ : وَمَا يَزَالُ عَبْدِي يَتَقَرَّبُ إليَّ بالنَّوَافِلِ حَتَّى أُحِبَّهُ ، فَإذَا أَحْبَبْتُهُ كُنْتُ سَمْعَهُ الَّذِي يَسْمَعُ به ، وَبَصَرَهُ الَّذِي يُبْصِرُ بِهِ ، وَيَدَهُ الَّتي يَبْطُشُ بِهَا ، وَرِجْلَهُ الَّتي يَمْشِي بها ، وَإِنْ سَأَلَني أَعْطَيْتُهُ ، وَلَئِنِ اسْتَعَاذَني لأُعِيذَنَّهُ » رواه البخاري

95. **Hazrat Abu Hurairah** (R.A.A.) relates that the Holy Prophet (S.A.W.) said: Allah says: 'Whoever is inimical to one whom I befriend, is at war with me. When a servant of Mine approaches Me through the medium of that which I like best, out of what I have declared obligatory for him, and continues to advance towards me through optional prayers (*Nawafil*), then I begin to love him. When I make him My beloved I become his ears to hear, and his eyes to see, and his hands to grasp, and his feet to walk. When he asks Me I grant him and when he seeks My protection I protect him. (*Bukhari*)

٩٦ ـ الثاني : عن أنس رضي الله عنه عن النبي صلى الله عليه وسلم فيما يَرْوِيه عَنْ رَبِّهِ عَزَّ وَجَلَّ قال : « إذَا تَقَرَّبَ العَبْدُ إليَّ شِبْراً تَقَرَّبْتُ إلَيْهِ ذِرَاعاً ، وَإِذَا تَقَرَّبَ إليَّ ذِرَاعاً تَقَرَّبْتُ مِنْهُ بَاعاً ، وَإِذَا أَتَاني يَمْشِي أَتَيْتُهُ هَرْوَلَةً » رواه البخاري

96. Hazrat Anas Bin Malik (R.A.A.) states that the Holy Prophet (S.A.W.) said: 'Allah says, when a servant of Mine proceeds towards Me a hand spread, I rush towards him an arm, and when he proceeds towards Me an arm, I advance towards him by the length of his arms spread out. When he comes to me walking, I advance to him running. (*Bukhari*).

٩٧ — الثالث : عن ابن عباس رضي الله عنهما قال : قال رسول الله صلى الله عليه وسلم : « نِعْمَتَانِ مَغْبُونٌ فِيهِمَا كَثِيرٌ مِنَ النَّاسِ : الصِّحَّةُ ، وَالْفَرَاغُ » رواه البخاري

97. Hazrat Ibn Abbas (R.A.A.) relates that the Holy Prophet (S.A.W.) said: 'People are great losers in respect of two bounties, i.e. health and affluence, as a result of which they do not worship Allah as much as they ought to do.' (*Bukhari*)

٩٨ — الرابع : عن عائشة رضى الله عنها أنَّ النَّبِيَّ صلى الله عليه وسلم كَانَ يَقُومُ مِنَ اللَّيْلِ حَتَّى تَتَفَطَّرَ قَدَمَاهُ ، فَقُلْتُ لَهُ : لِمَ تَصْنَعُ هَذَا يَا رَسُولَ اللهِ ، وَقَدْ غَفَرَ اللهُ لَكَ مَا تَقَدَّمَ مِنْ ذَنْبِكَ وَمَا تَأَخَّرَ؟ قَالَ : « أَفَلاَ أُحِبُّ أَنْ أَكُونَ عَبْداً شَكُوراً؟ » متفقٌ عليه . هذا لفظ البخاري ، ونحوه في الصحيحين من رواية المُغيرة بن شُعْبَةَ .

98. Hazrat Ayesha (R.A.A.) says: the Holy Prophet (S.A.W.) used to stand so long during his optional prayers at night, that the skin of his feet would erupt; therefore I said to him; Messenger of Allah, (S.A.W.) why do you stand so long in prayer when Allah has forgiven your past and future sins (if any)? He said: 'Then may I not become the most grateful servant of Allah?' (*Bukhari and Muslim*)

٩٩ — الخامس : عن عائشة رضي الله عنها أنها قالت : « كان رسول الله صلى الله عليه وسلم إِذَا دَخَلَ الْعَشْرَ أَحْيَا اللَّيْلَ ، وَأَيْقَظَ أَهْلَهُ ، وَجَدَّ وَشَدَّ المِئْزَرَ » متفقٌ عليه

99. Hazrat Ayesha (R.A.A.) relates: 'During the last ten days of the month of Ramazan the Holy Prophet (S.A.W.) used to keep awake the whole night and would call upon the members of his family to do the same, greatly intensifying for prayers. (*Bukhari and Muslim*)

١٠٠ — السادس : عن أبي هريرة رضي الله عنه قال : قال رسولُ الله صلى الله عليه وسلم : « المُؤْمِنُ الْقَوِيُّ خَيْرٌ وَأَحَبُّ إلى اللهِ مِنَ المُؤْمِنِ الضَّعِيفِ وَفي كُلٍّ خَيْرٌ . احْرِصْ عَلى مَا يَنْفَعُكَ ، وَاسْتَعِنْ بِاللهِ وَلاَ تَعْجَزْ وَإنْ أَصَابَكَ شَيْءٌ فَلاَ تَقُلْ : لَوْ أَنِّي فَعَلْتُ كَانَ كَذَا وَكَذَا ، وَلَكِنْ

قُلْ : قَدَّرَ اللهُ ، وما شاء فعَلَ ؛ فإنَّ لَوْ تفتحُ عَمَلَ الشَّيطَانِ ،
رواه مسلم

100. Hazrat Abu Huraira (R.A.A.) relates that the Holy Prophet (S.A.W.) said: Allah likes a strong believer more than the weak one. Out of all good things, ask for that which may be most beneficial to you. Keep imploring Allah for help and do not give up. Should you come across some mishap, do not say: Had I only done this and that things would have turned out so and so; but say only Allah so determines and did as he willed.'; because the phrase; 'Had I' only opens the gates of evil conduct. (*Muslim*).

١٠١ ـ السابع : عنه أنَّ رسول الله صلى الله عليه وسلم قال : « حُجِبَتِ النَّارُ بِالشَّهَوَاتِ ، وحُجِبَتِ الْجَنَّةُ بِالْمَكَارِهِ » متفقٌ عليه

وفي رواية لمسلم : « حُفَّت » بَدلَ « حُجِبَتْ » وهوَ بمَعْنَاهُ ؛ أيْ : بَيْنَهُ وبَيْنَهَا هذا الحِجَابُ ؛ فإذا فعَلَهُ دَخَلَهَا .

101. Hazrat Abu Hurairah (R.A.A.) relates that the Holy Prophet (S.A.W.) said: 'Hell lies hidden behind evil (wordly desires) and paradise is screened behind hard labour.' *(Agreed Upon)*.

١٠٢ ـ الثامن : عن أبي عبد الله حُذَيْفَةَ بنِ اليمانِ ، رضي الله عنهما . قال : صَلَّيْتُ مَعَ النَّبيِّ صلى الله عليه وسلم ذَاتَ لَيْلَةٍ ، فَافْتَتَحَ البَقَرَةَ ، فَقُلْتُ يَرْكَعُ عِنْدَ المائَةِ ، ثمَّ مَضَى ؛ فَقُلْتُ يُصَلِّي بهَا في رَكْعَةٍ ، فَمَضَى ؛ فَقُلْتُ يَرْكَعُ بهَا ، ثمَّ افْتَتَحَ النِّسَاءَ ؛ فَقَرَأَهَا ، ثمَّ افْتَتَحَ آلَ عِمْرَانَ فقرَأَهَا ، يقرأُ مُتَرَسِّلاً إذا مرَّ بآيةٍ فيها تَسْبِيحٌ سَبَّحَ ، وإذا مرَّ بسؤالٍ سَأَلَ ، وإذا مرَّ بتعوذٍ تعوَّذَ ، ثمَّ رَكَعَ فجعَلَ يَقُولُ : «سُبْحَانَ رَبِّيَ الْعَظِيمِ» فكَانَ رُكُوعُهُ نحواً مِنْ قِيَامِهِ ثمَّ قالَ : «سَمِعَ اللهُ لِمَنْ حَمِدَهُ ، رَبَّنَا لَكَ الْحَمْدُ » ثمَّ قامَ قِيَاماً طَوِيلاً قَرِيباً مِمَّا رَكَعَ ، ثمَّ سَجَدَ فقَالَ : « سُبْحَانَ رَبِّيَ الأَعْلَى » فكَانَ سُجُودُهُ قَرِيباً مِنْ قِيَامِهِ » رواه مسلم

102. Hazrat Huzaifah Ibn Yaman (R.A.A.) says: 'One night I joined the Holy Prophet (S.A.W.) in prayer. He began recitation of *Sura Al-Baqarah*. I thought he would go into *Ruku* (Bowing the head) after reciting a hundred verses, but he continued the recitation. Then I thought he would complete its recitation in one *Raka'at* (Bending, standing, bowing and lying prostrate at prayer) but he continued its recitation and then began to recite *Sura Al-e-Imran* and thereafter *Sura An-Nisa.* His oration was clear. When he recited a verse which contained glorification of Allah, he praised Him, where supplication was mentioned he supplicated and where 'seeking protection' was mentioned he sought protection. Then he went into *Ruku* (bending standing) and began repeating: 'Holy is my Lord, and Great;' and his *Ruku* was almost as long as his *Qiyam* (standing). Then he recited: 'Allah hears him who praises him. Thine is the praise O Lord.' He then went into prostration (*Sajdah*) and recited: 'Holy is my Lord, the High:' and his prostration was like his *Qiyam*. (*Muslim*).

١٠٣ – التاسع : عن ابن مسعود رضيَ الله عنه قال : صَلَّيْتُ مَعَ النَّبي صلى الله عليه وسلم لَيْلَةً ، فأطَالَ القِيَامَ حَتَّى هَمَمْتُ بِأمْرِ سُوء ! قيل : وَمَا هَمَمْتَ بِهِ ؟ قالَ : هَمَمْتُ أنْ أجْلِسَ وَأدَعَه . متفقٌ عليه

103. Hazrat Ibn Mas'ud (R.A.A.) relates: 'One night I joined the Holy Prophet (S.A.W.) in prayer. He prolonged the *Qiyam* so much that I made up my mind to commit an act amounting to impertinence.' He was asked: 'What was that bad act?' He said: 'To sit down and stop following him (in prayer).' (*Bukhari and Muslim*)

١٠٤ – العاشر : عن أنس رضي الله عنه عن رسول الله صلى الله عليه وسلم قال : « يَتْبَعُ المَيْتَ ثَلاثَةٌ : أهْلُهُ وَمَالُه وَعَمَلُه ، فَيَرْجِعُ اثْنَانِ وَيَبْقَى وَاحِدٌ : يَرْجِعُ أهْلُهُ وَمَالُهُ ، وَيَبْقَى عَمَلُهُ » متفقٌ عليه

104. Hazrat Anas Bin Malik (R.A.A.) relates that the Holy Prophet (S.A.W.) said: Three things follow a dead person; members of his family, his belongings and his deeds — The first two come back and the third remains with him. (*Bukhari and Muslim*)

١٠٥ – الحادي عشر : عن ابن مسعود رضي الله عنه قال : قال النبي صلى الله عليه وسلم : « الجَنَّةُ أقْرَبُ إلى أحَدِكُمْ مِنْ شِرَاكِ نَعْلِهِ وَالنَّارُ مِثْلُ ذَلِكَ » رواه البخاري

105. Hazrat Ibn Mas'ud (R.A.A.) relates that the Holy Prophet (S.A.W.) said: 'Paradise is closer to you than your shoe-lace, and similar is the case of Hell'. (*Bukhari*).

١٠٦ – الثاني عشر : عن أبي فِرَاسٍ رَبِيعَةَ بنِ كَعْبٍ الأسْلَمِيِّ خَادِمِ رسول الله صلى الله عليه وسلم ، وَمِنْ أهْلِ الصفَّةِ رضي الله عنه قال : « كُنْتُ أبِيتُ مَعَ رسول الله صلى الله عليه وسلم ، فَآتِيهِ بِوَضُوئِهِ ،

وَحَاجَتِهِ فَقَالَ : « سَلْنِي » فَقُلْتُ : أَسْأَلُكَ مُرَافَقَتَكَ فِي الجَنَّةِ . فَقَالَ : « أَوَ غَيْرَ ذَلِكَ ؟ » قُلْتُ : هُوَ ذَاكَ قَالَ : « فَأَعِنِّي عَلَى نَفْسِكَ بِكَثْرَةِ السُّجُودِ » رواه مسلم

106. Hazrat Abi Faras Rabi'ah Ibn K'ab (R.A.A.) a servant of the Holy Prophet (S.A.W.) and one of the *As'hab-e-Suffa* relates: 'I used to pass my night in the company of the Holy Prophet (S.A.W.) and used to supply water for his ablutions and toilet. One day he said to me: 'Ask me whatever thing you desire!' I said: 'I solicit for your companionship in Paradise.' He enquired: 'Anything more!' I said: 'Only your companionship' He said: 'Then help me by multiplying your prostration in prayers.' (*Muslim*)

١٠٧ – الثالث عشر : عن أبي عبد الله – وَيُقَالُ : أَبُو عَبْدِ الرَّحْمَنِ – ثَوْبَانَ مَوْلَى رسول الله صلى الله عليه وسلم قال : سَمِعْتُ رسول الله صلى الله عليه وسلم يقول : « عَلَيْكَ بِكَثْرَةِ السُّجُودِ ، فَإِنَّكَ لَنْ تَسْجُدَ لله سَجْدَةً إِلاَّ رَفَعَكَ اللهُ بِهَا دَرَجَةً . وَحَطَّ عَنْكَ بِهَا خَطِيئَةً » .

رواه مسلم

107. Hazrat Sauban (R.A.A.) relates that he heard the Holy **Prophet (S.A.W.) say: 'Multiply your prostrations** (optional prayers). **Every such prostration will raise your status** one degree and will remit **one of your sins.'** (*Muslim*)

١٠٨ – الرابع عشر : عن أَبِي صَفْوَانَ عبد الله بن بُسْرٍ الأَسْلَمِيِّ ، رضي الله عنه ، قال : قال رسول اللهِ صلى الله عليه وسلم : « خَيْرُ النَّاسِ مَنْ طَالَ عُمُرُه وَحَسُنَ عَمَلُهُ » رواه الترمذي ، وقال : حديثٌ حسنٌ .

108. Hazrat Abi Safvan Abdullah ibn Busr-il Aslami (R.A.A.) relates that the Holy Prophet (S.A.W.) said: 'The best person is he who has a long span of life and his action and conduct are good.' (*Tirmizi*)

١٠٩ – الخامس عشر : عن أنس رضي الله عنه ، قال : غَابَ عَمِّي أَنَسُ ابنُ النَّضْرِ رضي الله عنه ، عن قِتَالِ بَدْرٍ ، فقال : يا رسول الله غِبْتُ عَنْ أَوَّلِ قِتَالٍ قَاتَلْتَ المُشْرِكِينَ ، لَئِنِ اللهُ أَشْهَدَنِي قِتَالَ المُشْرِكِينَ لَيُرِيَنَّ اللهُ مَا أَصْنَعُ . فَلَمَّا كَانَ يَوْمُ أُحُدٍ انْكَشَفَ المُسْلِمُونَ ، فَقَالَ : اللَّهُمَّ أَعْتَذِرُ إِلَيْكَ مِمَّا صَنَعَ هَؤُلاَءِ – يَعْنِي أَصْحَابَه – وَأَبْرَأُ إِلَيْكَ مِمَّ

صَنَعَ هؤُلاءِ ـ يعني المُشرِكِينَ ـ ثُمَّ تَقَدَّمَ فاستَقْبَلَهُ سَعْدُ بنُ مُعاذٍ ، فقَالَ : يا سَعْدُ بنُ مُعَاذٍ الجَنَّةُ وَرَبِّ الكَعْبَةِ ، إنِّي أجِدُ رِيحَها مِنْ دُونِ أحُدٍ . قال سَعْدٌ : فَمَا استَطَعْتُ يا رَسولَ اللهِ ما صَنَعَ ! قال أنسٌ : فَوَجَدْنَا بِهِ بِضعاً وَثَمانِينَ ضَرْبَةً بِالسَّيفِ ، أوْ طَعْنَةً بِرُمْحٍ ، أوْ رَمْيَةً بِسَهْمٍ ، وَوَجَدْنَاهُ قَدْ قُتِلَ وَمَثَّلَ بِهِ المُشرِكُونَ فَمَا عَرَفَهُ أحَدٌ إلاّ أختُهُ بِبَنَانِهِ . قال أنس : كُنَّا نَرَى أوْ نَظُنُّ أنَّ هَذهِ الآيَةَ نَزَلَتْ فيهِ وفي أشْباهِهِ : مِنَ المُؤْمِنِينَ رِجَالٌ صَدَقُوا ما عَاهَدُوا اللهَ عَلَيْهِ [الأحزاب : ٢٣] إلى آخرها . متفقٌ عليه

109. Hazrat Anas bin Malik (R.A.A.) relates: 'My uncle Anas Ibn Nazar was not present in the battle of Badr. He said to the Holy Prophet (S.A.W.): O Messenger of Allah! I could not join you in your first battle with the pagans. If I had the chance to fight the pagans, Allah will (enable me) to show my performance. On the day of the battle of Uhud the Muslims apparently suffered a defeat. He said: 'Allah I plead with Thee concerning that which the Muslims have done and disassociate myself from that which the pagans have perpetrated.' Then he went forward and on the way met Sa'ad Ibn Mu'az. He said: "O Mu'az, By the Lord of Ka'ba, I smell the fragrance of Paradise from beyond Uhud.' S'ad said: Messenger of Allah, I have not the power to describe what he did (his chivalry). His nephew Hazrat Anas bin Malik says: 'We found on his person more than eighty injuries inflicted by swords, spears and arrows. In this way he was martyred; over and above this the infidels had mutilated his dead body by cutting his nose and ears, so much so that nobody could identify him except his sister who recognised him with the help of his fingers. He thought that the following verse referred to him and to those like him:

> 'Among the believers are men who have been true to the covenant they made with Allah. Some have fulfilled their vow and laid down their lives in battle and there are others who wait. They have not weakened in their resolve in the least." (8:24)

(*Bukhari and Muslim*)

١١٠ ـ السادس عشر : عن أبي مسعود عُقْبَةَ بنِ عمرٍو الأنصاريِّ البدريِّ رضي الله عنه قال : لَمَّا نَزَلَتْ آيَةُ الصَّدَقَةِ كُنَّا نُحَامِلُ عَلَى ظُهُورِنَا . فَجاءَ رَجُلٌ فَتَصَدَّقَ بِشَيْءٍ كَثِيرٍ فَقَالُوا : مُرَاءٍ ، وجاءَ رَجُلٌ آخَرُ فَتَصَدَّقَ بِصَاعٍ فقالُوا : إنَّ اللهَ لَغَنِيٌّ عَنْ صاعِ هَذا ! فَنَزَلَتْ الَّذِينَ

يَلْمِزُونَ الْمُطَّوِّعِينَ مِنَ الْمُؤْمِنِينَ فِي الصَّدَقَاتِ وَالَّذِينَ لاَ يَجِدُونَ إِلاَّ جُهْدَهُمْ الآية [التوبة : ٧٩] . متفقٌ عليه

110. **Hazrat Abu Mas'ud Uqbah Ibn 'Amr Ansari Al Badri** (R.A.A.) relates that when the verse enjoining alms-giving was revealed we used to carry loads on our backs to earn something that we could give away in charity. One of us presented a substantial amount for charity and the hypocrites remarked that he had done it only to show off. Another gave away a few pounds of dates and they said: 'Allah does not need his dates.' Thereupon was revealed:

> 'Those who point at such of the believers as give the alms willingly and such as can find naught to give but their endeavours, and deride them — Allah (Himself) derideth them. Theirs will be a painful doom." (9:79) (*Bukhari and Muslim*).

١١١ — السابعَ عشر : عن سعيد بن عبد العزيز ، عن ربيعة بن يزيد ، عن أبي إدريس الخولاني ، عن أبي ذرّ جُنْدُبِ بنِ جُنَادَةَ ، رضي الله عنه ، عن النبيِّ صلى الله عليه وسلم فيما يرْوِي عَنِ الله تبارك وتعالى أنه قال : « يا عِبَادِي إنّي حرّمْتُ الظُّلْمَ على نفْسِي وجعلْتُهُ بيْنكُمْ مُحرّماً فلاَ تظَالمُوا ، يا عِبادِي كُلُّكُمْ ضَالّ إلاَّ منْ هدَيْتُهُ ، فاسْتهْدُونِي أهْدِكُمْ ، يا عِبادِي كُلُّكُمْ جائِعٌ إلاَّ منْ أطْعَمْتُهُ ، فاسْتَطْعِمُونِي أُطْعِمْكُمْ ، يا عِبادِي كُلُّكُمْ عارٍ إلاَّ منْ كسوْتُهُ ، فاسْتكْسُونِي أكْسُكُمْ ، يا عِبادِي إنّكُمْ تُخْطِئُونَ باللّيْلِ والنّهارِ وأنا أغْفِرُ الذُّنُوبَ جمِيعاً ، فاسْتغْفِرُونِي أغْفِرْ لكُمْ ، يا عِبادِي إنّكُمْ لنْ تبْلُغُوا ضُرّي فتَضُرُّونِي ، ولنْ تبْلُغُوا نفْعِي فتنْفعُونِي ، يا عِبادِي لوْ أنّ أوّلكُمْ وآخِركُمْ ، وإنْسكُمْ وجِنّكُمْ ، كانُوا على أتْقى قلْبِ رجُلٍ واحِدٍ مِنْكُمْ ما زادَ ذلِكَ في مُلْكِي شيْئاً ، يا عِبادِي لوْ أنّ أوّلكُمْ وآخِركُمْ وإنْسكُمْ وجِنّكُمْ كانُوا على أفْجرِ قلْبِ رجُلٍ واحِدٍ مِنْكُمْ ما نقص ذلِكَ مِنْ مُلْكِي شيْئاً . يا عِبادِي لوْ أنّ أوّلكُمْ وآخِركُمْ وإنْسكُمْ وجِنّكُمْ قامُوا في صعِيدٍ واحِد ، فسألُونِي فأعْطيْتُ كُلّ إنْسانٍ مسْألتهُ ، ما نقص ذلِكَ مِمّا عِنْدِي إلاَّ كما ينْقُصُ المِخْيطُ إذا أُدْخِل البحْر ، يا عِبادِي إنّما هِيَ أعْمالُكُمْ أُحْصِيها لكُمْ ، ثُمّ أُوفّيكُمْ إيّاها ، فمنْ

وَجَدَ خَيْراً فَلْيَحْمَدِ اللهَ ، وَمَنْ وَجَدَ غَيْرَ ذَلِكَ فَلاَ يَلُومَنَّ إلَّا نَفْسَهُ » . قَالَ سعيدٌ : كان أبو إدريس إذا حدَّثَ بهذا الحديثِ جثَا على رُكبتيه ; واه مسلم . وروينا عن الإمام أحمد ن حنبل رحمه الله قال : ليس لأهل الشام حديث أشرف من هذا الحديث

111. Hazrat Sayeed Bin Abdul Aziz quotes from Hazrat Rabia bin Yazid and he quotes from **Hazrat Ali Idrees Al-Khaulani,** who quotes from Hazrat Abu Zar who relates that the Holy Prophet (S.A.W.) said: 'Allah admonishes you: O my servants, I have charged Myself to wrong no one and have forbidden it between you. So wrong not anyone; O My servants, all of you are not on the correct path except those whom I may guide; O My servants, all of you are hungry save those whom I should feed, then supplicate Me for food, I shall feed you; O My servants, all of you are unclothed save those whom I should clothe, then supplicate Me for clothes; I shall clothe you. O My servants, you misbehave night and day and I forgive all your sins, then supplicate Me for forgiveness; I shall forgive you. O My servants, you can have no power to do Me harm, nor can you have power to confer any benefit upon Me. O My servants, if the first of you and the last of you, and the whole lot of you, high and low, were to become like one who has most righteous soul among you, that would not add a whit to my kingdom: O My servants if the first of you and the last of you, and the whole lot of you, high and low, were to become like the one who has the most vicious soul among you, that would not detract a whit from my kingdom. O My servants, if the first of you and the last of you, and the whole lot of you, high and low, were to assemble in one large plain and were to beg Me for whatever they desire and I were to bestow upon each of you all that he had asked for, that would not detract from My treasures any more than a needle could diminish from the ocean, by touching its surface by its point. O My servants, I understand your actions and shall make a full repayment for the same to you. Then he who gets good reward should praise Allah for it; and he who receives something else should blame only himslef .' (*Muslim*)

Hazrat Sayeed says that while Hazrat Abu Idrees Khaulani used to narrate this tradition, he would kneel down in awe and reverence for Allah, the Almighty.

Note: *Mujahida* means striving and struggling for a good cause or for the sake of Allah e.g. spreading and preaching His commands: And according to *Ulema* this is the best kind of *Jihad.* According to some traditions of the Holy Prophet (S.A.W.) to fight against ones own evil intentions, is the best *Jihad.*

* * * * * * * * * *

CHAPTER 12

On Doing Virtuous Deeds Increasingly Towards the Closing Years of One's Life and Urging Others for the Same.

قال الله تعالى : أَوَ لَمْ نُعَمِّرْكُم مَّا يَتَذَكَّرُ فِيهِ مَن تَذَكَّرَ وَجَاءَكُمُ النَّذِيرُ [فاطر : ٣٧]

Allah, the Exalted, has said:

48. **Did** not we grant you a life long enough for him who reflected to repent therein? And the Warner came unto you? (35:37)

Imam Nawavi says that according to Hazrat Ibn-i-Abbas and other scholars, long life means the age of 60 years. Some-have assessed it at 18 years. Imams Hasan, Kalabi and Masrooq have taken it as 40 years. In Madina it is said when a person reached the age of 40 years, he used to dedicate himself to prayers.

١١٢ ـ وأمّا الأحاديث فالأوّل : عن أبي هريرة رضي الله عنه ، عن النبيّ صلى الله عليه وسلم قال : « أعْذَرَ الله إلى امرِئٍ أخَّرَ أجَلَه حتى بلَغَ ستِّينَ سَنَةً » رواه البخاري

112. Hazrat Abu Hurairah (R.A.A.) relates that the Holy Prophet (S.A.W.) said: 'Allah continues to forgive a person till he attains the age of sixty years'. *(Bukhari)*

١١٣ ـ الثاني : عن ابن عباس ، رضي الله عنهما ، قال : كان عمر رضي الله عنه يُدْخِلُني مَعَ أشياخِ بَدْرٍ ، فكأنَّ بَعضَهُمْ وَجَدَ في نفْسِه فقال : لِمَ يدخُلُ هذا معنا ولَنا أبْناءٌ مثلُه !؟ فقال عمر : إنَّه مَنْ حيثُ علِمتُمْ ! فدَعاني ذاتَ يوْمٍ فأدْخَلَني مَعَهُمْ ، فما رأيتُ أنَّه دعاني يومئذٍ إلاَّ ليُريَهُمْ قال : ما تقولون في قول الله تعالى : إذا جاءَ نَصْرُ اللهِ والفَتْحُ ؟ [الفتح : ١] فقال بعضهم : أُمِرْنا نَحْمَدُ اللهَ ونَستَغفِره إذا نَصَرَنا وفَتَحَ علَيْنا . وسَكَتَ بعضهُمْ فلم يقُلْ شيئاً . فقال لي : أكذلكَ تقول يا ابن عباس ؟ فقلت : لا . قال : فما تقول ؟ قلت : هُوَ أجَلُ رسولِ الله صلى الله عليه وسلم ، أعْلَمَه له قال : إذا جاءَ نَصْرُ اللهِ والفَتْحُ وذلك علامة أجَلِك فَسَبِّحْ بِحَمْدِ ربِّكَ واستَغْفِرْهُ إنَّه كانَ تَوَّاباً . [الفتح : ٣] فقال عمر

رضى الله عنه : ما أَعْلَمُ منها إلاَّ ما تَقُول . رواه البخاري

113. Hazrat-Ibn-Abbas (R.A.A.). relates: Hazrat Umar (R.A.A.) used to associate him in consultation alongwith the elders who had taken part in the battle of Badr. Some companions (senior participants) resented this and remarked: ' Why does (Hazrat) Umar allow this boy to join us in council, although our sons are of his age.' Hazrat Umar told them: 'He belongs to the source of your knowledge.' (the House of the Holy Prophet) (S.A.W.). He called me one day to his Council alongwith them, and I guessed that he had done so simply to show to them my skill and knowledge. He asked them: 'What is the meaning of:

'When Allah's succour and triumph cometh? (110:1)

Some of them said: In this verse we have been asked to praise Allah and supplicate for His forgiveness when He helps us and grants victory. Some remained quiet and said nothing. Hazrat Umar (R.A.A.) said to me: Ibn-e-Abbas ?' Do you agree I said: 'No'. He then enquired as to what I have to say, I said: 'This was an intimation of the approach of the death of the Holy Prophet (S.A.W.) which Allah conveyed to him. Allah said: The help from Allah and succour having come," this is said to be an advance information of the death of the Holy Prophet (S.A.W.),

"then hymn the praises of thy Lord and seek forgiveness of Him;
Lo! He is ever ready to show mercy." (110:3). (110:3).

Hazrat Umar (R.A.A.) said to Hazrat Ibn-i-Abbas: Nobody knows more than what you have said *(Bukhari)*

١١٤ ـ الثالث : عن عائشة رضي الله عنها قالت : ما صَلَّى رسول الله صلى الله عليه وسلم صلاةً بَعْدَ أَنْ نَزَلَتْ عَلَيْهِ (إذَا جَاءَ نَصْرُ اللهِ وَالْفَتْحُ) إلاَّ يقول فيها : « سُبْحَانَكَ رَبَّنَا وَبِحَمْدِكَ ، اللَّهُمَّ اغفِرْ لي » متفق عليه

وفي رواية في الصحيحين عنها: كان رسول الله صلى الله عليه وسلم يُكْثِر أَنْ يَقُولَ في رُكُوعِهِ وسُجُودِهِ : « سُبْحَانَكَ اللَّهُمَّ رَبَّنَا وَبِحَمْدِكَ ، اللَّهُمَّ اغفِرْ لي » يَتَأَوَّلُ القُرْآنَ .

وفي رواية لمسلم: كان رسول الله صلى الله عليه وسلم يُكْثِر أَنْ يَقُولَ قَبْلَ أَنْ يَمُوتَ : « سُبْحَانَكَ اللَّهُمَّ وبِحَمْدِكَ ، أَسْتَغْفِرُكَ وَأَتُوبُ إِلَيْكَ » . قالت عائشة : قلت : يا رسول الله ما هَذِهِ الكَلِمَاتُ الَّتي أَرَاكَ أَحْدَثْتَهَا تقولها ؟ قال: «جُعِلَتْ لي علامةٌ في أُمَّتي إذَا رَأَيْتُها قُلْتُها إذَا جَاءَ نَصْرُ اللهِ وَالْفَتْحُ إلى آخر السورة» .

وفي رواية له : كان رسول الله صلى الله عليه وسلم يُكْثِر مِنْ قَوْلِ :

« سُبْحَانَ اللهِ وبِحَمْدِهِ . أَسْتَغْفِرِ اللهَ وَأَتُوبُ إِلَيْهِ » . قالت : قلت : يا رسولَ الله ! أَرَاكَ تُكْثِر مِنْ قَوْلِ : سُبْحَانَ اللهِ وَبِحَمْدِهِ ، أَسْتَغْفِر اللهَ وَأَتُوبُ إِلَيْهِ ؟ فقال : « أَخْبَرَنِي رَبِّي أَنِّي سَأَرَى عَلَامَةً فِي أُمَّتِي فَإِذَا رَأَيْتُها أَكْثَرْتُ مِنْ قَوْلِ : سُبْحَانَ اللهِ وبِحَمْدِهِ ، أَسْتَغْفِرُ اللهَ وَأَتُوبُ إِلَيْهِ ، فَقَدْ رَأَيْتُهَا : (إِذَا جَاءَ نَصْرُ اللهِ وَالْفَتْحُ) فَتْحُ مَكَّةَ ، (وَرَأَيْتَ النَّاسَ يَدْخُلُونَ فِي دِينِ اللهِ أَفْوَاجاً . فَسَبِّحْ بِحَمْدِ رَبِّكَ وَاسْتَغْفِرْهُ إِنَّهُ كَانَ تَوَّاباً) .

114. Hazrat Ayesha (R.A.A.) relates that after the revelation of this *Surah (An-Nasr)* the Holy Prophet (S.A.W.) used to recite in every *Salat:*

'Holy Art Thou, our Lord, and all praise is Thine; Forgive me, O Allah. (*Bukhari and Muslim*)

According to another version of *Bukhari and Muslim*, the Holy Prophet (S.A.W.) used to recite repeatedly in his *Ruku* and *Sajdah:* (bending and prostration in prayer) 'Holy art Thou O Allah our Lord, and all praise is Thine; forgive me O Allah; as directed in the Quran.

Yet another version in *Muslim* says: Before his death the Holy Prophet (S.A.W.) often recited: 'Holy art Thou and all praise is Thine, I seek Thy forgiveness and repent before Thee.' I (Hazrat Ayesha) asked him 'Messenger of Allah', what are these new phrases which I hear you recite? He said: 'Allah has fixed a sign concerning my Ummah, that when I should see that signal I should recite these phrases.' Then he recited *Sura An-Nasr.*

According to another version, 'The Holy Prophet (S.A.W.) often recited: 'Holy is Allah and His is all praise: I seek forgiveness of Allah and turn to Him in repentance.' Hazrat Ayesha said to him: 'Messenger of Allah, I hear you recite often: 'Holy is Allah and His is all Praise: I seek forgiveness of Allah and turn to him in repentance.' He elucidated: 'My Lord told me that I will soon see indications relating to my *Ummah* and that when I see it, I should often proclaim His holiness and praise, and seek His forgiveness and turn to Him. Now I have already seen this sign. The coming of Allah's help and victory was the fall of Mecca, and the sign was seeing people joining the religion of Allah in large numbers. The command is: Proclaim the Holiness of Allah alongwith His praise and ask forgiveness of Him. He is the Most Merciful and Forgiving.

١١٥ ـ الرابع : عن أنس رضي الله عنه قال : إِنَّ اللهَ عَزَّ وَجَلَّ تَابَعَ الوَحْيَ عَلَى رسول الله صلى الله عليه وسلم قَبْلَ وَفَاتِهِ ، حَتَّى تُوُفِّيَ أَكْثَرَ مَا كَانَ الوَحْيُ . متفقٌ عليه

115. Hazrat Anas (R.A.A.) relates: 'Allah, the Most Glorious and Respected sent revelation to the Holy Prophet (S.A.W.) more frequently towards the close of his years till he passed away.'

(*Bukhari and Muslim*)

١١٦ ـ الخامس : عن جابر رضي الله عنه قال : قال رسول الله صلى الله عليه وسلم : « يُبْعَثُ كُلُّ عَبْدٍ عَلَى مَا مَاتَ عَلَيْهِ » رواه مسلم

116. Hazrat Jabir (R.A.A.) relates that the Holy Prophet (S.A.W.) said that 'Everyone will be resurrected in the condition in which he died.

(*Muslim*)

* * * * * * * * * *

CHAPTER 13

On Different Ways of Doing Good

قال الله تعالى: وَمَا تَفْعَلُوا مِنْ خَيْرٍ فَإِنَّ اللهَ بِهِ عَلِيمٌ [البقرة: ٢١٥]

وقال تعالى : وَمَا تَفْعَلُوا مِنْ خَيْرٍ يَعْلَمْهُ اللهُ [البقرة : ١٩٧] وقال تعالى : فَمَنْ يَعْمَلْ مِثْقَالَ ذَرَّةٍ خَيْرًا يَرَهُ [الزلزلة : ٧] وقال تعالى: مَنْ عَمِلَ صَالِحًا فَلِنَفْسِهِ [الجاثية : ١٥] والآيات في الباب كثيرةٌ

وأمّا الأحاديث فكثيرة جداً ، وهي غير منحصرة ، فنذكر طرفاً منها :

Allah, the Exalted, has said:

49. And Whatsoever good ye do, lo! Allah is aware of it. (2:215)
50. And whatsoever good ye do Allah knoweth it (2:197)
51. And whoso doeth good an atom's weight will see it then (99:7)
52. Whoso doeth right, it is for his soul. (45:15).
And there are a number of verses on this topic, and several sayings of the Holy Prophet (S.A.W.).

١١٧ ـ الأوّل : عن أبي ذرٍ جُنْدَبِ بن جُنَادَةَ رضي الله عنه قال : قلت يا رسول الله ،أيُّ الأعْمَالِ أفضَلُ ؟ قال : « الإيمانُ بالله ، وَالجِهَادُ في سَبِيلِهِ ». قُلْتُ : أيُّ الرِّقَابِ أفضَلُ ؟ قال : «أنفَسُهَا عِنْدَ أهْلِهَا ، وَأكْثَرُهَا ثَمَنًا». قُلْتُ : فَإنْ لَمْ أفعَلْ ؟ قال :«تُعِينُ صَانِعاً أوْ تَصنَعُ لأخْرَقَ » . قُلْتُ : يا رَسول الله أرَأيْتَ إنْ ضَعُفْتُ عَنْ بَعْضِ العَمَلِ ؟ قال : تَكُفُّ شَرَّكَ عَنِ النَّاسِ فَإنَّها صَدَقَةٌ مِنْكَ عَلَى نَفْسِكَ »

متفقٌ عليه

117. Hazrat Abu Zarr (R.A.A.) relates: I requested the Holy Prophet (S.A.W.) as to what act is most meritorious? He said: 'Faith in Allah and *Jihad* (striving) in His way.' I asked, 'the liberation of which kind of slave is better?' He said, 'Of the one who is the most iiked by the master and whose price is the highest.' I asked: 'If I am unable to do that (on account of lack of money).' He said 'Then help someone in his work or make something for someone who is not able to make it himself.' I asked: 'If one should not have the capacity.' He said: 'Restrain thyself from doing harm to anyone for that is also charity towards thyself'. (*Bukhari and Muslim*)

١١٨ – الثاني : عن أبي ذرٍّ أيضاً رضي اللهُ عنه أنَّ رَسُولَ الله صلى الله عليه وسلم قال : « يُصْبِحُ عَلَى كُلِّ سُلاَمَى مِنْ أَحَدِكُمْ صَدَقَةٌ ، فَكُلُّ تَسْبِيحَةٍ صَدَقَةٌ ، وكُلُّ تَحْمِيدَةٍ صَدَقَةٌ ، وكُلُّ تَهْلِيلَةٍ صَدَقَةٌ ، وكُلُّ تَكْبِيرَةٍ صَدَقَةٌ ، وأَمْرٌ بالمَعْرُوفِ صَدَقَةٌ ، وَنَهْيٌ عَنِ المُنْكَرِ صَدَقَةٌ . ويُجْزِىءُ مِنْ ذَلكَ رَكْعَتَانِ يَرْكَعُهُمَا مِنَ الضُّحَى » رواه مسلم

118. Hazrat Abu Zarr (R.A.A.) relates tha the Holy Prophet (S.A.W.) has said: 'When you get up in the morning charity is due from every part of your body. All glorification of Allah (to say *subhan-Allah*) is charity; all praise of Allah (to say *Al Hamdo Lillah*) is charity, (to say *La Ilaha Illallah*) is charity, enjoining good is charity; (to say *AllahoAkbar*) is charity, forbidding somebody from evil is charity. Two *Raka'ts* of prayer offered early after sunrise equal all this.' (*Muslim*).

١١٩ – الثالثُ عَنْهُ قال : قال النبي صلى الله عليه وسلم : « عُرِضَتْ عَلَيَّ أَعْمَالُ أُمَّتِي حَسَنُهَا وَسَيِّئُهَا ، فَوَجَدْتُ فِي مَحَاسِنِ أَعْمَالِهَا الأَذَى يُمَاطُ عَنِ الطَّرِيقِ ، وَوَجَدْتُ فِي مَسَاوِىءِ أَعْمَالِهَا النُّخَاعَةَ تَكُونُ فِي المَسْجِدِ لاَ تُدْفَنُ » رواه مسلم

119. Hazrat Abu Zarr (R.A.A.) relates that the Holy Prophet (S.A.W.) said: "The good and bad deeds of my *Ummah* were shown to me. Among the good deeds, I found the removal of obstacles and articles which might cause inconvenience to the passers-by from a path, and among the bad spittal lying unburried in the mosque.' (*Muslim*)

١٢٠ – الرابع عنه : أنَّ ناساً قالوا : يا رسُول الله ، ذَهَبَ أَهْلُ الدُّثُورِ بِالأُجُورِ ، يُصَلُّونَ كَمَا نُصَلِّي ، وَيَصُومُونَ كَمَا نَصُومُ ، وَيَتَصَدَّقُونَ بِفُضُولِ أَمْوَالِهِمْ قال : « أَوَ لَيْسَ قَدْ جَعَلَ اللهُ لَكُمْ مَا تَصَدَّقُونَ بِهِ : إنَّ بِكُلِّ تَسْبِيحَةٍ صَدَقَةً ، وكُلِّ تَكْبِيرَةٍ صدقة ، وكل تَحْمِيدَةٍ

صدقةٌ ، وكلُّ تَهْلِيلَةٍ صدقةٌ ، وَأَمْرٌ بالمعْرُوفِ صدقةٌ ، ونَهْيٌ عَنِ المُنْكَرِ صدقةٌ وفي بُضْعِ أَحَدِكُمْ صدقةٌ » قالوا : يا رسُولَ اللهِ أيَأتي أحَدُنَا شَهْوَتَهُ ، ويَكُونُ لَه فيها أجْرٌ ؟ ! قال: « أرَأَيْتُمْ لَوْ وَضَعَهَا في حرَامٍ أَكَانَ عَلَيهِ وِزْرٌ ؟ فكذلكَ إذا وضَعَهَا في الحَلاَلِ كانَ لَهُ أَجْرٌ »

رواه مسلم

120. Hazrat Abu Zarr (R.A.A.) relates that some companions said to the Holy Prophet (S.A.W.): The rich people have taken away a good deal of merit. They pray and fast as we do, but they are in a position to distribute in charity a part of their wealth (which we are unable to do.) He said 'Has not Allah given you things which you can employ for charity? All glorification of Allah (saying *Subhan Allah*) is charity. All praise of Allah (to say *Al Hamdo Lillah*) is charity, all affirmation of Allah's Unity (To say *La Ilaha Illallah*) is charity, all affirmation of Allah's Greatness (To say *Allaho Akbar*) is charity; calling upon somebody to do good is charity; prohibiting somebody from doing evil is charity; to cohabit with your wife is charity.' They asked: 'Messenger of Allah (S.A.W.), is it possible that one of us should satisfy his desire and he would be rewarded?' He said: 'If he satisfied his urge through illicit means, would it not be sinful? Therefore when he satisfies it lawfully it is deserving reward.' (*Muslim*)

١٢١ ــ الخامس : عنه قال : قال لي النبيُّ صلى الله عليه وآله وسلم :

« لاَ تَحقِرَنَّ مِنَ المَعْرُوفِ شَيْئاً ولَوْ أنْ تَلْقَى أخَاكَ بِوَجْهٍ طَلِيقٍ »

رواه مسلم.

121. Hazrat Abu Zarr relates that the Holy Prophet (S.A.W.) said: 'Do not consider even the smallest good deed as insignificant; even meeting your brother with a cheerful face (is a good deed).

(*Muslim*)

١٢٢ ــ السادس : عن أبي هريرة رضي الله عنه قال : قال رسُولُ الله صلى الله عليه وسلم : « كُلُّ سُلاَمَى مِنَ النَّاسِ عَلَيْهِ صَدَقَةٌ كُلَّ يَوْمٍ تَطْلُعُ فيه الشَّمْسُ : تَعْدِلُ بَيْنَ الاثْنَيْنِ صَدَقَةٌ ، وَتُعِينُ الرَّجُلَ في دَابَّتِهِ ، فَتَحْمِلُهُ عَلَيْهَا ، أَوْ تَرفَعُ لَهُ عَلَيْهَا مَتَاعَهُ صدقةٌ ، والكلِمَةُ الطَّيِّبَةُ صَدَقَةٌ ، وَبِكُلِّ خَطْوَةٍ تَمْشِيها إلى الصَّلاَةِ صَدَقَةٌ ، وتُمِيطُ الأَذَى عَنِ الطَّرِيقِ صَدَقَةٌ » متفق عليه

ورواه مسلم أيضاً من رواية عائشة رضي الله عنها قالت : قال رسول الله صلى الله عليه وسلم : « إنَّهُ خُلِقَ كُلُّ إنسانٍ مِنْ بَني آدَمَ عَلى سِتِّينَ وثلاثمائةِ مَفْصِلٍ ، فَمَنْ كَبَّرَ اللهَ ، وَحَمِدَ اللهَ ، وَهَلَّلَ اللهَ ، وَسَبَّحَ اللهَ واسْتَغْفَرَ اللهَ ، وَعَزَلَ حَجَراً عَنْ طَريقِ النَّاسِ أَوْ شَوْكَةً أَوْ عَظْماً عن طَرِيقِ النَّاسِ ، أَوْ أَمَرَ بِمَعْرُوفٍ أَوْ نَهى عَنْ مُنْكَرٍ ، عَدَدَ السِّتِّينَ وَالثَّلاثمائةِ ، فَإِنَّهُ يُمْسِي يَوْمَئِذٍ وَقَدْ زَحْزَحَ نَفْسَهُ عَنِ النَّارِ » .

122. **Hazrat Abu Hurairah** (R.A.A.) relates that the Holy Prophet (S.A.W.) said: 'Charity is due from every part of a person's body. Every day on which the sun rises, doing justice between two persons is charity; to extend a helping hand to a person in riding his mount or to put his baggage on it is charity; a pleasant word is charity; every step taken to join in the *salat* is charity; removing anything which causes harm from a path is charity.' (*Bukhari and Muslim*).

Muslim has also reported on the authority of **Hazrat Ayesha** (R.A.A.) that the Holy Prophet (S.A.W.) said: 'Everyone has been created with three hundred and sixty joints; then whoever affirms Allah's greatness (says *Allah-o-Akbar*) praises Allah (says *Al Hamdo Lillah*) affirms his unity (*La Ilaha Il-lal-lah*), proclaims His holiness (says *Subhan Allah*), asks his forgiveness, removes a stone or thorn or bone from a path frequented by people, enjoins doing good, or forbids from doing a bad thing, and all these acts number three hundred and sixty, such a person becomes immune from the fire of Hell.'

١٢٣ — السابع : عنه عن النبي صلى الله عليه وسلم قال : « مَنْ غَدَا إلى المَسْجِدِ أَوْ رَاحَ ، أَعَدَّ اللهُ لَهُ في الجَنَّةِ نُزُلاً كُلَّما غَدَا أَوْ رَاحَ » متفق عليه

123. **Hazrat Abu Hurairah** (R.A.A.) relates that the Holy Prophet (S.A.W.) said: 'Whoever goes to the mosque for prayer in the morning or in the evening then Allah, the Almighty prepares a feast for him in Paradise, everytime he so walks.' (*Bukhari and Muslim*)

١٢٤ — الثامن : عنه قال : قال رسول الله صلى الله عليه وسلم : « يا نِسَاءَ المُسْلِماتِ لا تَحْقِرَنَّ جارَةٌ لِجارَتِها وَلَوْ فِرْسِنَ شاةٍ » متفق عليه

124. **Hazrat Abu Hurairah** (R.A.A.) relates that the Holy Prophet (S.A.W.) addressing the women said: 'O Muslim women do not feel small in sending her neighbour even the smallest thing, it may be goats shank as present to her neighbour.' (*Bukhari and Muslim*)

١٢٥ — التاسع : عنه عن النبي صلى الله عليه وسلم قال : « الإيمانُ بِضْعٌ وَسَبْعُونَ ، أَوْ بِضْعٌ وَسِتُّونَ شُعْبَةً : فَأَفْضَلُها قَوْلُ لا إلهَ إلاَّ اللهُ ،

وَأَدْنَاهَا إِمَاطَةُ الأَذَى عَنِ الطَّرِيقِ ، وَالحَيَاءُ شُعْبَةٌ مِنَ الإِيمَانِ » متفقٌ عليه

125. Hazrat Abu Hurairah (R.A.A.) relates that the Holy Prophet (S.A.W.) said: 'Faith has more than sixty or seventy kinds; the noblest of which is the affirmation that there is no god but Allah; and the least of which is to remove from a path that which causes inconvenience. Modesty is also a branch of faith.' (*Bukhari and Muslim*)

١٢٦ — العاشر : عنه أن رسول الله صلى الله عليه وسلم قال : « بَيْنَمَا رَجُلٌ يَمْشِي بِطَرِيقٍ اشْتَدَّ عَلَيْهِ الْعَطَشُ ، فَوَجَدَ بِئْراً فَنَزَلَ فِيهَا فَشَرِبَ ، ثُمَّ خَرَجَ فإذا كَلْبٌ يَلْهَثُ يَأْكُلُ الثَّرَى مِنَ الْعَطَشِ ، فقال الرَّجُلُ : لَقَدْ بَلَغَ هَذَا الْكَلْبَ مِنَ الْعَطَشِ مِثْلَ الَّذِي كَانَ قَدْ بَلَغَ مِنِّي ، فَنَزَلَ الْبِئْرَ فَمَلأَ خُفَّهُ مَاءً ثُمَّ أَمْسَكَهُ بِفِيهِ ، حَتَّى رَقِيَ فَسَقَى الْكَلْبَ ، فَشَكَرَ اللهُ لَهُ فَغَفَرَ لَهُ » قَالُوا : يا رسول الله إِنَّ لَنَا فِي الْبَهَائِمِ أَجْراً؟ فَقَالَ : « فِي كُلِّ كَبِدٍ رَطْبَةٍ أَجْرٌ » متفقٌ عليه

وفي روايةٍ للبخاري : « فَشَكَرَ اللهُ لَهُ فَغَفَرَ لَهُ . فَأَدْخَلَهُ الْجَنَّةَ » .

وفي روايةٍ لَهُمَا : « بَيْنَمَا كَلْبٌ يُطِيفُ بِرَكِيَّةٍ قَدْ كَادَ يَقْتُلُهُ الْعَطَشُ إِذْ رَأَتْهُ بَغِيٌّ مِنْ بَغَايَا بَنِي إِسْرَائِيلَ ، فَنَزَعَتْ مُوقَهَا فَاسْتَقَتْ لَهُ بِهِ ، فَسَقَتْهُ فَغُفِرَ لَهَا بِهِ » .

126. Hazrat Abu Hurairah (R.A.A.) relates that the Holy Prophet (S.A.W.) said: 'A man walking along a path felt very much thirsty, reaching a well he descended into it, drank water to his fill and came out, when he saw a dog with its tongue bulging out and trying to lick up mud to quench his thirst. The man said to himself that the dog was feeling the same extreme thirst as he had felt a little while ago. So he descended once more into the well, filled his leather hosier with water and came up holding it by his teeth and gave the dog a drink. Allah appreciated this act of this man and forgave his sins. The Holy Prophet (S.A.W,) was asked: 'Messenger of Allah, are we rewarded for kindness towards animals as well? He said. 'There is recompense for kindness to every living thing.' (*Bukhari and Muslim*)

Bukhari's version concludes with 'Allah appreciated his action and admitted him to Paradise.'

Another version says: 'A dog was circling round the brink of a well in an extreme thirst, when a bad character Jewess saw the animal, lowered her leather sock into the well, drew up some water and gave the dog a drink. Allah the Most Merciful, forgave her simply on account of this kindness.

١٢٧ – الحَادِي عَشَرَ: عَنْهُ عن النبي صلى الله عليه وسلم قال : « لَقَدْ رَأَيْتُ رَجُلاً يَتَقَلَّبُ فِي الْجَنَّةِ فِي شَجَرَةٍ قَطَعَهَا مِنْ ظَهْرِ الطَّرِيقِ كَانَتْ تُؤْذِي الْمُسْلِمِينَ » . رواه مسلم

وفي رواية : « مَرَّ رَجُلٌ بِغُصْنِ شَجَرَةٍ عَلَى ظَهْرِ طَرِيقٍ فَقَالَ : وَاللهِ لأُنَحِّيَنَّ هذا عَنِ الْمُسْلِمِينَ لا يُؤْذِيهِمْ ، فَأُدْخِلَ الْجَنَّةَ » .

وفي رواية لهما : « بَيْنَمَا رَجُلٌ يَمْشِي بِطَرِيقٍ وَجَدَ غُصْنَ شَوْكٍ عَلَى الطَّرِيقِ ، فَأَخَّرَهُ فَشَكَرَ اللهُ لَهُ ، فَغَفَرَ لَهُ »

127 Hazrat Abu Hurairah (R.A.A.) relates that the Holy Prophet (S.A.W.) said: I saw a man strolling in Paradise, because he had cut down a tree from the side of a road which caused inconvenience to the Muslims. (*Muslim*)

According to another version 'A man passed by a branch of a tree obstructing a road. He thought that he must cut it down so that it may not cause inconvenience to the Muslims. He was admitted to Paradise on account of this good act.

Yet another version says: 'A man passing along a road found a thorny branch leaning over the road and pushed it away. Allah appreciated his action and forgave his sins.' (*Bukhari and Muslim*)

١٢٨ – الثَّانِي عَشَرَ : عَنْهُ قَالَ : قَالَ رسول الله صلى الله عليه وسلم : « مَنْ تَوَضَّأَ فَأَحْسَنَ الْوُضُوءَ ، ثُمَّ أَتَى الْجُمُعَةَ ، فَاسْتَمَعَ وَأَنْصَتَ ، غُفِرَ لَهُ مَابَيْنَهُ وَبَيْنَ الْجُمُعَةِ وَزِيَادَةُ ثَلاثَةِ أَيَّامٍ ، وَمَنْ مَسَّ الْحَصَا فَقَدْ لَغَا » رواه مسلم

128. **Hazrat Abu Hurairah** (R.A.A.) relates that the Holy Prophet (S.A.W.) said: 'One who makes his ablutions carefully and comes to the Friday prayer and listens to the sermon attentively, has his sins from the previous Friday and three days more remitted, and one who occupies himself with pebbles during the sermon has not done well. (*Muslim*)

١٢٩ – الثَّالِثَ عَشَرَ : عَنْهُ أن رسول الله صلى الله عليه وسلم قال : « إِذَا تَوَضَّأَ الْعَبْدُ الْمُسْلِمُ ، أَوِ الْمُؤْمِنُ فَغَسَلَ وَجْهَهُ خَرَجَ مِنْ وَجْهِهِ كُلُّ خَطِيئَةٍ نَظَرَ إِلَيْهَا بِعَيْنَيْهِ مَعَ الْمَاءِ ، أَوْ مَعَ آخِرِ قَطْرِ الْمَاءِ ، فَإِذَا غَسَلَ يَدَيْهِ خَرَجَ مِنْ يَدَيْهِ كُلُّ خَطِيئَةٍ كَانَ بَطَشَتْهَا يَدَاهُ

عَ الْمَاء ، أَوْ مَعَ آخِرِ قَطْرِ الْمَاء ، فَإِذَا غَسَلَ رِجْلَيْهِ خَرَجَتْ كُل خَطِيئَةٍ مَشَتْهَا رِجْلاهُ مَعَ الْمَاء أَوْ مَعَ آخِرِ قَطْرِ الْمَاء حَتَّى يَخْرُجَ نَقِيّاً مِنَ الذُّنُوبِ » رواه مسلم

129. **Hazrat Abu Hurairah** (R.A.A.) relates that the Holy Prophet (S.A.W.) said: 'When a Muslim or a believer makes his ablutions and washes his face, the water carries away all sins committed by his eyes and, when he washes his hands the water removes sins committed by his hands, and when he washes his feet the water washes away all sins towards which his feet had taken him, and he emerges cleansed of all his (minor) sins. (*Muslim*)

١٣٠ — الرَّابعَ عَشَرَ : عنه عن رسول الله صلى الله عليه وسلم قال :

« الصَّلَوَاتُ الْخَمْسُ ، وَالْجُمُعَةُ إِلَى الْجُمُعَةِ ، وَرَمَضَانُ إِلَى رَمَضَانَ مُكَفِّرَاتٌ لِمَا بَيْنَهُنَّ إِذَا اجْتُنِبَتْ الْكَبَائِرُ » رواه مسلم

130. **Hazrat Abu Hurairah** (R.A.A.) relates that the Holy Prophet (S.A.W.) said: (Regular and punctual) performing of five daily prayers will make amends for minor sins provided no major sins are committed between two Fridays and two Ramazans. (*Muslim*)

١٣١ — الْخَامِسَ عَشَرَ : عنه قال : قال رسول الله صلى الله عليه وسلم :

« ألا أَدُلُّكُم عَلَى مَا يَمْحُو اللهُ بِهِ الْخَطَايَا ، وَيَرْفَعُ بِهِ الدَّرَجَاتِ ؟ » قالوا : بَلَى يَا رَسُولَ اللهِ ، قال : « إِسْبَاغُ الْوُضُوءِ عَلَى الْمَكَارِهِ وَكَثْرَةُ الْخُطَا إِلَى الْمَسَاجِدِ ، وَانْتِظَارُ الصَّلاةِ بَعْدَ الصَّلاةِ ، فَذَلِكُمُ الرِّبَاطُ » رواه مسلم

131. **Hazrat Abu Hurairah** (R.A.A.) relates that the Holy Prophet (S.A.W.) said: 'May I tell you something thereby: 'Allah will remit your sins, and thereby your position will be raised. The Companions said, 'Do tell us 'O Messenger of Allah.' He said: Performing the ablution properly, going to the mosque frequently for prayers even in difficult and distressing circumstances and waiting for the next prayer after one is over. This is your *Jihad* in the cause of Allah.' (*Muslim*)

Note: Cleanliness, prayers and worshipping of Allah with perseverance, is as good as *Jihad* in the cause of *Allah*.

١٣٢ — السَّادسَ عَشَرَ : عن أبي موسى الأَشْعَرِيِّ رضي اللهُ عنه قال :

قال رسول الله صلى الله عليهِ وسلم : « مَنْ صَلَّى الْبَرْدَيْنِ دَخَلَ الْجَنَّةَ » متفقٌ عليه

132. **Hazrat Abu Musa Ash'ari** (R.A.A.) relates that the Holy Prophet (S.A.W.) said: One who regularly and punctually offers the Morning (*Fajr*) and afternoon (*Asr*) Prayers will enter Paradise.'

(*Bukhari and Muslim*)

١٣٣ ـ السَّابِعَ عَشَرَ : عنه قال : قال رسول الله صلى الله عليه وسلم : « إذَا مَرِضَ الْعَبْدُ أوْ سَافَرَ كُتِبَ لَهُ مِثْلُ مَا كَانَ يَعْمَلُ مُقِيماً صَحِيحاً» رواه البخاري

133. **Hazrat Abu Musa Ash'ari** (R.A.A.) also relates the Holy Prophet (S.A.W.) said: 'When a servant of Allah falls ill or goes on a journey, he is credited with an equal amount of recompense as he used to do in his state of health or when he was at home.' (*Bukhari*)

١٣٤ ـ الثَّامِنَ عَشَرَ : عَنْ جَابِرٍ رضي الله عنه قال : قال رسول الله صلى الله عليه وسلم : « كُلُّ مَعْرُوفٍ صَدَقَةٌ » رواه البخاري ، ورواه مسلم مِن رواية حُذَيْفَةَ رضي الله عنه

134. **Hazrat Jabir** (R.A.A.) relates that the Holy Prophet (S.A.W.) said: 'Every good deed is a charity.' (*Bukhari*)

Muslim has reported the same on the authority of **Hazrat Huzaifah** (R.A.A.).

١٣٥ ـ التَّاسِعَ عَشَرَ : عَنْهُ قال : قال رسول الله صلى الله عليه وسلم : « مَا مِنْ مُسْلِمٍ يَغْرِسُ غَرْساً إلاَّ كَانَ مَا أُكِلَ مِنْهُ لَهُ صَدَقَةً ، وَمَا سُرِقَ مِنه له صَدَقَة ، ولا يَرْزَؤه أحَدٌ إلاَّ كَانَ لَه صَدَقَةٌ » رواه مسلم.

وفي رواية له : « فَلا يَغْرِسُ الْمُسْلِمُ غَرْساً، فيَأْكُلَ مِنه إنسَانٌ وَلا دَابَّةٌ وَلا طَيْرٌ إلاَّ كَانَ لَه صَدَقَةً إلَى يَوْمِ الْقِيَامَةِ » .

وفي رواية له : « لايَغْرِسُ مُسْلِمٌ غَرْساً ، وَلا يَزْرَعُ زَرْعاً ، فَيَأْكُلَ مِنه إنسَانٌ وَلا دَابَّةٌ وَلا شَيْءٌ إلاَّ كَانَتْ له صَدَقَةً » وَرَوَيَاه جَمِيعاً مِنْ رواية أنَسٍ رضي الله عنه

135. **Hazrat Jabir** (R.A.A.) relates that the Holy Prophet (S.A.W.) said: 'If a Muslim plants a tree then whatever is eaten from it (by the birds and animals) is a charity on his part and whatever is stolen is also charity, and whatever is lost from it, is charity.' (*Muslim*)

Another version relates: 'A Muslim does not plant a sapling but a man or an animal or a bird eats of it, it is a charity for him till the Day of Resurrection. Another version says: whatever a Muslim plants, or cultivates a crop, then whatever a man or animal or anything eats, it is a charity for him. Both the versions have been related on the authority of **Hazrat Anas** (R.A.A.)

١٣٦ ــ الْعِشْرُونَ : عَنْهُ قَالَ : أَرَادَ بَنُو سَلِمَةَ أن يَنْتَقِلُوا قُرْبَ الْمَسْجِدِ فَبَلَغَ ذلكَ رسولَ الله صلى الله عليه وسلم ، فَقَالَ لَهُمْ : « إِنَّهُ قَدْ بَلَغَنِي أَنَّكُمْ تُرِيدُونَ أَنْ تَنْتَقِلُوا قُرْبَ الْمَسْجِدِ ؟ » فَقَالُوا : نَعَمْ يَارسول اللهِ قَدْ أَرَدْنَا ذلكَ ، فَقَالَ : « بَنِي سَلِمَةَ دِيَارَكُمْ ، تُكْتَبْ آثَارُكُمْ ، دِيَارَكُمْ ، تُكْتَبْ آثَارُكُمْ » رواه مسلم .

وفي روايةٍ : « إِنَّ بِكُلِّ خَطْوَةٍ دَرَجَةً » رواه مسلم . ورواه البخاري أيضاً بِمَعْنَاهُ مِنْ رواية أنس رضي الله عنه

136. Hazrat Jabir (R.A.A.) relates that the (tribe of) Bani Salimah intended to move closer to the mosque (of the Holy Prophet S.A.W.) On learning this the Holy Prophet (S.A.W.) said to them: 'I have come to know that you intend moving closer to the Mosque'. They said: 'Yes, O Messenger of Allah, we want to do that.' He said: Bani Salimah, Stay in your homes, your footprints are noted. (*Muslim*)

Another version says. 'Your every step towards the mosque enhances your position.' Bukhari also reported to the same meaning on the authority of Hazrat Anas (R.A.A.)

١٣٧ ــ الْحَادي وَالْعِشْرُونَ : عَنْ أبي الْمُنْذِرِ أُبَيِّ بن كَعب رضي الله عنه قال : كَانَ رَجُلٌ لا أَعْلَمُ رَجُلاً أَبْعَدَ مِنَ الْمَسْجِدِ مِنْهُ ، وكَانَ لاتُخْطِئُهُ صَلاةٌ فَقِيلَ لَهُ ، أَوْ فَقُلْتُ لَهُ : لَو اشْتَرَيْتَ حِمَاراً تَرْكَبُهُ فِي الظَّلْمَاءِ ، وَفِي الرَّمْضَاءِ ؟ فَقَالَ : مَا يَسُرُّنِي أَنَّ مَنْزِلي إلَى جَنْبِ الْمَسْجِدِ ، إِنِّي أُرِيدُ أَنْ يُكْتَبَ لِي مَمْشَايَ إلَى الْمَسْجِد ، وَرُجُوعِي إذَا رَجَعْتُ إلَى أَهْلِي ، فَقَالَ رسول الله صلى الله عليه وسلم: « قَدْ جَمَعَ اللهُ لَكَ ذلِكَ كُلَّهُ » رواه مسلم

وفي روايةٍ : « إِنَّ لَكَ مَا احْتَسَبْتَ » « الرَّمْضَاءُ » : الأَرْضُ الَّتِي أَصَابَهَا الْحَرُّ الشَّدِيدُ .

137. Hazrat Abu Munzir Ubayy ibn K'ab (R.A.A.) relates: There was a person whose house was at a considerable distance from the mosque but he never missed a prayer (in congregation). It is said to him or I said to ohim 'Why do you not purchase a donkey that you could ride in the dark and in the hot weather? He said: I do not like that my house should be closer to the Mosque. I would like that my going to the mosque and my return therefrom should be recorded in my account as for the sake of Allah. The Holy Prophet (S.A.W.) said to him 'Allah has credited all that to your account.' (*Muslim*)

Another version adds: All that virtuous acts are recorded as good deeds in your account.

١٣٨ — الثَّانِي وَالْعِشْرُونَ : عَنْ أَبِي مُحمدٍ عبدِ اللهِ بنِ عمرو بن العاص رضي الله عنهما قال : قال رسول الله صلى الله عليه وسلم : « أَرْبَعُونَ خَصْلَةً أَعْلاهَا مَنِيحَةُ الْعَنْزِ ، مَا مِنْ عَامِلٍ يَعْمَلُ بِخَصْلَةٍ مِنْهَا رَجَاءَ ثَوَابِهَا وَتَصْدِيقَ مَوْعُودِهَا إِلاَّ أَدْخَلَهُ اللهُ بِهَا الْجَنَّةَ » رواه البخاري

138. Hazrat Abdullah ibn 'Amr Ibn 'Aas (R.A.A.) relates that the Holy Prophet (S.A.W.) said: 'There are forty kinds of good deeds — the highest being the loaning of a she-camel giving milk, whichever of these acts is practised in hoping for its reward and offering the promise mentioned therein, would lead its practitioner to Paradise.' (*Bukhari*)

١٣٩ — الثَّالثُ وَالْعِشْرُونَ : عَنْ عَدِيِّ بنِ حَاتِمٍ رضي الله عنه قال : سَمِعْتُ النَّبِيَّ صلى الله عليه وسلم يقول : « اتَّقُوا النَّارَ وَلَوْ بِشِقِّ تَمْرَةٍ » متفقٌ عليه .

وفي رواية لهما عنه قال : قال رسول الله صلى الله عليه وسلم : « مَا مِنْكُمْ مِنْ أَحَدٍ إِلاَّ سَيُكَلِّمُهُ رَبُّهُ لَيْسَ بَيْنَهُ وَبَيْنَهُ تَرْجُمَانٌ ، فَيَنْظُرُ أَيْمَنَ مِنْهُ فَلا يَرَى إِلاَّ مَا قَدَّمَ ، وَيَنْظُرُ أَشْأَمَ مِنْهُ فَلا يَرَى إِلاَّ مَا قَدَّمَ ، وَيَنْظُرُ بَيْنَ يَدَيْهِ فَلا يَرَى إِلاَّ النَّارَ تِلْقَاءَ وَجْهِهِ ، فاتَّقُوا النَّارَ وَلَوْ بِشِقِّ تَمْرَةٍ ، فَمَنْ لَمْ يَجِدْ فَبِكَلِمَةٍ طَيِّبَةٍ »

139. Hazrat Adi Ibn Hatim (R.A.A.) relates that he heard the Holy Prophet (S.A.W.) say: 'Protect yourselves against the fire (of Hell), even by giving away half piece of a date (in charity).' (*Bukhari and Muslim*)

Another version from Hazrat Adi is that the Holy Prophet (S.A.W.) said: 'There is none of you but that his Lord will speak to him without the help of an interpreter. He will look to his right and will find only his deeds; he will look to his left and see only his deeds. He will look in front of him and will only see the Fire (of the Hell) in front of him. Therefore protect yourselves against the fire (of Hell), even if it may be possible by giving away half piece of a date in charity, and if even that may not be available, by saying a pleasant word.'

١٤٠ — الرَّابِعُ وَالْعِشْرُونَ : عَنْ أَنَسٍ رضي الله عنه قال : قال رسول

الله صلى الله عليه وسلم : « إنَّ اللهَ لَيَرْضَى عَنِ العَبْدِ أنْ يَأْكُلَ الأَكْلَةَ فَيَحْمَدَهُ عَلَيْهَا ، أوْ يَشْرَبَ الشَّرْبَةَ فَيَحْمَدَهُ عَلَيْهَا » رواه مسلم

140. **Hazrat Anas** (R.A.A.) relates that the Holy Prophet (S.A.W.) said: When a servant of Allah eats something and he thanks Him and when he drinks something and he praises Allah, this pleases Allah. (*Muslim*)

١٤١ – الخَامِسُ وَالعِشْرُونَ : عن أبي موسى رضي الله عنه ، عن النبي صلى الله عليه وسلم قال : « عَلَى كُلِّ مُسْلِمٍ صَدَقَةٌ » قالَ : أرَأيْتَ إنْ لَمْ يَجِدْ ؟ قالَ : « يَعْمَلُ بِيَدَيْهِ فَيَنْفَعُ نَفْسَهُ وَيَتَصَدَّقُ » : قالَ : أرَأيْتَ إنْ لَمْ يَسْتَطِعْ ؟ قالَ : « يُعِينُ ذَا الحَاجَةِ المَلْهُوفَ » قالَ : أرَأيْتَ إنْ لَمْ يَسْتَطِعْ قالَ : « يَأْمُرُ بِالمَعْرُوفِ أوِ الخَيْرِ » قالَ : أرَأيْتَ إنْ لَمْ يَفْعَلْ ؟ قالَ : « يُمْسِكُ عَنِ الشَّرِّ فَإنَّهَا صَدَقَةٌ » متفقٌ عليه

141. **Hazrat Abu Musa Ash'ari** (R.A.A.) relates that the Holy Prophet (S.A.W.) said: 'Charity is necessary for every Muslim. He was asked: If a person may have nothing? The Holy Prophet replied: 'He should work with his own hands for his benefit and also give (something out of such earnings in charity). The companions said that if he may not be able to work. The Holy Prophet (S.A.W.) said: 'He should help poor and needy persons. The companions further said that if he cannot do even that? The Holy Prophet (S.A.W.) said that he should urge others to do good. The companions submitted that if he lacks that slso? The Holy Prophet (S.A.W.) said that he should check himslef from doing an evil. That is also charity.' (*Bukhari and Muslim*)

* * * * * * * * * *

CHAPTER 14

Following a Middle Course in Prayer

قال الله تعالى : طه ١ مَا أنزَلْنَا عَلَيْكَ القُرْآنَ لِتَشْقَى [طه : ١-٢] وقال تعالى : يُرِيدُ اللهُ بِكُمُ اليُسْرَ وَلا يُرِيدُ بِكُمُ العُسْرَ [البقرة : ١٨٥]

Allah, the Exalted, has said:

53. We have not revealed unto thee (O Muhammad) the Quran that thou shouldest be distressed' (20:2).
54. Allah desireth for you ease; He desireth not hardship for you; (2:185)

١٤٢ – عن عائشةَ رضي الله عنها أن النبي صلى الله عليه وسلم دَخَلَ عَلَيْهَا وَعِنْدَهَا امْرَأَةٌ قال : مَنْ هَذِهِ ؟ قالت : هَذِهِ فُلانَة تَذْكُرُ مِنْ صَلاتِهَا قالَ : « مه عَلَيْكُمْ بِمَا تُطِيقُونَ ، فَوَاللهِ لا يَمَلُّ اللهُ حَتَّى تَمَلُّوا » وكَانَ أَحَبُّ الدِّينِ إِلَيْهِ ما دَاوَمَ صَاحِبُهُ عَلَيْهِ . متفقٌ عليه

142. **Hazrat Ayesha** (R.A.A.) relates that the Holy Prophet (S.A.W.) once came to me when a woman was sitting with me. He asked: 'Who is she?' *Hazrat Ayesha* (R.A.A.) said: 'She is the same woman known for her (excessive) prayers: Addressing her he said: 'Just listen to me'. You are called upon to pray only as much as you can do easily. By Allah'. Allah does not tire of you until you yourself get tired. Allah likes those prayers which a devotee can perform easily and regularly. (*Agreed upon*).

١٤٣ – وعن أنسٍ رضي الله عنه قال : جاءَ ثلاثَةُ رَهْطٍ إلَى بُيُوتِ أزْوَاجِ النَّبيِّ صلى الله عليه وسلم ، يَسْأَلُونَ عَنْ عِبَادَةِ النبيِّ صلى الله عليه وسلم ، فلَمَّا أُخْبِرُوا كأنَّهُمْ تَقَالُّوهَا وقَالُوا : ايْنَ نَحْنُ مِنَ النبيِّ صلى الله عليه وسلم قَدْ غُفِرَ لَهُ ما تَقَدَّمَ مِنْ ذَنْبِهِ ومَا تَأَخَّرَ قالَ أَحَدُهُمْ : أمَّا أنَا فأُصَلِّي اللَّيْلَ أبداً . وقَالَ الآخَرُ : وأنا أصُومُ الدَّهْرَ ولا أُفْطِر ، وقَالَ الآخَرُ : وأنا أعْتَزِلُ النِّسَاءَ فَلا أتَزَوَّج أبَداً ، فَجَاءَ رسول الله صلى الله عليه وسلم إلَيْهِمْ فقالَ : « أنْتُمُ الَّذينَ قُلْتُمْ كَذا وكَذا ؟! أمَا واللهِ إنِّي لأخْشَاكُمْ لِلهِ وَأَتْقَاكُمْ لَه لَكِنِّي أصُومُ وَأُفْطِرُ ، وَأُصَلِّي وَأَرْقُدُ ، وَأتَزَوَّجُ النِّسَاءَ . فَمَنْ رَغِبَ عَنْ سُنَّتِي فَلَيْسَ مِنِّي » .

متفق عليه

143. **Hazrat Anas** (R.A.A.) relates: Once three persons came to enquire from the household of the Holy Prophet (S.A.W.) about the routine of his prayers. When they were apprised of the same, they felt that the same was insufficient so far as they were concerned. They remarked that there is no comparison between the Holy Prophet (S.A.W.) and us. He has been forgiven by Allah for all his omissions and shortcomings — past or future. One of them declared: I shall, in future, spend the whole night in praying. The second said: I shall continuously fast without interruption'. The third said: 'I shall abstain from women and shall never marry. In the meantime the Holy Prophet (S.A.W.) arrived and asked them: 'Did you say this and this? Listen, I fear Allah

more than all of you do, and I am more conscious of my duty to Him than all of you are, I observe a fast, but do break; I offer prayers at night and have a sleep as well, and I marry the woman. And this is my way of living. One who turns away from my practices (*Sunnah*) does not belong to me.' (*Bukhari and Muslim*)

١٤٤ — وعن ابن مسعودٍ رضي الله عنه أن النبي صلى الله عليه وسلم قال « هَلَكَ الْمُتَنَطِّعُونَ » قالها ثلاثاً ، رواه مسلم

144. Hazrat Ibn Mas'ud (R.A.A.) relates that the Holy Prophet (S.A.W.) said: 'Those persons who go to extremes (in practising their religion) were killed and destroyed.' He repeated this thrice. (*Muslim*)

١٤٥ — عن أبي هريرة رضي الله عنه عن النبي صلى الله عليه وسلم قال : « إنَّ الدِّينَ يُسْرٌ ، وَلَنْ يُشَادَّ الدِّينُ إلاَّ غَلَبَهُ ، فَسَدِّدُوا وَقَارِبُوا وَأَبْشِرُوا ، وَاسْتَعِينُوا بِالْغَدْوَةِ وَالرَّوْحَةِ وَشَيْءٍ مِنَ الدُّلْجَةِ » رواه البخاري .

وفي رواية له : « سَدِّدُوا وَقَارِبُوا وَاغْدُوا وَرُوحُوا ، وَشَيْءٌ مِنَ الدُّلْجَةِ ، الْقَصْدَ الْقَصْدَ تَبْلُغُوا » .

145. Hazrat Abu Hurairah (R.A.A.) relates that the Holy Prophet (S.A.W.) said: The pracitising of their religion is easy and nobody indulges in extremes in matters of faith, but one who is overpowered by the same. Therefore be moderate and practice the same in proportion to your capacity, have good tidings and seek Allah's help through extra prayers in the morning and evening and some parts of the night.

(*Bukhari*)

According to another version of *Bukhari:* Be moderate. Practise religion commensurate with your physical strength. Offer prayers in morning and evening and in some parts of evening and in some parts of the night. Follow the middle course, you will reach (the goal).

Note: By suggesting morning, evening and night prayers it is meant that during these hours one will be able to pray better and with concentration and achieve his object. Otherwise excessive prayers during all the time will deprive him of the required peace and concentration, and as such he will not be able to do full justice either to his religion or worldly matters.

١٤٦ — وعن أنس رضي الله عنه قال : دَخَلَ النبيُّ صلى الله عليه وسلم الْمَسْجِدَ فَإذَا حَبْلٌ مَمْدُودٌ بَيْنَ السَّارِيَتَيْنِ فقالَ : « مَا هَذَا الْحَبْلُ ؟ » قالُوا : هَذَا حَبْلٌ لِزَيْنَبَ ، فإذا فَتَرَتْ تَعَلَّقَتْ بِهِ . فقالَ النَّبِيُّ صلى الله عليه وسلم : « حُلُّوهُ ، لِيُصَلِّ أَحَدُكُمْ نَشَاطَهُ ، فَإذَا فَتَرَ

فَلْيَرْقُدْ » متفقٌ عليه

146. Hazrat Anas, (R.A.A.) relates that once when the Holy Prophet (S.A.W.) came to the mosque, he noticed a rope strung between two columns. He inquired as to why that rope was so fastened between two columns. The Companions said: that Hazrat Zainab had tied this rope only to take rest when tired in the course of her prayers. The Holy Prophet (S.A.W.) said: 'Untie it. You should pray so long as you feel pleasant. When you feel tired you should go to rest.

(*Bukhari and Muslim*)

١٤٧ — وعن عائِشَةَ رضي الله عنها أن رسول الله صلى الله عليه وسلم قال : « إذَا نَعَسَ أَحَدُكُمْ وَهُوَ يُصَلِّي ،فَلْيَرْقُدْ حتَّى يَذْهَبَ عَنْهُ النَّوْمُ ، فإنَّ أَحَدَكم إذَا صَلَّى وهُوَ نَاعِسٌ لايَدْرِي لَعَلَّهُ يَذْهَبُ يَسْتَغْفِرُ فَيَسُبُّ نَفْسَهُ » متفقٌ عليه

147. Hazrat Ayesha (R.A.A.) relates that the Holy Prophet (S.A.W.) said: If any one of you may be heavy with sleep while praying, he ought to go to sleep, till he reawakens fully conscious; because if he continues to pray while in a state of drowsiness, he does not know what words he is uttering; he may be cursing instead of seeking Allah's forgiveness. (*Bukhari and Muslim*)

١٤٨ — وعن أبي عبد الله جابر بن سَمُرَةَ رضي الله عنهما قال : « كُنْتُ أُصَلِّي مَعَ النبيِّ صلى الله عليه وسلم الصَّلَوَاتِ ،فَكَانَتْ صَلاتُهُ قَصْداً وخُطْبَتُهُ قَصْداً » رواه مسلم

148. Hazrat Abu Abdullah Jabir bin Samurah (R.A.A.) relates: I occassionally joined the Holy Prophet (S.A.W.) in prayers. Both his prayers and sermons used to be of moderate duration. (*Muslim*)

١٤٩ — وعن أبي جُحَيْفَةَ وَهْبِ بْنِ عبد الله رضي الله عنه قال : آخَى النَّبيُّ صلى الله عليه وسلم بَيْنَ سَلْمَانَ وأبي الدَّرْدَاءِ ، فَزَارَ سَلْمَانُ أَبَا الدَّرْدَاءِ ، فَرَأَى أمَّ الدَّرْدَاءِ مُتَبَذِّلَةً فقالَ : ماشَأْنُكِ ؟ قالَتْ : أَخُوكَ أَبُو الدَّرْدَاءِ لَيْسَ لَه حَاجَةٌ في الدُّنْيَا فَجاءَ أَبُو الدَّرْدَاءِ فَصَنَعَ لَه طَعَاماً، فقالَ لَهُ : كُلْ فَإنِّي صَائِمٌ ، قالَ : ما أنا بآكل حَتَّى تَأْكُلَ ، فأَكَلَ ، فلَمَّا كانَ اللَّيْلُ ذَهَبَ أبُو الدَّرْدَاء يَقُوم فقالَ لَه : نَمْ فنَامَ ، ثُمَّ ذَهَبَ يَقُوم فقالَ لَه : نَمْ ،فَلَمَّا كانَ من آخر اللَّيْلِ قالَ سَلْمَانُ :

قُمِ الآنَ ،فَصَلَّيَا جَمِيعاً ، فقالَ لَهُ سَلْمَانُ : إنَّ لِرَبِّكَ عَلَيْكَ حَقّاً ، وَإنَّ لِنَفْسِكَ عَلَيْكَ حَقّاً ، وَلِأهْلِكَ عَلَيْكَ حَقّاً ، فَأعْطِ كُلَّ ذِي حَقٍّ حَقَّهُ ، فَأتَى النبيَّ صلى الله عليه وسلم فَذَكَرَ ذلكَ لَهُ ، فقالَ النبيُّ صلى الله عليه وسلم : « صَدَقَ سَلْمَانُ » رواه البخاري .

149. **Hazrat Abu Juhaifah Wahab bin Abdullah** (R.A.A.) relates that the Holy Prophet (S.A.W.) had established a union of brotherhood between Hazrat Salman and Hazrat Abu Darda (R.A.A.). Once Salman (R.A.A.) went to see Hazrat Abu Darda (R.A.A.) and found Umme Darda, his wife in shabby dress. He asked her as to what was the matter with her? She said: 'Your brother Abu Darda has nothing to do with the world (and the women implying that he is always busy in prayers.). In the meantime Hazrat Abu Darda (R.A.A.) came and cooked some food for Hazrat Salman (R.A.A.) and asked him to start eating and said: 'I will not join you as I am fasting.' Hazrat Salman (R.A.A.) said to him that I will only eat the fare, if you join me. So Hazrat Abu Darda (R.A.A.) had to eat with him. At night, Hazrat Abu Darda (R.A.A.) got up for voluntary prayers. Hazrat Salman asked him to continue sleeping and he did so. After sometime Hazrat Abu Darda got up again for prayers but once again was made to sleep by Hazrat Salman (R.A.A.). In the later part of the night Hazrat Salman (R.A.A.) said: 'Awake now is the time for prayers, and the two prayed together. After this Hazrat Salman (R.A.A.) said: 'No doubt you have a duty to your Sustainer; likewise you owe a duty to yourself and a duty to your family. You should discharge your duty to everybody.' Both of them went to the Holy Prophet (S.A.W.) and related all this to him. The Holy Prophet (S.A.W.) said: 'What Salman says is correct.' (*Bukhari*)

١٥٠ — وعن أبي محمدٍ عبدِ اللهِ بنِ عَمْرِو بنِ العاصِ رضي الله عنهما قال : أُخْبِرَ النبي صلى الله عليه وسلم أنِّي أقُول : وَاللهِ لَأصُومَنَّ النَّهارَ ، وَلَأقُومَنَّ اللَّيْلَ مَا عِشْتُ ، فَقَالَ رسُول الله صلى الله عليه وسلم : أنْتَ الَّذي تَقُول ذلكَ ؟ فَقُلْتُ لَه : قَدْ قُلْتُه بِأبي أنْتَ وَأمِّي يَا رسول الله . قَالَ : « فإنك لا تَسْتَطِيع ذلكَ ؛ فَصُمْ وَأفْطِرْ ،وَنَمْ وَقُمْ ، وَصُمْ مِنَ الشَّهْرِ ثَلاثَةَ أيَّامٍ فَإنَّ الحَسَنَةَ بِعَشْرِ أمْثَالِهَا ، وَذلكَ مِثْلُ صِيَامِ الدَّهْرِ » قُلْت : فَإنِّي أُطيق أفْضَلَ مِنْ ذلكَ قَالَ : فَصُمْ يَوْماً وَأفْطِر يَوْمَيْنِ ، قُلْت : فَإنِّي أُطيق أفْضَلَ مِنْ ذلكَ . قَالَ : «فَصُمْ يَوْماً وَأفْطِرْ يَوْماً ، فَذلكَ صِيَام دَاودَ صلى الله عليه وسلم ،وَهُوَ أعْدَل الصِّيَامِ » . وَفي رِوايَة : « هوَ أفْضَلُ

الصِّيَام » فَقُلْتُ : فَإِنِّي أُطِيقُ أَفْضَلَ مِنْ ذَلِكَ . فَقَالَ رسول الله صلى الله عليه وسلم : « لا أَفْضَلَ مِنْ ذَلِكَ » وَلأَنْ أَكُونَ قَبِلْتُ الثَّلاثَةَ الأَيَّامِ الَّتِي قال رسول الله صلى الله عليه وسلم أَحَبُّ إِلَيَّ مِنْ أَهْلِي وَمَالِي .

وَفي رِوايةٍ :« أَلَمْ أُخْبَرْ أَنَّكَ تَصُومُ النَّهَارَ وَتَقُومُ اللَّيْلَ ؟» قلت: بَلَى يَا رسولَ اللهِ قال : « فَلا تَفْعَلْ: صُمْ وَأَفْطِرْ ، وَنَمْ وَقُمْ فَإِنَّ لِجَسَدِكَ عَلَيْكَ حَقّاً ، وَإِنَّ لِعَيْنَيْكَ عَلَيْكَ حَقّاً ، وَإِنَّ لِزَوْجِكَ عَلَيْكَ حَقّاً . وَإِنَّ لِزَوْرِكَ عَلَيْكَ حَقّاً ، وَإِنَّ بِحَسْبِكَ أَنْ تَصُومَ فِي كُلِّ شَهْرٍ ثَلاثَةَ أَيَّامٍ ،فَإِنَّ لَكَ بِكُلِّ حَسَنَةٍ عَشْرَ أَمْثَالِهَا ، فَإِنَّ ذَلِكَ صِيَامُ الدَّهْرِ » فَشَدَّدْتُ فَشُدِّدَ عَلَيَّ، قُلْتُ : يارسول الله إِنِّي أَجِدُ قُوَّةً ، قال : « صُمْ صِيَامَ نَبِيِّ اللهِ دَاوُدَ وَلا تَزِدْ عَلَيْهِ » قلت: وَمَا كَانَ صِيَامُ داود ؟ قال : « نِصْفُ الدَّهْرِ » فَكَانَ عَبْدُ اللهِ يقول بَعْدَ مَا كَبِرَ : يَالَيْتَنِي قَبِلْتُ رُخْصَةَ رسول اللهِ صلى الله عليه وسلم .

وفي روايةٍ : « أَلَمْ أُخْبَرْ أَنَّكَ تَصُومُ الدَّهْرَ ، وَتَقْرَأُ القُرْآنَ كُلَّ لَيْلَةٍ ؟ » فَقُلْتُ : بَلَى يا رسولَ اللهِ ، وَلَمْ أُرِدْ بِذَلِكَ إِلاَّ الْخَيْرَ ، قَالَ : « فَصُمْ صَوْمَ نَبِيِّ اللهِ دَاوُدَ ، فَإِنَّهُ كَانَ أَعْبَدَ النَّاسِ ، وَاقْرَأِ الْقُرْآنَ فِي كُلِّ شَهْرٍ » قُلْت : يَا نَبِيَّ اللهِ إِنِّي أُطِيق أَفْضَلَ مِنْ ذَلِكَ ؟ قَالَ : « فَاقْرَأْهُ فِي كُلِّ عِشْرِينَ » قُلْت : يَا نبيَّ اللهِ إِنِّي أطيق أَفْضَل مِنْ ذَلِكَ ؟ قَالَ: « فَاقْرَأْهُ في كُلِّ عَشْرٍ » قُلْت : يَا نَبِيَّ اللهِ إِنِّي أُطيق أَفْضَلَ مِنْ ذَلِكَ ؟ قَالَ : « فَاقْرَأْهُ فِي كُلِّ سَبْعٍ وَلا تَزِدْ عَلَى ذَلِكَ » فَشَدَّدْتُ فَشُدِّدَ عَلَيَّ ، وَقَالَ لِي النَّبِيُّ صلى الله عليه وسلم: « إِنَّكَ لاتَدْرِي لَعَلَّكَ يَطُول بِكَ عُمُرٌ » قَالَ: فَصِرْتُ إِلَى الَّذِي قَالَ لِي النَّبِيُّ صلى الله عليه وسلم ، فَلَمَّا كَبِرْتُ وَدِدْتُ أَنِّي كُنْتُ قَبِلْتُ رخصةَ نَبِيِّ اللهِ صلى الله عليه وسلم .

وفي رِوايةٍ : « وَإِنَّ لِوَلَدِكَ عَلَيْكَ حَقّاً » وفي رِوايةٍ : « لا صَامَ مَنْ

صَامَ الأَبَدَ» ثلاثاً . وفي رِوايةٍ : «أَحَبُّ الصِّيَامِ إِلَى اللهِ تَعَالَى صِيَامُ دَاوُدَ ، وَأَحَبُّ الصَّلاةِ إِلَى اللهِ تَعَالَى صَلاةُ دَاوُدَ : كَانَ يَنَامُ نِصْفَ اللَّيْلِ ، وَيَقُومُ ثُلُثَهُ ، وَيَنَامُ سُدُسَهُ ، وَكَانَ يَصُومُ يَوْماً وَيُفْطِرُ يَوْماً ، وَلا يَفِرُّ إِذَا لاقَى » .

وفي رِوايةٍ قَالَ : أَنْكَحَنِي أَبِي امْرَأَةً ذَاتَ حَسَبٍ ، وَكَانَ يَتَعَاهَدُ كَنَّتَهُ - أَي : امْرَأَةَ وَلَدِهِ - فَيَسْأَلُهَا عَنْ بَعْلِهَا ، فَتَقُولُ لَهُ : نِعْمَ الرَّجُلُ مِنْ رَجُلٍ لَمْ يَطَأْ لَنَا فِرَاشاً وَلَمْ يُفَتِّشْ لَنَا كَنَفاً مُنْذُ أَتَيْنَاهُ . فَلَمَّا طَالَ ذَلِكَ عَلَيهِ ذَكَرَ ذَلِكَ لِلنَّبِيِّ صلى الله عليه وسلم . فَقَالَ : « الْقَنِي بِهِ » فَلَقِيتُهُ بَعْدَ ذلك فَقَالَ : « كَيْفَ تَصُومُ ؟ » قُلْتُ كُلَّ يَوْمٍ ، قَالَ : « وَكَيْفَ تَخْتِمُ ؟ » قلتُ : كُلَّ لَيْلَةٍ ، وَذَكَرَ نَحْوَ مَاسَبَقَ - وَكَانَ يَقْرَأُ عَلَى بَعْضِ أَهْلِهِ السُّبُعَ الَّذِي يَقْرَؤُهُ ، يَعْرِضُهُ مِنَ النَّهَارِ لِيَكُونَ أَخَفَّ عَلَيْهِ بِاللَّيْلِ ، وَإِذَا أَرَادَ أَنْ يَتَقَوَّى أَفْطَرَ أَيَّاماً وَأَحْصَى وَصَامَ مِثْلَهُنَّ كَرَاهِيَةَ أَنْ يَتْرُكَ شَيْئاً فَارَقَ عَلَيْهِ النَّبِيَّ صلى الله عليه وسلم .

كُلُّ هَذِهِ الرِّوَايَاتِ صَحِيحَةٌ مُعْظَمُهَا فِي الصَّحِيحَيْنِ وَقَلِيلٌ مِنْهَا فِي أَحَدِهِمَا .

150. Hazrat Abu Muhammad Abdullah bin 'Amr bin 'Aas, says that the Holy Prophet (S.A.W.) was informed that I had vowed to keep fast during the day and offer voluntary prayers during the whole night for the whole life. The Holy Prophet (S.A.W.) asked me: 'Do you say this?' I replied: 'O Messenger of Allah, may my parents be sacrificed for you, I did say like this' He (S.A.W.) said: 'You will not be able to withstand this. You may fast but break it. Sleep and you may get up (in the night for voluntary prayers). Fast for three days in a month, as the value of a good deed is tenfold, thus it would be equal to a month's fasting, and as such it would mean perpetual fasting. I said: 'I am strong enough to do more than this.' He (S.A.W.) said: 'Then fast for a day and break on two days.' I said: 'I am strong enough to do better'. He said 'Well, then fast on alternate days.' This was the fast of prophet David, and it is a moderate fast and according to another version it is the best fast.' I said: 'I am strong enough to do still better,' The Holy Prophet (S.A.W.) said: 'There is no virtue better than this.' When Hazrat

Abdullah had grown old he lamented that he ought to have agreed to the suggestion of the Holy Prophet (S.A.W.) to fast on three days in a month. This would have been dearer to him than all his assets and his children (*Bukhari and Muslim*).

Another version says that the Holy Prophet (S.A.W.) said: 'Have I not been informed that you observe the fast every day and offer voluntary prayers for the whole night?' I affirmed: 'O Messenger of Allah it is so'. He said: 'Do not do this. Observe the fast and break it; sleep and stand in prayers. Your body has a right on you, your eyes have a right on you, your wife has a right on you. and your guest has a right on you. It would be sufficient if you fast on three days in a month; since every virtue has a tenfold value; this would amount to a whole month of fasting. This means perpetual fasting.' Hazrat Abdullah (R.A.A.) says: 'I was hard on myself and thus caused hardship for myself. I said to the Messenger of Allah (S.A.W.) 'I feel strong to fast more frequently. He said, 'Then, observe the fast of David, the Prophet of Allah, and do not exceed.' I asked: 'What was the fast of Prophet David?' He said 'Half the perpetual fasting — one day fasting and one day break.' In his old age Hazrat Abdullah used to say: 'I wish I would have accepted the concession proposed by the Holy Prophet (S.A.W.) (of moderation in fasting and prayers).'

Yet another version says that the Holy Prophet said: Have I not been apprised that you fast daily and recite the whole Quran in one night? I said: 'This is correct O Messenger of Allah and thereby I hope to do only good.' He said: 'Observe the fast of David, the Prophet of Allah, because he was the most ardent devotee of Allah, and completed the recitation of the Quran in one month.' I submitted, 'O Prophet of Allah, I am strong enough to do better than that. He said: 'Then recite it in ten days.' I said: 'Prophet of Allah, I have strength enough to do better.' He said: 'Well, then read it in seven days and do not complete its reading earlier than that.' Thus I subjected myself to hardship and suffered. The Holy Prophet (S.A.W.) said to me: 'You know not you may have a longer life.' Then in fact it so happened as the Holy Prophet (S.A.W.) had said: I had a long span of life. When I became old I realised that I ought to have accepted the concession made by the Holy Prophet (S.A.W.)

According to another version he said: 'Your son has a right on you.' And yet another version, says that the Holy Prophet (S.A.W.) said: 'One who perpetually fasts does not fast at all', and repeated this thrice.

One more version adds: 'The fast of Prophet David was the most favoured by Allah, and the prayer (*Salat*) of Prophet David was the most favoured by Allah. He rested in the first half of the night, then would offer his *Tahajjud* — midnight prayers in one third of it, and then would sleep through the remaining one-sixth. Similarly he used to fast on alternate days. He never yielded ground when he had to face an enemy.

In another account Hazrat Abdullah is reported to have said that his father had married him to a woman belonging to a respectable family, and that his father used to ask her about her husband. She used to say that he was a good man, and that ever since she was married to him, he had neither slept with her, nor had uncovered her private parts. When this state of affairs prolonged, Hazrat Abdullah's father brought the matter to the notice of the Holy Prophet (S.A.W.) who asked my father to send me to him. When I presented my self to the Holy Prophet (S.A.W.), he asked me as to how often I fast? I said: 'I fast daily.' He then asked me as to how long I take to finish the Holy Quran? I replied that I finish the Holy Book in one night, and related the story already mentioned.

When Hazrat Abdullah became old he used to rehearse the seventh part of the Holy Quran to some members of his family during the day time so that his labour for the night might be reduced. Likewise, when he needed some relief from his continuous fasting he used to omit fasting for a few days, but would make up for the missing days subsequently. He could not give up the practice altogether as he disliked going back on what he had been practising upto the last days of the Holy Prophet (S.A.W.).

Imam Nawawi says that all these traditions are true and most of them have been reported by *Bukhari and Mulsim.*

١٥١ – وعن أبي رِبْعِيٍّ حَنْظَلَةَ بنِ الرَّبيعِ الأُسَيْدِيِّ الْكَاتِبِ أَحَدِ
كُتَّابِ رسول الله صلى الله عليه وسلم قال : لَقِيَنِي أَبُو بَكْرٍ رضي الله عنه فقال :
كَيْفَ أَنْتَ يا حَنْظَلَةُ ؟ قُلْتُ : نَافَقَ حَنْظَلَةُ ! قَالَ : سُبْحَانَ الله
مَا تَقُولُ ؟ ! قُلْتُ : نَكُونُ عِنْدَ رسول الله صلى الله عليه وسلم يُذَكِّرُنَا
بالْجَنَّةِ وَالنَّارِ كأنَّا رَأْيَ عَيْنٍ ، فَإِذَا خَرَجْنَا مِنْ عِنْدِ رسول الله صلى
الله عليه وسلم عَافَسْنَا الأزْوَاجَ وَالأَوْلادَ وَالضَّيْعَاتِ نَسِينَا كَثِيراً . قالَ أَبُو
بَكْرٍ رضي الله عنه : فَوَاللهِ إِنَّا لَنَلْقَى مِثْلَ هَذَا ؛ فَانْطَلَقْتُ أنَا وَأَبُو
بَكْرٍ حَتَّى دَخَلْنَا عَلَى رسول الله صلى الله عليه وسلم . فَقُلْتُ : نَافَقَ حَنْظَلَةُ
يا رسول الله ! فقالَ رسولُ الله صلى الله عليه وسلم : « وَمَا ذَاكَ ؟ » قُلْتُ :
يا رسولَ اللهِ نَكُونُ عِنْدَكَ تُذَكِّرُنَا بالنَّارِ وَالْجَنَّةِ كأنَّا رَأْيَ العَيْنِ ،
فَإِذَا خَرَجْنَا مِنْ عِنْدِكَ عَافَسْنَا الأَزْوَاجَ وَالأَوْلادَ والضَّيْعَاتِ نَسِينَا
كَثِيراً . فقال رسولُ الله صلى الله عليه وسلم : « وَالَّذِي نَفْسِي بِيَدِهِ لَوْ
تَدُومُونَ عَلَى مَا تَكُونُونَ عِنْدِي وَفي الذِّكْرِ لَصَافَحَتْكُمُ الملائكةُ

عَلَى فُرُشِكُمْ وَفِي طُرُقِكُمْ ، وَلَكِنْ يَا حَنْظَلَةُ سَاعَةً وَسَاعَةً ثَلاثَ مَرَّاتٍ ، رواه مسلم

151. Hazrat Abi Ribyee Hanzala bin Rabi al Usaidi, one of the copyists of the Holy Prophet (S.A.W.) reported that Hazrat Abu Bakr Siddiq once met him and enquired, 'How are you, Hanzala'?. He said: 'Hanzala has turned hypocrite.' Hazrat Abu Bakr (R.A.A.) said: 'Glory be to Allah'. What are you saying Hanzala?' Hanzala asserted: 'When we were before the Holy Prophet (S.A.W.) and he sermonized us and mentioned the Hell and Heaven, we would feel as if these were before our eyes. But when we left him and got busy with our wives, children, lands and gardens, we used to forget much of the Holy Prophet's advices.' Hazrat Abu Bakr (R.A.A.) said: 'By Allah'. We are all in the same condition.' Thereafter, both of them presented themselves before the Holy Prophet (S.A.W.). Then Hazrat Hanzala said, 'O Messenger of Allah, 'Hanzala has turned hypocrite.' The Holy Prophet (S.A.W.) asked him, as to what did he mean. I said: 'O Messenger of Allah, when we are in your company and you talk to us about Heaven and Hell, then we feel as if they are before our eyes. But as soon as we leave your company we get busy with our wives, children, gardens and lands and thereafter we forget much of your advices.' The Holy Prophet (S.A.W.) said: 'By Allah, in Whose hands lies my life, if you were to continue in the same state as you are when with me, remembering Allah, angels would come down to shake hands with you when you are in your beds and in the streets. But Hanzala, such things happen occasionally.' He repeated this sentence thrice. *(Muslim)*

١٥٢ ــ وعن ابن عباس رضي الله عنهما قال : بَيْنَمَا النَّبِيُّ صلى الله عليه وسلم يَخْطُبُ إِذَا هُوَ بِرَجُلٍ قَائِمٍ ، فَسَأَلَ عَنْهُ فَقَالُوا : أَبُو إِسْرَائِيلَ نَذَرَ أَنْ يَقُومَ فِي الشَّمْسِ وَلا يَقْعُدَ ، وَلا يَسْتَظِلَّ وَلا يَتَكَلَّمَ ، وَيَصُومَ فَقَالَ النَّبِيُّ صلى الله عليه وسلم : « مُرُوهُ فَلْيَتَكَلَّمْ وَلْيَسْتَظِلَّ وَلْيَقْعُدْ وَلْيُتِمَّ صَوْمَهُ » رواه البخاري

152. Hazrat Ibn Abbas (R.A.A.) relates: Once when the Holy Prophet (S.A.W.) was delivering the sermon, he saw a man standing, (among those who were sitting in the meeting). Accordingly he made enquiries about him. He was told that his name was Abu Israel and he had vowed that he would remain standing in the sun and would not sit down nor go under shade and would not talk with anybody, and would observe a fast. The Holy Prophet (S.A.W.) said: 'Ask him to talk, to go into the shade and sit down. But let him complete his fast.' *(Bukhari)*

* * * * * * * * * * *

CHAPTER 15

To Be Steady and Regular in Virtuous Deeds

قال الله تعالى : أَلَمْ يَأْنِ لِلَّذِينَ آمَنُوا أَنْ تَخْشَعَ قُلُوبُهُمْ لِذِكْرِ اللهِ وَمَا نَزَلَ مِنَ الْحَقِّ وَلا يَكُونُوا كَالَّذِينَ أُوتُوا الْكِتَابَ مِنْ قَبْلُ فَطَالَ عَلَيْهِمُ الأَمَدُ فَقَسَتْ قُلُوبُهُمْ [الحديد: ١٦] . وقال تعالى : « وَقَفَّيْنَا بِعِيسَى ابْنِ مَرْيَمَ وَآتَيْنَاهُ الإِنْجِيلَ وَجَعَلْنَا فِي قُلُوبِ الَّذِينَ اتَّبَعُوهُ رَأْفَةً وَرَحْمَةً وَرَهْبَانِيَّةً ابْتَدَعُوهَا مَا كَتَبْنَاهَا عَلَيْهِمْ إِلاَّ ابْتِغَاءَ رِضْوَانِ اللهِ فَمَا رَعَوْهَا حَقَّ رِعَايَتِهَا [الحديد : ٢٧] ، وقال تعالى: وَلا تَكُونُوا كَالَّتِي نَقَضَتْ غَزْلَهَا مِنْ بَعْدِ قُوَّةٍ أَنْكَاثاً [النمل: ٩٢]، وقال تعالى : وَاعْبُدْ رَبَّكَ حَتَّى يَأْتِيَكَ الْيَقِينُ [الحجر : ٩٩] .

Allah, the Exalted, has said:

55. Is not the time ripe for the hearts of those who believe to submit Allah's reminder, and to the truth which is revealed, that they become not as those who received the scripture of the old but the term was prolonged for them and so their hearts were hardened and many of them are evil doers. (25:16)
56. And we caused Jesus, son of Mary, to follow, and gave him the Gospel, and placed compassion and mercy in the hearts of those who followed him. But monasticism they invented. We ordained it not for them only for seeking Allah's Pleasure, and they observed it not with right observance. (25:27)
57. And be not like unto her who unravelleth the thread, after she hath made it strong, to thin filaments, making your oaths a deceit between you because of a nation being more numerous than (another) nation. (16:92)
58. And serve thy Lord till the inevitable (i.e. death) cometh unto thee. (15:99)

One of the traditions in this connection is one by Hazrat Ayesha (R.A.A.) to the effect that the Holy Prophet (S.A.W.) has said that Allah likes most the consistency and regularity in the performance of religion (Islam). This tradition has been reported in detail earlier.

١٥٣ — وعن عمر بنِ الخطابِ رضي الله عنه قال : قال رسول الله صلى الله عليه وسلم : « مَنْ نَامَ عَنْ حِزْبِهِ مِنَ اللَّيْلِ ، أَوْ عَنْ شَيْءٍ مِنْهُ فَقَرَأَهُ

مَا بَيْنَ صَلاةِ الْفَجْرِ وَصَلاةِ الظهْرِ ، كُتِبَ لَهُ كَأنمَا قَرَأَهُ مِنَ اللَّيْلِ »
رواه مسلم

153. Hazrat Umar bin Khattab (R.A.A.) relates that the Holy Prophet (S.A.W.) said: 'If a person has forgotten to recite religious chants (his voluntary prayers) or a part of it, at night, and went to sleep, will get the same recompense if he recites it at any time between *Fajr* (early morning) and *Zohr* (mid-day) prayers next day.' (*Muslim*)

١٥٤ – وعن عبدِ اللهِ بن عمرو بن العاصِ رضي الله عنهما قال : قال لي رسول الله صلى الله عليه وسلم : « يَا عَبْدَ اللهِ لا تَكُنْ مِثْلَ فُلانٍ ، كَانَ يَقُومُ اللَّيْلَ فَتَرَكَ قِيَامَ اللَّيْلِ » متفقٌ عليه

154. Hazrat Abdullah bin Amr bin 'Aas (R.A.A.) relates that the Holy Prophet (S.A.W.) said to me: 'O Abdullah, do not be like so and so, who used to get up at night for voluntary prayers but discontinued it after sometime.' (*Bukhari and Muslim*)

١٥٥ – وعن عائشة رضي الله عنها قالت : كان رسول الله صلى الله عليه وسلم إذَا فَاتَتْهُ الصَّلاةُ مِنَ اللَّيْلِ مِنْ وَجَعٍ أوْ غَيْرِهِ، صَلَّى مِنَ النَّهَارِ ثنتَيْ عَشَرَةَ رَكْعَةً » رواه مسلم

155. Hazrat Ayesha (R.A.A.) relates that when the Holy Prophet (S.A.W.) could not perform his nightly optional prayer due to some cause like sickness he would offer twelve *raka'at* during the day. (*Muslim*)

Note: This is the greatest kind heartedness of the Holy Prophet (S.A.W.) that he taught and guided his followers (*Ummat*) to practice good deeds and virtues with an open mind and easy mood and to worship Allah without any exertion, physical torture or handicap, and earn His blessings. As against those persons who abandon this method and involve themselves in religious penance and physical hardhsips in their worship of Allah, become tired of these torments and tortuous methods and give up this practice and thus deprive themselves of great recompense. The Holy Quran has condemned this loss. The practices and precepts of the Holy Prophet (S.A.W.) taught us to pray in the proper manner and become entitled to be stride on the right path.

* * * * * * * * * * *

CHAPTER 16

Injunctions for Regular Observation of the Holy Prophet's (S.A.W.) Practice and its Conditions

قاله الله تعالى : وَمَا آتَاكُمُ الرَّسُولُ فَخُذُوهُ وَمَا نَهَاكُمْ عَنْهُ فَانْتَهُوا [الحشر : ٧] ، وقال تعالى : وَمَا يَنْطِقُ عَنِ الْهَوَى . إِنْ هُوَ إِلاَّ وَحْيٌ يُوحَى [النجم : ٣ ، ٤] ، وقال تعالى : قُلْ إِنْ كُنْتُمْ تُحِبُّونَ اللهَ فَاتَّبِعُونِي يُحْبِبْكُمُ اللهُ وَيَغْفِرْ لَكُمْ ذُنُوبَكُمْ [آل عمران : ٣١] وقال تعالى : لَقَدْ كَانَ لَكُمْ فِي رَسُولِ اللهِ أُسْوَةٌ حَسَنَةٌ لِمَنْ كَانَ يَرْجُو اللهَ وَالْيَوْمَ الآخِرَ [الأحزاب : ٢١] ، وقال تعالى : فَلا وَرَبِّكَ لا يُؤْمِنُونَ حَتَّى يُحَكِّمُوكَ فِيمَا شَجَرَ بَيْنَهُمْ ثُمَّ لا يَجِدُوا فِي أَنْفُسِهِمْ حَرَجاً مِمَّا قَضَيْتَ وَيُسَلِّمُوا تَسْلِيماً [النساء : ٦٥] ، وقال تعالى : فَإِنْ تَنَازَعْتُمْ فِي شَيْءٍ فَرُدُّوهُ إِلَى اللهِ وَالرَّسُولِ [النساء : ٥٩] ، قال الْعُلَمَاءُ : مَعْنَاهُ إِلَى الْكِتَابِ وَالسُّنَّةِ . وقال تعالى : مَنْ يُطِعِ الرَّسُولَ فَقَدْ أَطَاعَ اللهَ [النساء : ٨٠] وقال تعالى : وَإِنَّكَ لَتَهْدِي إِلَى صِرَاطٍ مُسْتَقِيمٍ [الشورى : ٥٢ ،] ، وقال تعالى : فَلْيَحْذَرِ الَّذِينَ يُخَالِفُونَ عَنْ أَمْرِهِ أَنْ تُصِيبَهُمْ فِتْنَةٌ أَوْ يُصِيبَهُمْ عَذَابٌ أَلِيمٌ [النور : ٦٣] ، وقال تعالى : وَاذْكُرْنَ مَا يُتْلَى فِي بُيُوتِكُنَّ مِنْ آيَاتِ اللهِ وَالْحِكْمَةِ [الأحزاب : ٣٤] والآيات في الباب كثيرة

Allah, the Exalted, has said:

59. And whatsoever the Messenger giveth you, take it. And whatsoever he forbiddeth, abstain (from it) (59:7)
60. Nor doth he speak of (his own) desire. It is naught save an inspiration that is inspired. (53:3—4)
61. Say (O Muhammad, to mankind) If you love Allah, follow me: Allah will love you and forgive you your sins. Allah is Forgiving, Merciful. (3:31)
62. Verily in the Messenger of Allah ye have a good example for 'him who looketh Allah and the last day, and remembereth Allah much. (33:21)
63. We sent no messenger save that he should be obeyed by Allah's leave. And if, when they had wronged themselves, they had but come unto thee and asked forgiveness of Allah, and asked forgiveness of the messenger they would have found Allah Forgiving Merciful (4:65)

64. O ye who believe! Obey Allah, and obey the messenger and those of you who are in authority and if ye have a dispute concerning any matter, refer it to Allah and the Messenger, if ye are (in truth) believers in Allah and the Last Day. That is better and more seemly in the end. (4:59)

65. Whoso obeyeth the Messenger, obeyeth Allah, and whoso turneth away: We have not sent thee as a warder over them (4:80)

66. And Lo! thou verily dost guide unto a right path. (42:52)

67. And let those who conspire to evade orders beware lest grief or painful punishment befall them. (24:64)

68. And stay in your houses. Bedizen not yourselves with the bedizement of the time of ignorance. Be regular in prayer and pay the poor due and obey Allah and his messenger (33:34)

١٥٦ ـ فالأوَّلُ : عَنْ أبي هُرَيْرَةَ رضي الله عنه عن النبي صلى الله عليه
وسلم قال : « دَعُونِي ماتَرَكْتُكُمْ : إنَّمَا أهْلَكَ مَنْ كانَ قَبْلَكُمْ كَثْرَةَ
سُؤَالِهِمْ ، وَاخْتِلافُهُمْ عَلَى أنْبِيَائِهِمْ ، فَإذَا نَهَيْتُكُمْ عَنْ شَيْءٍ
فاجْتَنِبُوهُ ، وَإذَا أمَرْتُكُمْ بِأمْرٍ فَأْتُوا مِنْهُ ما اسْتَطَعْتُمْ » متفقٌ عليه

156. **Hazrat Abu Hurairah** (R.A.A.) relates that the Holy Prophet (S.A.W.) said: Don't bother me with questions on such matters which I do not mention to you because the nations who preceded you, were ruined due to their asking too many unnecessary questions and having the audacity to differ from their prophets. Therefore when I forbid you from doing anything, totally abstain from doing the same and when I prescribe anything for you, carry it out according to your capacity. (*Bukhari and Muslim*)

١٥٧ ـ الثَّانِي : عَنْ أبي نَجِيحٍ الْعِرْبَاضِ بنِ سَارِيَةَ رضي الله عنه
قال : « وَعَظَنَا رسول اللهِ صلى الله عليه وسلم مَوْعِظَةً بليغَةً وَجِلَتْ مِنْهَا
الْقُلُوبُ وَذَرَفَتْ مِنهَا الْعُيُونُ ، فقُلْنَا : يا رَسولَ اللهِ كأنَّهَا مَوْعِظَةُ
مُوَدِّعٍ فَأوْصِنَا . قال : « أُوصيكُمْ بِتَقْوَى اللهِ ، وَالسَّمْعِ وَالطَّاعَةِ وَإنْ
تَأمَّرَ عَلَيْكُمْ عَبْدٌ ، وَإنَّهُ مَنْ يَعِشْ مِنكُمْ فَسَيَرَى اخْتِلافاً كَثِيراً .
فَعَلَيْكُمْ بسُنَّتِي وَسُنَّةِ الْخُلَفَاءِ الرَّاشِدِينَ الْمَهْدِيِّينَ ، عَضُّوا عَلَيْهَا
بالنَّوَاجِذِ ، وَإيَّاكُمْ ومُحْدَثَاتِ الأُمُورِ فَإنَّ كُلَّ بِدْعَةٍ ضَلالَةٌ » رواه
أبو داود ، والترمِذِي وقال : حديث حسن صحيح

157. Hazrat Abu Najih Irbaz Bin Sariah (R.A.A.) relates: The Holy Prophet (S.A.W.) delivered a moving speech which greatly moved us and sent a wave of fear into our hearts. We said to him that this sermon appears like the last advice, then tell us some thing more as advice; whereupon he said: I advise you to be afraid of Allah (because of your obligations to Allah) and to hear and obey even a slave who may be put in authority over you. Those of you who survive me will notice a lot of differences. It will be incumbent upon you to follow my *Sunnah* (practice) and the practices of my rightly guided successors (Caliphs) and hold fast with these precepts and traditions and beware of innovations and inventions in religion. Because every innovation leads to wrong path. (*Abu Dawood*)

According to *Imam Tirmizi* this is an authentic tradition.

١٥٨ ـ الثَّالِثُ : عَنْ أَبِي هريرة رضي الله عنه أن رسول الله صلى الله عليه وسلم قالَ : « كُلُّ أُمَّتِي يَدْخُلُونَ الْجَنَّةَ إلاَّ مَنْ أبِى » . قِيلَ : وَمَنْ يَأبَى يارسول اللهِ ؟ قالَ : « مَنْ أَطَاعَنِي دَخَلَ الجَنَّةَ ، وَمَنْ عَصَانِي فَقَدْ أبَى » رواه البخاري

158. Hazrat Abu Hurairah (R.A.A.) relates that the Holy Prophet (S.A.W.) said: All my followers will go to heaven, except those who defied me. He was asked: 'O Messenger of Allah, who will be such persons?' The Holy Prophet (S.A.W.) elucidated: 'One who obeys me will enter Paradise and the one who disobeys me defies me (i.e., will not enter paradise).' (*Bukhari*)

١٥٩ ـ الرَّابعُ : عن أَبي مسلمٍ ، وقِيلَ : أبي إيَاسٍ سَلَمَةَ بْنِ عَمْرو ابْنِ الأَكْوَعِ رضي الله عنه ، أَنَّ رَجُلاً أَكَلَ عِنْدَ رسول الله صلى الله عليه وسلم بِشِمَالِهِ فقال : « كُلْ بِيَمِينِكَ » قالَ : لا أَسْتَطِيعُ . قالَ : « لا اسْتَطَعْتَ » ما مَنَعَهُ إلاَّ الْكِبْرُ ، فَمَا رَفَعَهَا إلَى فِيهِ رواه مسلم

159. Hazrat Abu Muslim also called Abu Ayaz (R.A.A.) relates that a person started eating with his left hand in the presence of the Holy Prophet (S.A.W.) who asked him to eat with his right hand. He said: 'I am unable to do so'. It was simply his insolence that prevented him to obey the orders of the Holy Prophet (S.A.W.). After this it so happened that the said man could not raise his hand upto his mouth. (*Muslim*)

١٦٠ ـ الْخَامِسُ : عَنْ أَبي عبدِ الله النُّعْمَانِ بْن بَشير رضي الله عنهما ، قال : سَمِعْتُ رسول الله صلى الله عليه وسلم يقولُ : « لَتُسَوُّنَّ صُفُوفَكُمْ

أوْ لَيُخَالِفَنَّ اللهُ بَيْنَ وُجُوهِكُمْ » متفقٌ عليه

وفي رِوايةٍ لِمسلمٍ : كانَ رسولُ الله صلى الله عليه وسلم يُسَوِّي صُفُوفَنَا حتَّى كأنَّما يُسَوِّي بهَا القِدَاحَ حتَّى إذَا رَأى أنَّا قدْ عقَلْنَا عنْهُ ثُمَّ خرَجَ يوماً ، فقامَ حتَّى كَادَ أنْ يُكَبِّرَ ، فرَأى رَجُلاً بَادِياً صَدْرُهُ فقَالَ : «عِبَادَ الله لتُسَوُّنَّ صُفوفَكُمْ أوْ ليُخَالِفَنَّ اللهُ بيْنَ وُجُوهِكُمْ» .

160. Hazrat Nu'man bin Bashir (R.A.A.) relates, 'I heard the Holy Prophet directing: 'You must properly align your rows (in prayer), failing which Allah will create differences among you (i.e. It will create enmity among you).' (*Bukhari and Muslim*)

According to another version of Muslim, 'The Holy Prophet (S.A.W.) insisted on keeping our rows straight, so much so as if he would straighten them by arrows. He continued to emphasise this till he felt that we had recognized its importance. One day he came into the mosque to lead the prayer and the *Takbir* was about to be called when he noticed the chest of one of the worshippers jutting out of the line, on which he said: 'Allah's bondsmen, keep your rows straight, else Allah will create dissensions among you.'

١٦١ — السَّادِسُ : عن أبي موسى رضي الله عنه قال : احتَرَق بيْتٌ بالمَدِينَةِ علَى أهْلِهِ مِنَ اللَّيْلِ ،فلَمَّا حُدِّثَ رسول الله صلى الله عليه وسلم بِشأْنِهِمْ قال : « إنَّ هذهِ النَّار عدُوٌّ لكُمْ ،فإذَا نِمْتُمْ فأطْفِئُوهَا عنكُمْ » متفقٌ عليه

161. Hazrat Abu Musa (R.A.A.) relates that a house in Medina caught fire at night and the same fell down upon the occupants. When this was brought to the notice of the Holy Prophet (S.A.W.) He said: 'Fire is your enemy when you go to sleep, put it out.'

(*Bukhari and Muslim*)

١٦٢ — السَّابِعُ : عَنْهُ قال : قال رسول الله صلى الله عليه وسلم : « إنَّ مثَلَ ما بعَثَنِي الله بِهِ مِنَ الهُدَى والعلْمِ كمَثَلِ غيْثٍ أصابَ أرْضاً فكَانَتْ مِنهَا طائِفَةٌ طَيِّبَةٌ ، قبِلَتِ المَاءَ فأنْبتَتِ الكَلأَ والعُشْبَ الكَثِيرَ ، وكَانَ مِنهَا أجَادِبُ أمْسَكَتِ المَاءَ ، فنَفَعَ اللهُ بِها النَّاسَ فشَرِبُوا مِنهَا وسَقَوْا وزَرَعُوا . وأصابَ طائِفَةً مِنهَا أُخرَى ، إنَّمَا هِيَ

قِيعَانٌ لا تُمْسِكُ مَاءً وَلا تُنْبِتُ كَلأً . فَذَلِكَ مَثَلُ مَنْ فَقُهَ في دِينِ اللهِ ، وَنَفَعَهُ بِمَا بَعَثَنِي اللهُ بِهِ ، فَعَلِمَ وَعَلَّمَ ، وَمَثَلُ مَنْ لَمْ يَرْفَعْ بِذلِكَ رَأْساً ، وَلَمْ يَقْبَلْ هُدَى اللهِ الَّذي أُرْسِلْتُ بِهِ » متفقٌ عليه

162. Hazrat Abu Musa (R.A.A.) also relates that the Holy Prophet (S.A.W.) remarked: The case of the guidance and knowledge with which Allah has endowed me (and sent for your enlightenment) is like the rain which falls on land, part of which is good and fertile where dry grass turns green and considerable fresh vegetation is grown; and part of it is dry and it stores up the water and Allah makes it beneficial for the human being; they drink from it and get saturated and use it for cultivation. This rain water also reached a piece of land which is wide open plain, where the water was neither retained nor it could help produce grass. Similar is the case of those who understand the knowledge of religion which Allah has sent (to the people) through me, and benefitted themselves from it; and also of those who learnt it and taught it to others. Another example is of those persons who neither raised their heads and learnt it nor accepted Allah's guidance, sent to them through me. *(Bukhari and Muslim)*

١٦٣ ــ الثَّامِنُ : عن جابرٍ رضي الله عنه قال : قال رسول الله صلى الله عليه وسلم : « مَثَلِي وَمَثَلُكُمْ كَمَثَلِ رَجُلٍ أَوْقَدَ نَاراً فَجَعَلَ الْجَنَادِبُ وَالْفَرَاشُ يَقَعْنَ فيها وَهُوَ يَذُبُّهُنَّ عَنْهَا وَأَنَا آخذٌ بِحُجَزِكُمْ عَنِ النَّارِ ، وَأَنْتُمْ تَفَلَّتُونَ من يَدَيَّ » رواه مسلم

163. Hazrat Jabir (R.A.A.) relates that the Holy Prophet (S.A.W.) has said: 'I and you are like a person who ignites a fire and moths and other insects started running to it and falling into it and the man, who started the fire, was trying to stop them. I am like this man trying to hold you by your waists (to save you) from Hell, but you are escaping from my hands. *(Muslim)*

١٦٤ ــ التَّاسِعُ : عَنْهُ أَنْ رسول الله صلى الله عليه وسلم ، أَمَرَ بِلَعْقِ الأَصَابِعِ وَالصَّحْفَةِ وَقَالَ : « إِنَّكُمْ لاتَدْرُونَ في أَيِّهَا الْبَرَكَةَ » رواه مسلم .

وفي رواية لَهُ : « إِذَا وَقَعَتْ لُقْمَةُ أَحَدِكُمْ . فَلْيَأْخُذْهَا فَلْيُمِطْ مَا كَانَ بِهَا مِنْ أَذىً ، وَلْيَأْكُلْهَا ، وَلا يَدَعْهَا لِلشَّيْطَانِ ، وَلا يَمْسَحْ يَدَهُ بِالْمَنْدِيلِ حَتَّى يَلْعَقَ أَصَابِعَهُ ؛ فَإِنَّهُ لا يَدْرِي في أَيِّ طَعَامِهِ الْبَرَكَةُ » .

وفي رواية له : « إنَّ الشَّيْطَانَ يَحْضُرُ أَحَدَكُمْ عِنْدَ كُلِّ شَيْءٍ مِنْ شَأْنِهِ حَتَّى يَحْضُرَهُ عِنْدَ طَعَامِهِ ، فَإِذَا سَقَطَتْ مِنْ أَحَدِكُمْ اللُّقْمَةُ فَلْيُمِطْ مَا كَانَ بِهَا مِنْ أَذىً ، فَلْيَأْكُلْهَا ، وَلا يَدَعْهَا لِلشَّيْطَانِ

164. Hazrat Jabir (R.A.A.) relates that the Holy Prophet (S.A.W.) ordained his followers to lick the fingers and clean the plates (after having eaten the meals.) He added: You do not know which part of the food is blessed. (*Muslim*)

Another version in *Muslim* says: 'If any of you may drop a morsel, he should pick it up, cleanse it of dust etc., and eat it and not leave it for the devil. Nor should he wipe his hands with a handkerchief without licking (the remnants of food off) his fingers, for he knows not which part of the food is blessed.

Another version in *Muslim* says: that the Holy Prophet (S.A.W.) revealed that the Satan is always present with you in all things and on all occasions, even when you are having your meal. Therefore, If some of you may drop a morsel you should pick it up, cleanse it of dust etc., and eat it and not leave it for the evil spirit.

١٦٥ ـ الْعَاشِرُ : عن ابنِ عباسٍ ، رضيَ للهُ عنهما ، قال : قَامَ فينَا رسولُ للهِ صلى الله عليه وسلم بِمَوْعِظَةٍ فقال : « يَا أَيُّهَا النَّاسُ إِنَّكُمْ مَحْشُورُونَ إِلَى اللهِ تَعَالى حُفَاةً عُرَاةً غُرْلاً (كَمَا بَدَأْنَا أَوَّلَ خَلْقٍ نُعِيدُهُ وَعْداً عَلَيْنَا إِنَّا كُنَّا فَاعِلِينَ) [الأنبياء : ١٠٣] أَلا وَإِنَّ أَوَّلَ الْخَلائِقِ يُكْسَى يَوْمَ الْقِيَامَةِ إِبْرَاهِيمُ ، صلى الله عليه وسلم ، أَلا وَإِنَّهُ سَيُجَاءُ بِرِجَالٍ مِنْ أُمَّتِي ، فَيُؤْخَذُ بِهِمْ ذَاتَ الشِّمَالِ ، فَأَقُولُ : يَارَبِّ أَصْحَابِي ؛ فَيُقَالُ : إِنَّكَ لا تَدْرِي مَا أَحْدَثُوا بَعْدَكَ ، فَأَقُول كَمَا قَالَ الْعَبْدُ الصَّالِحُ : (وَكُنْتُ عَلَيْهِمْ شَهِيداً مَا دُمْتُ فِيهِمْ) إِلَى قولِهِ : (الْعَزِيزُ الْحَكِيمُ) [المائدة : ١١٧ ، ١١٨] فَيُقَالُ لِي : إِنَّهُمْ لَمْ يَزَالُوا مُرْتَدِّينَ عَلَى أَعْقَابِهِمْ مُنْذُ فَارَقْتَهُمْ » متفقٌ عليه

165. Hazrat Ibn Abbas (R.A.A.) relates: The Holy Prophet (S.A.W.) once stood up to sermonise us and said: 'O' people! you will be resurrected and gathered before Allah barefooted, naked and uncircumcised.'

Allah the Almighty says:

'As We began the first creation, so shall We resurrect them, We have charged ourselves with it, and so shall We do'. (21:104)

Beware! First of all, it will be Prophet Abraham (A.S.) who will be dressed. And that some persons from amongst my followers will be brought who will be held on the left side near the Hell. I shall say, 'O' Lord, these are my companions'. then I will be told: 'You do not know what innovations did they perpetrate after you.' Then I will repeat what a pious servant Prophet Christ submitted to Allah:

> I was a witness of them while I dwelt among them, and when thou tookest me thou wast the Watcher over them. Thou art witness over all things. If Thou punish them, Lo, they are Thy slaves, and if Thou forgive them (Lo! they are Thy slaves.) Lo! Thou, only Thou art the Mighty, the Wise. (5:117–118)

I shall further be told that after I left them (my demise) they continued to turn renegades.' (*Agreed upon*).

١٦٦ – الحَادِي عشَرَ : عَنْ أَبي سعيدِ عبدِ اللهِ بنِ مُغَفَّلٍ ، رضي الله عَنْه ، قال : نَهَى رسولُ الله ، صلى الله عليه وسلم عَنِ الخَذْفِ ، وقالَ : « إنَّهُ لا يَقْتُلُ الصَّيْدَ ، ولا يَنْكَأُ العَدُوَّ ، وإنَّهُ يَفْقَأُ العَيْنَ ، ويَكْسِرُ السِّنَّ » متفقٌ عليه

وفي رواية : أنَّ قَريباً لِابْنِ مُغَفَّلٍ خَذَفَ ؛ فَنَهَاهُ وقال : إن رسول الله صلى الله عليه وسلم نَهَى عن الخَذْفِ وَقالَ : « إنَّهَا لاتَصِيدُ صَيْداً » ثُمَّ عادَ فقالَ : أُحَدِّثُكَ أن رسول الله ، صلى الله عليه وسلم ، نَهَى عَنْهُ ، ثُمَّ عُدْتَ تَخْذِفُ ! ؟ لا أُكَلِّمُكَ أبَداً

166. Hazrat Abu Sa'eed Abdullah bin Mughaffal (R.A.A.) relates that the Holy Prophet (S.A.W.) prohibited stoning with the help of the thumb and forefinger, as a missile and said: 'Such a shot does neither kill a game nor harm the enemy, but it injures the eye and breaks a tooth.' (*Bukhari and Muslim*)

Another version says: A close relative of Hazrat Abdullah bin Mughaffal shot somebody with a stone in this way. The latter admonished the former saying: 'The Holy Prophet (S.A.W.) has forbidden this practice and said that it does not kill the game.' But the man did not listen and continued throwing stones whereupon Hazrat Abdullah bin Mughaffal (R.A.A.) said to him: 'I told you that the Holy Prophet (S.A.W.) had forbidden such throwing of stones and yet you repeated it. I shall never speak to you again.'

١٦٧ – وعن عابِسِ بنِ ربيعةَ قال : رَأيْتُ عُمَرَ بنَ الخطابِ ، رضي الله عنه ، يُقَبِّلُ الحَجَرَ – يَعْني الأَسْوَدَ – ويَقُولُ : إني أَعْلَمُ أنَّكَ حَجَرٌ

مَاتَنْفَعُ وَلا تَضُرُّ ، وَلَوْلا أَنِّي رَأَيْتُ رسول الله ، صلى الله عليه وسلم ، يُقَبِّلُكَ مَاقَبَّلْتُكَ متفقٌ عليه

167. Hazrat 'Aabiṣ bin Rabi (R.A.A.) relates: I saw Hazrat Umar bin Khattab (R.A.A.) kissing the Black Stone (in the Holy K'aba) and I heard him say: I know well thou art simply a piece of rock, and has no power to confer a benefit or to do harm. Had I not seen the Holy Prophet (S.A.W.) kiss thee I would never have kissed thee.'

(*Agreed upon*)

Note: The preservation and protection of the *Sunnat* (practices and precepts) of the Holy Prophet (S.A.W.) and its voluntary acceptance and acting upon it is incumbent upon every Muslim for all time to come, as is evident from the Quranic verses. Allah the Almighty has not deputed his prophets only to convey His Divine message to His servants (people) but they have to behave and act like a teacher, guide, reformer, and patron and to present themselves as embodiment of virtues and model of good deeds, so that their actions and words may serve as a beacon light and example for their followers. This is necessary so that people may know that in obeying the prophet is the worship of Allah. Allah Himself says: 'One who obeys the Prophet, obeys Allah.'

* * * * * * * * * *

CHAPTER 17

Significance of Obedience of the Commands of Allah and the One Who Invited to it, or Ordained for Good and Forbade from Evil.

قال الله تعالى : فَلا وَرَبِّكَ لايُؤْمِنُونَ حَتَّى يُحَكِّمُوكَ فِيمَا شَجَرَ بَيْنَهُمْ ثُمَّ لايَجِدُوا في أَنْفُسِهِمْ حَرَجاً مِمَّا قَضَيْتَ وَيُسَلِّمُوا تَسْلِيماً [النساء : ٦٥] وقال تعالى : إِنَّمَا كَانَ قَوْلَ الْمُؤْمِنِينَ إِذَا دُعُوا إِلى اللهِ وَرَسُولِهِ لِيَحْكُمَ بَيْنَهُمْ أَنْ يَقُولُوا سَمِعْنَا وَأَطَعْنَا وَأُولَئِكَ هُمُ الْمُفْلِحُونَ [النور : ٥١] .

Allah, The Exalted, has said:

69. But nay, thy Lord, they will not believe (in truth) until they make thee judmge of what is in dispute between them and find within themselves no dislike of that which thou decidest, and submit with full submission. (4:65)

70. The saying of (all true) believers when they appeal unto Allah and His Messenger to judge between them is only that they say: We hear and we obey. And such are the successful. (24:51)

١٦٨ – عن أبي هريرة ، رضي الله عنه ، قال : لَمَّا نَزَلَتْ عَلَى رسول الله ، صلى الله عليه سلم : (لِلهِ ما في السَّمٰوَاتِ وَمَا في الأَرْضِ وَإِنْ تُبْدُوا مَا في أَنْفُسِكُمْ أَوْ تُخْفُوهُ يُحَاسِبْكُمْ بِهِ اللهُ) الآيَةَ [البقرة: ٢٨٤] اشْتَدَّ ذلِكَ عَلَى أَصْحَابِ رسول الله، صلى الله عليه وسلم ، فَأَتَوْا رسول الله ، صلى الله عليه وسلم ، ثُمَّ بَرَكُوا عَلَى الرُّكَبِ فَقَالُوا : أَيْ رسولَ الله كُلِّفْنَا مِنَ الأَعْمَالِ مَا نُطِيقُ : الصَّلاةَ وَالْجِهَادَ وَالصِّيَامَ وَالصَّدَقَةَ ، وَقَدْ أُنْزِلَتْ عَلَيْكَ هَذِهِ الآيَةُ وَلا نُطِيقُهَا . قال رسولُ الله ، صلى الله عليه وسلم : « أَتُرِيدُونَ أَنْ تَقُولُوا كَمَا قَالَ أَهْلُ الْكِتَابَيْنِ مِنْ قَبْلِكُمْ : سَمِعْنَا وَعَصَيْنَا ؟ بَلْ قُولُوا : سَمِعْنَا وَأَطَعْنَا غُفْرَانَكَ رَبَّنَا وَإِلَيْكَ الْمَصِيرُ » فَلَمَّا اقْتَرَأَهَا الْقَوْمُ ، وَذَلَّتْ بِهَا أَلْسِنَتُهُمْ ، أَنْزَلَ اللهُ تَعَالَى في إِثْرِهَا : (آمَنَ الرَّسُولُ بِمَا أُنْزِلَ إِلَيْهِ مِنْ رَبِّهِ وَالْمُؤْمِنُونَ كُلٌّ آمَنَ بِاللهِ وَمَلائِكَتِهِ وَكُتُبِهِ وَرُسُلِهِ لا نُفَرِّقُ بَيْنَ أَحَدٍ مِنْ رُسُلِهِ وَقَالُوا سَمِعْنَا وَأَطَعْنَا غُفْرَانَكَ رَبَّنَا وَإِلَيْكَ الْمَصِيرُ) فَلَمَّا فَعَلُوا ذلِكَ نَسَخَهَا اللهُ تَعَالَى ، فَأَنْزَلَ اللهُ عَزَّ وَجَلَّ : (لا يُكَلِّفُ اللهُ نَفْساً إِلاَّ وُسْعَهَا لَهَا مَا كَسَبَتْ وَعَلَيْهَا مَا اكْتَسَبَتْ، رَبَّنَا لا تُؤَاخِذْنَا إِنْ نَسِينَا أَوْ أَخْطَأْنَا) قَالَ : نَعَمْ (رَبَّنَا وَلا تَحْمِلْ عَلَيْنَا إِصْراً كَمَا حَمَلْتَهُ عَلَى الَّذِينَ مِنْ قَبْلِنَا) قَالَ : نَعَمْ (رَبَّنَا وَلا تُحَمِّلْنَا مَا لا طَاقَةَ لَنَا بِهِ) قَالَ : نَعَمْ (وَاعْفُ عَنَّا وَاغْفِرْ لَنَا وَارْحَمْنَا أَنْتَ مَوْلانَا فَانْصُرْنَا عَلَى الْقَوْمِ الْكَافِرِينَ) قَالَ : نَعَمْ » رواه مسلم

168. **Hazrat Abu Hurairah** (R.A.A.) relates that when the following verse was revealed to the Holy Prophet (S.A.W.).

'Unto Allah (belongeth) whatsoever is in the heavens and whatsoever is in the earth; and whether ye make known what is in your minds or hide it, Allah will bring you to account for it. He will forgive whom He will and He will punish whom He will. Allah is able to do all things. (2:284):

His companions were much perturbed and went to him and kneeling down on their knees, said to him 'Messenger of Allah! we have already been charged with (duties) which are within our power i.e. *Salat,*

Jihad, Fasting, poor due and charity. Now this verse has been revealed to you and what it charges us with is beyond our capacity. He said: Do you want to say what the People of the two Books have said earlier i.e.

'We have heard, but we shall disobey?

Instead, you ought to say:

'We hear, and we obey.' (Grant us) Thy forgiveness, our Lord, Unto thee is the journeying.' (2:285)

When they had recited this and their tongues had adapted themselves to it, Allah revealed:

"The Messenger believeth in that which hath been unto him from his Lord and (so do) the believers. Each one believeth in Allah and His angels and His Scriptures and His Messengers — We make no distinction between any of His Messengers — and they say:

We hear, and we obey. (Grant us) Thy forgiveness, our Lord. Unto Thee is the journeying (2:285).

When they had done this Allah cancelled this command and He then revealed: 'Allah tasketh not a soul beyond its scope. For it (is only) that which it hath earned, and against it (only) that which it hath deserved. Our Lord! Condemn us not if we forget, or miss the mark.' (he said yes be so.). Our Lord! Lay not on us such a burden as Thou didst lay on those before us' (he said, yes be so). Our Lord! Impose not on us that which we have not the strength to bear! (He said, yes be so) Pardon us, absolve us and have mercy on us. Thou, our Protector, and give us victory over the disbelieving folk. (2:286) (he said, yes be so) (*Muslim*)

* * * * * * * * * * *

CHAPTER 18

Innovation in Religion and Heresy Prohibited.

قال الله تعالى: فَمَاذَا بَعْدَ الْحَقِّ إِلاَّ الضَّلالُ ﴿ [يونس : ٣٢] وقال تعالى : مَافَرَّطْنَا فِي الْكِتَابِ مِنْ شَيْءٍ [الأنعام : ٣٨] وقال تعالى : فَإِنْ تَنَازَعْتُمْ فِي شَيْءٍ فَرُدُّوهُ إِلَى اللهِ وَالرَّسُولِ [النساء : ٥٩] أي : الْكِتَابِ وَالسُّنَّةِ وَقَالَ تَعَالَى : وَأَنَّ هَذَا صِرَاطِي مُسْتَقِيماً فَاتَّبِعُوهُ وَلا تَتَّبِعُوا السُّبُلَ فَتَفَرَّقَ بِكُمْ عَنْ سَبِيلِهِ [الأنعام : ١٥٣] وقال تعالى : قُلْ إِنْ كُنْتُمْ تُحِبُّونَ اللهَ فَاتَّبِعُونِي يُحْبِبْكُمُ اللهُ وَيَغْفِرْ لَكُمْ ذُنُوبَكُمْ [آل عمران : ٣١] وَالآيَاتُ فِي الْبَاب كَثِيرَةٌ مَعْلُومَةٌ

Allah, the Exalted, has said:

71. So what remains there after the Truth (is manifest) save the stray (10:32)
72. We have neglected nothing in the Book (of our decrees). (6:38)
73. And if ye have a dispute concerning any matter, refer it to Allah and the Messenger. (4:59)
74. This is my path, so follow it. Follow not other ways lest ye be parted from his way (6:153)
75. Say, (O Muhammad, to mankind): If you love Allah, follow me. Allah will love you and forgive you your sins. (3:31)

١٦٩ — عن عائشةَ ، رضي الله عنها ، قالت : قال رسولُ الله ، صلى الله عليه وسلم : « مَنْ أَحْدَثَ في أَمْرِنا هذا ما لَيْسَ مِنْهُ فَهُوَ رَدٌّ » متفقٌ عليه

وفي رواية لمسلم : « مَنْ عَمِلَ عَمَلاً لَيْسَ عَلَيْهِ أَمْرُنا فَهُوَ رَدٌّ »

169. Hazrat Ayesha (R.A.A.) relates that the Holy Prophet (S.A.W.) said: 'If somebody tries to introduce into this faith of ours (Islam) something which is not a part of it, is to be rejected (and that person is condemned) (*Bukhari andMuslim*)

Another tradition by *Muslim* says if anybody introduces some innovation or practice, which is not authenticated by me, is to be rejected (i.e. the person responsible or the innovation is to be condemned.)

١٧٠ — وعن جابرٍ ، رضي الله عنه ، قال : كان رسول الله ، صلى الله عليه وسلم ، إذا خَطَبَ احْمَرَّتْ عَيْنَاهُ ، وَعَلا صَوْتُهُ ، وَاشْتَدَّ غَضَبُهُ ، حتّى كأنَّهُ مُنْذِرُ جَيْشٍ يَقُولُ : « صَبَّحَكُمْ وَمَسَّاكُمْ » ويقولُ : « بُعِثْتُ أنا وَالسَّاعَةُ كَهَاتَيْنِ » وَيَقْرِنُ بَيْنَ أُصْبُعَيْهِ ؛ السَّبابَةِ وَالوُسْطَى ، وَيَقُولُ : « أَمَّا بَعْدُ ؛ فَإِنَّ خَيْرَ الحَدِيثِ كِتابُ الله ، وَخَيْرَ الهَدْيِ هَدْيُ مُحَمَّدٍ ، صلى الله عليه وسلم ، وَشَرَّ الأُمُورِ مُحْدَثَاتُها ، كُلَّ بِدْعَةٍ ضَلالَةٌ » ثُمَّ يَقُولُ : « أنا أَوْلَى بِكُلِّ مُؤْمِنٍ مِنْ نَفْسِهِ . مَنْ تَرَكَ مالاً فَلأَهْلِهِ ، وَمَنْ تَرَكَ دَيْناً أَوْ ضَيَاعاً ، فَإِلَيَّ وَعَلَيَّ » رواه مسلم

170. Hazrat Jabir (R.A.A.) relates: 'When the Holy Prophet (S.A.W.) addressed us, his eyes used to become red, the tone of his voice would rise and he would be somewhat excited as if he was cautioning us against some hostile army poised against us. He would say: 'The enemy would attack you in the morning or the enemy would advance advance against you in the evening.' He would further say: 'My advent and the advent of the Day of Judgment are placed together as my two fingers (He would show his fore finger and the middle finger crossed): He would say that the best word is the Book of Allah, and the best guidance is the guidance shown by Muhammad (S.A.W.). The worst practice is the introduction of new elements in the Islamic faith and every innovation amounts to heresy. He would say I have more claim on every Muslim than his own self (i.e. I am greater well-wisher of the Muslims). (In spite of this) if a Muslim leaves behind some property, the same belongs to his family members. If he dies leaving debts, survived by dependants, I hold myself responsible for the payment of his debts and maintnance of his dependants.' (*Muslim*)

The tradition quoted by Hazrat Irbaz bin Saria (R.A.A.) reproduced vide S.No. 157 under Ch. No. 16 may also be seen.

Note: Hazrat Qazi Ayaz (R.A.A.) says that a person who invents or introduces in Islam something new which is not to be found in the Book of Allah (Holy Quran) or the traditions of the Holy Prophet (S.A.W.) is condemned (or is to be treated as a renegade); because Islam is now complete in all respects and there is no necessity for any addition, innovation or deletion. As such, such a person attempts to introduce something unpleasant and unwanted in the *Sharia*. Faith comprises belief in the divine revelations and practices and precepts of the Holy Prophet (S.A.W.) and his (immediate) followers. Therefore such a person is to be considered as having betrayed Islam.

* * * * * * * * * * *

CHAPTER 19

Inventing New Ways of Virtue and Vice

قال الله تعالى : وَالَّذِينَ يَقُولُونَ رَبَّنَا هَبْ لَنَا مِنْ أَزْوَاجِنَا وَذُرِّيَّاتِنَا

قُرَّةَ أَعْيُنٍ وَاجْعَلْنَا لِلْمُتَّقِينَ إِمَاماً [الفرقان : ٧٤] وقال تعالى :

وَجَعَلْنَاهُمْ أَئِمَّةً يَهْدُونَ بِأَمْرِنَا [الأنبياء : ٧٣]

Allah, the Exalted, has said:

76. And who say: Our Lord! Vouchsafe us comfort of our wives and of our offspring, and make us pattern for (all) those who ward of (evil) (25:74)
77. And we made them chiefs who guide people by our Command. (21:73)

١٧١ ــ عَنْ أبي عَمْرو ، جَرير بن عبد الله ، رضي الله عنه ، قال : كُنَّا في صَدْر النَّهَار عِنْدَ رسول الله ، صلى الله عليه وسلم ، فَجَاءَهُ قَوْمٌ عُرَاةٌ مُجْتَابي النِّمَارِ ، أو الْعَبَاءِ ، مُتَقَلِّدِي السُّيُوف ، عَامَّتُهُمْ مِنْ مُضَرَ ، بَلْ كُلُّهُمْ مِنْ مُضَرَ ؛ فَتَمَعَّرَ رسول الله ، صلى الله عليه وسلم ، لِمَا رَأى بِهِمْ مِنَ الْفَاقَةِ ؛ فَدَخَلَ ثُمَّ خَرَجَ ، فَأَمَرَ بِلالاً فَأَذَّنَ وَأَقَامَ ، فَصَلَّى ثُمَّ خَطَبَ ؛ فَقَالَ : (يَا أَيُّهَا النَّاسُ اتَّقُوا رَبَّكُمُ الَّذِي خَلَقَكُمْ مِنْ نَفْسٍ وَاحِدَةٍ) إِلَى آخرِ الآية : (إنَّ الله كَانَ عَلَيْكُمْ رَقِيباً) ، وَالآيَةُ الأُخْرَى الَّتِي في آخرِ الحَشْرِ : (يَا أَيُّهَا الَّذِينَ آمَنُوا اتَّقُوا الله وَلْتَنْظُرْ نَفْسٌ مَا قَدَّمَتْ لِغَد) تَصَدَّقَ رَجُلٌ مِنْ دِينَارِهِ مِنْ دِرْهَمِهِ مِنْ ثَوْبِهِ مِنْ صَاعِ بُرِّهِ مِنْ صَاعِ تَمْرِهِ ، حَتَّى قَالَ : وَلَوْ بِشِقِّ تَمْرَةٍ ، فَجَاءَ رَجُلٌ مِنَ الأَنْصَارِ بِصُرَّةٍ كَادَتْ كَفُّهُ تَعْجِزُ عَنْهَا ، بَلْ قَدْ عَجَزَتْ ، ثُمَّ تَتَابَعَ النَّاسُ حَتَّى رَأَيْتُ كَوْمَيْنِ مِنْ طَعَامٍ وَثِيَابٍ ، حَتَّى رَأَيْتُ وَجْهَ رسولِ الله ، صلى الله عليه وسلم ، يَتَهَلَّلُ كَأَنَّهُ مُذْهَبَةٌ ؛ فقال رسولُ اللهِ ، صلى الله عليه وسلم : « مَنْ سَنَّ في الإِسْلامِ سُنَّةً حَسَنَةً فَلَهُ أَجْرُهَا ، وَأَجْرُ مَنْ عَمِلَ بِهَا مِنْ بَعْدِهِ مِنْ غَيْرِ أَنْ يَنْقُصَ مِنْ أُجُورِهِمْ شَيْءٌ ، وَمَنْ سَنَّ في الإِسْلام سُنَّةً سَيِّئَةً كَانَ عَلَيْهِ وِزْرُهَا وَوِزْرُ مَنْ عَمِلَ بِهَا مِنْ بَعْدِهِ مِنْ غَيْرِ أَنْ يَنْقُصَ مِنْ أَوْزَارِهِمْ شَيْءٌ » رواه مسلم

171. **Hazrat Jarir bin Abdullah** (R.A.A.) relates: We were present in an audience with the Holy Prophet (S.A.W.)on one day in the forenoon. In the meantime some people came there who had nothing but pieces of sackcloth on their bodies, some of them had robelike garments with their swords dangling on one side. Almost all of them belonged to the Muzar tribe. The Holy Prophet (S.A.W.) was greatly moved on seeing them with their emaciated and starved bodies. He got up and went into his chamber then came out and asked Hazrat Bilal (R.A.A.) to call the *Azan* as it was the time for prayer. He led the prayer and at the end addressed that assembly:

"O mankind be careful of your duty to your Lord Who created you from a single soul and from it created its mate and from them twin, hath spread abroad a multitude of men and women. Be careful of your duty toward Allah in whom ye claim (your rights) of one another, and towards the wombs (that bore you). Lo! Allah hath been a watcher over you.' (4:1) And then he read another verse from *Surah Hashr*, "O ye who believe! Observe your duty to Allah. And let every soul look to that which it sendeth on before for the morrow. And observe your duty to Allah: Lo! Allah is informed of what ye do." (59:18)

After this the Holy Prophet (S.A.W.) asked those present to make contribution towards charity out of his dinars and dirhams, cloths, wheat and dates; although it may be only half a date. Hearing this one of the Ansars brought a heavy bag, the weight of which became difficult for him to hold; then others followed one after the other till the collections made two heaps of eatbles and clothes. Then I saw that the face of the Holy Prophet (S.A.W.) was shining like gold.

The Holy Prophet (S.A.W.) then said: Whoever introduces in Islam a good measure, will have his reward for it and also a reward for those who act upon it without reducing anything from this reward: likewise one who introduces an evil practice in Islam, will be punished for this and all those who act upon that evil practice will be punished without diminishing in any way the burden of their evil deeds (*Muslim*)

١٧٢ — وعن ابن مسعودٍ رضي الله عنه أنَّ النَّبيَّ صلى الله عليه وسلم قال « ليس مِنْ نَفْسٍ تُقْتَلُ ظُلْماً إلاَّ كَان عَلَى ابْنِ آدم الأوَّلِ كِفْلٌ مِنْ دمِهَا لأنَّهُ كَان أوَّل مَنْ سَنَّ الْقَتْلَ » متفقٌ عليه

172. Hazrat Ibn Mas'ud (R.A.A.) relates that the Holy Prophet (S.A.W.) said: For all the murders committed in the world without any justification, Prophet Adam's eldest son, Cain will get a share of punishment, because it was he who invented the method of killing by murdering his brother Abel. (*Bukhari and Muslim*)

* * * * * * * * * *

CHAPTER 20

Recommending for Good, Inducement for Doing Good and Tempting Towards Vice

قال تعالى : وَادْعُ إلَى رَبِّكَ [القصص: ٨٧] وقال تعالى : ادْعُ إلَى سَبِيلِ رَبِّكَ بالْحِكْمَةِ وَالْمَوْعِظَةِ الْحَسَنَةِ [النحل : ١٢٥] وقال تعالى : وَتَعَاوَنُوا عَلَى الْبِرِّ وَالتَّقْوَى [المائدة : ٢] وقال تعالى : وَلْتَكُنْ مِنْكُمْ أُمَّةٌ يَدْعُونَ إلَى الْخَيْرِ [آل عمران : ٨٤]

Allah, the Exalted, has said:

78. But call (mankind) unto thy Lord. (28:87)
79. Call unto the way of thy Lord with wisdom and fair exhortation, and reason with them in the better way (16:125)
80. But help ye one another unto righteousness and pious duty. (5:2)
81. And there may spring from you a nation who invite to goodness. (3:104).

١٧٣ ـ وعن أبي مسعودٍ عُقْبَةَ بْن عمرو الأنصاريّ البَدْرِي رضي الله عنه قال: قال رسول الله صلى الله عليه وسلم: « مَنْ دَلَّ عَلَى خَيْرٍ فَلَهُ مِثْلُ أَجْرِ فَاعِلِهِ » رواه مسلم

173. Hazrat Abu Mas'ud 'Uqbah ibn 'Amr Ansari al Badri relates: 'that the Holy Prophet (S.A.W.) said: The recompense of one who directs somebody to do good deed will be equal to the reward of the latter (*Muslim*)

١٧٤ ـ وعن أبي هريرة رضي الله عنه أن رسول الله صلى الله عليه وسلم قال: « مَنْ دَعَا إِلَى هُدَىً كَانَ لَهُ مِنَ الأَجْرِ مِثْلُ أُجُورِ مَنْ تَبِعَهُ لاَ يَنْقُصُ ذلكَ مِنْ أُجُورِهِمْ شَيْئاً، وَمَنْ دَعَا إِلَى ضَلالَةٍ كَانَ عَلَيْهِ مِنَ الإِثْمِ مِثْلُ آثَامِ مَنْ تَبِعَهُ لا يَنْقُصُ ذلكَ مِنْ آثَامِهِمْ شَيْئاً » رواه مسلم

174. Hazrat Abu Hurairah (R.A.A.) relates that the Holy Prophet (S.A.W.) said: 'A person who calls people towards doing good deed will get the same reward as those who follow him and do good; and nothing will be diminished from the requittal of the latter. Similarly those, who call the people towards vice'will have the same punishment as those who follow him without any diminution in the punishment of the perpetrators. (*Muslim*)

١٧٥ ـ وعن أبي العباس سَهْلِ بن سعدٍ السَّاعِدِيِّ رضي الله عنه أن رسول الله صلى الله عليه وسلم قال يَوْمَ خَيْبَرَ: « لأُعْطِيَنَّ الرَّايَةَ غَداً رَجُلاً يَفْتَحُ اللهُ عَلَى يَدَيْهِ، يُحِبُّ اللهَ وَرَسُولَهُ، وَيُحِبُّهُ اللهُ وَرَسُولُهُ » فَبَاتَ النَّاسُ يَدُوكُونَ لَيْلَتَهُمْ أَيُّهُمْ يُعْطَاهَا. فَلَمَّا أَصْبَحَ النَّاسُ غَدَوْا عَلَى رسول الله صلى الله عليه وسلم: كُلُّهُمْ يَرْجُو أَنْ يُعْطَاهَا، فقال: « أَيْنَ عَلِيُّ بن أبي طالبٍ؟ » فَقِيلَ: يارسول الله هُوَ يَشْتَكِي عَيْنَيْهِ

قال : « فَأَرْسِلُوا إِلَيْهِ » فَأُتِيَ بِهِ ، فَبَصَقَ رسول الله صلى الله عليه وسلم في عَيْنَيْهِ ، وَدَعَا لَهُ ، فَبَرَأَ حَتَّى كَأَنْ لَمْ يَكُنْ بِهِ وَجَعٌ ، فَأَعْطَاهُ الرَّايَةَ . فقال عليٌّ رضي الله عنه : يارسول الله أُقَاتِلُهُمْ حَتَّى يَكُونُوا مِثْلَنَا ؟ فَقَالَ : « انْفُذْ عَلَى رِسْلِكَ حَتَّى تَنْزِلَ بِسَاحَتِهِمْ ، ثُمَّ ادْعُهُمْ إِلَى الإِسْلَامِ ، وَأَخْبِرْهُمْ بِمَا يَجِبُ عَلَيْهِمْ مِنْ حَقِّ اللهِ تَعَالَى فِيهِ ، فَوَاللهِ لَأَنْ يَهْدِيَ اللهُ بِكَ رَجُلاً وَاحِداً خَيْرٌ لَكَ مِنْ حُمْرِ النَّعَمِ » .
متفقٌ عليه

175. Hazrat Abu Abbas Sahl ibn Sa'ad (R.A.A.) relates that before launching an attack on the day of the battle of Khaibar the Holy Prophet (S.A.W.) declared: Tomorrow I shall hand over the standard to a person, through whom Allah will bestow victory upon us; and it is significant that such a person would be immensely loving Allah and His Messenger and Allah and His Messenger would be loving him.' The people spent the night in suspense guessing and discussing as to who would get the distinction of receiving the standard. Next morning they went to the Holy Prophet (S.A.W.) each expected to be himself getting the honour. The Holy Prophet (S.A.W.) enquired about Hazrat Ali bin Abu Talib. He was told that he had sore eyes. The Holy Prophet (S.A.W.) asked the people to send for him. When he came, the Holy Prophet (S.A.W.) put his saliva in his eyes and prayed for him; He was cured of his eyesore then and there as if he had never had any trouble at all. Then the Holy Prophet (S.A.W.) handed over the standard to him. Hazrat Ali asked: 'Messenger of Allah, shall I fight them till they become Muslim like us?' The Holy Prophet (S.A.W.) answered: 'Continue advancing with your normal speed till you reach their plain and encamp there. Then invite them to embrace Islam and apprise them their obligations and duties to Allah. By Allah even if Allah guides a single person through you, that would be much better for you than a whole lot of red camles (a costly specie of the camels). *(Bukhari and Muslim)*

١٧٦ — وعن أنس رضي الله عنه أنَّ فَتًى مِنْ أَسْلَمَ قال : يا رَسُولَ الله إِنِّي أُرِيدُ الْغَزْوَ وَلَيْسَ مَعِي مَا أَتَجَهَّزُ بِهِ ؟ قَالَ : « ائْتِ فُلاناً فإنه قَدْ كَانَ تَجَهَّزَ فَمَرِضَ » فَأَتَاهُ فقال : إِنَّ رسول الله صلى الله عليه وسلم يُقْرِئُكَ السَّلَامَ وَيَقُولُ : أَعْطِنِي الَّذِي تَجَهَّزْتَ بِهِ ، فقال : يَافُلَانَةُ أَعْطِيهِ الَّذِي تَجَهَّزْتُ بِهِ ، وَلَا تَحْبِسِي مِنْهُ شَيْئاً ، فَوَاللهِ لَا تَحْبِسِينَ مِنْهُ شَيْئاً فَيُبَارَكَ لَكِ فِيهِ . رواه مسلم

176. Hazrat Anas bin Malik (R.A.A.) relates that a young-man belonging to the tribe of Bani Aslam, came to the Holy Prophet (S.A.W.) and said to him 'Messenger of Allah, I want to join in the jihad, but I have nothing with me to procure necessary equipment (for the *Jihad*).' The Holy Prophet (S.A.W.) said: Go to so and so, he had made full preparation for *Jihad*, but has fallen sick. The youngman went to this man and said: 'The Holy Prophet (S.A.W.) sends you greetings and says that you should hand over to me the equipment that you have arranged for *Jihad*. This gentleman asked his wife to hand over all his equipment for participation in *Jihad* to the youngman and not to hold back anything from him. By Allah, if you do not hold back anything, Allah will bless you for it. (*Muslim*)

* * * * * * * * * *

CHAPTER 21

Cooperation in Good and Virtuous Deeds

قال الله تعالى : وتعاونوا على البر والتقوى [المائدة : ٣] وقال تعالى :
والعصر . إن الإنسان لفي خسر . إلا الذين آمنوا وعملوا الصالحات
وتواصوا بالحق وتواصوا بالصبر [العصر : ١ - ٣] .

Allah, the Exalted, has said:

82. But help ye one another unto good and righteousness (5:2)
83. By the declining day, Lo! Man is in a state of loss, those who believe and do good works, and exhort one another to truth and exhort one another to endurance. (103:1—3)

Imam Shafie has said that some people do not ponder over the significance of this Chapter (*Surah*).

١٧٧ — عن أبي عبد الرحمن زيد بن خالد الجهني رضي الله عنه قال :
قال رسول الله صلى الله عليه وسلم : « من جهز غازياً في سبيل الله فقد
غزا ومن خلف غازياً في أهله بخير فقد غزا » متفق عليه

177. Hazrat Abu Abdur Rahman Zaid bin Khalid Juhni (R.A.A.) relates that the Holy Prophet (S.A.W.) said: 'One who furnishes a *mujahid* with equipment for *Jihad* in the cause of Allah, is as if he himself participated in *Jihad* (frighting in the cause of Allah) and one who looks after the dependants of a fighter, in his absence, is as if he fights himself (*Bukhari and Muslim*)

١٧٨ — وعن أبي سعيد الخدري رضي الله عنه أن رسول الله صلى الله
عليه وسلم ، بعث بعثاً إلى بني لحيان من هذيل فقال : « لينبعث

مِنْ كُلِّ رَجُلَيْنِ أَحَدُهُمَا وَالأَجْرُ بَيْنَهُمَا » رواه مسلم

178. **Hazrat Abu Sa'id Khurdri** (R.A.A.) relates that the Holy Prophet (S.A.W.) deputed a detachment of fighters to fight against the tribe of Bani Lahyan of Hudail and directed: Every second man should get ready to proceed on *Jihad*, but both will get the same amount of recompense *(Muslim)*

١٧٩ – وعن ابنِ عباسٍ رضي الله عنهما أنَّ رسُولَ الله صلى الله عليه وسلم لَقِيَ رَكْباً بالرَّوْحاءِ فقال : « مَنِ القَوْمُ ؟ » قَالُوا : المُسْلِمُونَ ، فَقَالُوا : مَنْ أَنْتَ ؟ قال : « رسول الله » فرَفَعَتْ إليهِ امرَأَةٌ صَبياً فقالَتْ: أَلِهَذَا حجٌّ ؟ قال : « نعَمْ وَلَكِ أَجْرٌ » رواه مسلم .

179. **Hazrat Ibn Abbas** (R.A.A.) relates that the Holy Prophet (S.A.W.) came across a party of mounted men at Rauha and asked them as to who they were. They said that they were Muslims. They further asked as to who he was. He said 'Prophet of Allah'. A woman from them came forward and produced a child and asked: Can this go on Haj? He said: 'Yes, and you will have the reward thereof. *(Muslim)*

١٨٠ – وعَنْ أبي موسى الأشعَرِيِّ رضي الله عنه ، عن النبيِّ صلى الله عليه وسلم أنَّهُ قال : « الخَازِنُ المُسْلِمُ الأمينُ الَّذي يُنَفِّذُ ما أُمِرَ بِهِ ، فيُعْطيهِ كامِلاً مُوَفَّراً ، طَيِّبَةً بِهِ نَفْسُهُ فيَدْفَعُهُ إلى الَّذي أُمِرَ لَهُ بِهِ أحَدُ المُتَصَدِّقِينِ » متفقٌ عليه .

وفي رواية : « الَّذي يُعْطِي مَا أُمِرَ بِهِ » وضبَطوا « المُتَصدِّقَيْنِ » بفتح القاف مع كسر النون على التَّثْنِيَةِ ، وعَكْسُهُ عَلى الجَمْعِ وكلاهُمَا صَحيحٌ .

180. **Hazrat Abu Musa Ash'ari** (R.A.A.) relates that the Holy Prophet (S.A.W.) said 'A trustworthy Muslim treasurer, is one who carries out his duties honestly and issues what he is ordered to, and hands it over in full to the person entitled to recite the same with the complete cheerfulness of his heart, such a treasurer is like a person who himself donated something.' *(Bukhari and Muslim)*

According to another tradition, a person who hands over a thing to another person, as ordered, is also entitled to recompense of charity.

* * * * * * * * * * *

CHAPTER 22

Tendering Good Advice

قال تعالى : ﴿ إنما المُؤْمِنُونَ إخْوَةٌ ﴾ [الحجرات : ١٠] وقال تعالى

إخباراً عن نُوحٍ صلى الله عليه وسلم : ﴿ وَأَنْصَحُ لَكُمْ ﴾ [الأعراف : ٦٢]

وعَنْ هُودٍ صلى الله عليه وسلم: ﴿ وَأَنا لَكُمْ نَاصِحٌ أَمينٌ ﴾ [الأعراف : ٦٨] .

Allah, the Exalted, has said:

84. The believers are naught else then brothers (49:10)

85. Prophet Noah said : I give good counsel unto you. (7:62).

85a. Prophet Hud said : I am for you trur adviser. (7:68).

١٨١ – فَالأوّلُ : عن أبي رُقَيَّةَ تَميمِ بنِ أوْسٍ الدّاريِّ رضي الله عنه أنَّ النَّبيَّ صلى الله عليه وسلم قال : « الدِّينُ النَّصيحَةُ » قُلْنَا : لِمَنْ ؟ قَالَ « للهِ وَلِكِتَابِهِ وَلِرَسُولِهِ وَلأئمَّةِ المُسْلِمينَ وَعَامَّتِهِمْ » رواه مسلم

181. Abu Ruqaiya Tamim bin Aus-ad-Dari relates that the **Holy** Prophet (S.A.W.) said: The basis of faith is sincerity. We submitted: "O Prophet of Allah! For whom?" He said: Towards Allah, the Holy Quran, His Prophet and the Muslims — both leaders masses' (*Muslim*)

١٨٢ – الثّاني : عَنْ جَريرِ بْنِ عبد الله رضي الله عنه قال : بَايَعْتُ رَسولَ اللهِ صلى الله عليه وسلم عَلى إقَامِ الصَّلاةِ ، وإيتَاءِ الزَّكَاةِ ، وَالنُّصْحِ لِكُلِّ مُسْلِمٍ . متفقٌ عليه

182. Hazrat Jarir bin Abdullah (R.A.A.) relates: 'I took oath of allegiance with the Holy Prophet (S.A.W.) that I would establish (offer) prayer, pay the *Zakat* (the poor due) and am a well-wisher of every Muslim. (*Bukhari and Muslim*)

١٨٣ – الثّالثُ : عَنْ أنَس رضي الله عنه عن النبي صلى الله عليه وسلم قال : « لا يُؤْمِنُ أحَدُكُمْ حَتّى يُحِبَّ لأخيهِ ما يُحِبُّ لِنَفْسِهِ » متفقٌ عليه

183. Hazrat Anas (R.A.A.) relates that the Holy Prophet said: 'A person can not be a perfect Muslim unless he desires for his brother (in faith) that which he desires for himself.' (*Bukhari and Muslim*)

* * * * * * * * * * *

CHAPTER 23

Enjoining Virtue and Forbidding Evil

قال الله تعالى : وَلْتَكُنْ مِنْكُمْ أُمَّةٌ يَدْعُونَ إلى الخَيْرِ وَيَأْمُرُونَ بِالمَعْرُوفِ وَيَنْهَوْنَ عَنِ المُنْكَرِ وأُولَئِكَ هُمُ المُفْلِحُونَ [آل عمران: ١٠٤] وقال تعالى : كُنْتُمْ خَيْرَ أُمَّةٍ أُخْرِجَتْ لِلنَّاسِ تَأْمُرُونَ بالمَعْرُوفِ وتَنْهَوْنَ عَنِ المُنْكَرِ [آل عمران : ١١٠] وقال تعالى : خُذِ العَفْوَ وَأْمُرْ بِالعُرْفِ وأَعْرِضْ عَنِ الجَاهِلِينَ [الأعراف : ١٩٩] وقال تعالى : والمُؤْمِنُونَ والمُؤْمِنَاتُ بَعْضُهُمْ أَوْلِيَاءُ بَعْضٍ يَأْمُرُونَ بِالمَعْرُوفِ وَيَنْهَوْنَ عَنِ المُنْكَرِ [التوبة : ٧١] وقال تعالى : لُعِنَ الَّذِينَ كَفَرُوا مِنْ بَنِي إِسْرَائِيلَ عَلَى لِسَانِ دَاوُدَ وعِيسَى ابْنِ مَرْيَمَ ذَلِكَ بِمَا عَصَوْا وكَانُوا يَعْتَدُونَ ، كَانُوا لا يَتَنَاهَوْنَ عَنْ مُنْكَرٍ فَعَلُوهُ لَبِئْسَ مَا كَانُوا يَفْعَلُونَ [المائدة: ٧٨-٧٩] وقال تعالى : وقُلِ الحَقُّ مِنْ رَبِّكُمْ فَمَنْ شَاءَ فَلْيُؤْمِنْ وَمَنْ شَاءَ فَلْيَكْفُرْ [الكهف : ٢٩] وقال تعالى : فَاصْدَعْ بِمَا تُؤْمَرُ [الحجر : ٩٤] وقال تعالى : (فَأَنْجَيْنَا الَّذِينَ يَنْهَوْنَ عَنِ السُّوءِ وأَخَذْنَا الَّذِينَ ظَلَمُوا بِعَذَابٍ بَئِيسٍ بِمَا كَانُوا يَفْسُقُونَ [الأعراف : ١٦٥] والآياتُ في الباب كَثِيرَةٌ مَعلومةٌ .

Allah, the Exalted, has said:

86. And there may spring from you a nation who invite to goodness and enjoin right conduct and forbid indecency. Such are they who are successful (3:104)
87. You are the best community that hath been raised for mankind. Ye enjoin right conduct and forbid indecency. (3:110)
88. Keep to forgiveness (O Muhammad), and enjoin kindness, and turn away from the ignorants (7:199)
89. And the believers, men and women, are protecting friends one of another. They enjoin the right and forbid the wrong. (9:71)
90. Those of the children of Israel who went astray were cursed by the tongue of David, and of Jesus, Son of Mary. That was because they rebelled and used to transgress. They restrained

not one another from the wickedness they did. Verily evil was that they used to do! (5:78—79)

91. Say: (It is) the truth from the Lord of you (all). Then whosoever will let him believe, and whosoever will let him disbelieve. (18:30)

92. So proclaim that which thou art command. (15:94)

93. And when they forgot that whereof they had been reminded. We rescued those who forbade wrong, and visited those who did wrong with dreadful punishment because they were evil livers. (7:165)

١٨٤ ـ فالأوَّلُ : عن أبي سعيدٍ الخُدْرِيِّ رضيَ الله عنه قالَ : سَمِعْتُ رسُولَ الله صلى الله عليه وسلم يَقُولُ : « مَنْ رَأى مِنكُم مُنكَراً فَلْيُغَيِّرْهُ بِيَدِهِ ، فإنْ لَمْ يَسْتَطِعْ فَبِلِسَانِهِ ، فإنْ لَمْ يَسْتَطِعْ فَبِقَلْبِهِ وَذَلِكَ أَضْعَفُ الإيمانِ » رواه مسلم

184. Hazrat Abu Sa'id Khudri (R.A.A.) relates that he heard the Holy Prophet (S.A.W.) saying: 'Anybody amongst you notices something evil, should correct it with his own hands, and if he is unable to do so, he should prohibit the same with his tongue; if he is unable even to do this, he should at least consider it as bad in his heart; this is the lowest degree of faith. (*Muslim*)

١٨٥ ـ الثاني : عن ابنِ مسْعُودٍ رضي الله عنه أنَّ رسول اللهِ صلى اللهُ عليه وسلم قال : « مَا مِنْ نَبيٍّ بَعَثَهُ الله في أُمَّةٍ قَبْلي إلاَّ كان لَه مِنْ أُمَّتِهِ حَوَارِيُّون وَأَصْحابٌ يَأْخُذُون بِسُنَّتِهِ ويَقْتَدُون بِأَمْرِهِ ، ثُمَّ إنها تَخْلُفُ مِنْ بَعْدِهِم خُلُوفٌ يقُولُون مَا لاَ يَفْعَلُون ، ويَفْعَلُون مَا لا يُؤْمَرُون ، فَمَنْ جَاهَدَهُم بِيَدِهِ فَهُو مُؤْمِنٌ ، ومَنْ جَاهَدَهُمْ بِقَلْبِهِ فَهُو مُؤْمِنٌ ، ومَنْ جَاهَدَهُم بِلِسَانِهِ فَهُو مُؤْمِنٌ . وليس وراء ذلك من الإيمان حَبَّةُ خَرْدَل » رواه مسلم

185. Hazrat Ibn Mas'ud (R.A.A.) relates that he heard the Holy Prophet (S.A.W.) said: 'All the prophets sent by Allah before me had some devoted disciples and companions, who followed his practice and obeyed his orders. After them their followers professed contrary to their actions, and did that which they were not asked to do. As such one who practices *Jihad* against them with his hands is a believer; one who practices *Jihad* against them with his heart is a *Momin* and one who fights them with his tongue is a believer. Except this, there is not a grain of faith. (*Muslim*)

١٨٦ ـ الثالثُ : عن أبي الوليدِ عُبادَةَ بنِ الصَّامِتِ رضي الله عنه قال :

« بايَعْنَا رسولَ الله صلى الله عليه وسلم عَلَى السَّمْعِ والطَّاعَةِ في العُسْرِ وَالْيُسْرِ وَالْمَنْشَطِ وَالْمَكْرَهِ ، وَعَلَى أثَرَةٍ عَلَيْنَا ، وَعَلَى أنْ لاَ نُنَازِعَ الأمْرَ أهْلَهُ إلاَّ أنْ تَرَوْا كُفْراً بَوَاحاً عِنْدَكُمْ مِنَ اللهِ تَعَالَى فِيهِ بُرْهَانٌ ، وَعَلَى أنْ نَقُولَ بالْحَقِّ أيْنَمَا كُنَّا لاَ نَخَافُ في اللهِ لَوْمَةَ لاَئِمٍ » متفقٌ عليه

186. Hazrat Abul Waleed Ubadah bin Samit (R.A.A.) relates: 'We covenanted with the Holy Prophet (S.A.W.) to hear and to obey under all circumstances whether adverse or favourable, pleasant or unpleasant; to put up when discriminated against and superseded, and never to dispute the command of the men of authority except in a case of open infidelity, violation of faith, you will have sanction from Allah to tell the truth in all circumstances and to care in the cause of Allah any censure or rebuke.' (*Bukhari and Muslim*)

١٨٧ ـ الرَّابعُ : عن النعْمانِ بنِ بَشيرٍ رضي الله عنهما عن النبي صلى اللهُ عليه وسلم قال : « مَثَلُ القَائِمِ في حُدودِ اللهِ ، وَالْوَاقِعِ فيها كَمَثَلِ قَوْمٍ اسْتَهَمُوا عَلَى سَفِينَةٍ ، فَصَارَ بَعْضُهُمْ أعْلاهَا وَبَعْضُهُمْ أسْفَلَهَا ، وَكانَ الَّذِينَ في أسْفَلِهَا إذَا اسْتَقَوْا مِنَ الماءِ مَرُّوا عَلَى مَنْ فَوْقَهُمْ فَقَالُوا : لَوْ أنَّا خَرَقْنَا في نَصِيبِنَا خَرْقاً وَلَمْ نُؤْذِ مَنْ فَوْقَنَا ، فَإنْ تَرَكُوهُمْ وَمَا أرَادُوا هَلَكُوا جَمِيعاً . وإنْ أخَذُوا عَلَى أيْدِيهِمْ نَجَوْا وَنَجَوْا جَمِيعاً »

رواهُ البخاري

187. Hazrat Nu'man ibn Bashir (R.A.A.) relates that the Holy Prophet (S.A.W.) said: The example of a person who obeys injunctions of Allah and the one who dis-regards these limits is like passengers on a boat who decide by drawing lots as to who should occupy the upper deck and who should go to the lower deck. Those in the lower deck had to pass through the upper deck to fetch water which caused some inconvenience to the occupants of the upper deck. So they suggested to the occupants of the upper deck to allow them to bore a hole in the lower deck and to draw water without causing any inconvenience to them. If the occupants of the upper deck were to leave the others to carry out their design, they would all perish together; but if they were to stop them from carrying it out they would save themselves and all others." (*Bukhari*)

١٨٨ ـ الخامسُ : عَنْ أمِّ المُؤْمِنِين أمِّ سَلَمَةَ هِنْدِ بنتِ أبي أُمَيَّةَ حُذيفَةَ رضي الله عنها ، عن النبي صلى الله عليه وسلم أنه قال : « إنَّهُ يُسْتَعْمَلُ عَلَيْكُمْ أمرَاءُ فتَعرِفُونَ وَتُنْكِرُونَ فَمَنْ كَرِهَ فَقَدْ بَرِئَ ، وَمَنْ أنْكَرَ فَقَدْ سَلِمَ ،وَلَكِنْ مَنْ رَضِيَ وَتَابَعَ » قالوا : يَا رَسُولَ اللهِ ألاَ نُقَاتِلُهُمْ ؟ قَالَ : « لاَ ، مَا أقَامُوا فِيكُمُ الصَّلاَةَ » رواه مسلم

188. Ummul Mommieneen Hazrat Umme Salamah (R.A.A.)' wife of the Holy Prophet (S.A.W.) says that the Holy Prophet (S.A.W.) said: 'Some persons will be appointed in authority over you; you will find actions of some of them in agreement with the *Shariat;* and some of their actions, you will find contrary to *Shariah.* Therefore one who expressed abhorrence, he is absolved of (accounting), and one who resents their action, will be safe (from accounting) but one who agreed with them and followed them, will have to account for. The people said "O Prophet of Allah, shall we not fight against them." He said: 'Not so long as they continue to establish the prayer among you.'

(*Muslim*)

١٨٩ ـ السَّادِسُ : عَن أمِّ المُؤْمِنِين أمِّ الحَكَمْ زَيْنَبَ بنت جحش رضي الله عنها أنَّ النَّبِيَّ صلى الله عليه وسلم دَخَلَ عَلَيْهَا فَزِعاً يقُولُ : « لا إلهَ إلاَّ اللهُ، وَيْلٌ لِلْعَرَبِ مِنْ شَرٍّ قَدِ اقْتَرَبَ، فُتِحَ الْيَوْمَ مِن رَدْمِ يَأْجُوجَ وَمَأْجُوجَ مِثْلُ هذِهِ » وَحَلَّقَ بأصْبُعَيْهِ الإبْهَامِ وَالَّتِي تَلِيهَا . فَقُلْتُ : يَارسول اللهِ أنَهْلِكُ وَفِينَا الصَّالِحُونَ ؟ قال : « نَعَمْ إذَا كَثُرَ الْخَبَثُ » متفقٌ عليه

189. Ummul Mommieneen Hazrat Zainab bint Jah'sh (R.A.A.) relates: 'Once the Holy Prophet (S.A.W.) came to her in much worried state and said: 'There is no god save Allah. Fie upon the Arabs for the evil consequence of which is approaching. A breach has been made in the wall holding back Gog and Magog. The hole is of this size; and he made a circle with thumb and forefinger." I said to him. "O Prophet of Allah, shall we be destroyed and killed while there are still a number of virtuous persons among us?" He said: 'Yes: when evil and corruption become widespread.' (Agreed upn). (*Agreed Upon*).

Note: Imam Nawawi elucidating this tradition has said: "The person who considered, in his heart, this act as bad, but has no power to stop it with the help of his hands and tongue, is guiltless, as he has discharged his duty; and the person who counteracted it as best as he could, is immune; but the one who agreed with this act, and expressed his pleasure, is a sinner."

١٩٠ ـ السَّابِعُ : عَنْ أَبِي سَعِيد الْخُدْرِيِّ رضي الله عنه عن النَّبِيِّ صلى الله عليه وسلم قال : « إِيَّاكُمْ وَالْجُلُوسَ فِي الطرُقَاتِ » فَقَالُوا : يَارَسُولَ الله مَالَنَا مِنْ مَجَالِسِنَا بُدٌّ ، نَتَحَدَّثُ فِيهَا ! فقال رسول الله صلى الله عليه وسلم : « فَإِذَا أَبَيْتُمْ إِلاَّ الْمَجْلِسَ فَأَعْطُوا الطَّرِيقَ حَقَّهُ » قالوا : وَمَا حَقُّ الطَّرِيقِ يَا رسولَ الله ؟ قال : « غَضُّ الْبَصَرِ ، وَكَفُّ الأَذَى ، وَرَدُّ السَّلامِ ، وَالأَمْرُ بِالْمَعْرُوفِ ، وَالنَّهْيُ عَنِ الْمُنْكَرِ » متفقٌ عليه

190. Hazrat Abu Sa'eed Khudri (R.A.A.) relates that the Holy Prophet (S.A.W.) directed us: 'Refrain from sitting in the streets.' The Companions submitted: 'O Prophet of Allah, we have no alternative, there is no other place where we can sit and discuss matters.' He said: 'If it is so, then in that case, discharge your responsibilities due to the street.' The Companions asked as to what was due to the street? He said: Keeping your eyes down, clearing the streets of obstacles, responding to Salam greetings, enjoining virtuous deeds and forbidding evil (*Agreed Upon*).

١٩١ ـ الثَّامِنُ : عن ابن عباس رضي الله عنهما أن رسول الله صلى الله عليه وسلم رَأَى خَاتَماً مِنْ ذَهَبٍ فِي يَدِ رَجُلٍ ، فَنَزَعَهُ فَطَرَحَهُ وَقَالَ : « يَعْمِدُ أَحَدُكُمْ إِلَى جَمْرَةٍ مِنْ نَارٍ فَيَجْعَلُهَا فِي يَدِهِ ! » فَقِيلَ لِلرَّجُلِ بَعْدَ مَا ذَهَبَ رسول الله صلى الله عليه وسلم : خُذْ خَاتَمَكَ ، انْتَفِعْ بِهِ . قَالَ : لا وَاللهِ لا آخُذُهُ أَبَداً وَقَدْ طَرَحَهُ رسول الله صلى الله عليه وسلم. رواه مسلم

191. Hazrat Ibn Abbas (R.A.A.) relates that the Holy Prophet (S.A.W.) noticed a man wearing a golden ring on his finger. The Holy Prophet (S.A.W.) removed the ring from his finger and threw it away, saying: 'Any one would like to put a piece of burning coal on his hand, so put it on.' After the Holy Prophet (S.A.W.) left, the man was told to pick up the ring and make use of it in some other way. Thereupon he said: "By Allah, since the Holy Prophet (S.A.W.) has thrown away the ring I shall never pick it up." (*Muslim*)

١٩٢ ـ التَّاسِعُ : عَنْ أَبِي سَعِيدِ الْحَسَنِ الْبَصْرِيِّ أَنَّ عَائِذَ بن عَمْرٍو رضي الله عنه دَخَلَ عَلَى عُبَيْدِ اللهِ بن زِيَادٍ فَقَالَ : أَيْ بُنَيَّ : إِنِّي سَمِعْتُ رسول الله صلى الله عليه وسلم يَقُولُ : « إِنَّ شَرَّ الرِّعَاءِ الْحُطَمَةُ » فَإِيَّاكَ

أنْ تَكُونَ مِنهُمْ. فَقَالَ لَهُ : اجْلِسْ فَإنَّمَا أنتَ مِنْ نُخَالَةِ أصْحَابِ مُحَمَّدٍ صلى الله عليه وسلم ، فقال : وَهَلْ كَانَتْ لَهُمْ نُخَالَةٌ ، إنَّمَا كَانَتِ النُّخَالَةُ بَعْدَهُمْ وَفي غَيْرِهِمْ ! رواه مسلم

192. Hazrat Abu Sa'eed Hasan Basri (R.A.A.) relates that Hazrat 'Aaiz Ibn 'Amr (R.A.A.) visited Ubaidullah Ibn Ziyad and said to him: 'O Son, I heard the Prophet say: The worst ruler is one who deals with people harshly. Be careful lest you should be one such (functionary). He said to him: 'Sit down you are like chaff among the Companions of the Holy Prophet (S.A.W.) Hazrat 'Aaiz bin 'Amr asked: "were such humble persons present among the companions of the Holy Prophet (S.A.W.)? Certainly not, such persons would come after them not belonging to them." (*Muslim*)

١٩٣ ـ الْعَاشِرُ : عَنْ حُذَيْفَةَ رضيَ اللهُ عنهُ عنِ النبي صلى الله عليه وسلم قال : « وَالَّذي نَفْسي بِيَدِهِ لَتَأْمُرُنَّ بِالْمَعْرُوفِ ، وَلَتَنْهَوُنَّ عَنِ الْمُنْكَرِ ، أوْ لَيُوشِكَنَّ الله أنْ يَبْعَثَ عَلَيْكُمْ عِقَاباً مِنْهُ ، ثُمَّ تَدْعُونَهُ فلا يُسْتَجَابُ لَكُمْ » رواه الترمذي وقال : حديثٌ حسنٌ .

193. Hazrat Huzaifah (R.A.A.) says that the Holy Prophet (S.A.W.) said: By him in whose hands is my, life (Allah the Almighty), necessarily you should enjoin virtue and check evil, or else Allah will certainly send chastisement upon you. And then you will pray but your supplications will not be accepted. Imam Tirmizi has said that this is a genuine and authentic tradition. (*Tirmizi*)

١٩٤ ـ الْحَادي عَشَرَ : عَنْ أبي سَعيدٍ الْخُدْرِيِّ رضي الله عنه عن النبي صلى الله عليه وسلم قال : « أفْضَلُ الْجِهَادِ كَلِمَةُ عَدْلٍ عِنْدَ سُلْطَانٍ جَائِرٍ » رواه أبو داود ، والترمذي وقال : حديثٌ حسنٌ .

194. Hazrat Abu Sa'eed Khudri (R.A.A.) relates that the Holy Prophet (S.A.W.) said: 'The best *Jihad* (struggle in the cause of Allah) is to speak just before a tyrannical ruler. (*Abu Daud and Tirmizi*)

This means one should not hesitate to speak truth due to fear. Imam Tirmizi holds this tradition as genuine and authentic.

١٩٥ ـ الثَّاني عَشَرَ : عَنْ أبي عبدِ الله طَارِقِ بن شِهَابِ الْبَجَليِّ الأحْمَسِيِّ رضي الله عنه أنَّ رَجُلاً سَأَلَ النَّبيَّ صلى الله عليه وسلم ، وَقَدْ وَضَعَ رِجْلَه في الْغَرْزِ : أيُّ الْجِهَادِ أفْضَل ؟ قَالَ : « كَلِمَةُ حَقٍّ عِنْدَ سُلْطَانٍ جائرٍ » رَوَاهُ النسائيُّ بإسنادٍ صحيحٍ .

195. Hazrat Abu Abdullah Tariq Ibn Shihab al-Bajli al-Ahmasi (R.A.A.) relates that a person asked the Holy Prophet (S.A.W.) when he was just mounting the camel, as to what is best type of *Jihad.* He said: 'Speaking truth before a tyrant ruler. (*Nisai*). *Imam Nisai* has related with perfect chain.

١٩٦ – الثَّالِثَ عَشَرَ : عن ابن مَسْعُودٍ رضي الله عنه قال : قال رسول الله صلى الله عليه وسلم : « إنَّ أوَّلَ مَا دَخَلَ النَّقْصُ عَلَى بَنِي إسْرَائِيلَ أنَّه كَانَ الرَّجُلُ يَلْقَى الرَّجُلَ فَيَقُولُ : يَا هذَا اتَّقِ الله وَدَعْ مَا تَصْنَعُ فَإنَّهُ لا يَحِلُّ لَكَ ، ثُمَّ يَلْقَاهُ مِنَ الغَدِ وهُوَ عَلَى حَالِهِ ،فَلا يَمْنَعُهُ ذلك أنْ يَكُونَ أكِيلَهُ وَشَرِيبَهُ وَقَعِيدَهُ ، فَلَمَّا فَعَلُوا ذلكَ ضَرَبَ الله قُلُوبَ بَعْضِهِمْ بِبَعْضٍ » ثُمَّ قال : (لُعِنَ الَّذينَ كَفَرُوا مِنْ بَنِي إسْرَائِيلَ عَلَى لِسَانِ دَاوُدَ وَعِيسَى ابْنِ مَرْيَمَ ذلكَ بِمَا عَصَوْا وَكَانُوا يَعْتَدُونَ . كَانُوا لا يَتَنَاهَوْنَ عَنْ مُنْكَرٍ فَعَلُوهُ لَبِئْسَ مَا كَانُوا يَفْعَلُونَ . تَرَى كَثِيراً مِنْهُمْ يَتَوَلَّوْنَ الَّذينَ كَفَرُوا لَبِئْسَ مَا قَدَّمَتْ لَهُمْ أنْفُسُهُمْ) إلى قولِهِ : (فَاسِقُونَ) [المائدة : ٧٨ ، ٨١] ثُمَّ قَالَ : « كَلاَّ ، وَالله لَتَأْمُرُنَّ بالمَعْرُوفِ ، وَلَتَنْهَوُنَّ عَنِ المُنْكَرِ ،ولَتَأخُذُنَّ عَلَى يَدِ الظَّالِمِ ، وَلَتَأْطِرُنَّهُ عَلَى الحَقِّ أطْراً ، وَلَتَقْصُرُنَّهُ عَلَى الحَقِّ قَصْراً ، أوْ لَيَضْرِبَنَّ الله بِقُلُوبِ بَعْضِكُمْ عَلَى بَعْضٍ ، ثُمَّ لَيَلْعَنَنْكُمْ كَمَا لَعَنَهُمْ » رواه أبو داود ، والترمذي وقال : حديث حسن.

هذا لفظ أبي داود ، وَلفظ الترمذي : قال رسول الله صلى الله عليه وسلم : « لَمَّا وَقَعَتْ بَنُو إسْرَائيلَ في المَعَاصِي نَهَتْهُمْ عُلَمَاؤُهُمْ فَلَمْ يَنْتَهُوا ، فَجَالَسُوهُمْ في مَجَالِسِهِمْ وَوَاكَلُوهُمْ وَشَارَبُوهُمْ ، فَضَرَبَ الله قُلُوبَ بَعْضِهِمْ بِبَعْضٍ ، وَلَعَنَهُمْ عَلَى لِسَانِ دَاوُدَ وَعِيسَى ابنِ مَرْيَمَ ذلِكَ بمَا عَصَوْا وكَانُوا يَعْتَدُونَ » فَجَلَسَ رسول الله صلى الله عليه وسلم ، وكَانَ مُتَّكِئاً فَقَالَ : « لا وَالَّذي نَفْسي بِيَدِهِ حَتَّى تَأْطِرُوهُمْ عَلَى الحَقِّ أطْراً » .

196. Hazrat Abdullah Ibn Masud (R.A.A.) relates that the Holy Prophet (S.A.W.) said: The very first failing that developed among the Jews was that a person when meeting another would say 'Fear Allah and eschew what you are doing unlawful? But meeting the erring person next day he could find no change in him, but this time the very person would not say anything to him because this time he did not refrain from eating, drinking and sitting with him. As such, Allah perverted the hearts of such persons also on account of their association with others (with black hearts). Then the Holy Prophet (S.A.W.) recited:

"Those of the children of Israel who went astray were cursed by the tongue of David, and of Jesus, son of Mary. That was because they rebelled and used to transgress. They restrained not one another from the wickedness they did. Verily evil was that they used to do! Thou seest many of them making friends with those who disbelieve. Surely all for them is that which they themselves send on before them, that Allah will be worth with them and in the doom they will abide. If they believed in Allah and the Prophet and that which is revealed unto him, they would not choose them for their friends. But many of them are of evil conduct."(5:78—81)

The Holy Prophet (S.A.W.) continuing said: "Certainly it is not so as you think: By Allah, you must enjoin good and forbid evil and hold the hand of the aggressors and persuade them to act justly and make them steadfast on truth, failing which Allah will punish you alongwith others (wrong doers) and you will be cursed like the Jews.

(*Abu Daud and Tirmizi*)

According to Imam Tirmizi this is a good tradition, and is in the words of Imam Abu Daud. The version of Tirmizi says:

The Holy Prophet (S.A.W.) said: 'When the chidren of Israel were involved in sin, first their divines tried to prevent them, but they did not heed. Their divines also got themselves associated with them and joined them in eating and drinking. So they were cursed by Prophets David and Jesus son of Mary, because they were disobedient and were given to excesses. The narrator says that the Holy Prophet (S.A.W.) who had been reclining on a pillow sat up and said: By Allah in whose hands is my life, (you will not be able to achieve redemption) unless you persuade them to follow the truth.

١٩٧ ـ الرَّابعَ عَشَرَ : عن أَبي بَكْرٍ الصِّدِّيق ، رضي الله عنه ، قال : يَا أَيُّهَا النَّاسُ إِنَّكُمْ لَتَقْرَؤُونَ هَذِهِ الآيَةَ : (يَا أَيُّهَا الَّذينَ آمَنُوا عَلَيْكُمْ أَنْفُسَكُمْ لا يَضُرُّكُمْ مَنْ ضَلَّ إِذَا اهْتَدَيْتُمْ) [النساء : ٨٥] وإني سَمِعت رسول الله ، صلى الله عليه وسلم ، يَقُولُ : « إِنَّ النَّاسَ إِذَا رَأَوْا الظَّالِمَ فَلَمْ يَأْخُذُوا عَلَى يَدَيْهِ أَوْشَكَ أَنْ يَعُمَّهُمُ الله بِعِقَابٍ مِنْهُ »

رواه أبو داود ، والترمذي ، والنسائي بأسانيد صحيحة .

197. Hazrat Abu Bakr Siddiq (R.A.A.) says 'O Muslims, you recite this verse:

'O ye who believe! Ye have charge of your own souls. He who

erreth cannot injure you if ye are rightly guided. Unto Allah ye will all return; and then He will inform you of what ye used to do. (5:105)

I have heard the Holy Prophet (S.A.W.) saying: When the people see a cruel person is committing aggression, and do not prevent him, it is likely that Allah would afflict them with His chastisement.
(*Abu Daud*، *Tirmizi and Nisai*). Nisai has quoted this tradition with authentic authorities.

Note: It is incumbent upon everybody to ask people to do good, irrespective of the fact whether he be a virtuous person or a wrong doer. The learned persons are required to act upon the things themselves which they ask other persons to do.

* * * * * * * * * *

CHAPTER 24

Divine Wrath on a Person Who Verbally Enjoins Virtue and Prohibits Vice, but Acts Contrarily.

قال الله تعالى : أَتَأْمُرُونَ النَّاسَ بِالْبِرِّ وَتَنْسَوْنَ أَنْفُسَكُمْ وَأَنْتُمْ تَتْلُونَ الْكِتَابَ أَفَلا تَعْقِلُونَ [البقرة : ٤٤] وقال تعالى : يَا أَيُّهَا الَّذِينَ آمَنُوا لِمَ تَقُولُونَ مَالا تَفْعَلُونَ كَبُرَ مَقْتاً عِنْدَ الله أَنْ تَقُولُوا مَا لا تَفْعَلُونَ [الصف : ٢ ، ٣] وقال تعالى إخباراً عَنْ شُعَيْبٍ ، صلى الله عليه وسلم : وَمَا أُرِيدُ أَنْ أُخَالِفَكُمْ إِلَى مَا أَنْهَاكُمْ عَنْهُ [هود : ٨٨] .

Allah, the Exalted, has said:

94. Enjoin ye righteousness upon mankind while ye yourselves forget (to practise it)? And ye are readers of the scriptures have ye then no sense? (2:44)
95. O ye who believe! Why say ye that which ye do not? It is most hateful in the sight of Allah that ye say that which ye do not` (61:2—3)
96. I do desire not to do behind your backs which I ask you not to do (11:88)

١٩٨ ــ وعن أبي زيدٍ أُسامَةَ بنِ زيدِ بنِ حَارِثَةَ ، رضي الله عنهما ، قال : سَمِعْتُ رسول الله ، صلى الله عليه وسلم ، يَقُولُ : « يُؤْتَى بالرَّجُلِ يَوْمَ الْقِيامَةِ فَيُلْقَى في النَّار ، فَتَنْدَلِقُ أَقْتَابُ بَطْنِهِ ، فَيَدُورُ بِهَا كَمَا يَدُورُ الحِمَارُ في الرَّحَا ، فَيَجْتَمِعُ إِلَيْهِ أَهْلُ النَّار فَيَقُولُونَ :

يَا فُلانُ مَالَكَ ؟ أَلَمْ تَكُ تَأْمُرُ بِالمَعْرُوفِ وَتَنْهَى عَنِ المُنْكَرِ ؟ فَيَقُولُ :
بَلَى ، كُنْتُ آمُرُ بِالمَعْرُوفِ وَلا آتِيهِ ، وَأَنْهَى عَنِ المُنْكَرِ وَآتِيهِ » متفق عليه .

198. Hazrat Abu Zaid Usamah Bin Zaid Harisa (R.A.A.) says that he heard the Holy Prophet (S.A.W.) saying 'On the day of judgement a man will be brought and thrown into the Hell, as a result of this his intestines will come out of his belly, and he will go circling holding his intestines like a donkey running a mill. His companions in the Hell will come to him: O! So and So! What is this? Did you not ask people to do good and avoid vice?' He will say: 'That is so. I enjoined others to do good, but did not do it myself; and I forbade them to do evil but did it myself.' (*Agreed upon*)

* * * * * * * * * * *

CHAPTER 25

Return of Deposits to Owners

قال الله تعالى : إِنَّ اللهَ يَأْمُرُكُمْ أَنْ تُؤَدُّوا الأَمَانَاتِ إِلَى أَهْلِهَا
[النساء : ٥٨] وقال تعالى : إِنَّا عَرَضْنَا الأَمَانَةَ عَلَى السَّمٰوَاتِ وَالأَرْضِ
وَالجِبَالِ فَأَبَيْنَ أَنْ يَحْمِلْنَهَا وَأَشْفَقْنَ مِنْهَا وَحَمَلَهَا الإِنْسَانُ إِنَّهُ
كَانَ ظَلُوماً جَهُولاً [الأحزاب : ٧٢] .

Allah, the Exalted, has said:

97. Lo! Allah Commandeth you that ye restore deposits to their owners (4:58)
98. Lo! We offered the trust unto the heavens and the earth and the hills, but they shrank from bearing it and were afraid of it. And man assumed it. Lo! he hath proved a tyrant and a fool. (33:72)

١٩٩ — عن أبي هريرة ، رضي الله عنه ، أن رسولَ الله ، صلى الله عليه
وسلم ، قال : « آيَةُ المُنَافِقِ ثَلاثٌ : إِذَا حَدَّثَ كَذَبَ ، وَإِذَا وَعَدَ أَخْلَفَ ،
وَإِذَا اؤْتُمِنَ خَانَ » متفقٌ عليه
وفي رواية : « وَإِنْ صَامَ وَصَلَّى وَزَعَمَ أَنَّهُ مُسْلِمٌ » .

199. Hazrat Abu Hurairah (R.A.A.) relates that the Holy Prophet (S.A.W.) said: A hypocrite has three distinguishing signs; first when he talks he talks a lie; second when he makes a promise he breaks it; and third when something is entrusted to him he misappropriates it. (*Bukhari and Muslim*)

According to another version: Even if he offers *Salat* (Prayer) and keeps fast and considers himself a Muslim.

٢٠٠ – وعن حُذَيْفَةَ بنِ الْيَمَانِ . رضي الله عنه ، قال : حدثنا رسول الله ، صلى الله عليه وسلم ، حَدِيثَيْنِ قَدْ رَأَيْتُ أحَدَهُمَا ، وَأَنَا أَنْتَظِرُ الآخَرَ : حدَّثَنَا أنَّ الأمَانَةَ نَزَلَتْ في جَذْرِ قُلُوبِ الرِّجَال ، ثُمَّ نَزَلَ القُرآنُ فَعَلِمُوا مِنَ القُرْآنِ ، وَعَلِمُوا مِنَ السُّنَّةِ ، ثُمَّ حَدَّثَنَا عَنْ رَفْعِ الأمَانَةِ فَقَالَ : « يَنَامُ الرَّجل النَّوْمَةَ فَتُقْبَضُ الأمَانَةُ مِنْ قَلْبِهِ ، فَيَظَلُّ أثَرُهَا مِثْلَ الوَكْتِ ، ثُمَّ يَنَامُ النَّوْمَةَ فَتُقْبَضُ الأمَانَةُ مِنْ قَلْبِهِ ، فَيَظَلُّ أثَرُهَا مِثْلَ أثَرِ المَجْلِ ، كَجَمْرٍ دَحْرَجْتَهُ عَلَى رِجْلِكَ ، فَنَفِطَ فَتَرَاه مُنْتَبِراً وَلَيْسَ فِيهِ شَيْءٌ » ثُمَّ أخَذَ حَصَاةً فَدَحْرَجَهُ عَلَى رِجْلِهِ « فَيُصْبِحُ النَّاسُ يَتَبَايَعُونَ ، فَلا يَكَادُ أحَدٌ يُؤَدِّي الأمَانَةَ حَتَّى يُقَالَ : إنَّ في بَنِي فُلانٍ رَجُلاً أَمِيناً ، حَتَّى يُقَالَ لِلرَّجُلِ : مَا أجْلَدَهُ مَا أظْرَفَهُ ، مَا أعْقَلَهُ ! وَمَا في قَلْبِهِ مِثْقَالُ حَبَّةٍ مِنْ خَرْدَلٍ مِنْ إيمَانٍ . وَلَقَدْ أتَى عَلَيَّ زَمَانٌ وَمَا أُبَالِي أيَّكُمْ بَايَعْتُ ، لَئِنْ كَانَ مُسْلِماً لَيَرُدَّنَّهُ عَلَيَّ دِينُهُ ، وَلَئِنْ كَانَ نَصْرَانِياً أوْ يَهُودِيّاً لَيَرُدَّنَّهُ عَلَيَّ سَاعِيهِ ، وَأمَّا اليَوْمَ فَمَا كُنْتُ أُبَايِعُ مِنْكُمْ إلاَّ فُلاناً وَفُلاناً » متفقٌ عليه

200. Hazrat Huzaifah bin Al-Yaman (R.A.A.) says: "The Holy Prophet (S.A.W.) told us two things, one of which I have seen (having come true) and as regards the other, I am awaiting its materialisation. The Holy Prophet (S.A.W.) informed us that trustworthiness was embeded in the hearts of the people. And when the Holy Quran was revealed, they learnt about it (also), learnt about my practice. Then he told us about the taking away of trust from us that a man will go to sleep and when he will get up, he will find trustworthiness taken away, leaving only a shadow of the same in his heart; and when he goes to sleep, the remaining portion of trust will vanish, leaving behind a small mark like a boil on the heart, like one you get if you put a spark on your foot, and you get boil which is erupted but empty from inside. (Then the Holy Prophet (S.A.W.) picked up a pebble and started striking at his foot). Then the people get up in the morning and will go on with their buying and selling, but none of them will be a man who will dischargo his trust, so much so that it will be said: there is only one trustworthy person in such and such a tribe. (On the contrary) it will be said of a man who will be well versed in worldly affairs; How clever, how handsome and how intelligent he is; although he will be void of a grain of faith. Hazrat Huzaifah (R.A.A.) further says: Time was when I did not mind with whom I did business, for if he happened to be Muslim, his faith was sufficient guarantee, and if he was a Jew or a Christian, his guardian (surety) was a good guarantee. But today I do not do business except with So and So *(Bukhari and Muslim)*

٢٠١ – وعن حُذَيْفَةَ ، وأبي هريرة ، رضي الله عنهما ، قالا : قال رسول الله ، صلى الله عليه وسلم : « يَجْمَعُ اللهُ ، تَبَارَكَ وَتَعَالَى ، النَّاسَ فَيَقُومُ الْمُؤْمِنُونَ حَتَّى تُزْلَفَ لَهُمُ الْجَنَّةُ ، فَيَأْتُونَ آدَمَ ، صَلَوَاتُ اللهِ عَلَيْهِ ، فَيَقُولُونَ : يَا أَبَانَا اسْتَفْتِحْ لَنَا الْجَنَّةَ ، فَيَقُولُ : وَهَلْ أَخْرَجَكُمْ مِنَ الْجَنَّةِ إِلاَّ خَطِيئَةُ أَبِيكُمْ ! لَسْتُ بِصَاحِبِ ذَلِكَ ، اذْهَبُوا إِلَى ابْنِي إِبْرَاهِيمَ خَلِيلِ اللهِ ، قال : فَيَأْتُونَ إِبْرَاهِيمَ ، فَيَقُولُ إِبْرَاهِيمُ : لَسْتُ بِصَاحِبِ ذَلِكَ إِنَّمَا كُنْتُ خَلِيلاً مِنْ وَرَاءِ وَرَاءِ ، اعْمِدُوا إِلَى مُوسَى الَّذِي كَلَّمَهُ اللهُ تَكْلِيماً ، فَيَأْتُونَ مُوسَى ، فَيَقُولُ : لَسْتُ بِصَاحِبِ ذَلِكَ ؛ اذْهَبُوا إِلَى عِيسَى كَلِمَةِ اللهِ وَرُوحِهِ فَيَقُولُ عِيسَى : لَسْتُ بِصَاحِبِ ذَلِكَ . فَيَأْتُونَ مُحَمَّداً ، صلى الله عليه وسلم ، فَيَقُومُ فَيُؤْذَنُ لَهُ ، وَتُرْسَلُ الأَمَانَةُ وَالرَّحِمُ فَيَقُومَانِ جَنَبَتَي الصِّرَاطِ يَمِيناً وَشِمَالاً ، فَيَمُرُّ أَوَّلُكُمْ كَالْبَرْقِ » قُلْتُ : بِأَبِي وَأُمِّي ، أَيُّ شَيْءٍ كَمَرِّ الْبَرْقِ ؟ قال : « أَلَمْ تَرَوْا كَيْفَ يَمُرُّ وَيَرْجِعُ فِي طَرْفَةِ عَيْنٍ ؟ ثُمَّ كَمَرِّ الرِّيحِ ، ثُمَّ كَمَرِّ الطَّيْرِ ، وَأَشَدِّ الرِّجَالِ تَجْرِي بِهِمْ أَعْمَالُهُمْ ، وَنَبِيُّكُمْ قَائِمٌ عَلَى الصِّرَاطِ يَقُولُ : رَبِّ سَلِّمْ سَلِّمْ ، حَتَّى تَعْجِزَ أَعْمَالُ الْعِبَادِ ، حَتَّى يَجِيءَ الرَّجُلُ لا يَسْتَطِيعُ السَّيْرَ إِلاَّ زَحْفاً ، وَفِي حَافَتَي الصِّرَاطِ كَلالِيبُ مُعَلَّقَةٌ مَأْمُورَةٌ بِأَخْذِ مَنْ أُمِرَتْ بِهِ ، فَمَخْدُوشٌ نَاجٍ ، وَمُكَرْدَسٌ فِي النَّارِ » وَالَّذِي نَفْسُ أَبِي هُرَيْرَةَ بِيَدِهِ إِنَّ قَعْرَ جَهَنَّمَ لَسَبْعُونَ خَرِيفاً . رواه مسلم

201. **Hazrat Huzaifah and Hazrat Abu Hurairah** (R.A.A.) relate that the Holy Prophet (S.A.W.) said: On the Day of Judgement Allah, the Glorified and Exalted, will collect the entire humanity, and the believers will be made to stand closer to the Paradise. They will first approach Prophet Adam, (Blessings of Allah be upon him) and will ask him,"Father, please get the Paradise opened for us". He will reply. "It is the fault of your father which caused your expulsion from the paradise. I am unable to help you; Go to my son, Prophet Abraham, the Friend of Allah." Then they will go to Prophet Abraham, who will tell them "I am not competent to do this; the task is very difficult. I was (simply) the friend of Allah. (He will say this by way of humility). Go to Prophet Moses with whom Allah spoke well." Moses will say to them: 'I am not competent for this; go to Jesus, word of Allah and a spirit for Him." He will also say "I am not fit for this job". Then they will come to the Holy Prophet Muhammad (S.A.W.). He will come forward and Allah the Almighty will allow him (to intercede). The integrity and mercy will be released and right and left will stand on either side of the Bridge of *Sirat* (the Bridge over which all will have to pass on the Day of Judgement). The first party from amongst you will pass over the Bridge like lightning. I enquired'(May my parents be sacrificed on you,) what does this mean?' He said: 'Have you not noticed how the lightning flashes forth and back in the twinkling of an eye? Then the next group will pass over the bridge like the wind, then the third party will pass like flying birds, and will rush through with the speed of running men, and this difference will be according to the merit of their deeds. At this time your Prophet will remain standing at the Bridge soliciting Allah's mercy and reciting: 'O Sustainer keep them safe,' keep them safe.' As the standard of the virtues of people falls, the speed will get slower and slower till a man will come, who will not be able to walk but will crawl along with the help of his buttocks. Some hand-grips will be hanging on both sides of the Bridge. These grips with the Command of Allah will catch hold of those whom He will like to help. One who is merely scratched, will be redeemed and some will be thrown into the Hell. Hazrat Abu Hurairah (R.A.A.) says: "By Allah in Whose hands lies the life of Abu Hurairah, depth of Hell is equal to the distance which could be covered in seventy years' journey (*Muslim*)

٢٠٢ ـ وعن أبي خُبَيْبٍ ـ بضم الخاء المعجمة ـ عبد الله بنِ الزبَيْرِ ، رضيَ الله عنهما ، قال : لَمَّا وَقَفَ الزبَيْرُ يَوْمَ الجَمَلِ دَعَانِي فَقُمْتُ إلَى جَنْبِهِ ، فَقَالَ : يَابُنَيَّ إنَّهُ لا يُقْتَلُ اليَوْمَ إلاَّ ظَالِمٌ أَوْ مَظْلُومٌ ، وَإنِّي لا أُرَانِي إلاَّ سَأُقْتَلُ اليَوْمَ مَظْلُوماً ، وَإنَّ مِنْ أَكْبَرِ هَمِّي لَدَيْنِي ، أَفَتَرَى دَيْنَنَا يُبْقِي مِنْ مَالِنَا شَيْئاً ؟ ثُمَّ قَالَ : يَابُنَيَّ بِعْ مَالَنَا وَاقْضِ دَيْنِي ، وَأَوْصَى بالثُّلُثِ ، وَثُلُثِهِ لِبَنِيهِ ، يَعْنِي لِبَنِي عَبْدِ الله بن الزبير

ثُلُثُ الثُّلُث . قَالَ : فَإِنْ فَضَلَ مِنْ مَالِنَا بَعْدَ قَضَاءِ الدَّيْنِ شَيْءٌ فَثُلُثُهُ لِبَنِيكَ ، قَالَ هِشَامٌ : وَكَانَ وَلَدُ عَبْدِ اللهِ قَدْ وازَى بَعْضَ بَنِي الزُّبَيْرِ خُبَيبٍ وَعَبَّادٍ ، وَلَهُ يَوْمَئِذٍ تِسْعَةُ بَنِينَ وَتِسْعُ بَنَاتٍ . قَالَ عَبْدُ اللهِ : فَجَعَلَ يُوصِينِي بِدَيْنِهِ وَيَقُولُ : يَابُنَيَّ إِنْ عَجَزْتَ عَنْ شَيْءٍ مِنْهُ فَاسْتَعِنْ عَلَيْهِ بِمَوْلَايَ . قَالَ : فَوَاللهِ مَادَرَيْتُ مَا أَرَادَ حَتَّى قُلْتُ : يَا أَبَتِ مَنْ مَوْلَاكَ ؟ قَالَ : اللهُ . قال : فَوَاللهِ مَا وَقَعْتُ فِي كُرْبَةٍ مِنْ دَيْنِهِ إِلَّا قُلْتُ : يَامَوْلَى الزُّبَيْرِ اقْضِ عَنْهُ دَيْنَهُ ، فَيَقْضِيهِ . قَالَ : فَقُتِلَ الزُّبَيْرُ وَلَمْ يَدَعْ دِينَاراً وَلَا دِرْهَماً إِلَّا أَرَضِينَ ، مِنْهَا الْغَابَةُ وَإِحْدَى عَشْرَةَ دَاراً بِالْمَدِينَةِ ، وَدَارَيْنِ بِالْبَصْرَةِ ، وَدَاراً بِالْكُوفَةِ وَدَاراً بِمِصْرَ . قال : وَإِنَّمَا كَانَ دَيْنُهُ الَّذِي كَانَ عَلَيْهِ أَنَّ الرَّجُلَ كَانَ يَأْتِيهِ بِالمال ، فَيَسْتَوْدِعُهُ إِيَّاهُ ، فَيَقُولُ الزُّبَيْرُ : لا وَلَكِنْ هُوَسَلَفٌ إِنِّي أَخْشَى عَلَيْهِ الضَّيْعَةَ . وَمَا وَلِيَ إِمَارَةً قَطُّ وَلَا جِبَايَةً وَلَاخَرَاجاً وَلَاشَيْئاً إِلَّا أَنْ يَكُونَ فِي غَزْوٍ مَعَ رسول الله صلى الله عليه وسلم ، أَوْ مَعَ أَبِي بَكْرٍ وَعُمَرَ وَعُثْمَانَ رضي الله عنهم ، قَالَ عَبْدُ اللهِ : فَحَسَبْتُ مَا كَانَ عَلَيْهِ مِنَ الدَّيْنِ فَوَجَدْتُهُ أَلْفَيْ أَلْفٍ وَمِائَتَيْ أَلْفٍ ! فَلَقِيَ حَكِيمُ بْنُ حِزَامٍ عَبْدَ اللهِ بْنَ الزُّبَيْرِ فَقَالَ : يَا ابْنَ أَخِي كَمْ عَلَى أَخِي مِنَ الدَّيْنِ ؟ فَكَتَمْتُهُ وَقُلْتُ : مِائَةُ أَلْفٍ . فَقَالَ حَكِيمٌ : وَاللهِ مَا أَرَى أَمْوَالَكُمْ تَسَعُ هَذِهِ ! فَقَالَ عَبْدُ اللهِ : أَرَأَيْتُكَ إِنْ كَانَتْ أَلْفَيْ أَلْفٍ ؟ وَمِائَتَيْ أَلْفٍ ؟ قَالَ : مَا أَرَاكُمْ تُطِيقُونَ هَذَا ، فَإِنْ عَجَزْتُمْ عَنْ شَيْءٍ مِنْهُ فَاسْتَعِينُوا بِي . قَالَ : وَكَانَ الزُّبَيْرُ قَدِ اشْتَرَى الْغَابَةَ بِسَبْعِينَ وَمِائَةِ أَلْفٍ ، فَبَاعَهَا عَبْدُ اللهِ بِأَلْفِ أَلْفٍ وَسِتِّمِائَةِ أَلْف ، ثُمَّ قَامَ فَقَال : مَنْ كَانَ لَهُ عَلَى الزُّبَيْرِ شَيْءٌ فَلْيُوافِنَا بِالْغَابَةِ ، فَأَتَاهُ عَبْدُ اللهِ بْنُ جَعْفَرٍ ، وَكَانَ لَهُ عَلَى الزُّبَيْرِ أَرْبَعُمِائَةِ أَلْفٍ ، فَقَالَ لِعَبْدِ اللهِ : إِنْ شِئْتُمْ تَرَكْتُهَا لَكُمْ ؟ قَالَ عَبْدُ اللهِ : لا ، قال : فَإِنْ شِئْتُمْ جَعَلْتُمُوهَا

فِيمَا تُؤَخِّرُونَ إِنْ أَخَّرْتُمْ ، فقال عَبْدُ اللهِ : لا ، قال : فَاقْطَعُوا لِي قِطْعَةً ، قال عَبْدُ اللهِ : لَكَ مِنْ هٰهُنَا إِلَى هٰهُنَا . فَبَاعَ عَبْدُ اللهِ مِنْهَا ، فَقَضَى عَنْهُ دَيْنَهُ ، وَأَوْفَاهُ وَبَقِيَ مِنْهَا أَرْبَعَةُ أَسْهُمٍ وَنِصْفٌ ، فَقَدِمَ عَلَى مُعَاوِيَةَ وَعِنْدَهُ عَمْرُو بْنُ عُثْمَانَ ، وَالْمُنْذِرُ بْنُ الزُّبَيْرِ ، وَابْنُ زَمْعَةَ . فقال لَهُ مُعَاوِيَةُ : كَمْ قُوِّمَتِ الْغَابَةُ ؟ قال : كُلُّ سَهْمٍ بِمِائَةِ أَلْفٍ قال : كَمْ بَقِيَ مِنْهَا ؟ قال : أَرْبَعَةُ أَسْهُمٍ وَنِصْفٌ ، فقال الْمُنْذِرُ بْنُ الزُّبَيْرِ : قَدْ أَخَذْتُ مِنْهَا سَهْماً بِمِائَةِ أَلْفٍ ، قال عَمْرُو بْنُ عُثْمَانَ : قَدْ أَخَذْتُ مِنْهَا سَهْماً بِمِائَةِ أَلْفٍ . وقال ابْنُ زَمْعَةَ : قَدْ أَخَذْتُ سَهْماً بِمِائَةِ أَلْفٍ ، فَقَالَ مُعَاوِيَةُ : كَمْ بَقِيَ مِنْهَا ؟ قال : سَهْمٌ وَنِصْفُ سَهْمٍ ، قَالَ : قَدْ أَخَذْتُهُ بِخَمْسِينَ وَمِائَةِ أَلْفٍ. قَالَ: وَبَاعَ عَبْدُ اللهِ بْنُ جَعْفَرٍ نَصِيبَهُ مِنْ مُعَاوِيَةَ بِسِتِّمِائَةِ أَلْفٍ . فَلَمَّا فَرَغَ ابْنُ الزُّبَيْرِ مِنْ قَضَاءِ دَيْنِهِ قَالَ بَنُو الزُّبَيْرِ : اقْسِمْ بَيْنَنَا مِيرَاثَنَا . قَالَ : وَاللهِ لا أَقْسِمُ بَيْنَكُمْ حَتَّى أُنَادِيَ بِالْمَوْسِمِ أَرْبَعَ سِنِينَ : أَلا مَنْ كَانَ لَهُ عَلَى الزُّبَيْرِ دَيْنٌ فَلْيَأْتِنَا فَلْنَقْضِهِ . فَجَعَلَ كُلَّ سَنَةٍ يُنَادِي فِي الْمَوْسِمِ ، فَلَمَّا مَضَى أَرْبَعُ سِنِينَ قَسَمَ بَيْنَهُمْ وَدَفَعَ الثُّلُثَ . وَكَانَ لِلزُّبَيْرِ أَرْبَعُ نِسْوَةٍ ، فَأَصَابَ كُلَّ امْرَأَةٍ أَلْفُ أَلْفٍ وَمِائَتَا أَلْفٍ ، فَجَمِيعُ مَالِهِ خَمْسُونَ أَلْفَ أَلْفٍ وَمِائَتَا أَلْفٍ ، رواه البخاري

202. Hazrat Abu Khubaib Abdullah Bin Zubair (R.A.A.) states when (in the month of *Jamadi-ul-Awwal* of 36 A.H.) Hazrat Zubair was going to fight in the battle of Jamal, he sent for me, and I went, and stood by his side. He told me "My son either the aggressor or the aggressed one would be killed today. I am sure today I shall be killed as an aggressed. I am much concerned about the disposal of property. Do you think something will be left over from my estate after the payment of debts? My son, pay my debts after selling my property. Should anything be left over after the discharge of my debts, I bequeth **for one** Third, One third of it i.e. one ninth of it (total left over) will be for the sons of Abdullah Bin Zubair. After this if anything more is left over, then one third of this residue is for your (Abdullah's) sons. Hisham says that some sons of Abdullah were of the same age as Khubaib and Abbad, the sons of Hazrat Zubair, and he had 9 sons and

9 daughters. He kept on instructing me about the disposal of his assets, and then said: 'My son, should you find any difficulty in the discharge of my debt, then have recourse to my master and implore his help. I did not understand what he meant by master and asked: 'Father who is your master?' He said: 'Allah' Accordingly whenever I faced a difficulty in discharging any portion of his debt, I would supplicate: "O Master of Zubair discharge his debt:" and He discharged it.' Hazrat Zubair was martyred. He left no Dirhams and Dinars (Cash) but he left some lands, one of them in Ghabah, eleven houses in Medina, two in Basra, one in Kufa and one in Egypt. The cause of his indebtedness was that if a person would come to him, asking him to keep something of his in trust for him. Hazrat Zubair (R.A.A.) would not agree to accept it as a trust, apprehending it might be lost, but would take it as a loan. He never accepted an Office of authority or a post of tax collector. He had the privilege of having participated in *Jihad* with the Holy Prophet (S.A.W.) Hazrat Abu Bakr, Hazrat Umar and Hazrat Usman (and got his share in booty).

I prepared a statement of his debts and they amounted to two million and two hundred thousand. Hazrat Hakeem Ibn Hizam met me and asked me: 'Nephew, how much is due from my brother as debt?' Concealing the real state of affairs I said: 'A hundred thousand,' Hazrat Hakeem said 'I do not think your assets will cover that much.' I said: What would you think if the amount were two million and two hundred thousand? He said: I would not think that this would be within your capacity. Should you be unable to discharge any portion of it, call upon me for help.'

Hazrat Zubair (R.A.A.) had purchased the land in Ghabah for a hundred and seventy thousand. Abdullah sold it for a million and six hundred thousand, and thereafter announced that whoever had a claim against Hazrat Zubair (R.A.A.) should come forward and meet him in Ghabah. Hazrat Abdullah Bin Jafar came to him and said: Hazrat Zubair owed me four hundred thousand, but I would release the debt if you wish. Abdullah said: 'No I do not want to get it written off.' Hazrat Ibn Jafar said: Then if you would like sometime, I am prepared to delay the recovery. Abdullah said: 'No. I do not want even this. Hazrat Ibn Jafar then said: As such demarcate a piece of land for me. Abdullah accordingly marked out a plot for him. In this way Abdullah paid his father, Hazrat Zubair's debt by selling his lands. After payment of his father's debt there still remained a piece of land measuring four and half sihams. After this Hazrat Abdullah visited Amir Mu'awiah, who had with him at the time Amr Ibn Usman, Munzir Ibn Zubair and Ibn Zamah. Amir Mu'awiah asked Hazrat Abdullah (R.A.A.) as to what price he had fixed for the land in Ghabah? He replied one hundred thousand for a sahm (or part). Amir Mu'awiah enquired as to how much land was still left. Hazrat Abdullah said: Four and half Sahms. Hazrat Munzir Ibn Zubair said: 'I take one Sahm for a hundred thousand.' Hazrat 'Amr Ibn Usman said: 'I would also like to take one Sahm for a hundred thousand.' Hazrat Ibn Zam'ah said: that he would also take one Sahm for a hundred thousand. Then Amir Mu'awiah asked: How much land is now left?' Hazrat Abdullah said: that One and a half Sahms was left. Amir Mu'awiah purchased this piece of land for one hundred and fifty thousand. Later, Hazrat Abdullah Bin Jafar sold his share of land to Amir Mu'awiah for six hundred thousand.

(Narrators further report that this piece of 'and which Hazrat Abdullah Ibn Jafar had taken from Hazrat Abdullah Ibn Zubair in lieu of his dues outstanding against late Hazrat Zubair sold to Amir Mu'awiah for six hundred thousand thereby earning a profit of two hundred thousand). When Hazrat Abdullah Bin Zubair had completed the settlement of the whole affair, the heirs of Hazrat Zubair (R.A.A.) asked him to distribute the remaining inheritance among them. But Hazrat Abdullah Bin Zubair said, By Allah I will not distribute the inheritance till after I had announced during four successive *Hajj* (Pilgrimage) seasons calling upon persons who might have claim against Hazrat Zubair to come forward and get their dues if any. Accordingly he made this announcement during four seasons and then distributed the remaining inheritance among the heirs of Hazrat Zubair (R.A.A.) according to his directions. Hazrat Zubair had four wives: each of them received a million and two hundred thousand. Thus Hazrat Zubair's total estate amounted to fifty million and two hundred thousands Dirhams. (*Bukhari*).

Note: The discharge of trust is the chief point in business transactions. The object is to make a person fully conscious of his obligations as regards honesty and fair play. One should pay the dues of other persons pie to pie. This is called in Arabic *Amanat* or Trust.

Allah, the Almighty, has called the worldly affairs entrusted by Him to the human beings as "*Amanat*" or "trust". This means that the entire world system has been entrusted to us by Allah as a trust. We are, therefore, required to discharge our responsibilities to our Lord (Allah) honesty and judiciously, failing which we will be treated as untrustworthy.

* * * * * * * * * *

CHAPTER 26

Prohibition of Cruelty and Injustice and Their Eradication.

قال الله تعالى: مَا لِلظَّالِمِينَ مِنْ حَمِيمٍ وَلَا شَفِيعٍ يُطَاعُ [غافر: ١٨]

وقال تعالى: وَمَا لِلظَّالِمِينَ مِن نَّصِيرٍ [الحج: ٧١].

Allah, the Exalted has said:

99. (When) there will be no friend for the wrong doers, nor any intercessor who will be heard (40:18)

100. For evil-doers there is no helper (22:71)

٢٠٣ ــ وعن جابرٍ رضي الله عنه أن رسول الله صلى الله عليه وسلم قال : « اتَّقُوا الظُّلْمَ ، فَإِنَّ الظُّلْمَ ظُلُمَاتٌ يَوْمَ الْقِيَامَةِ ، واتَّقُوا الشُّحَّ فَإِنَّ الشُّحَّ أَهْلَكَ مَنْ كَانَ قَبْلَكُمْ ، حَمَلَهُمْ عَلَى أَنْ سَفَكُوا دِمَاءَهُم وَاسْتَحَلُّوا مَحَارِمَهُمْ » رواه مسلم

203. Hazrat Jabir Bin Abdullah (R.A.A.) relates that the Holy Prophet (S.A.W.) said: Avoid cruelty and injustice for, on the Day of Judgement, the same will turn into several darknesses; and guard yourselves against miserliness; for this has ruined nations who lived before you. Miserliness led them to bloodshed and to treat unlawful as lawful. (*Muslim*)

٢٠٤ ــ وعن أبي هريرة رضي الله عنه أن رسول الله صلى الله عليه وسلم قال : « لَتُؤَدُّنَّ الْحُقُوقَ إِلَى أَهْلِهَا يَوْمَ الْقِيَامَةِ حَتَّى يُقَادَ لِلشَّاةِ الْجَلْحَاءِ مِنَ الشَّاةِ الْقَرْنَاءِ » رواه مسلم

204. Hazrat Abu Hurairah (R.A.A.) relates that the Holy Prophet (S.A.W.) said: Allah will definitely enforce the settlement of all the dues to those entitled to receive them on the Day of Judgement; even the wrong done to a hornless goat by a horned goat, will be redressed. (*Muslim*)

٢٠٥ ــ وعن ابن عمر رضي الله عنهما قال : كُنَّا نَتَحَدَّثُ عَنْ حَجَّةِ الْوَدَاعِ ، وَالنَّبِيُّ صلى الله عليه وسلم بَيْنَ أَظْهُرِنَا ، وَلا نَدْرِي مَا حَجَّةُ الْوَدَاعِ ، حَتَّى حَمِدَ اللهَ رسول الله صلى الله عليه وسلم ، وَأَثْنَى عَلَيْهِ ، ثُمَّ ذَكَرَ الْمَسِيحَ الدَّجَّالَ فَأَطْنَبَ فِي ذِكْرِهِ ، وَقَالَ : « مَا بَعَثَ اللهُ مِنْ نَبِيٍّ إِلاَّ أَنْذَرَهُ أُمَّتَهُ : أَنْذَرَهُ نُوحٌ وَالنَّبِيُّونَ مِنْ بَعْدِهِ ، وَإِنَّهُ إِنْ يَخْرُجْ فِيكُمْ فَمَا خَفِيَ عَلَيْكُمْ مِنْ شَأْنِهِ فَلَيْسَ يَخْفَى عَلَيْكُمْ : إِنَّ رَبَّكُمْ لَيْسَ بِأَعْوَرَ ، وَإِنَّهُ أَعْوَرُ عَيْنِ الْيُمْنَى ، كَأَنَّ عَيْنَهُ عِنَبَةٌ طَافِيَةٌ . ألا إِنَّ اللهَ حَرَّمَ عَلَيْكُمْ دِمَاءَكُمْ وَأَمْوَالَكُمْ ، كَحُرْمَةِ يَوْمِكُمْ هَذَا ، فِي بلدكُمْ هذا ، فِي شَهْرِكُمْ هذا ، ألاهَلْ بَلَّغْتُ ؟ » قَالُوا : نَعَمْ ، قال :

«اللّهُمَّ اشْهَدْ–ثلاثاً–وَيْلَكُمْ ، أوْ:وَيْحَكُمْ ، انْظُرُوا : لاتَرْجِعُوا بَعْدِي كُفَّاراً يَضْرِبُ بَعْضُكُمْ رِقَابَ بَعْضٍ » رواه البخاري ، وروى مسلم بعضه

205. Hazrat Ibn 'Umar (R.A.A.) relates: One day, in a gathering in which the Holy Prophet (S.A.W.) was also present, we were discussing about the Last Pilgrimage, not knowing what it meant, till the Holy Prophet (S.A.W.) recited Allah's praise and dwelt at length about the role of Maseeh-ad-Dajjal (Roaming Devil) and said: All Prophets sent by Allah have been warning their followers against (the wickedness) of him, later Prophet Noah did warn his people and so did all the Prophets who came after him. If he will rise amongst you, his condition will not remain hidden to you. You know it well your Lord is not one-eyed while the Dajjal's right eye is defective. His eye is deformed and looks like a swollen grape. Beware, Allah has prohibited you from shedding each other's blood, ransacking belongings; these are sacrosanct like the sanctity of this (sacred) day of this sacred month in this sacred place. Be on guard! Have I not conveyed (and taught all the divine commands to you). The Companions submitted: 'Yes'. The Holy Prophet (S.A.W.) said: 'O Allah Be my witness' and repeated these words thrice and concluded by saying: 'Understand it well that you should not turn an unbeliever when I am no more (among you) and start killing and shedding blood among yourselves (*Bukhari and Muslim* has also mentioned some parts).

٢٠٦ – وعن عائشة رضي الله عنها أن رسول الله صلى الله عليه وسلم قال : « مَنْ ظَلَمَ قِيدَ شِبْرٍ مِنَ الأَرْضِ طُوِّقَهُ مِنْ سَبْعِ أَرَضِينَ » متفقٌ عليه

206. Hazrat Ayesha (R.A.A.) relates that the Holy Prophet (S.A.W.) said, 'One who usurped the smallest piece of land, be punished by Allah by having seven earths suspended around his neck.'

(*Bukhari and Muslim*)

٢٠٧ – وعن أبي موسى رضي الله عنه قال : قال رسول الله صلى الله عليه وسلم : « إنَّ اللهَ لَيُمْلِي لِلظَّالِمِ فَإذَا أخَذَهُ لَمْ يُفْلِتْهُ » ثُمَّ قَرَأَ : (وَكَذَلِكَ أخْذُ رَبِّكَ إذَا أخَذَ القُرَى وَهِيَ ظَالِمَةٌ إنَّ أخْذَهُ أَلِيمٌ شَدِيدٌ) [هود : ١٠٢] متفق عليه

207. Hazrat Abu Musa Ash'ari (R.A.A.) relates that the Holy Prophet (S.A.W.) said: Allah postpones taking any action against a tyrant (so that the cup of his sins may get full), and thereafter when he takes him to task, he does not let him escape. Then he read this Quranic verse:

Even thus is the grasp of thy Lord when He graspeth the

townships (or communities) while they are doing wrong. Lo! His grasp is painful, very strong, (11:102) (*Bukhari and Muslim*)

٢٠٨ – وعن مُعَاذٍ رضي الله عنه قال : بَعَثَنِي رسول الله صلى الله عليه وسلم فقال : « إنَّكَ تَأْتِي قَوْماً مِنْ أَهْلِ الْكِتَابِ ، فادْعُهُمْ إلَى شَهَادَةِ أَنْ لا إلَهَ إلاَّ الله ، وَأَنِّي رسول الله ، فَإِنْ هُمْ أَطَاعُوا لِذَلِكَ ، فَأَعْلِمْهُمْ أَنَّ الله قَدِ افْتَرَضَ عَلَيْهِم خَمْسَ صَلَوَاتٍ في كُلِّ يَوْمٍ وَلَيْلَةٍ ، فَإِنْ هُمْ أَطَاعُوا لِذلكَ ، فَأَعْلِمْهُمْ أَنَّ الله قَدِ افْتَرَضَ عَلَيْهِمْ صَدَقَةً تُؤْخَذُ مِنْ أَغْنِيَائِهِمْ فَتُرَدُّ عَلَى فُقَرَائِهِمْ ، فَإِنْ هُمْ أَطَاعُوا لِذلكَ ، فَإِيَّاكَ وَكَرَائِمَ أَمْوَالِهِمْ . وَاتَّقِ دَعْوَةَ الْمَظْلُومِ فَإِنَّهُ لَيْسَ بَيْنَهَا وَبَيْنَ الله حِجَابٌ » متفقٌ عليه

208. Hazrat Mu'az (R.A.A.) relates: 'The Holy Prophet (S.A.W.) nominated me as (Governor of Yemen) and said: 'Bear in mind! a group of the people of the Book (followers of the revealed religions) will come to you, therefore ask them to bear witness that there is no god save Allah, and that I am His Messenger. When they have accepted this, inform them that Allah has prescribed for them five prayers (*Salat*) in a day and night. When they accept this then tell them that Allah has made it compulsory for them *Zakat* (poor due) which will be realised from those who are wealthy among them, and will be distributed to poor persons among you. When they agree to this, do not to take their best articles as *Zakat*. Fear the call of an oppressed person, because there is no barrier between the complaint of an oppressed person and Allah! (*Bukhari and Muslim*)

٢٠٩ – وعن أبي حُمَيْدٍ عَبْدِ الرَّحْمن بن سعدٍ السَّاعِدِيِّ رضي الله عنه قال : اسْتَعْمَلَ النَّبِيُّ صلى الله عليه وسلم رَجلاً مِنَ الأَزْدِ يُقَالُ لَهُ : ابْنُ اللُّتْبِيَّةِ عَلَى الصَّدَقَةِ ، فَلَمَّا قَدِمَ قال : هذا لَكُمْ ، وهَذَا أُهْدِيَ إِلَيَّ ، فَقَامَ رسول الله صلى الله عليه وسلم عَلَى الْمِنْبَرِ ، فَحَمِدَ الله وَأَثْنَى عَلَيْهِ ، ثُمَّ قال : « أَمَّا بَعْدُ فَإِنِّي أَسْتَعْمِلُ الرَّجُلَ مِنْكُمْ عَلَى الْعَمَلِ مِمَّا وَلاَّنِي الله ، فَيَأْتِي فَيَقُولُ : هَذَا لَكُمْ ، وَهَذَا هَدِيَّةٌ أُهْدِيَتْ إِلَيَّ ، أَفَلا جَلَسَ في بيتِ أَبِيهِ أَوْ أُمِّهِ حَتَّى تَأْتِيَهُ هَدِيَّتُهُ إِنْ كَانَ صَادِقاً . والله لا يَأْخُذُ أَحَدٌ مِنْكُمْ شَيْئاً بِغَيْرِ حَقِّهِ إِلاَّ لَقِيَ الله تَعَالَى ،

يَحْمِلُهُ يَوْمَ الْقِيَامَةِ ، فَلا أعرِفَنَّ أحَداً مِنْكُمْ لَقِيَ الله يَحْمِلُ بَعِيراً لَهُ رُغاءٌ ، أوْ بَقَرَةً لَهَا خُوَار ، أوْ شَاةً تَيْعَر » ثُمَّ رَفَعَ يَدَيْهِ حَتَّى رُؤِيَ بَيَاضُ إبْطَيْهِ فقال : « اللَّهُمَّ هَلْ بَلَّغْتُ » ثلاثاً متفقٌ عليه

209. Hazrat Abu Humaid Abdur Rahman Bin Sadis Sa'di (R.A.A.) said: The Holy Prophet (S.A.W.) appointed a man belonging to Azd Tribe named Ibn-ul-Lutbiyyah as collector of *Zakat*. When he returned (to Medina) he said that so much is yours, which I have collected as *Zakat*, and so much is given to me by way of gifts. On hearing this the Holy Prophet (S.A.W.) mounted the pulpit and delivered a sermon. He first praised and glorified Allah and then said. I have deputed a person from among you to do some duty on my behalf for which I have been assigned by Allah. On the completion of his mission that man comes back and says: 'This is your property, and that has been presented to me as a gift.' If he is telling the truth then why does he not stay in the house of his father or mother, till some body comes to him and presents him gifts. By Allah, if any one of you takes anything without any rights, he will have to face Allah on the Day of Judgement, with the burden of such things. Therefore I would not like to see any one of you face Allah carrying a grunting camel, a mooing cow or a bleeding goat (laden with illegally acquired goods). Then raising his arms so high that the whiteness of his armpits could be seen he said: 'O Allah, I have conveyed Thy command and repeated it thrice.'

(*Bukhari and Muslim*)

٢١٠ – وعن أبي هُرَيْرَةَ رضي الله عنه عن النَّبيِّ صلى الله عليه وسلم قال : « مَنْ كَانَتْ عِنْدَهُ مَظْلِمَةٌ لأخِيهِ ، مِنْ عِرْضِهِ أوْ مِنْ شَيْءٍ ، فَلْيَتَحَلَّلْه مِنْه الْيَوْمَ قَبْلَ أنْ لا يَكُونَ دِينَارٌ وَلا دِرْهَمٌ ؛ إنْ كَانَ لَهُ عَمَلٌ صَالِحٌ أخِذَ مِنْهُ بِقَدْرِ مَظْلِمَتِهِ ، وَإنْ لَمْ يَكُنْ لَهُ حَسَنَاتٌ أخِذَ مِنْ سَيِّئَاتِ صَاحِبِهِ فَحُمِلَ عَلَيْهِ » رواه البخاري

210. Hazrat Abu Hurairah (R.A.A.) relates that the Holy Prophet (S.A.W.) said: 'If any Muslim has oppressed his brother concerning his honour or anything else, let him obtain his pardon today (in this world) before the time comes when he will have neither Dinars nor Dirhams (i.e. he will be penniless). If the agressor may have some good deeds (in his account) the same would be deducted in equal proportion to his wrongs, if the aggressor will have no good deeds in his account, the wrongs of the aggrieved would be added to the account of the aggressor in equal proportion.' (*Bukhari*)

٢١١ – وعن عبد الله بن عَمْرو بن الْعَاص رضي الله عنهما عن النَّبيِّ صلى الله عليه وسلم قال : « الْمُسْلِمُ مَنْ سَلِمَ الْمُسْلِمُونَ مِنْ لِسَانِهِ وَيَدِهِ ، وَالْمُهَاجِرُ مَنْ هَجَرَ مَا نَهَى اللهُ عَنْهُ » متفقٌ عليه

211. **Hazrat Abdullah Ibn 'Amr Ibn Al'Aas** relates that the Holy Prophet (S.A.W.) said: 'A Muslim is a person who does not harm another Muslim with his tongue or hands and an emigrant, is one who leaves that which Allah has forbidden.' (*Bukhari and Muslim*)

٢١٢ – وعنه رضي الله عنه قال : كَانَ عَلَى ثَقَلِ النَّبيِّ صلى الله عليه وسلم رَجُلٌ يُقَالُ لَهُ كِرْكِرَةُ ، فَمَاتَ ، فقال رسول الله صلى الله عليه وسلم : « هُوَ فِي النَّارِ » فَذَهَبُوا يَنْظُرُونَ إِلَيْهِ فَوَجَدُوا عَبَاءَةً قَدْ غَلَّهَا رواه البخاري

212. The above mentioned companion narrated: A man named Kirkira who was in charge of the personal effects of the Holy Prophet (S.A.W.) died, and the Holy Proplet (S.A.W.) said: 'He is suffering the Hell.' The companions of the Holy Prophet (S.A.W.) went to the house of the deceased, to ascertain the cause and found therein a cloak that he had misappropriated. (*Bukhari*)

٢١٣ – وعن أبي بَكْرَةَ نُفَيْعِ بنِ الحارثِ رضيَ الله عنهُ عنِ النبي صلى الله عليه وسلم قال : « إنَّ الزَّمَانَ قَدِ اسْتَدَارَ كَهَيْئَتِهِ يَوْمَ خَلَقَ اللهُ السَّمٰوَاتِ وَالأَرْضَ : السَّنَةُ اثْنَا عَشَرَ شَهْراً ، مِنْهَا أَرْبَعَةٌ حُرُمٌ : ثَلاثٌ مُتَوَالِيَاتٌ : ذُو الْقَعْدَة ، وَذُو الْحِجَّةِ ، وَالْمُحَرَّم ، وَرَجَبُ مُضَرَ الَّذي بَيْنَ جُمَادَى وَشَعْبَانَ ، أيُّ شَهْرٍ هَذَا ؟ » قُلْنَا : اللهُ وَرَسُولُهُ أَعْلَمُ ، فَسَكَتَ حَتَّى ظَنَنَّا أَنَّهُ سَيُسَمِّيهِ بِغَيْرِ اسْمِهِ ، قال : أَلَيْسَ ذَا الْحِجَّةِ ؟ قُلْنَا : بَلَى . قال : « فَأَيُّ بَلَدٍ هَذَا ؟ » قُلْنَا : اللهُ وَرَسُولُهُ أَعْلَمُ ، فَسَكَتَ حَتَّى ظَنَنَّا أَنَّهُ سَيُسَمِّيهِ بِغَيْرِ اسْمِهِ . قال : « أَلَيْسَ الْبَلْدَةَ ؟ » قُلْنَا : بَلَى . قال : « فَأَيُّ يَوْمٍ هَذَا ؟ » قُلْنَا : اللهُ وَرَسُولُهُ أَعْلَمُ . فَسَكَتَ حَتَّى ظَنَنَّا أنه سَيُسَمِّيهِ بِغَيْرِ اسمِهِ . قال : « أَلَيْسَ يَوْمَ النَّحْرِ ؟ » قُلْنَا : بَلَى . قال : « فَإِنَّ دِمَاءَكُمْ وَأَمْوَالَكُمْ وَأَعْرَاضَكُمْ عَلَيْكُمْ حَرَامٌ ، كَحُرْمَةِ يَوْمِكُمْ هَذَا فِي بَلَدِكُمْ هَذَا

فِي شَهْرِكُم هَذَا ، وَسَتَلْقَوْنَ رَبَّكُمْ فَيَسْأَلُكُمْ عَنْ أَعْمَالِكُمْ ، أَلا فَلا تَرْجِعُوا بَعْدِي كُفَّاراً يَضْرِبُ بَعْضُكُمْ رِقَابَ بَعْضٍ ، أَلا لِيُبَلِّغِ الشَّاهِدُ الْغَائِبَ ، فَلَعَلَّ بَعْضَ مَنْ يَبْلُغُهُ أَنْ يَكُونَ أَوْعَى لَهُ مِن بَعْضِ مَنْ سَمِعَهُ » ثُمَّ قَالَ: « أَلا هَلْ بَلَّغْتُ، أَلا هَلْ بَلَّغْتُ ؟ » قُلْنَا : نَعَمْ . قَالَ : « اللَّهُمَّ اشْهَدْ » مُتَّفَقٌ عَلَيه

213. Hazrat Abu Bakr Nufai' Ibn Haris relates that the Holy Prophet (S.A.W.) said: Time is running in the same manner as it was on the day, Allah fashioned the universe. A year comprises of twelve months, four of which are sacred three in succession i.e. *Zul Qa'ad, Zul Hajj* and *Muharram*, and *Rajab* the most sacred month of Muzar Tribe which falls between *Jamadi* and *Sha'aban.* The Holy Prophet then asked 'Which month is this?' We submitted: 'Allah and His Messenger know better.' Hearing this he kept quiet for a while, and we thought he was going to give a new name to this month. Then he said: 'It is not *Zul Hajj?*' We said: 'Yes, it is! Then he asked: 'What is the name of this city? We said: 'Allah and His Prophet know better'. He paused a while and we thought he would give it a new name. Then he said: 'Is it not the sacred city?' We submitted: 'Of course, it is.' Then he asked: 'Which day is this?' We said: 'Allah and His Messenger know better.' He again paused a while and we thought he would give it a new name. Then be said: Your blood, your belongings and your honour are sacred to each other, as sacred as this day, this city and this month. The day is not far off when you will face Allah and He will call upon you to account for your actions in this world. Therefore, beware and do not turn as disbelievers, when I am no more, by killing each other. Let all those who are present here should convey this message to those who are absent. Because some of those who receive this message indirectly my remember it better than those who hear it directly. Then he asked twice: have I communicated to you (Allah's command)?' We said: 'Yes Sir,'. He then submitted: 'O Allah, be Thou witness.'

(*Bukhari and Muslim*)

٢١٤ – وعن أبي أُمَامَةَ إِيَاسِ بن ثَعْلَبَةَ الْحَارِثِيِّ رضي الله عنه أن رسول الله صلى الله عليه وسلم قال : « مَنِ اقْتَطَعَ حَقَّ امْرِىءٍ مُسْلِمٍ بِيَمِينِهِ فَقَدْ أَوْجَبَ اللهُ لَهُ النَّارَ ، وَحَرَّمَ عَلَيْهِ الْجَنَّةَ » فقال رَجُلٌ : وَإِنْ كَانَ شَيْئاً يَسِيراً يا رسولَ اللهِ ؟ فقال : « وَإِنْ قَضِيباً مِنْ أَرَاكٍ » رواه مسلم

214. Hazrat Abu Umamah Iyas Ibn Sa'albah Harisi relates that the Holy Prophet (S.A.W.) said: Allah has decreed the Fire of Hell for a

person who usurps the property of a Muslim through false oath and debarred him from Paradise. A companion asked: O Messenger of Allah! even if it may be the twing of a bush.' (*Muslim*)

٢١٥ – وعن عَدِي بن عُمَيْرَةَ رضي الله عنه قال : سَمِعْتُ رسول الله صلى الله عليه وسلم يَقُول : « مَنِ اسْتَعْمَلْنَاهُ مِنْكُمْ عَلَى عَمَلٍ فَكَتَمَنَا مِخْيَطاً فَمَا فَوْقَهُ ، كَانَ غُلُولاً يَأْتِي بِهِ يَوْمَ الْقِيَامَةِ » فَقَامَ إِلَيْهِ رَجُلٌ أَسْوَدُ مِنَ الأَنْصَارِ ، كَأَنِّي أَنْظُرُ إِلَيْهِ ، فقال : يارسول الله اقْبَلْ عَنِّي عَمَلَكَ ، قال : « وَمَا لَكَ ؟ » قال : سَمِعْتُكَ تَقُولُ كَذَا وَكَذَا ، قال : « وَأَنَا أَقُولُهُ الآنَ : مَنِ اسْتَعْمَلْنَاهُ عَلَى عَمَلٍ فَلْيَجِيءْ بِقَلِيلِهِ وَكَثِيرِهِ ، فَمَا أُوتِيَ مِنْهُ أَخَذَ ، وَمَا نُهِيَ عَنْهُ انْتَهَى » رواه مسلم

215. Hazrat Adiyy Ibn Umairah (R.A.A.) relates that he heard the Holy Prophet (S.A.W.) say: 'When I nominate a person from amongst you on some job, and if that person hides even a needle or anything lesser than that from me, then this act will amount to misappropriation; and he will have to produce such thing on the Day of Judgement. On this a black-skinned Ansar stood up before the Holy Prophet (S.A.W), as if I am seeing him, and who said: 'O Messenger of Allah, please relieve me from the assignment given to me.' The Holy Prophet (S.A.W.) asked the said man as to what was the matter. The man said: 'I have just heard you saying this thing.' The Holy Prophet (S.A.W.) said: 'I once more say this that the person whom I appoint to any (public) office must render account of his charge in full whether by or small. What he has been allowed to receive, many and from what he has been restrained, he must avoid. (*Muslim*)

٢١٦ – وعن عمر بن الخطاب رضي الله عنه قال : لَمَّا كَانَ يَوْمُ خَيْبَرَ أَقْبَلَ نَفَرٌ مِنْ أَصْحَابِ النَّبِيِّ صلى الله عليه وسلم فَقَالُوا : فُلانٌ شَهِيدٌ ، وفُلانٌ شَهِيدٌ ، حَتَّى مَرُّوا عَلَى رَجُلٍ فقالوا : فُلانٌ شَهِيدٌ . فقال النَّبِيُّ صلى الله عليه وسلم : « كَلاَّ إِنِّي رَأَيْتُهُ فِي النَّارِ فِي بُرْدَةٍ غَلَّهَا – أَوْ عَبَاءَةٍ – » رواه مسلم

216. Hazrat 'Umar Ibn Khattab (R.A.A.) relates that on the day when the battle of Khaibar was being fought a party of the companions of the Holy Prophet (S.A.W.) came and started naming one by one persons who fell in the engagement and became a martyr. Soon they passed by a person (dead) and exclaimed that he too was a martyr.

The Holy Prophet (S.A.W.) thereupon said: Certainly not. I have just seen him in the Fire of Hell, in a sheet or cloak which he had misappropriated (*Muslim*)

٢١٧ – وعن أبي قَتَادَةَ الْحارث بن رِبْعِيٍّ رضي الله عنه عن رسول الله صلى الله عليه وسلم أَنَّهُ قَامَ فِيهِمْ ، فَذَكَرَ لَهُمْ أَنَّ الْجِهَادَ في سَبِيلِ الله، وَالإِيمَانَ بِاللهِ أَفْضَلُ الأَعْمَالِ ، فَقَامَ رَجُلٌ فقال : يارسول الله أَرَأَيْتَ إِنْ قُتِلْتُ في سَبِيلِ الله ، تُكَفَّرُ عَنِّي خَطَايَايَ ؟ فَقَالَ لَهُ رسول الله صلى الله عليه وسلم : « نَعَمْ إِنْ قُتِلْتَ في سَبِيلِ الله وَأَنْتَ صَابِرٌ مُحْتَسِبٌ، مُقْبِلٌ غَيْرُ مُدْبِرٍ » ثُمَّ قال رسول الله صلى الله عليه وسلم : « كَيْفَ قُلْتَ؟»

قال : أَرَأَيْتَ إِنْ قُتِلْتُ في سَبِيلِ الله ، أَتُكَفَّرُ عَنِّي خَطَايَايَ ؟ فقال رسول الله صلى الله عليه وسلم : « نَعَمْ وَأَنْتَ صَابِرٌ مُحْتَسِبٌ ، مُقْبِلٌ غَيْرُ مُدْبِرٍ . إِلاَّ الدَّيْنَ فَإِنَّ جِبْرِيلَ قَالَ لِي ذَلِكَ » رواه مسلم

217. Hazrat Abu Qatadah Haris Bin Ribi relates that the Holy Prophet (S.A.W.) stood up to deliver a sermon to his companions, and said that faith in Allah and *Jihad* in His cause, were the highest type of virtuous deeds. From among the audience a man stood up and said: 'O Messenger of Allah: Do you think that if I were killed fighting in the cause of Allah, will my sins be atoned. He answered: 'Yes, if you were to be killed in the cause of Allah and you be patient, self scrutinising continue marching forward and not fleeing back. Then, the Holy Prophet (S.A.W,) asked him to repeat what he said: The man repeated: Do you think that if I were to be killed while fighting in the cause of Allah, would all my sins be remitted?' He answered 'Yes, if you are killed while you are steadfast and patient self scrutinising, marching forth and not turning away and fleeing. However, your debts will not be remitted. Angel Gabriel has just informed me of this. (*Muslim*)

٢١٨ – وعن أبي هريرة رضي الله عنه ، أن رسول الله صلى الله عليه وسلم قال: « أَتَدْرُونَ مَا الْمُفْلِسُ ؟ » قَالُوا : الْمُفْلِسُ فِينَا مَنْ لا دِرْهَمَ لَهُ وَلا مَتَاعَ فقال : « إِنَّ الْمُفْلِسَ مِنْ أُمَّتِي مَنْ يَأْتِي يَوْمَ الْقِيَامَةِ بِصَلاةٍ وَصِيَامٍ وَزَكَاةٍ . وَيَأْتِي قَدْ شَتَمَ هذَا ، وَقَذَفَ هذَا وَأَكَلَ مَالَ هذَا . وَسَفَكَ دَمَ هذَا ، وَضَرَبَ هذَا ، فَيُعْطَى هذَا مِنْ

حَسَنَاتِهِ . وَهذَا مِنْ حَسَنَاتِهِ . فَإِنْ فَنِيَتْ حَسَنَاتُهُ قَبْلَ أَنْ يَقْضِي مَاعَلَيْهِ . أُخِذَ مِنْ خَطَايَاهُمْ فَطُرِحَتْ عَلَيْهِ ، ثُمَّ طُرِحَ فِي النَّارِ

رواه مسلم

218. Hazrat Abu Hurairah (R.A.A.) relates that the Holy Prophet (S.A.W.) once asked his companions: Do you know who is a pauper. The companions replied that a pauper is a person who had no money or property. The Holy Prophet (S.A.W.) elucidated the point said: 'a pauper from among my followers (*Ummah*) is one who will come on the Day of Judgement with a good record of *Salat* (prayers) and *Saum* (fasting) and *Zakat* (payment of poor due) but also he had abused somebody; Slandered against someone; unsurped the goods of another person, had killed someone or beaten yet another person. Then all the oppressed persons will receive a part of the aggressors' good deeds. Should they fall short of his aggression, then the aggrieved person's sins and defaults, will be transferred from them to him, and he will be thrown into the Fire (Hell)*'* (*Muslim*)

٢١٩ – وعن أُمِّ سَلَمَةَ رضي الله عنها ، أن رسول الله صلى الله عليه وسلم قال : « إِنَّمَا أَنَا بَشَرٌ ، وَإِنَّكُمْ تَخْتَصِمُونَ إِلَيَّ ، وَلَعَلَّ بَعْضَكُمْ أَنْ يَكُونَ أَلْحَنَ بِحُجَّتِهِ مِنْ بَعْضٍ ، فَأَقْضِيَ لَهُ بِنَحْوِ مَا أَسْمَعُ ، فَمَنْ قَضَيْتُ لَهُ بِحَقِّ أَخِيهِ فَإِنَّمَا أَقْطَعُ لَهُ قِطْعَةً مِنَ النَّارِ » متفقٌ عليه

219. Hazrat Umme Salamah (R.A.A.) relates that the Holy Prophet (S.A.W.) said: 'I am after all a human being. Your disputes come to me for decision. It is just possible that one party might be well versed in the art of argumentation and be adept in presenting his case. Accordingly I decide the case in his favour. But if I decide in favour of a person not entitled to the thing, I do not allow him but a price of fire (i.e. the person receiving it will go to Hell)*'* (*Bukhari and Muslim*)

٢٢٠ – وعن ابن عمر رضي الله عنهما قال : قال رسول الله صلى الله عليه وسلم. « لَنْ يَزَالَ الْمُؤْمِنُ فِي فُسْحَةٍ مِنْ دِينِهِ مَالَمْ يُصِبْ دَمَاً حَرَاماً »

رواه البخاري .

220. Hazrat Ibn Umar (R.A.A.) relates that the Holy Prophet (S.A.W.) said: A Muslim remains enjoying the safety and protection of his faith, so long as he does not commit an unlawful murder. (*Bukhari*)

٢٢١ – وعن خَوْلَةَ بِنْتِ عَامِرٍ الأَنْصَارِيَّةِ ، وَهِيَ امْرَأَةُ حَمْزَةَ رضي الله عنه وعنها ، قالت : سَمِعْتُ رسول الله صلى الله عليه وسلم يَقُولُ : « إِنَّ

رِجَالاً يَتَخَوَّضُونَ فِي مَالِ اللهِ بِغَيْرِ حَقٍّ ، فَلَهُمُ النَّارُ يَوْمَ الْقِيَامَةِ »

رواه البخاري

221. Hazrat Khaula Bint Amir Al-Ansariya (the wife of Hazrat Hamza, the uncle of the Holy Prophet (S.A.W.) relates that she heard the Holy Prophet (S.A.W.) say: Many people misappropriate Allah's property, (such as *Bait-ul-Mal* or public treasury), Such people are destined for the fire of Hell on the Day of Judgement. (*Bukhari*)

Note: The word tyranny or injustice (*Zulm*) is a widely used word. It is also extensively used to denote paganism, profanity and irreligiousness; Polytheism or belief in plurality of God, and Sin. But in the above chapter it is used for the oppression or highhandedness of a person over another. If this tendency is not checked it will destroy the peace and tranquility of the whole country and the nation. The first step to check it, is to recognise the rights of the aggrieved person or persons to avenge the wrong done to him or them, so that the people, keeping in view the consequences of this Social evil, may desist from oppressing each other.

* * * * * * * * * * *

CHAPTER 27

Respecting the Dignity of Muslims, Their Rights and Compassion for Them.

قال الله تعالى : وَمَنْ يُعَظِّمْ حُرُمَاتِ اللهِ فَهُوَ خَيْرٌ لَهُ عِنْدَ رَبِّهِ

[الحج : ٣٠] وقال تعالى : وَمَنْ يُعَظِّمْ شَعَائِرَ اللهِ فَإِنَّهَا مِنْ تَقْوَى

الْقُلُوبِ [الحج : ٣٢] وقال تعالى : وَاخْفِضْ جَنَاحَكَ لِلْمُؤْمِنِينَ

[الحجر : ٨٨] وقال تعالى : مَنْ قَتَلَ نَفْساً بِغَيْرِ نَفْسٍ أَوْ فَسَادٍ فِي

الأَرْضِ فَكَأَنَّمَا قَتَلَ النَّاسَ جَمِيعاً ، وَمَنْ أَحْيَاهَا فَكَأَنَّمَا أَحْيَا النَّاسَ

جَمِيعاً [المائدة : ٣٢]

Allah, the Exalted has said:

101. That (is the command). And whoso magnifieth the sacred things of Allah, it will be well for him in the sight of his Lord. (22:30)

102. That (is the command). And whoso magnifieth the offerings consecrated to Allah, it surely is from devotion of the hearts. (22:32)

103. And lower thy wing (in tenderness) for the believers (15:88)
104. For that cause We decreed for the children of Israel that whosoever killeth a human being for other than man slaughter or corruption in the earth, it shall be as if he had killed all mankind, and whoso saveth the life of one, it shall be as if he had saved the life of all mankind. (5:32)

٢٢٢ – وعن أبي موسى رضي الله عنه قال : قال رسول الله صلى الله عليه وسلم : « الْمُؤْمِنُ لِلْمُؤْمِنِ كَالْبُنْيَانِ يَشُدُّ بَعْضُهُ بَعْضاً » وَشَبَّكَ بَيْنَ أَصَابِعِهِ . متفقٌ عليه

222. Hazrat Abu Musa Ash'ari (R.A.A.) relates that the Holy Prophet (S.A.W.) said: The bonds of brotherhood between two Muslims are like parts of a house, one part strengthens and holds the other. He crossed the fingers of one hand between those of the other, to elucidate and illustrate the point *(Bukhari and Muslim)*

٢٢٣ – وعنه قال : قال رسول الله صلى الله عليه وسلم : « مَنْ مَرَّ في شَيْءٍ مِنْ مَسَاجِدِنَا ، أَوْ أَسْوَاقِنَا ، وَمَعَهُ نَبْلٌ فَلْيُمْسِكْ ، أَوْ لِيَقْبِضْ عَلَى نِصَالِهَا بِكَفِّهِ أَنْ يُصِيبَ أَحَداً مِنَ الْمُسْلِمِينَ مِنْهَا بِشَيْءٍ » متفقٌ عليه

223. Hazrat Abu Musa Ash'ari (R.A.A.) relates that the Holy Prophet (S.A.W.) said: 'A person who passes through our mosques or streets carrying something, and may have an arrow with him, he should be stopped or asked to cover its pointed end with his hand so that it may not hurt a Muslim.' *(Bukhari and Muslim)*

٢٢٤ – وعن النُّعْمَانِ بْنِ بَشِيرٍ رضي الله عنهما قال : قال رسول الله صلى الله عليه وسلم : « مَثَلُ الْمُؤْمِنِينَ في تَوَادِّهِمْ وَتَرَاحُمِهِمْ وَتَعَاطُفِهِمْ ، مَثَلُ الْجَسَدِ إِذَا اشْتَكَى مِنْهُ عُضْوٌ تَدَاعَى لَهُ سَائِرُ الْجَسَدِ بِالسَّهَرِ وَالْحُمَّى » متفقٌ عليه

224. Hazrat N'uman Ibn Bashir (R.A.A.) relates that the Holy Prophet (S.A.W.) said: The Muslims in their mutual love, kindness and compassion, are like the human body where when one of its parts is in agony the entire body feels the pain both in sleeplessness and fever. *(Bukhari and Muslim)*

٢٢٥ – وعن أبي هُرَيْرَةَ رضي الله عنه قال : قَبَّلَ النَّبِيُّ صلى الله عليه وسلم الْحَسَنَ بْنَ عَلِيٍّ رضي الله عنهما ، وَعِنْدَهُ الأَقْرَعُ بْنُ حَابِسٍ ،

فقال الأَقْرَعُ : إنَّ لِي عَشَرَةً مِنَ الوَلَدِ مَا قَبَّلْتُ مِنهُمْ أَحَداً . فَنَظَرَ إِلَيْهِ رسولُ الله صلى الله عليه وسلم فقال : « مَنْ لا يَرْحَمْ لا يُرْحَمْ » متفقٌ عليه

225. **Hazrat Abu Hurairah** (R.A.A.) relates that once the Holy Prophet (S.A.W.) kissed his grandson Hazrat Hasan Ibn Ali. Hazrat Aqr'a Ibn Habis (R.A.A.), who was sitting with him, saw this, and remarked: I have ten sons and have never kissed any of them. The Prophet (S.A.W.) looked at him and said: 'One who has no compassion for others is not entitled for compassion (from Allah).'

(*Bukhari and Muslim*)

٢٢٦ – وعن عائشةَ رضي الله عنها قالت : قَدِمَ نَاسٌ مِنَ الأَعْرَابِ عَلَى رسول الله صلى الله عليه وسلم ، فقالوا : أَتُقَبِّلُونَ صِبْيَانَكُمْ ؟ فقال : « نَعَمْ » قالوا : لَكِنَّا والله مَا نُقَبِّلُ ! فقال رسول الله صلى الله عليه وسلم : « أوَ أَمْلِكُ إنْ كَانَ اللهُ نَزَعَ مِنْ قُلُوبِكُمُ الرَّحْمَةَ ! » متفقٌ عليه

226. **Hazrat Ayeshah** (R.A.A.) relates that some Arabs from villages came to the Holy Prophet (S.A.W.) and asked him as to whether he kisses his children. He (S.A.W.) answered: 'Yes'. They said: But we never kiss them. 'He said: How can I be held responsible if Allah has deprived you of love and affection.' (*Bukhari and Muslim*)

٢٢٧ – وعن جرير بن عبد الله رضي الله عنه قال : قال رسول الله صلى الله عليه وسلم : « مَنْ لا يَرْحَمْ النَّاسَ لا يَرْحَمْهُ اللهُ » متفقٌ عليه

227. **Hazrat Jarir Ibn Abdullah** (R.A.A.) relates that the Holy Prophet (S.A.W.) said: 'Allah the Dignified has no mercy for one who has no mercy for others.' (*Bukhari and Muslim*)

٢٢٨ – وعن أبي هُريرة رضي الله عنه ، أنَّ رسول الله صلى الله عليه وسلم قال : « إذا صلى أَحَدُكُمْ للنَّاسِ فَلْيُخَفِّفْ ، فَإِنَّ فِيهِمُ الضَّعِيفَ وَالسَّقِيمَ وَالكَبِيرَ . وَإِذَا صَلَّى أَحَدُكُمْ لِنَفْسِهِ فَلْيُطَوِّلْ مَا شَاءَ » متفقٌ عليه

وفي رواية : « وَذَا الحَاجَةِ » .

228. **Hazrat Abu Hurairah** (R.A.A.) relates that the Holy Prophet (S.A.W.) said: 'When any one of you may have an occasion to lead the people in prayer, he should make it short (i.e. he should not recite long sural), for among those praying behind him may be some who are weak, ill or old. However, when praying alone you can recite as long as you like.'

(*Bukhari and Muslim*)

According to another version among the congregation may also be some persons who may have to attend some other jobs.

٢٢٩ – وعن عَائشَةَ رضي الله عنها قَالَتْ : إنْ كَانَ رسول الله صلى الله عليه وسلم لَيَدَعُ الْعَمَلَ ، وَهُوَ يُحِبُّ أَنْ يَعْمَلَ بِهِ ، خَشْيَةَ أَنْ يَعْمَلَ بِهِ النَّاسُ فَيُفْرَضَ عَلَيْهِمْ » متفقٌ عليه

229. Hazrat Ayesha (R.A.A.) relates that the Holy Prophet (S.A.W.) sometimes used to avoid doing something, although he liked to do the same, fearing that his followers might start doing it and it might become obligatory for them. (*Bukhari and Muslim*)

٢٣٠ – وَعَنْهَا رضي الله عنها قَالَتْ : نَهَاهُمُ النَّبِيُّ صلى الله عليه وسلم عَنِ الْوِصَالِ رَحْمَةً لَهُمْ ، فقالوا : إِنَّكَ تُوَاصِلُ ؟ قال : « إِنِّي لَسْتُ كَهَيْئَتِكُمْ ، إِنِّي أَبِيتُ يُطْعِمُنِي رَبِّي وَيَسْقِينِي » متفقٌ عليه

230. Hazrat Ayeshah (R.A.A.) relates that the Holy Prophet (S.A.W.) as a gesture of love and mercy prohibited his companions continuously fasting. They submitted: 'But, Sir, you fast continuously.' He replied: 'I am not like you. In the night my Sustainer furnishes me with food and drink.' (*Bukhari and Muslim*)

That is Allah bestows upon him the energy of a man who eats and drinks.

٢٣١ – وعن أبي قَتَادَةَ الْحَارِثِ بن رِبْعِيٍّ رضي الله عنه قال : قال رسول الله صلى الله عليه وسلم : « إِنِّي لأَقُومُ إِلَى الصَّلَاةِ ، وَأُرِيدُ أَنْ أُطَوِّلَ فِيهَا ، فَأَسْمَعَ بُكَاءَ الصَّبِيِّ ، فَأَتَجَوَّزَ فِي صَلَاتِي كَرَاهِيَةَ أَنْ أَشُقَّ عَلَى أُمِّهِ » رواه البخاري

231. Hazrat Abu Qatadah Haris Ibn Ribi (R.A.A.) relates that the Holy Prophet (S.A.W.) said: I stand up for Prayers (*Salat*) intending to prolong it. In the meantime I hear the wailings of a baby and I have to shorten my prayer, being apprehensive lest my recitation of a long verse may tell upon the baby's mother. (*Bukhari*)

٢٣٢ – وعن جُنْدُبِ بن عبد الله رضي الله عنه قال : قال رسول الله صلى الله عليه وسلم : « مَنْ صَلَّى صَلَاةَ الصُّبْحِ فَهُوَ فِي ذِمَّةِ الله فَلا يَطْلُبَنَّكُمُ الله مِنْ ذِمَّتِهِ بِشَيْءٍ ، فَإِنَّهُ مَنْ يَطْلُبْهُ مِنْ ذِمَّتِهِ بِشَيْءٍ يُدْرِكْهُ ، ثُمَّ يَكُبَّهُ عَلَى وَجْهِهِ فِي نَارِ جَهَنَّمَ » رواه مسلم

232. **Hazrat Jundub Bin Abdullah** (R.A.A.) relates that the Holy Prophet (S.A.W.) said: 'One who offers early morning prayers (*Fajr Salat*) goes under the protection of Allah. You should therefore maintain yourself in such a way, that Allah may not have to call upon you to account for; if Allah calls upon somebody to account for and he is found wanting, then he would be straight away sent to Hell.'

(*Muslim*)

٢٣٣ ــ وعن ابنِ عمر رضي الله عنهما أنَّ رسول الله صلى الله عليه وسلم قال : « المُسْلِمُ أخو المُسْلِمِ ، لا يَظْلِمُه ، ولا يُسْلِمُهُ مَنْ كَانَ في حَاجَةِ أخيهِ كَانَ اللهُ في حَاجَتِهِ ، وَمَنْ فَرَّجَ عَنْ مُسْلِمٍ كُرْبَةً فَرَّجَ اللهُ عَنْهُ بِهَا كُرْبَةً مِنْ كُرَبِ يَوْمِ القِيَامَةِ ، وَمَنْ سَتَرَ مُسْلِماً سَتَرَهُ اللهُ يَوْمَ القِيَامَةِ » متفقٌ عليه

233. **Hazrat Ibn Umar** (R.A.A.) relates that the Holy Prophet (S.A.W.) said: 'A Muslim is the brother of another Muslim; he does not harm him nor does he hand him over to his enemy. One who fulfils the need of another Muslim, Allah the Supreme, will fulfil the former's need. One who removes the difficulty of a Muslim, Allah the Almighty will remove one of his troubles on the Day of Judgement. Similarly one who covers (clothes) the faults of another Muslim, Allah the Almighty will cover the former's faults on the Day of Judgement.'

(*Bukhari and Muslim*)

٢٣٤ ــ وعن أبي هريرة رضي الله عنه قال : قال رسول اللهِ صلى الله عليه وسلم : « المُسْلِمُ أخو المُسْلِمِ لا يَخُونُه ولا يَكْذِبُهُ ولا يَخْذُلُهُ كُلُّ المُسْلِمِ عَلَى المُسْلِمِ حَرَامٌ عِرْضُهُ وَمَالُه ودَمُهُ ، التَّقْوَى هٰهُنَا . بِحَسْبِ امْرِئٍ مِنَ الشَّرِّ أنْ يَحْقِرَ أخَاهُ المسلم » رواه الترمذيُّ وقال : حديث حسن .

234. **Hazrat Abu Hurairah** (R.A.A.) relates that the Holy Prophet (S.A.W.) said: A Muslim is the brother of another Muslim. He neither betrays him nor tells him a lie, nor humiliates him. Everything belonging to a Muslim, his honour, his property and his blood, is sacrosanct to another Muslim; and the piety is here (pointing towards heart). It is fairly serious evil to consider a Muslim, 'mean'. (*Imam Tirmizi* has mentioned this tradition and called it good)

٢٣٥ ــ وعنه قال : قال رسول الله صلى الله عليه وسلم : « لا تَحَاسَدُوا وَلا تَنَاجَشُوا وَلا تَبَاغَضُوا وَلا تَدَابَرُوا وَلا يَبِعْ بَعْضُكُمْ عَلَى بَيْعِ

بَعْضٍ ، وَكُونُوا عِبَادَ اللهِ إِخْوَاناً . الْمُسْلِمُ أَخو الْمُسْلِمِ : لا يَظْلِمُهُ وَلا يَحْقِرُهُ وَلا يَخْذُلُهُ . التَّقْوَى هٰهُنَا ـ وَيُشِيرُ إِلَى صَدْرِهِ ثَلاثَ مَرَّاتٍ ـ بِحَسْبِ امْرِئٍ مِنَ الشَّرِّ أَنْ يَحْقِرَ أَخَاهُ الْمُسْلِمَ . كُلُّ الْمُسْلِمِ عَلَى الْمُسْلِمِ حَرَامٌ دَمُهُ وَمَالُهُ وَعِرْضُه » رواه مسلم .

235. Hazrat Abu Hurairah (R.A.A.) relates that the Holy Prophet (S.A.W.) said: do not be envious of other Muslims; do not overbid at auctions (in business) against another Muslim; do not have malice against a Muslim; do not go against a Muslim and forsake him; do not make an offer during a pending transaction. 'O' the servants of Allah! be like brother with each other; A Muslim is the brother of another Muslim; do not hurt him, or look down upon him or bring shame on him. Piety is a matter of heart (The Holy Prophet (S.A.W.) repeated it thrice). It is enough evil for a person to look down upon him, Muslim brother. The Blood property and honour of a Muslim is inviolable to a Muslim (*Muslim*)

٢٣٦ ـ وعن أنسٍ رضي الله عنه عن النبي صلى الله عليه وسلم قال : « لايُؤْمِنُ أَحَدُكُمْ حَتَّى يُحِبَّ لِأَخِيهِ مَا يُحِبُّ لِنَفْسِهِ » متفقٌ عليه

236. Hazrat Anas Bin Malik (R.A.A.) relates that the Holy Prophet (S.A.W.) said: 'None of you is perfect Muslim until he desires for his brother Muslim that which he desires for himself.'

(*Bukhari and Muslim*)

٢٣٧ ـ وعنه قال : قال رسول الله صلى الله عليه وسلم : « انْصُرْ أَخَاكَ ظَالِماً أَوْ مَظْلُوماً » فَقَالَ رَجُلٌ : يَا رسول الله أَنْصُرُهُ إِذَا كَانَ مَظْلُوماً أَرَأَيْتَ إِنْ كَانَ ظَالِماً كَيْفَ أَنْصُرُهُ ؟ قال : « تَحْجُزُهُ ـ أَوْ تَمْنَعُهُ ـ مِنَ الظُّلْمِ فَإِنَّ ذَلِكَ نَصْرُهُ » رواه البخاري

237. Hazrat Anas Bin Malik (R.A.A.) also relates that the Holy Prophet (S.A.W.) said: Help your brother whether he is an oppressor or oppressed person. A companion asked: 'Messenger of Allah (It is true) I will help him if he is an oppressed person, but please tell me how I am to help him if he happens to be an oppressor. The Holy Prophet (S.A.W.) answered: check him from doing injustice. Because preventing him from committing aggression is a help to him (*Bukhari*)

٢٣٨ ـ وعن أبي هريرة رضي الله عنه أنَّ رسول الله صلى الله عليه وسلم قال :

« حَقُّ الْمُسْلِمِ عَلَى الْمُسْلِمِ خَمْسٌ : رَدُّ السَّلامِ ، وَعِيَادَةُ الْمَرِيضِ ،

وَاتِّبَاعُ الْجَنَائِزِ وَإِجَابَةُ الدَّعْوَةِ ، وَتَشْمِيتُ الْعَاطِسِ » متفقٌ عليه

وفي رواية لمسلم : « حقُّ الْمُسْلِمِ سِتٌّ : إذَا لَقِيتَهُ فَسَلِّمْ عَلَيْهِ ، وَإِذَا دَعَاكَ فَأَجِبْهُ ، وَإِذَا اسْتَنْصَحَكَ فَانْصَحْ لَهُ ، وإذَا عَطَسَ فَحَمِدَ اللهَ فَشَمِّتْهُ ، وَإِذَا مَرِضَ فَعُدْهُ ، وَإِذَا مَاتَ فَاتْبَعْهُ »

238. Hazrat Abu Hurairah (R.A.A.) relates that the Holy Prophet (S.A.W.) said: 'A Muslim has five duties to another Muslim. viz. (1) Reciprocating his salutation (2) paying him a visit when he is sick (3) accompanying his funeral procession (i.e. offering *Janaza* prayers) for him (4) accepting invitation from him, and (5) on sneezing, when he says *Alham-du-Lillah* (all praise to Allah) you should respond with '*Yar hamuk-Allah*' (Allah have mercy on you). (*Bukhari and Muslim*)

According to another version of Muslim, a Muslim owes six obligations towards another Muslim viz. (1) When you meet him, salute him saying 'Peace be on you; (2) when he invites you, you should accept his invitation; (3) when he solicits your advice, advise him sincerely; (4) when he sneezes and praises Allah, respond with the supplication '*Yar hamuk-Allah*' i.e. 'Allah have mercy on you'; (5) when he falls sick you should visit him; and (6) on his death join his funeral.

٢٣٩ ــ وعن أبي عُمَارَةَ الْبَرَاءِ بن عازبٍ رضي الله عنهما قال : أَمَرَنَا رسول الله صلى الله عليه وسلم بِسَبْعٍ ، وَنَهَانَا عَنْ سَبْعٍ : أَمَرَنَا بِعِيَادَةِ الْمَرِيضِ ، وَاتِّبَاعِ الْجَنَازَةِ ، وَتَشْمِيتِ الْعَاطِسِ ، وَإِبْرَارِ الْمُقْسِمِ ، وَنَصْرِ الْمَظْلُومِ ، وَإِجَابَةِ الدَّاعِي ، وَإِفْشَاءِ السَّلَامِ . وَنَهَانَا عَنْ خَوَاتِيمِ أَوْ تَخَتُّمٍ بِالذَّهَبِ ، وَعَنْ شُرْبٍ بِالْفِضَّةِ ، وَعَنِ الْمَيَاثِرِ الْحُمْرِ ، وَعَنِ الْقَسِّيِّ ، وَعَنْ لُبْسِ الْحَرِيرِ وَالإِسْتَبْرَقِ وَالدِّيبَاجِ . متفق عليه

وفي روايةٍ : وَإِنْشَادِ الضَّالَّةِ فِي السَّبْعِ الأُوَلِ .

239. Hazrat Abu Umara al-Bara'a Ibn 'Azib, relates: 'The Holy Prophet (S.A.W.) prescribed seven duties for us, and has forbidden us from seven things.

He orderd us (1) to visit the sick; (2) to follow funerals; (3) to invoke Allah's mercy on one who sneezes; (4) to carry out vows; (5) to help the oppressed; (6) to accept an invitation; and (7) to propagate (mutual) greetings.

He prohibited us (1) from manufacturing or wearing gold rings; (2) drinking from silver cups, sitting on red silk cushioned saddles (it was customary to put on silken cushions on horses and camels), and wearing clothes made from a kind of cloth with mixed silken and cotton yarns, and pure silk, heavy silk and brocade.

One version substitutes in the first seven edicts the recovery of (the person or thing) which is lost, instead of fulfilment of vows.

(*Bukhari and Muslim*)

Note: Things which are of some use or benefit to human beings are called their rights; and the obligations imposed upon them are called duties. Both rights and duties are inter-related. The first teaching of Islam lays down that every person has certain duties towards other human beings, even towards animals and inanimate things; they have their rights and every person is required to discharge these rights as much as he can. These rights and corresponding duties are the very first principles of Islamic moral code.

* * * * * * * * * * *

CHAPTER 28

Covering Shortcomings of Muslims.

قال الله تعالى : إِنَّ الَّذِينَ يُحِبُّونَ أَنْ تَشِيعَ الْفَاحِشَةُ فِي الَّذِينَ آمَنُوا لَهُمْ عَذَابٌ أَلِيمٌ فِي الدُّنْيَا وَالآخِرَةِ [النور : ١٩] .

Allah, the Exalted, has said:

105. Lo! Those who love that slander should be spread concerning those who believe, their will be painful punishment in the world and Hereafter (24:19)

٢٤٠ – وعن أبي هريرة رضي الله عنه عن النبي صلى الله عليه وسلم قال : « لا يَسْتُرُ عَبْدٌ عَبْداً فِي الدُّنْيَا إِلاَّ سَتَرَهُ اللهُ يَوْمَ الْقِيَامَةِ » رواه مسلم

240. Hazrat Abu Hurairah (R.A.A.) relates that the Holy Prophet (S.A.W.) said: 'One who covers up the failings of somebody in this world, will have his short-comings covered up by Allah on the Day of Judgment.' (*Muslim*)

٢٤١ – وعنه قال : سمعت رسول اللهِ صلى الله عليه وسلم يقول : « كُلُّ أُمَّتِي مُعَافَى إِلاَّ الْمُجَاهِرِينَ ، وَإِنَّ مِنَ الْمُجَاهَرَةِ أَنْ يَعْمَلَ الرَّجُلُ بِاللَّيْلِ عَمَلاً ، ثُمَّ يُصْبِحَ وَقَدْ سَتَرَهُ اللهُ عَلَيْهِ فَيَقُولُ : يَافُلانُ عَمِلْتُ الْبَارِحَةَ كَذَا وَكَذَا ، وَقَدْ بَاتَ يَسْتُرُهُ رَبُّهُ ، وَيُصْبِحُ يَكْشِفُ سِتْرَ اللهِ عنه » متفق عليه

241. **Hazrat Abu Hurairah** (R.A.A.) relates that he heard the Holy Prophet (S.A.W.) saying, "Everyone of my followers will be forgiven except those who make public faults of other people." Making public includes a person disclosing his own misbehaviour which he committed during the night and which Allah had concealed. In the morning he says: 'Well, so and so I did such and such thing last night. He passed the night, when Allah had concealed the shortcomings, whereas in the morning he himself was disclosing everything'. *(Bukhari and Muslim)*

٢٤٢ – وعنه عن النبي صلى الله عليه وسلم قال : « إذَا زَنَتِ الأَمَةُ فَتَبَيَّنَ زِنَاهَا فَلْيَجْلِدْهَا الحَدَّ ، وَلا يُثَرِّبْ عَلَيْهَا ، ثُمَّ إنْ زَنَتِ الثَّانِيَةَ فَلْيَجْلِدْهَا الحَدَّ وَلا يُثَرِّبْ عَلَيْهَا ، ثُمَّ إنْ زَنَتِ الثَّالِثَةَ فَلْيَبِعْهَا وَلَوْ بِحَبْلٍ مِنْ شَعَرٍ » متفق عليه

242. **Hazrat Abu Hurairah** (R.A.A.) relates that the Holy Prophet (S.A.W.) said: 'If a maid servant is proved guilty of adultery, she should be punished but should not be chided; if she commits the offence a second time, the same punishment be awarded to her but if she offends a third time, she should be sold, even for a hair rope i.e. for the smallest price'. *(Bukhari and Muslim)*

٢٤٣ – وعنه قال : أُتِيَ النَّبِيُّ صلى الله عليه وسلم بِرَجُلٍ قَدْ شَرِبَ خَمْراً قال : « اضْرِبُوهُ » قال أبو هُرَيْرَةَ : فَمِنَّا الضَّارِبُ بِيَدِهِ ، وَالضَّارِبُ بِنَعْلِهِ ، وَالضَّارِبُ بِثَوْبِهِ . فَلَمَّا انْصَرَفَ قَالَ بَعْضُ القَوْمِ : أَخْزَاكَ اللهُ قال : « لا تَقُولُوا هكَذَا لا تُعِينُوا عَلَيْهِ الشَّيْطَانَ » رواه البخاري

243. **Hazrat Abu Hurairah** (R.A.A.) relates: A drunkard was produced before the Holy Prophet (S.A.W.). He ordered him to be beaten. Hazrat Abu Hurairah reports that 'some of us started beating him with our hands, some with shoes and some with clothes.' When he returned to his people, someone said: 'May Allah humiliate you'. The Holy Prophet (S.A.W.) said: 'Do not say like this; and have the Devil over-power him'. *(Bukhari)*

* * * * * * * * * *

CHAPTER 29

Helping the Needy Muslims

قالَ اللهُ تعالى : وَافْعَلُوا الخَيْرَ لَعَلَّكُمْ تُفْلِحُونَ [الحج : ٧٧]

Allah, the Exalted, has said:

106. And do good, that haply ye may prosper (22:77)

٢٤٤ ــ وعن ابن عمر رضي الله عنهما أن رسول الله صلى الله عليه وسلم قال :

« المُسْلِمُ أخُو المُسْلِمِ لا يَظْلمه ولا يُسْلِمُهُ . مَنْ كَانَ في حَاجَةِ أخيه كَانَ اللهُ في حَاجَتِهِ ، ومَنْ فَرَّجَ عَنْ مُسْلِمٍ كُرْبَةً فَرَّجَ الله عَنْهُ بِهَا كُرْبَةً مِنْ كُرَبِ يَوْمِ القِيَامَةِ ، وَمَنْ سَتَرَ مُسْلِماً سَتَرَهُ اللهُ يَوْمَ القِيامَةِ » متفق عليه

244. This has already been cited in S.No. 233. In this Hadis Hazrat Ibn 'Umar (R.A.A.) reports the Holy Prophet (S.A.W.) saying that Muslims are like brothers who do not harm each other nor hand over any Muslim to his enemy. One who fulfills the demand and redresses the difficulty of another Muslim, will get Allah's help in his difficulty; similarly, a Muslim, who covers the faults of another Muslim, will have Allah's cover for his own faults. (*Bukhari and Muslim*)

٢٤٥ ــ وعن أبي هُرَيرَةَ رَضِيَ الله عنهُ ، عن النبيّ صلى الله عليه وسلم قالَ : « مَن نَفَّسَ عَنْ مُؤْمِنٍ كُرْبَةً مِنْ كُرَبِ الدُّنْيَا ، نَفَّسَ الله عَنْهُ كُرْبَةً مِنْ كُرَبِ يَوْمِ القِيامَةِ ، وَمَنْ يَسَّرَ عَلَى مُعْسِرٍ يَسَّرَ الله عَلَيْهِ في الدُّنْيا والآخِرَةِ ، وَمَنْ سَتَرَ مُسْلِماً سَتَرَهُ الله في الدُّنْيا والآخِرَةِ ، والله في عَوْنِ العَبدِ ماكَانَ العَبْدُ في عَوْنِ أخيهِ ، وَمَنْ سَلَكَ طَرِيقاً يَلْتَمِسُ فيهِ عِلْماً سَهَّلَ الله لَهُ طَرِيقاً إلَى الجَنَّةِ . وَمَا اجْتَمَعَ قَوْمٌ في بَيْتٍ مِنْ بُيُوتِ الله تَعَالَى ، يَتْلُونَ كِتَابَ الله ، وَيَتَدَارَسُونَهُ بَيْنَهُمْ إلاَّ نَزَلَتْ عَلَيْهِمُ السَّكِينَةُ ، وَغَشِيَتْهُمُ الرَّحْمَةُ ، وَحَفَّتْهُمُ المَلائِكَةُ ، وَذَكَرَهُمُ الله فِيمَنْ عِنْدَهُ . وَمَنْ بَطَّأَ بِهِ عَمَلُهُ لَمْ يُسْرِعْ بِهِ نَسَبُهُ » رواه مسلم

245. Hazrat Abu Hurairah (R.A.A.) relates that the Holy Prophet (S.A.W.) said: One who helps a fellow Muslim in removing his difficulty in this world, Allah will remove the former's distress on the Day of Judgment. He, who helps to remove the hardship of another, will have his difficulties removed by Allah in this world and the Hereafter. One, who covers the shortcomings of another Muslim, will have his faults covered up in this world, and the next by Allah. Allah continues to help a servant so long as he goes on helping his own brother. One who treads a path in search of knowledge,* has his path to Paradise made easy by Allah, thereby. Whenever devotees gather in a house of Allah (Mosque) for the purpose of reciting the Book of Allah (Holy Quran) and share its reading among themselves, will be blessed with tranquality. (Allah's) mercy covers them, angels cover them with their wings, Allah talks about them with the angels around Him. He who is slow in his conduct, will not make good the deficiency by the nobility of his birth (*Muslim*)

* * * * * * * * * *

CHAPTER 30

Recommendation

قال الله تعالى : مَنْ يَشْفَعْ شَفَاعَةً حَسَنَةً يَكُنْ لَهُ نَصِيبٌ مِنْهَا [النساء : ٨٥] .

Allah, the Exalted, has said:

107. Whoso interveneth in a good cause will have the reward thereof. (4:85)

٢٤٦ — وعن أبي موسى الأشعري رضيَ الله عنه قال : كان النبي صلى الله عليه وسلم إذَا أَتَاهُ طَالِبُ حَاجَةٍ أَقْبَلَ عَلَى جُلَسَائِهِ فقال : « اشْفَعُوا تُؤْجَرُوا وَيَقْضِي الله عَلَى لِسَانِ نَبِيِّهِ مَا أَحبَّ » متفقٌ عليه .

وفي رواية : « مَا شَاءَ » .

246. Hazrat Abu Musa Ash'ari (R.A.A.) relates that whenever a person, in need of something, approached the Holy Prophet (S.A.W.), he would ask those present and say: 'Recommend his case, you will have your reward (from Allah) and Allah makes His Prophet (S.A.W.) to say what He wants and Wills. (*Bukhari and Muslim*)

٢٤٧ — وعن ابن عباس رضي الله عنهما في قِصَّةِ بَرِيرَةَ وَزَوْجِهَا . قال : قال لَهَا النَّبيُّ صلى الله عليه وسلم : « لَوْ رَاجَعْتِهِ ؟ » قَالَتْ : يَا رَسُولَ الله تَأْمُرُنِي ؟ قال : « إِنَّمَا أَشْفَعُ » قَالَتْ : لا حَاجَةَ لي فيهِ . رواه البخاري .

247. Hazrat Ibn Abbas (R.A.A.) relates, in the matter of dispute between Burairah and her husband, that the Holy Prophet (S.A.W.) said to her: 'It would be better if you go back to him.' She said: 'Messenger of Allah (S.A.W.). 'Is it your recommendation or order?' He replied: 'I only recommend.' She said: 'I do not need him.' (*Bukhari*)

* * * * * * * * * *

CHAPTER 31

Reforming and Reconciling People

قال الله تعالى : لا خَيْرَ في كَثِيرٍ مِنْ نَجْوَاهُمْ إلاَّ مَنْ أَمَرَ بِصَدَقَةٍ أَوْ مَعْرُوفٍ أَوْ إِصْلاحٍ بَيْنَ النَّاسِ [النساء : ١١٤] وقال تعالى : وَالصُّلْحُ خَيْرٌ [النساء : ١٢٨] وقال تعالى : فَاتَّقُوا اللهَ وَأَصْلِحُوا ذَاتَ بَيْنِكُمْ) [الأنفال : ١] وقال تعالى : إِنَّمَا المُؤْمِنُونَ إِخْوَةٌ فَأَصْلِحُوا بَيْنَ أَخَوَيْكُمْ [الحجرات : ١٠] .

Allah, the Exalted, has said:

108. There is no good in much of their secret conferences save (in) him who enjoineth almsgiving and kindness and peace-making among the people (4:114)
109. Peace is better (4:128)
110. So fear Allah, and adjust the matter of your difference (8:1)
111. The believers are naught else than brothers. Therefore make peace between your brethren (49:10)

٢٤٨ — وعن أبي هريرة رضي الله عنه قال : قال رسول الله صلى الله عليه وسلم : « كُلُّ سُلامَى مِنَ النَّاسِ عَلَيْهِ صَدَقَةٌ كُلَّ يَوْمٍ تَطْلُعُ فِيهِ الشَّمْسُ : تَعْدِلُ بَيْنَ الاثْنَيْنِ صَدَقَةٌ ، وَتُعِينُ الرَّجُلَ في دَابَّتِهِ فَتَحْمِلُهُ عَلَيْهَا ، أَوْ تَرْفَعُ لَهُ عَلَيْهَا مَتَاعَهُ صَدَقَةٌ . وَالْكَلِمَةُ الطَّيِّبَةُ صَدَقَةٌ ، وَبِكُلِّ خَطْوَةٍ تَمْشِيهَا إلَى الصَّلاةِ صَدَقَةٌ ، وَتُمِيطُ الأَذَى عَنِ الطَّرِيقِ صَدَقَةٌ » متفقٌ عليه

248. Hazrat Abu Hurairah (R.A.A.) relates that the Holy Prophet (S.A.W.) said: 'Charity is due from every part of human body, day on which the sun rises. (To pay this due) bring about a fair reconciliation between two opposing parties (and it) is charity: helping somebody to mount his animal, or to load his baggage on the animal, is also a charity; a polite word is a charity, every step taken to the mosque for prayers (*Salat*) is charity; to remove something, which cause hindrance, (to the way farers) from the road, is charity.' (*Bukhari and Muslim*)

٢٤٩ — وعن أمِّ كُلْثُومٍ بنتِ عُقْبَةَ بن أبي مُعَيط رضي الله عنها قالت : سمعْتُ رسول الله صلى الله عليه وسلم يَقُولُ : « لَيْسَ الْكَذَّابُ الَّذِي يُصْلِحُ بَيْنَ النَّاسِ فَيَنْمِي خَيْراً ، أَوْ يَقُولُ خَيْراً » متفقٌ عليه

وفي رواية مسلم زيادة ، قالت : وَلَمْ أَسْمَعْهُ يُرَخِّصُ في شَيْءٍ مِمّا يَقُولُهُ النَّاسُ إلاَّ في ثَلاثٍ ؛ تعني : الحَرْبَ ، وَالإصْلاحَ بَيْنَ النَّاسِ ، وَحَدِيثَ الرَّجُلِ امْرَأَتَهُ ، وَحَدِيثَ المَرْأَةِ زَوْجَهَا .

249. Hazrat Umm Kulsum bint Uqbah Bin Abi Moyeet (R.A.A.) relates that she heard the Holy Prophet (S.A.W.) say: 'He is not a liar who brings about peace between people and attains good or says that which is good through falsehood' (*Bukhari and Muslim*).

Muslim's another version adds: 'I did not hear him let people have a latitude in what they said, except in three situations: war, making peace, and talking husband to wife, 'or wife to husband.'

(*Bukhari and Muslim*)

٢٥٠ – وعن عائشة رضي الله عنها قالت : سمع رسول الله صلى الله عليه وسلم صَوْتَ خُصُومٍ بِالْبَابِ عَالِيَةٍ أَصْوَاتُهُمَا ، وإذا أَحَدُهُمَا يَسْتَوْضِعُ الآخَرَ وَيَسْتَرْفِقُهُ في شَيْءٍ ، وَهُوَ يَقُولُ : واللهِ لا أَفْعَلُ ، فَخَرَجَ عَلَيْهِمَا رسولُ اللهِ صلى الله عليه وسلم فقال : « أَيْنَ الْمُتَأَلِّي عَلَى اللهِ لا يَفْعَلُ المَعْرُوفَ ؟ » فقال : أَنَا يَارسولَ اللهِ ، فَلَهُ أَيُّ ذلكَ أَحَبَّ . متفقٌ عليه

250. Hazrat Ayesha (R.A.A.) relates that Holy Prophet (S.A.W.) heard two men trying conclusions with each other loudly, outside his door. One of them begged the other to agree to reduce the amount of the debt he owed him and to deal with him kindly. The other siad: 'By Allah, I shall not do it.' The Holy Prophet (S.A.W.) went out to them and asked: 'Who is the person who swears by Allah that he will not act kindly?' The man submitted: 'It is I 'Messenger of Allah, and for him (his opponent) is whatever he prefers.' (*Bukhari and Muslim*)

٢٥١ – وعن أبي العباس سهل بن سعدٍ السَّاعِدِيِّ رضي الله عنه، أن رسول الله صلى الله عليه وسلم بَلَغَهُ أَنَّ بَنِي عَمْرِو بن عَوْفٍ كَانَ بَيْنَهُمْ شَرٌّ ، فَخَرَجَ رسولُ الله صلى الله عليه وسلم يُصْلِحُ بَيْنَهُمْ في أُنَاسٍ مَعَهُ ، فَحُبِسَ رسولُ اللهِ صلى الله عليه وسلم وَحَانَتِ الصَّلاةُ ، فَجَاءَ بِلالٌ إلَى أبي بكرٍ رضي الله عنهما فقال : يَا أَبَا بَكْرٍ إنَّ رسول اللهِ صلى الله عليه وسلم قَدْ حُبِسَ ، وَحَانَتِ الصَّلاةُ ، فَهَلْ لَكَ أَنْ تَؤُمَّ النَّاس ؟ قال : نَعَمْ إنْ شِئْتَ، فَأَقَامَ بِلالٌ الصَّلاةَ ، وَتَقَدَّمَ أبو بَكْرٍ فَكَبَّرَ وَكَبَّرَ النَّاسُ ، وَجَاءَ رسول الله صلى الله عليه وسلم يَمْشِي في الصُّفُوفِ حَتَّى قَامَ في الصَّفِّ ، فَأَخَذَ النَّاسُ

فِي التَّصْفِيقِ ، وَكَانَ أَبُو بَكْرٍ رضي الله عنه لا يَلْتَفِتُ فِي صَلاتِهِ ، فَلَمَّا أَكْثَرَ النَّاسُ التَّصْفِيقَ الْتَفَتَ ، فَإِذَا رسول الله صلى الله عليه وسلم ، فَأَشَارَ إِلَيْهِ رسول الله صلى الله عليه وسلم ، فَرَفَعَ أَبُو بَكْرٍ رضي الله عنه يَدَهُ فَحَمِدَ اللهَ ، وَرَجَعَ الْقَهْقَرَى وَرَاءَهُ حَتَّى قَامَ فِي الصَّفِّ ، فَتَقَدَّمَ رسول الله صلى الله عليه وسلم . فَصَلَّى لِلنَّاسِ ، فَلَمَّا فَرَغَ أَقْبَلَ عَلَى النَّاسِ فقال : « أَيُّهَا النَّاسُ مَالَكُمْ حِينَ نَابَكُمْ شَيْءٌ فِي الصَّلاةِ أَخَذْتُمْ فِي التَّصْفِيقِ ؟! إِنَّمَا التَّصْفِيقُ لِلنِّسَاءِ . مَنْ نَابَهُ شَيْءٌ فِي صَلاتِهِ فَلْيَقُلْ : سُبْحَانَ اللهِ ، فَإِنَّهُ لا يَسْمَعُهُ أَحَدٌ حِينَ يَقُولُ : سُبْحَانَ اللهِ ، إِلاَّ الْتَفَتَ . يَا أَبَا بَكْرٍ : مَا مَنَعَكَ أَنْ تُصَلِّيَ بِالنَّاسِ حِينَ أَشَرْتُ إِلَيْكَ ؟ » فقال أَبُو بَكْرٍ : مَا كَانَ يَنْبَغِي لابْنِ أَبِي قُحَافَةَ أَنْ يُصَلِّيَ بِالنَّاسِ بَيْنَ يَدَيْ رسول الله صلى الله عليه وسلم . متفقٌ عليه

251. **Hazrat Abul Abbad Sahl Ibn S'ad As Sa'edi** (R.A.A.) relates that the Holy Prophet (S.A.W.) learnt that a dispute had arisen between members of the Bani Amr and Ibn Auf tribes. He went there with some of his companions to reconcile them. After the settlement of the dispute he had to stay there to reciprocate their hospitablity. In the meantime the time for Prayer arrived and Hazrat Bilal (R.A.A.) approached Hazrat Abu Bakr (R.A.A.) and said to him: The Holy Prophet (S.A.W.) has been detained (there) and it is time for Prayer. Will you lead the Prayer?' He said: 'Yes, if you wish.' Hazrat Bilal (R.A.A.) called the *Iqamah* and Hazrat Abu Bakr (R.A.A.) stepped forward and said the *Takbir*. Just then the Holy Prophet (S.A.W.) arrived, and, walking through the rows, stood in the first row. Thereupon the worshippers began to clap (signalling Hazrat Abu Bakr that the Holy Prophet had come). Hazrat Abu Bakr (R.A.A.) used to get engrossed while praying, and therefore he paid no attention to clapping. As the clapping increased, he noticed the Holy Prophet (S.A.W.), who, however, motioned to him by a sign to remain in his place, and continue leading the *Salat*. But Hazrat Abu Bakr (R.A.A.) raised his hands, praised Allah, and retreated backwards to take his stand in the row. The Holy Prophet (S.A.W.) then went forward to lead the prayer. When it was over, he faced towards the companions and said: Why is it that when something happens in the course of the *Salat* you start clapping your thighs? Clapping thighs is customary only with the women. When any of you is faced with a situation in the course of the *Salat*, he should say: 'Holy is Allah'. This is bound to draw attention. And O Abu Bakr (R.A.A.)

what prevented you from continuing to lead the prayer after I had signalled you? He said: 'It did not behove the son of Abu Quhafah (i.e. Hazrat Abu Bakr) to lead the Prayer in the presence of the Holy Prophet (S.A.W.)!' (*Bukhari and Muslim*)

Note: Abu Quhafa is the name of Hazrat Abu Bakr's father.

* * * * * * * * * *

CHAPTER 32

Superiority of the Poor and Weak among Muslims.

قال الله تعالى : ﴿ وَاصْبِرْ نَفْسَكَ مَعَ الَّذِينَ يَدْعُونَ رَبَّهُمْ بِالْغَدَاةِ وَالْعَشِيِّ يُرِيدُونَ وَجْهَهُ وَلَا تَعْدُ عَيْنَاكَ عَنْهُمْ ﴾ [الكهف : ٢٨]

Allah, the Exalted, has said:

112. Restrain thyself along with those who cry unto on their Lord at morn and evening seeking His countenances, and let not thine eyes overlook them (18:28)

٢٥٢ – عن حَارِثَة بْنِ وَهْبٍ رضي الله عنه قال : سمعت رسول الله صلى الله عليه وسلم يقولُ : « ألا أُخْبِرُكُمْ بِأَهْلِ الجَنَّةِ ؟ كُلُّ ضَعِيفٍ مُتَضَعَّفٍ، لَوْ أَقْسَمَ عَلَى اللهِ لأَبَرَّهُ، ألا أُخْبِرُكُمْ بِأَهْلِ النَّارِ ؟ كُلُّ عُتُلٍّ جَوَّاظٍ مُسْتَكْبِرٍ » متفقٌ عليه

252. Hazrat Harisa bin Wahb relates that he heard the Holy Prophet (S.A.W.) say: 'May I tell you as to who are the dwellers of Paradise? It is every person who is considered weak and is despised, and who, if he takes an oath of reliance upon Allah, then He would fulfil it. Now shall I tell you as to who are the persons destined for the hell? It is one who is ignorant, impertinent, proud and arrogant.' (*Bukhari and Muslim*)

٢٥٣ – وعن أبي العباس سهل بن سعدٍ الساعِديّ رضي الله عنه قال : مَرَّ رَجُلٌ على النبيّ صلى الله عليه وسلم، فقال لرَجُلٍ عِنْدَهُ جَالِسٍ : « مَارَأْيُكَ في هذا ؟ » فقال : رَجُلٌ مِنْ أَشْرَافِ النَّاسِ ، هذا وَاللهِ حَرِيٌّ إنْ خَطَبَ أنْ يُنْكَحَ وَإنْ شَفَعَ أنْ يُشَفَّعَ . فَسَكَتَ رسولُ الله صلى الله عليه وسلم، ثُمَّ مَرَّ رَجُلٌ آخَرُ ، فقال له رسولُ الله صلى الله عليه وسلم : « مَارَأْيُكَ في

هذا ؟ » فقال : يارسول الله هذا رجلٌ مِنْ فُقَرَاءِ المُسْلِمِينَ هذا حَرِيٌّ انْ خَطَبَ أَنْ لايُنْكَحَ ، وَإِنْ شَفَعَ أَنْ لا يُشَفَّعَ ، وَإِنْ قَالَ أَنْ لا يُسْمَعَ لِقَوْلِهِ . فقال رسول الله صلى الله عليه وسلم : « هذا خَيْرٌ مِنْ مِلْءِ الأَرْضِ مِثْلَ هذا » متفقٌ عليه .

253. Hazrat Abul Abbas Sahl Ibn Sa'ad As Sa'edi (R.A.A.) relates that a person passed by the Holy Prophet (S.A.W.). The Holy Prophet (S.A.W.) asked his companion sitting with him:' 'What do you think of this man, who has just passed this way. The companion said: 'He is one of the gentlest; and by God, if he proposes marriage with any woman, his proposal should be accepted, and if he should recommend, his recommendation should prove, effective'. The Holy Prophet (S.A.W.) kept quiet. Then another man passed, and he asked: 'What is your opinion about this man?' He answered: 'Holy Prophet (S.A.W.), he belongs to the class of poor Muslims. If he goes for marriage, his proposal would not be accepted; if he were to intercede on behalf of any person, his intercession would be rejected, and if he were to speak, nobody would listen to him.' 'The Holy Prophet (S.A.W.) said: This man (the Muslim *faqir*) is better than all the persons of the world, like those whom you have just praised. (*Bukhari and Muslim*)

٢٥٤ – وعن أبي سعيدٍ الخدري رضي الله عنه عن النبي صلى الله عليه وسلم قال : « احتَجَّتِ الجَنَّةُ وَالنَّارُ فقالتِ النَّارُ : فِيَّ الجَبَّارُونَ وَالمُتَكَبِّرُونَ ، وَقَالَتِ الجَنَّةُ : فِيَّ ضُعَفَاءُ النَّاسِ وَمَسَاكِينُهُمْ ، فَقَضَى اللهُ بَيْنَهُمَا : إِنَّكِ الجَنَّةُ رَحْمَتِي أَرْحَمُ بِكِ مَنْ أَشَاءُ ، وَإِنَّكِ النَّارُ عَذَابِي أُعَذِّبُ بِكِ مَنْ أَشَاءُ ، وَلِكِلَيْكُمَا عَلَيَّ مِلْؤُهَا » رواه مسلم

254. Hazrat Abu Sa'id Khudri (R.A.A.) relates that the Holy Prophet (S.A.W.) said: 'A debate took place between the Heaven and the Hell. The latter said: In me, shall enter tyrant and the arrogant persons; and the Heaven said: In me shall enter the weak and the lowly.' Allah decided the issue by, saying: You are Heaven, My mercy; through you I shall have mercy on whomsoever I please; and you are Hell, a place of punishment, through you I shall chastise whomsoever I like. It is incumbent upon Me to fill both of you!' (*Muslim*)

٢٥٥ – وعن أبي هريرةَ رضي الله عنه عن رسول الله صلى الله عليه وسلم قال : « إِنَّهُ لَيَأْتِي الرَّجُلُ السَّمِينُ العَظِيمُ يَوْمَ القِيَامَةِ لايَزِنُ عِنْدَ اللهِ جَنَاحَ بَعُوضَةٍ » متفقٌ عَلَيْه

255. Hazrat Abu Hurairah (R.A.A.) relates that the Holy Prophet (S.A.W.) said: A great and fat man will be produced before Allah on the Day of Judgement, but his worth, in the sight of Allah, will be no more than the wing of a mosquito.' *(Bukhari and Muslim)*

٢٥٦ – وعنه أنَّ امْرَأَةً سَوْدَاء كَانَتْ تَقُمُّ الْمَسْجِدَ ، أَوْ شَابّاً ، فَفَقَدَهَا ، رسول الله صلى الله عليه وسلم ، فَسَأَلَ عَنْهَا أَوْ عَنْهُ ، فقالوا : مَاتَ . قال : « أَفَلا كُنْتُمْ آذَنْتُمُونِي » فَكَأَنَّهُمْ صَغَّرُوا أَمْرَهَا ، أَوْ أَمْرَهُ ، فقال : « دُلُّونِي عَلَى قَبْرِهِ » فَدَلُّوهُ فَصَلَّى عَلَيْهَا ، ثُمَّ قال : « إنَّ هَذِهِ الْقُبُورَ مَمْلُوءَةٌ ظُلْمَةً عَلَى أَهْلِهَا ، وَإِنَّ الله تعالى يُنَوِّرُهَا لَهُمْ بِصَلاتِي عَلَيْهِمْ » متفقٌ عليه .

256. Hazrat Abu Hurairah (R.A.A.) relates that a dark-skinned woman (or perhaps a young man, the reporter is not definite) used to take care of the mosque. One day the Holy Prophet (S.A.W.) did not see her (or him) serving the mosque, and enquired about her (or him), and was informed that she (or he) had died. Whereupon the Holy Prophet (S.A.W.) said that as to why he was not apprised of this fact as if the companions had not thought the matter of any importance. Thereafter he asked them to show him (S.A.W.) the grave of the deceased. On being shown the grave, he prayed over it and said: These graves are full of darkness for their inmates, and Allah illuminates them for their occupants as a result of my prayers for them. *(Bukhari and Muslim)*

٢٥٧ – وعنه قال : قال رسول الله صلى الله عليه وسلم : « رُبَّ أَشْعَثَ مَدْفُوعٍ بالأَبْوَابِ لَوْ أَقْسَمَ عَلَى الله لأَبَرَّهُ » رواه مسلم .

257. Hazrat Abu Hurairah (R.A.A.) relates that the Holy Prophet (S.A.W.) said: There are many persons who look much disturbed with ruffled hair and boggard face and are scornfully pushed away from people's doors, yet if they were to say in the name of Allah, the same would be fulfilled. *(Muslim)*

٢٥٨ – وعن أُسَامَةَ رضي الله عنه عن النبي صلى الله عليه وسلم قال : « قُمْتُ عَلَى بَابِ الْجَنَّةِ ، فَإِذَا عَامَّةُ مَنْ دَخَلَهَا الْمَسَاكِينُ ، وَأَصْحَابُ الْجَدِّ مَحْبُوسُونَ ، غَيْرَ أَنَّ أَصْحَابَ النَّارِ قَدْ أُمِرَ بِهِمْ إِلَى النَّارِ . وَقُمْتُ عَلَى بَابِ النَّارِ فَإِذَا عَامَّةُ مَنْ دَخَلَهَا النِّسَاءُ » متفقٌ عليه .

258. Hazrat Usamah Bin Zaid (R.A.A.) relates that the Holy Prophet (S.A.W.) said: On the night of *Meraj* (Ascension) when I stood at the gate of Paradise, I observed that the bulk of those who entered it were poor persons. The rich people had been refused entry. Thereafter people condemned to Hell were ordered to be pushed there, and noticed that majority of those who entered it were women.' (*Bukhari and Muslim*)

٢٥٩ ــ وعن أبي هريرة رضي الله عنه عن النبي صلى الله عليه وسلم قال :

« لَمْ يَتَكَلَّمْ فِي المَهْدِ إِلاَّ ثَلاثَةٌ : عِيسَى ابْنُ مَرْيَمَ ، وَصَاحِبُ جُرَيْجٍ ، وَكَانَ جُرَيْجٌ رَجُلاً عَابِداً ، فَاتَّخَذَ صَوْمَعَةً فَكَانَ فِيهَا ، فَأَتَتْهُ أُمُّهُ وَهُوَ يُصَلِّي فَقَالَتْ : يَاجُرَيْجُ ، فقال : يَارَبِّ أُمِّي وَصَلاتِي فَأَقْبَلَ عَلَى صَلاتِهِ فَانْصَرَفَتْ . فَلَمَّا كَانَ مِنَ الْغَدِ أَتَتْهُ وهُوَيُصَلِّي ، فَقَالَتْ : يَاجُرَيْجُ ، فقال : أَيْ رَبِّ أُمِّي وَصَلاتِي . فَأَقْبَلَ عَلَى صَلاتِهِ ، فَلَمَّا كَانَ مِنَ الْغَدِ أَتَتْهُ وَهُوَ يُصَلِّي فَقَالَتْ : يَاجُرَيْجُ ، فقال : أَيْ رَبِّ أُمِّي وَصَلاتِي ، فَأَقْبَلَ عَلَى صَلاتِهِ ، فَقَالَتْ : اللَّهُمَّ لاتُمِتْهُ حَتَّى يَنْظُرَ إِلَى وُجُوهِ المُومِسَاتِ . فَتَذَاكَرَ بَنُو إِسْرَائِيلَ جُرَيْجاً وَعِبَادَتَهُ ، وكَانَتِ امْرَأَةٌ بَغِيٌّ يُتَمَثَّلُ بِحُسْنِهَا ، فَقَالَتْ : إِنْ شِئْتُمْ لأَفْتِنَنَّهُ ، فَتَعَرَّضَتْ لَهُ ، فَلَمْ يَلْتَفِتْ إِلَيْهَا ، فَأَتَتْ رَاعِياً كَانَ يَأْوِي إِلَى صَوْمَعَتِهِ ، فَأَمْكَنَتْهُ مِنْ نَفْسِهَا فَوَقَعَ عَلَيْهَا . فَحَمَلَتْ ، فَلَمَّا وَلَدَتْ قَالَتْ : هُوَ مِنْ جُرَيْجٍ ، فَأَتَوْهُ فَاسْتَنْزَلُوهُ وَهَدَمُوا صَوْمَعَتَهُ ، وَجَعَلُوا يَضْرِبُونَهُ ، فقال : مَاشَأْنُكُمْ ؟ قالوا : زَنَيْتَ بِهَذِهِ الْبَغِيِّ فَوَلَدَتْ مِنْكَ . قال : أَيْنَ الصَّبِيُّ ؟ فَجَاؤُوا بِهِ فقال : دَعُونِي حَتَّى أُصَلِّيَ ، فَصَلَّى . فَلَمَّا انْصَرَفَ أَتَى الصَّبِيَّ فَطَعَنَ فِي بَطْنِهِ وقَالَ : يَاغُلامُ مَنْ أَبُوكَ ؟ قال : فُلانٌ الرَّاعِي ، فَأَقْبَلُوا عَلَى جُرَيْجٍ يُقَبِّلُونَهُ وَيَتَمَسَّحُونَ بِهِ وَقَالُوا : نَبْنِي لَكَ صَوْمَعَتَكَ مِنْ ذَهَبٍ ، قال : لا ، أَعِيدُوهَا مِنْ طِينٍ كَمَا كَانَتْ ، فَفَعَلُوا . وَبَيْنَا صَبِيٌّ يَرْضَعُ مِنْ أُمِّهِ ، فَمَرَّ رَجُلٌ رَاكِبٌ عَلَى دَابَّةٍ فَارِهَةٍ وَشَارَةٍ حَسَنَةٍ ، فقالت أُمُّهُ : اللَّهُمَّ اجْعَلِ ابْنِي مِثْلَ هذَا ، فَتَرَكَ الثَّدْيَ وَأَقْبَلَ إِلَيْهِ فَنَظَرَ إِلَيْهِ

فقال: اللَّهُمَّ لاتَجعَلْنِي مِثْلَهُ، ثُمَّ أقبَلَ عَلَى ثَدْيِهِ فَجَعَلَ يَرْتَضِعُ،
فَكَأَنِّي أَنْظُرُ إِلَى رسول الله صلى الله عليه وسلم وَهُوَ يَحكِي ارْتِضاعَهُ بِأُصْبُعِهِ
السَّبَّابَةِ فِي فِيهِ ، فَجَعَلَ يَمُصُّهَا ، قال : « وَمَرُّوا بِجَارِيَةٍ وَهُمْ
يَضْرِبُونَهَا ، وَيَقُولُونَ : زَنَيْتِ سَرَقْتِ ، وَهِيَ تَقُولُ : حَسْبِيَ اللهُ
وَنِعْمَ الوَكِيلُ . فقالت أُمُّهُ : اللَّهُمَّ لا تَجْعَلْ ابْنِي مِثْلَهَا ، فَتَرَكَ
الرَّضَاعَ وَنَظَرَ إِلَيْهَا فقال : اللَّهُمَّ اجْعَلْنِي مِثْلَهَا، فَهُنَالِكَ تَرَاجَعَا
الحَدِيثَ فقالت : مَرَّ رَجُلٌ حَسَنُ الهَيْئَةِ فَقُلْتُ : اللَّهُمَّ اجْعَلْ ابْنِي
مِثْلَهُ فَقُلْتَ : اللَّهُمَّ لا تَجْعَلْنِي مِثْلَهُ، وَمَرُّوا بِهَذِهِ الأَمَةِ وَهُمْ
يَضْرِبُونَهَا وَيَقُولُونَ: زَنَيْتِ سَرَقْتِ، فَقُلْتُ: اللَّهُمَّ لا تَجْعَلْ ابْنِي
مِثْلَهَا فَقُلْتَ: اللَّهُمَّ اجْعَلْنِي مِثْلَهَا ؟ ! قالَ: إِنَّ ذلِكَ الرَّجُلَ كانَ جَبَّاراً
فَقُلْتُ: اللَّهُمَّ لا تَجْعَلْنِي مِثْلَهُ، وَإِنَّ هَذِهِ يَقُولُونَ لَهَا زَنَيْتِ، وَلَمْ تَزْنِ
وَسَرَقْتِ، وَلَمْ تَسْرِقْ، فَقُلْتُ : اللَّهُمَّ اجْعَلْنِي مِثْلَهَا » متفقٌ عليه

259. Hazrat Abu Hurairah (R.A.A.) relates that the Holy Prophet (S.A.W.) said: (Among the Bani Israels) only three persons talked in their cradles. One was Hazrat Isa son of Mary (Jesus Christ); another was Juraij, who was a pious man and had built a monastery in which he led a retired life and given to worship. One day when he was engaged in his prayers, his mother came and called him; he prayed in his heart, 'Lord, my mother and my prayers. (i.e. enlighten me as to which should I prefer), and continued in his prayers and his mother went away. Next day his mother came again and called him, "O Juraij", and he supplicated once more: Lord my mother and my prayers, and continued in his prayers. The mother came on the third day and called her son 'O Juraij'. Juraij once again prayed to Allah. "O my Sustainer my mother and my prayers,' and remained busy in his worship The mother said: 'Allah he may not die till he has seen the face of prostitutes. Juraij and his devotion now became famous and the chief topics of conversation among the Bani Israel. There was among them a harlot also, whose beauty was being cited example. She said: 'If you like, I can involve Juraij in some scandal.' Thereafter she tried to seduce him but Juraij did not pay any attention to her. Then she approached a shepherd who lived near the monastery of Juraij, and surrendered herself to him and thus got conceived from him. When her child was born, she declared that it was from Juraij. The Bani Israel came to

Juraij, degraded him, and pulled him down from his retreat, demolished it and started beating him. Juraij asked the reason for all this. They said: 'You have committed adultery with this harlot and she has given birth to your child'. He said: 'Where is the Child?' They brought it to him. He said: 'Now leave me alone so that I may pray.' Then he prayed, and when he finished his prayers, he came to the child, seated it in his lap and asked it: 'Who is thy father?' The child replied: 'So and So, the shepherd.' Then the Bani Israelis all turned to Juraij, kissing him and seeking his blessing and said: 'We shall build thy monastery of gold.' Juraij said: 'Build it of clay as it was. So they built it.

The Third case was that of an infant who was being suckled by his mother. At this time a man passed by riding a fast and handsome horse and the rider was wearing fine clothes. The mother prayed 'Allah, do Thou make my son like this man. The infant left his mother's breast, and moving his face glanced at the man and said: 'Allah, do not make me like this man.' Then he turned to his mother's breast and resumed the suckling. Here the Holy Prophet (S.A.W.) demonstrated the suckling of the child by putting his forefinger into his mouth and sucking it. Then he continued: 'Then some people and maid servant passed by and the men were beating the maid servant charging her for having committed adultery and theft; 'and in reply she was saying: 'Sufficient for me is Allah and an Excellent Guardian is He.' The mother prayed: 'Allah, do not make my son like this maid servant. 'Thereupon the baby left suckling, looked upon the young woman and said: 'Allah, do make me like this.' Now a dialogue began between the mother and the child. She said: 'A handsome person passed and I supplicated: 'Allah, make my son like him, but you said: Allah do not make me like him. Then some persons passed with a maid servant, whom they were beating accusing her of adultery and theft. I supplicated: Allah, do not make my son like this maid servant, but you said: 'Allah, do make me like her.' The boy replied that man was a cruel person, so I contradicted you and said: 'Allah, do not make me like this person. As to the girl, they said: you committed adultry; but actually she had not. They charged 'you stole'; but she had not stolen,' I therefore, said: Allah, make me like her.' *(Bukhari and Muslim)*

Note: Both the Holy Quran and Traditions of the Holy Prophet (S.A.W.) have spoken in very high terms about poor persons who lead a pious life, and those who are meek and humble. According to a Tradition reported by Tirmizi, all these persons will enter the Heaven 500 years before the affluent persons. The former will get due recompense for their having been deprived of easy life and comforts in this world.

* * * * * * * * * * *

CHAPTER 33

Kind Treatment of Orphans, Girls, the Weak, the Poor and Lowly, and Mercy and Affection upon Them, Generosity and Soft Treatment with Them.

قال الله تعالى : وَاخْفِضْ جَنَاحَكَ لِلْمُؤْمِنِينَ [الحجر : ٨٨] وقال تعالى : وَاصْبِرْ نَفْسَكَ مَعَ الَّذِينَ يَدْعُونَ رَبَّهُمْ بِالْغَدَاةِ وَالْعَشِيِّ يُرِيدُونَ وَجْهَهُ وَلَا تَعْدُ عَيْنَاكَ عَنْهُمْ تُرِيدُ زِينَةَ الْحَيَاةِ الدُّنْيَا [الكهف : ٢٨] وقال تعالى : فَأَمَّا الْيَتِيمَ فَلَا تَقْهَرْ وَأَمَّا السَّائِلَ فَلَا تَنْهَرْ [الضحى : ٩ ، ١٠] وقال تعالى : أَرَأَيْتَ الَّذِي يُكَذِّبُ بِالدِّينِ فَذَلِكَ الَّذِي يَدُعُّ الْيَتِيمَ وَلَا يَحُضُّ عَلَى طَعَامِ الْمِسْكِينِ [الماعون:٣]

Allah, the Exalted has said:

113. and lower thy wing (in tenderness) for the believers (15:88)
114. Restrain thyself alongwith those who cry unto their Lord at morn and evening, seeking his countenance; and not thine eyes overlook them desiring the pomp of the life of the world. (18:28)
115. Thereafter the orphan oppress not. Therefore the beggar drive not away (93:9—10)
116. Hast thou observed him who belieth religion? That is he who repelleth the orphan, And urgeth not the feeding of the needy (107:1—3)

٢٦٠ — عن سعد بن أبي وَقّاصٍ رضي الله عنه قال : كُنَّا مَعَ النَّبِيِّ صلى الله عليه وسلم سِتَّةَ نَفَرٍ ، فقال الْمُشْرِكُونَ للنَّبِيِّ صلى الله عليه وسلم : اطْرُدْ هَؤُلاء لا يَجْتَرِئُونَ عَلَيْنَا . وكُنْتُ أنا وَابْنُ مَسْعُودٍ وَرَجُلٌ مِنْ هُذَيْلٍ وَبِلالٌ وَرَجُلانِ لَسْتُ أُسَمِّيهِمَا . فَوَقَعَ في نَفْسِ رسول الله صلى الله عليه وسلم مَاشَاءَ اللهُ أَنْ يَقَعَ فَحَدَّثَ نَفْسَهُ ، فَأَنْزَلَ اللهُ تعالى: (وَلا تَطْرُدِ الَّذِينَ يَدْعُونَ رَبَّهُمْ بِالْغَدَاةِ وَالْعَشِيِّ يُرِيدُونَ وَجْهَهُ) [الأنعام : ٥٢] رواه مسلم

260. Hazrat S'ad Ibn Abi Waqqas (R.A.A.) relates: 'Six of us were (sitting) with the Holy Prophet (S.A.W.) when he (S.A.W.) offered Islam to the disbelievers) they (disbelievers) asked him: 'Remove these persons away, lest they should begin to over-power us.' The six were myself, Ibn Mas'ud, a man of the Huzail tribe, Bilal, and two other persons whose names I do not know. The Holy Prophet (S.A.W.) felt badly what Allah wished him to feel. He mediated, and Allah revealed to him: 'Repel not those who call upon their Lord at morn and evening seeking His countenance.' (6:52) (*Muslim*)

٢٦١ – وعن أبي هُبَيْرَةَ عَائِذِ بن عَمْرٍو المُزَنِيِّ وَهُوَ مِنْ أهْلِ بَيْعَةِ الرِّضْوَانِ رضي الله عنه . أنَّ أبَا سُفْيَانَ أتَى عَلَى سَلْمَانَ وَصُهَيْبٍ وَبِلالٍ في نَفَرٍ فقالوا : مَا أخَذَتْ سُيُوفُ الله مِنْ عَدُوِّ الله مَأخَذَهَا ، فقال أبُو بَكْرٍ رضي الله عنه : أتَقُولُونَ هَذَا لِشَيْخِ قُرَيْشٍ وَسَيِّدِهِمْ ؟ فَأتَى النَّبِيَّ صلى الله عليه وسلم . فَأخْبَرَهُ فقال : يَا أبَا بَكْرٍ لَعَلَّكَ أغْضَبْتَهُمْ ؟ لَئِنْ كُنْتَ أغْضَبْتَهُمْ لَقَدْ أغْضَبْتَ رَبَّكَ ؟ فَأتَاهُمْ فقال : يَا إخْوَتَاهُ آغْضَبْتُكُمْ ؟ قالوا : لا ، يَغْفِرُ اللهُ لَكَ يَا أخِيَّ . ورواه مسلم

261. Hazrat Abu Hurairah Aiz Ibn Amr Muzani (R.A.A.), who had taken the Bai'at Rizwan(i.e. one of those blessed persons who had taken oath for the pleasure of Allah at Hodaibiyah) relates that Abu Sufyan came to Hazrat Salman, Hazrat Suhaib and Hazrat Bilal (R.A.A.) who said to him: 'We have settled accounts with the enemy of Allah with the swords of Allah'. Hazrat Abu Bakr (R.A.A.) said to them: Do you speak like this to the Sheikh and Chief of the Quraish? Then he (Hazrat Abu Bakr) went to the Holy Prophet (S.A.W.) and related this to him. He said: 'Abu Bakr, perhaps, you have offended these (august) persons. If so, you have offended your Lord.' Hazrat Abu Bakr (R.A.A.) went back to them and said: 'Brothers, did I offend you? 'They replied: 'No. May Allah forgive you, brother.' (*Muslim*)

٢٦٢ – وعن سهل بن سعدٍ رضي الله عنه قال : قال رسول الله صلى الله عليه وسلم : « أنَا وَكَافِلُ اليَتِيمِ في الجَنَّةِ هَكَذَا » وَأشَارَ بِالسَّبَّابَةِ وَالوُسْطَى ، وَفَرَّجَ بَيْنَهُمَا . رواه البخاري

262. Hazrat Sahl Ibn S'ad (R.A.A.) relates that the Holy Prophet (S.A.W.) said: 'I and one who takes care of an orphan, will enter Paradise together like this' and he raised his forefinger and middle finger jointly leaving space between them (by way of illustration). (*Bukhari*)

٢٦٣ – وعن أبي هريرة رضي الله عنه قال : قال رسول الله صلى الله عليه وسلم : « كَافِلُ الْيَتِيمِ لَهُ أَوْ لِغَيْرِهِ أَنَا وَهُوَ كَهَاتَيْنِ فِي الْجَنَّةِ » وَأَشَارَ الرَّاوِي وَهُوَ مَالِكُ بْنُ أَنَسٍ بِالسَّبَّابَةِ وَالْوُسْطَى . رواه مسلم

263. Hazrat Abu Hurairah (R.A.A.) relates that the Holy Prophet (S.A.W.) said: 'I and one who takes care of an orphan, whether related to him or a stranger, will be like these two in Paradise;' and the narrator (i.e. Hazrat Anas Bin Malik) raised his forefinger and middle finger to illustrate this. *(Muslim)*

٢٦٤ – وعنه قال : قال رسول الله صلى الله عليه وسلم : « لَيْسَ الْمِسْكِينُ الَّذِي تَرُدُّهُ التَّمْرَةُ وَالتَّمْرَتَانِ ، وَلا اللُّقْمَةُ وَاللُّقْمَتَانِ إِنَّمَا الْمِسْكِينُ الَّذِي يَتَعَفَّفُ » متفق عليه

وفي رواية في « الصحيحين » : « لَيْسَ الْمِسْكِينُ الَّذِي يَطُوفُ عَلَى النَّاسِ تَرُدُّهُ اللُّقْمَةُ وَاللُّقْمَتَانِ ، وَالتَّمْرَةُ وَالتَّمْرَتَانِ ، وَلَكِنَّ الْمِسْكِينَ الَّذِي لا يَجِدُ غِنىً يُغْنِيه ، وَلا يُفْطَنُ بِهِ فَيُتَصَدَّقَ عَلَيْهِ ، وَلا يَقُومُ فَيَسْأَلَ النَّاسَ »

264. Hazrat Abu Hurairah (R.A.A.) relates that the Holy Prophet (S.A.W.) said: 'A needy and poor person is not one who can be turned back with a date or two or a morsel or two: the real poor person is one who, despite his poverty, abstains from asking.' *(Bukhari and Muslim)*

Another version by these two narrators is: 'A poor person is not one who goes round abegging and who can be turned away with a morsel or two or a date or two. A truly poor person is one who does not accumulate enough to suffice him, and does not disclose his poverty so that he might be given alms, and does not stand up to beg.'

٢٦٥ – وعنه عن النبي صلى الله عليه وسلم : « السَّاعِي عَلَى الأَرْمَلَةِ وَالْمِسْكِينِ كَالْمُجَاهِدِ فِي سَبِيلِ اللهِ » وَأَحْسَبُهُ قال : « وَكَالْقَائِمِ الَّذِي لا يَفْتُرُ ، وَكَالصَّائِمِ لا يُفْطِرُ » متفقٌ عليه

265. Hazrat Abu Hurairah (R.A.A.) relates that the Holy Prophet (S.A.W.) said: He who works hard on behalf of old women and the indigent, is like a *Mujahid* (a warrior) in the cause of Allah; and the narrator thinks, he (S.A.W.) added: 'and like the person standing in prayer and who never tires, and like one who observes the fast and does not break it.' *(Bukhari and Muslim)*

٢٦٦ – وعنه عن النبي صلى الله عليه وسلم قال: «شَرُّ الطَّعَامِ طَعَامُ الْوَلِيمَةِ، يُمْنَعُهَا مَنْ يَأْتِيهَا، وَيُدْعَى إِلَيْهَا مَنْ يَأْبَاهَا، وَمَنْ لَمْ يُجِبِ الدَّعْوَةَ فَقَدْ عَصَى اللهَ وَرَسُولَهُ» رواه مسلم

وفي رواية في الصحيحين عن أبي هريرة من قوله: «بِئْسَ الطَّعَامُ طَعَامُ الْوَلِيمَةِ يُدْعَى إِلَيْهَا الأَغْنِيَاءُ وَيُتْرَكُ الْفُقَرَاءُ»

266. Hazrat Abu Hurairah (R.A.A.) relates that the Holy Prophet (S.A.W.) said: The worst food is the food served at a *Walima* (After-marriage dinner) to which such persons are denied who would like to come, and to which such persons are invited who do not like to come; and one who turns down an invitation, disobeys Allah and His Messenger' (*Muslim*)

Another version in *Bukhari and Muslim* is: 'The worst food is the food served at a *Walima* to which the rich persons are invited and from which the poor people are excluded.'

٢٦٧ – وعن أنس رضي الله عنه عن النبي صلى الله عليه وسلم قال: «مَنْ عَالَ جَارِيَتَيْنِ حَتَّى تَبْلُغَا جَاءَ يَوْمَ الْقِيَامَةِ أَنَا وَهُوَ كَهَاتَيْنِ» وَضَمَّ أَصَابِعَهُ. رواه مسلم

267. Hazrat Anas (R.A.A.) relates that the Holy Prophet (S.A.W.) said: 'One, who brings up two girls right from their childhoold till their maturity, will appear on the Day of Judgement attached to me like two fingers of hand and he joined his two fingers.' (*Muslim*)

٢٦٨ – وعن عائشة رضي الله عنها قالت: دَخَلَتْ عَلَيَّ امْرَأَةٌ وَمَعَهَا ابْنَتَانِ لَهَا تَسْأَلُ، فَلَمْ تَجِدْ عِنْدِي شَيْئاً غَيْرَ تَمْرَةٍ وَاحِدَةٍ، فَأَعْطَيْتُهَا إِيَّاهَا فَقَسَمَتْهَا بَيْنَ ابْنَتَيْهَا وَلَمْ تَأْكُلْ مِنْهَا، ثُمَّ قَامَتْ فَخَرَجَتْ، فَدَخَلَ النَّبِيُّ صلى الله عليه وسلم عَلَيْنَا، فَأَخْبَرْتُهُ فقال: «مَنِ ابْتُلِيَ مِنْ هَذِهِ الْبَنَاتِ بِشَيْءٍ فَأَحْسَنَ إِلَيْهِنَّ كُنَّ لَهُ سِتْراً مِنَ النَّارِ» متفقٌ عليه

268. Hazrat Ayesha (R.A.A.) relates: 'A woman came to me along with her two daughters asking something for them. I did not have anything at that time except a single date, which I gave to her. She divided it between her daughters and did not eat herself. Thereafter she

got up and went away. When the Holy Prophet (S.A.W.) came, I told him about this. He said: 'One who is tried with the bringing up of daughters and treats them well, will find that they will become his shield from the fire of Hell.' (*Bukhari and Muslim*)

٢٦٩ – وعن عائشة رضي الله عنها قالت : جاءتني مِسْكِينَةٌ تَحْمِلُ ابْنَتَيْنِ لها ، فَأَطْعَمْتُهَا ثَلاثَ تَمَرَاتٍ ، فَأَعْطَتْ كُلَّ وَاحِدَةٍ مِنْهُمَا تَمْرَةً وَرَفَعَتْ إلى فيها تَمْرَةً لِتَأْكُلَهَا ، فَاسْتَطْعَمَتْهَا ابْنَتَاهَا ، فَشَقَّتِ التَّمْرَةَ الَّتي كَانَتْ تُرِيدُ أَنْ تَأْكُلَهَا بَيْنَهُمَا ، فَأَعْجَبَنِي شَأْنُهَا ، فَذَكَرْتُ الَّذي صَنَعَتْ لرسول الله صلى الله عليه وسلم فقال : « إنَّ الله قَدْ أَوْجَبَ لَهَا بِهَا الجَنَّةَ ، أَوْ أَعْتَقَهَا بِهَا مِنَ النَّارِ » رواه مسلم

269. Hazrat Ayesha (R.A.A.) relates: 'A poor woman came to me with her two daughters. I gave her three dates. She gave one to each girl and wanted the third to eat herself. The two girls asked her for this also. So she divided it into two parts and gave one to each of the girls. I was much impressed by her action and mentioned all this to the Holy Prophet (S.A.W.). He said: 'Allah has ordained Paradise for her in consequence of this action; or 'Allah freed her from the Hell on account of this gesture.' (*Muslim*)

٢٧٠ – وعن أبي شُرَيْحٍ خُوَيْلِدِ بْنِ عَمْرٍو الخُزَاعِيِّ رضي الله عنه قال : قال النبي صلى الله عليه وسلم : « اللَّهُمَّ إنِّي أُحَرِّجُ حَقَّ الضَّعِيفَيْنِ اليَتِيمِ وَالمَرْأَةِ » حديث حسن رواه النسائي بإسناد جيد

270. Hazrat Abu Shuraih Khuwailid Ibn Amr Khuza'i (R.A.A.) relates that the Holy Prophet (S.A.W.) said: 'Allah, I declare sinful any failure to safeguard the rights of two weak ones namely orphans and women.' (*Nasai*)

Note: *Imam Nasai* has declared this Tradition as good.

٢٧١ – وعن مُصْعَبِ بنِ سعد بن أبي وَقَّاصٍ رضي الله عنهما قال : رَأَى سَعْدٌ أَنَّ لَهُ فَضْلاً عَلَى مَنْ دُونَهُ ، فقال النبيُّ صلى الله عليه وسلم : « هَلْ تُنْصَرُونَ وَتُرْزَقُونَ إلَّا بِضُعَفَائِكُمْ » رواه البخاري. هكَذَا مُرْسَلاً ، فَإنَّ مُصْعَبَ بن سعدٍ تَابِعِيٌّ ، ورواه الحافِظُ أبو بكر البَرْقَانِي في صحيحِهِ مُتَّصِلاً عن مُصْعَب عن أبيه رضي الله عنه .

271. **Hazrat Mus'ab Bin S'ad Bin Abi Waqqas** relates: 'Hazrat Sa'ad haa a notion that he had a superiority over those who were not so well off as he was. Holy Prophet (S.A.W.) said: You are helped and provided for the sake of weaks. (*Bukhari*)

٢٧٢ — وعن أبي الدَّرْداء عُوَيْمِرٍ رضي الله عنه قال : سمِعْتُ رسولَ اللهِ صلى الله عليه وسلم يقول : « ابغُونِي الضُّعفَاء ، فإنَّما تُنْصَرُونَ ، وتُرْزَقُونَ بضُعفَائِكُمْ » رواه أبو داود بإسناد جيد .

272. **Hazrat Abu Darda 'Ovaimer** (R.A.A.) relates that he heard the Holy Prophet (S.A.W.) say: Look for my pleasure among the weak ones, for you are helped (against your enemies) and provided (your subsistence) on account of the weak ones among you,' (*Abu Daud*)

Imam Daud has quoted this Tradition on the authority of excellent testimony.

Note: The sum and substance of the Quranic verses and Traditions referred to above is hospitality and humility, because greatness is the chief characteristic of Allah, the Almighty and Supreme alone, in which He has no associates or partners. As such it does not be-fit Allah's servants to portray themselves as great. As bonds men of Allah it is their duty to be hospitable and humble, and that they should treat each other with civility and kindness. Alongwith this, mercy and affection are such traits which are found not only in human beings but in living creatures. These characteristics play an important role in the administration of the universe. According to the Holy Quran, the appointment of the Holy Prophet Muhammad (S.A.W.) as the Messenger of Allah is the result of Allah's mercy and bounty for his bondsmen.

* * * * * * * * * * * *

CHAPTER 34

Kind Treatment of Women

قال الله تعالى: وَعَاشِرُوهُنَّ بِالمَعْرُوفِ [النساء : ١٩] وقال تعالى : وَلَنْ تَسْتَطِيعُوا أَنْ تَعْدِلُوا بَيْنَ النِّسَاءِ وَلَوْ حَرَصْتُمْ فَلا تَمِيلُوا كُلَّ المَيْلِ فَتَذَرُوهَا كَالمُعَلَّقَةِ وَإِنْ تُصْلِحُوا وَتَتَّقُوا فَإِنَّ اللهَ كَانَ غَفُوراً رَحِيماً [النساء : ١٢٩]

Allah, the Exalted, has said:

117. But consort with them in kindness. (4:19)

118. Ye will not be able to deal equally between (your) wives,

however, much ye wish (to do so). But turn not altogether away (from one), leaving her as in suspense. If ye do good and keep away from evil, Lo! Allah is ever Forgiving, Merciful. (4:129)

٢٧٣ – وعن أبي هريرة رضي الله عنه قال : قال رسول الله صلى الله عليه وسلم : « استَوْصُوا بِالنِّساء خيْراً ؛ فإنَّ المَرْأَةَ خُلِقَتْ مِنْ ضِلَعٍ ، وإنَّ أعوجَ مافي الضِّلَعِ أعلاهُ ، فإنْ ذَهَبْتَ تُقِيمُهُ كَسَرْتَهُ ، وإنْ تَرَكْتَهُ ، لَمْ يَزَلْ أعْوَجَ ، فاستَوْصُوا بِالنِّساءِ » متفقٌ عليه

وفي روايةٍ في الصحيحينِ : « المَرْأَةُ كالضِّلَعِ إنْ أقَمْتَهَا كَسَرْتَهَا ، وإنِ استَمْتَعْتَ بِهَا ، استَمْتَعْتَ وَفِيهَا عِوَجٌ » .

وفي روايةٍ لمسلمٍ : « إنَّ المَرْأَةَ خُلِقَتْ مِنْ ضِلَعٍ ، لَنْ تَسْتَقِيمَ لَكَ عَلَى طَرِيقَةٍ ، فإنْ استَمْتَعْتَ بِهَا ، استَمْتَعْتَ بِهَا وَفِيهَا عِوَجٌ ، وإنْ ذَهَبْتَ تُقِيمُهَا كَسَرْتَهَا ، وكَسْرُهَا طَلاقُهَا » .

273. **Hazrat Abu Hurairah** (R.A.A.) relates that the Holy Prophet (S.A.W.) said: Treat women kindly. Woman has been created from a rib (the rib is crooked), and the most crooked part of the rib is in the upper region. If you try to make it straight you will break it, and if you leave it as it is, it will remain curved. So treat women kindly.

(*Bukhari and Muslim*)

Another version from Bukhari and Muslim says: A woman is like a rib; if you try to straighten it, you might break it and if you wish to draw benefit from it, you can do so inspite of its being curved.

Yet another version of Muslim is: Woman has been created from a rib and you cannot straighten her. If you wish to draw benefit from her, do so despite her crookedness. If you try to straighten her you will break her, and breaking her means divorcing her.

٢٧٤ – وعن عبد الله بن زَمْعَةَ رضي الله عنه ، أنه سَمِعَ النبيَّ صلى الله عليه وسلم يخطُبُ ، وذَكَرَ النَّاقَةَ والَّذي عقَرَهَا ، فقال رسول الله صلى الله عليه وسلم : (إذِ انبَعَثَ أشْقَاهَا) انبَعَثَ لَهَا رَجُلٌ عَزِيزٌ ، عارِمٌ مَنِيعٌ في رَهْطِهِ ، ثُمَّ ذَكَرَ النِّساءَ ، فوَعَظَ فِيهِنَّ ، فقَالَ : « يَعْمِدُ أحَدُكُم فيَجْلِدُ امرَأَتَهُ جَلْدَ العَبْدِ فلَعَلَّهُ يُضَاجِعُهَا مِنْ آخِرِ يَوْمِهِ » ثُمَّ وَعَظَهُمْ في ضَحِكِهِمْ مِنَ الضَّرْطَةِ وقال : « لِمَ يَضْحَكُ أحَدُكُمْ مِمَّا يَفْعَلُ ؟ » متفقٌ عليه

274 **Hazrat Abdullah Ibn Zam'a** (R.A.A.) relates that he heard the Holy Prophet (S.A.W.) delivering an address, in the course of which, he (S.A.W.) mentioned the case of the she-camel (of Prophet Saleh), and the person who killed her. In the course of his sermon he said: "When the basest of them broke forth" (91:13), means that a leading, but wicked and the most powerful chief of the tribe of Samud came forward to cut the feet of the she-camel. Thereafter he tendered advice about the women and said: Some among you beats his wife treating her like a slave, and then towards the close of the day cohabits with her. Then he admonished the audience against laughing at somebody passing the wind, saying: 'Why do you laugh at another person, doing the same thing which he himself does.' *(Bukhari and Muslim)*

٢٧٥ – وعن أبي هريرة رضي الله عنه قال : قال رسول الله صلى الله عليه
وسلم : « لا يَفْرَكْ مُؤْمِنٌ مُؤْمِنَةً إنْ كَرِهَ مِنْهَا خُلُقاً رَضِيَ مِنْهَا آخَرَ ،
أوْ قَالَ : « غَيْرَهُ » رواه مسلم

275. **Hazrat Abu Hurairah** (R.A.A.) relates that the Holy Prophet (S.A.W.) said: Let no Muslim male entertain any malice against a Muslim female. He may dislike one habit in her, but may find another in her which is pleasing. *(Muslim)*

٢٧٦ – وعن عَمْرِو بن الأحْوَصِ الجُشَمِيِّ رضي الله عنه أنَّهُ سَمِعَ
النَّبيَّ صلى الله عليه وسلم في حَجَّةِ الوَدَاعِ يَقُولُ بَعْدَ أنْ حَمِدَ الله تعالى ،
وأثْنَى عَلَيْهِ وذَكَّرَ وَوَعَظَ ، ثُمَّ قال : « ألا وَاسْتَوْصُوا بِالنِّسَاءِ خَيْراً ،
فإنَّمَا هُنَّ عَوَانٍ عِنْدَكُمْ لَيْسَ تَمْلِكُونَ مِنْهُنَّ شَيْئاً غَيْرَ ذلِكَ
إلاَّ أنْ يَأْتِينَ بِفَاحِشَةٍ مُبَيِّنَةٍ ، فإنْ فَعَلْنَ فَاهْجُرُوهُنَّ في المَضَاجِعِ ،
وَاضْرِبُوهُنَّ ضَرْباً غَيْرَ مُبَرِّحٍ ، فإنْ أطَعْنَكُمْ فَلا تَبْغُوا عَلَيْهِنَّ سَبِيلاً ؛
ألا إنَّ لَكُمْ عَلَى نِسَائِكُمْ حَقّاً ، وَلِنِسَائِكُمْ عَلَيْكُمْ حَقّاً ؛ فَحَقُّكُمْ
عَلَيْهِنَّ أنْ لا يُوطِئْنَ فُرُشَكُمْ مَنْ تَكْرَهُونَ ، وَلا يَأْذَنَّ في بُيُوتِكُمْ
لِمَنْ تَكْرَهُونَ ، ألا وَحَقُّهُنَّ عَلَيْكُمْ أنْ تُحْسِنُوا إلَيْهِنَّ في كِسْوَتِهِنَّ
وَطَعَامِهِنَّ » رواه الترمذي وقال : حديث حسن صحيحٌ

276. Hazrat 'Amr Ibn Ahwas Jushami (R.A.A.) relates that he heard the Holy Prophet (S.A.W.) say in his farewell address on the eve of his last Pilgrimage, after he had glorified and praised Allah, he cautioned his followers: 'Listen! Treat women kindly; they are like prisoners in your hands. Beyond this you do not owe anything from them. Should they be guilty of flagrant misbehaviours, you may remove them from your beds, and beat them but do not inflict upon them any severe punishment. Then if they obey you, do not have recourse to anything else against them. Listen! You have your rights upon your wives and they have their rights upon you. Your right is that they shall not allow anyone, you dislike, to trample your bed and do not permit them to enter your home whom you dislike, and their right is that you should treat them well in the matter of food and clothing.' (*Tirmizi*)

According to *Imam Tirmizi* this is a good Tradition.

٢٧٧ ـ وعن مُعَاوِيَةَ بن حَيْدَةَ رضي الله عنه قال : قلت يا رسولَ اللهِ ما حَقُّ زَوْجَةِ أحَدِنَا عَلَيْهِ ؟ قال : « أنْ تُطْعِمَهَا إذَا طَعِمْتَ ، وتَكْسُوهَا إذَا اكْتَسَيْتَ وَلا تَضْرِبِ الوَجْهَ ، وَلا تُقَبِّحْ ، وَلا تَهْجُرْ إلاَّ في البَيْتِ » حديثٌ حسنٌ رواه أبو داود

277. Hazrat Muawiah Ibn Haidah (R.A.A.) relates I requested the Holy Prophet (S.A.W.) as to what is the right of a wife upon her husband? He said: 'Feed her as and when you feed yourself; clothe her as and when you clothe yourself; do not beat on her face; do not abuse (or curse) her and do not separate yourself from her except inside the house.' (*Abu Daud*)

This is also a good Tradition.

٢٧٨ ـ وعن أبي هريرة رضي الله عنه قال : قال رسول الله صلى الله عليه وسلم : « أكْمَلُ المُؤْمِنِينَ إيمَاناً أحْسَنُهُمْ خُلُقاً ، وَخِيَارُكُمْ خِيَارُكُمْ لِنِسَائِهِمْ » رواه التِّرمذي وقال : حديثٌ حسنٌ صحيح

278. Hazrat Abu Hurairah (R.A.A.) relates that the Holy Prophet (S.A.W.) said: The most perfect Muslim in the matter of faith is one who has an excellent behaviour; and the best among you are those who behave best towards their wives. (*Tirmizi*). This is a good and authentic Tradition.

٢٧٩ – وعن إياس بن عبد الله بن أبي ذُبابٍ رضي الله عنه قال : قال رسول الله صلى الله عليه وسلم : «لاتَضرِبُوا إمَاءَ الله » فَجاءَ عُمَرُ رضي الله عنه إلى رسول الله صلى الله عليه وسلم ، فَقَالَ : ذَئِرْنَ النِّسَاءُ عَلَى أَزْوَاجِهِنَّ ، فَرَخَّصَ في ضَرْبِهِنَّ ، فَأَطَافَ بِآلِ رسولِ الله صلى الله عليه وسلم نِساءٌ كَثِيرٌ يَشْكُونَ أَزْوَاجَهُنَّ ، فقال رسول الله صلى الله عليه وسلم : « لَقَدْ أَطَافَ بِآلِ بَيْتِ مُحَمَّدٍ نِسَاءٌ كَثِير يَشْكُونَ أَزْوَاجَهُنَّ لَيْسَ أُولَئِكَ بِخِيَارِكُمْ » رواه أبو داود بإسناد صحيح .

279. **Hazrat Iyas Ibn Abdullah Bin Abu Zubah** (R.A.A.) relates that the Holy Prophet (S.A.W.) warned (the Muslims) not to ill-treat the handmaidens of Allah (females). After some time Hazrat Umar (R.A.A.) approached the Holy Prophet (S.A.W.) and said: The women folk have become very daring and dominating as against their husbands: On hearing this the Holy Prophet (S.A.W.) allowed their punishment. After this a large number of women approached the Holy wives of the Holy Prophet (S.A.W.) and complained against their husbands. Thereafter the Holy Prophet (S.A.W.) said: a number of women have approached my wives complaining against the ill treatment by their husbands. Such persons among you are not good persons. (*Abu Daud*)

٢٨٠ – وعن عبد الله بن عمرو بن العاص رضي الله عنهما أن رسولَ الله صلى الله عليه وسلم قال « الدُّنْيَا مَتَاعٌ ، وَخَيْرُ مَتَاعِهَا المَرْأَةُ الصَّالِحَةُ » رواه مسلم

280. **Hazrat Abdullah Ibn 'Amr Ibn 'Aas** (R.A.A.) relates that the Holy Prophet (S.A.W.) said: The whole world is a place of useful things and the best thing of this world is a virtuous woman (wife). (*Muslim*)

****

CHAPTER 35

A Husband's Rights on His Wife

قال الله تعالى : الرِّجَالُ قَوَّامُونَ عَلَى النِّسَا بِما فَضَّلَ اللهُ بَعْضَهُمْ عَلَى بَعْضٍ وَبِمَا أَنفَقُوا مِنْ أَمْوَالِهِم فالصَّالِحَاتُ قَانِتَاتٌ حَافِظَاتٌ لِلْغَيْبِ بِمَا حَفِظَ الله [النساء : ٣٤]

Allah, the Exalted, has said:

119. Men are incharge of women, because Allah hath made the one of them to excel the other, and because they spend their property (for the support of women). So good women are the obedient, guarding in secret that which Allah hath guarded (4:34)

٢٨١ – وعن أبي هريرة رضي الله عنه قال : قال رسول الله صلى الله عليه وسلم : « إذَا دَعَا الرَّجُلُ امْرَأَتَهُ إلَى فِرَاشِهِ فَلَمْ تَأْتِهِ فَبَاتَ غَضْبَانَ عَلَيْهَا لَعَنَتْهَا المَلائِكَةُ حَتَّى تُصْبِحَ » متفقٌ عليه

وفي روايةٍ لهما « إذا بَاتَتْ المَرْأَةُ هَاجِرَةً فِرَاشَ زَوْجِهَا لَعَنَتْهَا المَلائِكَةُ حَتَّى تُصْبِحَ »

وفي روايةٍ قال رسول الله صلى الله عليه وسلم : « والَّذِي نَفْسِي بِيَدِهِ مَامِنْ رَجُلٍ يَدْعُو امْرَأَتَهُ إلَى فِرَاشِهِ فَتَأْبَى عَلَيْهِ إلاَّ كَانَ الَّذِي فِي السَّمَاءِ سَاخِطاً عَلَيْهَا حَتَّى يَرْضَى عَنْهَا » .

281. **Hazrat Abu Hurairah** (R.A.A.) relates that the Holy Prophet (S.A.W.) said: 'When the husband calls his wife to his bed and she disobeys, and he spends the night in anger against her, the angels keep cursing her till the morning' (*Bukhari and Muslim*)

Another version from Bukhari and Muslim is: When a woman spends the night not on her husband's bed, the angels keep cursing her all the night.

Yet another versions: The Holy Prophet (S.A.W.) said: By Allah, in whose hands is my life, when a husband calls his wife to his bed, and she refuses him then He who is in heaven (i.e. Allah) remains displeased with her till her husband is reconciled with her.

٢٨٢ – وعن أبي هريرة رضي الله عنه أيضاً أن رسول الله صلى الله عليه وسلم قال : « لا يَحِلُّ لامْرَأَةٍ أَنْ تَصُومَ وَزَوْجُهَا شَاهِدٌ إلا بِإِذْنِهِ ، وَلا تَأْذَنَ فِي بَيْتِهِ إلاَّ بإذنه » متفقٌ عليه وهذا لفظ البخاري

282. **Hazrat Abu Hurairah** (R.A.A.) relates that the Holy Prophet (S.A.W.) said: A woman should not observe an optional fast when her husband is present at home, except with his permission. She should also not permit anyone to enter his house without his consent. (*Bukhari and Muslim*, wording is of *Bukhari*)

٢٨٣ ـ وعن ابن عمر رضي الله عنهما عن النبي صلى الله عليه وسلم قال :
« كُلُّكُمْ رَاعٍ ، وَكُلُّكُمْ مَسْؤُولٌ عَنْ رَعِيَّتِهِ ، وَالأَمِيرُ رَاعٍ ، وَالرَّجُلُ
رَاعٍ عَلَى أَهْلِ بَيْتِهِ ؛ وَالمَرْأَةُ رَاعِيَةٌ عَلَى بَيْتِ زَوْجِها وَوَلَدِهِ ،
فَكُلُّكُمْ رَاعٍ ، وَكُلُّكُمْ مَسْؤُولٌ عَنْ رَعِيَّتِهِ » متفقٌ عليه

283. Hazrat Ibn Umar (R.A.A.) relates that the Holy Prophet (S.A.W.) said: 'Every-one of you is a protector and guardian (of his immediate charge and is responsible for the action of those persons who are committed to his charge. A ruler is also a steward (and is accountable for those who are put under his charge) a man is steward in respect of his family members of his house, a woman is a steward in respect of her husband's house and his children. In short everyone of you is a steward and is accountable for those who are placed under his care.' (*Bukhari and Muslim*)

٢٨٤ ـ وعن أبي عَلي طلق بن علي رضي الله عنه أن رسولَ اللهِ صلى الله
عليه وسلم قال : « إذَا دَعَا الرَّجُلُ زَوْجَتَهُ لِحَاجَتِهِ فَلْتَأْتِهِ وَإِنْ كَانَتْ
عَلَى التَّنُّورِ » رواه الترمذي والنسائي وقال الترمِذي . حديث حسن صحيح .

284. Hazrat Abu Ali Talq Ibn Ali (R.A.A.) relates that the Holy Prophet (S.A.W.) said: 'When a man sends for his wife for the satisfaction of his need, she should go to him even if she may be occupied in baking bread (cooking food)' (*Tirmizi and Nisai*). This is an authentic Tradition.

٢٨٥ ـ وعن أبي هريرة رضي الله عنه عن النبي صلى الله عليه وسلم قال :
لَوْ كُنْتُ آمِراً أَحَداً أَنْ يَسْجُدَ لِأَحَدٍ لَأَمَرْتُ المَرْأَةَ أَنْ تَسْجُدَ
لِزَوْجِهَا » رواه الترمذي وقال : حديث حسن صحيح .

285. Hazrat Abu Hurairah (R.A.A.) relates that the Holy Prophet (S.A.W.) said: 'Had it been permissible that a person may prostrate himself before another, I would have ordered that a wife should prostrate herself before her husband' (*Tirmizi*). This is an authentic Tradition.

٢٨٦ ـ وعن أمِّ سَلَمَةَ رضيَ الله عنها قالت : قال رسول الله صلى الله عليه
وسلم : « أَيُّمَا امْرَأَةٍ مَاتَتْ ، وَزَوْجُهَا عَنْهَا رَاضٍ دَخَلَتِ الجَنَّةَ » رواه
الترمذي . قال حديث حسن

286. Hazrat Umm Salamah (R.A.A.) relates that the Holy Prophet (S.A.W.) said: if a woman dies while her husband was pleased with her, she will enter Paradise (*Tirmizi*). This is a good Tradition.

٢٨٧ – وعن معاذ بن جبل رضي الله عنه عن النبي صلى الله عليه وسلم قال : « لا تُؤْذِي امْرَأَةٌ زَوْجَهَا في الدُّنْيَا إلاَّ قَالَتْ زَوْجَتُهُ مِنَ الحُورِ الْعِينِ لا تُؤْذِيهِ قَاتَلَكِ الله ! فَإنَّما هُوَ عِنْدَكِ دَخِيلٌ يُوشِكُ أَنْ يُفَارِقَكِ إلَيْنَا » رواه الترمذيُّ وقال حديث حسن .

287. Hazrat Mu'az Ibn Jabal (R.A.A.) relates that the Holy Prophet (S.A.W.) said: Whenever a woman causes annoyance and torture to her husband in this world, his mate from among the houris of Paradise, says to her: May Allah ruin thee, do not cause your husband annoyance, for, he is only thy guest, and will soon leave thee to join us in paradise (*Tirmizi*). This is also a good Tradition.

٢٨٨ – وعن أسامة بن زيد رضي الله عنهما عن النبي صلى الله عليه وسلم قال : « مَا تَرَكْتُ بَعْدِي فِتْنَةً هِيَ أَضَرَّ عَلَى الرِّجَالِ مِنَ النِّسَاءِ » متفقٌ عليه

288. Hazrat Usamah Ibn Zaid (R.A.A.) relates that the Holy Prophet (S.A.W.) said: I am not leaving behind a more harmful trial (cause of mischief) for men than women (*Bukhari and Muslim*)

* * * * * * * * * *

CHAPTER 36

Spending for the Members of the Family

قال الله تعالى : وَعَلَى المَوْلُودِ لَهُ رِزْقُهُنَّ وَكِسْوَتُهُنَّ بالمَعْرُوف [البقرة : ٢٣٣] وقال تعالى : لِيُنْفِقْ ذُو سَعَةٍ مِنْ سَعَتِهِ وَمَنْ قُدِرَ عَلَيْهِ رِزْقُهُ فَلْيُنْفِقْ مِمَّا آتَاهُ الله لا يُكَلِّفُ الله نَفْساً إلاَّ مَا آتَاهَا [الطلاق : ٧] وقال تعالى : وَمَا أَنْفَقْتُمْ مِنْ شَيْءٍ فَهُوَ يُخْلِفُهُ [سبأ : ٣٩] .

Allah, the Exalted has said:

120. The duty of feeding, and clothing nursing mothers in a seemly manner is upon the father of the child (2:233)

121. Let him, who hath abundance, spend of his abundance, and he, whose provision is measured, let him spend of that which Allah hath given him. Allah asketh naught of any soul save that which He hath given it. (65:7)

122. And whatsoever ye spend (for good) He replaceth it (34:39)

٢٨٩ — وعن أبي هريرة رضي الله عنه قال : قال رسول الله صلى الله عليه وسلم : « دِينَارٌ أَنفَقْتَهُ فِي سَبِيلِ اللهِ وَدِينَارٌ أَنفَقْتَهُ فِي رَقَبَةٍ وَدِينَارٌ تَصَدَّقْتَ بِهِ عَلَى مِسْكِينٍ ، وَدِينَارٌ أَنفَقْتَهُ عَلَى أَهْلِكَ ، أَعْظَمُهَا أَجْرًا الَّذِي أَنفَقْتَهُ عَلَى أَهْلِكَ » رواه مسلم

289. Hazrat Abu Hurairah (R.A.A.) relates that the Holy Prophet (S.A.W.) said: Of the dinar you spend in the way of Allah, the dinar you spend for the freedom of slave, the dinar you give away in charity to the poor, and the dinar you spend on your wife and children, the highest in respect of reward is the one you spend on your family (*Muslim*)

٢٩٠ — وعن أبي عبد الله وَيُقَالُ له : أبي عبدِ الرَّحمنِ ثَوْبَانَ بنِ بُجْدُدَ مَوْلَى رسول الله صلى الله عليه وسلم قال : قال رسول الله صلى الله عليه وسلم : « أَفْضَلُ دِينَارٍ يُنْفِقُهُ الرَّجُلُ دِينَارٌ يُنْفِقُهُ عَلَى عِيَالِهِ ، وَدِينَارٌ يُنْفِقُهُ عَلَى دَابَّتِهِ فِي سَبِيلِ اللهِ ، وَدِينَارٌ يُنْفِقُهُ عَلَى أَصْحَابِهِ فِي سَبِيلِ اللهِ » رواه مسلم

290. Hazrat Abu Abdullah who was also called Abu Abdur Rahman Sauban Ibn Yuhdud (R.A.A.), who was a freed slave of Holy Prophet (S.A.W.) relates that the Holy Prophet (S.A.W.) said: The best dinar is that which a person spends on his family; and the dinar he sends on his horse in the cause of Allah (*Jihad*), and the dinar he spends on his companions for the sake of Allah are also the best spending. (*Muslim*)

٢٩١ — وعن أمِّ سَلَمَةَ رضي الله عنها قالَتْ : قلتُ يارسولَ الله ، هَلْ لِي أَجْرٌ فِي بَنِي أَبِي سَلَمَةَ أَنْ أُنفِقَ عَلَيْهِمْ ، وَلَسْتُ بِتَارِكَتِهِمْ هَكَذَا وَهَكَذَا إِنَّمَا هُمْ بَنِيَّ ؟ فقال : « نَعَمْ لَكِ أَجْرُ مَا أَنْفَقْتِ عَلَيْهِمْ » متفقٌ عليه

291. Hazrat Umm Salamah (R.A.A.) relates: I asked the Holy Prophet (S.A.W.) Shall I get a recompense if I spend on the children (from my first husband Abu Salamah?) They cannot be left uncared, running about here and there (in search of a living). They are after all my children. He answered: Yes, you will have reward for whatever you spend on them. (*Bukhari and Muslim*)

٢٩٢ — وعن سعدِ بن أبي وقّاصٍ رضي الله عنه في حديثِهِ الطّويلِ الذي قدّمناهُ في أوّلِ الكتابِ في بابِ النيّةِ أنّ رسول الله صلى الله عليه وسلم قال له : « وإنّكَ لَنْ تُنفِقَ نفقةً تبتغِي بِهَا وجهَ اللهِ إلاّ أُجِرْتَ بِهَا حتّى مَا تجعَلُ في فِي امرَأتِكَ » متفقٌ عليه

292. **Hazrat Sa'ad Ibn Abi Waqqas** (R.A.A.) relates in the course of a long *Hadis* which we have quoted earlier in the chapter on intentions that the Holy Prophet (S.A.W.) said: Whatever you spend for the pleasure of Allah, will have its recompense, even if you put a morsel in the mouth of your wife (will be a meritorious act). (*Bukhari and Muslim*)

٢٩٣ — وعن أبي مَسْعُودٍ البَدْرِيّ رضي الله عنه ، عن النبي صلى الله عليه وسلم قال : « إذا أنفقَ الرَّجُلُ عَلَى أهْلِهِ نفقةً يحتسِبُهَا فهِيَ لَهُ صَدَقةٌ » متفقٌ عليه

293. **Hazrat Ibn Mas'ud Al-Badri** (R.A.A.) relates that the Holy Prophet (S.A.W.) said: When a person spends on his family, hoping for a recompense, the same is counted as charity on his part. (*Bukhari and Muslim*)

٢٩٤ — وعن عبد الله بن عمرو بن العاص رضي الله عنهما قال : قال رسول الله صلى الله عليه وسلم : « كَفَى بِالمرْءِ إثماً أنْ يُضَيِّعَ مَنْ يَقُوتُ » حديثٌ صحيحٌ رواه أبو داود وغيره .

ورواه مسلم في صحيحه بمعناهُ قال : « كفَى بِالمرْءِ إثماً أن يَحْبِسَ عمّنْ يَمْلِكُ قُوتَهُ » .

294. **Hazrat Abdullah Bin 'Amr Bin Al'Aas** relates that the Holy Prophet (S.A.W.) said: It suffices a man to be a sinner that he ruins him whom he supports. (*Abu Daud*)

Muslim's version is: it is indeed a sin for a person to hold back the sustenance of one whose living depends on him.

٢٩٥ — وعن أبي هريرة رضي الله عنه أن النبي صلى الله عليه وسلم قال : « مَا مِنْ يَوْمٍ يُصْبِحُ العِبادُ فِيهِ إلاّ مَلَكَانِ يَنْزِلانِ ، فيَقُولُ أحَدُهُمَا : اللّهُمّ أعْطِ مُنْفِقاً خلَفاً ، ويَقُولُ الآخرُ : اللّهُمّ أعْطِ مُمْسِكاً تلَفاً » متفقٌ عليه

295. **Hazrat Abu Hurairah** (R.A.A.) relates that the Holy Prophet (S.A.W.) said: Everyday, two angels descend, one of them saying: *Allah*, bestow a (good) return upon the spender: and the other saying: *Allah*, Destroy the goods of the miser (*Bukhari and Muslim*)

٢٩٦ ــ وعنه عن النبي صلى الله عليه وسلم قال : « الْيَدُ الْعُلْيَا خَيْرٌ مِنَ الْيَدِ السُّفْلَى وَابْدَأْ بِمَنْ تَعُولُ ، وَخَيْرُ الصَّدَقَةِ مَا كَانَ عَنْ ظَهْرِ غِنىً ، وَمَنْ يَسْتَعْفِفْ ، يُعِفَّهُ اللهُ ، وَمَنْ يَسْتَغْنِ ، يُغْنِهِ اللهُ » رواه البخاري

296. **Hazrat Abu Hurairah** (R.A.A.) relates that the Holy Prophet (S.A.W.) said: The upper hand (the giver) is better than the lower hand (the receiver) and start (your generosity) with your dependants; and the best kind of charity is from your surplus; and one who wants to become virtuous, Allah will make him so, and one who desires abundance will be made so by Allah. (*Bukhari*)

****

CHAPTER 37

Spending the Most Cherished and the Best Thing for the Sake of Allah

قال الله تعالى : لَنْ تَنَالُوا الْبِرَّ حَتَّى تُنْفِقُوا مِمَّا تُحِبُّونَ [آل عمران : ٩٢] وقال تعالى : يَا أَيُّهَا الَّذِينَ آمَنُوا أَنْفِقُوا مِنْ طَيِّبَاتِ مَا كَسَبْتُمْ وَمِمَّا أَخْرَجْنَا لَكُمْ مِنَ الأَرْضِ وَلَا تَيَمَّمُوا الْخَبِيثَ مِنْهُ تُنْفِقُونَ [البقرة : ٢٦٧]

Allah, the Exalted, has said:

123. Ye will not attain unto piety until ye spend of that which ye love. (3:92)

124. O ye who believe! Spend of the good things which ye have earned, and of that which we bring forth from the earth for you, and seek not the bad (with intent) to spend thereof (in chairty) (2:267)

٢٩٧ ــ عن أنس رضي الله عنه قال : كَانَ أَبُو طَلْحَةَ رضي الله عنه أَكْثَرَ الأَنْصَارِ بِالْمَدِينَةِ مَالاً مِنْ نَخْلٍ ، وَكَانَ أَحَبُّ أَمْوَالِهِ إِلَيْهِ بَيْرَحَاء ، وَكَانَتْ مُسْتَقْبِلَةَ الْمَسْجِدِ وَكَانَ رسول الله صلى الله عليه

وسلم يَدْخُلُهَا وَيَشْرَبُ مِنْ مَاءٍ فِيهَا طَيِّبٍ قَالَ أَنَسٌ : فَلَمَّا نَزَلَتْ
هَذِهِ الآيَةُ : (لَنْ تَنَالُوا الْبِرَّ حَتَّى تُنْفِقُوا مِمَّا تُحِبُّونَ) قام أَبُو
طَلْحَةَ إلى رسول الله صلى الله عليه وسلم فقال : يا رسول الله إنَّ الله تَعَالَى
أَنزَلَ عَلَيْكَ : (لَنْ تَنَالُوا الْبِرَّ حَتَّى تُنْفِقُوا مِمَّا تُحِبُّونَ) وَإِنَّ أَحَبَّ
مَالِي إِلَيَّ بَيْرَحَاءَ ، وَإِنَّهَا صَدَقَةٌ لِلَّهِ تَعَالَى أَرْجُو بِرَّهَا وَذُخْرَهَا
عِنْدَ الله تعالى، فَضَعْهَا يا رسول الله حَيْثُ أَرَاكَ الله ، فقال رسول الله صلى الله
عليه وسلم : « بَخٍ ! ذلِكَ مَالٌ رَابِحٌ ، ذلِكَ مَالٌ رَابِحٌ ، وَقَدْ سَمِعْتُ
مَا قُلْتَ ، وَإِنِّي أَرَى أَنْ تَجْعَلَهَا فِي الأَقْرَبِينَ » فقال أَبُو طَلْحَةَ : أَفْعَلُ
يا رسول الله، فَقَسَّمَهَا أَبُو طَلْحَةَ فِي أَقَارِبِهِ ، وَبَنِي عَمِّهِ . متفقٌ عليه

297. **Hazrat Anas Bin Malik** (R.A.A.) relates that Hazrat Abu Talha (R.A.A.) was the richest person among the Ansars in Medina so far as landed property and date gardens were concerned. He liked his garden of Bairaha the best of all his properties. It was just in front of the Mosque of the Holy Prophet (S.A.W.) The Holy Prophet (S.A.W.) used to visit this garden and drink its sweet water. When the verse cited above was revealed: (3:92), Hazrat Abu Talha (R.A.A.) went to the Holy Prophet (S.A.W.) and submitted: 'Messenger of Allah! Allah has sent down to you this verse, (Ye will not attain piety until ye spend of that which ye love) and the property I like most is Bairaha. I, therefore, offer it in charity for the pleasure of Allah, hoping for its recompense from Him. You may dispose it of, as Allah might direct you. The Holy Prophet (S.A.W.) said: 'Well, well, this is a very profitable property, this is a very profitable property. I have heard what you have said, and I think you should divide it among your relatives.' *Hazrat Abu Talha* (R.A.A.) said: 'So shall I do, Messenger of Allah!' and he divided it among his cousins and relatives. (*Bukhari and Muslim*)

Note: Man is a social being and life in society is mutual give and take — of service. Cooperation, which is at the base of social life, is impossible, if men refuse to cooperate or render service to those who need it, to the best of their ability and capacity. However, that service is only great, mertorious and efficacious which is rendered under the spirit of self sacrifice and not for any worldly and but for the pleasure of Allah only.

The basis of the entire human virtues are fellow-feeling, sublimity and high thinking. With this end in view Islam has laid great emphasis on distribution of wealth or commodities among one's kith and kin, and the human beings at large. While giving things to others, special care is to be taken to give the best quality of commodities even as charity. The doling out of inferior quality of things creates displeasure and repugnance. Thereof, to generate healthy fellow-ship and development of lofty ideas, Islam has encouraged the distribution of the very best articles in charity.

* * * * * * * * * *

CHAPTER 38

Obligation of a Person to Enjoin the Obedience of Allah on His Family Members, Grown up,, the Children and all the Subordinates and to Forbid the Disobedience and to Chastise and Check from its Contraventions

قال الله تعالى : وَأْمُرْ أَهْلَكَ بِالصَّلاةِ وَاصْطَبِرْ عَلَيْهَا [طه : ١٣٢]

وقال تعالى : يَا أَيُّهَا الَّذِينَ آمَنُوا قُوا أَنْفُسَكُمْ وَأَهْلِيكُمْ نَاراً [التحريم : ٦] .

Allah, the Exalted has said:

125. And enjoin upon thy people worship, and be constant therein (20:132)

126. O ye who believe! Ward off from yourselves and your families a fire whereof the fuel is men and stones (66:6)

٢٩٨ – عن أبي هريرة رضي الله عنه قال : أخذ الحسن بن علي رضي الله عنهما تَمْرَةً مِنْ تَمْرِ الصَّدَقَةِ فَجَعَلَهَا في فِيهِ فقال رسولُ اللهِ صلى الله عليه وسلم : « كُخْ كُخْ، إرْمِ بِهَا، أمَا عَلِمْتَ أنَّا لانأْكُلُ الصَّدَقَةَ !؟ » متفقٌ عليه

وفي روايةٍ « أنَّا لا تَحِلُّ لَنَا الصَّدَقَةُ » وقوله : « كِخْ كِخْ » يُقَال بإسْكَانِ الخَاء، ويُقَالُ بكَسْرِهَا مَعَ التَّنْوِينِ وهيَ كَلِمَةُ زَجْرٍ للصَّبيِّ عَن المُسْتَقْذَرَاتِ ، وكَانَ الحَسَنُ رضي الله عنه صبياً .

298. Hazrat Abu Hurairah (R.A.A.) relates that Hazrat Hasan Ibn Ali (R.A.A.) while he was a child, picked up a date from the lot of dates collected as charity, and put it in his mouth. Noticing this, the Holy Prophet (S.A.W.) expressing his displeasure said: Kukh! Kukh! and asked him to throw it out, and said: Did you not know that we do not eat alms?" (*Bukhari and Muslim*)

According to another version he said that for us (the family of the Holy Prophet (S.A.W.) *Sadaqa* (charity) is not lawful for us.

٢٩٩ ـ وعن أبي حَفْصٍ عُمَرَ بن أبي سَلَمَةَ عبد الله بن عبدِ الأسدِ رَبِيبِ رسول الله صلى الله عليه وسلم قال: كُنْتُ غُلاماً في حَجْرِ رسول الله صلى الله عليه وسلم وكَانَتْ يَدِي تَطِيشُ في الصَّحْفَةِ، فقال لي رسول الله صلى الله عليه وسلم: «يَاغُلامُ سَمِّ الله تعالى، وكُلْ بِيَمِينِكَ، وكُلْ مِمَّا يَلِيكَ» فَمَا زَالَتْ تِلْكَ طِعْمَتِي بَعْدُ. متفقٌ عليهِ

299. Abi Hafs Umar Bin Abi Salamah Hazrat Abdullah Bin Abdul Asad, who is the son of Hazrat Umm Salamah (R.A.A.) the wife of the Holy Prophet (S.A.W.) from her previous husband, relates: when I was child under the guardianship of the Holy Prophet (S.A.W.), I used to run my hand inside the bowl when eating. He said to me: 'O 'Boy, take the name of Allah, the Almighty and eat with your right hand, and from the stuff which is in front of you.' This then became my practice in eating thereafter. (*Bukhari and Muslim*)

٣٠٠ ـ وعن ابن عمر رضي الله عنهما قال: سمعت رسول الله صلى الله عليه وسلم يقول: كُلُّكُمْ رَاعٍ، وكُلُّكُمْ مَسْؤُولٌ عَنْ رَعِيَّتِهِ، الإمَامُ رَاعٍ، وَمَسْؤُولٌ عَنْ رَعِيَّتِهِ، والرَّجُلُ رَاعٍ في أهْلِهِ وَمَسْؤُولٌ عَنْ رَعِيَّتِهِ، وَالمَرْأةُ رَاعِيَةٌ في بَيْتِ زَوْجِهَا وَمَسْؤُولَةٌ عَنْ رَعِيَّتِهَا، وَالخَادِمُ رَاعٍ في مَالِ سَيِّدِهِ وَمَسْؤُولٌ عَنْ رَعِيَّتِهِ، فَكُلُّكُمْ رَاعٍ وَمَسْؤُولٌ عَنْ رَعِيَّتِهِ» متفقٌ عليه

300. This is a repetition and the subject matter has already been covered vide S.No.283.

٣٠١ ـ وعن عمرو بن شُعَيْب، عن أبيه، عن جَدِّهِ رضي الله عنه قال: قال رسول الله صلى الله عليه وسلم: «مُرُوا أوْلادَكُمْ بِالصَّلاةِ وَهُمْ أبْنَاءُ سَبْعِ سِنِينَ، وَاضْرِبُوهُمْ عَلَيْهَا، وَهُمْ أبْنَاءُ عَشْرٍ وَفَرِّقُوا بَيْنَهُمْ في المَضَاجِعِ» حديثٌ حسنٌ رواه أبو داود بإسنادٍ حسنٍ.

301. Hazrat 'Amr Ibn Shuaib (R.A.A.) relates from his father and the latter from his father, that the Holy Prophet (S.A.W.) said: when your children attain the age of seven years, ask them to perform the *Salat* and chastise them in respect of any fault in this behalf, when they are ten years old, and let them sleep in separate beds.' (*Abu Daud*)

This is a good Tradition and *Imam Daud* has mentioned it with sound authorities.

٣٠٢ – وعن أبي ثُرَيَّةَ سَبْرَةَ بن مَعْبَدٍ الجُهَنِيِّ رضي الله عنه قال: قال رسول الله صلى الله عليه وسلم: «عَلِّمُوا الصَّبِيَّ الصَّلاةَ لِسَبْعِ سِنِينَ، وَاضْرِبُوهُ عَلَيْهَا ابْنَ عَشْرِ سِنِينَ» حديث حسن رواه أبو داود، والترمذي وقال حديث حسن.

وَلَفْظُ أبي دَاوُدَ: «مُرُوا الصَّبِيَّ بِالصَّلاةِ إذَا بَلَغَ سَبْعَ سِنِينَ».

302. **Hazrat Abi Suraiyah Sabrah Ibn Ma'abad Al-Juhni** (R.A.A.) relates that the Holy Prophet (S.A.W.) said: when a boy reaches the age of seven years, teach him *Salat*, and punish him, when he commits a default (in his prayers) at the age of ten years

(*Abu Daud and Tirmizi*)

Abu Daud's version is: Order a boy to perform the *Salat* when he reaches seven years of age. This is a good Tradition.

* * * * * * * * * * *

CHAPTER 39

Rights of the Neighbour and Good Treatment of Him.

قال الله تعالى: ﴿وَاعْبُدُوا اللهَ وَلا تُشْرِكُوا بِهِ شَيْئاً وَبِالْوَالِدَيْنِ إحْسَاناً وَبِذِي الْقُرْبَى وَالْيَتَامَى وَالْمَسَاكِينِ وَالْجَارِ ذِي الْقُرْبَى وَالْجَارِ الْجُنُبِ وَالصَّاحِبِ بِالْجَنْبِ وَابْنِ السَّبِيلِ وَمَا مَلَكَتْ أَيْمَانُكُمْ﴾ [النساء: ٣٦].

Allah, the Exalted, has said:

127. And serve Allah. Ascribe nothing as partner unto Him. (Show) kindness unto parents, and unto near kindered, and orphans, and the needy, and unto the neighbour who is of kin (unto you) and the neighbour who is not of kin, and the fellow traveller and the wayfarer and (the slaves) whom your right hand possesses (4:36)

٣٠٣ – وعن ابنِ عمر وعائشة رضي الله عنهما قالا: قال رسول الله صلى الله عليه وسلم: «مَازَالَ جِبْرِيلُ يُوصِينِي بِالْجَارِ حَتَّى ظَنَنْتُ أَنَّهُ سَيُوَرِّثُهُ» متفق عليه

303. Hazrat Ibn Umar (R.A.A.) and **Hazrat Ayesha** (R.A.A.) relate that the Holy Prophet (S.A.W.) said: 'Angel Gabriel kept exhorting me about (obligations towards) the neighbour, so much so that I imagined that he might be included as one of the heirs. (*Bukhari and Muslim*)

٣٠٤ ــ وعن أبي ذرٍّ رضي الله عنه قال : قال رسول الله صلى الله عليه وسلم « يَا أبَا ذرٍّ إذا طَبَخْتَ مَرَقَةً ، فَأكْثِرْ مَاءَهَا ، وَتَعَاهَدْ جِيرَانَكَ » رواه مسلم

وفي رواية له عن أبي ذرٍّ قال : إن خليلي صلى الله عليه وسلم أوْصَاني : « إذا طَبَخْتَ مَرَقاً فَأكْثِرْ مَاءَه ، ثُمَّ انْظُرْ أهْلَ بَيْتٍ مِنْ جِيرَانِكَ ، فَأصِبْهُمْ مِنْهَا بِمَعْرُوفٍ » .

304. Hazrat Abu Zarr (R.A.A.) relates that the Holy Prophet (S.A.W.) said: 'O! Abu Zarr! when you prepare soup put a little more water in it, and see if your neighbour needs some. (*Muslim*)

Another version says: 'My friend (well wisher) the Holy Prophet (S.A.W.) advised me: 'When you prepare soup put plenty of water in it, then find out about (state of affairs of) the families of your neighbour, and give some soup to them as well.

٣٠٥ ــ وعن أبي هريرة رضى الله عنه أن النبى صلى الله عليه وسلم قال : « واللهِ لا يُؤْمِنُ ، وَاللهِ لا يُؤْمِنُ ، وَاللهِ لا يُؤْمِنُ ! » قِيلَ : مَنْ يا رسول الله ؟ قال : « الَّذي لا يَأمَنُ جَارُهُ بَوَائِقَهُ ! » متفق عليه

وفي روايةٍ لمسلمٍ : « لا يَدْخُلُ الجَنَّةَ مَنْ لا يَأمَنُ جَارُهُ بَوَائِقَهُ »

« البَوَائِقُ » : الغَوَائِلُ وَالشُّرُورُ .

305. Hazrat Abu Hurairah (R.A.A.) relates that the Holy Prophet (S.A.W.) declared 'By Allah, his faith is incomplete', 'By Allah, he is not a perfect Muslim', "By Allah, he does not believe". He was asked: 'O! Messenger of Allah! who is he' He said: 'One whose neighbour is not immune against his mischief.' (*Bukhari and Muslim*)

Muslim's version is: That person will not enter Paradise whose neighbour is not safe against his mischief.

٣٠٦ ــ وعنه قال : قال رسول الله صلى الله عليه وسلم : « يَانِسَاءَ المُسْلِمَاتِ لا تَحْقِرَنَّ جَارَةٌ لِجَارَتِهَا وَلَوْ فِرْسِنَ شَاةٍ » متفقٌ عليه

306. **Hazrat Abu Hurairah** (R.A.A.) relates that the Holy Prophet (S.A.W.) said: 'O Muslim women! Do not consider your neighbours despicable even though she may send you a piece of goat's shank as present.' (*Bukhari and Muslim*)

٣٠٧ ـ وعنه أن رسول الله صلى الله عليه وسلم قال: « لا يَمْنَعْ جَارٌ جَارَهُ أَنْ يَغْرِزَ خَشَبَةً فِي جِدَارِهِ » ثُمَّ يَقُولُ أبو هريرة: مَالِي أَرَاكُمْ عَنْهَا مُعْرِضِينَ! واللهِ لأَرْمِيَنَّ بِهَا بَيْنَ أَكْتَافِكُمْ. متفقٌ عليه

307. **Hazrat Abu Hurairah** (R.A.A.) relates that the Holy Prophet (S.A.W.) said: 'let no neighbour forbid his immediate neighbour placing his rafter on his own wall.' Hazrat Abu Hurairah (R.A.A.) added: 'Now I see you turning away from this, but I shall continue to proclaim it. (*Bukhari and Muslim*)

٣٠٨ ـ وعنه أن رسول الله صلى الله عليه وسلم قال: « مَنْ كَانَ يُؤْمِنُ بِاللهِ وَالْيَوْمِ الآخِرِ، فَلا يُؤْذِ جَارَهُ، وَمَنْ كَانَ يُؤْمِنُ بِاللهِ وَالْيَوْمِ الآخِرِ، فَلْيُكْرِمْ ضَيْفَهُ، وَمَنْ كَانَ يُؤْمِنُ بِاللهِ وَالْيَوْمِ الآخِرِ، فَلْيَقُلْ خَيْراً أَوْ لِيَسْكُتْ » متفق عليه

308. **Hazrat Abu Hurairah** (R.A.A.) relates that the Holy Prophet (S.A.W.) said: One who believes in Allah and the Day of Judgement must not cause hardship and inconvenience to his neighbour; and he who believes in Allah and the Last Day must respect his guest; and he, who believes in Allah and the Day of Judgement must speak well or keep quiet! (*Bukhari and Muslim*)

٣٠٩ ـ وعن أبي شُرَيْح الخُزَاعِيِّ رضي الله عنه أن النبي صلى الله عليه وسلم قال: « مَنْ كَانَ يُؤْمِنُ بِاللهِ وَالْيَوْمِ الآخِرِ، فَلْيُحْسِنْ إلى جَارِهِ، وَمَنْ كَانَ يُؤْمِنُ بِاللهِ واليَوْمِ الآخِرِ، فَلْيُكْرِمْ ضَيْفَهُ، وَمَنْ كَانَ يُؤْمِنُ بِاللهِ وَالْيَوْمِ الآخِرِ، فَلْيَقُلْ خَيْراً أَوْ لِيَسْكُتْ » رواه مسلم بهذا اللفظ، وروى البخاري بعضه

309. **Hazrat Abu Shuraih Al Khuzaee** (R.A.A.) relates that the Holy Prophet (S.A.W.) said: 'One who believes in Allah and the Last Day, should treat his neighbour kindly; and one who believes in Allah and the Day of Judgement should honour his guest; and one who believes in Allah and the Last Day, should speak well or should keep quiet.' (*Muslim* reported with these words while *Bukhari* reports some of these words).

٣١٠ — وعن عائشة رضي الله عنها قالت : قلت : يارسول الله إنَّ لي جارَيْنِ ، فإلى أيِّهما أُهْدِي ؟ قال : « إلى أقربِهما منكِ باباً » رواه البخاري

310. Hazrat Ayesha (R.A.A.) relates that she asked the Holy Prophet (S.A.W.) 'I have two neighbours, to whom shall I send a present?' He said: 'To the one whose door is nearer to yours.' *(Bukhari)*

٣١١ — وعن عبدِ الله بن عمر رضي الله عنهما قال : قال رسول الله صلى الله عليه وسلم : «خيرُ الأصحابِ عِندَ الله تعالى خيرُهُمْ لصاحبِهِ ، وخيرُ الجيرانِ عِندَ الله تعالى خيرُهُمْ لجارِهِ » رواه الترمذي وقال :حديثٌ حسن .

311. Hazrat Abdullah Ibn 'Umar (R.A.A.) relates that the Holy Prophet (S.A.W.) said: The best friend in the sight of Allah is he who is the well-wisher of his companions, and the best neighbour is one who behaves best towards his neighbours.' *(Tirmizi)*

Note: The neighbours are two such persons who live very close to each other; in such a situation one of them apprehends some trouble from the other, as they reside nearer to each other. It is, therefore, the foremost duty of a true, rational and divine religion like Islam to regulate the relations of such persons in a manner as to eradicate all possibilities of any mishap or clash between the two, so that they may live a peaceful and harmonious life.

* * * * * * * * * * *

CHAPTER 40

Benevolence towards Parents and Good Treatment of the Relatives.

قال الله تعالى : وَاعبُدُوا اللهَ وَلا تُشرِكوا بِهِ شَيئاً وَبِالوالِدَينِ إحساناً وَبِذي القُربى واليَتامى والمَساكِينِ والجارِ ذي القُربى والجارِ الجُنُبِ والصاحِبِ بِالجَنبِ وابنِ السَّبِيلِ وَمَا مَلَكَتْ أيمانُكُم [النساء : ٣٦]

وقال تعالى : وَاتَّقُوا اللهَ الَّذي تَساءَلُونَ بِهِ وَالأرحامَ [النساء : ١]

وقال تعالى: وَالَّذينَ يَصِلُونَ مَا أمَرَ اللهُ بِهِ أنْ يُوصَلَ ، الآية [الرعد: ٢١]

وقال تعالى : وَوَصَّيْنَا الإنسانَ بِوالِدَيهِ حُسناً ، [العنكبوت : ٨]

وقال تعالى : ، وَقَضى رَبُّكَ أن لا تَعبُدُوا إلاَّ إيّاهُ وَبِالوالِدَينِ إحساناً إمّا يَبلُغَنَّ عِندَكَ الكِبَرَ أحَدُهُما أوْ كِلاهُما فَلا تَقُلْ لَهُما أُفٍّ

وَلا تَنْهَرْهُمَا وَقُلْ لَهُمَا قَوْلاً كَرِيماً . وَاخْفِضْ لَهُمَا جَنَاحَ الذُّلِّ مِنَ
الرَّحْمَةِ وَقُلْ رَبِّ ارْحَمْهُمَا كَمَا رَبَّيَانِي صَغِيراً [الإسراء : ٢٤ ، ٢٣]
وقال تعالى : وَوَصَّيْنَا الإِنْسَانَ بِوَالِدَيْهِ حَمَلَتْهُ أُمُّهُ وَهْناً عَلَى وَهْنٍ
وَفِصَالُهُ فِي عَامَيْنِ أَنِ اشْكُرْ لِي وَلِوَالِدَيْكَ [لقمان : ١٤] .

Allah, the Exalted has said:

128. And serve Allah. Ascribe nothing as partner unto Him. (Show) kindness unto parents, and unto near kindered, and orphans, and the needy, and unto the neighbour who is of kin (unto you) and the neighbour who is not of kin, and the fellow traveller and the wayfarer and (the slaves) whom your right hand possesses. (4:36)
129. Be careful of your duty towards Allah in Whom ye claim (your rights) of one another, and toward the wombs (that bore you) (4:1)
130. Such as unite that which Allah hath commanded should be joined. (13:21)
131. We have enjoined on man, kindness to parents. (29:8)
132. Thy Lord has decreed that ye worship none save Him, and (that ye show) kindness to parents. If one of them or both of them to attain old age with thee, say not "fie" unto them, nor repulse them, but speak unto them a gracious word. And lower unto them the wing of submission through mercy, and say: My Lord! Have mercy on them both as they did care for me when I was little (17:23–24)
133. And We have enjoined upon man concerning his parents — his mother beareth him in weakness upon weakness, and his weaning is in two years — give thanks unto Me and unto thy parents. (31:14)

٣١٢ — عن أبي عبد الرحمن عبد الله بن مسعود رضي الله عنه قال : سَأَلْتُ
النبي صلى الله عليه وسلم : أَيُّ الْعَمَلِ أَحَبُّ إِلَى اللهِ تَعَالَى ؟ قال « الصَّلاةُ عَلَى
وَقْتِهَا » قُلْتُ : ثُمَّ أَيٌّ ؟ قال : « بِرُّ الْوَالِدَيْنِ » قلتُ : ثُمَّ أَيٌّ ؟ قال :
« الْجِهَادُ فِي سَبِيلِ اللهِ » متفقٌ عليه

312. Hazrat Abu Abdur Rehman Abdullah Bin Mas'ud (R.A.A.) says that he asked the Holy Prophet (S.A.W.): which action is most favourite with Allah the Almighty. He answered: 'Performing the *Salat* (or offering Prayers) in time.' I asked: Thereafter? He said: 'Good treatment of parents.' I submitted; 'Then which next?' He said: Fighting or struggling in the way of Allah.' *(Bukhari and Muslim)*

٣١٣ – وعن أبي هريرة رضي الله عنه قال : قال رسولُ الله صلى الله عليه وسلم : « لا يَجْزِي وَلَدٌ وَالِداً إلاَّ أنْ يَجِدَهُ مَمْلُوكاً ، فَيَشْتَرِيَهُ ، فَيَعْتِقَهُ » رواه مسلم

313. Hazrat Abu Hurairah (R.A.A.) relates that the Holy Prophet (S.A.W.) said: No son can repay his father (for his affection and love), unless he finds him a slave and purchases him and sets him free (*Muslim*)

٣١٤ – وعنه أيضاً رضي الله عنه أن رسولَ الله صلى الله عليه وسلم قال : « مَنْ كَانَ يُؤْمِنُ بِاللهِ وَالْيَوْمِ الآخِرِ ، فَلْيُكْرِمْ ضَيْفَهُ ، وَمَنْ كَانَ يُؤْمِنُ بِاللهِ وَالْيَوْمِ الآخِرِ . فَلْيَصِلْ رَحِمَهُ ، وَمَنْ كَانَ يُؤْمِنُ بِاللهِ وَالْيَوْمِ الآخِرِ ، فَلْيَقُلْ خَيْراً أَوْ لِيَصْمُتْ » متفقٌ عليه

314. This is the repetition and the subject matter has been narrated under S. No. 309.

٣١٥ – وعنه قال : قال رسول الله صلى الله عليه وسلم : « إنَّ الله تَعَالَى خَلَقَ الخَلْقَ حَتَّى إذا فَرَغَ مِنْهُمْ قَامَتِ الرَّحِمُ ، فَقَالَتْ : هذا مُقَامُ العَائِذِ بِكَ مِنَ القَطِيعَةِ ، قال : نَعَمْ أمَا تَرْضَيْنَ أَنْ أَصِلَ مَنْ وَصَلَكِ ، وَأَقْطَعَ مَنْ قَطَعَكِ ؟ قالت : بَلَى ، قال : فَذَلِكِ لَكِ ، ثم قال رسول الله صلى الله عليه وسلم : « اقرَؤُوا إنْ شِئْتُمْ : (فَهَلْ عَسَيْتُمْ إنْ تَوَلَّيْتُمْ أنْ تُفْسِدُوا في الأرْضِ وَتُقَطِّعُوا أرْحَامَكُمْ . أُولئكَ الَّذِينَ لَعَنَهُمُ اللهُ فَأَصَمَّهُمْ وَأَعْمَى أبْصَارَهُمْ) [محمد : ٢٢ ، ٢٣] متفقٌ عليه

وفي رواية للبخاري : فقال الله تعالى : « مَنْ وَصَلَكِ ، وَصَلْتُهُ ، وَمَنْ قَطَعَكِ ، قَطَعْتُهُ

315. Hazrat Abu Hurairah (R.A.A.) relates that the Holy Prophet (S.A.W.) said: After Allah had created all the creatures, the womb (the blood relation) stood up and submitted: Is this the place of the person who asks for Thy protection against being cut (discarded) (i.e. I seek Thy protection). Allah said: 'yes, would thee be content that I should be kind to him who holds (regards) with thee, and should cut off from him who cuts thee off?' The womb said: 'I am content.' Allah said: 'Then this is the place for thee.' The Holy Prophet (S.A.W.) said: Read if you like the verse:

'Would ye then, if ye were given the command, work corruption in the land and sever your ties. Such are they whom Allah curseth so that he deafeneth them and maketh blind their eyes.' (47:22-23).

(*Bukhari and Muslim*)

And a version in *Bukhari* says, Allah the Almighty said, whoso joins with thee joins with Me. Whoso cuts off thee cuts off with Me.'

٣١٦ — وعنه رضي الله عنه قال : جَاءَ رَجُلٌ إلى رسولِ الله صلى الله عليه وسلم فقال : يارسول الله مَنْ أَحَقُّ النَّاسِ بِحُسْنِ صَحَابَتِي ؟ قال : « أُمُّكَ » قال : ثُمَّ مَنْ ؟ قال : « أُمُّكَ » قال : ثُمَّ مَنْ ؟ قال : « أُمُّكَ » قال : ثُمَّ مَنْ ؟ قال : « أَبُوكَ » متفقٌ عليه .

وفي رواية : يارسول الله مَنْ أَحَقُّ بِحُسْنِ الصُّحْبَةِ ؟ قال : « أُمُّكَ ، ثُمَّ أُمُّكَ ، ثُمَّ أُمُّكَ ، ثُمَّ أَبَاكَ ، ثُمَّ أَدْنَاكَ أَدْنَاكَ » .

316. Hazrat Abu Hurairah (R.A.A.) relates that a man came to the Holy Prophet (S.A.W.) and asked: 'O Messenger of Allah, which person of all the people is best entitled to kind treatment and the good companionship from me? He answered? 'Your mother.' The man asked: And then? He said: 'Your mother.' And after her? He said: 'Your mother.' and after her? The Holy Prophet (S.A.W.) said: 'Your father.'

(*Bukhari and Muslim*)

According to another version the man asked: 'O Messenger of Allah, who is best entitled to kind treatment and good companionship from me? He answered: 'Your mother, and then your mother, and then your mother, and then your father, and then your nearer relations, your nearer relations.'

٣١٧ — وعنه عن النبي صلى الله عليه وسلم قال : « رَغِمَ أَنْفُ ، ثُمَّ رَغِمَ أَنْفُ ، ثُمَّ رَغِمَ أَنْفُ مَنْ أَدْرَكَ أَبَوَيْهِ عِنْدَ الْكِبَرِ، أَحَدَهُمَا أَوْ كِلاهُمَا ، فَلَمْ يَدْخُلِ الجَنَّةَ » رواه مسلم

317. Hazrat Abu Hurairah (R.A.A.) relates that the Holy Prophet (S.A.W.) said: 'May his nose be rubbed in dust, may his nose be rubbed in dust, may his nose be rubbed in dust i.e. May he be humiliated, (He said this thrice), who found his parents, one or both, approaching old age, but did not enter Paradise, (by serving them).' (*Muslim*)

٣١٨ — وعنه رضي الله عنه أن رجلاً قال : يا رسول الله إنَّ لي قَرَابَةً أَصِلُهُمْ وَيَقْطَعُونِي ، وَأُحْسِنُ إِلَيْهِمْ وَيُسِيئُونَ إِلَيَّ ، وَأَحْلُمُ عَنْهُمْ وَيَجْهَلُونَ عَلَيَّ ، فقال : « لَئِنْ كُنْتَ كَمَا قُلْتَ ، فَكَأَنَّمَا تُسِفُّهُمُ

المَلَّ ، ولا يَزَالُ مَعَكَ مِنَ اللهِ ظَهِيرٌ عَلَيْهِم مَادُمْتَ عَلَى ذَلِكَ

رواه مسلم

318. **Hazrat Abu Hurairah** (R.A.A.) relates that a man said to the Holy Prophet (S.A.W.): 'O Messenger of Allah, my relatives are such that I cooperate with them, but they cut off; I am kind to them but they illtreat me: I forbear and they are rude with me? The Holy Prophet (S.A.W.) said: 'If you are as you say, you are feeding them with hot ash; and so long as you continue as you are, Allah will always help you and He will protect you against their mischief.' (*Muslim*)

٣١٩ – وعن أنسٍ رضي الله عنه أن رسولَ الله صلى الله عليه وسلم قال : « مَنْ أَحَبَّ أنْ يُبْسَطَ له في رِزْقِهِ ، ويُنْسَأَ لَهُ في أثَرِهِ ، فَلْيَصِلْ رحِمَهُ » متفقٌ عليه

319. **Hazrat Anas** (R.A.A.) relates that the Holy Prophet (S.A.W.) said: 'A person who wants that there may be abundance in his provision, and that his age be lengthened, then he should do favour to his blood relations.' (*Bukhari and Muslim*)

٣٢٠ – وعنه قال : كَانَ أَبُو طَلْحَةَ أَكْثَرَ الأَنْصَارِ بالمَدِينَةِ مَالاً مِنْ نَخْلٍ ، وكَانَ أَحبَّ أمْوَالِهِ إلَيْهِ بِيرحَاءُ ، وكَانَتْ مُسْتَقْبِلَةَ المَسْجِدِ ، وكَانَ رسولُ الله صلى الله عليه وسلم يَدْخُلُهَا ، ويَشْرَبُ مِنْ مَاءٍ فِيها طَيِّبٍ ، فَلَمَّا نَزَلَتْ هذهِ الآيَةُ : (لَنْ تَنَالُوا البِرَّ حَتَّى تُنْفِقُوا مِمَّا تُحِبُّونَ) [آل عمران : ٩٢] قَامَ أَبُو طَلْحَةَ إلى رسول الله صلى الله عليه وسلم فقال : يا رسولَ الله إنَّ اللهَ تَبَارَكَ وتعالى يقول : (لَنْ تَنَالُوا البِرَّ حَتَّى تُنْفِقُوا مِمَّا تُحِبُّونَ) وإنَّ أَحبَّ مَالي إليَّ بَيْرحَاءُ ، وإنَّهَا صَدَقَةٌ لله تعالى ، أرْجُو بِرَّهَا وَذُخْرَهَا عِنْدَ اللهِ تعالى ، فَضَعْهَا يا رسول الله حَيْثُ أَرَاكَ الله . فقال رسولُ الله صلى الله عليه وسلم : « بَخٍ ! ذلِكَ مَالٌ رَابِحٌ ، ذلِكَ مَالٌ رَابحٌ ! وقَدْ سَمِعْتُ ما قُلْتَ ، وإنِّي أرَى أنْ تَجْعَلَهَا في الأقْرَبِينَ » فقال أَبُو طَلْحَةَ : أَفْعَلُ يا رسول الله ، فَقَسَمَهَا أَبُو طَلْحَةَ في أَقَارِبِهِ وبَنِي عَمِّهِ . متفقٌ عليه

320. This the repetition of the Hadis already covered under S.No. 297.

٣٢١ – وعن عبد الله بن عمرو بن العاص رضي الله عنهما قال : أَقْبَلَ رَجُلٌ إلى نَبِيِّ الله صلى الله عليه وسلم ، فقال : أُبَايِعُكَ عَلَى الهِجْرَةِ وَالجِهَادِ أَبْتَغِي الأَجْرَ مِنَ الله تعالى . قال : « فَهَلْ لَكَ مِنْ وَالِدَيْكَ أَحَدٌ حَيٌّ ؟ » قال : نَعَمْ بَلْ كِلاهُمَا قال : « فَتَبْتَغِي الأَجْرَ مِنَ اللهِ تعالى ؟ » قال : نَعَمْ . قال « فَارْجِعْ إلى وَالِدَيْكَ ، فَأَحْسِنْ صُحْبَتَهُمَا » متفقٌ عليه وهذا لَفْظُ مسلِمٍ .

وفي روايةٍ لَهُمَا : جَاءَ رَجُلٌ فَاسْتَأْذَنَهُ في الجِهَادِ فقال « أَحَيٌّ وَالِدَاكَ ؟ قال : نَعَمْ ، قال : « فَفِيهِمَا فَجَاهِدْ »

321. Hazrat Abdullah Ibn 'Amr Ibn 'Al'Aas relates that a man approached the Holy Prophet (S.A.W.) and said: I wish to take the oath of allegiance with you, to emigrate and fight in the cause of Allah, seeking reward from Him.' The Holy Prophet (S.A.W.) enquired: 'Is either of your parents alive.' The man said: yes, both of them are living.' The Holy Prophet (S.A.W.) asked him: 'Do you seek reward from Allah?' The man said: 'Yes, Sir'. The Holy Prophet (S.A.W.) said: 'Then go back to your parents and serve them well

(*Bukhari and Muslim*)

Another version is: A man came and sought permission for *Jihad* (fighting in the way of Allah). The Holy Prophet (S.A.W.) asked him: 'Are your parents living?' The man said: 'yes, Sir.' He said: 'Then carry on *Jihad* in serving them: this service is as good as *Jihad*.'

٣٢٢ – وعنه عن النبي صلى الله عليه وسلم قال : « لَيْسَ الوَاصِلُ بِالمُكَافِىءِ وَلَكِنَّ الوَاصِلَ الَّذِي إذا قَطَعَتْ رَحِمُهُ وَصَلَهَا » رواه البخاري .

322. Hazrat Abdullah Ibn 'Amr Bin Al'Aas (R.A.A.) relates that the Holy Prophet (S.A.W.) said: A person who reciprocates in doing good is not the one who joins his blood relations generously; but he is one who joins with his blood relations when they cut with him.

(*Bukhari*)

٣٢٣ – وعن عائشة قالت : قال رسول الله صلى الله عليه وسلم: « الرَّحِمُ مُعَلَّقَةٌ بِالعَرْشِ تَقُولُ : مَنْ وَصَلَنِي ، وَصَلَهُ الله ، وَمَنْ قَطَعَنِي ، قَطَعَهُ الله » متفقٌ عليه

323. Hazrat Ayesha (R.A.A.) relates that the Holy Prophet (S.A.W.) said: The womb i.e. blood relation, is suspended from the Throne of Allah and announces: 'Allah will hold by him who holds

by me; and Allah will cut asunder from him who cuts asunder from me.'
(*Bukhari and Muslim*)

٣٢٤ ـ وعن أُمِّ المُؤْمِنِينَ مَيْمُونَةَ بِنْتِ الحَارِثِ رضي الله عنها أَنَّهَا أَعْتَقَتْ وَلِيدَةً وَلَمْ تَسْتَأْذِنِ النَّبِيَّ صلى الله عليه وسلم ، فَلَمَّا كَانَ يَوْمُهَا الَّذي يَدُورُ عَلَيْهَا فيه ، قالت : أَشَعَرْتَ يا رسولَ الله أَنِّي أَعْتَقْتُ وَلِيدَتِي ؟ قال : « أَوَفَعَلْتِ ؟ » قالت : نَعَمْ . قال : « أَمَا إِنَّكِ لو أَعْطَيْتِهَا أَخْوَالَكِ كان أَعْظَمَ لِأَجْرِكِ » متفقٌ عليه

324. Ummul Momineen Hazrat Maimunah Bint Haris (R.A.A.) (wife of the Holy Prophet S.A.W.), says that she freed her slave girl without soliciting the permission of the Holy Prophet (S.A.W.). When he visited her, in her turn, she said to him: 'O Messenger of Allah; do you know that I have freed my slave girl'. He said: 'Is it so'? She said: 'Yes, Sir'. He said: 'But if you had given her to your maternal uncles, it would have been still better.'
(*Bukhari and Muslim*)

٣٢٥ ـ وعن أَسْمَاءَ بِنْتِ أَبي بَكْرٍ الصِّدِّيقِ رضي الله عنهما قالت : قَدِمَتْ عَلَيَّ أُمِّي وَهِيَ مُشْرِكَةٌ في عَهْدِ رسول الله صلى الله عليه وسلم ، فَاسْتَفْتَيْتُ رسول الله صلى الله عليه وسلم قلتُ : قَدِمَتْ عَلَيَّ أُمِّي وَهِيَ رَاغِبَةٌ ، أَفَأَصِلُ أُمِّي ؟ قال : « نَعَمْ صِلِي أُمَّكِ » متفقٌ عليه .

325. Hazrat Asma'a bint Abu Bakr Siddiq (R.A.A.) relates: My mother came to Medina from Mecca to see me, while she was still an unbeliever. She had come to demand something from me. I enquired from the Holy Prophet (S.A.W.): 'My mother has come to see me and she is expecting something from me. May I oblige her?' He said: 'Yes. Be kind to your mother.'
(*Bukhari and Muslim*)

٣٢٦ ـ وعن زَيْنَبَ الثَّقَفِيَّةِ امْرَأَةِ عبدِ اللهِ بن مسعودٍ رضي الله عنه وعنها قالت : قال رسولُ الله صلى الله عليه وسلم « تَصَدَّقْنَ يَامَعْشَرَ النِّسَاءِ وَلَوْ مِن حُلِيِّكُنَّ » قالت : فَرَجَعْتُ إلى عبدِ الله بنِ مسعودٍ فقلتُ له : إِنَّكَ رَجُلٌ خَفِيفُ ذَاتِ اليَدِ وَإِنَّ رسولَ اللهِ صلى الله عليه وسلم قد أَمَرَنَا بِالصَّدَقَةِ فَأْتِهِ ، فاسأله ، فَإِن كَانَ ذلِكَ يُجْزِىءُ عَنِّي وَإِلاَّ صَرَفْتُهَا إلى غَيْرِكُمْ . فقالَ عبدُ اللهِ : بَلِ ائتيه أَنتِ ، فانْطَلَقْتُ ، فَإِذَا امْرَأَةٌ

مِنَ الأَنْصَارِ بِبَابِ رسول الله صلى الله عليه وسلم حَاجَتِي حَاجَتُهَا ، وكَانَ رسولُ الله صلى الله عليه وسلم قد أُلقِيَتْ عَلَيهِ المَهابَةُ ، فَخَرَجَ عَلَيْنَا بِلالٌ ، فَقُلْنَا له : ائتِ رسولَ الله صلى الله عليه وسلم ، فَأَخْبِرْهُ أَنَّ امْرَأَتَيْنِ بِالبَابِ تَسأَلانِكَ : أَتُجزِىءُ الصَّدَقَةُ عَنْهُمَا على أَزْوَاجِهِمَا وَعَلى أَيْتَامٍ في حُجُورِهِمَا ؟ ولا تُخْبِرْهُ مَنْ نَحنُ ، فَدَخَلَ بِلالٌ عَلى رسول الله صلى الله عليه وسلم ، فَسَأَلَهُ ، فقال لهُ رسولُ الله صلى الله عليه وسلم « من هُمَا؟» قَالَ : امْرَأَةٌ مِنَ الأَنْصَارِ وَزَيْنَبُ . فقال رسول الله صلى الله عليه وسلم « أيُّ الزَّيَانِبِ هِيَ ؟ » قال : امْرَأَةُ عبدِ اللهِ ، فقال رسول الله صلى الله عليه وسلم : « لَهُمَا أَجْرَانِ : أَجْرُ القَرَابَةِ وَأَجْرُ الصَّدَقَةِ » متفقٌ عليه

326. Hazrat Zainab as Saqafia (R.A.A.) wife of **Hazrat Abdullah Bin Mas'ud** (R.A.A.), says: 'The Holy Prophet (S.A.W.) addressing a group of women said: 'Spend in charity, O women, even out of your ornaments.' On hearing this I went to my husband and said to him: 'You are a poor and needy person, and the Holy Prophet (S.A.W.) has enjoined us to spend in charity. So you go to his august presence and ask him if my giving you something will be treated as charity, otherwise I may give to someone else.' Hazrat Abdullah Bin Mas'ud said: You should go yourself and enquire from him.' So I went there and found an Ansari woman already at the door of the Holy Prophet (S.A.W.) who had come for the same purpose as myself. But we were reluctant to enter on account of dignity and magnificence of the Holy Prophet (S.A.W.). In the meantime Hazrat Bilal (R.A.A.) came out and we said to him: 'Please go to the Holy Prophet (S.A.W.) and tell him that two women had come and want to know whether it would be charity if they spend on their husbands and on the orphans under their care, but do not tell him as to who we are.' Hazrat Bilal (R.A.A.) went to the Holy Prophet (S.A.W.) and presented our case to him. He enquired 'Who are they?' Hazrat Bilal (R.A.A.) said: 'An Ansari woman and the other is named Zainab.' He asked 'which Zainab is she?' Hazrat Bilal (R.A.A.) said: 'The wife of Hazrat Abdullah (R.A.A.).' The Holy Prophet (S.A.W.) said: 'They will get twofold recompense, one for kindness towards relatives, and the other for charity.

(*Bukhari and Muslim*)

٣٢٧ ـ وعن أَبي سُفْيَانَ صَخْرِ بنِ حَرْبٍ رضي الله عنه في حَدِيثِهِ الطَّوِيل في قِصَّةِ هِرَقْلَ أَنَّ هِرَقْلَ قال لأَبِي سُفْيَان : فَمَاذَا يَأْمُرُكُمْ بِهِ ؟

يَعْنِي النَّبِيَّ صلى الله عليه وسلم قال : قلت : يقولُ : « اعبُدُوا الله وَحْدَهُ ، وَلا تُشْرِكُوا بِهِ شَيْئاً ، واترُكُوا ما يَقُولُ آباؤُكُمْ ، وَيأمُرُنَا بالصَّلاة ، والصِّدْقِ ، والعَفَافِ ، والصِّلَةِ » متفقٌ عليه

327. **Hazrat Abu Sufyan Sakhr Bin Harb** (R.A.A.) states that during his meeting with Hiraclius, the Roman Ruler, the latter asked him:, "What does your Prophet (S.A.W.) ask you to do?' I said: 'He asks us to worship the only One Allah, and not to associate anybody with Him; not to follow the habits and practices of our ancestors; he further enjoins us to perform the *Salat*, tell the truth, keep chaste and to treat our blood relations well.' (*Bukhari and Muslim*)

٣٢٨ – وعن أبي ذرّ رضي الله عنه قال : قال رسولُ الله صلى الله عليه وسلم : « إنَّكُمْ ستَفتَحُونَ أرْضاً يُذْكَرُ فيها القيرَاطُ » .

وفي روايةٍ : « ستَفتَحُونَ مصرَ وهِيَ أرضٌ يُسَمَّى فيها القيرَاطُ ، فَاستَوْصُوا بِأهْلِهَا خيْراً ، فإنَّ لَهُم ذِمَّةً ورَحِماً » .

وفي روايةٍ : « فإذا افتَتَحتُمُوهَا، فَأَحْسِنُوا إلى أهْلِهَا،فإنَّ لَهُمْ ذمَّةً وَرَحِماً » أو قال « ذِمَّةً وَصِهراً » رواه مسلم

328. **Hazrat Abu Zarr** (R.A.A.) relates that the Holy Prophet (S.A.W.) said: 'You will soon conquer a land where '*Qairat*' is much spoken off.'

And another tradition says that he said that you will shortly conquer Egypt where there is a land called Qairat. Then treat its people kindly, for there are ties of kin-ship and our responsibility with them. (*Muslim*). Another tradition says, 'When you conquer it, treat its inhabitants well, for them we have responsibility and kinship, or he said we have responsibility and maternal relations. (*Muslim*)

Imam Nawawi elucidating this kinship with the Egyptians refers to the historical fact that Hazrat Hajra, the mother of Prophet Ismail (Ishmael) was an Egyptian, and Hazrat Maria Qibtia (R.A.A.) the mother of Hazrat Ibrahim, the son of the Holy Prophet (S.A.W.) was also an Egyptian.

٣٢٩ – وعن أبي هريرة رضي الله عنه قال : لما نَزَلَتْ هذهِ الآيَةُ : ﴿ وَأَنذِرْ عَشِيرَتَكَ الأَقْرَبِينَ ﴾ [الشعراء : ٢١٤] دَعَا رسولُ الله صلى الله عليه وسلم قُرَيْشاً ، فَاجْتَمَعُوا فعَمَّ ، وخَصَّ وقال : « يَابَنِي عَبْدِ شَمْسٍ ، يَا بَنِي كَعْبِ بنِ لُؤَيٍّ ،أنقِذُوا أنفُسَكُمْ مِنَ النَّارِ، يَابَنِي مُرَّةَ بنِ كَعْبٍ،

أنقِذُوا أنفُسَكُمْ مِنَ النَّار ، يَابَنِي عَبْدِ مَنَافٍ ، أَنقِذُوا أَنفُسَكُمْ
مِنَ النَّارِ ، يَابَنِي هاشِمٍ أنقِذُوا أنفُسَكُمْ مِنَ النَّارِ ، يَابَنِي عَبْدِ المُطَّلِبِ
أَنقِذُوا أَنفُسَكُمْ مِنَ النَّارِ ، يَافَاطِمَةُ أَنقِذِي نَفْسَكِ مِنَ النَّار ، فَإنِّي
لا أَمْلِكُ لَكُمْ مِنَ اللهِ شَيْئاً ، غَيْرَ أَنَّ لَكُمْ رَحِماً سَأَبُلُّهَا بِبِلالِهَا »
رواه مسلم

329. Hazrat Abu Hurairah (R.A.A.) relates that when this verse was revealed:

'And warn thy tribe of near kindred.' (26:214)

The Holy Prophet (S.A.W.) summoned the (tribe of) Quraish, and they all came, commons and chiefs. He said to them 'O the descendants of Abd Shams! O the children of Ka'ab Bin Luwaiye.' protect yourselves against the Fire (of Hell); O the progeny of Abd Manaf! safeguard yourselves against the Fire (of Hell) 'O the Hashemites'. get yourselves released from the Fire (of Hell); O the offsprings of Abdul Muttalib! protect yourselves against the Fire (of Hell)! O Fatimah secure yourself from the Fire, for, on the Day of Judgement I shall not be able to interfere with the will of Allah. Of course I am related to you and on this account I will continue to fulfil my obligations. (*Muslim*)

Note: *Imam Nawawi* explains that in this tradition the cutting or disregard of blood relations has been likened by Fire, which can be extinguished with water or discharging ones obligations towards his kinsmen.

٣٣٠ — وعن أبي عبد الله عمرو بن العاص رضي الله عنهما قال : سمعتُ
رسول الله صلى الله عليه وسلم جِهاراً غَيْرَ سِرٍّ يقولُ : « إنَّ آلَ بَنِي
فُلانٍ لَيْسُوا بأوْلِيائي ، إنَّما وَلِيِّيَ اللهُ وصَالِحُ المُؤْمِنِينَ ، وَلَكِنْ لَهُمْ
رَحِمٌ أَبُلُّها ببلالِهَا ، » متفق عليه . واللَّفْظُ للبخاري .

330. Hazrat Abu Abdullah 'Amr Ibn Al'Aas (R.A.A.) relates that he heard the Holy Prophet (S.A.W.) say openly without any reservation: 'The children of So and So are not my friends; or relative; but my friends are Allah and the virtuous Muslims. No doubt I have ties of kinship with them which I shall continue to fulfil. (*Bukhari and Muslim*)

٣٣١ — وعن أبي أيُّوبَ خالدِ بن زيدٍ الأنصاري رضي الله عنه أن رجلاً
قال : يا رسولَ الله أخْبِرْني بِعَمَلٍ يُدْخِلُنِي الجَنَّةَ ، وَيُبَاعِدُنِي مِنَ النَّارِ .
فقال النبيُّ صلى الله عليه وسلم : « تَعبُدُ اللهَ ، وَلا تُشْرِكُ بِهِ شَيْئاً ، وتُقِيمُ
الصَّلاةَ ، وَتُؤْتِي الزَّكَاةَ ، وَتَصِلُ الرَّحِمَ » متفق عليه

331. **Hazrat Abu Ayub Khalid Ibn Zaid Al-Ansari** (R.A.A.) relates that a man requested; 'Messenger of Allah! tell me the action which will get me admitted to Paradise and keep me away from the Hell.' He answered: 'Worship Allah and do not associate anybody with Him: establish Prayer; pay the *Zakat* and join the ties of kinship.'

(*Bukhari and Muslim*)

٣٣٢ ـ وعن سَلْمَانَ بنِ عامرٍ رضي الله عنه، عن النبيِّ صلى الله عليه وسلم قال: «إذا أفْطَرَ أحدُكُم، فَلْيُفْطِرْ على تَمْرٍ، فإنَّهُ بَرَكَةٌ، فإنْ لَمْ يَجِدْ تَمْراً، فالماءُ، فإنَّهُ طَهُورٌ» وقال: «الصَّدَقَةُ على المِسْكِينِ صَدَقَةٌ، وَعَلى ذي الرَّحِمِ ثِنْتَانِ: صَدَقَةٌ وَصِلَةٌ»

رواه الترمذي وقال: حديث حسن.

332. **Hazrat Salman Ibn Amir** (R.A.A.) relates that the Holy Prophet (S.A.W.) said: 'When you break the fast, break it with a date, for there is a blessing in it, and if you do not find a date, break it with water for water purifies. He added: Giving alms to a poor is one charity, and for a relative it amounts to two good deeds i.e. charity and benevolence to kinsmen.' (*Tirmizi*)

٣٣٣ ـ وعن ابن عمرَ رضي الله عنهما قال: كانَتْ تَحْتي امرَأةٌ، وكُنْتُ أُحِبُّها، وكانَ عُمَرُ يَكْرَهُهَا، فقال لي: طَلِّقْهَا، فأبَيْتُ، فأتى عُمَرُ رضي الله عنه النبيَّ صلى الله عليه وسلم، فَذَكَرَ ذلكَ لَهُ، فقال النبيُّ صلى الله عليه وسلم: «طَلِّقْهَا» رواه أبو داود، والترمذي وقال: حديث حسن صحيح.

333. **Hazrat Ibn Umar** (R.A.A.) relates: I had a wife whom I like but my father disliked her. He therefore asked me to divorce her, which I refused. Hazrat Umar (R.A.A.) brought this fact to the notice of the Holy Prophet (S.A.W.) who asked me: 'Divorce her.'

(*Abu Daud and Tirmizi*)

Tirmizi said this tradition is sound and authentic.

٣٣٤ ـ وعن أبي الدَّرْدَاء رضي الله عنه أن رَجُلاً أتاهُ فقال: إنَّ لي امرَأةً وإنَّ أُمّي تأمُرُني بِطَلاقِها؟ فقال: سَمِعْتُ رسولَ اللهِ صلى الله عليه وسلم يقول: «الوَالِدُ أوْسَطُ أبْوَابِ الجَنَّةِ، فإنْ شِئْتَ، فأضِعْ ذلكَ البابَ، أوِ احْفَظْهُ» رواه الترمذي وقال: حديثٌ حسنٌ صحيح.

334. **Hazrat Abu Darda'** (R.A.A.) relates that a man came to him and said: 'I have a wife and my mother asks me to divorce her.' Hazrat Abu Darda' (R.A.A.) said to him that he had heard the Holy Prophet

(S.A.W.) saying: 'A father is one of the strongest doors of Paradise. If you wish you may pull it down, or if you wish you may protect it.' (*Tirmizi*)

٣٣٥ ـ وعنِ البَرَاء بن عازِبٍ رضي الله عنهما ، عن النبي صلى الله عليه وسلم قال : « الخَالَةُ بِمَنْزِلَة الأُمِّ » رواه الترمذي وقال : حديثٌ حسن صحيح

335. Hazrat Bra'a Ibn 'Aazib (R.A.A.) relates that the Holy Prophet (S.A.W.) said: A mother's sister is equal to mother. *Imam Tirmizi* has mentioned this Tradition and has called it as authentic.

Hazrat Amr-Ibn-'Ambasa (R.A.A.) in a lengthy tradition, inter alia, reports that once he visited the Holy Prophet (S.A.W.) during the early days of Prophethood at Mecca. He says: 'I asked him, 'who are you'? The Holy Prophet (S.A.W.) replied, A Prophet.' I then asked "What is a Prophet'. He replied, 'Allah has sent me.' I further asked him: 'With what thing (message) Allah has sent you?' He answered that 'Allah has ordered me to be generous towards blood relations, to demolish (man-made) idols and to proclaim Allah's oneness and not to associate anybody with Him. (*Bukhari*)

Note: In the religious codes (*Shariat*) of the Prophets Moses (A.S.) Jesus (A.S.) and Muhammad (S.A.W.) the service and obedience of the parents have been declared as compulsory and obligatory. In fact the status and position of the parents has been classified as supreme and the highest among the human relations and only second after Allah. Along with the obedience of Allah, the obedience of the parents has also been emphasised, as is evident from the Quranic verses and traditions of the Holy Prophet (S.A.W.) cited above. Those fortunate persons who discharge their duties towards their parents, treat them well and are obedient to them, get their sins remitted and are rewarded with Allah's pleasure, innumerable blessings and favours.

* * * * * * * * * *

CHAPTER 41

Prohibition of Disobedience of Parents and Repudiation of Ties of Blood Relation.

قال الله تعالى : فَهَلْ عَسَيْتُمْ إنْ تَوَلَّيْتُمْ أَنْ تُفْسِدُوا فِي الأَرْضِ وَتُقَطِّعُوا أَرْحَامَكُمْ أُولئِكَ الَّذِينَ لَعَنَهُمُ اللهُ فَأَصَمَّهُمْ وَأَعْمَى أَبْصَارَهُمْ [محمد : ٢٢ ، ٢٣] وقال تعالى : وَالَّذِينَ يَنْقُضُونَ عَهْدَ اللهِ مِنْ بَعْدِ مِيثَاقِهِ وَيَقْطَعُونَ مَا أَمَرَ اللهُ بِهِ أَنْ يُوصَلَ وَيُفْسِدُونَ فِي

الأَرْضِ ، أولئِكَ لَهُمُ اللَّعْنَةُ وَلَهُمْ سُوءُ الدَّارِ [الرعد : ٢٥] وقال تعالى :
وَقَضَى رَبُّكَ أَلاَّ تَعْبُدُوا إلاَّ إِيَّاهُ وَبِالْوَالِدَيْنِ إِحْسَاناً إِمَّا يَبْلُغَنَّ عِنْدَكَ
الْكِبَرَ أَحَدُهُمَا أَوْ كِلاهُمَا فَلا تَقُلْ لَهُمَا أُفٍّ وَلا تَنْهَرْهُمَا وَقُلْ لَهُمَا
قَوْلاً كَرِيماً وَاخْفِضْ لَهُمَا جَنَاحَ الذُّلِّ مِنَ الرَّحْمَةِ وَقُلْ رَبِّ ارْحَمْهُمَا
كَمَا رَبَّيَانِي صَغِيراً [الإسراء : ٢٣ ، ٢٤] .

Allah, the Exalted, has said:

134. Would ye then, if ye were given the command, work corruption in the land and sever your ties of kinship. Such are they whom Allah curseth so that He deafeneth them and maketh blind their eyes (47:22—23)

135. And those who break the convenant of Allah after retifying it, and sever that which Allah hath commanded, should be joined, and make mischief in the earth: theirs is the curse and theirs the ill abode (13:25)

136. Thy Lord hath decreed that ye worship none save Him, and (that ye show) kindness to parents. If one of them or both of them to attain old age with thee, say not "Fie" unto them nor repulse them, but speak unto them a gracious word. And lower unto them the wing of submission through mercy, and say: My Lord! Have mercy on them both as they did care for me when I was little (17:23—24)

٣٣٦ ـ وعن أبي بكْرَةَ نُفَيْعِ بن الحارثِ رضي الله عنه قال : قال رسولُ
الله صلى الله عليه وسلم : « ألا أُنَبِّئُكُمْ بِأَكْبَرِ الْكَبَائِرِ ؟ » ـ ثلاثاً ـ قُلْنَا :
بَلَى يا رسول الله : قال : « الإِشْرَاكُ بِاللهِ ، وَعُقُوقُ الْوَالِدَيْنِ » وكَانَ
مُتَّكِئاً فَجَلَسَ ، فقال : « ألا وَقَوْلُ الزُّورِ وَشَهَادَةُ الزُّورِ » فَمَا زَالَ يُكَرِّرُهَا
حَتَّى قُلْنَا : لَيْتَهُ سَكَتَ . متفقٌ عليه

336. Hazrat Abu Bakarah Nufai Ibn Haris (R.A.A.) relates that the Holy Prophet (S.A.W.) said: 'May I tell you what are the major sins? (He repeated this thrice). We said: 'Certainly, O! Messenger of Allah.' He said: 'Association of others with Allah; disobedience of parents, (he had been resting on a pillow, then he sat up and continued) 'and telling lie and giving false testimony. He repeated this sentence so may times that we wished he should stop. (*Bukhari and Muslim*)

٣٣٧ – وعن عبد الله بن عمرو بن العاص رضي الله عنهما عن النبي صلى الله عليه وسلم قال : « الْكَبَائِرُ : الإِشْرَاكُ بِاللهِ ، وَعُقُوقُ الْوَالِدَيْنِ ، وَقَتْلُ النَّفْسِ ، وَالْيَمِينُ الْغَمُوسُ » رواه البخاري

337. Hazrat Abdullah Ibn 'Amr Ibn 'Al'Aas (R.A.A.) relates that the Holy Prophet (S.A.W.) said: Among the major sins are: Association of anybody with Allah, disobedience of parents, killing of a person and taking a false oath. (*Bukhari*)

٣٣٨ – وعنه أن رسول الله صلى الله عليه وسلم قال : « مِنَ الْكَبَائِرِ شَتْمُ الرَّجُلِ وَالِدَيْهِ ! » قالوا : يارسول الله وَهَلْ يَشْتُمُ الرَّجُلُ وَالِدَيْهِ ؟! قال « نَعَمْ ، يَسُبُّ أَبَا الرَّجُلِ ، فَيَسُبُّ أَبَاهُ ، وَيَسُبُّ أُمَّهُ ، فَيَسُبُّ أُمَّهُ » متفقٌ عليه

وفي روايةٍ : « إِنَّ مِنْ أَكْبَرِ الكَبَائِرِ أَنْ يَلْعَنَ الرَّجُلُ وَالِدَيْهِ ! » قِيلَ : يا رسولَ اللهِ كَيْفَ يَلْعَنُ الرَّجُلُ والِدَيْهِ ؟! قال « يَسُبُّ أَبَا الرَّجُلِ ، فَيَسُبُّ أَبَاهُ ، وَيَسُبُّ أُمَّهُ ، فَيَسُبُّ أُمَّهُ » .

338. Hazrat Abdullah Ibn 'Amr Ibn Al'Aas (R.A.A.) relates that the Holy Prophet said: 'Abusing one's parents is a major sin. People said: 'O Messenger of Allah! could a person abuse his own parents?' He answered: 'Yes, if he abuses another person's father, the latter would in retaliation abuse his father; if he abuses another person's mother, the latter would in turn abuse his mother.' (*Bukhari and Muslim*)

Another version says: 'One of the most heinous sins is that a person should curse his parents.' He was asked: 'O Messenger of Allah! How could a person curse his own parents? He said: 'When he abuses another's father, who, in turn, abuses his father, and when he abuses another's mother, who, in turn, abuses his mother.'

٣٣٩ – وعن أبي محمد جُبَيْرِ بن مُطْعِمٍ رضي الله عنه أن رسولَ الله صلى الله عليه وسلم قال : « لا يَدْخُلُ الجَنَّةَ قَاطِعٌ » قال سفيان في روايتِهِ : يَعْني : قَاطِعُ رَحِمٍ . متفق عليه

339. Hazrat Jubair Ibn Mut'im (R.A.A.) relates that the Holy Prophet (S.A.W.) said: 'One who disregards blood ties of kinship, will not enter Paradise.' (*Bukhari and Muslim*)

٣٤٠ – وعن أبي عِيسى المُغيرَةِ بن شُعْبَةَ رضي الله عنه عن النبيِّ صلى الله

عليه وسلم قال : «إنَّ اللهَ تعَالى حرَّمَ علَيْكُم عُقُوقَ الأُمَّهاتِ، ومَنْعاً وهاتِ، ووَأْدَ البَنَاتِ ، وكَرِهَ لَكُمْ قيلَ وقالَ ، وكَثْرَةَ السُّؤَالِ ، وإِضَاعَةَ المَالِ »
متفقٌ عليه .

340. Hazrat Abu Isa Mughirah Ibn Shu'bah (R.A.A.) relates that Holy Prophet (S.A.W.) said: 'Allah has forbidden you from the disobedience of your parents, parsimony, usurping the property of others, and the burying alive of female infants; and has disapproved for you useless talking, excessive questioning and waste of property.'
(*Bukhari and Muslim*)

* * * * * * * * * * *

CHAPTER 42

Virtue of Doing Good to Friends of Parents and Relations and Wives and Others, who are Entitled to Respect.

٣٤١ — عن ابنِ عمر رضي الله عنهما أن النبي صلى الله عليه وسلم قال : « إن أبرَّ البرِّ أنْ يَصِلَ الرَّجُلُ وُدَّ أبيهِ » .

341. Hazrat Ibn Umar (R.A.A.) relates that the Holy Prophet (S.A.W.) said: The noblest deed is that a person should be benevolent towards his father's friends. (*Muslim*)

٣٤٢ — وعن عبد الله بن دينارٍ عن عبد الله بن عمر رضي الله عنهما أنَّ رَجُلاً مِنَ الأعْرَابِ لَقِيَهُ بِطَرِيقِ مَكَّةَ ، فَسَلَّمَ عَلَيْهِ عَبْدُ الله بْنُ عُمَرَ ، وحَمَلَهُ عَلى حِمَارٍ كَانَ يَرْكَبُهُ ، وأَعْطَاهُ عِمَامَةً كَانَتْ عَلى رَأْسِهِ ، قال ابنُ دينارٍ : فَقُلْنَا لَهُ : أَصْلَحَكَ الله إنَّهُمُ الأَعْرَابُ وهُمْ يَرْضَوْنَ باليَسِيرِ فقال عبدُ الله بنُ عمر : إنَّ أَبَا هذا كَانَ وُدّاً لِعُمَرَ بن الخطاب رضي الله عنه وإنِّي سَمِعْتُ رسول الله صلى الله عليه وسلم يقول : « إنَّ أَبَرَّ البِرِّ صِلَةُ الرَّجُلِ أَهْلَ وُدِّ أَبِيهِ »

وفي روايةٍ عن ابن دينارٍ عن ابن عُمَرَ أنَّهُ كَانَ إذَا خَرَجَ إلى مَكَّةَ كَانَ لَهُ حِمارٌ يَتَرَوَّحُ عَلَيْهِ إذا مَلَّ رُكُوبَ الرَّاحِلَةِ ، وعِمَامَةٌ يَشُدُّ بها رَأْسَهُ ، فَبَيْنَا هُوَ يَوْماً عَلى ذلِكَ الحِمَارِ إذْ مَرَّ بِهِ أَعْرَابِيٌّ ، فقال : أَلَسْتَ

فُلانَ بْنَ فُلانٍ ؟ قال : بَلَى . فَأَعْطَاهُ الحِمَارُ ، فقال : ارْكَبْ هذا ، وأَعْطَاهُ العِمَامَةَ وقال : اشْدُدْ بِهَا رَأْسَكَ ، فقال لَهُ بَعْضُ أَصْحَابِهِ : غَفَرَ الله لَكَ أَعْطَيْتَ هذَا الأَعْرَابِيَّ حِمَاراً كُنْتَ تَرَوَّحُ عَلَيْهِ ، وعِمَامَةً كُنْتَ تَشُدُّ بِها رَأْسَكَ ؟ فقال : إنِّي سَمِعْتُ رسولَ الله صلى الله عليه وسلم يَقُولُ : «إنَّ مِنْ أَبَرِّ البِرِّ أَنْ يَصِلَ الرَّجُلُ أَهْلَ وُدِّ أَبِيهِ بَعْدَ أَنْ يُوَلِّيَ» وإنَّ أَبَاهُ كَانَ صَدِيقاً لِعُمَرَ رضي الله عنه ، روى هذِهِ الرِّوَايَاتِ كُلَّهَا مسلم

342. Hazrat Abdullah Ibn Dinar (R.A.A.) relates about Abdullah Ibn Umar that a villager Arab met him on his way to Mecca. Abullah Ibn Umar greeted him, asking him to ride with him on the donkey he was riding and also presented him the turban he was putting on. Hazrat Abdullah Ibn Dinar (R.A.A.) relates: 'I (Dinar) said to him: Ibn Umar May Allah be kind to you, these villagers can be pleased with small things (then why you do much to placate him). Hazrat Abdullah Ibn Umar (R.A.A.) said: 'This man's father was my father's (Hazrat Umar Ibn Khattab's) friend and I have heard the Holy Prophet (S.A.W.) say: The highest merit is that a person should be kind and generous towards his father's friend (*Muslim*)

Another tradition says: Hazrat Ibn Dinar (R.A.A.) says about Hazrat Abdullah Ibn Umar (R.A.A.) that 'when the latter travelled to Mecca and got tired riding a camel, he would ride on his donkey for an easy ride, and would put a turban round his head. When one day he was riding on his donkey, a village Arab passed by him and he (Abdullah Bin Umar) said to him: 'Are you not so and so, son of So and So?' The man said: 'Yes, I am.' Hazrat Abdullah (R.A.A.) gave him donkey and said: 'Ride it; and gave him his turban also and said: 'Wrap it round your head. Some of his companions said to him. 'May Allah pardon you; you have given this villager the donkey, on which you were riding with ease and the turban with which you had covered your head'. He said: 'I have heard the Holy Prophet (S.A.W.) say: It is the supreme virtue that a person should be benevolent towards the members of the families of the friends of his father after the latter's death. This man's father was a friend of my father (Hazrat Umar Ibn Khattab).' (*Muslim*)

٣٤٣ – وعن أبي أُسَيْدٍ – بضم الهمزة وفتح السين – مالِك بن رَبِيعَةَ السَّاعِدِيِّ رضي الله عنه قال : بَيْنَا نَحْنُ جُلُوسٌ عِنْدَ رسول اللهِ صلى الله عليه وسلم إذ جَاءَهُ رَجُلٌ مِنْ بَنِي سَلَمَةَ فقالَ : يارسولَ اللهِ هَلْ بَقِي

مِنْ بِرِّ أَبَوَيَّ شَيْءٌ أَبَرُّهُمَا بِهِ بَعْدَ مَوْتِهِمَا ؟ فقال : « نَعَمْ ، الصَّلاةُ عَلَيْهِمَا ، وَالاسْتِغْفَارُ لَهُمَا ، وَإِنْفَاذُ عَهْدِهِمَا مِنْ بَعْدِهِمَا ، وَصِلَةُ الرَّحِمِ الَّتِي لا تُوصَلُ إِلاَّ بِهِمَا ، وَإِكْرَامُ صَدِيقِهِمَا » رواه أبو داود

343. **Hazrat Abu Usaid Malik Ibn Rabia Sa'di** (R.A.A.) relates that they were sitting with the Holy Prophet (S.A.W.) when a man of the Bani Salamah tribe came and said: 'O Messenger of Allah! Is there anything, by means of which, I can now do something by way of benevolence towards my parents after their death?' The Holy Prophet (S.A.W.) answered: 'Yes, by praying for them and soliciting (Allah's) mercy and forgiveness for them, fulfilling their promises and undertakings, doing kindness to those who may be related to you through them, and respecting their friends.' *(Abu Daud)*

٣٤٤ – وعن عائشةَ رضي الله عنها قالت : مَا غِرْتُ عَلَى احدٍ مِنْ نِسَاءِ النبي صلى الله عليه وسلم مَا غِرْتُ عَلَى خديجةَ رضي الله عنها ، وَمَا رَأَيْتُهَا قَطُّ ، وَلكِنْ كَانَ يُكْثِرُ ذِكْرَهَا ، وَرُبَّمَا ذَبَحَ الشَّاةَ ، ثُمَّ يُقَطِّعُهَا أَعْضَاءً ، ثُمَّ يَبْعَثُهَا فِي صَدَائِقِ خَدِيجَةَ ، فَرُبَّمَا قلتُ لَهُ : كَأَنْ لَمْ يَكُنْ فِي الدُّنْيَا إِلاَّ خَدِيجَةُ ! فيقولُ : « إِنَّهَا كَانَتْ وَكَانَتْ وَكَانَ لِي مِنْهَا وَلَدٌ » متفقٌ عليه

وفي روايةٍ وإِنْ كَانَ لَيَذْبَحُ الشَّاءَ ، فَيُهْدِي فِي خَلائِلِهَا مِنْهَا مَا يَسَعُهُنَّ .

وفي روايةٍ كَانَ إِذَا ذَبَحَ الشَّاةَ يَقُولُ : « أَرْسِلُوا بِهَا إِلَى أَصْدِقَاءِ خَدِيجَةَ » .

وفي روايةٍ قالت : اسْتَأْذَنَتْ هَالَةُ بِنْتُ خُوَيْلِدٍ أُخْتُ خَدِيجَةَ عَلَى رسول الله صلى الله عليه وسلم ، فَعَرَفَ اسْتِئْذَانَ خَدِيجَةَ ، فَارْتَاحَ لِذلِكَ فقالَ : « اللَّهُمَّ هَالَةُ بِنْتُ خُوَيْلِدٍ » .

344. **Hazrat Ayesha** (R.A.A.) says: 'I was not so much jealous of the wives of the Holy Prophet (S.A.W.) as much as I grudged (Hazrat) Khadijah (R.A.A.), though I had no chance to see her. The Holy Prophet (S.A.W.) remembered her very often. Whenever a goat was slaughtered, he would cut its limbs and send them to (Hazrat) Khadijah's companions. Sometimes I would say to him: 'You talk of her as if there never was any woman in the world except (Hazrat) Khadijah!' and he would say: 'She was a noble woman', and I had my children too from her.' (*Bukhari and Muslim*)

According to another version whenever he used to slaughter a goat, he would invariably send pieces of meat to her friends as a present as much as was available.

Another version says: When a goat was slaughtered he would say: 'Send out of it to Khadijah's friends.'

On one occasion, Halah Bin Khuwailid, sister of Hazrat Khadijah (R.A.A.) asked permission of the Holy Prophet (S.A.W.) to come in. He thought it might be (Hazrat) Khadijah, and was deeply moved (as both the sisters had similar voice). He exclaimed, O Allah, she is Halah Bint Khuwailad.

٣٤٥ ـ وعن أنس بن مالك رضي الله عنه قال : خرجت مع جرير بن عبد الله البجلي رضي الله عنه في سفر ، فكان يخدمني فقلت له : لا تفعل ، فقال : إني قد رأيت الأنصار تصنع برسول الله صلى الله عليه وسلم شيئاً آليت على نفسي أن لا أصحب أحداً منهم إلا خدمته . متفق عليه

345. Hazrat Anas Ibn Malik (R.A.A.) says: Once I went on a journey along with Hazrat Jarir Ibn Abdullah Bujali (R.A.A.). In the course of this journey the latter used to serve me, though he was older than me (Hazrat Anas (R.A.A.). So I (Hazrat Anas R.A.A.) said to him: 'Please do not do so.' He replied: 'I saw the Ansar (the original inhabitants of Medina) serve the Holy Prophet (S.A.W.) with such devotion that I made a vow that whenever I am in the company of any of them I will serve him.' (*Bukhari and Muslim*)

* * * * * * * * * * *

CHAPTER 43

Honouring the Members of the Family of the Holy Prophet (S.A.W.) and Their Virtues.

قال الله تعالى : إنما يريد الله ليذهب عنكم الرجس أهل البيت ويطهركم تطهيراً [الأحزاب : ٣٣] وقال تعالى : ومن يعظم شعائر الله فإنها من تقوى القلوب [الحج : ٣٢] .

Allah, the Exalted, has said:

137. Allah's wish is but to remove uncleanness, far from you, O Folk of the Household, and cleanse you with a thorough

cleansing. (33:33)

138. And whoso magnifieth the offerings consecrated to Allah, it surely is from devotion of the hearts. (22:32)

٣٤٦ – وعن يزيد بن حَيَّانَ قال : انطَلَقْتُ أنا وَحُصَيْنُ بنُ سَبْرَةَ ، وَعَمْرُو بنُ مُسْلِمٍ إلى زَيْدِ بنِ أرْقَمَ رضي الله عنهم ، فَلَمَّا جَلَسْنَا إلَيْهِ قال له حُصَيْنٌ : لَقَدْ لَقِيتَ يا زَيْدُ خيراً كثيراً ، رأيْتَ رسولَ الله صلى الله عليه وسلم ، وسَمِعْتَ حديثَهُ ، وَغَزَوْتَ مَعَهُ ، وَصَلَّيْتَ خَلْفَهُ : لَقَدْ لَقِيتَ يا زَيْدُ خيراً كثيراً ، حَدِّثْنَا يا زَيْدُ ما سَمِعْتَ مِنْ رسول الله صلى الله عليه وسلم قال : يا ابنَ أخي والله لَقَدْ كَبِرَتْ سِنِّي ، وَقَدُمَ عَهْدِي ، وَنَسِيتُ بعضَ الَّذي كُنْتُ أعِي مِنْ رسولِ الله صلى الله عليه وسلم ، فما حَدَّثْتُكُمْ ، فاقْبَلُوا ، وما لا فلا تُكَلِّفُونِيهِ ثُمَّ قال : قامَ رسولُ الله صلى الله عليه وسلم يوماً فينا خطيباً بماءٍ يُدْعَى خُمّاً بَيْنَ مَكَّةَ والمدينةِ ، فَحَمِدَ اللهَ ، وأثْنَى عَلَيْهِ ، وَوَعَظَ ، وَذَكَّرَ ، ثُمَّ قال : « أمَّا بَعْدُ : ألا أيُّها النَّاسُ ، فإنَّما أنا بَشَرٌ يُوشِكُ أنْ يَأتِيَ رسولُ رَبِّي فَأُجِيبَ ، وأنا تارِكٌ فيكُمْ ثَقَلَيْنِ : أوَّلُهُما كِتابُ اللهِ ، فيه الهُدَى والنُّورُ ، فَخُذُوا بِكِتابِ اللهِ ، واسْتَمْسِكُوا به . فَحَثَّ على كِتابِ اللهِ ، وَرَغَّبَ فيه ثُمَّ قالَ « وأهْلُ بَيْتِي أُذَكِّرُكُمُ اللهَ في أهْلِ بَيْتِي ، أُذَكِّرُكُمُ اللهَ في أهْلِ بَيْتِي » فقالَ لَهُ حُصَيْنٌ : وَمَنْ أهْلُ بَيْتِهِ يا زَيْدُ ، ألَيْسَ نِساؤُهُ مِنْ أهْلِ بَيْتِهِ ؟ قالَ : نِساؤُهُ مِنْ أهْلِ بَيْتِهِ ، وَلَكِنْ أهْلُ بَيْتِهِ مَنْ حُرِمَ الصَّدَقَةَ بَعْدَهُ ، قالَ : وَمَنْ هُمْ ؟ قالَ : هُمْ آلُ عَلِيٍّ ، وآلُ عَقِيلٍ ، وآلُ جَعْفَرٍ ، وآلُ عَبَّاسٍ قالَ : كُلُّ هؤلاءِ حُرِمَ الصَّدَقَةَ ؟ قالَ : نَعَمْ . رواه مسلم .

وفي روايةٍ : « ألا وإنِّي تارِكٌ فيكُمْ ثَقَلَيْنِ : أحَدُهُما كِتابُ اللهِ وَهُوَ حَبْلُ اللهِ ، مَنِ اتَّبَعَهُ كانَ عَلَى الهُدَى ، وَمَنْ تَرَكَهُ كانَ عَلَى ضَلالَةٍ »

346. Hazrat Yazid Ibn Hayyan (R.A.A.) relates that: I, Hazrat Husain Ibn Sabrah and Hazrat 'Amr Ibn Muslim went to Hazrat Zaid

Ibn Arqam (R.A.A.) and when we had taken our seats (Hazrat) Husain said to him: '(Hazrat) Zaid, you have collected a good amount of merit as you have seen the Holy Prophet (S.A.W.); you have heard him talk; you have fought along with him; you have offered your prayers (*Salat*) behind him. Undoubtedly you have gained a great amount of virtue. O Zaid! please let us know what you have heard from the Holy Prophet (S.A.W.). He said: 'Nephew, I have become very old and have become antiquated; some of the things that I heard from the Holy Prophet (S.A.W.), I have forgotten. So what I may narrate, please accept that and do not compel me to recall that which I have forgotten. The Holy Prophet (S.A.W.) once addressed us at Khuma, a spring between Mecca and Medina. He praised and glorified Allah and then admonished us by inviting our attention to divine punishment and reward and then again eulogised Allah, and said: 'Listen O people, I am but a man (like you) and soon the messenger of my Sustainer will come, and I shall have to obey His command. I shall leave behind two important things. The first is the Holy Quran, the Book of Allah; this contains instructions and guidance for you, and it has got light. Hold fast this Book, and adhere to it.' He laid great stress on this point and urged his followers to act upon the same. Then he said: 'The second thing, are the *Ahle-e-Baitor*, members of my family.' I call upon you in the name of Allah, to have due regard of my family members, and I once more urge upon you in the name of Allah, about my family. Hazrat Husain Bin Sabrah said: 'Zaid, who are the members of the Holy Prophet's family? Are not his wives the members of his family?' Hazrat Zaid replied: 'His wives are members of his family, and also those who are not allowed to accept *Sadqa* or alms after him.' Hazrat Hussain Bin Sabrah asked: 'Who are they?' Hazrat Zaid said: 'They are the descendants of Hazrat Ali, Hazrat Aqil, Hazrat J'afar and Hazrat Abbas. They have all been disallowed to accept alms?' Hazrat Zaid said: 'Yes' (*Muslim*)

Another tradition says: The Holy Prophet (S.A.W.) said: 'Listen I am leaving for you two great things. One of them is the Book of Allah; it is like the rope of Allah. One who folllows it, will be rightly guided; and he who discards it, will go astray.'

Note: This tradition, interalia, emphasises the human nature of the personality of the Holy Prophet (S.A.W.) who himself declares that he was a human being like us except that he received the divine message from Allah.

٣٤٧ – وعَنِ ابنِ عُمَرَ رضي الله عنهما ، عن أبي بَكْرٍ الصِّدِّيق رضي الله عنه موقُوفاً عَلَيْهِ أنَّهُ قالَ : ارقُبُوا مُحَمَّداً صلى الله عليه وسلم في أهْلِ بَيْتِهِ ، رواه البخاري

347. Hazrat Ibn Umar (R.A.) relates that Hazrat Abu Bakr Siddiq (R.A.A.) said: 'Honour (the most venerated master Hazrat) Muhammad, (the Holy Prophet of Allah (S.A.W.) by honouring the members of his family.' (*Bukhari*)

Note: Holy and pious persons and respectable theologians of the past have held the view that to respect the august children and the venerated wives of the Holy Prophet (S.A.W.) and to serve them and to love them, amounts to respecting the Holy Prophet (S.A.W.) himself.

CHAPTER 44

Honouring the Ulama, the Pious and the Learned Persons, to Prefer Them on Others and to Express Their Dignity.

قال الله تعالى: قُلْ هَلْ يَسْتَوِي الَّذِينَ يَعْلَمُونَ وَالَّذِينَ لا يَعْلَمُونَ إِنَّمَا يَتَذَكَّرُ أُولُوا الألْبَابِ [الزمر : ٩] .

Allah, the Exalted, has said:

139. Say (unto them, O Muhammad): Are those who know, equal with those who know not? But only men of understanding will pay heed. (39:9)

٣٤٨ – وعن أبي مسعودِ عقبةَ بنِ عمرو البدري الأنصاري رضي الله عنه قال : قال رسول الله صلى الله عليه وسلم : « يَؤُمُّ القَوْمَ أَقْرَؤُهُمْ لكِتَابِ الله ، فَإنْ كَانُوا في القِرَاءةِ سَوَاءً ، فَأَعْلَمُهُمْ بِالسُّنَّةِ ، فَإنْ كَانُوا في السُّنَّةِ سَوَاءً ، فَأَقْدَمُهُم هِجْرَةً ، فَإنْ كَانُوا في الهِجْرَةِ سَوَاءً ، فَأَقْدَمُهُمْ سِنّاً وَلا يَؤُمَّنَّ الرَّجُلُ الرَّجُلَ في سُلْطَانِهِ ، وَلا يَقْعُدُ في بَيْتِهِ عَلَى تَكْرِمَتِهِ إلاَّ بِإذْنِهِ » رواه مسلم

وفي روايةٍ لَهُ : « فَأَقْدَمُهُمْ سِلْماً » بَدَلَ « سِنّاً » : أَوْ إسْلاماً .

وفي روايةٍ : يَؤُمُّ القَوْمَ أَقْرَؤُهُمْ لِكِتَابِ الله ، وَأَقْدَمُهُمْ قِرَاءةً ، فَإنْ كَانَتْ قِرَاءتُهُمْ سَوَاءً فَيَؤُمُّهُمْ أَقْدَمُهُمْ هِجْرَةً ، فَإنْ كَانُوا في الهِجْرَةِ سَوَاءً ، فَلْيَؤُمَّهُمْ أَكْبَرُهُمْ سِنّاً » .

348. Hazrat Abu Masood 'Uqbah Ibn 'Amr Al-Badri Al-Ansari (R.A.A.) relates that the Holy Prophet (S.A.W.) said: 'The person most suited to lead the (congregational) prayers is one who is best versed in the recitation of the Holy Quran; if all those present, be equal in that respect, then the one who is the most learned of them in Sunnah; if they happen to be equal in this respect as well then the one of them who migrated earliest; and should they be all equal in this respect as well, then the oldest of them in age should lead the prayer. One should not lead the prayer in place of another person without his consent, nor he should take another's seat in his house without his permission'.*(Muslim)*

Another tradition by Muslim says: 'The senior most of them in accepting Islam, in place of the oldest of them in age.'

Yet another version is: The leader in prayer should be one who reads the Holy Quran the most and is the best reciter; should they be all equal in that respect then the senior most of them in migration; and should they be all equal in that respect, the oldest of them in age.'

٣٤٩ – وعنه قال : كان رسولُ الله صلى الله عليه وسلم يَمْسَحُ مَنَاكِبَنَا في الصَّلاةِ وَيَقُولُ : « اسْتَوُوا وَلا تَخْتَلِفُوا ، فَتَخْتَلِفَ قُلُوبُكُمْ ، لِيَلِنِي مِنْكُمْ أُولُوا الأَحْلامِ وَالنُّهَى ، ثُمَّ الَّذِينَ يَلُونَهُمْ » رواه مسلم

349. Hazrat Abu Mas'ud 'Uqbah Ibn 'Amr Al-Badri Al-Ansari (R.A.A.) also relates that the Holy Prophet (S.A.W.) would place his hands upon our shoulders when we were lining up for prayer and would say: 'Stand in straight lines and do not differ among yourselves, otherwise your hearts will differ with each other due to disaccord. Let those be nearest to me who are of age and possess knowledge, then those who are closest to them in these respects, and then those who are closest to them.' *(Muslim).*

٣٥٠ – وعن عبد الله بن مسعودٍ رضي الله عنه قال : قال رسول الله صلى الله عليه وسلم : « لِيَلِنِي مِنْكُمْ أُولُوا الأَحْلامِ وَالنُّهَى ، ثُمَّ الَّذِينَ يَلُونَهُمْ » ثلاثاً « وَإِيَّاكُمْ وَهَيْشَاتِ الأَسْوَاقِ » رواه مسلم

350. Hazrat Abdullah Ibn Mas'ud (R.A.A.) relates that the Holy Prophet (S.A.W.) said: In prayer let those be nearest to me who are adults and possess knowledge, then those who are closest to them in these respect, (he repeated this thrice) and added: 'Be careful and do not indulge in the loose talks of the market when you are in the mosque.' *(Muslim).*

٣٥١ – وعن أبي يَحْيَى وَقِيلَ : أبي مُحَمَّدٍ سَهْلِ بن أبي حَثْمَةَ – بفتح الحاء المهملة وإسكان الثاء المثلثة – الأنصاري رضي الله عنه قال : انْطَلَقَ عَبْدُ اللهِ ابن سَهْلٍ وَمُحَيِّصَةُ بْنُ مَسْعُودٍ إلى خَيْبَرَ وَهِيَ يَوْمَئِذٍ صُلْحٌ ، فَتَفَرَّقَا ، فأتى مُحَيِّصَةُ إلى عبدِ الله بنِ سهلٍ وهو يَتَشَحَّطُ في دَمِهِ قَتِيلاً ، فَدَفَنَهُ ، ثُمَّ قَدِمَ المَدِينَةَ فَانْطَلَقَ عَبْدُ الرحمنِ بْنُ سَهْلٍ وَمُحَيِّصَةُ وَحُوَيِّصَةُ ابْنَا مَسْعُودٍ إلى النَّبِيِّ صلى الله عليه وسلم ، فَذَهَبَ عَبْدُ الرَّحْمنِ يَتَكَلَّمُ فقال : « كَبِّرْ كَبِّرْ » وَهُوَ أَحْدَثُ القَوْمِ ، فَسَكَتَ ، فَتَكَلَّمَا فقال : « أَتَحْلِفُونَ وَتَسْتَحِقُّونَ قَاتِلَكُمْ ؟ وَذَكَرَ تَمَامَ الحَدِيث. متفقٌ عليه

351. Hazrat Abi Yahya or Abi Muhammad Sahl Ibn Abi Hasmah relates that **Abdullah Ibn Sahl** and **Muhayysah Ibn Mas'ud** went to Khaibar, during the period of truce, and got separated in pursuit of their respective business. Then Muhayysah came back to Abdullah and found him dead, drenched in his blood. He arranged his burial and returned to Madina. Then Abdur Rahman Ibn Sahl and Muhayysah and Huwayysah, sons of Mas'ud, approached the Holy Prophet (S.A.W.) and Abdur Rahman who was the best speaker among them began to speak; whereupon the Holy Prophet (S.A.W.), said: 'The eldest should speak; thereupon Abdur Rahman being the youngest of the three stopped talking and the other two addressed the Holy Prophet (S.A.W.), who said: 'Do you swear to this and demand justice against the murderer and narrated the entire Hodis. *(Bukhari and Muslim).*

٣٥٢ – وعن جابرٍ رضي الله عنه أنَّ النبي صلى الله عليه وسلم كَانَ يَجْمَعُ بَيْنَ الرَّجُلَيْنِ مِنْ قَتْلَى أُحُدٍ يَعْنِي فِي القَبْرِ ، ثُمَّ يَقُولُ : أَيُّهُمَا أَكْثَرُ أَخْذاً لِلْقُرْآنِ ؟ » فَإِذَا أُشِيرَ لَهُ إِلَى أَحَدِهِمَا قَدَّمَهُ فِي اللَّحْدِ . رواه البخاري

352. Hazrat Jabir (R.A.A.) relates that after the battle of Uhud was over, the Holy Prophet (S.A.W.) arranged the burial of two of the martyrs in one grave. In each case he would enquired: 'Which of these had memorised more of the Quran by heart.' Whoever was thus pointed out to him, was placed by him first in the grave. *(Bukhari).*

٣٥٣ – وعن ابن عمر رضي الله عنهما أنَّ النبي صلى الله عليه وسلم قال : « أَرَانِي فِي المَنَامِ أَتَسَوَّكُ بِسِوَاكٍ ، فَجَاءَنِي رَجُلَانِ ، أَحَدُهُمَا أَكْبَرُ مِنَ الآخَرِ ، فَنَاوَلْتُ السِّوَاكَ الأَصْغَرَ ، فَقِيلَ لِي : كَبِّرْ ، فَدَفَعْتُهُ إِلَى الأَكْبَرِ مِنْهُمَا » رواه مسلم مُسْنَداً والبخاري تعليقاً

353. Hazrat Ibn 'Umar (R.A.A.) relates that the Holy Prophet (S.A.W.) said: 'I dreamt that I was brushing my teeth with miswak— a fresh twig — when two men came to me, one being older than the other; I handed over the miswak to the younger, but I was asked to give it to the older, which I did.' *(Bukhari and Muslim).*

٣٥٤ – وعن أبي موسى رضي الله عنه قال : قال رسول الله صلى الله عليه وسلم : « إِنَّ مِنْ إِجْلَالِ اللهِ تعالى إِكْرَامَ ذِي الشَّيْبَةِ المُسْلِمِ ، وَحَامِلِ القُرْآنِ غَيْرِ الغَالِي فِيهِ ، وَالجَافِي عَنْهُ وإِكْرَامَ ذِي السُّلْطَانِ المُقْسِطِ » . حديثٌ حسنٌ رواه أبو داود

354. Hazrat Abu Musa (R.A.A.) relates that the Holy Prophet (S.A.W.) said: 'It is in fact the glorification of Allah to honour an aged Muslim; to honour one who has learnt the Quran by heart or is its interpreter, provided he makes no interpolations in it and does not contradict it by his conduct; and to respect a just ruler. ' *(Abu Daud).*

This is a good tradition.

٣٥٥ ــ وعن عَمْرِو بن شُعَيْبٍ ، عن أبيهِ ، عن جده رضي الله عنهم قال: قال رسول الله صلى الله عليه وسلم: «لَيْسَ مِنَّا مَنْ لَمْ يَرْحَمْ صَغيرَنَا، ويَعْرِفْ شَرَفَ كَبيرِنَا » حديثٌ صحيحٌ رواه أبو داود والترمذي ، وقال الترمذي : حديثٌ حسنٌ صحيحٌ .

وفي رِوَايَة أبي داود « حَقَّ كَبيرِنَا » .

355. Hazrat 'Amr Ibn Shuaib (R.A.A.) relates on the authority of his father who heard it from his father, that the Holy Prophet (S.A.W.) said: A person who has no compassion for our children and does not honour our elders is not from us. *(Abu Daud and Tirmizi).*

Tirmizi says that it is a sound tradition. Imam Daud says the right of the elders instead of the honour of the elders.

٣٥٦ ــ وعن مَيْمُونَ بن أبي شَبيبٍ رحمه الله أن عَائشَةَ رضي الله عنها مَرَّ بها سَائِلٌ، فَأَعْطَتْهُ كِسْرَةً ، وَمَرَّ بِهَا رَجُلٌ عَلَيْهِ ثِيَابٌ وَهَيْئَةٌ . فَأَقْعَدَتْهُ ، فَأَكَلَ فَقِيلَ لَهَا في ذلكَ ؟ فقالت: قال رسول الله صلى الله عليه وسلم : « أَنْزِلُوا النَّاسَ مَنَازِلَهُمْ » رواه أبو داود . لكِنْ قال : مَيْمُونُ لَمْ يُدْرِك عائِشَةَ .

وَقَدْ ذَكَرَهُ مُسْلِمٌ في أَوَّلِ صَحِيحِهِ تَعْليقاً فقال : وَذَكَرَ عَنْ عائِشَةَ رضي الله عنها قالت : أمرنا رسولُ الله صلى الله عليه وسلم أَنْ نُنْزِلَ النَّاسَ مَنَازِلَهُمْ ، وَذَكَرَهُ الحَاكِمُ أَبُو عبدِ اللهِ في كِتابِهِ « مَعْرِفَة عُلُومِ الحَدِيث » وقال : هوحديثٌ صحيح .

356. Hazrat Maimun Ibn Abi Shabib (R.A.A.) relates that a person asked Hazrat Ayesha (R.A.A.) for charity and she gave him a piece of bread. Later when one better person asked her for charity, she invited him to sit down and served him food. When asked the reason for the different treatment meted out, she said: 'The Holy Prophet (S.A.W.) has directed us: Entertain people according to their standing.' *(Abu Daud).*

٣٥٧ – وعن ابن عباس رضي الله عنهما قال : قَدِمَ عُيَيْنَةُ بْنُ حِصْنٍ ، فَنَزَلَ عَلَى ابْنِ أَخِيهِ الحُرِّ بْنِ قَيْسٍ ، وَكَانَ مِنَ النَّفَرِ الَّذِينَ يُدْنِيهِم عُمَرُ رضي الله عنه ، وَكَانَ القُرَّاءُ أَصْحَابَ مَجْلِسِ عُمَرَ وَمُشَاوَرَتِهِ ، كُهُولاً كَانُوا أَوْ شُبَّاناً ، فقال عُيَيْنَةُ لابْنِ أَخِيهِ : يَاابْنَ أَخِي لَكَ وَجْهٌ عِنْدَ هذَا الأَمِيرِ ، فَاسْتَأْذِنْ لِي عَلَيْهِ . فَاسْتَأْذَنَ لَهُ . فَأَذِنَ لَهُ عُمَرُ رضي الله عنه ، فلما دَخَلَ : قال هِيِ يَاابْنَ الخَطَّابِ : فَوَالله مَاتُعْطِينَا الجَزْلَ ، وَلا تَحْكُمُ فِينَا بِالعَدْلِ ، فَغَضِبَ عُمَرُ رضي الله عنه حَتَّى هَمَّ أَنْ يُوقِعَ بِهِ . فقال لَهُ الحُرُّ : يَاأَمِيرَ المُؤْمِنِينَ إِنَّ الله تعالى قال لِنَبِيِّهِ صلى الله عليه وسلم (خُذِ العَفْوَ وَأْمُرْ بِالعُرْفِ وَأَعْرِضْ عَنِ الجَاهِلِينَ)وإن هذا مِنَ الجَاهِلِينَ. والله مَا جَاوَزَهَا عُمَرُ حِينَ تَلاهَا عَلَيْهِ ، وَكَانَ وَقَّافاً عِنْدَ كِتَابِ الله تعالى . رواه البخاري .

357. The subject matter of this tradition has already been narrated under S.No. 50.

٣٥٨ – وعن أبي سعيد سَمُرَةَ بن جُنْدبٍ رضي الله عنه قال : لَقَدْ كُنْتُ عَلَى عَهْدِ رسول الله صلى الله عليه وسلم غُلاماً ، فَكُنْتُ أَحْفَظُ عَنْهُ ، فَمَا يَمْنَعُنِي مِنَ القَوْلِ إِلاَّ أَنَّ هَهُنَا رِجَالاً هُمْ أَسَنُّ مِنِّي . متفقٌ عليه .

358. Hazrat Abu Sa'id Samurah Ibn Jundub (R.A.A.) relates: 'I was only a boy during the time of the Holy Prophet (S.A.W.) and used to memorise the traditions of the Holy Prophet (S.A.W.) but I do not relate what I have preserved, because we have among us, people older than myself.' *(Bukhari and Muslim).*

٣٥٩ – وعن أنس رضي الله عنه قال : قال رسول الله صلى الله عليه وسلم : « مَا أَكْرَمَ شَابٌّ شَيْخاً لِسِنِّهِ إِلاَّ قَيَّضَ الله لَهُ مَنْ يُكْرِمُهُ عِنْدَ سِنِّهِ » رواه الترمذي وقال : حديث غريب .

359. Hazrat Anas Bin Malik (R.A.A.) relates that the Holy Prophet (S.A.W.) said: 'If a young-man honours an older person on account of his age, Allah will appoint someone who would honour him, when he attains old age.' *(Tirmizi).*

Iman: Tirmizi says that this tradition is not sound.

CHAPTER 45

Visiting Holy and Virtuous Persons and Keeping Company with Them Soliciting Their Favour and Visiting Sacred Places.

قال الله تعالى : وَإِذْ قَالَ مُوسَى لِفَتَاهُ لا أَبْرَحُ حَتَّى أَبْلُغَ مَجْمَعَ الْبَحْرَيْنِ أَوْ أَمْضِيَ حُقُباً إلى قوله تعالى: قَالَ لَهُ مُوسَى : هَلْ أَتَّبِعُكَ عَلَى أَنْ تُعَلِّمَنِ مِمَّا عُلِّمْتَ رُشْداً ؟ [الكهف:٦٠-٦٦] وقال تعالى وَاصْبِرْ نَفْسَكَ مَعَ الَّذِينَ يَدْعُونَ رَبَّهُمْ بِالْغَدَاةِ وَالْعَشِيِّ يُرِيدُونَ وَجْهَهُ [الكهف : ٢٨] .

Allah, the Exalted, has said:

140. And when Moses said unto his servant: I will not give up I reach the point where the two rivers meet, though I march on for ages *upto* Moses said unto him: May I follow thee, to the end that thou mayst teach me right conduct of that which thou hast been taught. (18:60-66).

141. Restrain thyself alongwith those who cry unto their Lord at morn and evening, seeking His countenance. (18:28).

٣٦٠ – وعن أنس رضي الله عنه قال : قال أبو بكر لعمر رضي الله عنهما بعدَ وَفَاةِ رسول الله صلى الله عليه وسلم : انْطَلِقْ بِنَا إلى أمِّ أَيْمَنَ رضي الله عنها نَزُورُهَا كَمَا كَانَ رسول الله صلى الله عليه وسلم يَزُورُهَا . فَلَمَّا انْتَهَيَا إلَيْهَا ، بَكَتْ ، فَقَالا لَهَا : مَا يُبْكِيكِ أمَا تَعْلَمِينَ أنَّ مَا عِنْدَ الله خَيْرٌ لِرَسُولِ الله صلى الله عليه وسلم؟ فقالت : إنِّي لا أَبْكِي أنِّي لا أعْلَمُ أنَّ مَا عِنْدَ الله تعالى خَيْرٌ رسول الله صلى الله عليه وسلم ، وَلَكِنْ أَبْكِي أنَّ الوَحْيَ قَدِ انْقَطَعَ مِنَ السَّمَاءِ، فَهَيَّجَتْهُمَا عَلَى البُكَاءِ، فَجَعَلا يَبْكِيَانِ مَعَهَا . رواه مسلم .

360 Hazrat Anas bin Malik (R.A.A.) relates that after the passing away of the Holy Prophet (S.A.W.), Hazrat Abu Bakr (R.A.A.) said to Hazrat Umar (R.A.A.): 'Let us visit Hazrat Umm Aiman (R.A.A.) a the Holy Prophet (S.A.W.) used to do. 'Accordingly when we came to her she started weeping.' They asked her; 'What makes you weep Do you not know that Allah has better recompense for the Holy Prophet (S.A.W.) than what he had in this world. She said: 'I know this well that what Allah has for the Holy Prophet (S.A.W.) with Him is the best recompense. I do not weep for this. I shed tears because Revelation has now stopped. This moved the two distinguished persons so much so that they too started weeping alongwith her. *(Muslim).*

Note: Hazrat Umm Aiman(R.A.A.) was a maid servant and foster mother of the Holy Prophet (S.A.W.). Subsequently he had freed her and married her with Hazrat Zaid Bin Harisa (R.A.A.). The Holy Prophet (S.A.W.) used to respect her much and frequently visited her, and would say that she was his mother.

٣٦١ – وعن أبي هريرة رضي الله عنه عن النبي صلى الله عليه وسلم ، أنَّ رَجُلاً زَارَ أخاً لَهُ في قَرْيَةٍ أُخْرَى ، فَأَرْصَدَ الله تعالى على مَدْرَجَتِهِ مَلَكاً. فلَمَّا أتَى عَلَيْهِ قال : أيْنَ تُرِيدُ ؟ قال : أُرِيدُ أخاً لي في هذهِ القَرْيَةِ . قال : هَلْ لَكَ عَلَيْهِ مِنْ نِعْمَةٍ تَرُبُّهَا عَلَيْهِ ؟ قال : لا ، غَيْرَ أنِّي أحْبَبْتُهُ في اللهِ تعالى ، قال : فَإنِّي رسول الله إلَيْكَ بأنَّ الله قَدْ أحَبَّكَ كَمَا أحْبَبْتَهُ فيهِ ، رواه مسلم .

361. Hazrat Abu Hurairah (R.A.A.) relates that the Holy Prophet (S.A.W.) said: 'A man set out to visit a brother in the neighbouring town. Allah deputed an angel (for his protection) on his way. When the said man met the angel en route the latter asked him: 'Where you are going?' He answered: 'I want to visit my brother who lives in this town.' The angel asked: Are you going to take some valuable thing for him? The man answered:'No. I have no desire except to visit him, because I love him for the sake of Allah only.' The Angel said to him: 'I am a messenger from Allah sent to tell you that Allah loves you as you love your brother for His sake.' *(Muslim).*

٣٦٢ – وعنه قال : قال رسولُ الله صلى الله عليه وسلم : « مَنْ عَادَ مَرِيضاً أوْ زَارَ أخاً لَهُ في الله ، نَادَاه مُنَادٍ : بِأنْ طِبْتَ ، وَطَابَ مَمْشَاكَ ، وَتَبَوَّأْتَ مِنَ الجَنَّةِ مَنْزِلاً » رواه الترمذي وقال : حديثٌ حسنٌ ،وفي بعض النسخ غريبٌ .

362. Hazrat Abu Hurairah (R.A.A.) relates that the Holy Prophet (S.A.W.) said: If a person visits a sick person or a brother of his simply for the sake of Allah, a caller announces, 'May you be happy, may your going be blessed and may you be awarded a pleasant residence in Paradise! *(Tirmizi)*

٣٦٣ – وعن أبي موسى الأشعَرِيِّ رضيَ اللهُ عنه أن النَّبي صلى الله عليه وسلم قال : « إنَّمَا مَثَلُ الجَلِيسِ الصَّالِحِ وَجَلِيسِ السُّوء . كَحَامِلِ

المِسْكِ ، وَنَافِخِ الكِيرِ ، فَحَامِلُ المِسْكِ ، إِمَّا أَنْ يُحْذِيَكَ ، وَإِمَّا أَنْ تَبْتَاعَ مِنْهُ وَإِمَّا أَنْ تَجِدَ مِنْهُ رِيحاً طَيِّبَةً ، وَنَافِخُ الكِيرِ . إِمَّا أَنْ يُحْرِقَ ثِيَابَكَ ، وَإِمَّا أَنْ تَجِدَ مِنْهُ رِيحاً مُنْتِنَةً » متفقٌ عليه .

363. Hazrat Abu Musa Ash'ari (R.A.A.) relates that the Holy Prophet (S.A.W.) said: 'The case of a good companion and that of a bad companion is like that of one who has *musk* (perfume) and of one who blows a furnace (or an iron smith). The owner of musk might give you some as gift, or you might buy some from him, or at least you might smell its fragrance. As regards the other, he might set your clothes a fire, or at least you will breathe fumes from the furnace.

(Bukhari and Muslim).

Note: According to Mullah Ali Qari in this tradition the Muslims have been encouraged to have company with the learned Ulama and virtuous persons, because the same is beneficial, and they have been dissuaded from associating with mischievous persons, as it is injurious.

٣٦٤ – وعن أبي هريرة رضي الله عنه، عن النبي صلى الله عليه وسلم قال: « تُنْكَحُ المَرْأَةُ لِأَرْبَعٍ : لِمَالِهَا ، وَلِحَسَبِهَا ، وَجَمَالِهَا ، وَلِدِينِهَا ، فَاظْفَرْ بِذَاتِ الدِّينِ تَرِبَتْ يَدَاكَ » متفقٌ عليه .

364. Hazrat Abu Hurairah (R.A.A.) relates that the Holy Prophet (S.A.W.) said: A man marries a woman for four reasons i.e. either for the sake of her wealth, her family chain, her charms or her love of religion. Try to get one for the sake of her religiousness, may you be blessed. *(Bukhari and Muslim).*

٣٦٥ – وعنْ ابنِ عباسٍ رضي الله عنهما قال : قال النبيُّ صلى الله عليه وسلم لجبريلَ : « مَا يَمْنَعُكَ أَنْ تَزُورَنَا أَكْثَرَ مِمَّا تَزُورُنَا ؟ » فَنَزَلَتْ : (وَمَا نَتَنَزَّلُ إِلاَّ بِأَمْرِ رَبِّكَ لَهُ مَا بَيْنَ أَيْدِينَا وَمَا خَلْفَنَا وَمَا بَيْنَ ذَلِكَ) رواه البخاري .

365. Hazrat Ibn Abbas (R.A.A.) relates that the Holy Prophet (S.A.W.) once said to Angel Gabriel: 'Why do you not visit us more than you do?' Whereupon the verse was revealed:

"We (angels)come not down save by commandment of thy Lord. Unto Him belongeth all that is before us and all that is behind us and all that is between those two."*(19:64)* *(Bukhari).*

٣٦٦ – وعنْ أبي سعيدٍ الخُدْرِيّ رضي الله عنه ، عن النبي صلى الله عليه وسلم قال : « لا تُصَاحِبْ إلاَّ مُؤْمِناً ، ولا يأْكُلْ طَعَامَكَ إلاَّ تَقِيٌّ » .

رواه أبو داود ، والترمذي بإسْنَادٍ لا بأس بِهِ .

366. Hazrat Abu Sa'id Khudri relates that the Holy Prophet (S.A.W.) said: 'Keep company with a believer only, and let your food be eaten only by the righteous.' *(Abu Daud and Tirmizi).*

This is an authentic tradition.

٣٦٧ – وعن أبي هريرة رضي الله عنه أن النبي صلى الله عليه وسلم قال : « الرَّجُلُ علَى دِينِ خَلِيلِهِ ، فَلْيَنْظُرْ أحَدُكُمْ مَنْ يُخَالِلُ » .

رواه أبو داود ، والترمذي بإسناد صحيح ، وقال الترمذي : حديثٌ حسن .

367. Hazrat Abu Hurairah (R.A.A.) relates that the Holy Prophet (S.A.W.) said: 'A person is likely to follow the faith of his friend, so look whom you be friend.' *(Abu Daud and Tirmizi).*

٣٦٨ – وعن أبي موسى الأشْعَرِيّ رضي الله عنه أن النبي صلى الله عليه وسلم قال : « المَرْءُ مَعَ مَنْ أحَبَّ » متفقٌ عليه .

وفي رواية قال : قِيلَ للنبيّ صلى الله عليه وسلم ، الرَّجُلُ يُحِبُّ القَوْمَ وَلَمَّا يَلْحَقْ بِهِمْ ؟ قال : « المَرْءُ مَعَ مَنْ أحَبَّ » .

368. Hazrat Abu Musa Ash'ari (R.A.A.) relates that the Holy Prophet (S.A.W.) said: 'A person will be considered to with one whom he loves.' *(Bukhari and Muslim).*

According to another version: 'The Holy Prophet (S.A.W.) was asked: 'What about a person who likes a people but does not associate with them.' He answered: 'A person will be with those he loves.'

٣٦٩ – وعن أنس رضي الله عنه أن أعرابياً قال لرسول الله صلى الله عليه وسلم : مَتَى السَّاعَةُ ؟ قال رسولُ الله صلى الله عليه وسلم : مَا أعْدَدْتَ لَهَا ؟ قال : حُبُّ اللهِ ورسولِهِ قال : « أنْتَ مَعَ مَنْ أحْبَبْتَ »

متفقٌ عليه ، وهذا لفظ مسلم .

وفي روايةٍ لهما : مَا أعْدَدْتُ لَهَا مِنْ كَثِيرِ صَوْمٍ ، ولا صَلاةٍ ، ولا صَدَقَةٍ ، وَلَكِنِّي أُحِبُّ اللهَ وَرَسُولَهُ .

369. Hazrat Anas Bin Malik (R.A.A.) relates that a villager asked the Holy Prophet (S.A.W.): 'When will the Day of Judgement come?' He asked the questioner: 'What preparations have you made for it?'

The man said: '(Only) the love of Allah and His Messenger (S.A.W.)'. The Holy Prophet (S.A.W.) said: 'You will be with those you love.'

(Bukhari and Muslim).

According to another version the villager said: 'I have not prepared for it with plenty of prayers, fasts and alms giving; but I love Allah and His Messenger (S.A.W.).'

٣٧٠ – وعن ابنِ مسعودٍ رضي الله عنه قال : جاءَ رَجُلٌ إلى رسول الله صلى الله عليه وسلم فقال : يارسول الله كَيْفَ تَقُولُ في رَجُلٍ أَحَبَّ قَوْماً وَلَمْ يَلْحَقْ بِهِمْ ؟ فقال رسولُ الله صلى الله عليه وسلم : « المَرْءُ مَعَ مَنْ أَحَبَّ » متفقٌ عليه .

370. Hazrat Ibn Mas'ud (R.A.A.) relates that a man came to the Holy Prophet (S.A.W.) and said: 'O Messenger of Allah! What would you say about a person who loves people but does not associate with them.' He said: 'A person will be with those he loves.'

(Bukhari and Muslim).

٣٧١ – وعن أبي هُرَيرة رضي الله عنه عن النبيِّ صلى الله عليه وسلم قال : « النَّاسُ مَعَادِنُ كَمَعَادِنِ الذَّهَبِ وَالفِضَّةِ ، خِيَارُهُمْ في الجَاهِلِيَّةِ خِيَارُهُمْ في الإِسْلَامِ إِذَا فَقِهُوا ، وَالأَرْوَاحُ جُنُودٌ مُجَنَّدَةٌ ، فَمَا تَعَارَفَ مِنْهَا ، ائْتَلَفَ، وَمَا تَنَاكَرَ مِنْهَا ، اخْتَلَفَ ، رواه مسلم

وروى البخاري قوله : « الأَرْوَاحُ » الخ من رواية عائشة رضي الله عنها .

371. Hazrat Abu Hurairah (R.A.A.) relates that the Holy Prophet (S.A.W.) said: 'People are like mines of gold and silver. Those of them who are best before Islam are best in Islam, if they have religious knowledge and understanding; and the spirits are like gathering armies, among these who are similar in qualities, they get mixed up with each other and those who are not, they drift away from each other.'

(Bukhari and Muslim).

Imam Bukhari cites Hazrat Ayeshah as the narrator of the last sentence of this tradition.

٣٧٢ – وعن أُسَيْرِ بنِ عَمْرٍو وَيُقَالُ : ابْنُ جابِرٍ وهو « بضم الهمزةِ وفتح السين المهملة » قال : كَانَ عُمَرُ بْنُ الخَطَّابِ رضي الله عنه إذا أَتَى عَلَيْهِ أَمْدَادُ أَهْلِ اليَمَنِ سَأَلَهُمْ : أَفِيكُمْ أُوَيْسُ بْنُ عَامِرٍ ؟ حَتَّى أتى على أُوَيْسٍ رضي الله عنه ، فقال له : أَنْتَ أُوَيْسُ بْنُ عامِرٍ ؟ قال : نَعَمْ ، قال : مِنْ مُرَادٍ ثُمَّ مِنْ قَرَنٍ ؟ قال : نَعَمْ قال : فَكَانَ بِكَ بَرَصٌ ، فَبَرَأْتَ

مِنهُ إلاَّ مَوضعَ دِرْهَمٍ ؟ قال : نَعَمْ قال : لَكَ وَالِدَةٌ ؟ قال : نَعَمْ ، قال سَمِعْتُ رسول الله صلى الله عليه وسلم يقول : « يَأْتي عَلَيْكُمْ أُوَيْسُ بْنُ عامِرٍ مَعَ أَمْدادِ أَهْلِ اليَمَنِ مِنْ مُرادٍ ، ثُمَّ مِنْ قَرَنٍ كَانَ بِهِ بَرَصٌ ، فَبَرَأَ مِنهُ إلاَّ مَوْضعَ دِرْهَمٍ ، لَهُ وَالِدَةٌ هُوَ بِها بَرٌّ لَوْ أَقسَمَ عَلى الله لأَبرَّهُ ، فَإنِ استَطَعْتَ أَنْ يَستَغفِرَ لَكَ فَافْعَلْ » فَاستَغفِرْ لي فَاستَغفَرَ لَهُ ، فقال له عُمَرُ : أَيْنَ تُرِيدُ ؟ قال : الكُوفَةَ ، قال : ألا أَكْتُبُ لَكَ إلى عَامِلِهَا ؟ قال : أَكُونُ في غَبْرَاءِ النَّاسِ أَحَبُّ إليَّ ، فَلَمَّا كَانَ مِنَ العَامِ المُقْبِلِ حَجَّ رَجُلٌ مِنْ أَشْرافِهِمْ ، فَوَافَى عُمَرَ ، فَسَأَلَهُ عَنْ أُوَيْسٍ ،فقال : تَرَكْتُهُ رَثَّ البَيْتِ قَلِيلَ المَتاعِ ،قال : سَمِعْتُ رسول الله صلى الله عليه وسلم يقول : يَأْتي عَلَيْكُمْ أُوَيْسُ بْنُ عَامِرٍ مَعَ أَمْدادٍ مِنْ أَهْلِ اليَمَنِ مِنْ مُرادٍ ، ثُمَّ مِنْ قَرَنٍ ، كَانَ بِهِ بَرَصٌ فَبَرَأَ مِنهُ إلاَّ مَوضِعَ دِرْهَمٍ ،لَهُ وَالِدَةٌ هُوَ بِها بَرٌّ لَوْ أَقسَمَ عَلى الله لأَبَرَّهُ ، فَإنِ استَطَعْتَ أَنْ يَستَغفِرَ لَكَ ، فَافْعَلْ ،فَأَتى أُوَيساً ، فقال : استَغفِرْ لي قال : أَنتَ أَحدَثُ عَهْداً بِسَفَرٍ صَالِحٍ ،فَاستَغفِرْ لي. قال : لَقِيتَ عُمَرَ ؟ قال : نَعَمْ ، فَاستَغفَرَ لَهُ ، فَفَطِنَ لَهُ النَّاسُ ، فَانطَلَقَ عَلى وَجهِهِ

رواه مسلم

وفي روايةٍ لمسلم أيضاً عن أُسَيْر بن جابر رضيَ الله عنه أنَّ أهلَ الكُوفةِ وَفَدُوا على عُمَرَ رضيَ اللهُ عنهُ ، وَفِيهِم رَجُلٌ مِمَّنْ كَانَ يَسْخَرُ بِأُوَيسٍ . فقال عُمَرُ : هَلْ هاهُنا أَحَدٌ مِنَ القَرَنِيِّينَ ؟ فَجَاءَ ذلكَ الرَّجُلُ ، فقالَ عُمَرُ : إنَّ رَسُولَ اللهِ صلى اللهُ عليه وسلم قد قال: « إنَّ رَجُلاً يَأْتِيكُمْ مِنَ اليَمَنِ يُقالُ لَهُ :أُوَيسٌ ، لا يَدَعُ بِاليَمَنِ غَيْرَ أُمٍّ لَهُ ، قَدْ كانَ بِهِ بَيَاضٌ فَدَعا اللهَ تعالى، فَأَذْهَبَهُ إلاَّ مَوضِعَ الدِّينارِ أَوِ الدِّرْهَمِ ، فَمَنْ لَقِيَهُ مِنكُمْ ، فَلْيَستَغفِرْ لَكُمْ » .

وفي روايةٍ له عَن عمر رضي الله عنه قال : إنِّي سَمِعْتُ رسول الله صلى الله

عليه وسلم يقول : « إنَّ خَيْرَ التَّابِعِينَ رَجُلٌ يُقَالُ لَهُ : أُوَيْسٌ ، وَلَهُ وَالِدَةٌ وَكَانَ بِهِ بَيَاضٌ ، فَمُرُوهُ ، فَلْيَسْتَغْفِرْ لَكُمْ » .

372. Hazrat 'Usair Ibn 'Amr (R.A.A.) also known as Ibn-i-Jabir relates that whenever a delegation came form Yemen to Hazrat Umar Ibn Khattab (R.A.A.) he would enquire from them: Is Uwais Ibn Aamir among you? At last in one of the delegations included Hazrat Uwais (R.A.A.) and the Caliph Hazrat Umar (R.A.A.) asked him. Are you Uwais Ibn Aamir? Hazrat Uwais replied: 'Yes'. He was then asked if he belonged to the Qarn branch of the tribe of Murad? He affirmed this. The Caliph then asked: 'Did you suffer from leprosy and recovered from it, except in respect of a space equal to the size of a *dirham* (a coin)!' He said: 'Yes! 'Is your mother alive?! asked the Caliph. He said 'Yes.' Then Hazrat Umar (R.A.A.) said:' I heard the Holy Prophet (S.A.W.) say: 'Uwais Ibn Aamir will come to you alongwith a delegation from Yemen. He is from the Qarn branch of the Murad tribe. He suffered from leprosy but he would have recovered from it, except for a space the size of a *dirham* (a coin). He has his mother whom he loved and obeyed. If he were to swear, relying upon Allah, for something, He would fulfil his oath. If you can prevail upon him to pray for you for your forgiveness, you must do so. As such I request you to pray to Allah for my forgiveness. Accordingly Hazrat Uwais (R.A.A.) prayed for Hazrat Umar's forgiveness. Hazrat Umar (R.A.A.) then asked him, where are you going? He said: 'Towards Kufa'. Hazrat 'Umar (R.A.A.) then asked him: 'May I write to the Governor of Kufa to help you?'Hazrat Uwais (R.A.A.) said: 'I prefer to live among the poor people.' Next year one of the nobles of Kufa came on pilgrimage and met Hazrat Umar (R.A.A.). Who enquired from him about Hazrat Uwais (R.A.A.). He said: 'I left him in a ramshackle house with few articles of furniture. Hazrat Umar (R.A.A.) said to him: 'I have heard the Holy Prophet (S.A.W.) say: Uwais Ibn Aamir of the Qarn branch of the Murad tribe will come to you in a delegation from Yemen. He would have suffered from leprosy but would have recovered except for a space equal to the size of a *dirham* (a coin). He would have his mother whom he would love immensely. If he would swear, relying upon Allah, for anything, Allah would fulfil his oath. If you can prevail upon him to pray for your forgiveness please, do so. Accordingly this man (the noble man) went to Hazrat Uwais (R.A.A.) and asked him to pray for his forgiveness. Hazrat Uwais (R.A.A.) said to him: 'You have just returned from a sacred journey (place); therefore it is you who should pray for my forgiveness.' He further asked the noble: Did you meet Hazrat Umar (R.A.A.)? The man said: 'Yes, I did meet him.' Hazrat Uwais (R.A.A.) then prayed for the noble's forgiveness. Thereafter the people became aware of the virtues (spiritual powers) of Hazrat Uwais (R.A.A.) and consequently he departed from that place following his impulse. *(Muslim).*

Another version of Muslim says: The inhabitants of Kufa waited upon Hazrat Umar (R.A.A.). Among them was one who was quite free with Hazrat Uwais (R.A.A.). Hazrat Umar (R.A.A.) enquired: 'Is there any one among you from the (sub-tribe of) Qarn?' So this man came forward. Then Hazrat Umar (R.A.A.) said: 'The Holy Prophet (S.A.W.) had said: 'A man will come to you from Yemen whose name would be Uwais. He would have left behind in Yemen only his mother. He had suffered from leprosy and had prayed to Allah to be cured from the disease. Consequently he was cured except for a space equal to the size of a dinar or dirham (a coin). Any of you should meet him, should ask him to pray for his forgiveness.' Yet another version says: Hazrat Umar (R.A.A.) said: 'I have heard the Holy Prophet (S.A.W.) say: 'The best one of the Tabi'ins. Those Muslims who had seen one or more of the companions of the Holy Prophet (S.A.W.) is a man called Owais; he has a mother and has got white spots on his body (leprosy). Go to him and request him to pray for your forgiveness.

٣٧٣ — وعن عمر بن الخطاب رضي الله عنه قال : اسْتَأْذَنْتُ النَّبيَّ صلى الله عليه وسلم في العُمْرَةِ ، فَأَذِنَ لي ، وقال : « لا تَنْسَنَا يَا أُخَيَّ مِنْ دُعَائِكَ » فقال كَلِمَةً مَا يَسُرُّنِي أَنَّ لي بِها الدُّنْيَا .

وفي روايةٍ قال : « أَشْرِكْنَا يَا أُخَيَّ في دُعَائِكَ »

حديثٌ صحيحٌ رواه أبوداود ، والترمذي وقال : حديثٌ حسنٌ صحيحٌ.

373. Hazrat Umar bin Khattab (R.A.A.) relates: ' I solicited leave of the Holy Prophet(S.A.W.) to perform the Umra.' He granted me leave and said: 'My Brother!. Please remember me while praying.' Hazrat Umar (R.A.A.) says: 'This is something which I would not like exchange for the whole world.' *(Abu Daud and Tirmizi).*

According to another version Hazrat Umar said: 'Also pray for me, my Brohter! in your supplications.'

٣٧٤ — وعن ابن عُمَرَ رضي الله عنهما قال : كَانَ النَّبيُّ صلى الله عليه وسلم يَزُورُ قُبَاءَ رَاكِباً وَمَاشِياً ، فَيُصَلِّي فيهِ رَكْعَتَيْنِ ، متفقٌ عليه .

وفي روايةٍ : كان النَّبيُّ صلى الله عليه وسلم يَأْتِي مَسْجِدَ قُبَاءَ كُلَّ سَبْتٍ رَاكِباً وَمَاشِياً وَكَانَ ابْنُ عُمَرَ يَفْعَلُهُ .

374. Hazrat Ibn Umar (R.A.A.) relates: 'The Holy Prophet (S.A.W.) used to visit (the mosque of) Quba both riding or on foot and would offer two *raka'at* of prayer there. *(Bukhari and Muslim).*

According to another version 'The Holy Prophet (S.A.W.) visited the mosque at Quba every Saturday, riding or on foot and Hazrat Ibn Umar (R.A.A.) following in his footsteps did the same.

****

CHAPTER 46

Virtues, Importance and Etiquette of Sincere Love for the Sake of Allah.

قال الله تعالى : مُحَمَّدٌ رَسُولُ اللهِ والَّذِينَ مَعَهُ أَشِدَّاءُ عَلَى الكُفَّارِ رُحَمَاءُ بَيْنَهُمْ [الفتح : ٢٩] إلى آخرِ السورة .وقال تعالى : وَالَّذِينَ تَبَوَّؤُا الدَّارَ والإيمَانَ مِنْ قَبْلِهِم يُحِبُّونَ مَنْ هاجَرَ إلَيْهِم [الحشر : ٩] .

Allah, the Exalted, has said:

142. Muhammad is the Messenger of Allah. And those with him are hard against the disbelievers, and merciful among themselves (48:29).

143. Those who entered the city and the faith before them love those who flee unto them for refuge. (59:9).

٣٧٥ – وعن أنس رضي الله عنه عن النبي صلى الله عليه وسلم قال : « ثلاثٌ مَنْ كُنَّ فيهِ وَجَدَ بِهِنَّ حَلاوَةَ الإيمَانِ : أَنْ يَكُونَ اللهُ وَرَسُولُهُ أَحبَّ إلَيْهِ مِمَّا سِواهُما ، وَأَنْ يُحِبَّ المَرْءَ لا يُحِبُّهُ إلاَّ لِلهِ ، وَأَنْ يَكْرَهَ أَنْ يَعُودَ فِي الكُفْرِ بَعْدَ أَنْ أَنْقَذَهُ اللهُ مِنْهُ ، كَمَا يَكْرَهُ أَنْ يُقْذَفَ فِي النَّارِ » متفقٌ عليه

375. **Hazrat Anas Bin Malik** (R.A.A.) relates that the Holy Prophet (S.A.W.) said: 'There are three qualities whosoever have them, may taste the sweetness of Faith: firstly one who loves Allah and His Messenger (S.A.W.) above all else; secondly one who loves some one simply for the sake of Allah, and thirdly, one who abhors return to disbelief, after Allah has rescued him from it, as he would abhor being thrown into the Fire (the Hell).' *(Bukhari and Muslim).*

٣٧٦ – وعن أبي هريرة رضي الله عنه عن النبي صلى الله عليه وسلم قال : « سَبْعَةٌ يُظِلُّهُمُ اللهُ في ظِلِّهِ يَوْمَ لاظِلَّ إلاَّ ظِلُّهُ : إمَامٌ عَادِلٌ ، وَشَابٌّ نَشَأَ في عِبادَةِ اللهِ عزَّ وجلَّ ، وَرَجُلٌ قَلْبُهُ مُعَلَّقٌ بالمَسَاجِدِ . وَرَجُلان تَحَابَّا في اللهِ اجْتَمَعَا عَلَيْهِ ، وَتَفَرَّقَا عَلَيْهِ ، وَرَجُلٌ دَعَتْهُ امْرَأَةٌ ذَاتُ حُسْنٍ وَجَمَالٍ ، فقالَ : إِنِّي أخافُ اللهَ ، وَرَجُلٌ تَصَدَّقَ بِصَدَقَةٍ ، فَأَخْفَاهَا حَتَّى لاتَعْلَمَ شِمَالُهُ ما تُنْفِقُ يَمِينُهُ ، وَرَجُلٌ ذَكَرَ

اللهَ خَالِياً فَفَاضَتْ عَيْنَاهُ » متفقٌ عليه

376. Hazrat Abu Hurairah (R.A.A.) relates that the Holy Prophet (S.A.W.) said: 'Seven persons are those who will be sheltered under the shade of Allah on the Day of Judgement when there will be no other shade, besides His shade. They are! A just ruler; a youngman who passed his youth with the worship and service of Allah — the Lord of honour and glory, one whose heart is perpetually attached with the mosque; two such persons who love each other for the sake of Allah, they joined together for His sake and parted for His sake; a man who is invited for sin by a charming and beautiful woman but declines, saying I fear Allah; one who spends in charity in a secret way without making a show, so that his left hand may not know that his right hand spent ; and one who remembers Allah in solitude so that his eyes overflow.

(Bukhari and Muslim).

٣٧٧ ــ وعنه قال : قال رسول الله صلى الله عليه وسلم : « إن الله تعالى يقولُ يَوْمَ القِيَامَةِ : أيْنَ المُتَحَابُّونَ بِجَلالي ؟ اليَوْمَ أُظِلُّهُمْ في ظِلِّي يَوْمَ لا ظِلَّ إلاَّ ظِلِّي » رواه مسلم

377. Hazrat Abu Hurairah (R.A.A.) relates that the Holy Prophet (S.A.W.) said: 'On the Day of Judgment, Allah, the most High, will announce where are those persons who love each other for the sake of My pleasure? This day I am going to shelter them in the shade provided by Me. Today there is no shade except My shade. *(Muslim).*

٣٧٨ ــ وعنه قال : قال رسولُ الله صلى الله عليه وسلم : « وَالَّذي نَفْسِي بِيَدِهِ لا تَدْخُلُوا الجَنَّةَ حَتَّى تُؤْمِنُوا ، وَلا تُؤْمِنُوا حَتَّى تَحَابُّوا ، أَوَلا أَدُلُّكُمْ عَلَى شَيْءٍ إذَا فَعَلْتُمُوهُ تَحَابَبْتُمْ ؟ أَفْشُوا السَّلامَ بينكم » رواه مسلم .

378. Hazrat Abu Hurairah (R.A.A.) relates that the Holy Prophet (S.A.W.) said: 'By Allah in whose hands is my life, you will not enter the Paradise unless you believe (in Islam), and you will not believe unless you love one another. May I tell you something so that you may love one another? Spread greeting and saluting between yourselves.'

(Muslim).

٣٧٩ ــ وعنه عن النبي صلى الله عليه وسلم : « أنَّ رَجُلاً زَارَ أخاً لَه في قَرْيَةٍ أُخْرَى ، فَأَرْصَدَ اللهُ لَهُ عَلَى مَدْرَجَتِهِ مَلَكاً » وذكر الحديث إلى قوله :

« إنَّ اللهَ قَدْ أَحَبَّكَ كَمَا أَحْبَبْتَهُ فِيهِ » رواه مسلم . وقد سبق بالباب قبله

379. This Hadis has already been covered in item No. 361.

٣٨٠ — وعن البَرَاءِ بن عَازِبٍ رضي الله عنهما عن النبي صلى الله عليه وسلم
أنه قال في الأَنْصَارِ : « لا يُحِبُّهُمْ إلاَّ مُؤْمِنٌ ، وَلا يُبْغِضُهُمْ إلاَّ مُنَافِقٌ .
مَنْ أَحَبَّهُمْ أَحَبَّهُ اللهُ ، وَمَنْ أَبْغَضَهُمْ أَبْغَضَهُ الله » متفقٌ عليه .

380. Hazrat Bra'a Ibn 'Aazib (R.A.A.) relates that the Holy Prophet (S.A.W.) said that only a believer loves the Ansar and only a deceitful person dislikes them. Allah lvoes him who loves them and Allah dislikes him who dislikes them. *(Bukhari and Muslim).*

٣٨١ — وعن مُعَاذٍ رضي الله عنه قال : سَمِعتُ رسول الله صلى الله عليه
وسلم يقول : « قَالَ اللهُ عَزَّ وَجَلَّ : المُتَحَابُّونَ فِي جَلالِي ، لَهُمْ مَنَابِرُ
مِنْ نُورٍ يَغْبِطُهُمُ النَّبِيُّونَ وَالشُّهَدَاءُ »
رواه الترمذي وقال : حديثٌ حسنٌ صحيحٌ

381. Hazrat Mu'az Bin Jabal (R.A.A.) relates that he heard the Holy Prophet (S.A.W.) say: Allah, the master of honour says: For those who love one another for the sake of Fear My majesty and magnificence, there will be high seats of light, that will be the envy of prophets and martyrs. *(Tirmizi).*

٣٨٢ — وعن أبي إدريس الخَوْلانيِّ رَحِمَهُ الله قال : دَخَلْتُ مَسْجِدَ
دِمَشْقَ ، فَإِذَا فَتًى بَرَّاقُ الثَّنَايَا وَإِذَا النَّاسُ مَعَهُ ، فَإِذَا اخْتَلَفُوا في
شَيْءٍ ، أَسْنَدُوهُ إِلَيْهِ ، وَصَدَرُوا عَنْ رَأْيِهِ ، فَسَأَلْتُ عَنْهُ ، فَقِيلَ :
هَذَا مُعَاذُ بْنُ جَبَلٍ رضي الله عنه ، فَلَمَّا كَانَ مِنَ الْغَدِ ، هَجَّرْتُ ،
فَوَجَدْتُهُ قَدْ سَبَقَنِي بِالتَّهْجِيرِ ، وَوَجَدْتُهُ يُصَلِّي ، فَانْتَظَرْتُهُ حَتَّى
قَضَى صَلاتَهُ ، ثُمَّ جِئْتُهُ مِنْ قِبَلِ وَجْهِهِ ، فَسَلَّمْتُ عَلَيْهِ ، ثُمَّ قُلْتُ :
وَاللهِ إِنِّي لأُحِبُّكَ للهِ ، فَقَالَ : آللهِ ؟ فَقُلْتُ : أَللهِ ، فقال : آللهِ ؟ فَقُلْتُ :
أللهِ ، فَأَخَذَنِي بِحَبْوَةِ رِدَائِي ، فَجَبَذَنِي إِلَيْهِ ، فَقَالَ : أَبْشِرْ ، فَإِنِّي
سَمِعْتُ رسول الله صلى الله عليه وسلم يقول : « قال الله تعالى وَجَبَتْ مَحَبَّتِي
لِلْمُتَحَابِّينَ فِيَّ ، وَالمُتَجَالِسِينَ فِيَّ ، وَالمُتَزَاوِرِينَ فِيَّ ، وَالمُتَبَاذِلِينَ فِيَّ »

حديث صحيح رواه مالك في الموطأ بإسناده الصحيح

382. Hazrat Abu Idris Al-Khaulani (R.A.A.) says: (Once) I entered the mosque in Damascus and by chance I saw a youth who had brilliant teeth, and a number of people were sitting with him. When they disagreed on some topic they would refer it to him and accepted his opinion. I asked as to who he was, and was told that he was Hazrat Mu'az Ibn Jabal (R.A.A.). Next day I hastened to the mosque, but found that he had already arrived there and was busy in prayer. I waited till he had finished his prayer and then went to him from the front; and after saluting him said: By Allah I love you. He said: 'For the sake of Allah?' I answered: 'Yes for the sake of Allah:' He again said'For the sake of Allah? I answered yes for the sake of Allah.' Then he took hold of the fold of my sheet, drew me closer to himself and said: 'Hear the glad tidings!' for I have heard the Holy Prophet (S.A.W.) say: 'Allah has decided: It is incumbent upon Me to bestow My love on those who love one another for My sake, meet one another for My sake, visit one another for My sake, and spend for each other for my sake.'
(Malik).

٣٨٣ – عن أبي كَرِيمَةَ المِقْدَادِ بْنِ مَعْدِيكَرِبَ رضي الله عنه عن النبيِّ صلى الله عليه وسلم قال: «إذا أَحَبَّ الرَّجُلُ أخاهُ، فَلْيُخْبِرْهُ أَنَّهُ يُحِبُّهُ» رواه أبو داود، والترمذي وقال: حديثٌ حسنٌ.

383. Hazrat Abu Karima-al-Miqdad Ibn Ma'dikarib (R.A.A.) relates that the Holy Prophet (S.A.W.) said: If a person loves his brother, he should apprise him of this fact. *(Abu Daud and Tirmizi).*

٣٨٤ – وعن مُعاذٍ رضي الله عنه، أنَّ رسول الله صلى الله عليه وسلم، أخذَ بيدِهِ وقال: «يامُعاذُ، واللهِ، إنِّي لأُحِبُّكَ، ثُمَّ أُوصيكَ يامُعاذُ لا تَدَعَنَّ في دُبُرِ كُلِّ صلاةٍ تقولُ: اللَّهُمَّ أَعِنِّي على ذِكْرِكَ وَشُكْرِكَ، وَحُسْنِ عِبادَتِكَ».

حديثٌ صحيحٌ، رواه أبو داود والنسائي بإسناد صحيح.

384. Hazrat Mu'az Bin Jabal (R.A.A.) relates that the Holy Prophet (S.A.W.) caught his hand and said: 'Mu'az, by Allah I love you and advise you that you should not forget praying after every *farz* (obligatory) salat: Allah, help me in worshipping you, and thanking you and praying in the proper way. *(Abu Daud and Nisai).*

٣٨٥ – وعن أنس ، رضي الله عنه ، أن رجلاً كان عند النبي ، صلى الله عليه وسلم ، فمر رجل به ، فقال : يارسول الله إني لأحب هذا ، فقال له النبي صلى الله عليه وسلم : « أأعلمته ؟ » قال : لا : قال : « أعلمه » فلحقه ، فقال : إني أحبك في الله ، فقال : أحبك الذي أحببتني له .

رواه أبو داود بإسناد صحيح .

385. **Hazrat Anas Bin Malik** (R.A.A.) relates that a man was sitting with the Holy Prophet (S.A.W.) when another person passed by him, and the former said: 'Messenger of Allah (S.A.W.), I love this man.' The Holy Prophet (S.A.W.) asked: 'Have you apprised him of this fact?' He said: 'No.' The Holy Prophet (S.A.W.) said: 'Do tell him.' So he went to the man and said to him: 'I love you for the sake of Allah;' and the other replied: 'May Allah, for whose sake you love me love you.'

(Abu Daud).

****

CHAPTER 47

Signs of Allah's Love for His Servants and the Efforts for Its Adoption and Struggle for its Achievement.

قال الله تعالى : قُلْ إِنْ كُنْتُمْ تُحِبُّونَ اللهَ فَاتَّبِعُونِي يُحْبِبْكُمُ اللهُ وَيَغْفِرْ لَكُمْ ذُنُوبَكُمْ واللهُ غَفُورٌ رَحِيمٌ [آل عمران : ٣١] ، وقال تعالى : يَا أَيُّهَا الَّذِينَ آمَنُوا مَنْ يَرْتَدَّ مِنْكُمْ عَنْ دِينِهِ فَسَوْفَ يَأْتِي اللهُ بِقَوْمٍ يُحِبُّهُمْ وَيُحِبُّونَهُ أَذِلَّةٍ عَلَى الْمُؤْمِنِينَ أَعِزَّةٍ عَلَى الكَافِرِينَ يُجَاهِدُونَ فِي سَبِيلِ اللهِ وَلا يَخَافُونَ لَوْمَةَ لائِمٍ ذَلِكَ فَضْلُ اللهِ يُؤْتِيهِ مَنْ يَشَاءُ واللهُ وَاسِعٌ عَلِيمٌ [المائدة : ٥٤] .

Allah, the Exalted, has said:

144. Say, (O Muhammad to mankind): If ye love Allah, follow me; Allah will love you and forgive you for your sins. Allah is Forgiving, Merciful. (3:31).
145. O ye who believe! Whoso of you becometh a renegade from his religion, (know that in his stead) Allah will bring a people whom He loveth and who love Him, humble toward believers, stern towards disbelievers, striving in the way of Allah, and fearing not the blame of any blamer. Such is the grace of Allah

which He giveth unto whom He will. Allah is All-embracing, All-knowing. (5:54).

٣٨٦ – وعن أبي هريرة رضي الله عنه قال : قال رسول الله صلى الله عليه وسلم : « إنَّ الله تعالى قال : مَنْ عادَى لي وَليّاً ، فَقَدْ آذَنْتُهُ بالحَرْبِ . وَما تَقَرَّبَ إليَّ عَبْدِي بِشَيْءٍ أَحَبَّ إليَّ مِمَّا افْتَرَضْتُ عَلَيْهِ وَمَا يَزالُ عَبْدِي يَتَقَرَّبُ إليَّ بالنَّوافِلِ حَتَّى أُحِبَّهُ ، فَإِذا أَحْبَبْتُهُ ، كُنْتُ سَمْعَهُ الَّذي يَسْمَعُ بِهِ ، وَبَصَرَهُ الَّذي يُبْصِرُ بِهِ ، وَيَدَهُ الَّتي يَبْطِشُ بِها ، وَرِجْلَهُ الَّتي يَمْشي بِها وإنْ سَأَلَني ، أَعْطَيْتُهُ ، وَلَئِنِ اسْتَعاذَني ، لأُعيذَنَّهُ » رواه البخاري

386. Hazrat Abu Hurairah (R.A.A.) relates that the Holy Prophet (S.A.W.) said: ‘Allah, the Exalted, says: I declare war against one who bears enmity towards a friend of Mine. When a servant of Mine comes closer to Me, with a thing which I love, out of the things which I have prescribed; and when he seeks my favour through optional prayers *(Nawafil)* I start loving him and when I love him, I become his ear with which he hears and his eyes with which he sees and his hand with which he grasps and his foot with which he walks, and when he requests Me for anything I grant him and when he seeks protection I give him protection.’ *(Bukhari).*

٣٨٧ – وعنه عن النبي ، صلى الله عليه وسلم ، قال : « إذا أَحَبَّ اللهُ تعالى العَبْدَ ، نادَى جِبْريلَ : إنَّ اللهَ تعالى يُحِبُّ فُلاناً ، فَأَحْبِبْهُ ، فَيُحِبُهُ جِبْريلُ ، فَيُنادي في أَهْلِ السَّماءِ : إنَّ اللهَ يُحِبُّ فُلاناً ، فَأَحِبوهُ ، فَيُحِبُّهُ أَهْلُ السَّماءِ ، ثُمَّ يُوضَعُ له القَبُولُ في الأَرْضِ » متفقٌ عليه .

وفي روايةٍ لمسلمٍ : قال رسولُ الله ، صلى الله عليه وسلم : « إنَّ اللهَ تعالى إذا أَحَبَّ عَبْداً دَعا جِبْريلَ ، فقال : إنّي أُحِبُّ فُلاناً فَأَحْبِبْهُ ، فَيُحِبُهُ جِبْريلُ ، ثُمَّ يُنادي في السَّماءِ ، فَيَقُولُ : إنَّ اللهَ يُحِبُّ فُلاناً ، فَأَحِبُّوهُ فَيُحِبُّهُ أَهْلُ السَّماءِ ، ثُمَّ يُوضَعُ له القَبُولُ في الأَرْضِ ، وإذا أَبْغَضَ عَبْداً دَعا جِبْريلَ ، فَيَقُولُ : إنّي أُبْغِضُ فُلاناً ، فَأَبْغِضْهُ ، فَيُبْغِضُهُ جِبْريلُ ، ثُمَّ يُنادي في أَهْلِ السَّماءِ : إنَّ اللهَ يُبْغِضُ فُلاناً ، فَأَبْغِضُوهُ ، فَيُبْغِضُهُ أَهْلُ السَّماءِ ثُمَّ تُوضَعُ له البَغْضاءُ في الأَرْضِ » .

387. **Hazrat Abu Hurairah** (R.A.A.) relates that the Holy Prophet (S.A.W.) said: When Allah loves a servant, Angel Gabriel is apprised and informed that : 'Allah, the Exalted, loves So and So, do thou love him also.' Then Angel Gabriel also starts loving him and sends a call through out the Heavens calling upon the dwellers that 'Allah loves So and So, so you also love him.' Then the dwellers of the Heavens also start loving him, and then he is made popular in the world (as well).

(Bukhari and Muslim).

Another version of Muslim says: The Holy Prophet (S.A.W.) said: when Allah, the Exalted loves a person, He calls Angel Gabriel and says: I love So and So, so love him. Hence Angel Gabriel loves him. Then it is announced in the heavens and said: Allah loves such and such person so love him, thence the dwellers of heaven love him. 'When Allah is displeased with a servant, He calls Angel Gabriel and says to him: ' I am angry with So and So as such you should also be displeased with him, and Angel Gabriel also gets angry with him. Then he sends a call all over the Heavens: 'Allah is offended with So and So, you should also be get offended with him.' Thereafter hatred against him is spread in the earth (as well).

٣٨٨ – وعن عائشة رضي الله عنها ، أن رسول الله صلى الله عليه وسلم ، بَعَثَ رَجُلاً عَلَى سَرِيَّةٍ ، فَكَانَ يَقْرَأُ لِأَصْحَابِهِ فِي صَلَاتِهِمْ ، فَيَخْتِمُ بِـ (قُلْ هُوَ اللهُ أَحَدٌ) فَلَمَّا رَجَعُوا ، ذَكَرُوا ذَلِكَ لرسول الله ، صلى الله عليه وسلم ، فقال : « سَلُوهُ لِأَيِّ شَيْءٍ يَصْنَعُ ذَلِكَ ؟ » فَسَأَلُوهُ ، فَقَالَ : لِأَنَّهَا صِفَةُ الرَّحْمَنِ ، فَأَنَا أُحِبُّ أَنْ أَقْرَأَ بِهَا ، فقال رسول الله ، صلى الله عليه وسلم : « أَخْبِرُوهُ أَنَّ اللهَ تعالى يُحِبُّهُ » متفقٌ عليه

388. Hazrat Ayesha (R.A.A.) relates that the Holy Prophet (S.A.W.) appointed a man in charge of a *Lashkar* (army) sent for a battle. He also led his men in prayers and always concluded his recitation with *sura Al-Ikhlas* (Chapter 112)! When the Lashkar returned to Medina they apprised the Holy Prophet (S.A.W.) of this practice, who said: 'Ask him why he does so?' Accordingly he was asked and said in reply: 'This chapter sets out the qualities of Allah the Exalted, and I love to recite it often. The Holy Prophet (S.A.W.) on being told this said: 'Tell him that Allah too loves him.' *(Bukhari and Muslim).*

****

CHAPTER 48

Caution Against Persecution of the Virtuous, Aged and Poor and Needy Persons.

قال الله تعالى : ﴿ وَالَّذِينَ يُؤْذُونَ الْمُؤْمِنِينَ وَالْمُؤْمِنَاتِ بِغَيْرِ مَا اكْتَسَبُوا فَقَدِ احْتَمَلُوا بُهْتَاناً وَإِثْماً مُبِيناً ﴾ [الأحزاب : ٥٨] وقال تعالى : ﴿ فَأَمَّا الْيَتِيمَ فَلا تَقْهَرْ وَأَمَّا السَّائِلَ فَلا تَنْهَرْ ﴾ [الضحى : ٩ ، ١٠] .

Allah, the Exalted, has said:

146. And those who malign believing men and believing women undeservedly, they bear the guilt of slander and manifest sin. (33:58).
147. Therefore the orphan oppress not. Therefore the beggar drive not away. (93:9—10).

Imam Nawawi (R.A.) says that there are numerous traditions on this topic. Among these one reported by Hazrat Abu Hurairah (R.A.A.) has already been mentioned earlier (S.No. 386). Another is one reported by Hazrat Sa'ad Bin Abi Waqqas (R.A.A.) (S.No. 258). And the Holy Prophet (S.A.W.) said to Hazrat Abu Bakr (R.A.A.) that 'O Bakr if you offend these persons then you will incur the displeasure of your Sustainer (S.No. 261).

٣٨٩ - وعن جندب بن عبد الله رضي الله عنه قال : قال رسول الله صلى الله عليه وسلم : « مَنْ صَلَّى صَلاةَ الصُّبْحِ ، فَهُوَ فِي ذِمَّةِ الله ، فَلا يَطْلُبَنَّكُمُ اللهُ مِنْ ذِمَّتِهِ بِشَيْءٍ ، فَإِنَّهُ مَنْ يَطْلُبْهُ مِنْ ذِمَّتِهِ بِشَيْءٍ ، يُدْرِكْهُ ، ثُمَّ يَكُبُّهُ عَلَى وَجْهِهِ فِي نَارِ جَهَنَّمَ » رواه مسلم

389. Hazrat Jundub Ibn Abdullah (R.A.A.) relates that the Holy Prophet (S.A.W.) said: 'One who performs the Salat at *Fajr* (morning prayers) comes under the security of Allah; therefore take care lest Allah may call you to account for anything concerning His undertaking, for if He were to call any of you to account for any short coming concerning His Guarantee, and find him wanting, that one would be hurled down to the Fire of Hell. *(Muslim).*

****

CHAPTER 49

Assessing People as Regards Their Apparent Conduct and Entrusting Their Hidden Secrets to Allah.

قال الله تعالى : ﴿ فَإِنْ تَابُوا وَأَقَامُوا الصَّلاةَ وَآتَوا الزَّكَاةَ فَخَلُّوا سَبِيلَهُمْ ﴾ [التوبة :] .

Allah, the Exalted, has said:

148. But if they repent and establish worship and pay the poor-due, then leave their way free. (9:5).

٣٩٠ — عن ابن عمر رضي الله عنهما ، أن رسولَ الله صلى الله عليه وسلم قال : « أُمِرتُ أنْ أُقاتِلَ النَّاسَ حتَّى يَشْهَدُوا أنْ لاإلهَ إلاَّ الله ، وأنَّ مُحمّداً رسولُ الله ، ويُقيموا الصَّلاةَ ، ويُؤتُوا الزَّكاةَ ، فإذا فعَلُوا ذلكَ ، عَصَمُوا مِنّي دِماءَهُم وأموالَهُمْ إلاّ بِحَقِّ الإسلامِ ، وحِسابُهُمْ على الله تعالى » متفقٌ عليه .

390. Hazrat Ibn 'Umar (R.A.A.) relates that the Holy Prophet (S.A.W.) said: I have been commanded (by Allah) that I should continue my contention with the people till they bear witness that there is none worthy of worship, except Allah, and that Muhammad (S.A.W.) is His Messenger; and (they) establish Prayer and pay the Zakat (the poor-due). When they have done this, they and their properties will be secured against me, subject to their obligations under Islam and their accounting is with Allah. *(Bukhari and Muslim)*

٣٩١ — وعن أبي عبدِ الله طارِقِ بن أشْيَمٍ ، رضي الله عنه ، قال : سمعتُ رسول الله صلى الله عليه وسلم يقُولُ : « مَنْ قال لاإلهَ إلاَّ الله محمداً رسول الله ، وكَفَرَ بِمَا يُعْبَدُ مِنْ دُونِ الله ، حَرُمَ مالُهُ ودَمُهُ ، وحِسابُهُ على الله تعالى » رواه مسلم .

391. Hazrat Abu Abdullah Tariq Ibn Ushaim (R.A.A.) relates that he heard the Holy Prophet(S.A.W.) say: 'One who affirms that there is no god save Allah and Muhammad (S.A.W.) is the Messenger of Allah, and rejects all that is worshipped beside Him, secured his life and property (from us) and is accountable only to Allah for actions.' *(Muslim)*

٣٩٢ — وعن أبي مَعْبَدٍ المقْدَادِ بن الأسْوَدِ ، رضي الله عنه ، قال : قلت لِرسُولِ الله صلى الله عليه وسلم : أرأيْتَ إنْ لقيتُ رَجُلاً مِنَ الكُفَّارِ ، فاقْتَتَلْنا ، فضَرَبَ إحدَى يدَيَّ بالسَّيْفِ ، فقطَعَها ، ثُمَّ لاذَ مِنّي بِشَجَرةٍ ، فقال : أسْلَمْتُ للهِ ، أأقتُلُهُ يارسول الله بعْدَ أنْ قالها ؟ فقَال : « لاتقْتُلْهُ » فقُلْتُ : يا رَسُولَ الله قَطَعَ إحدَى يدَيَّ ، ثُمَّ قال ذلكَ

بَعْدَ مَا قَطَعَهَا؟ ! فقال : « لاتَقْتُلْهُ ، فَإِنْ قَتَلْتَهُ ، فَإِنَّهُ بِمَنْزِلَتِكَ قَبْلَ أَنْ تَقْتُلَهُ ، وَإِنَّكَ بِمَنْزِلَتِهِ قَبْلَ أَنْ يَقُولَ كَلِمَتَهُ الَّتِي قال » متفقٌ عليه

392. Hazrat Abu Maabad Miqdad Ibn Al-Aswad (R.A.A.) relates: 'I submitted to the Holy Prophet (S.A.W.: "Please let me know if I am fighting a disbeliever and he cuts off one of my hands with his sword, and then taking cover behind a tree to protect himself from my assault, says: 'I bow to Allah' (i.e. I accept Islam) is it permissible for me to kill him after he has said this? He said: 'No, do not kill him.' I submitted "O Messenger of Allah (S.A.W.), even after he cuts off one of my hands and thereafter says this?" He said: 'Do not kill him, for if you kill him, he will be in the position in which you were before you killed him, and you will be in the position in which he was before he uttered these words:

(Bukhari and Muslim).

٣٩٣ - وعن أُسامَةَ بنِ زَيْدٍ ، رضي الله عنهما ، قال : بَعَثَنَا رسولُ الله صلى الله عليه وسلم ، إلى الحُرَقَةِ مِنْ جُهَيْنَةَ ، فَصَبَّحْنا القَوْمَ عَلَى مِياهِهِمْ ، وَلَحِقْتُ أنا وَرَجُلٌ مِنَ الأَنْصارِ رَجُلاً مِنْهُمْ ، فَلَمَّا غَشِيناهُ قال : لا إلهَ إلاَّ اللهُ ، فَكَفَّ عَنْهُ الأَنْصارِيُّ ، وَطَعَنْتُهُ بِرُمْحِي حَتَّى قَتَلْتُهُ ، فَلَمَّا قَدِمْنا المَدِينَةَ ، بَلَغَ ذلِكَ النَّبِيَّ ، صلى الله عليه وسلم ، فقال لي : « يا أُسامَةُ أَقَتَلْتَهُ بَعْدَ ما قالَ : لا إلهَ إلاَّ اللهُ ؟ قلتُ : يارسولَ الله إنَّما كانَ مُتَعَوِّذاً ، فَقالَ : « أَقَتَلْتَهُ بَعْدَ مَا قالَ لا إلهَ إلاَّ اللهُ ؟ ! » فَمَا زَالَ يُكَرِّرُهاعَلَيَّ حَتَّى تَمَنَّيْتُ أَنِّي لَمْ أَكُنْ أَسْلَمْتُ قَبْلَ ذلِكَ اليَوْمِ متفقٌ عليه

وفي روايةٍ : فَقالَ رَسولُ الله ، صلى الله عليه وسلم : « أَقالَ : لا إلهَ إلاَّ اللهُ وَقَتَلْتَهُ ؟ ! قلتُ : يا رسولَ اللهِ ، إنَّمَا قالَهَا خَوْفاً مِنَ السِّلاحِ ، قال : « أفَلا شَقَقْتَ عَنْ قَلْبِهِ حَتَّى تَعْلَمَ أَقالَهَا أَمْ لا ؟ ! » فَمَا زَالَ يُكَرِّرُهَا حَتَّى تَمَنَّيْتُ أَنِّي أَسْلَمْتُ يَوْمَئِذٍ

393. Hazrat Usamah Ibn Zaid (R.A.A.) relates: Once the Holy Prophet (S.A.W.) sent us on expedition against the tribe of Juhainah living in the Oasis of Huraqah. We reached their (water) springs in the

morning. Ansar and I caught hold of one of their men, and when we had over-powered him, he recited *La-ilaha-il-lal-lah* (the *kalima*). 'There is no god save Allah.' On hearing this the Ansari held back, but I killed him with a stroke of my spear. On our return to Medina, this incident was brought to the knowledge of the Holy Prophet (S.A.W.). He asked me: 'O Usamah, did you kill him even after he had said *La ilaha -il-lal-lah*. (There is no god save Allah?)' I said: 'Messenger of Allah (S.A.W.), he made the declaration only to save his life.' He said again: 'Did you kill him after he had affirmed: There is no god save Allah?' He sent on repeating this sentence till I felt that it would have been lesser if I had not accepted Islam before that day. *(Bukhari and Muslim)*.

Another version is: The Holy Prophet (S.A.W.) said: Did he affirm: 'There is no god save Allah;' and even then you killed him?' I said: 'Messenger of Allah (S.A.W.), he had said this only out of fear of our arms.' He said: 'Why did you not get his heart dissected to discover whether he had said these words from his heart or not?' He kept on repeating it till I wished I had accepted Islam only that day.

٣٩٤ ـ وعن جُنْدُبِ بنِ عبد الله ، رضي الله عنه ، أنَّ رسولَ الله ، صلى الله عليه وسلم ، بعَثَ بعثاً مِنَ المُسْلِمِينَ إلى قومٍ مِنَ المُشْرِكِينَ ، وأنَّهُمْ التقَوْا ، فكانَ رَجُلٌ مِنَ المُشْرِكِينَ إذا شاءَ أنْ يقْصِدَ إلى رَجُلٍ مِنَ المُسْلِمِينَ قصَدَ لهُ فقَتَلَهُ ، وأنَّ رَجُلاً مِنَ المُسْلِمِينَ قصَدَ غفْلَتَهُ ، وكُنَّا نَتَحَدَّثُ أنَّهُ أُسامةُ بْنُ زَيْدٍ ، فلَمَّا رفَعَ السَّيْفَ ، قال : لا إلهَ إلاَّ اللهُ ، فقَتَلَهُ ، فجاءَ البَشِيرُ إلى رسول الله ، صلى الله عليه وسلم ، فسأَلَهُ ، وأخْبَرَهُ ، حتَّى أخْبَرَهُ خبَرَ الرَّجُلِ كَيْفَ صنَعَ ، فدَعاهُ فسأَلَهُ ، فقال : « لِمَ قتَلْتَهُ ؟ فقَالَ : يارسولَ الله أوْجَعَ في المُسْلِمِينَ ، وقَتَلَ فُلاناً وفُلاناً ـ وسَمَّى له نفراً ـ وإنِّي حمَلْتُ علَيْهِ ، فلَمَّا رأى السَّيْفَ قال : لاإلهَ إلاَّ اللهُ . قال رسول الله صلى الله عليه وسلم : « أقتَلْتَهُ ؟ » قالَ : نعَمْ ، قال : « فكَيْفَ تصْنَعُ بلا إلهَ إلاَّ اللهُ ، إذا جاءَتْ يوْمَ القِيامةِ ؟ قالَ : يارسولَ الله استَغْفِرْ لي . قال : « وكيفَ تصْنَعُ بِلاإلهَ إلاَّ اللهُ إذا جاءَتْ يوْمَ القِيامَةِ ؟ » فجَعَلَ لايزيدُ على أنْ يقُولَ : « كَيْفَ تصْنَعُ بِلا إلهَ إلاَّ اللهُ إذا جاءَتْ يوْمَ القِيامَةِ » رواه مسلم

394. Hazrat Jundub Ibn Abdullah (R.A.A.) relates that the Holy Prophet (S.A.W.) despatched a Muslim force to fight against a disbelieving community. When the two forces met in combat, one of the desperado disbeliever was so adapt in the art of fighting that he could kill any Muslim whom he wanted. One of the Muslims was also after him, and we said, that it must be Hazrat Usamah Ibn Zaid (R.A.A.) on the look out for an opportunity to kill him. When he raised his sword over him, the unbeliever at once said: 'There is no god save Allah' Inspite of this Hazrat Usamah Ibn Zaid (R.A.A.) killed him. When the Muslims achieved victory and this good news reached the Holy Prophet (S.A.W.), he was also apprised of this particular incident. He sent for Hazrat Usamah (R.A.A.) and asked him: 'Why did you kill this man?' He answered: 'Messenger of Allah (S.A.W.) this man had created panic among the Muslims, and slain so and so, (naming a few). Accordingly I advanced upon him and when he saw (my drawn) sword he said: 'There is no god save Allah.' The Holy Prophet (S.A.W.) asked: 'Did you kill him?' He said: 'Yes, Sir' The Holy Prophet (S.A.W.) said: 'On the Day of Judgement, what you will say in reply to his reciting La ilaha il-lal-lah?" Hazrat Usamah (R.A.A.) submitted 'O Messenger of Allah (S.A.W.), please pray for my forgiveness.' The Holy Prophet (S.A.W.) kept on repeating the same sentence i.e. 'What will you say in reply to his recitation of *la ilaha-il-lal-lah?* on the Day of Judgment?. *(Muslim).*

٣٩٥ – وعن عبدِ الله بنِ عُتْبَةَ بنِ مسعودٍ قال : سَمِعْتُ عُمَرَ بْنَ الخطَّابِ ، رضي الله عنه ، يقولُ : « إنَّ نَاساً كَانُوا يُؤْخَذُونَ بِالوَحْيِ فِي عَهْدِ رسول الله ، صلى الله عليه وسلم ، وإنَّ الوَحْيَ قَدِ انْقَطَعَ ، وإنَّما نَأْخُذُكُمُ الآنَ بِمَا ظَهَرَ لَنَا مِنْ أَعْمَالِكُمْ ، فَمَنْ أَظْهَرَ لَنَا خَيْراً ، أَمَّنَّاهُ وقَرَّبْنَاهُ ، وَلَيْسَ لَنَا مِنْ سَرِيرَتِهِ شَيْءٌ ، الله يُحَاسِبُهُ فِي سَرِيرَتِهِ ، وَمَنْ أَظْهَرَ لَنَا سُوءاً ، لَمْ نَأْمَنْهُ ، وَلَمْ نُصَدِّقْهُ وإنْ قالَ : إنْ سَرِيرَتَهُ حَسَنَةٌ » رواه البخاري

395. Hazrat Abdullah Ibn Utbah Bin Mas'ud (R.A.A.) relates that he heard Hazrat Umar Ibn Khattab (R.A.A.) say: Dring the life time of the Holy Prophet (S.A.W.) people were called upon to account (for their wrongs) through revelation. Now since revelation has stopped therefore we shall call you to account on the basis of your visible actions. As such now whoever exhibits or shows to us good we shall take it as such, and accept it, and we shall not enquire into his hidden activities or motive; with a view to disapprove it. Allah will take notice of his hidden activities and call him to account for the same; but whoever exhibits or shows to us evil we shall not accept it and shall not confirm it, although he may claim that his intention was good. *(Bukhari).*

****

CHAPTER 50

Fear (of Allah)

قال الله تعالى : وإِيَّايَ فَارْهَبُونِ [البقرة : ٤٠]وقال تعالى : إِنَّ بَطْشَ رَبِّكَ لَشَدِيدٌ [البروج : ١٢] وقال تعالى : وكَذَلِكَ أَخْذُ رَبِّكَ إِذا أَخَذَ القُرَى وهِيَ ظَالِمَةٌ إِنَّ أَخْذَهُ أَلِيمٌ شَدِيدٌ إِنَّ فِي ذَلِكَ لآيَةً لِمَنْ خَافَ عَذَابَ الآخِرَةِ ذَلِكَ يَوْمٌ مَجْمُوعٌ لهُ النَّاسُ وذَلِكَ يَوْمٌ مَشْهُودٌ وَمَا نُؤَخِّرُهُ إِلاَّ لأَجَلٍ مَعْدُودٍ يَوْمَ يَأْتِ لاتَكَلَّمُ نَفْسٌ إِلاَّ بِإِذْنِهِ فَمِنْهُمْ شَقِيٌّ وَسَعِيدٌ فَأَمَّا الَّذِينَ شَقُوا فَفِي النَّارِ لَهُمْ فِيهَا زَفِيرٌ وَشَهِيقٌ [هود : ١٠٢ – ١٠٦] وقال تعالى : وَيُحَذِّرُكُمُ اللهُ نَفْسَهُ [آل عمران : ٢٨] وقال تعالى : يَوْمَ يَفِرُّ المَرْءُ مِنْ أَخِيهِ وَأُمِّهِ وَأَبِيهِ وَصَاحِبَتِهِ وَبَنِيهِ لِكُلِّ امْرِئٍ مِنْهُمْ يَوْمَئِذٍ شَأْنٌ يُغْنِيهِ [عبس : ٣٤ – ٣٧] ، وقال تعالى : يَا أَيُّهَا النَّاسُ اتَّقُوا رَبَّكُمْ إِنَّ زَلْزَلَةَ السَّاعَةِ شَيْءٌ عَظِيمٌ . يَوْمَ تَرَوْنَهَا تَذْهَلُ كُلُّ مُرْضِعَةٍ عَمَّا أَرْضَعَتْ وَتَضَعُ كُلُّ ذَاتِ حَمْلٍ حَمْلَهَا وَتَرَى النَّاسَ سُكَارَى وَمَا هُمْ بِسُكَارَى وَلَكِنَّ عَذَابَ اللهِ شَدِيدٌ [الحج : ١ ، ٢] ، وقال تعالى : وَلِمَنْ خَافَ مَقَامَ رَبِّهِ جَنَّتَانِ [الرحمن : ٤٦] الآيات. وقال تعالى : وَأَقْبَلَ بَعْضُهُمْ عَلَى بَعْضٍ يَتَسَاءَلُونَ قَالُوا إِنَّا كُنَّا قَبْلُ فِي أَهْلِنَا مُشْفِقِينَ فَمَنَّ اللهُ عَلَيْنَا وَوَقَانَا عَذَابَ السَّمُومِ . إِنَّا كُنَّا مِنْ قَبْلُ نَدْعُوهُ إِنَّهُ هُوَ البَرُّ الرَّحِيمُ [الطور : ٢٥ ، ٢٨] والآيات في الباب كثيرة جداً معلوماتٌ، والغرضُ الإشارةُ إلى بعضها وقد حَصَلَ

Allah, the Exalted, has said:

149. (O Children of Israil!) fear Me. (2:40)
150. Lo! the punishment of thy Lord is stern. (85:12)
151. Even thus is the grasp of thy Lord when He graspeth the townships (or communities) while they are doing wrong. Lo! His grasp is painful very strong. Lo! herein verily there

is a portent for those who fear the doom of the Hereafter. That is a day unto which mankind will be gathered and that is a day that will be witnessed. And we defer it only as a term already reckoned. On the day when it cometh no soul will speak except by His permission; some among them will be wretched, (others) glad. As for those who will be wretched (on that day) they will be in the Fire; sighing and wailing will be their portion therein. (11:102—106).

152. Allah biddeth you beware (only) of Himself. (3:28).

153. On the day when a man flees from his brother, and his mother and his father, and his wife, and his children. Every man that day everyone will have concern enough to make him heedless (of others) alone. (80:34—37).

154. O mankind! Fear your Lord. Lo! the earthquake of the Hour (of Doom) is a tremendous thing. On the day when ye behold it, every nursing mother will forget her nursing and every pregnant one will be delivered of her burden, and thou (Muhammad) will see mankind as drunken, yet they will not be drunken, but the Doom of Allah will be strong (upon them) (22:1—2).

155. But for him who feareth the standing before his Lord there are two Gardens. (55:46).

156. And some of them draw near unto others questioning. Saying: Lo! of old, when we were with our families, we were ever anxious. But Allah has been gracious unto us, and hath preserved us from the torment of the breath of Fire. Lo! we used to pray unto Him of old. Lo! He is the Benign, the Merciful. (52:25—28).

٣٩٦ — عنِ ابنِ مسعودٍ ، رضي الله عنه ، قال : حدثنا رسولُ الله صلى الله عليه وسلم ، وهو الصَّادِقُ المصدوقُ : « إنَّ أحَدَكُمْ يُجْمَعُ خَلْقُهُ في بَطْنِ أمِّهِ أرْبَعينَ يَوْماً نُطْفَةً ، ثمَّ يَكُونُ عَلَقَةً مِثْلَ ذلِكَ ، ثُمَّ يَكُونُ مُضْغَةً مِثْلَ ذلِكَ ، ثُمَّ يُرْسَلُ المَلَكُ ، فَيَنْفُخُ فيهِ الرُّوحَ ، وَيُؤْمَرُ بِأرْبَعِ كَلِماتٍ : بِكَتْبِ رِزْقِهِ ، وأَجَلِهِ ، وَعَمَلِهِ ، وَشَقِيٌّ أوْ سَعِيدٌ . فَوَالَّذي لا إلهَ غَيْرُهُ إنَّ أحَدَكُمْ لَيَعْمَلُ بِعَمَلِ أهْلِ الجَنَّةِ حَتَّى ما يَكُونُ بَيْنَهُ وَبَيْنَهَا إلاَّ ذِراعٌ ، فَيَسْبِقُ عَلَيْهِ الكِتابُ ، فَيَعْمَلُ بِعَمَلِ أهْلِ النَّارِ ، فَيَدْخُلُها ، وَإنَّ أحَدَكُمْ لَيَعْمَلُ بِعَمَلِ أهْلِ النَّارِ حَتَّى ما يَكُونُ بَيْنَهُ وَبَيْنَها إلاَّ ذِراعٌ ، فَيَسْبِقُ عَلَيْهِ الْكِتابُ فَيَعْمَلُ بِعَمَلِ أهْلِ الجَنَّةِ فَيَدْخُلُها » متفقٌ عليه

396. Hazrat Abdullah Ibn Mas'ud (R.A.A.) relates that the Holy Prophet (S.A.W.) who is the truest and acclaimed as the truest said: Every of you remains in the form of a spern-drop in the womb of his mother for forty days, and then as a clot for next forty days and then again as a lump of flesh for another forty days, and lastly an angel is sent who breathes the soul into it, and is also directed to record four orders governing its destiny in this world that is its subsistence, its length of life, its behaviour and activities and whether it will be wretched or happy (good) person. Then by Him there is no god save Him, (i.e. Allah) one of you acts like the inmates of Paradise till there is left between him and the heaven but the space of a hand and then that which has already been recorded, overtakes him and he begins to act like the denizens of the Hell and eventually enters it. On the other hand, one of you acts like the denizens of the Hell till there is left between him and the Hell only the space of hand, then that which has already been recorded overtakes him and he begins to act like the dwellers of Paradise and eventually enters it. *(Bukhari and Muslim).*

٣٩٧ ــ وعنه قال : قال رسولُ الله ، صلى الله عليه وسلم : « يُؤْتَى بِجَهَنَّمَ يَوْمَئِذٍ لَهَا سَبْعُونَ أَلْفَ زِمَامٍ ، مَعَ كُلِّ زِمَامٍ سَبْعُونَ أَلْفَ مَلَكٍ يَجُرُّونَهَا » رواه مسلم .

397. Hazrat Ibn Mas'ud (R.A.A.) relates that the Holy Prophet (S.A.W.) said: On the Day of Judgement Hell will be dragged and it will have seventy thousand bridles, each bridle being pulled by seventy thousand angels. *(Muslim).*

٣٩٨ ــ وعن النُّعْمَانِ بنِ بَشِيرٍ ، رضي الله عنهما ، قال : سمِعتُ رسول الله ، صلى الله عليه وسلم ، يقول : « إنَّ أَهْوَنَ أَهْلِ النَّارِ عَذَاباً يَوْمَ الْقِيامَةِ لَرَجُلٌ يُوضَعُ في أَخْمَصِ قَدَمَيْهِ جَمْرَتَانِ يَغْلِي مِنْهُمَا دِمَاغُهُ مَا يَرَى أَنَّ أَحَداً أَشَدُّ مِنْه عَذَاباً ، وَإِنَّه لأَهْوَنُهُمْ عَذَاباً » متفق عليه

398. Hazrat Nu'man Ibn Bashir (R.A.A.) relates that he heard the Holy Prophet (S.A.W.) say that the least torture in the Hell will be that two embers of fire will be put under the feet of the guilty person whereby his brain will be boiling. He will consider himself the most severely punished person and yet he will be the least punished person. *(Bukhari and Muslim).*

٣٩٩ ــ وعن سَمُرَةَ بنِ جُنْدُبٍ ، رضي الله عنه ، أن نبيَّ الله، صلى الله عليه وسلم قال : « مِنْهُمْ مَنْ تَأْخُذُهُ النَّارُ إلى كَعْبَيْهِ ، وَمِنْهُمْ مَنْ

تَأْخُذُهُ إلى رُكْبَتَيْهِ ، وَمِنْهُمْ مَنْ تَأْخُذُهُ إلى حُجْزَتِهِ ، وَمِنْهُمْ مَنْ تَأْخُذُهُ إلى تَرْقُوَتِهِ » رواه مسلم

399. Hazrat Samurah Bin Jundub (R.A.A.) relates that the Holy Prophet (S.A.W.) said: Some persons, sentenced to Hell will be caught in the fire up to their ankles, some up to their knees, some up to their waists and some up to their throats (in commensurate with their acts and sins). *(Muslim).*

٤٠٠ — وعن ابنِ عمر رضي الله عنهما أن رسولَ الله ، صلى الله عليه وسلم ، قال : « يَقُومُ النَّاسُ لِرَبِّ العَالَمِينَ حَتَّى يَغِيبَ أَحَدُهُمْ في رَشْحِهِ إلى أَنْصَافِ أُذُنَيْهِ » متفقٌ عليه

400. Hazrat Ibn-i-Umar (R.A.A.) relates that the Holy Prophet (S.A.W.) said that on the Day (of Judgement) when people will stand before Almighty Allah some of them will be immersed in their sweat upto middle of their ears. *(Bukhari and Muslim).*

٤٠١ — وعن أنس ، رضي الله عنه ، قال : خَطَبَنَا رَسول الله ، صلى الله عليه وسلم ، خُطْبَةً ما سَمِعْتُ مِثْلَهَا قَطُّ ، فقال: « لَوْ تَعْلَمُونَ مَا أَعْلَمُ لَضَحِكْتُمْ قَلِيلاً وَلَبَكَيْتُمْ كَثِيراً » فَغَطَّى أَصْحَابُ رسول الله ، صلى الله عليه وسلم وجُوهَهُمْ ، وَلَهُمْ خَنِينٌ . متفقٌ عليه

وفي رواية : بَلَغَ رسولَ الله ، صلى الله عليه وسلم عَنْ أَصْحَابِهِ شيءٌ فَخَطَبَ ، فقال : « عُرِضَتْ عَلَيَّ الجَنَّةُ وَالنَّارُ ، فَلَمْ أَرَ كَاليَوْمِ في الخَيْرِ وَالشَّرِّ ، وَلَوْ تَعْلَمُونَ ما أَعْلَمُ لَضَحِكْتُمْ قَلِيلاً ، وَلَبَكَيْتُمْ كَثِيراً » فَمَا أَتَى عَلَى أَصْحَابِ رسول الله ، صلى الله عليه وسلم يَوْمٌ أَشَدُّ مِنْهُ غَطَّوْا رُؤُوسَهُمْ وَلَهُمْ خَنِينٌ

401. Hazrat Anas Bin Malik (R.A.A.) relates: 'The Holy Prophet (S.A.W.) delivered before us a sermon, the like of which I had never heard form him before. In course of it he said: 'If you could know what I know, you would laugh little and weep much.' Thereupon those present covered their faces and began to sob loudly. *(Bukhari and Muslim).*

Another version says: Some reports from the companions reached the Holy Prophet (S.A.W.). He therefore addressed them and said:

Heaven and Hell were shown I have never seen the like of (the these two) till this day in good and in evil. If you could know what I know, you would laugh little and weep much. That was the hardest day for the companions of the Holy Prophet (S.A.W.). They covered their faces and started weeping loudly.

٤٠٢ – وعن المِقْدَادِ ، رضيَ اللهُ عنه ، قال : سمعتُ رسولَ الله . صلى الله عليه وسلم ، يقُولُ : « تُدْنَى الشَّمْسُ يَوْمَ القِيامَةِ مِنَ الخَلْقِ حتَّى تَكُونَ مِنهُم كَمِقْدَارِ ميل » قالَ سُلَيْمُ بنْ عامرٍ الرَّاوي عَنْ المِقْدَادِ : فوَاللهِ ما أَدْرِي ما يعْني بِالمِيلِ ، أمَسَافَةَ الأرْضِ أمِ المِيلَ الَّذي تُكْتَحَلُ بهِ العَيْنُ « فيَكُونُ النَّاسُ عَلى قَدْرِ أعْمَالِهِم في العَرَقِ . فَمِنْهُمْ مَنْ يَكُونُ إلى كَعْبَيْهِ ، وَمِنهُمْ مَنْ يَكُونُ إلى رُكْبَتَيْهِ ، وَمِنهُمْ مَنْ يَكونُ إلى حِقْوَيْهِ ومِنهُمْ مَنْ يُلْجِمُهُ العَرَقُ إلجاماً » وَأشارَ رسول الله . صلى الله عليه وسلم . بيدهِ إلى فيهِ . رواه مسلم

402. Hazrat Miqdad (R.A.A.) relates that he heard the Holy Prophet (S.A.W.) say: On the Day of Judgement the sun will be so close to the people, as if it were only a meel away from them. Sulaim Bin Aamir who narrated this Hadis from Hazrat Miqdad says, 'By Allah I do not know what was meant by meel — a mile or the antimony applying stick. The people will perspire according to the quality of their actions. The perspiration of some will rise to their ankles, of others to their knees, of some to their waists and some will be bridled by their perspirations. The Holy Prophet(S.A.W.) pointed to his mouth by way of illustration. *(Muslim).*

٤٠٣ - وعن أبي هريرة ، رضيَ اللهُ عنه ، أنَّ رسولَ اللهِ ، صلى الله عليه وسلم ، قال : « يَعْرَقُ النَّاسُ يَوْمَ القِيامَةِ حتَّى يَذْهَبَ عَرَقُهُمْ في الأرْضِ سَبْعِينَ ذِرَاعاً ، وَيُلْجِمُهُمْ حتَّى يَبْلُغَ آذانَهُمْ » متفقٌ عليه

403. Hazrat Abu Hurairah (R.A.A.) relates that the Holy Prophet (S.A.W.) said: 'People will perspire so much on the Day of Judgement, that the earth will be drenched with it to a depth of seventy yards and people will be bridled with it after it has come up to their ears. *(Bukhari and Muslim).*

٤٠٤ – وعنه قال : كنا مع رسول الله ، صلى الله عليه وسلم ، إذ سَمِعَ وَجْبَةً فقال : « هَلْ تَدْرُونَ ما هذا ؟ » قُلْنَا : اللهُ وَرَسُولُهُ أعْلَمُ .

قال : هذا حَجَرٌ رُمِيَ بِهِ فِي النَّارِ مُنْذُ سَبْعِينَ خَرِيفاً فَهُوَ يَهْوِي فِي النَّارِ الآنَ حَتَّى انْتَهَى إلى قَعْرِهَا ، فَسَمِعْتُمْ وَجْبَتَهَا » رواه مسلم

404. Hazrat Abu Hurairah (R.A.A.) relates: Once upon a time we were with the Holy Prophet (S.A.W.) when we heard the sound of something falling. He asked us: 'Do you know what is this?' We said: 'Allah and His Messenger (S.A.W.) are better informed (than we people)' He said: 'This was a stone that had been hurled into the Hell seventy years ago; it kept rolling into it upto this time, and has now touched its bottom; you have (now) heard the sound of touching its base.'

(Muslim).

٤٠٥ ــ وعن عَدِيّ بنِ حَاتِمٍ ، رضي الله عنه ، قال : قال رسولُ الله ، صلى الله عليه وسلم : « مَا مِنْكُمْ مِنْ أَحَدٍ إلاَّ سَيُكَلِّمُهُ رَبُّهُ لَيْسَ بَيْنَهُ وَبَيْنَهُ تَرْجُمَانُ ، فَيَنْظُرُ أَيْمَنَ مِنْهُ ، فَلا يَرَى إلاَّ ما قَدَّمَ ، وَيَنْظُرُ أَشْأَمَ مِنْهُ ، فَلا يَرَى إلاَّ ما قَدَّمَ ، وَيَنْظُرُ بَيْنَ يَدَيْهِ ، فَلا يَرَى إلاَّ النَّارَ تِلْقَاءَ وَجْهِهِ ، فاتَّقُوا النَّارَ وَلَوْ بِشِقِّ تَمْرَةٍ » متفقٌ عليه .

405. This Hadis has already been covered vide No. 139.

٤٠٦ ــ وعن أبي ذرٍ ، رضي الله عنه ، قال : قال رسولُ الله ، صلى الله عليه وسلم : « إنِّي أَرَى مَا لا تَرَوْنَ ، أَطَّتِ السَّمَاءُ وَحُقَّ لَهَا أَنْ تَئِطَّ ، مَا فِيهَا مَوْضِعُ أَرْبَعِ أَصَابِعَ إلاَّ وَمَلَكٌ وَاضِعٌ جَبْهَتَهُ سَاجِداً لِلهِ تَعَالَى ، واللهِ لَوْ تَعْلَمُونَ مَا أَعْلَمُ ، لَضَحِكْتُمْ قَلِيلاً ، وَلَبَكَيْتُمْ كَثِيراً ، وَمَا تَلَذَّذْتُمْ بِالنِّسَاءِ عَلَى الْفُرُشِ وَلَخَرَجْتُمْ إلى الصُّعُدَاتِ تَجْأَرُونَ إلى اللهِ تَعَالَى » رواه الترمذي وقال : حديثٌ حسن .

406. Hazrat Abu Zarr (R.A.A.) relates, that the Holy Prophet (S.A.W.) said: I see that which you do not. The Heaven cries (on account of the heavy load of the angels prostrating) and is justified in doing so. There is not a space equal to four fingers in it but is occupied by angels who are prostrating before Allah. By Allah, if you could know what I know, you would laugh little and weep much; you would not enjoy your wives in beds, and would rush into streets and jungles in search of Allah's refuge.' *(Tirmizi).*

٤٠٧ ـــ وعن أبي برْزَةَ ـــ بِراءٍ ثم زايٍ ـــ نَضْلَةَ بنِ عُبَيْدٍ الأَسْلَمِيِّ ، رضي الله عنه ، قال : قال رسولُ اللهِ ، صلى الله عليه وسلم ، : « لا تَزُولُ قَدَمَا عَبْدٍ ، حتَّى يُسْأَلَ عَنْ عُمُرِهِ فِيمَ أفْنَاهُ . وَعَنْ عِلْمِهِ فِيمَ فَعَلَ فيهِ ، وَعَنْ مَالِهِ مِنْ أَيْنَ اكْتَسَبَهُ ، وَفِيمَ أَنْفَقَهُ . وَعَنْ جِسْمِهِ فِيمَ أَبْلاهُ » رواه الترمذي وقال : حديث حسن صحيح

407. Hazrat Abu Barzah Nazla Bin Ubaid-ul-Aslami (R.A.A.) relates that the Holy Prophet (S.A.W.) said: 'A servant of Allah will remain standing on the Day of Judgment till he is questioned about his age, how he spent it; and about his knowledge and how he utilised it; and about his wealth from where he acquired it and in what (activities) he spent it, and about his body as to how he consumed it.' *(Tirmizi).*

٤٠٨ ـــ وعن أبي هريرة ، رضي الله عنه ، قال : قرأ رسولُ اللهِ ، صلى الله عليه وسلم : (يَوْمَئِذٍ تُحَدِّثُ أَخْبَارَهَا) ثم قال : « أَتَدْرُونَ مَا أَخْبَارُهَا ؟ » قالوا : اللهُ وَرَسُولُهُ أَعْلَمُ . قال « فَإِنَّ أَخْبَارَها أَنْ تَشْهَدَ عَلى كُلِّ عَبْدٍ أَوْ أَمَةٍ بِمَا عَمِلَ عَلى ظَهْرِهَا تَقُولُ : عَمِلْتَ كَذا وَكَذَا في يَوْمِ كَذَا وَكَذَا ، فَهَذِهِ أَخْبَارُهَا » رواه التِّرْمِذِي وقال : حديثٌ حسنٌ .

408. Hazrat Abu Hurairah (R.A.A.) relates that the Holy Prophet (S.A.W.) recited the verse: 'That day she (earth) will relate her chronicles' *(99:4);* and enquired: 'Do you know what are its news?' His companions submitted: 'Allah and His Messenger (S.A.W.) know better'. He said: 'Its news is that it shall testify against every man and woman relating to that which he or she did on the earth. It will say that he or she did this and this on such and such day. This will be its news.' *(Tirmizi).*

٤٠٩ ـــ وعن أبي سعيد الخُدْرِيِّ ، رضي الله عنه ، قال : قال رسولُ الله ، صلى الله عليه وسلم : « كَيْفَ أَنْعَمُ ، وَصَاحِبُ الْقَرْنِ قَدِ الْتَقَمَ الْقَرْنَ ، وَاسْتَمَعَ الإِذْنَ مَتى يُؤْمَرُ بِالنَّفْخِ فَيَنْفُخُ » فَكَأَنَّ ذلِكَ ثَقُلَ عَلى أَصْحَابِ رسول الله ، صلى الله عليه وسلم ، فقال لَهُمْ : « قُولُوا : حَسْبُنَا الله وَنِعْمَ الْوَكِيلُ » رواه الترمذي وقال حديثٌ حسنٌ .

409. Hazrat Abu Sa'id Khudri (R.A.A.) relates that the Holy Prophet (S.A.W.) said: How can I feel happy when the Angel Israfil (the angel appointed to blow the Trumpet on the Day of Judgement) has put his lips to the Trumpet waiting to hear the Order to blow the trumpet. This very much distressed his companions, so he told them (to seek comfort through reciting *'Hasbunal-Laho wa naimal wakeel'* (Sufficient for us is Allah and an excellent Guardian is He). *(Tirmizi).*

٤١٠ — وعن أبي هريرة ، رضي الله عنه ، قال : قال رسول الله ، صلى الله عليه وسلم : « مَنْ خَافَ أَدْلَجَ . وَمَنْ أَدْلَجَ ، بَلَغَ المَنْزِلَ . أَلا إنَّ سِلْعَةَ اللهِ غَالِيَةٌ . أَلا إنَّ سِلْعَةَ اللهِ الجَنَّةُ » رواه الترمذي وقال : حديثٌ حسنٌ

410. Hazrat Abu Hurairah (R.A.A.) relates that the Holy Prophet (S.A.W.) said: One who is afraid of his enemy, sets out in the early part of the night; and one who sets out early, arrives at his destination. Beware that the property of allah is precious! Beware the belongings of Allah is precious. Be informed that the assets of Allah is Paradise. *(Tirmizi).*

٤١١ — وعن عائشةَ ، رضي الله عنها ، قالت : سمعتُ رسول الله ، صلى الله عليه وسلم ، يقول : « يُحْشَرُ النَّاسُ يَوْمَ القِيَامَةِ حُفَاةً عُرَاةً غُرْلاً » قُلْتُ : يارسول الله الرِّجَالُ وَالنِّسَاءُ جَمِيعاً يَنْظُرُ بَعْضُهُمْ إلى بَعضٍ !؟ قال : « يَا عَائِشَةُ الأَمرُ أَشَدُّ من أَنْ يُهِمَّهُم ذلكَ »

وفي روايةٍ : « الأَمْرُ أَهَمُّ مِن أن يَنْظُرَ بَعضُهم إلى بَعْضٍ » متفقٌ عليه

411. Hazrat Ayesha (R.A.A.) relates that she heard the Holy Prophet (S.A.W.) say: 'On the Day of Judgement people will be gathered together barefooted, unclothed and uncircumcised. I said: 'Messenger of Allah (S.A.W.), will men and women be together looking at one another?' He said: 'Ayesha, the occasion will be too grave and terrifying for them to be at ease to look at one another:

(Bukhari and Muslim).

Another version says that the occasion will be so serious that nobody (will dare) look at another.

Note: The fear of Allah's might is helpful in living a virtuous life and escaping from sins.

****

CHAPTER 51

Cherishing Hope and Expecting Good from Allah

قال الله تعالى : قُلْ يَا عِبَادِيَ الَّذِينَ أَسْرَفُوا عَلَى أَنْفُسِهِمْ لاَ تَقْنَطُوا مِنْ رَحْمَةِ اللهِ إِنَّ اللهَ يَغْفِرُ الذُّنُوبَ جَمِيعاً إِنَّهُ هُوَ الغَفُورُ الرَّحِيمُ [الزمر : ٥٣] وقال تعالى : وَهَلْ يُجَازَى إِلاَّ الكَفُورُ • [سبأ:١٧] وقال تعالى : إِنَّا قَدْ أُوحِيَ إِلَيْنَا أَنَّ العَذَابَ عَلَى مَنْ كَذَّبَ وَتَوَلَّى [طه : ٤٨] وقال تعالى : وَرَحْمَتِي وَسِعَتْ كُلَّ شَيْءٍ • [الأعراف : ١٥٦].

Allah, the Exalted, has said:

157. Say: O My slaves who have been prodigal to their own hurt! Despair not of the mercy of Allah, who forgiveth all sins. Lo! He is the Despair not of the mercy of Allah, who forgiveth all sins. Lo! He is the Forgiving, the Merciful. (39:53).

158. Punish We ever any save the ingrates? (34:17).

159. Lo! it hath been revealed unto us that the doom will be for him who denieth and turneth away. (20:48).

160. (He said:) and My mercy embraceth all things. (7:156).

٤١٢ — وعن عُبادةَ بنِ الصامِتِ ، رضي الله عنه ، قال : قال رسول الله ، صلى الله عليه وسلم : « مَنْ شَهِدَ أَنْ لا إلَهَ إلاَّ اللهُ وَحْدَهُ لاَ شَرِيكَ لَهُ ، وَأَنَّ مُحَمَّداً عَبْدُهُ وَرَسُولُهُ ، وَأَنَّ عِيسى عَبْدُ اللهِ وَرَسُولُهُ ، وَكَلِمَتُهُ أَلْقَاها إلى مَرْيَمَ وَرُوحٌ مِنْهُ ، والجَنَّةَ وَالنَّارَ حَقٌّ ، أَدْخَلَهُ اللهُ الجَنَّةَ عَلى ما كانَ مِنَ العَمَلِ » . متفقٌ عليه .

وفي رواية لمسلم : « مَنْ شَهِدَ أَنْ لا إلَهَ إلاَّ اللهُ ، وَأَنَّ مُحَمَّداً رَسُولُ اللهِ ، حَرَّمَ اللهُ عَلَيْهِ النَّارَ » .

412. **Hazrat Ubadah Ibn Samit** (R.A.A.) relates that the Holy Prophet (S.A.W.), Said: 'One who bears witness that there is no god save Allah, the one, without associate, and that Muhammad (S.A.W.) is His servant and Messenger, that Jesus is Allah's servant and Messenger, and His word that He conveyed to Mary and a spirit from Him, that Paradise is true and that the Hell is true, Allah will admit him to Paradise though whatever he does. *(Bukhari and Muslim).*

Another version of Muslim says: He who bears witness that there is no god save Allah and that Muhammad (S.A.W.) is the Messenger of Allah, Allah has forbidden the Fire of Hell on him.'

٤١٣ — وعن أبي ذرٍ ، رضيَ اللهُ عنه ، قال : قال النبيُّ ، صلى اللهُ عليه وسلم : « يقولُ اللهُ عزَّ وجلَّ : مَنْ جاءَ بِالحسَنَةِ ، فلَهُ عَشْرُ أمْثالِها أوْ أزيَدُ ، ومَنْ جاءَ بِالسَّيِّئَةِ ، فجزاءُ سيِّئَةٍ سيِّئَةٌ مثلُها أوْ أغفرُ . ومَنْ تقرَّبَ مِنِّي شِبْراً ، تقرَّبْتُ مِنهُ ذِراعاً ، ومَنْ تقرَّبَ مِنِّي ذِراعاً ، تقرَّبْتُ مِنهُ باعاً ، ومَنْ أتاني يَمْشي ، أتيتُهُ هرْوَلَةً ، ومَنْ لَقِيَني بِقُرابِ الأرْضِ خَطيئَةً لا يُشْرِكُ بي شيْئاً ، لَقيتُهُ بِمِثْلِها مَغْفِرَةً » . رواه مسلم .

413. Hazrat Abu Zarr (R.A.A.) relates that the Holy Prophet (S.A.W.) said: 'Allah, the Lord of honour and glory, says: One who does one good deed shall be rewarded ten times or more, and one who does an evil deed will be punished for only one sin, or he may be forgiven; and one who comes to Me by a hand's breadth I shall approach him an arm's and one who advances towards me by an arms length I shall approach him the length of two arms; and one who comes to Me walking, I shall go to him running; and one who meets Me with an earthful of sins, provided he has not associated anybody with Me, I shall meet him with an equal amount of pardon.' *(Muslim).*

٤١٤ — وعن جابرٍ ، رضيَ اللهُ عنه ، قالَ : جاءَ أعْرابيٌّ إلى النبيِّ ، صلى اللهُ عليهِ وسلم . فقال : يا رَسُولَ اللهِ ، ما المُوجِبَتانِ ؟ فقالَ : « مَنْ ماتَ لاَ يُشْرِكُ باللهِ شيْئاً دَخَلَ الجنَّةَ ، ومَنْ ماتَ يُشْرِكُ بهِ شيْئاً ، دَخَلَ النَّارَ » رواهُ مُسلم

414. Hazrat Jabir (R.A.A.) relates that a villager came to the Holy Prophet (S.A.W.) and said: O Messenger of Allah (S.A.W.), what are the two things which make Heaven or Hell necessary? He replied 'One who dies associating nobody with Allah, will enter Paradise, and one who dies associating anybody with Allah will enter the Hell. *(Muslim).*

٤١٥ — وعن أنسٍ ، رضي اللهُ عنه ، أنَّ النَّبيَّ صلى اللهُ عليه وسلم ، ومُعاذٌ رَديفُهُ علَى الرَّحْلِ قالَ : « يا مُعاذُ » قال : لبَّيْكَ يا رَسُولَ اللهِ وسَعْدَيْكَ ، قالَ : « يا مُعاذُ » قالَ : لبَّيْكَ يا رَسُولَ اللهِ وسَعْدَيْكَ . قالَ : يا مُعاذُ » قال : لبيكَ يا رَسُولَ اللهِ وسَعْدَيْكَ ثلاثاً ، قالَ : « ما مِنْ

عَبْدٍ يَشْهَدُ أَنْ لاَ إِلَهَ إِلاَّ اللهُ ، وأَنَّ مُحَمَّداً عَبْدُهُ وَرَسُولُهُ صِدْقاً مِنْ قَلْبِهِ إِلاَّ حَرَّمَهُ اللهُ عَلَى النَّارِ » قالَ : يَا رَسُولَ اللهِ أَفَلاَ أُخْبِرُ بها النَّاسَ فَيَسْتَبْشِرُوا ؟ قال : « إِذاً يَتَّكِلُوا » فَأَخْبَرَ بها مُعَاذٌ عِنْدَ مَوْتِهِ تَأَثُّماً

مُتفقٌ عليه

415. Hazrat Anas (R.A.A.) relates that Hazrat Mu'az was riding behind on the Holy Prophet (S.A.W.), Holy Prophet (S.A.W.) called him 'O Mu'az'. He responded: 'I am here, Messenger of Allah, may Allah bless you'. This was repeated thrice, and thereafter the Holy Prophet (S.A.W.) said: 'Any of the servants of Allah who affirms sincerely that there is no god save Allah and that Muhammad (S.A.W.) is His servant and His Messenger, Allah has forbidden the Fire of Hell on him. Hazrat Mu'az (R.A.A.) said: 'O Messenger of Allah, shall I announce this among the people so that they may be happy. He said: 'No, then they would depend wholly on (and would not offer prayers) this.' However, Hazrat Mu'az (R.A.A.) disclosed this only at the approach of his death, fearing lest he should be held guilty of holding back something that was within his knowledge.
(Bukhari and Muslim)

٤١٦ – وعَنْ أَبي هريرةَ – أَوْ أَبي سعيد الخُدْرِيِّ – رضيَ اللهُ عنهما : شَكَّ الرَّاوِي ، وَلا يَضُرُّ الشَّكُّ في عَيْنِ الصَّحابيِّ ؛ لأَنهُم كُلُّهُمْ عُدُولٌ ، قال : لما كانَ غَزْوَةُ تَبُوكَ ، أَصابَ النَّاسَ مَجَاعَةٌ ، فَقالُوا : يا رَسُولَ اللهِ لَوْ أَذِنْتَ لَنا فَنَحَرْنَا نَوَاضِحَنَا ، فَأَكَلْنا وَادَّهَنَّا ؟ فَقالَ رَسُولُ اللهِ ، صلى اللهُ عليهِ وسلم : « افْعَلُوا » فَجاءَ عُمَرُ رَضِيَ اللهُ عنهُ ، فقالَ : يا رَسُولَ اللهِ إِنْ فَعَلْتَ ، قَلَّ الظَّهْرُ ، وَلَكِنِ ادْعُهُمْ بِفَضْلِ أَزْوَادِهِمْ ، ثُمَّ ادْعُ اللهَ لَهُمْ عَلَيْها بِالبَرَكَةِ لَعَلَّ اللهَ أَنْ يَجْعَلَ في ذلكَ البَرَكَةَ . فَقالَ رَسُولُ اللهِ ، صلى اللهُ عليهِ وسلم : « نَعَمْ » فَدَعَا بِنِطَعٍ فَبَسَطَهُ ، ثُمَّ دَعَا بِفَضْلِ أَزْوَادِهِمْ ، فَجَعَلَ الرَّجُلُ يَجِيءُ بِكَفِّ ذُرَةٍ ، وَيَجِيءُ الآخَرُ بِكَفِّ تَمْرٍ ، وَيَجِيءُ الآخَرُ بِكِسْرَةٍ حَتى اجْتَمَعَ عَلَى النِّطَعِ مِنْ ذَلِكَ شَيْءٌ يَسِيرٌ ، فَدَعَا رَسُولُ اللهِ ، صلى اللهُ عليه وسلم بِالبَرَكَةِ ، ثُمَّ قالَ : « خُذُوا في أَوْعِيَتِكُمْ » ، فَأَخَذُوا في أَوْعِيَتِهِمْ حتى ما تَرَكُوا في العَسْكَرِ وِعاءً إِلاَّ مَلَؤُوهُ ، وَأَكَلُوا حتى شَبِعُوا وَفَضَلَ فَضْلَةٌ ،

فقالَ رَسُولُ اللهِ ، صلى اللهُ عليه وسلم : « أشْهَدُ أنْ لا إلَهَ إلاّ اللهُ ، وأنّي رَسُولُ اللهِ ، لا يَلْقَى اللهَ بهما عَبْدٌ غَيْرُ شاكٍ ، فيُحْجَبَ عَنِ الجَنَّةِ »
رواهُ مسلم .

416. Hazrat Abu Hurairah (R.A.A.) or Hazrat Abu Sa'eed Khudri (R.A.A.) The narrator is not definite as to who reported this tradition. Imam Nawawi holds that this fact does not affect the authenticity of the tradition as both the persons are just and honest persons)relates that on the occasion of the battle of Tabuk the Muslims were in difficulty due to hunger (as their rations had run short) and they requested the Holy Prophet (S.A.W.): 'O Messenger of Allah (S.A.W.) if you kindly permit us, we may slaughter our camels eat their flesh and make use of their fat.' The Holy Prophet (S.A.W.) permitted them to do so. On this Hazrat Umar (R.A.A.) came forward and submitted. 'O Messenger of Allah (S.A.W.), if this is done we will suffer from shortage of animals for transportation. Instead you ask them to bring the residue of their provisions and you pray and invoke Allah blessings; may He bestow His blessings upon the stuff.' The Holy Prophet (S.A.W.) agreed and called for his leather table cover and had it spread out and asked people to bring their left-over provisions. They started bringing their stuff. One brought a handful of beans, another brought a handful of dates, a third brought a piece of bread, and thus some eatables were collected on the table cover The Holy Prophet (S.A.W.) prayed and invoked for blessings, and then said: 'Now take it up in your pots. Everyone filled his pot with food, so that there was not left a single empty pot in the whole camp. All of them ate their fill and there was still something left over. The Holy Prophet (S.A.W.) said: 'I bear witness that there is no god save Allah, and that I am Allah's Messenger. No servant of Allah who meets Him' with these two affirmations,believing sincerely in them, would be denied the Paradise. *(Muslim)*.

٤١٧ – وعَنْ عِتْبانَ بنِ مالكٍ ، رضي الله عنه ، وهو ممَّنْ شَهِدَ بَدْراً . قالَ : كُنْتُ أُصَلّي لِقَوْمي بَني سالمٍ ، وكانَ يَحُولُ بيْني وبَيْنَهُم وادٍ إذا جاءَتِ الأمْطارُ ، فيَشُقُّ عَلَيَّ اجْتِيازُهُ قِبَلَ مَسْجِدِهِمْ ، فَجِئْتُ رَسُولَ اللهِ ، صلى اللهُ عليه وسلم ، فقلتُ له : إنّي أنْكَرْتُ بَصَري ، وإنَّ الوَادِيَ الّذي بيْني وبَيْنَ قَوْمي يَسيلُ إذا جاءَتِ الأمْطارُ ، فَيَشُقُّ عَلَيَّ اجْتِيازُهُ ، فَوَدِدْتُ أنَّكَ تَأتي ، فتُصَلّي في بَيْتي مَكاناً أتَّخِذُهُ مُصَلّىً ، فقال رسُولُ اللهِ ، صلى الله عليه وسلم : « سَأفْعَلُ » ، فَغَدا عليَّ رَسُولُ اللهِ ،

وأبُوبَكْرٍ ، رَضِيَ اللهُ عنه ، بَعْدَ مَا اشْتَدَّ النَّهارُ ، وَاسْتَأْذَنَ رَسُولُ اللهِ ، صلى اللهُ عليه وسلم ، فَأَذِنْتُ لَهُ ، فَلَمْ يَجْلِسْ حتى قالَ : « أَيْنَ تُحِبُّ أَنْ أُصَلِّيَ مِنْ بَيْتِكَ ؟ » فَأَشَرْتُ لَهُ إلى المَكانِ الَّذِي أُحِبُّ أَنْ يُصَلِّيَ فيه ، فَقَامَ رَسُولُ اللهِ ، صلى اللهُ عليهِ وسلم ، فَكَبَّرَ وصَفَفْنا وَرَاءَهُ ، فَصَلَّى رَكْعَتَيْنِ ، ثُمَّ سَلَّمَ وَسَلَّمْنا حِينَ سَلَّمَ ، فَحَبَسْتُهُ عَلى خَزيرَةٍ تُصْنَعُ لَهُ ، فَسَمِعَ أَهْلُ الدَّارِ أَنَّ رَسُولَ اللهِ ، صلى اللهُ عليه وسلم في بَيْتِي ، فَثَابَ رِجالٌ منهمْ حَتَّى كَثُرَ الرِّجالُ في البَيْتِ ، فَقَالَ رَجُلٌ : مَا فَعَلَ مالِكٌ لا أَرَاهُ ! فَقَالَ رَجُلٌ : ذلكَ مُنافِقٌ لا يُحِبُّ اللهَ ورَسُولَهُ ، فقالَ رَسُولُ اللهِ ، صلى اللهُ عليه وسلم : « لا تَقُلْ ذلِكَ ،ألا تَراهُ قالَ: لا إلَهَ إلاَّ اللهُ يَبْتَغِي بِذلِكَ وَجْهَ اللهِ تَعالى ؟!» . فَقَالَ :اللهُ وَرَسُولُهُ أَعْلَمُ ، أَمَّا نَحْنُ فَوَاللهِ ما نَرَى وُدَّهُ ،ولا حَدِيثَهُ إلاَّ إلى المُنافِقِينَ ! فقالَ رسولُ اللهِ، صلى اللهُ عليه وسلم : « فَإِنَّ اللهَ قَدْ حَرَّمَ على النَّارِ مَنْ قَالَ : لا إلَهَ إلاَّ اللهُ يَبْتَغِي بِذلِكَ وَجْهَ اللهِ » متفقٌ عليه .

417. Hazrat 'Itban Ibn Malik (R.A.A.) one of the martyrs of Badr, relates: I used to offer my Prayers alongwith my tribe, the Bani Salim, but there was a valley between my house and the mosque there; when it rained this valley becomes full of running water and it would be difficult for me to reach the mosque there. So I went to the Holy Prophet (S.A.W.) and said to him: 'My eyesight is weak and I am unable to cross the rivalet which separates me from my people. I earnestly desire that you may please come to my house and say your prayers there so that I might fix that spot as my place of prayer.' He said: 'I will do this.' Next day, when the sun had risen high, the Holy Prophet (S.A.W.) came to my house accompanied with Hazrat Abu Bakr (R.A.A.) and asked for permission to enter, which I granted. Thereafter without seating himself he asked: 'Where do you wish me to say my Prayer?' I pointed out the spot where I wanted to offer prayers. He stood for prayer and called out the *Takbir* (the call for prayer) and we lived behind him. He led the Prayer for two *raka'ats* and we prayed with him. When he finished we also finished with him, and then I detained him over a dish of concoction of sugar, milk and fine granules of flour that was prepared for him. When the neighbours heard that the Holy Prophet (S.A.W.) was in my house, they came and gathered in my house in large numbers. Someone said: What has happened to Malik Bin Dakhsham?

He is not here? Another said: 'He is a renegade, and neither loves Allah nor His Messenger (S.A.W.).' On this the Holy Prophet (S.A.W.) said: 'Do not say like this. Do you not know that he has recited the *Kalima* that there is no god save Allah, seeking thereby only the pleasure of Allah.' The man said: Allah and His Messenger (S.A.W.) know better but we see that his talk and friendship are confined with the hypocrites. The Holy Prophet (S.A.W.) said: 'Allah will forbid the Fire of Hell on one who affirms: 'There is no god save Allah; seeking thereby only the pleasure of Allah.'
(Bukhari and Muslim).

٤١٨ — وعن عمرَ بنِ الخطّابِ ، رضيَ اللهُ عنه ، قال : قَدِمَ رسُولُ اللهِ . صلّى اللهُ عليهِ وسلم ، بِسَبْيٍ ، فَإذا امْرَأَةٌ مِنَ السَّبْيِ تَسْعَى ، إذْ وَجَدَتْ صَبِيّاً في السَّبْيِ أخَذَتْهُ ، فَألزَقَتْهُ ببَطْنِها ، فَأرْضَعَتْهُ ، فقالَ رَسُولُ اللهِ ، صلى اللهُ عليهِ وسلَّم : « أتُرَوْنَ هَذِهِ المَرْأةَ طارِحَةً وَلَدَها في النَّارِ ؟ » قُلْنَا : لاَ وَاللهِ . فَقَالَ : « لَلَّهُ أرْحَمُ بِعِبادِهِ مِنْ هَذِهِ بِوَلَدِها » متّفقٌ عليه

418. Hazrat Umar Ibn Khattab (R.A.A.) says: Once some prisoners of war were produced before the Holy Prophet (S.A.W.). Among them was a woman running anxiously here and there, probably searching her missing child. When she found the child, she took it up in her lap, drew it close, and suckled it. The Holy Prophet (S.A.W.) said to his companions: 'Can you imagine this woman will ever throw her child in the Fire?' We said: 'By God not.' On this the Holy Prophet (S.A.W.) said: 'Allah is more kind towards His servants, than this woman is towards her child.'
(Bukhari and Muslim).

٤١٩ — وعن أبي هريرة ، رضيَ اللهُ عنه ، قال : قال رسُولُ اللهِ ، صلى اللهُ عليه وسلم : « لمَّا خَلَقَ اللهُ الخَلْقَ ، كَتَبَ في كِتابٍ ، فَهُوَ عِنْدَهُ فَوْقَ العَرْشِ : إنَّ رَحْمَتِي تَغْلِبُ غَضَبِي »

وفي روايةٍ « غَلَبَتْ غَضَبِي » وفي روايةٍ « سَبَقَتْ غَضَبِي » متفق عليه

419. Hazrat Abu Hurairah (R.A.A.) states that the Holy Prophet (S.A.W.) said: 'When Allah created the creatures He wrote in the book which is with Him on the highest heaven: 'My mercy shall prevail over My wrath.'

Another tradition say: 'My mercy covers My anger,' and yet another tradition says that: 'My compassion surpasses My anger.'
(Bukhari and Muslim).

٤٢٠ ــ وعنه قال : سمِعْتُ رسُولَ اللهِ ، صلى اللهُ عليه وسلم ، يقول : «جَعَلَ اللهُ الرَّحْمَةَ مائةَ جُزْءٍ ، فَأَمْسَكَ عِنْدَهُ تسعَةً وتِسْعِينَ، وأَنْزَلَ في الأَرْضِ جُزْءاً واحِداً ، فَمِنْ ذَلِكَ الجُزْءِ يَتَراحَمُ الخَلائِقُ حتى ترْفَعَ الدَّابَّةُ حَافِرَها عَنْ وَلَدِها خَشْيَةَ أَنْ تُصِيبَهُ» .

وفي روايةٍ : «إنَّ للهِ تعَالى مائةَ رَحْمَةٍ أَنْزَلَ مِنهَا رَحْمَةً واحِدَةً بَيْنَ الجِنِّ والإِنسِ والبَهائِمِ والهَوامِّ ، فَبِهَا يَتَعاطَفُونَ ، وَبِها يتَراحَمُونَ ، وَبِها تَعْطِفُ الوَحْشُ عَلى وَلَدِها ، وَأَخَّرَ اللهُ تَعَالى تِسعاً وتِسْعِينَ رَحْمَةً يَرْحَمُ بِها عِبادَهُ يَوْمَ القِيامَةِ» متفقٌ عليه

ورواهُ مسلم أيضاً من روايةِ سَلْمَانَ الفَارِسيِّ ، رضي اللهُ عنه ، قالَ : قالَ رسُولُ اللهِ ، صلى اللهُ عليه وسلم : «إنَّ للهِ تَعَالى مِائَةَ رَحْمَةٍ فَمِنْها رَحْمَةٌ يَتَراحَمُ بها الخَلْقُ بَيْنَهُمْ ، وَتِسْعٌ وَتِسْعُونَ لِيَوْمِ القِيامَةِ»

وفي روايةٍ : «إنَّ اللهَ تَعَالى خَلَقَ يَوْمَ خَلَقَ السَّمواتِ والأَرْضَ مائةَ رَحْمَةٍ كُلُّ رَحْمَةٍ طِبَاقُ ما بَيْنَ السَّماءِ إلى الأَرْضِ ، فَجَعَلَ مِنها في الأَرْضِ رَحْمَةً ، فَبِها تَعْطِفُ الوالِدَةُ عَلى وَلَدِها ، والوَحْشُ والطَّيْرُ بَعْضُها عَلى بَعْضٍ ، فَإِذَا كانَ يَوْمُ القِيامَةِ ، أَكْمَلَها بهذِهِ الرَّحْمَةِ»

420. Hazrat Abu Hurairah (R.A.A.) states that he heard the Holy Prophet (S.A.W.) say: 'Allah divided mercy into one hundred parts, out of which He retained ninety-nine parts with Him, and sent down one part to the earth. From this one part emanates all the compassion that the entire creation exercises towards one another, so much so that an animal lifts its hoof above its young lest it should get hurt.'

Another version says: 'Allah has one hundred mercies, out of which He has sent down only one for human beings, venies, animals and insects, by virtue of which they love one another and have compassion for one another, and even wild animals care for their young. Allah has retained the remaining ninety-nine mercies to deal kindly with His servants on the Day of Judgement.' *(Bukhari and Muslim).*

Another version Imam Muslim has quoted on the authority of Hazrat Salman Farsi (R.A.A.) which says: 'Allah has hundred mercies. Out of these one mercy is used by all the creatures for kindness between them and ninety-nine are for use on the Day of Judgment.'

Still another version says: 'Allah created one hundred units of mercy on the day on which He created the heavens and the earth; each unit is equal to the space between heaven and earth. Of them, He put one part in the earth, by virtue of which a mother has compassion for her children and animals and birds have compassion for one another (of their kinds). On the Day of Judgement He will perfect and complete His mercy. (That is He will use all the hundred parts of mercy for His servants on that day.)'

٤٢١ — وعنه عن النبي ، صلى الله عليه وسلم ، فيما يحكي عن ربه ، تبارك وتعالى ، قال : « أذنب عبد ذنباً ، فقال : اللهم اغفر لي ذنبي ، فقال الله تبارك وتعالى : أذنب عبدي ذنباً ، فعلم أن له رباً يغفر الذنب ، ويأخذ بالذنب ، ثم عاد فأذنب ، فقال : أي رب اغفر لي ذنبي ، فقال تبارك وتعالى : أذنب عبدي ذنباً ، فعلم أن له رباً يغفر الذنب ، ويأخذ بالذنب ، ثم عاد فأذنب ، فقال : أي رب اغفر لي ذنبي ، فقال ، تبارك وتعالى : أذنب عبدي ذنباً ، فعلم أن له رباً يغفر الذنب ، ويأخذ بالذنب ، قد غفرت لعبدي فليفعل ماشاء » متفق عليه .

421. Hazrat Abu Hurairah (R.A.A.) relates that the Holy Prophet (S.A.W.) conveys from his Lord: 'A servant of Allah committed a sin and then prayed:'Allah, pardon me for my mistake.' On which Allah the Blessed and Exalted, said: 'My servant committed a sin and subsequently realised that he has a sustainer Who forgives wrong and also calls to account for it.' The servant committed the sin again and supplicated:'O my sustainer, forgive me for my sin,.' The Blessed and Exalted Allah said: 'My servant committed a wrong and subsequently realised that he has a sustainer who forgives sin and also calls to account for it.' The servant again committed a sin and then supplicated: 'Allah, forgive me for my sin.' The Blessed and the Exalted Allah said: 'My servant committed a sin and then realised that he has a sustainer who forgives sin and also calls to account for it.' I have excused My servant; so let him do what he likes i.e. so long as he repents he will be forgiven, because — repentance wipes out all previous sins.)

(Bukhari and Muslim).

٤٢٢ — وعنه قال : قال رسول الله ، صلى الله عليه وسلم : « والذي نفسي بيده لو لم تذنبوا ، لذهب الله بكم ، وجاء بقوم يذنبون ، فيستغفرون الله تعالى ، فيغفر لهم » رواه مسلم

422. Hazrat Abu Hurairah (R.A.A.) says that the Holy Prophet (S.A.W.) said: 'By Allah in Whose possession and control is my life, if you had not committed wrong. He would have replaced you by another people who would have committed wrong and then would have sought pardon from Allah, so that he would have forgiven them.' *(Muslim).*

٤٢٣ — وعن أبي أيُّوبَ خَالِدِ بنِ زيد ، رضي الله عنه ، قال : سمعتُ رسول الله ، صلى الله عليه وسلم ، يقول : « لَوْلا أنَّكُمْ تُذنِبُونَ ، لخَلَقَ اللهُ خَلقاً يُذنِبُونَ ، فيَستَغفِرُونَ ، فيَغفِرُ لَهُم » رواه مسلم

423. Hazrat Abu Ayub Khalid Bin Zaid (R.A.A.) relates that he heard the Holy Prophet (S.A.W.) say, Had you not sinned, Allah would have certainly created a people that would have sinned and asked for forgiveness from Him so that He would have forgiven them.' *(Muslim).*

٤٢٤ — وعن أبي هريرة ، رضي الله عنه ، قال : كُنَّا قُعُوداً مَعَ رسول الله صلى الله عليه وسلم ، مَعَنَا أبُو بكرٍ وَعُمَرُ ، رضي الله عنهما في نَفَرٍ . فقَامَ رسول الله ، صلى الله عليه وسلم ، مِنْ بَيْنِ أظهُرِنَا ، فأبطَأَ عَلَيْنَا . فخَشِينَا أنْ يُقتَطَعَ دُونَنَا ؛ ففَزِعنا ، فقُمْنَا ، فكُنْتُ أوَّلَ مَنْ فَزِعَ ، فخَرَجتُ أبْتَغِي رسول الله ، صلى الله عليه وسلم ، حتَّى أتَيتُ حَائِطاً لِلأنصارِ — وَذَكَرَ الحَدِيثَ بطُوله إلى قوله : فقال رسول الله ، صلى الله عليه وسلم : « اذهَبْ فمَنْ لَقِيتَ وَرَاءَ هَذَا الحَائِطِ يَشهَدُ أنْ لا إلهَ إلاَّ الله ، مُستَيقِناً بِهَا قَلبُهُ فَبَشِّرْهُ بِالجَنَّةِ » رواه مسلم .

424. Hazrat Abu Hurairah (R.A.A.) relates: 'Once we were sitting with the Holy Prophet (S.A.W.); among us also were Hazrat Abu Bakr (R.A.A.).The Holy Prophet(S.A.W.)got up and left the gathering and it took him long to return. As such we felt worried about his safety as we were not with him. On this apprehension we got up to go in his search, I was the first to get in anxiety and set out in his search, till I came to a garden belonging to an Ansar; here he narrated a long account, at the end of which he reports the Holy Prophet (S.A.W.) as having said: 'Go and whomsoever you meet outside this garden and who affirms with the depth of his heart, that there is no God save Allah, give him the glad tiding that he will be admitted into Paradise.' *(Muslim).*

٤٢٥ — وعن عبد الله بن عَمْرو بن العاص ، رضي الله عنهما ، أن النبي ، صلى الله عليه وسلم ، تَلا قَولَ اللهِ ، عَزَّ وَجَلَّ في إبراهيم ، صلى الله عليه وسلم :

﴿ رَبِّ إِنَّهُنَّ أَضْلَلْنَ كَثِيراً مِنَ النَّاسِ فَمَن تَبِعَنِي فَإِنَّهُ مِنِّي ﴾ [إبراهيم : ٣٦] ، وقَوْلَ عيسى ، صلى الله عليه وسلم : ﴿ إِن تُعَذِّبْهُم فَإِنَّهُم عِبَادُكَ وَإِن تَغْفِرْ لَهُم فَإِنَّكَ أَنتَ الْعَزِيزُ الْحَكِيمُ ﴾ [المائدة : ١١٨] ، فرَفَعَ يدَيْه وقال « اللّهُمَّ أُمَّتِي أُمَّتِي » وبَكَى ، فقال الله عزَّ وجَلَّ ، : « يَاجبريلُ اذهَبْ إلى مُحمَّدٍ وربُّكَ أعلَمُ ، فسَلْهُ ما يُبكِيهِ ؟ » فأتاهُ جبريلُ ، فأخبَرَهُ رسولُ الله ، صلى الله عليه وسلم بمَا قال : وَهُوَ أعلَمُ ، فقال اللهُ تعالى : « ياجبريلُ اذهَب إلى مُحمَّد فقُل : إنَّا سنُرضيكَ في أُمَّتِكَ ولا نَسُوؤُكَ » رواه مسلم

425. **Hazrat Abdullah Ibn 'Amr Al-'Aas** (R.A.A.) says that the Holy Prophet (S.A.W.) recited the words of Allah in the Holy Quran concerning Prophet Abraham that he prayed:

'My Lord! Lo! they (the idols) have led many of mankind astray. But those followeth me he verily is of me. And whoso disobeyth me — still thou art Most Forgiving. Merciful.' (14:36).

And the words of Prophet Christ:

'If Thou punishes them, Lo! they are Thy slaves, and if Thou forgives them Lo!, only Thou art the Mighty, the Wise.' (5:118).

And then the Holy Prophet (S.A.W.) raised his hands and said: O Allah, my Ummah, my Ummah, and wept. Allah commanded Angel Gabriel: 'Go to Muhammad (S.A.W.) and thy Lord knows all, and ask him, as to what makes him weep? So Angel Gabriel came to him and the Holy Prophet (S.A.W.) told him what he had said. (Allah already knew it). Allah, the Almighty, commanded Angel Gabriel: Go to Muhammad (S.A.W.) and tell him that we shall cause you to be pleased as regards your Ummah and shall not make you sorrowful.' *(Muslim)*

٤٢٦ ــ وعن مُعاذِ بنِ جبَلٍ ، رضي الله عنه ، قال : كُنتُ رِدْفَ النبيِّ ، صلى الله عليه وسلم ، على حِمار فقال : « يامُعاذ هَل تَدري ما حَقُّ الله على عبادِهِ ، وما حَقُّ العِبادِ على الله ؟ قلت : اللهُ ورَسُولُهُ أعلَمُ . قال : « فإنَّ حَقَّ الله على العِباد أن يَعبُدُوهُ ، ولا يُشرِكُوا بِهِ شَيئاً ، وحَقَّ العِبادِ على الله أنْ لا يُعَذِّبَ مَنْ لا يُشرِكُ بِهِ شَيئاً ، فقلتُ : يا رسولَ الله أفلا أُبَشِّرُ النَّاسَ ؟ قال لاتُبَشِّرْهُم فيَتَّكِلُوا » متفقٌ عليه

426. Hazrat Mu'az Bin Jabal (R.A.A.) relates: I was riding a donkey behind the Holy Prophet (S.A.W.) when he asked me: 'O Mu'az, do you know what is the right of Allah on His servants and what is the right of His servants on Allah?' I said: 'Allah and His Messenger (S.A.W.) know better.' He said: 'Allah's right on His servants is that they should worship Him alone and should not associate anything with Him; and the right of His servants, on Allah is that He should not punish those who do not associate anything with Him.' On this I said: 'O Messenger of Allah (S.A.W.) may I give people this happy news?' He said: 'Do not do so, lest the people should depend entirely on this.'

(Bukhari and Muslim).

٤٢٧ — وعن البَرَاءِ بن عازبٍ ، رضي الله عنهما ، عن النبي ، صلى الله عليه وسلم ، قال : « المُسلمُ إذَا سُئِلَ في القَبرِ يَشهَدُ أن لا إلهَ إلاّ الله ، وَأنَّ مُحمَّداً رسولُ الله ، فذلك قولُه تعالى : (يُثَبِّتُ اللهُ الَّذينَ آمَنُوا بِالقَوْلِ الثَّابِتِ في الحَياة الدُّنيَا وفي الآخِرَةِ) [إبراهيم : ٢٧] متفقٌ عليه

427. Hazrat Bra'a Bin 'Aazib (R.A.A.) reports from the Holy Prophet (S.A.W.) that: 'When a Muslim is questioned in his grave, he testifies that there is no god save Allah, and that Muhammad (S.A.W.) is His Messenger.' This is what Allah declared in the verse:

Allah confirmeth those who believe by a firm saying in the life of the world and in the Herwafter (14:27). *(Bukhari and Muslim).*

٤٢٨ — وعن أنسٍ ، رضي الله عنه ، عن رسولِ الله ، صلى اللهُ عليهِ وسلم ، قال : « إنَّ الكَافِرَ إذَا عَمِلَ حَسَنَةً ، أُطعِمَ بِهَا طُعمَةً مِنَ الدُّنيَا ، وَأمَّا المُؤمِنُ ، فَإنَّ الله تعالى يَدَّخِرُ لَهُ حَسَنَاتِه في الآخِرَةِ ، وَيُعْقِبُهُ رِزْقاً في الدُّنْيَا عَلى طَاعَتِهِ »

وفي روايةٍ : « إنَّ الله لا يَظْلِمُ مُؤْمِناً حَسَنَةً يُعْطَى بِهَا في الدُّنْيَا ، وَيُجزَى بِهَا في الآخِرَة ، وَأمَّا الكَافِرُ ، فَيُطْعَمُ بِحَسَنَاتِ مَا عَمِلَ لله ، تعالى ، في الدُّنيَا حَتَّى إذَا أفضَى إلى الآخِرَة ، لَمْ يَكُنْ لَهُ حَسَنَةٌ يُجزَى بِهَا » رواه مسلم

428. Hazrat Anas Bin Malik (R.A.A.) says that the Holy Prophet (S.A.W.) said: 'When a disbeliever does a good deed, he is given its return in this world, and in the case of a Muslim, Allah the Almighty stores up his good works for him in the Hereafter, and provides him with the sustenance in this life on account of his obedience.'

Another version says: 'Allah does no wrong to anyone. A believer is rewarded for his good deeds both here and the Hereafter. A disbeliever is rewarded in this world only, for his good works done for the sake of Allah; till he proceeds to the Hereafter, where there will be no good work to be rewarded to him there. *(Muslim).*

٤٢٩ — وعن جابرٍ ، رضي الله عنه قال : قال رسولُ اللهِ ، صلى الله عليه وسلم : « مَثَلُ الصَّلَوَاتِ الخَمْسِ كَمَثَلِ نَهَرٍ جَارٍ غَمْرٍ عَلَى بَابِ أَحَدِكُمْ يَغْتَسِلُ مِنْهُ كُلَّ يَوْمٍ خَمْسَ مَرَّاتٍ » رواه مسلم

429. Hazrat Jabir (R.A.A.) relates that the Holy Prophet (S.A.W.) said: The five daily Prayers are like a great canal running in front of your door in which you bathe five times a day thereby you are thoroughly cleansed removing all dirt from your person; similar is the case of a person who regularly offers his five daily prayers. *(Muslim).*

٤٣٠ — وعنِ ابنِ عباسٍ ، رضي الله عنهما ، قال : سمعتُ رسولَ الله ، صلى الله عليه وسلم ، يقول : « مَا مِنْ رَجُلٍ مُسْلِمٍ يَمُوتُ فَيَقُومُ عَلَى جَنَازَتِهِ أَرْبَعُونَ رَجُلاً لَا يُشْرِكُونَ بِاللهِ شَيْئاً إِلَّا شَفَّعَهُمُ اللهُ فِيهِ » رواه مسلم

430. Hazrat Ibn Abbas (R.A.A.) says that he heard the Holy Prophet (S.A.W.) say: 'If a Muslim dies and forty people; who do not associate anything with Allah, join in the funeral prayers for him, Allah accepts their prayers for him.' *(Muslim).*

٤٣١ — وعنِ ابنِ مسعودٍ ، رضيَ اللهُ عنه ، قال : كُنَّا مَعَ رسولِ اللهِ ، صلى الله عليهِ وسلم ، في قُبَّةٍ نحواً مِنْ أَرْبَعِينَ ، فقال : « أَتَرْضَوْنَ أَنْ تَكُونُوا رُبُعَ أَهْلِ الجَنَّةِ ؟ » قُلْنَا : نَعَمْ ، قال : « أَتَرْضَوْنَ أَن تَكُونُوا ثُلُثَ أَهْلِ الجَنَّةِ ؟ » قُلْنَا : نَعَمْ ، قال: « وَالَّذِي نَفْسُ مُحَمَّدٍ بِيَدِهِ إِنِّي لأَرْجُو أَن تَكُونُوا نِصفَ أَهْلِ الجَنَّةِ ، وَذَلِكَ أَنَّ الجَنَّةَ لَا يَدخُلُهَا إِلَّا نَفسٌ مُسلِمَةٌ ، وَمَا أَنتُم فِي أَهْلِ الشِّركِ إِلَّا كَالشَّعرةِ البَيضَاءِ فِي جِلدِ الثَّورِ الأَسوَدِ ، أَوْ كَالشَّعَرَةِ السَّودَاءِ فِي جِلدِ الثَّورِ الأَحمَرِ » متفقٌ عليه

431. Hazrat Ibn Mas'ud (R.A.A.) relates that : 'About forty of us were present in a tent alongwith the Holy Prophet (S.A.W.) when he asked us: 'Would you be pleased if you were to be a quarter of the dwellers of Paradise?' We answered: Yes Sir, Then he asked:'Would you be happy if you were to be a third of the dwellers of Paradise?' We answered: 'We are happy.' He said: 'By Allah in whose possession and control is the life of Muhammad (S.A.W.), I hope that you will be one half of the dwellers of Paradise. This is because none will enter Paradise except a soul that is a Muslim (in full submission) to Allah, and your ratio against the disbelievers is like that of white hair on the skin of a black ox, or that of black hair on the skin of a red ox.'

(Bukhari and Muslim).

٤٣٢ — وعن أبي موسى الأشعري ، رضي الله عنه ، قال : قال رسولُ الله . صلى الله عليه وسلم : « إذَا كَانَ يَوْمُ القِيامَةِ دَفَعَ اللهُ إلى كُلِّ مُسْلِمٍ يَهُودِيّاً أو نَصرَانِياً فَيَقُولُ : هَذَا فِكَاكُكَ مِنَ النَّارِ » .

وفي روايةٍ عنهُ عنِ النبيِّ ، صلى الله عليه وسلم قال : « يَجِيءُ يَوْمَ القِيامَةِ نَاسٌ مِنَ المُسْلِمِينَ بِذُنُوبٍ أَمْثَالِ الجِبَالِ يَغفِرُهَا اللهُ لَهُم » رواه مسلم

432. **Hazrat Abu Musa Ash'ari (R.A.A.)** relates that the Holy Prophet (S.A.W.) said: 'On the Day of Judgment, Allah will push for Muslim a Jew or a Christian, and will say: 'He is your ransom for your deliverance from the Fire of Hell.'

Another version says: 'On the Day of Judgment some Muslims will come with sins piled up like mountains and Allah will forgive them all.'

(Muslim).

٤٣٣ — وعن ابنِ عمرَ رضيَ الله عنهما قال : سمعتُ رسولَ الله ، صلى الله عليه وسلم ، يقول : « يُدْنَى المُؤْمِنُ يومَ القِيامَةِ مِنْ رَبِّهِ حتَّى يَضَعَ كَنَفَهُ عَلَيهِ ، فَيُقَرِّرُهُ بِذُنُوبِه ، فيقولُ : أتعرفُ ذَنْبَ كَذَا ؟ أتعرفُ ذَنْبَ كَذَا ؟ فيقول : رَبِّ أعْرِفُ، قال : فَإنِّي قَد سَتَرتُهَا عَلَيكَ في الدُّنيَا ، وَأنَا أغْفِرُهَا لَكَ اليَومَ ، فَيُعطَى صَحِيفَةَ حَسَنَاته » متفقٌ عليه .

433. **Hazrat Ibn Umar (R.A.A.)** relates that he heard the Holy Prophet (S.A.W.) say: 'A believer will approach his Lord (Allah) on the Day of Judgment and He will cover him with His mercy. He will question him about his sins: 'Do you recognise (remember) such and such this sin and this sin?' He will answer: 'Lord, I do recognise.' Then He will say: I kept it secret for you in the world, and I pardon you today. Then the record of his good works will be handed over to him.

(Bukhari and Muslim).

٤٣٤ — وعن ابنِ مسعودٍ . رضي الله عنه ، أنَّ رَجُلاً أصَابَ مِنِ امرَأةٍ قُبلَةً ، فَأتَى النَّبيَّ ، صلى الله عليه وسلم ، فأخبره ، فأنزل الله تعالى : (وَأَقِمِ الصَّلاةَ طَرَفَي النَّهَارِ وَزُلَفاً مِنَ اللَّيلِ إنَّ الحَسَنَاتِ يُذْهِبْنَ السَّيِّئَاتِ)

[هود : ١١٤] فقال الرجل : ألي هذا يارسول الله ؟ قال « لجميع أمتي كلهم » متفق عليه

434. Hazrat Ibn Mas'ud (R.A.A.) says that a man kissed a (stranger) woman and came to the Holy Prophet (S.A.W.) and confessed his guilt. At that time Allah revealed this verse:

'Establish Salat in the beginning and the end of the day in some time of the night. Lo! good deeds annul ill deeds.' (11:114).

The said man asked: 'Messenger of Allah (S.A.W.), is this verse for me?' He (S.A.W.) answered: 'For the whole of Ummat.' This is an agreed tradition. *(Bukhari and Muslim).*

٤٣٥ — وعن أنس ، رضي الله عنه ، قال : جاء رجل إلى النبي ، صلى الله عليه وسلم فقال : يا رسول الله أصبت حداً ، فأقمه علي ، وحضرت الصلاة ، فصلى مع رسول الله ، صلى الله عليه وسلم ، فلما قضى الصلاة قال : يا رسول الله إني أصبت حداً ، فأقم في كتاب الله . قال : « هل حضرت معنا الصلاة ؟ » قال : نعم . قال : قد غفر لك » متفق عليه

435. Hazrat Anas Bin Malik (R.A.A.) relates: A man came to the Holy Prophet (S.A.W.) and said:'O Messenger of Allah (S.A.W.), I have committed a great and punishable crime, so please punish me for the same. As it was the prayer time the man offered the prayer with the Holy Prophet (S.A.W.). After the prayer the man again said to the Holy Prophet (S.A.W.): 'O Messenger of Allah (S.A.W.), I have committed a serious crime, please enforce the punishment on me as prescribed in the Holy Quran. The Holy Prophet (S.A.W.) asked him: Have you offered *Salat* (the congregational prayer) with us?' He answered: 'Yes, Sir.' The Holy Prophet (S.A.W.) said: 'Then you have been excused (on account of excellence of this prayer).' *(Bukhari and Muslim)*

٤٣٦ — وعنه قال : قال رسول الله ، صلى الله عليه وسلم : « إن الله ليرضى عن العبد أن يأكل الأكلة ، فيحمده عليها ، أو يشرب الشربة ، فيحمده عليها » رواه مسلم

436. Hazrat Anas Bin Malik (R.A.A.) says that the Holy Prophet (S.A.W.) said: 'Allah is pleased with His servant who eats and priases Him for it, and drinks a water and praises Him for it.' *(Muslim).*

٤٣٧ — وعن أبي موسى ، رضي الله عنه ، عن النبي صلى الله عليه وسلم ، قال : « إن الله تعالى ، يبسط يده بالليل ليتوب مسيء النهار ، ويبسط

يَدهُ بِالنهارِ لِيَتُوبَ مُسِيءُ اللَّيلِ حتى تَطْلُعَ الشمسُ مِنْ مَغْرِبِها » رواه مسلم

437. This Hadis has already been covered in S.No. 16.

٤٣٨ — وعن أبي نجيحٍ عَمرو بن عَبَسَةَ — بفتحِ العين والباء — السُّلَمِيِّ ، رضيَ اللهُ عنه ، قال : كنتُ وَأنَا في الجَاهِلِيَّةِ أظُنُّ أنَّ النَّاسَ على ضَلالَةٍ ، وَأنَّهُمْ لَيْسُوا على شيءٍ ، وَهُمْ يَعْبُدُونَ الأوْثَانَ ، فَسَمِعْتُ بِرَجُلٍ بِمَكَّةَ يُخْبِرُ أخْباراً ، فَقَعَدْتُ على رَاحِلَتِي ، فَقَدِمْتُ عَلَيْهِ ، فإذا رسول الله ، صلى اللهُ عليه وسلم ، مُسْتَخْفِياً جُرَآءُ عليه قَوْمُهُ ، فَتَلَطَّفْتُ حتَّى دَخَلْتُ عَلَيهِ بِمَكَّةَ ، فقلتُ له : ما أنتَ ؟ قال : « أنا نَبِيٌّ » قلتُ : وما نبيٌّ ؟ قال : « أرْسَلَنِي اللهُ » قلت : « وبأيِّ شَيْءٍ أرْسَلَكَ ؟ قال « أرْسَلَنِي بِصِلَةِ الأرْحامِ ، وكسْرِ الأوْثانِ ، وَأنْ يُوَحَّدَ اللهُ لا يُشْرَكُ بهِ شَيْءٌ » قلت : فَمنْ مَعَكَ على هذا ؟ قال : « حُرٌّ وَعَبْدٌ » ومعهُ يَوْمَئِذٍ أبو بكرٍ وبِلالٌ ، رضي الله عنهما ، قلت : إنِّي مُتَّبِعُكَ ، قال : « إنَّكَ لَنْ تَسْتَطِيعَ ذلكَ يَوْمَكَ هذا ؛ ألا تَرَى حَالِي وحالَ النَّاسِ ؟ وَلَكِنِ ارْجِعْ إلى أهْلِكَ فَإذا سَمِعْتَ بي قد ظَهَرْتُ فَأْتِنِي » قال : فَذَهَبْتُ إلى أهْلِي ، وَقَدِمَ رسول الله صلى الله عليه وسلم ، المَدِينَةَ ، وكنتُ في أهْلِي ، فَجَعَلْتُ أتَخَبَّرُ الأخْبَارَ ، وَأسْألُ النَّاسَ حينَ قَدِمَ المدينةَ ، حتَّى قَدِمَ نَفَرٌ مِنْ أهْلِ المدينةَ ، فقلتُ : مَا فَعَلَ هذا الرَّجُلُ الذي قدم المدينةَ ؟ فقالوا : النَّاسُ إليهِ سِرَاعٌ وَقَدْ أرَادَ قَوْمُهُ قَتْلَهُ ، فَلَمْ يَسْتَطِيعُوا ذلِكَ ، فَقَدِمتُ المدينةَ ، فَدَخَلتُ عليهِ ، فقلتُ : يارسولَ الله أتَعرِفُنِي ؟ قال : « نعم أنتَ الَّذي لَقِيتَنِي بِمَكَّةَ » قال: فقلتُ : يا رسولَ اللهِ أخبِرْنِي عمَّا عَلَّمَكَ اللهُ وَأجْهَلُهُ ، أخبِرْنِي عَنِ الصَّلاةِ ؟ قال : « صَلِّ صَلاةَ الصُّبحِ ، ثُمَّ اقْصُرْ عَنِ الصَّلاةِ حتَّى تَرْتَفِعَ الشَّمْسُ قِيدَ رُمْحٍ ، فَإنَّهَا تَطْلُعُ حينَ تَطْلُعُ بَيْنَ قَرْنَيْ شَيْطَانٍ ، وَحِينَئِذٍ يَسْجُدُ لها الكُفَّارُ ، ثُمَّ صَلِّ ، فَإنَّ الصَّلاةَ مشهودةٌ مَحْضُورَةٌ

حتى يستقِلَّ الظِّلُّ بالرُّمحِ ، ثُمَّ اقْصُر عن الصَّلاةِ ، فإنه حينئذٍ تُسْجَرُ جَهَنَّمُ ؛ فإذا أقبلَ الفَيءُ فصَلِّ ؛ فإنَّ الصَّلاة مَشهودةٌ مَحضورة حتى تُصَلِّيَ العصرَ ، ثم اقْصُر عن الصلاةِ حتى تَغرُبَ الشمسُ ، فإنها تَغرُبُ بين قَرنَيْ شيطانٍ ، وحينئذٍ يسجدُ لها الكُفَّارُ » قال : فقلت : يانَبيَّ الله ؛ فالوضوءُ حدِّثني عنه ؟ فقال : « ما مِنكُم رجُلٌ يُقَرِّبُ وَضُوءَهُ ، فيَتَمَضْمَضُ ويستَنْشِقُ فيَنْتَثِرُ ، إلاَّ خَرَّتْ خطايَا وجهِه وفيهِ وخياشيمِهِ ، ثم إذا غَسَلَ وجهَهُ كما أمَرَهُ اللهُ ، إلاَّ خرّت خطايا وجهِهِ مِنْ أطرافِ لحْيَتِهِ مع الماء ، ثم يغسِل يديه إلى المِرفَقَينِ ، إلاَّ خرّت خطايا يديه من أنامِلِه مع الماء ، ثم يَمسحُ رَأسَهُ ، إلاَّ خَرَّتْ خطَايَا رَأسِهِ من أطرافِ شَعْرِهِ مع الماء ، ثم يَغْسِلُ قَدَمَيْهِ إلى الكَعْبَيْنِ ، إلاَّ خَرَّتْ خطايا رِجْلَيه من أناملِهِ مع الماء ، فإن هو قامَ فصلَّى ، فحمِدَ الله تعالى ، وأثْنَى عليه وَمَجَّدَهُ بالذي هو له أهلٌ ، وفَرَّغَ قلبه للهِ تعالى ، إلاَّ انصَرَفَ مِن خطيئَتِهِ كَهَيْئَتِهِ يوم وَلَدَتْهُ أُمُّهُ » .

فحدَّثَ عَمرُو بن عبَسَةَ بهذا الحديثِ أبَا أُمامَةَ صاحِبَ رسولِ الله ، صلى الله عليه وسلم ، فقال له أبو أُمامَةَ : ياعَمْرُو بن عَبَسَةَ ، انظُر ما تقولُ ! في مَقامٍ واحِدٍ يعطى هذا الرَّجُلُ ؟ فقال عَمْرُو : يا أبَا أمامة ، لقد كَبِرَتْ سِنِّي ، ورَقَّ عَظمِي ، وَاقْتَرَبَ أجَلِي ، وما بِيْ حَاجَةٌ أنْ أكذِبَ على الله تعالى ، ولا على رسول الله ، صلى الله عليه وسلم ، لو لم أسْمَعْهُ مِن رسول الله ، صلى الله عليه وسلم ، إلاَّ مَرَّةً أوْ مَرَّتَينِ أو ثلاثاً ، حتَّى عَدَّ سبعَ مَرَّاتٍ ، ما حَدَّثتُ أبداً بِهِ ، ولكنِّي سَمِعتُهُ أكثر من ذلك . رواه مسلم .

438. Hazrat Abu Najeeh 'Amr bin 'Abasah Sulami (R.A.A.) relates: 'In the days of Jahiliyah I used to think that people have gone astray and did not follow any true religion.. They used to worship idols. After sometime I heard about a man in Mecca who was telling something new. So mounting my camel I went to him. I found that it was the Holy Prophet (S.A.W.) (with the new ideas) and he used to live out of the sight of his people who used to persecute him. With some planning I managed to meet him in Mecca. I asked him: 'What are you?' He said:

'I am a Prophet.' then enquired 'What is a Prophet?' He said: 'Allah has sent me as His Messenger.' I further asked: 'With what (mission) has He sent you?' He said: 'He has sent me to tell the people to be kind to kins, to destroy the idols, and to proclaim that Allah is one, none to be associated with Him: I asked: 'Who are persons among your followers.' He said: On this occasion Hazrat Abu Bakr (R.A.A.) and Hazrat Bilal (R.A.A.) were with the Holy Prophet (S.A.W.). I said: 'I am also your follower and want to be with you.' He said: 'In the present situation it is not advisable for you to do so. You see my position and the attitude of the people?' Go back to your people and when you hear that I have succeeded in my mission then come to me.' 'Accordingly I returned to my people, and while I was with them, the Holy Prophet (S.A.W.) migrated to Medina. I continued asking people about him till some of my people visited Medina. When they returned back I asked them: 'How the man (the Holy Prophet (S.A.W.) who has just arrived in Medina is getting on?' They said: 'People are rushing to him (to accept his creed) Although his own people tried to kill him, yet they did not succeed.' Thereafter I proceeded to Madina and presented myself before the Holy Prophet (S.A.W.) and submitted 'O Messenger of Allah (S.A.W.), do you recognise me?' He said: 'Yes, you are the person who met me in Mecca.' I said: 'O Messenger of Allah (S.A.W.), tell me those things which Allah has taught you and which I do not know. First of all tell me about Salat (Prayer).' He said: Offer the early morning prayer and then keep away from it till the sun has risen equal to the length of a spear, for at that time it rises between the two horns of the devil when the disbelievers prostrate themselves before it. After this you may pray for (during this time) Salat is attended and testified to by angels, till the shadow of a spear equals (disappears in) the length of a spear. Again keep away from Prayer, the fire in Hell is fed with fuel that time.' When the shadow lengthens, you may pray, for salat is attended and testified to by angels till the time of Asr Prayer. After 'Asr Prayer refrain from Prayer till the sun has set, for it sets between two horns of devil and the disbelievers prostrate themselves before it at that time.

Then I said: 'O Prophet of Allah (S.A.W.) please tell me about ablution' He Said: 'When a person begins the ablution and washes out his mouth (gargles) and cleans his nose, the sins of his nose are washed out. Then as he washes his face as Allah has commanded, the sins of his face are washed out from the sides of his beard with the water. Then he washes his hands up to his elbows, and the sins of his hands are washed out through his fingers with the water. Then he runs his wet hands over his head and the sins of the head are washed out through the ends of his hair with the water. Then he washes his feet up to the ankles and the sins of his feet are washed out through his digits with the water. Then if he stands up for Prayer and praises Allah and glorifies Him, and devotes his heart wholly to Allah, he emerges absolved from his sins as on the day his mother bore him.

When **Hazrat Amr Ibn'Abasah** (R.A.A.) related this Hadis to **Hazrat**

Abu Umamah (R.A.A.), the companion of the Holy Prophet (S.A.W.), the latter said to him: 'O! Amr Ibn Abasah, be careful about what you relate at one place about all that is bestowed upon such a person? Hazrat Amr replied: 'Abu Umamah, I have reached the old age, my bones have become dry, my death is approaching near and there is no need for me to coin lies on Allah and His Messenger (S.A.W.) Had I not heard this from the Holy Prophet (S.A.W.) once, twice, thrice (and he counted up to seven) I would never have related it. Indeed I have heard this even more often.' *(Muslim).*

٤٣٩ — وعن أبي موسى الأشعَري . رضي الله عنه . عن النبي صلى الله عليه وسلم . قال : « إذا أرادَ اللهُ تعالى . رحمةَ أمَّةٍ ، قَبضَ نبيَّها قبلَها . فجعلَهُ لها فَرطا وسلَفاً بين يدَيها . وإذا أراد هلَكةَ أمَّةٍ . عذَّبها ونبيُّها حيٌّ . فأهلَكَها وهوَ حيٌّ ينظرُ ، فأقرَّ عينَهُ بِهلاكِها حين كذَّبوهُ وعصَوا أمرَهُ » رواه مسلم

439. Hazrat Abu Musa Ash'ari (R.A.A.) related that the Holy Prophet (S.A.W.) said: 'When Allah determines mercy for a people, He recalls the soul of its Prophet, before it, and makes him a herald and a storehouse (of good deeds) for it in the Hereafter; and when He determines upon the destruction of a people, He chastises it while its Prophet is alive, and destroys it during his life-time and watches it and delights in its destruction, because they rejected Him and disobeyed His commandments.' *(Muslim).*

****

CHAPTER 52

Virtues of Maintaining Good Opinion and High Hope from Allah

قال الله تعالى إخباراً عن العبدِ الصَّالحِ : « وَأُفَوِّضُ أَمْرِي إلى اللهِ إنَّ اللهَ بصيرٌ بالعبادِ فوقاهُ اللهُ سيئاتِ مَا مَكَرُوا [غافر : ٤٤ ، ٤٥] .

Allah, the Exalted, has said:

161. (The pious believer said) I confide my cause unto Allah. Lo! Allah is Seer of (His) slaves. So Allah warded off from him the evils which they plotted. (40:44–45).

٤٤٠ — وعن أبي هريرة ، رضيَ الله عنه . عن رسولِ اللهِ ، صلى الله عليه وسلم . أنهُ قال : « قال اللهُ ، عزَّ وجلَّ : أنا عِندَ ظَنِّ عَبْدي بي ، وأنا

مَعَهُ حَيْثُ يَذْكُرُنِي . وَاللهِ للهُ أَفْرَحُ بِتَوْبَةِ عَبْدِهِ مِنْ أَحَدِكُمْ يَجِدُ ضَالَّتَهُ بِالْفَلاةِ . وَمَنْ تَقَرَّبَ إِلَيَّ شِبْراً . تَقَرَّبْتُ إِلَيْهِ ذِرَاعاً ، وَمَنْ تَقَرَّبَ إِلَيَّ ذِرَاعاً . تَقَرَّبْتُ إِليه بَاعاً . وإذا أَقْبَلَ إِلَيَّ يَمْشِي . أَقْبَلْتُ إِلَيه أُهَرْوِلُ » متفقٌ عليه وهذا لفظ إحدى روايات مسلم .

440. Hazrat Abu Hurairah (R.A.A.) states that the Holy Prophet (S.A.W.) said: 'Allah says: I behave with My Servant, as he conceives Me to be. I am with him where he remembers Me.' The Holy Prophet (S.A.W.) continuing said that: 'By Allah! He is more pleased with the repentance of a servant of His than one of you who finds out something (camel) lost by him in the desert. Allah says: One who advances towards Me by a hand's breadth, I advance towards him by an arm's length, and he who advances towards Me by an arm's length, I advance towards him by two arm's length. If a servant of Mine comes to Me walking, I go to him running.' *(Bukhari and Muslim).*

٤٤١ — وعن جابرِ بنِ عبدِ اللهِ . رضيَ اللهُ عنهما . أنهُ سمعَ النبيَّ . صلّى الله عليه وسلم . قبلَ موتِهِ بثلاثةِ أيّامٍ يقولُ : « لا يَموتَنَّ أحدُكم إلاَّ وَهوَ يُحسِنُ الظَّنَّ باللهِ عزَّ وجلَّ » رواه مسلم

441. Hazrat Jabir Ibn Abdullah (R.A.A.) relates that he heard the Holy Prophet (S.A.W.) say, three days before his passing away. 'Let no one of you die except expecting for the best from Allah, the Almighty and exalted.' *(Muslim).*

٤٤٢ — وعن أنس . رضي الله عنه قال: سمعتُ رسولَ اللهِ . صلّى الله عليه وسلم . يقول : « قال الله تعالى : يَا ابْنَ آدَمَ . إِنَّكَ مَا دَعَوْتَنِي وَرَجَوْتَنِي غَفَرْتُ لَكَ عَلَى مَا كَانَ مِنكَ وَلا أُبَالِي . يَا ابْنَ آدَمَ . لَوْ بَلَغَتْ ذُنُوبُكَ عَنَانَ السماءِ . ثم اسْتَغْفَرْتَنِي غَفَرتُ لَكَ ، يَا ابْنَ آدَمَ . إِنَّكَ لَو أَتَيْتَنِي بِقُرابِ الأَرْضِ خطايا . ثُمَّ لَقِيتَنِي لا تُشرِكُ بِي شَيْئاً . لأَتَيْتُكَ بِقُرَابِهَا مَغْفِرَةً » رواه الترمذي . وقال : حديث حسن .

442. Hazrat Anas Bin Malik (R.A.A.) relates that he heard the Holy Prophet (S.A.W.) say:'Allah, the Exated, has said: O the son of Adam! Certainly I shall continue to pardon thee so long as thou supplicates Me and hopest (for My forgiveness), whatever may be thy faults and sins, I don't care. O Son of Adam, even if thy sins pile up as high as the sky, and thou asks for my forgiveness, I would forgive thee. O

Son of Adam, if thou comest to Me with an earthful of defaults and meetest Me, not associating anything with Me, I would come to thee, with an earthful of forgiveness.' *(Tirmizi).*

****

CHAPTER 53

Combining Hope and Fear

Imam Nawawi says that for a person — a servant of Allah the Almighty, it is desirable that while in good health he should fear Allah the Exalted, and should be an aspirant for good from Allah. Both these things are equally desired. And while ill, should have unflinching faith and hope. On this point the principles of Shariat, Quranic orders and the traditions of the Holy Prophet (S.A.W.) are clear.

قال الله تعالى: فَلا يَأْمَنُ مَكْرَ اللهِ إلاَّ الْقَوْمُ الخَاسِرُونَ [الأعراف: ٩٩] وقال تعالى: إنَّهُ لا يَيْأَسُ مِنْ رَوْحِ الله إلاَّ الْقَوْمُ الْكَافِرُونَ [يوسف: ٨٧] وقال تعالى: يَوْمَ تَبْيَضُّ وُجُوهٌ وتَسْوَدُّ وُجُوهٌ [آل عمران: ١٠٦] وقال تعالى: إنَّ رَبَّكَ لَسَرِيعُ العِقَابِ وَإنَّهُ لَغفورٌ رَحيمٌ [الأعراف: ١٦٧]. وقال تعالى: إنَّ الأبرارَ لَفي نعيمٍ وَإنَّ الْفُجَّارَ لَفي جَحِيمٍ) [الانفطار: ١٣، ١٤] وقال تعالى: فَأمَّا مَنْ ثَقُلَتْ مَوَازِينُهُ فَهُوَ في عِيشَةٍ راضيةٍ وَأمَّا مَنْ خَفَّتْ مَوَازِينُهُ فَأُمُّهُ هَاوِيَةٌ [القارعة: ٦-٩] والآيات في هذا المعنى كثيرة فَيَجْتَمِعُ الخوفُ والرجاءُ في آيتَيْنِ مُقْتَرِنَتَيْنِ أو آيات أو آية

Allah, the Exalted, has said:

162. None deemeth himself secure from Allah's scheme save folk that perish (7:99).
163. Lo! none despaireth of the Spirit of Allah save disbelieving folk. (12:87).
164. On the day when (some) faces will be whitened and (some) faces will be blackened. (3:106).
165. Lo! Verily thy Lord is swift in prosecution and Lo! Verily He is Forgiving, Merciful. (7:167).
166. Lo! The righteous verily will be in delight. And Lo! the wicked verily will be in Hell. (82: 13—14).
167. Then, as for him whose scales are heavy (with good works) he will live a pleasant life. But as for him whose scales are light, the Bereft and Hungry one will be his mother. (101: 6—9).

٤٤٣ ـ وعن أبي هريرة ، رضي اللهُ عنه ، أنّ رسُولَ اللهِ ، صلّى اللهُ عليه وسلم ، قال : « لَوْ يَعْلَمُ المُؤمِنُ ما عِنْدَ اللهِ مِنَ العُقُوبَةِ ، ما طَمِعَ بِجَنَّتِهِ أَحَدٌ ، وَلَوْ يَعْلَمُ الكافِرُ مَا عِنْدَ اللهِ مِنَ الرَّحْمَةِ ، مَا قَنِطَ مِنْ جَنَّتِهِ أَحَدٌ » رواه مسلم

443. Hazrat Abu Hurairah (R.A.A.) relates that the Holy Prophet (S.A.W.) said: 'Had a believer fully known what is the full extent of the chastisement with Allah, none would desire His Paradise; and if a disbeliever had known fully the extent of Allah's mercy, none would despair of His Paradise.' *(Muslim).*

٤٤٤ ـ وعن أبي سَعيدٍ الخدريّ ، رضي اللهُ عنه ، أنّ رسُولَ اللهِ ، صلى اللهُ عليه وسلم ، قال : « إذا وُضِعَتِ الجَنازَةُ واحْتَمَلَها النَّاسُ أَوِ الرِّجالُ عَلى أَعْناقِهِمْ ، فَإِنْ كانَتْ صالِحَةً قالَتْ : قَدِّمُوني قَدِّمُوني ، وَإِنْ كانَتْ غَيرَ صالِحَةٍ ، قالَتْ : يا وَيْلَها ! أَيْنَ تَذْهَبُونَ بها ؟ يَسْمَعُ صَوْتَها كُلَّ شَيْءٍ إلاَّ الإِنْسانُ ، وَلَوْ سَمِعَهُ صَعِقَ » رواهُ البخاري

444. Hazrat Abu Sa'eed Khudri (R.A.A.) relates that the Holy Prophet (S.A.W.) said: 'When the coffin is ready and is lifted by people above the shoulders then if the corpse is that of a virtuous person it urges: Take me ahead; Take me ahead; if it is that of a non-virtuous person, it says: 'Damn it, where are you taking it?' Its voice is heard by everything except the humans and if they could hear it they would have gone unconscious. *(Bukhari).*

٤٤٥ ـ وعن ابنِ مسعودٍ ، رضيَ اللهُ عنه ، قالَ : قالَ رسُولُ اللهِ ، صلى اللهُ عليه وسلم : « الجَنَّةُ أَقْرَبُ إلى أَحَدِكُمْ مِنْ شِراكِ نَعْلِهِ وَالنَّارُ مِثْلُ ذلك » رواه البخاري

445. This Hadis has already been covered vide No. 105.

****

CHAPTER 54

The Excellence of Being Moved and Weeping due to Fear of Allah and Love of Him.

قالَ اللهُ تعالى : وَيَخِرُّونَ لِلأَذْقَانِ يَبْكُونَ وَيَزِيدُهُمْ خُشُوعاً [الإسراء : ١٠٩] وقال تعالى: أَفَمِنْ هَذا الحَدِيثِ تَعْجَبُونَ . وتَضْحَكُونَ وَلاَ تَبْكُونَ [النجم : ٥٩ ـ ٦٠] .

Allah, the Exalted, has said:

168. They fall down on their faces, weeping and it increaseth humility in them (17:109).

169. Marvel ye, then, at this statement, and laugh and not weep. (53: 59—60).

٤٤٦ ـ وعَن أبي مَسعودٍ ، رضيَ اللهُ عنه ، قالَ : قال لي النبيُّ ، صلى اللهُ عليه وسلم : « اقرَأْ عليَّ القرآنَ » قلتُ : يا رسُولَ اللهِ ، أَقرَأُ عليكَ ، وَعليكَ أُنزِلَ ؟ ! قالَ : « إني أُحِبُّ أَنْ أَسمَعَهُ مِنْ غَيْرِي » فقرَأْتُ عليه سورَةَ النِّسَاء . حتى جِئْتُ إلى هذهِ الآية : (فَكَيْفَ إذا جِئْنا مِنْ كُلّ أُمَّةٍ بِشَهيدٍ وَجِئْنا بِكَ عَلى هَؤلاءِ شَهِيداً) [الآية : ٤١] قال : « حَسْبُكَ الآنَ » فَالْتَفَتُّ إلَيْهِ ، فَإذا عَيْناهُ تَذْرِفانِ . متفق عليه

446. Hazrat Abdullah Ibn Mas'ud (R.A.A.) states: 'The Holy Prophet (S.A.W.) said to me: Recite the Holy Quran before me. I said: 'O Messenger of Allah, may I recite the Quran before you, whereas it has been revealed on you?' He said: 'I like to hear the Holy Quran read out by another.' As such I recited before him Surah An-Nisa (the fourth Chapter) till I reached the verse:

'But how (will it be with them) when We bring of every people a witness, and We bring thee (O Muhammad) a witness against these?' (4:41).

On this he said: 'Now that is enough'. When I looked toward him I found that his eyes were flowing. *(Bukhari and Muslim).*

٤٤٧ ـ وعن أنسٍ ، رضيَ اللهُ عنه ، قالَ : خَطَبَ رَسُولُ اللهِ ، صلّى اللهُ عليه وسلم ، خُطْبَةً ما سَمِعْتُ مِثْلَها قَطُّ ، فقالَ : « لَوْ تَعْلَمُونَ ما أَعْلَمُ لَضَحِكْتُمْ قَلِيلاً وَلَبَكَيْتُمْ كثيراً » قال : فَغَطّى أَصْحابُ رَسُولِ اللهِ ، صلى اللهُ عليه وسلم ، وُجُوهَهُمْ ، ولهُمْ خَنِينٌ ، متفقٌ عليه ،

447. This Hadis is the same as covered in the first part of No.401 under Chapter 50.

٤٤٨ ـ وعن أبي هريرة ، رضي اللهُ عنه ، قالَ : قالَ رسُولُ اللهِ ، صلى اللهُ عليه وسلم ، « لاَ يَلِجُ النَّارَ (٥) رَجُلٌ بَكَى مِنْ خَشْيَةِ اللهِ حتَّى يَعُودَ اللَّبَنُ في الضَّرْعِ ، وَلاَ يَجْتَمِعُ غُبارٌ في سَبيلِ اللهِ وَدُخانُ جَهَنَّمَ » رواهُ الترمذي وقال : حديثٌ حسنٌ صحيحٌ .

448. Hazrat Abu Hurairah (R.A.A.) relates that the Holy Prophet (S.A.W.) said: The person, who sheds tears on account of fear of Allah, will not go to Hell till the milk returns into the breasts (that is it is impossible) and the dust produced in Jihad (that is fighting and struggling in the cause of Allah and the smoke of Hell will never exist together (this means that such a God-fearing person shall go to Paradise). *(Tirmizi).*

٤٤٩ ـ وعنه قالَ : قالَ رسُولُ اللهِ ، صلى اللهُ عليه وسلم : « سَبْعَةٌ يُظِلُّهُمُ اللهُ في ظِلِّهِ يَوْمَ لاَ ظِلَّ إلاَّ ظِلُّهُ : إمامٌ عادِلٌ ، وشَابٌّ نَشَأَ في عِبادَةِ اللهِ تَعالى ، ورَجُلٌ قَلْبُهُ مُعَلَّقٌ في المَسَاجِدِ ، ورَجُلانِ تَحابَّا في اللهِ ، اجتَمَعا عَلَيْهِ ، وتَفَرَّقا عَلَيْهِ ، ورَجُلٌ دَعَتْهُ امْرَأَةٌ ذاتُ مَنْصِبٍ وَجَمالٍ ، فَقالَ : إنِّي أخافُ اللهَ ، ورَجُلٌ تَصَدَّقَ بِصَدَقَةٍ فَأَخْفاها حتَّى لاَ تَعْلَمَ شِمالُهُ ما تُنْفِقُ يَمِينه ، ورَجُلٌ ذَكَرَ اللهَ خالِياً فَفاضَتْ عَيْناهُ » متفقٌ عليهِ

449. This Hadis has been covered in No. 376 under Chapter 46.

٤٥٠ ـ وعَن عبدِ اللهِ بنِ الشِّخِّيرِ ، رضيَ اللهُ عنه ، قال : أتَيْتُ رسُولَ اللهِ ، صلَّى اللهُ عليه وسلم ، وهُوَ يُصَلِّي ولِجَوْفِهِ أزيزٌ كَأَزيزِ المِرْجَلِ مِنَ البُكاءِ . حديث صحيح رواه أبو داود ، والتِّرْمذي في الشَّمائِلِ بإسنادٍ صحيحٍ .

450. Hazrat Abdullah Ibn Shakhkhair (R.A.A.) relates: 'Once I visited the Holy Prophet(S.A.W.) when he was offering Salat (Prayer). I heard the sound of his weeping coming out of his chest which was like the sound of a boiling pot *(Abu Daud and Tirmizi).*

٤٥١ ـ وعن أنسٍ ، رضي اللهُ عنه ، قالَ : قالَ رسُولُ اللهِ ، صلى اللهُ عليه وسلم ، لأُبَيِّ بنِ كَعْبٍ ، رضيَ اللهُ عنه : « إنَّ اللهَ ، عَزَّ وجَلَّ ، أمَرَني أنْ أقْرَأَ عَلَيْكَ : لَمْ يَكُنِ الَّذِينَ كَفَرُوا » قالَ : وَسَمَّاني ؟ قالَ : « نَعَمْ »

فَبَكَى أُبَيٌّ ، متفقٌ عليه

وفي روايةٍ : فَجَعَلَ أُبَيٌّ يَبْكِي .

451. **Hazrat Anas Bin Malik** (R.A.A.) relates that the Holy Prophet (S.A.W.) said to Hazrat Ubayy bin Ka'ab (R.A.A.). 'Allah the Almighty and Exalted has ordered me to read before Ayat: *Lam Yakunil Lazina Kafaroo* (Sur Al-Baiyyana — Chapter No. 98) 'Hazrat Ubayy Bin Ka'ab submitted: 'Did He name me?' The Holy Prophet (S.A.W.) said: 'Yes' Whereupon Hazrat Ubayy (R.A.A.) started weeping (due to fear of Allah). (*Bukhari and Muslim*).

٤٥٢ — وعنهُ قالَ : قالَ أبو بكرٍ لعمرَ ، رضيَ اللهُ عنهما ، بعدَ وفاةِ رسُولِ اللهِ ، صلى اللهُ عليه وسلَّم : انْطَلِقْ بِنا إلى أُمِّ أَيمَنَ ، رضيَ اللهُ عنهما ، نَزُورُها كما كانَ رسُولُ اللهِ ، صلى اللهُ عليه وسلم ، يَزُورُها ، فَلَمَّا انتَهَيْنا إلَيْها بَكَتْ ، فَقالا لها : ما يُبْكِيكِ ؟ أَمَا تَعْلَمِينَ أَنَّ ما عِنْدَ اللهِ تَعالى خَيْرٌ لِرَسُولِ اللهِ . صلى اللهُ عليهِ وسلَّم ! قالَتْ : إني لا أَبْكِي ، أني لا أَعْلَمُ أَنَّ ما عِنْدَ اللهِ خَيْرٌ لِرَسُولِ اللهِ صلى اللهُ عليه وسلم، ولكِنِّي أَبْكِي أَنَّ الوَحْيَ قَدِ انْقَطَعَ مِنَ السَّماءِ ؛ فَهَيَّجَتْهُما عَلى البُكاءِ ، فَجَعَلا يَبْكِيانِ مَعَها . رواهُ مسلم   وقد سبق في باب زيارةِ أهل الخير

452. This Hadis has already been covered in item No. 360 under Chapter 45.

٤٥٣ — وعن ابنِ عمَرَ ، رضيَ اللهُ عنهما ، قال : لمَّا اشْتَدَّ بِرَسُولِ اللهِ ، صلى اللهُ عليه وسلم ، وَجَعُهُ ، قيلَ لَهُ في الصَّلاةِ ، فقال : « مُرُوا أَبا بَكْرٍ فَلْيُصَلِّ بالنَّاسِ » فقالتْ عائشةُ ، رضيَ اللهُ عنها : إنَّ أَبا بَكْرٍ رَجُلٌ رَقيقٌ إذا قرَأَ القرآنَ غَلَبَهُ البُكاءُ ، فقالَ : « مُرُوهُ فَلْيُصَلِّ » .

وفي روايةٍ عن عائشةَ ، رضيَ اللهُ عنها ، قالَتْ : قلتُ : إنَّ أَبا بَكْرٍ إذا قامَ مَقامَكَ لمْ يُسْمِعِ النَّاسَ مِنَ البُكاءِ . متفقٌ عليه

453. **Hazrat Ibn Umar** (R.A.A.) relates that when the illness of the Holy Prophet (S.A.W.) became serious he was requested as to who should lead the prayers. He said: Abu Bakr may be asked to lead the people in Prayer. On this Hazrat Ayesha (R.A.A.) submitted: Hazrat

Abu Bakr (R.A.A.) is a man with tender-heart, he may break down and start weeping when he recites the Holy Quran.' The Holy Prophet (S.A.W.) repeated: 'Ask him (Hazrat Abu Bakr) to lead the Prayer.'

According to another version: Hazrat Ayesha (R.A.A.) said: 'When Hazrat Abu Bakr (R.A.A.) would stand in your place, the congregation will not be able to hear him on account of his sobbing.'

(*Bukhari and Muslim*).

٤٥٤ – وعن إبراهيمَ بنِ عبدِ الرَّحمنِ بنِ عوفٍ أنَّ عبدَ الرَّحمنِ بنَ عوفٍ ، رَضيَ اللهُ عنهُ ، أُتِيَ بطَعامٍ وكانَ صائماً ، فقالَ : قُتِلَ مُصْعَبُ بنُ عُميرٍ ، رضيَ اللهُ عنه ، وَهُوَ خيْرٌ منِّي ، فلَمْ يُوجَدْ لَهُ ما يُكفَّنُ فيهِ إلاَّ بُرْدَةٌ إنْ غُطِّيَ بها رَأسُهُ بَدَتْ رِجْلاهُ ، وإنْ غُطِّيَ بها رِجْلاهُ بَدَا رأسُهُ ، ثُمَّ بُسِطَ لنَا منَ الدُّنيا ما بُسِطَ – أوْ قالَ : أُعْطِينا منَ الدُّنيا ما أُعْطِينا – قدْ خشِينا أنْ تكُونَ حَسَناتُنا عُجِّلَتْ لنا . ثُمَّ جعَلَ يَبْكي حتَّى ترَكَ الطَّعامَ . رواهُ البخاري

454. **Hazrat Ibrahim bin Abdur Rahman bin Auf** (R.A.A.) says that once food was brought before Hazrat Abdur Rahman bin Auf (R.A.A.) when he had been fasting (and was going to break it). He then remarked, 'Mus'ab bin Umair was martyred (when he was fasting) and he was a better man than me. There was nothing available even for his shroud, except a sheet of cloth (so short) that if his head was concealed his feet remained bare and if his feet were covered his head remained unclothed. And now the world has been made wide open for us or we have been given wealth generously; we fear that our good deeds might have been rewarded quickly (that is in this world only). On this he began to weep and even did not eat. (*Bukhari*).

٤٥٥ – وعن أبي أمامة صُدَيِّ بنِ عجلانَ الباهليِّ ، رضيَ اللهُ عنه ، عن النبيِّ ، صلى الله عليه وسلم قال : « ليْسَ شيءٌ أحَبَّ إلى اللهِ تعالى من قَطْرتَيْنِ وأثرَيْنِ : قَطْرَةُ دُمُوعٍ من خَشْيَةِ اللهِ ، وقَطرةُ دمٍ تُهرَاقُ في سَبيلِ اللهِ . وأمَّا الأثرَانِ : فَأثرٌ في سَبيلِ اللهِ تعالى ، وأثرٌ في فَريضَةٍ منْ فرَائِضِ اللهِ تعالى » رواه الترمذي وقال : حديثٌ حسنٌ .

455. **Hazrat Abu Umamah Sudaiye Bin Ajlan Bahili** (R.A.A.) relates that the Holy Prophet (S.A.W.) said: That Allah likes most two drops, one of tears due to fear of Allah and a drop of blood shed for the sake of Allah; and two marks, one received (i.e. wounded) in the cause of

Allah, and a mark received in the course of discharging an obligation commanded by Allah. (*Tirmizi*).

٤٥٦ ـ حديث العرْباض بن ساريةَ ، رضي الله عنه ، قال : وَعَظنَا رسولُ الله ، صلى الله عليه وسلم ، موْعِظةً وَجِلَتْ منها القُلُوبُ ، وذَرَفَتْ منهَا العيُونُ

456. This Hadis has been dealt with in item No. 157 under Chapter 16.

****

CHAPTER 55

The Excellence of Indifference to the World and the Contentment on the Small Portion and Virtues of Poverty.

قالَ اللهُ تعالى : إنَّمَا مَثَلُ الحياةِ الدُّنْيا كَمَاءٍ أنزَلْنَاهُ منَ السَّمَاءِ فَاخْتَلَطَ بِهِ نَبَاتُ الأرْضِ مِمَّا يأكُلُ النَّاسُ وَالأنعامُ حتَّى إذا أخذَتِ الأرضُ زُخْرُفَهَا وَازَّيَّنَتْ وظَنَّ أهْلُهَا أنَّهُم قَادرُونَ عليْهَا أتاهَا أمرُنَا ليْلاً أوْ نَهاراً فجعَلْنَاهَا حَصِيداً كأنْ لمْ تَغْنَ بِالأمْسِ كذلِكَ نُفَصِّلُ الآياتِ لِقَوْمٍ يتَفكَّرُونَ [يونس : ٢٤] وقال تعالى : وَاضْرِبْ لَهُمْ مَثَلَ الحَيَوةِ الدُّنيَا كماءٍ أنزَلْنَاهُ منَ السَّمَاءِ فاخْتَلَطَ بِهِ نَبَاتُ الأرْضِ فأصْبَحَ هَشِيماً تَذْرُوهُ الرِّيَاحُ وكانَ اللهُ عَلى كُلِّ شيْءٍ مُقْتَدِراً . المالُ وَالبَنُونَ زِينَةُ الحياةِ الدُّنْيا والباقياتُ الصَّالحاتُ خيْرٌ عنْدَ رَبِّكَ ثَوَاباً وَخيْرٌ أمَلاً [الكهف : ٤٥ ، ٤٦] وقال تعالى : اعْلَمُوا أنَّمَا الحيَاةُ الدُّنْيَا لَعِبٌ وَلَهوٌ وَزِينَةٌ وَتَفَاخُرٌ بَيْنَكُمْ وَتَكَاثُرٌ في الأمْوَالِ وَالأولادِ كَمَثَلِ غَيْثٍ أعجبَ الكُفَّارَ نَبَاتُهُ ثُمَّ يَهِيجُ فتَرَاهُ مُصْفَرّاً ثُمَّ يكُونُ حُطَاماً، وَفي الآخرةِ عذَابٌ شديدٌ وَمَغْفِرَةٌ من اللهِ ورِضْوَانٌ وما الحيَاةُ الدُّنيَا إلاَّ مَتَاعُ الغُرُورِ [الحديد : ٢٠] وقال تعالى : زُيِّنَ لِلنَّاسِ حُبُّ الشَّهَوَاتِ مِنَ النِّسَاءِ وَالبَنِينَ والقَنَاطِيرِ المُقَنطَرَةِ مِنَ الذَّهَبِ وَالفِضَّةِ والخَيلِ المُسَوَّمَةِ وَالأنعامِ وَالحَرْثِ ذلكَ مَتَاعُ الحيَاةِ الدُّنيا واللهُ عنْدَهُ

حُسْنُ المآبِ [آل عمران : ١٤] وقال تعالى : يَاأَيُّهَا النَّاسُ إنَّ وَعْدَ اللهِ
حَقٌّ فَلا تغرُنَّكُمُ الحَيَاةُ الدُّنْيا وَلا يَغرُنَّكُم بِاللهِ الغَرُورُ [فاطر : ٥]
وقال تعالى : أَلهَاكُمُ التَّكَاثُرُ ، حَتَّى زُرْتُمُ المَقَابِرَ ، كَلاَّ سَوفَ
تَعْلَمُونَ ، ثُمَّ كَلَّا سَوْفَ تَعْلَمُونَ ، كَلَّا لَوْ تَعْلَمُونَ عِلْمَ اليَقِينِ
[التكاثر : ١ ــ ٥] وقال تعالى : وَمَا هَذِهِ الحَيَوةُ الدُّنيَا إلاَّ لَهْوٌ وَلَعِبٌ
وَإنَّ الدَّارَ الآخِرَةَ لَهِيَ الحَيَوانُ لَوْ كَانُوا يَعْلَمُونَ [العنكبوت : ٦٤]
والآيات في الباب كثيرة مشهورة .

Allah, the Exalted, has said:

170. The similitude of the life of the world is only as water which we send down from the sky, then the earth's growth of that which men and cattle eat mingleth with it till, when the earth hath taken on her ornaments and is embellished, and her people deem that they are masters of her, Our commandment cometh by night or by day and we make it as reaped corn as if it had not flourished yesterday. Thus do we expound the revelations for people who reflect (10:24)

171. And coin for them the similitude of the life of the world as water which we send down from the sky, and the vegetation of the earth mingleth with it and then becometh dry twigs that the winds scatter. Allah is able to do all things. Wealth and children are an ornament of life of the world. But the good deeds which endure are better in thy Lord's sight for reward, and better in respect of hope. (18:45—46).

172. Know that the life of this world is only play, and idle talk, and pageantry, and boasting among you, and rivalry in respect of wealth and children; as the likeness of vegetation after rain, whereof the growth is pleasing to the husband man, but afterward it drieth up and thou seest it turning yellow, then it becometh straw. And in the Hereafter there is grievous punishment, and (also) forgiveness from Allah and His good pleasure, whereas the life of the world is but matter of illusion. .(57.20)

173. Beautified for mankind is love of the joys (that come) from women and offspring, and stored-up heaps of gold and silver, and horses branded (with their mark), and cattle and land. That is comfort of the life of the world. Allah! with Him is a more excellent abode. (3:14).

174. O mankind! Lo! the promise of Allah is true. So let not the life of the world beguile you, and let not the (avowed) beguiler beguile you with regard to Allah. (35:5).

175. Rivalry in worldly increase distracteth you until ye come to the graves. Nay, but ye will come to know! Nay, but ye will come to know! Nay, would that ye knew (now) with a sure knowledge! (102: 1–5).

176. This life of th world is but a pastime and a game.Lo! the home of the Hereafter — that is Life, if they but knew. (29:64).

٤٥٧ ـ عن عمرو بن عوف الأنصاري ، رضي الله عنه ، أنَّ رسولَ الله ، صلّى الله عليه وسلم ، بعثَ أبا عُبيدةَ بنَ الجرَّاحِ ، رَضِيَ الله عنه ، إلى البحرينِ يأتي بجزيتها ، فقدمَ بمالٍ من البحرينِ ، فسمعتِ الأنصارُ بقدومِ أبي عبيدةَ ، فوافَوْا صلاةَ الفجرِ مع رسول الله ، صلى اللهُ عليه وسلم ، فلمَّا صلّى رسول الله ، صلى الله عليه وسلم ، انصرفَ ، فتعرَّضوا لهُ ، فتبسَّمَ رسول الله ، صلّى اللهُ عليه وسلم حينَ رآهمْ ، ثُمَّ قال : « أظنُّكُم سمعتُم أنَّ أبا عُبيدةَ قدمَ بشيءٍ منَ البحرينِ ؟ » فقالوا : أجلْ يا رسول الله ، فقال : « أبشِروا وأمِّلوا ما يسرُّكُمْ ، فوالله ما الفقرَ أخشى عليكُمْ ، ولكنِّي أخشى أنْ تُبسطَ الدُّنيا عليكُم كما بُسِطتْ على مَنْ كانَ قبلَكُمْ ، فتنافسوها كما تنافسوها ، فتهلِكَكُمْ كما أهلكتهُمْ » متفقٌ عليهِ

457. Hazrat 'Amr bin 'Auf Ansari (R.A.A.) says that the Holy Prophet (S.A.W.) sent Hazrat Abu Ubaidah Ibn Al-Jarrah (R.A.A.) to collect the capitation tax *(Jizya)* and as such he returned from Bahrain with the money. When the Ansars came to know about this they gathered in the morning prayer congregation with the Holy Prophet (S.A.W.). After the prayer was over, they appeared before him. On seeing them, he smiled and remarked: 'I think you have come to know that (Hazrat) Abu Ubaidah has brought something from Bahrain: They said: 'Yes, it is so, O Messenger of Allah (S.A.W.).' He said: 'Be happy, and expect the thing which will give you pleasure. By Allah! it is not your poverty for which I am worried about you. What I am concerned is that you will be endowed with landed property and riches in abundance, as the people before you had acquired, and then you will start longing for the same as the people before you did. The result will be that this world (your desire for worldly acquisitions) will destroy you, as it destoryed those people who preceded you.' *(Bukhari & Muslim)*.

٤٥٨ – وعن أبي سعيدٍ الخدريِّ ، رَضِيَ اللهُ عنه ، قالَ : جلَسَ رسول الله ، صلى الله عليه وسلم ، علَى المِنْبَرِ ، وَجلَسْنَا حَوْلَهُ ، فقال : « إنَّ مِمَّا أخَافُ علَيْكُم مِنْ بعْدِي مَا يُفْتَحُ علَيْكُمْ مِن زَهْرَةِ الدُّنْيَا وَزِينَتِهَا » . متفقٌ عليه

458. Hazrat Abu Sa'eed Al-Khudri (R.A.A.) says that once the Holy Prophet (S.A.W.) sat on the pulpit and we took our seats around him. He said: 'What I am worried about you after my leaving this world are the charms and attractions and riches of the world, that might be thrown wide open to you as a result of your conquests.

(Bukhari and Muslim).

٤٥٩ – وعنه أنَّ رسولَ الله ، صلّى الله عليهِ وسلمَ ، قال : « إنَّ الدُّنْيَا حُلْوَةٌ خَضِرَةٌ وإنَّ اللهَ تعالى مُسْتَخْلِفكُم فِيهَا ، فَيَنْظُرُ كَيْفَ تَعْمَلُونَ فَاتَّقُوا الدُّنْيَا وَاتَّقُوا النِّسَاءَ » رواه مسلم

459. Hazrat Abu S'aeed Al-Khudri (R.A.A.) relates that the Holy Prophet (S.A.W.) said: 'The world is green and sweet (i.e. it is full of riches and captivation) and Allah will appoint you (as His) vicegerent in it, and will see how you behave. Then beware of this world and the women (i.e. shun much indulgence in the world and sexual misbehaviour and licentiousness).

(Muslim).

٤٦٠ – وعن أنسٍ ، رضيَ الله عنه ، أنَّ النبيَّ ، صلى الله عليه وسلم ، قال : « اللّهُمَّ لا عَيْشَ إلاَّ عَيْشُ الآخِرَةِ » . متفقٌ عليه

460. Hazrat Anas Bin Malik (R.A.A.) relates that the Holy Prophet (S.A.W.) said: 'O Allah! there is no comfort, but the comfort of the Hereafter.'

(Bukhari and Muslim).

٤٦١ – وعنهُ عن رسول الله ، صلى الله عليه وسلم ، قال : « يَتْبَعُ المَيِّتَ ثلاثَةٌ : أهْلُهُ وَمَالُهُ وَعَمَلُهُ : فَيَرْجِعُ اثْنانِ ، وَيَبْقَى وَاحِدٌ : يَرْجِعُ أهْلُهُ وَمَالُهُ وَيَبْقَى عَمَلُهُ » . متفقٌ عليه

461. This Hadis has already been covered in item No. 104 under Chapter 11.

٤٦٢ – وعنه قال : قالَ رسولُ اللهِ ، صلى الله عليه وسلم : « يُؤْتَى بأنْعَمِ أهْلِ الدُّنْيَا مِنْ أهْلِ النَّارِ يَوْمَ القِيامَةِ . فَيُصْبَغُ في النَّارِ صَبْغَةً ، ثُمَّ يُقَالُ : يا ابْنَ آدَمَ هَلْ رَأيْتَ خَيْراً قَطُّ ؟ هَلْ مَرَّ بِكَ نَعِيمٌ قَطُّ ؟

فَيَقُولُ : لا واللهِ يا رَبِّ . وَيُؤْتَى بأشَدِّ النَّاسِ بُؤْساً في الدُّنْيا مِنْ أهْلِ الجَنَّةِ ، فَيُصْبَغُ صَبْغَةً في الجَنَّةِ ، فَيُقَالُ لَهُ : يا ابْنَ آدَمَ هَلْ رَأَيْتَ بُؤْساً قَطُّ ؟ هَلْ مَرَّ بِكَ شِدَّةٌ قَطُّ ؟ فيقولُ : لا ، وَاللهِ ، مَا مَرَّ بِي بُؤْسٌ قَطُّ ، وَلا رَأَيْتُ شِدَّةً قَطُّ » رواه مسلم

462. Hazrat Anas Bin Malik (R.A.A.) says that the Holy Prophet (S.A.W.) said: 'The richest person in the world who had been destined to hell will be brought up on the Day of Judgment and will be dipped once in the Fire of Hell and then asked: 'O! Son of Adam! Did you ever see any good, did you ever have any bliss?' He will say: 'By Allah! Never, O Sustainer! Then the one who was worst hit with adversity and penury in the world, and was destined to Paradise, will be brought up and given one dip (in the spring of) Paradise, and then asked: 'O Son of Adam! Did you ever face any adversity; did you ever have any hardship?' He will say: 'By Allah! I never experienced any adversity; I never passed through any hardship.' *(Muslim).*

٤٦٣ ــ وعن المُسْتَوْرِدِ بن شدَّادٍ رَضِيَ الله عنه ، قال : قالَ رسولُ الله ، صلى الله عليه وسلم : « مَا الدُّنْيَا في الآخِرَةِ إلاَّ مِثْلُ مَا يَجْعَلُ أحَدُكُمْ أُصْبُعَهُ في اليَمِّ ، فَلْيَنْظُرْ بِمَ يَرْجِعُ ؟ » رواه مسلم

463. Hazrat Mustaurid bin Shaddad (R.A.A.) relates that the Holy Prophet (S.A.W.) said: 'The worth of the world as compared with the Hereafter is as if one of you puts his finger in the ocean or a river and then examines as to how much water it brings when taken out? *(Muslim).*

٤٦٤ ــ وعن جابرٍ ، رَضِيَ اللهُ عنهُ أنَّ رسولَ اللهِ ، صلى الله عليه وسلم ، مَرَّ بِالسُّوقِ وَالنَّاسُ كَنَفَتَيْهِ ، فَمَرَّ بِجَدْيٍ أسَكَّ مَيِّتٍ ، فَتَنَاوَلَهُ ، فَأَخَذَ بأذُنِهِ ، ثُمَّ قال : « أيُّكُمْ يُحِبُّ أنْ يَكُونَ هذَا لَهُ بِدِرْهَمٍ ؟ » فقالوا : مَا نُحِبُّ أنَّهُ لَنَا بِشَيْءٍ وَمَا نَصْنَعُ بِهِ ؟ ثم قال : « أتُحِبُّونَ أنَّهُ لَكُمْ ؟ قالُوا : وَاللهِ لَوْ كَانَ حَيّاً كَانَ عَيْباً ، أنَّهُ أسَكُّ . فَكَيْفَ وَهو مَيِّتٌ ! فقال : « فَوَاللهِ لَلدُّنْيَا أهْوَنُ عَلَى اللهِ مِنْ هذا عَلَيْكُمْ » رواه مسلم

464. Hazrat Jabir Bin Abdullah (R.A.A.) relates that the Holy Prophet (S.A.W.) accompanied by his companions, was passing through the Bazar when he noticed a dead kid with cut ears lying there. He caught it by its ear and asked: Who would like to have it for a Dirham?' They said: 'We do not like to have this thing in return for anything; it is of no use to us?' He then asked: Any one of you would like to have it gratis?' He then asked: Any one of you would like to have it gratis? They replied: Had it been alive, even then it would have been defective being cut-eared, and of what use is it now when dead?' The Holy Prophet (S.A.W.) said: 'By Allah! the world is even more valueless in the sight of Allah, than this is in your eyes. *(Muslim).*

٤٦٥ — وعن أبي ذرٍ رَضِيَ اللهُ عنه ، قال : كُنْتُ أَمْشِي مَعَ النبيِّ ، صلى الله عليه وسلم ، في حَرَّةٍ بالمدينةِ ، فَاسْتَقْبَلَنَا أُحُدٌ فقال : « يا أَبَا ذَرٍّ » . قلت : لَبَّيْكَ يا رسول الله . فقال : « مَا يَسُرُّنِي أَنَّ عِنْدِي مِثْلَ أُحُدٍ هذا ذَهَبًا تَمْضِي عَلَيَّ ثَلاثَةُ أَيَّامٍ وَعِنْدِي مِنْهُ دِينَارٌ ، إلاَّ شَيْءٌ أُرْصِدُهُ لِدَيْنٍ ، إلاَّ أَنْ أَقُولَ بِهِ فِي عِبَادِ اللهِ هكَذَا ، وَهكَذَا وَهكَذَا » عن يَمِينِهِ وعن شماله وعن خلفه ؛ ثم سار فقال : « إنَّ الأَكْثَرِينَ هُمُ الأَقَلُّونَ يَوْمَ القِيامَةِ إلاَّ مَنْ قَالَ بالمَالِ هكَذَا وهكذا وهكذا » عن يمينِهِ ، وعن شمالِهِ ، ومِنْ خَلْفِه « وَقَلِيلٌ مَا هُمْ » . ثم قال لي : « مَكَانَكَ لاتَبْرَحْ حَتَّى آتِيَكَ » . ثم انْطَلَقَ في سَوَادِ اللَّيْلِ حتى تَوارَى ، فَسَمِعْتُ صَوْتاً قَدِ ارْتَفَعَ ، فَتَخَوَّفْتُ أَنْ يَكُونَ أَحَدٌ عَرَضَ للنَّبِيِّ ، صلى الله عليه وسلم ، فَأَرَدْتُ أَنْ آتِيَهُ فَذَكَرْتُ قوله : « لا تَبْرَحْ حَتَّى آتِيَكَ » فلم أَبْرَحْ حَتَّى أَتاني ، فَقُلْتُ : لقد سَمِعْتُ صَوْتاً تَخَوَّفْتُ منه ، فَذَكَرْتُ له ، فقال : « وَهَلْ سَمِعْتَهُ ؟ » قلت : نَعَمْ ، قال : « ذَاكَ جِبريلُ أَتاني فقال : مَنْ مات مِنْ أُمتِكَ لايُشْرِكُ بالله شَيْئاً دَخَلَ الجَنَّةَ ، قلتُ : وَإنْ زَنَى وَإنْ سَرَقَ ؟ قال : وَإنْ زَنَى وَإنْ سَرَقَ » متفقٌ عليه ، وهذا لفظ البخاري .

465. Hazrat Abu Zarr (R.A.A.) relates: 'I was walking alongwith the Holy Prophet (S.A.W.) in the rocky plain of Medina, when we reached in front of Mount Uhud, he called me and I responded: 'Yes, Sir, here I am at your service, O Messenger of Allah (S.A.W.).' He said: 'If I had as much gold as the weight of Uhud, it would not please me to have single dinar out of it with me after the passage of three days, except, I were to hold back something for the return of a debt. I would distribute it among the servants of Allah like this and this and this to the right and left and rear'. He then walked further and said: Those who have plenty of wealth will indeed own the least on the Day of Judgment save those persons who spend their wealth like this and this and this to the right, to the left and the rear but such persons are few.' Then he asked me: 'Stay here, do not move and wait for my return. Thereafter he walked into the dark and disappeared. Soon afterwards I heard a loud sound, and felt afraid lest the Holy Prophet (S.A.W.) might have come to grip. I wanted to go after him but remembered his direction not to move till he returned — so I did not move from my place till he came back to me and I said to Him: 'I heard a noise which made me afraid, but I remembered your instruction to me.' He asked: 'Did you hear him? I replied: 'Yes, Sir' He said: 'It was Angel Gabriel (A.S.) who had come to me, and said: One who dies from among your Ummah not having associated anything with Allah, will enter the Paradise; I submitted: Even if he had committed adultry and theft? He said: (Yes), even if he had committed adultery, or and theft. *(Bukhari and Muslim).*

٤٦٦ — وعن أبي هريرة ، رضي الله عنه ، عن رسول الله ، صلى الله عليه وسلم ، قال : « لو كان لي مثلُ أُحُدٍ ذَهَباً ، لَسَرَّني أنْ لا تَمُرَّ عَلَيَّ ثَلاثُ لَيَالٍ وَعِندي منه شيءٌ إلّا شيءٌ أرْصِدُهُ لِدَيْنٍ » متفقٌ عليه

466. Hazrat Abu Hurairah (R.A.A.) says that the Holy Prophet (S.A.W.) said if I had gold equal in weight to Uhud mountain, it would have delighted me that I should have nothing left of it with me after three nights, save something that I might hold back for the return of a debt. *(Bukhari and Muslim).*

٤٦٧ — وعنه قال : قال رسول الله ، صلى الله عليه وسلم : انْظُرُوا إلى مَنْ هُوَ أسفَلَ مِنكُم ولا تَنظُرُوا إلى مَنْ هُوَ فَوقَكُم فَهُوَ أجدَرُ أن لا تَزدَرُوا نعمةَ اللهِ عَلَيكُم » متفق عليه وهذا لفظ مسلم .

وفي رواية البخاري ، « إذا نَظَرَ أحَدُكُم إلى مَنْ فَضَلَ عليهِ في المال وَالخَلقِ . فَلْيَنظُرْ إلى مَنْ هو أسفَلُ مِنهُ » .

467. Hazrat Abu Hurairah (R.A.A.) relates that the Holy Prophet (S.A.W.) said: 'Look at the person who is inferior to you, and do not look at one who is superior to you. Thereby you would be able to appreciate better the benevolences of Allah bestowed upon you.' *(Bukhari and Muslim).*

This is the wording of *Muslim*. Anothr version in *Bukhari* says: 'When any of you happens to see one whom Allah has given more riches and made him more beautiful than him, he should look at one who is inferior to him.'

٤٦٨ ــ وعنه عن النبي ، صلى الله عليه وسلم ، قال : « تَعِسَ عَبْدُ الدِّينَارِ وَالدِّرْهَمِ وَالْقَطِيفَةِ وَالْخَمِيصَةِ ، إنْ أُعْطِيَ رَضِيَ ، وَإنْ لَمْ يُعْطَ لَمْ يَرْضَ » رواه البخاري

468. Hazrat Abu Hurairah (R.A.A.) relates that the Holy Prophet (S.A.W.) said: Cursed are those person who are after Dinars and Dirhams and of black and striped sheets of cloth (i.e. precious cloth). If they are given, they feel happy and if they are not given they are displeased.' *(Bukhari and Muslim).*

٤٦٩ ــ وعنه ، رضي الله عنه . قال : لَقَدْ رَأَيْتُ سَبْعِينَ مِنْ أَهْلِ الصُّفَّةِ ، مَا مِنْهُمْ رَجُلٌ عليه رداءٌ ؛ إمَّا إزَارٌ، وإمَّا كِسَاءٌ ، قَدْ رَبَطُوا في أَعْنَاقِهِمْ ، فَمِنْهَا مَا يَبْلُغُ نِصْفَ السَّاقَيْنِ ، وَمِنْهَا مَا يَبْلُغُ الكَعْبَيْنِ ، فَيَجْمَعُهُ بِيَدِهِ كَرَاهِيَةَ أَنْ تُرَى عَوْرَتُهُ » رواه البخاري

469. Hazrat Abu Hurairah (R.A.A.) relates: 'I have seen seventy of the poor and homeless but very pious companions of the Holy Prophet (S.A.W.) (known as *Aṣhab-i-Suffa*) none of whom had a full sheet of cloth to cover the body, only a loin cloth or a small blanket, which they tied with their necks; and some had their loin cloth reach down half way to their calf of the legs or to their ankles. Some of them who had their loin clothes shorter, used catch if with their hands lest their private parts might be exposed.' *(Bukhari).*

٤٧٠ ــ وعنه قال : قال رسول الله ، صلى الله عليه وسلم : « الدُّنْيَا سِجْنُ المُؤْمِنِ وَجَنَّةُ الكَافِرِ » رواه مسلم

470. Hazrat Abu Hurairah (R.A.A.) relates that the Holy Prophet (S.A.W.) said: 'The world is the prison for the believer and the paradise for the disbeliever.' *(Muslim).*

٤٧١ ــ وعن ابن عمر ، رضي الله عنهما ، قال : أخذ رسول الله ، صلى الله عليه وسلم ، بِمَنْكِبَيَّ ، فقال : « كُنْ في الدُّنْيَا كَأَنَّكَ غَرِيبٌ ، أَوْ عَابِرُ سَبِيلٍ » .

وكَانَ ابنُ عمرَ ، رضي الله عنهما ، يقول : إذَا أَمْسَيْتَ ، فَلا تَنْتَظِرِ الصَّبَاحَ ، وَإذَا أَصْبَحْتَ ، فَلا تَنْتَظِرِ المَسَاءَ ، وَخُذْ مِنْ صِحَّتِكَ لِمَرَضِكَ وَمِنْ حَيَاتِكَ لِمَوْتِكَ . رواه البخاري

471. Hazrat Ibn Umar (R.A.A.) states that once the Holy Prophet (S.A.W.) caught hold of his shoulders and said: Live in this world as if you are a stranger or a traveller.'

Hazrat Ibn Umar (R.A.A.) used to say:'When you (pass the day) arrive at the evening do not expect that you will pass night and hope to reach morning, and when you arrive in morning do not look forward to the evening. While in health, be ready for illness, and while alive prepare for death.' *(Bukhari).*

٤٧٢ – وعن أبي العَبَّاسِ سَهْلِ بنِ سَعْدٍ السَّاعديِّ ، رضي اللهُ عنهُ ، قالَ : جاءَ رَجُلٌ إلى النبيِّ صلى الله عليه وسلم ، فقالَ : يا رسولَ الله دُلَّني على عَمَلٍ إذا عَمِلْتُهُ أَحَبَّني اللهُ . وَأَحبَّني النَّاسُ ، فقال : « ازْهَدْ في الدُّنْيا يُحِبَّكَ اللهُ ، وَازْهَدْ فيما عِنْدَ النَّاسِ يُحِبَّكَ النَّاسُ » حديثٌ حسنٌ رواه ابن ماجه وغيره بأسانيد حسنةٍ .

472. Hazrat Abdul Abbas Sahl Bin Sa'ad Al-Sa'idi (R.A.A.) says that a man came to the Holy Prophet (S.A.W.) and requested him: 'Messenger of Allah (S.A.W.), tell me something by doing which, I should win the love of Allah and the People.' The Holy Prophet told him: 'Do not love the world, and Allah will love you; and do not have a longing for that which people have, and they will love you.'

This tradition has been reported by *Ibn-i-Majah* and others on reliable authorities.

٤٧٣ – وعن النُّعْمَانَ بنِ بَشيرٍ ، رضيَ اللهُ عنهما . قالَ : ذَكَرَ عُمَرُ ابنُ الخطَّاب ، رضي الله عنه ، مَا أَصَابَ النَّاسُ مِنَ الدُّنْيَا ، فقال : لَقَدْ رَأَيْتُ رسول اللهِ ، صلى الله عليه وسلم ، يَظَلُّ اليَوْمَ يَلْتَوِي مَا يَجِدُ مِنَ الدَّقَلِ مَا يَمْلأُ بِهِ بَطْنَهُ . رواه مسلم

473. Hazrat N'uman Bin Bashir (R.A.A.) relates that Hazrat Umar Bin Khattab (R.A.A.) said when the people had become rich and prosperous (during his tenure as caliph of Islam)referring to the austere life the Muslims led said: 'I have seen the Holy Prophet (S.A.W.) pass his days in acute hunger when he could not get even rotten dates to satisfy his hunger'. *(Muslim).*

٤٧٤ – وعن عائشةَ ، رضي الله عنها ، قالتْ : تُوُفِّيَ رسولُ اللهِ ، صلى الله عليه وسلم . وَمَا في بَيْتِي مِنْ شَيْءٍ يَأْكُلُهُ ذُو كَبِدٍ إلاَّ شَطْرُ شَعِيرٍ في رَفٍّ لِي ، فَأَكَلْتُ مِنْهُ حَتَّى طَالَ عَلَيَّ ، فَكِلْتُهُ فَفَنِيَ . متفقٌ عليه

« شَطْرُ شَعِيرٍ » أَيْ : شَيْءٌ مِنْ شَعِيرٍ ، كَذا فَسَّرَهُ التِّرْمِذِيُّ .

474. Hazrat Ayesha (R.A.A.) relates: 'When the Holy Prophet (S.A.W.) passed away, there was nothing worth eating in the house, except a small quantity of barley, in the store upon which I subsisted for a considerable time. After sometime I wanted to measure the stuff but was soon finished.' *(Bukhari and Muslim).*

٤٧٥ — وعن عمرو بن الحارث أخي جُوَيْرِيَةَ بنتِ الحارث أُمّ المُؤْمنينَ، رضي الله عنهما ، قال : مَاتَرَكَ رسولُ الله ، صلى الله عليه وسلم ، عِنْدَ مَوْتِهِ دِينَاراً ، وَلا دِرْهَماً ، وَلا عَبْداً ، وَلا أَمَةً ، وَلا شَيْئاً إلاَّ بَغْلَتَهُ البَيْضَاءَ الَّتِي كَانَ يَرْكَبُهَا ، وَسِلاحَهُ ، وَأَرْضاً جَعَلَهَا لابْنِ السَّبِيلِ صَدَقَةً » رواه البخاري

475. Hazrat 'Amr Bin Haris (R.A.A.) brother of Ummul Momnin Hazrat Juweria (R.A.A.) states that when the Holy Prophet (S.A.W.) passed away he left no dinar or dirham or slave or bondwoman, or anything, except his white riding mule, his arms and his land which he had given in charity for the (the use and convenience) of the travellers *(Bukhari).*

٤٧٦ — وعن خَبَّابِ بنِ الأَرَتِّ ، رضي الله عنه ، قال : هَاجَرْنَا مَعَ رسولِ الله ، صلَّى الله عليه وسلم ، نَلْتَمِسُ وَجْهَ اللهِ تعالى ؛ فَوَقَعَ أَجْرُنَا عَلَى اللهِ . فَمِنَّا مَنْ مَاتَ وَلَمْ يَأْكُلْ مِنْ أَجْرِهِ شَيْئاً . مِنْهُمْ مُصْعَبُ بنُ عُمَيْرٍ . رضي الله عنه ، قُتِلَ يَوْمَ أُحُدٍ ، وَتَرَكَ نَمِرَةً . فَكُنَّا إذَا غَطَّيْنَا بِهَا رَأْسَهُ ، بَدَتْ رِجْلاهُ . وَإِذَا غَطَّيْنَا بِهَا رِجْلَيْهِ ، بَدَا رَأْسُهُ . فَأَمَرَنَا رسولُ اللهِ ، صلَّى اللهُ عليه وسلم ، أَنْ نُغَطِّيَ رَأْسَهُ ، وَنَجْعَلَ عَلَى رِجْلَيْهِ شَيْئاً مِنَ الإِذْخِرِ ، وَمِنَّا مَنْ أَيْنَعَتْ لَهُ ثَمَرَتُهُ . فَهُوَ يَهْدِبُهَا متفقٌ عليه

476. Hazrat Khabbab Bin Arat (R.A.A.) says that We migrated with the Holy Prophet (S.A.W.) simply to please Allah only, and as such our recompense in the Hereafter is certain. Some of us died soon without enjoying anything out of their recompense (in this world). One of them was Hazrat Mus'ab Bin Umair (R.A.A.) who received martyrdom in the battle of Uhud; he left only a small sheet of blanket after his death. It was so small that if we covered his head with it, his feet were bared and if we covered his feet, his head was left uncovered. So the Holy Prophet (S.A.W.) directed us to cover his head and to cover his feet with grass. There are some others among us who are enjoying the life with abundance (i.e. they are now leading a happy and prosperous life). *(Bukhari and Muslim).*

٤٧٧ – وعن سَهْلِ بن سَعْدٍ السّاعديّ ، رضي الله عنه . قال : قال رسول الله ، صلى الله عليه وسلم : « لَوْ كَانَتِ الدُّنْيَا تَعدِلُ عِنْدَ الله جَنَاحَ بَعُوضَةٍ ، مَا سقَى كَافراً مِنْهَا شَرْبَةَ مَاءٍ » .

رواه الترمذي وقال : حديث حسن صحيحٌ .

477. Hazrat Sahl Bin Sa'ad Al-Sa'idi (R.A.A.) states that the Holy Prophet (S.A.W.) said: If'in the sight of Allah the world had the value equal to that of the wing of a mosquito, He would not have allowed a disbeliver even to drink a mouthful of water out of it. *(Tirmizi).*

٤٧٨ – وعن أَبي هُرَيْرَةَ ، رضي الله عنه . قال : سمعتُ رسولَ اللهِ . صلى الله عليه وسلم ، يقول : « أَلا إنَّ الدُّنْيَا مَلْعُونَةٌ ، مَلْعُونٌ مَا فيها . إلاَّ ذِكْرَ اللهِ تَعَالَى . وَمَا وَالاهُ . وَعالماً وَمُتَعَلِّماً » .

رواه الترمذي وقال : حديثٌ حسنٌ .

478. Hazrat Abu Hurairah (R.A.A.) relates that he heard the Holy Prophet (S.A.W.) say: This world is cursed and so are all the things in it except the remembrance of Allah and that which He likes, and the scholars and the students.*(Tirmizi).* This is an authentic tradition.

٤٧٩ – وعن عَبْدِ اللهِ بنِ مسعودٍ ، رضيَ الله عنه ، قال : قال رسول الله ، صلى الله عليه وسلم : « لاتَتَّخِذُوا الضَّيعَةَ فَتَرْغَبُوا في الدُّنْيَا » .

رواه الترمذي وقال : حديثٌ حسنٌ

479. Hazrat Abdullah Ibn Mas'ud (R.A.A.) states that the Holy Prophet (S.A.W.) said: 'Do not try too much to acquire property (real estate) or else you will be absorbed too much enamoured with the world.' *(Tirmizi).*

This is an authentic tradition.

٤٨٠ – وعن عبدِ اللهِ بنِ عمروِ بنِ العاصِ ، رضيَ اللهُ عنهما ، قال : مَرَّ عَلَيْنَا رسولُ الله . صلى الله عليه وسلم . ونحنُ نعالِجُ خُصّاً لَنَا فقال : « ما هذا ؟ » فَقُلْنَا : قَدْ وَهَى . فَنَحْنُ نُصْلِحُه . فقال : « ما أَرَى الأمْرَ إلاَّ أَعْجَلَ مِنْ ذلكَ » .

رواه أبو داود . والترمذي بإسناد البخاري ومسلم ، وقال الترمذي حديثٌ حسنٌ صحيحٌ .

480. Hazrat Abdullah Ibn 'Amr Bin Al'Aas (R.A.A.) states that we were repairing our thatched roof, when the Holy Prophet (S.A.W.) came there and asked us: 'What are you doing?' We submitted 'The roof had become week and therefore we are repairing it.' He said: 'I see the order (the Day of Judgment) approaching faster than this.' *(Abu Daud and Tirmizi).*

This is also an authentic tradition.

٤٨١ – وعن كَعْبِ بن عِيَاضٍ ، رضي الله عنه ، قال : قالَ سمعتُ رسولَ الله ، صلى الله عليه وسلم ، يقول : « إنَّ لِكُلِّ أُمَّةٍ فِتْنَةً . وفِتْنَةُ أُمَّتِي المَالُ » رواه الترمذي قال : حديثٌ حسنٌ صحيحٌ .

481. Hazrat K'ab Bin Ayaz (R.A.A.) states that he heard the Holy Prophet (S.A.W.) say: 'Every Ummah (nation) has a test to undergo, my Ummah (nation) will be tried through the wealth. *(Tirmizi)*

This is an authentic tradition.

٤٨٢ – وعن أبي عَمْرٍو، ويقالُ :أبوعبدِ الله ، ويقال: أبو لَيْلَى عُثْمَانَ ابنَ عفَّانَ ، رَضي لله عنه ، أنَّ النبيَّ ، صلَّى لله عليه وسلم ، قال : « لَيْسَ لابْنِ آدَمَ حَقٌّ في سِوى هَذِهِ الخِصَالِ : بَيْتٌ يَسْكُنُهُ ، وثَوْبٌ يُوَارِي عَوْرَتَهُ وَجِلْفُ الخُبْزِ ، والمَاءِ » رواه الترمذي وقال : حديث صحيح .

482. Hazrat Abu 'Amr who was called Abu Abdullah or Abu Laila Usman Ibn Affan (R.A.A.) also relates that the Holy Prophet (S.A.W.) said: 'A Son of Adam (man) has a right to have only three things; a house to live in a dress to cover his body and private parts and a piece of bread and water.' *(Tirmizi).*

Imam Tirmizi says that he heard this from Abu Daud Sulaiman Bin Salim Al-Balkhi who heard it from Nazar Bin Shumail that this tradition is true).

٤٨٣ – وعنْ عبدِ الله بنِ الشِّخِّيرِ « بكسر الشينِ والخاء المشددةِ المعجمتين» رضيَ الله عنه ، أنَّهُ قالَ : أتَيْتُ النَّبيَّ ، صلّى الله عليه وسلم ، وَهُوَ يقرأُ : (ألهَاكُمُ التَّكَاثُرُ) قال : « يَقُولُ ابنُ آدَم : مَالي ، مَالي . وَهَلْ لكَ يَا ابنَ آدَمِ مِنْ مالِكَ إلاَّ ما أكَلْتَ . فأفنَيْتَ ، أوْ لبِسْتَ فأبْلَيْتَ . أوْ تَصَدَّقْتَ فأمْضَيْتَ ؟ ! » رواه مسلم .

483. Hazrat Abdullah Bin Shikhkhair (R.A.A.) says that I presented myself before Holy Prophet (S.A.W.) when he was reciting Sura Al-Takasur i.e. "Rivalry in worldly increase distracteth you." (102:1)

He added: 'Man says: My property, my property; but O Son of Adam what is for thee that is out of thy property only which thou ate and it vanished, which thou wore and made it worn out and spent in charity and sent it ahead.' *(Muslim).*

٤٨٤ — وعن عبدِ الله بن مُغَفَّلٍ . رضيَ الله عنه. قال قال رَجُلٌ للنَّبيِّ ، صلى الله عليه وسلم : يا رسولَ اللهِ . واللهِ إنّي لأُحِبُّكَ ، فقال : « انْظُرْ ماذا تَقُولُ ؟ » قال : وَاللهِ إنّي لأُحِبُّكَ . ثَلاثَ مَرّاتٍ . فقال : « إنْ كُنْتَ تُحِبُّني فَأَعِدَّ لِلفَقرِ تِجفَافاً ، فإنَّ الفَقرَ أَسْرَعُ إلى من يُحِبُّني مِنَ السَّيْلِ إلى مُنْتَهاهُ » رواه الترمذي وقال حديث حسن .

484. Hazrat Abdullah Bin Mughaffal (R.A.A.) says: 'A man said to the Holy Prophet (S.A.W.): 'By Allah, O Messenger of Allah (S.A.W.) I do love you.' The Holy Prophet (S.A.W.) said 'Look, what you are saying.' The man said: 'By Allah, I love you;' and repeated this sentence thrice. The Holy Prophet (S.A.W.) said: 'If you really love me, then he prepared for acute poverty, for extreme poverty rushes more rapidly towards a person who loves me, than a flood flows towards its goal. (*Imam Tirmizi* has cited this tradition and has declared it authentic).

٤٨٥ — وعن كَعبِ بنِ مالكٍ ، رضيَ الله عنه ، قال : قال رسول الله صلى الله عليه وسلم : « ما ذِئبانِ جائِعانِ أُرْسِلا في غَنَمٍ بِأَفْسَدَ لها مِنْ حِرْصِ المَرءِ على المالِ وَالشَّرَفِ. لِدِينِهِ » رواه الترمذي وقال: حديث حسن صحيح.

485. Hazrat K'ab Bin Malik (R.A.A.) relates that the Holy Prophet (S.A.W.) said: Two hungry wolves if let loose among a flock of sheep, will not do more damage than that is caused by a man's avarice for wealth and status to his religion.

(*Imam Tirmizi* has quoted this tradition and called it authentic).

٤٨٦ — وعن عبد الله بن مَسْعُودٍ . رضي الله عنه ، قال : نامَ رسولُ الله صلى الله عليه وسلم . على حَصيرٍ . فَقَامَ وَقَدْ أَثَّرَ في جَنْبِهِ . قُلْنَا : يارَسُولَ الله لو اتَّخَذْنَا لَكَ وِطاءً . ! . فقال : « مالي وَللدُّنْيا ؟ ما أنا في الدُّنْيا إلاَّ كَراكِبٍ اسْتَظَلَّ تَحْتَ شَجَرَةٍ ثُمَّ رَاحَ وَتَرَكَهَا »

رواه الترمذي وقال : حديث حسن صحيح

486. Hazrat Abdullah Ibn Mas'ud (R.A.A.) says that (once) the Holy Prophet(S.A.W.) slept on a mat made of date palm leaves and when he awoke the impressions of the mat were visible on his body.

We said: 'O Messenger of Allah (S.A.W.) may we prepare a soft bedding for you?' He said: I have got nothing to do with the world, I am in this world like a rider who halts in the shade of a tree for a short time and after taking some rest resumes his journey leaving the tree behind.

(*Imam Tirmizi* has reported this tradition calling it as authentic).

٤٨٧ – وعن أبي هريرة ، رضي الله عنه ، قال : قال رسول الله ، صلّى الله عليه وسلم : « يَدْخُلُ الفُقَرَاءُ الجَنَّةَ قَبْلَ الأَغْنِيَاءِ بِخَمْسِمائَةِ عَامٍ » رواه الترمذي وقال : حديث صحيح .

487. Hazrat Abu Hurairah (R.A.A.) relates that the Holy Prophet (S.A.W.) said: The poor persons will enter Paradise five hundred years earlier than the rich.'

(*Imam Tirmizi* has reported this tradition and said that it is authentic).

٤٨٨ – وعن ابنِ عبَّاسٍ ، وعمرَانَ بنِ الحُصَيْنِ ، رضيَ الله عنهم ، عن النبي ، صلى الله عليه وسلم ، قال « اطَّلَعْتُ في الجَنَّةِ فرَأَيْتُ أَكْثَرَ أَهلِهَا الفُقَرَاءَ ، واطَّلَعْتُ في النَّارِ فرَأَيْتُ أَكْثَرَ أَهْلِهَا النِّسَاءَ » متفقٌ عليه من رواية ابن عباس .

ورواه البخاري أيضاً من روايةِ عمرَانَ بنِ الحُصَيْنِ .

488. Hazrat Ibn Abbas (R.A.A.) and Hazrat Imran bin Husain (R.A.A.) relate that the Holy Prophet (S.A.W.) said: When I had a look at Paradise, I saw that most of its dwellers were the poor; and when I had a glance of the Hell I saw that most of its dwellers were women.

(Bukhari and Muslim).

٤٨٩ – وعن أسامةَ بنِ زيدٍ ، رضيَ الله عنهما ، عنِ النبيِّ صلى الله عليه وسلم ، قال : « قُمْتُ عَلى بَابِ الجَنَّةِ ، فكَانَ عَامَّةَ مَنْ دَخَلَهَا المَسَاكِينُ . وَأَصحَابُ الجَدِّ مَحبُوسُونَ ، غَيْرَ أَنَّ أَصحَابَ النَّار قد أُمِرَ بِهِم إلى النَّارِ » متفقٌ عليه

489. Hazrat Usama bin Zaid (R.A.A.) relates that the Holy Prophet (S.A.W.) said: (On the eve of *lailatul-Meraj*) when I was standing at the gate of Paradise, I saw that most of the persons who entered it were poor, while the rich were not allowed to enter there. But those condemned to Hell were ordered to be taken there.

(Bukhari and Muslim).

٤٩٠ — وعن أبي هريرة ، رضي الله عنه ، عن النبيّ ، صلى الله عليه وسلم ، قال : « أَصْدَقُ كَلِمَةٍ قَالَهَا شَاعِرٌ كَلِمَةُ لَبِيدٍ :

أَلا كُلُّ شَيْءٍ ما خَلا اللهَ بَاطِلُ

متفقٌ عليه

490. Hazrat Abu Hurairah (R.A.A.) relates that the Holy Prophet (S.A.W.) said: 'The most accurate thing which has been said is the verse said by poet Labid: 'Everything beside Allah is false.'

(Bukhari and Muslim).

****

CHAPTER 56

The Excellence of Hunger and Leading a Life of Abstinence, Subsisting on Meagre Food and Clothing and Abstaining from Luxuries of Life and Sex.

قال الله تعالى : فَخَلَفَ مِنْ بَعْدِهِم خَلْفٌ أَضَاعُوا الصَّلَوةَ وَاتَّبَعُوا الشَّهَوَاتِ فَسَوْفَ يَلقَوْنَ غَيّاً إِلاَّ مَنْ تابَ وَآمَنَ وَعَمِلَ صَالِحاً فَأُولئكَ يَدْخُلُونَ الجَنَّةَ وَلا يُظْلَمُونَ شَيْئاً [مريم : ٥٩ ، ٦٠] وقال تعالى فَخَرَجَ عَلَى قَوْمِهِ في زِينَتِهِ قال الَّذِينَ يُرِيدُونَ الحَيَوةَ الدُّنْيَا يالَيْتَ لَنَا مِثْلَ ما أُوتِيَ قارُونُ إِنهُ لَذُو حَظٍّ عَظِيمٍ . وَقَالَ الَّذِينَ أُوتُوا العِلْمَ وَيْلَكُمْ ثَوَابُ اللهِ خَيْرٌ لِمَنْ آمَنَ وَعَمِلَ صَالِحاً [القصص : ٧٩ — ٨٠ وقال تعالى : ثُمَّ لَتُسْأَلُنَّ يَوْمَئِذ عَنِ النَّعِيمِ [التكاثر : ٨] وقال تعالى : مَنْ كَانَ يُرِيدُ العَاجِلَةَ عَجلْنَا لَهُ فِيها ما نَشَاءُ لِمَن نُرِيدُ ثُمَّ جَعَلْنَا لَهُ جَهَنَّمَ يَصْلاهَا مَذْمُوماً مَدْحُوراً [الإسراء : ١٨]

والآياتُ في الباب كثيرةٌ مَعْلُومَةٌ

Allah, the Exalted, has said:

177. Now there hath succeeded them a later generation who have ruined worship and have followed lusts. But they will meet deception. Save him who shall repent and believe and do right. Such will enter the Garden and they will not be wronged in aught. (19:59—60).

178. Then went he (Korah) forth before his people in his pomp. Those who were desirous of the life of the world said: Ah, Would that unto us had been given the like of what hath been given unto Korah! Lo! he is lord of rare good fortune. But those who had been given knowledge said: Woe unto you! The reward of Allah for him who believeth and doeth right is better. (28:79—80).

179. Then, on that day, ye will be asked concerning pleasure. (102:8).

180. Whose desireth that (life) which hasteneth away, We hasten for him therein that we will for whom We please. And afterward We have appointed for him Hell; he will endure the heat thereof, condemned, rejected. (17:18).

٤٩١ — عن عائشةَ ، رضي الله عنها ، قالت : مَا شَبِعَ آلُ مُحمَّد صلى الله عليه وسلم ، مِنْ خُبْزِ شَعِير يَوْمَيْنِ مُتَتَابِعَيْنِ حتَّى قُبِضَ متفقٌ عليه

وفي رواية : مَا شَبِعَ آلُ مُحمَّد ، صلى الله عليه وسلم . مُنْذُ قَدِمَ المَدِينَةَ مِنْ طَعَامِ البُرِّ ثَلاثَ لَيَالٍ تِبَاعاً حتَّى قُبِضَ .

491. Hazrat Ayesha (R.A.A.) relates: The family members of the Holy Prophet (S.A.W.) never ate their fill of barley bread for two continuous days till he passed away. *(Bukhari and Muslim).*

Another version says: 'Ever since his migration to Medina, the family of the Holy Prophet (S.A.W.) never ate their fill of wheat bread for three continuous nights till he passed away.'

٤٩٢ — وعن عُرْوَةَ عَنْ عائشة ، رضي الله عنها ، أَنَّهَا كَانَتْ تَقُولُ : وَالله يَاابْنَ أُخْتِي إنْ كُنَّا لَنَنْظُرُ إلى الهِلالِ ، ثُمَّ الهِلالِ : ثَلاثَةَ أَهِلَّةٍ في شَهْرَيْنِ ، وَمَا أُوقِدَ في أبيَاتِ رسولِ الله ، صلى الله عليه وسلم ، نَارٌ . قُلْتُ : يَا خالَةُ فَمَا كَانَ يُعِيشُكُمْ ؟ قالتْ : الأَسْوَدَانِ : التَّمْرُ وَالمَاءُ ، إلاَّ أَنَّهُ قَدْ كانَ لرسول الله صلى الله عليه وسلم جِيرانٌ مِنَ الأَنْصَارِ ، وَكانَتْ لَهُم مَنَائِحُ وَكانُوا يُرْسِلُونَ إلى رسول الله صلى الله عليه وسلم مِنْ أَلبَانِها فَيَسْقِينَا . متفق عليه

492. Hazrat 'Urwah (R.A.A.) relates from Hazrat Ayesha (R.A.A.) that she used to say: O my Nephew, we would sight three moons in two months, without burning fire in the homes of the Holy Prophet (S.A.W.) I asked: 'Aunt, how did you subsist?' She said: 'On two black things, that is dates and water, except that the Holy Prophet (S.A.W.) had some Ansar as neighbours who had milk giving she-camels. They used to send some milk to the Holy Prophet (S.A.W.) who used to give that milk to us for drinking.' *(Bukhari and Muslim).*

٤٩٣ — وعن أبي سعيدٍ المَقْبُرِيِّ عَنْ أبي هُرَيْرَةَ رضي الله عنه ، أنه مَرَّ بِقَوْمٍ بَيْنَ أَيْدِيهِمْ شَاةٌ مَصْلِيَّةٌ ، فَدَعَوْهُ فَأَبَى أَنْ يَأْكُلَ ، وقال : خَرَجَ رسول الله صلى الله عليه وسلم مِنَ الدُّنيا وَلَمْ يَشْبَعْ مِنْ خُبْزِ الشَّعِيرِ .

رواه البخاري

493. Hazrat Abu Sa'id Maqburi (R.A.A.) reports from Hazrat Abu Hurairah (R.A.A.) that (once) Hazrat Abu Hurairah passed by some people who had a roasted goat before them. They asked him to join them in the fare, but he refused to partake saying: 'The Holy Prophet (S.A.W.) passed away from this world without having eaten his fill of even barley bread.' *(Bukhari).*

٤٩٤ — وعن أنسٍ رضي الله عنه . قال : لَمْ يَأْكُلِ النَّبِيُّ صلى الله عليه وسلم عَلَى خِوَانٍ حَتَّى مَاتَ ، وَما أَكَلَ خُبْزاً مرقَّقاً حَتَّى مَاتَ ؛

رواه البخاري

وفي روايةٍ له : وَلا رَأَى شَاةً سَمِيطاً بِعَيْنِهِ قطُّ

494. Hazrat Anas Bin Malik (R.A.A.) relates that the Holy Prophet (S.A.W.) never had the chance of eating on a table-cloth till he passed away, nor did he ever eat bread made of fine flour. *(Bukhari).*

Another version says: He never even saw whole roasted goat.

٤٩٥ — وعن النُّعمانِ بن بشيرٍ رضي الله عنهما قال : لَقَدْ رَأَيْتُ نَبِيَّكُمْ صلى اللهُ عليه وسلم، وَما يَجِدُ مِنَ الدَّقَلِ ما يَمْلأُ بِهِ بَطْنَهُ، رواه مسلم

495. Hazrat Nu'man Ibn Bashir (R.A.A.) relates: 'I have seen your Prophet (S.A.W.) who did not get enough of even the ordinary quality of dates with which he could have satisfied his hunger. *(Muslim).*

٤٩٦ — وعن سهلِ بنِ سعدٍ رضي اللهُ عنه ، قال : ما رَأَى رَسُولُ اللهِ صلى اللهُ عليه وسلم النَّقِيَّ مِنْ حِينَ ابْتَعَثَهُ اللهُ تعالى حتّى قَبَضَهُ اللهُ تعالى . فَقِيلَ لَهُ : هَلْ كانَ لَكُمْ في عَهْدِ رسول اللهِ صلى اللهُ عليه وسلَّم مَناخِلُ ؟ قالَ : ما رَأَى رسولُ اللهِ صلى اللهُ عليه وسلم مُنْخلاً مِنْ حِينَ ابْتَعَثَهُ اللهُ

تَعالى حتّى قَبَضَهُ اللهُ تعالى ، فَقِيلَ لَهُ : كَيْفَ كُنْتُمْ تَأكُلُونَ الشَّعِيرَ غَيْرَ مَنْخُولٍ ؟ قالَ : كُنَّا نَطْحَنُهُ ونَنْفُخُهُ ، فَيَطيرُ ما طارَ ، وما بَقِيَ ثَرَّيْنَاهُ . رواهُ البخاري

496. Hazrat Sahl bin Sa'ad (R.A.A.) relates that the Holy Prophet (S.A.W.) never even saw the bread of fine flour since he was commissioned as Prophet till he was recalled by Allah the Almighty. He was asked: 'Did you not have sieves in the time of the Holy Prophet (S.A.W.) (to take out fine flour). Ever since his appointment as Prophet the Holy Prophet (S.A.W.) never saw a sieve, till he was recalled by Allah. He was further asked: 'How could you manage to eat bread made from unsieved barley flour?' He replied: 'We ground it and then remove the chaff by blowing; the husk is in this way blown off, and the grounded kernal remained there, kneaded into dough.' *(Bukhari).*

٤٩٧ — وعن أبي هُرَيرة رضي اللهُ عنه قال : خَرَجَ رَسُولُ اللهِ صلى اللهُ عليه وسلم ذاتَ يَوْمٍ أَوْ لَيْلَةٍ ، فَإذا هُوَ بأبي بَكْرٍ وعُمَرَ رضيَ اللهُ عنهما ، فقال : « ما أَخْرَجَكُما مِنْ بُيُوتِكُما هذهِ السَّاعَةَ ؟ » قالا : الجُوعُ يا رَسُولَ اللهِ . قالَ : « وَأَنا ، والَّذي نَفْسي بيَدِهِ ، لأَخْرَجَني الَّذي أخْرَجَكُما . قُوما » فَقاما مَعَهُ ، فَأَتى رَجُلاً مِنَ الأَنْصارِ ، فَإذا هُوَ لَيْسَ في بَيْتِهِ ، فَلَمَّا رَأَتْهُ المَرْأَةُ قالَتْ : مَرْحَباً وَأَهْلاً . فقال لها رَسُولُ اللهِ صلى اللهُ عليه وسلم : « أَيْنَ فُلانُ ؟ » قالَتْ : ذَهَبَ يَسْتَعْذِبُ لَنَا الماءَ ، إذْ جاءَ الأَنْصارِيُّ ، فَنَظَرَ إلى رَسُولِ الله صلى اللهُ عليه وسلم وصاحِبَيْهِ ، ثُمَّ قالَ : الحَمْدُ لله ، ما أَحَدٌ اليَوْمَ أكْرَمَ أَضْيافاً مِنِّي . فانْطَلَقَ فَجاءَهُمْ بِعِذْقٍ فيهِ بُسْرٌ وَتَمْرٌ ورُطَبٌ ، فقالَ : كُلُوا ، وَأَخَذَ المُدْيَةَ ، فَقالَ لَهُ رسُولُ اللهِ صلى اللهُ عليهِ وسلَّم : « إيَّاكَ وَالحَلُوبَ » فَذَبَحَ لَهُمْ ، فَأَكَلُوا مِنَ الشَّاةِ وَمِنْ ذلكَ العِذْقِ وشَرِبُوا . فَلَمَّا أَنْ شَبِعُوا وَرَوُوا قال رسولُ اللهِ صلى اللهُ عليه سلم لأبي بكْرٍ وعُمَرَ رضيَ اللهُ عنهما : « وَالَّذي نَفْسي بِيَدِهِ ، لَتُسْأَلُنَّ عَنْ هذا النَّعِيمِ يَوْمَ القيامَةِ ، أَخْرَجَكُمْ مِنْ بُيُوتِكُمُ الجُوعُ ، ثُمَّ لَمْ تَرْجِعُوا حتى أصابَكُمْ هذا النَّعيمُ » رواهُ مسلم

497. Hazrat Abu Hurairah (R.A.A.) relates: 'The Holy Prophet (S.A.W.) came out one day or one night when Hazrat Abu Bakr and Hazrat Umar (R.A.A.) were also present there. He asked them: 'What have made you both come out of your houses at this hour?' They said: 'O Messenger of Allah (S.A.W.) due to hunger'. He (S.A.W.) seconded: 'By Allah in whose hands lies my life, due to the same reason I too have come out. Get up (and let us go)' Hazrat Abu Bakr and Hazrat Umar stood up and all the three went to the house of an Ansar, but he was not present at his house. When his wife saw the Holy Prophet (S.A.W.) she said: 'Most welcome, blessed you are.He (S.A.W.) asked her: 'Where is So and So?' She replied:'He has gone to fetch fresh and sweet water for us.' In the meantime the Ansari also arrived there. Seeing the Holy Prophet (S.A.W.) and his two companions, he said: Allah be Praised. Today nobody has more honourable and distinguished guests than I have.' He immediately went out and brought a branch bearing ripe and semi-ripe date fruits and requested his august visitors to eat. He then took a knife in order to slaughter a goat for the dinner of the guests When the Holy Prophet (S.A.W.) asked him: 'Do not slaughter a goat that is yielding milk'. However he slaughtered a (non milk-giving) goat for the distinguished guests and they ate the goat meat and dates and drank water. When they had eaten to their fill and were refreshed, the Holy Prophet (S.A.W.) said to his two companions: 'By Allah in whose hands is my life, on the day of judgment you will be questioned for these munificence. You came out of your homes due to hunger, but before you returned (to your homes) you had enjoyed these delicacies'
(Muslim).

Note: Imam Nawawi elucidates that by calling to account on the Day of Judgment, means that they will have to enumerate these bounties by way of thanking Allah for the same.

٤٩٨ ـ وعن خالدِ بن عُمَرَ العَدَوِيِّ قال : خَطَبَنا عُتْبَةُ بنُ غَزْوانَ ، وكانَ أميراً على البَصْرَةِ ، فَحَمِدَ اللهَ وأثنى عَلَيْهِ ، ثُمَّ قالَ : أمّا بَعْدُ ، فَإنَّ الدُّنيا قَدْ آذَنَتْ بِصُرْمٍ ، وَوَلَّتْ حَذّاءَ ، وَلَمْ يَبْقَ مِنْها إلاَّ صُبابَةٌ كَصُبابَةِ الإناءِ يَتَصابُّها صاحِبُها ، وإنكُمْ مُنْتَقِلُونَ مِنْها إلى دارٍ لا زَوالَ لَهَا ، فانْتَقِلُوا بِخَيْرِ ما بِحَضْرَتِكُمْ ، فَإنَّهُ قَدْ ذُكِرَ لَنا أنَّ الحَجَرَ يُلْقَى مِنْ شَفِيرِ جَهَنَّمَ فَيَهْوِي فِيها سَبْعِينَ عاماً ، لا يُدْرِكُ لَهَا قَعْراً ، واللهِ لَتُمْلأنَّ . أفَعَجِبْتُمْ !؟ ولَقَدْ ذُكِرَ لَنا أنَّ ما بَيْنَ مِصْراعَيْنِ مِنْ مَصارِيعِ الجَنَّةِ مَسيرَةَ أرْبَعِينَ عاماً ، وَلَيَأتِيَنَّ عَلَيْهِ يَوْم وهُوَ كَظِيظٌ مِنَ الزِّحامِ ، وَلَقَدْ رَأيْتُنِي سابِعَ سَبْعَةٍ مَعَ رَسُولِ اللهِ ، صلى اللهُ

عليه وسلم ، ما لنا طعام إلاَّ ورقُ الشجرِ ، حتى قرحت أشداقنا ، فالتقطتُ بُرْدَةً فشققتُها بيني وبينَ سعدِ بنِ مالك ، فاتزرتُ بنصفها ، واتزر سعدٌ بنصفها ، فما أصبحَ اليومَ منا أحدٌ إلاَّ أصبح أميراً على مصرٍ منَ الأمصارِ . وإني أعوذُ باللهِ أنْ أكونَ في نفسي عظيماً ، وعندَ اللهِ صغيراً . رواهُ مسلم

498. Hazrat Khalid Ibn Umar Adavi (R.A.A.) relates: (Once) Hazrat Utbah Ibn Ghazwan (R.A.A.), Governor of Basrah, delivered a speech before us. After enumerating eulogies of Allah and glorifying Him, he said: 'The world is announcing its end (doom) has turned its face and running fast. Very little of the world left. It is (so small) like the few drops of water left after drinking at the bottom of the pot. It is these drops which the world lovers are dirnking. You will certainly be shifted from this world to a home which is ever lasting. Therefore, make sure that you go there with the best things you have. We have been informed that a stone will be dropped from the mouth of Hell which will continue falling for seventy years and even then will not reach its bottom. But by Allah it will have to be filled (by the sinners). Do you wonder at it? We have also been told that the distance between the two shutters of the gate of Paradise is equal to a journey covering a period of over forty years. Inspite of this a day will come when it will be over crowded with human beings. I remember being one of seven persons alongwith the Holy Prophet (S.A.W.) when we could not get anything to eat except tree leaves which enquired the sides of our mouths. Somehow I got a sheet which I cut in two, using one myself, and giving the other to Hazrat Sa'ad Ibn Malik (R.A.A.). Today everyone of us is administrator of a city. Although I may be an important person in my own estimation for which I seek Allah's forgiveness yet I am very small in the sight of Allah. *(Muslim).*

٤٩٩ ــ وعن أبي موسى الأشعريِّ رضي اللهُ عنه قال : أخرجتْ لنا عائشةُ رضيَ اللهُ عنها كساءً وإزاراً غليظاً قالتْ : قُبِضَ رسولُ اللهِ صلى اللهُ عليه وسلم في هذينِ . متفقٌ عليه

499. Hazrat Abu Musa Ash'ari (R.A.A.) says: 'Hazrat Ayesha (R.A.A.) showed us a sheet and a coarse loin-cloth, and said that these were the only two pieces of clothes which the Holy Prophet (S.A.W.) had on his person when he passed away. *(Bukhari and Muslim)*

٥٠٠ ــ وعنْ سعد بنِ أبي وقّاصٍ ، رضيَ اللهُ عنه ، قال : إنّي لأوّلُ العربِ رمى بسهمٍ في سبيلِ اللهِ ، ولقدْ كنا نغزو معَ رسولِ اللهِ

صلى اللهُ عليه وسلم ما لَنَا طَعامٌ إلاَّ وَرَقُ الحُبْلَةِ ، وَهذا السمُرُ ، حتَى إنْ كانَ أحَدُنا لَيَضعُ كما تَضعُ الشاةُ ما لَهُ خَلْطٌ . متفقٌ عليه

500. Hazrat S'ad Ibn Abi Waqqas (R.A.A.) relates: 'I am the first among the Arabs who used arrows in fighting in the cause of Allah. We had to carry on Jihad alongwith the Holy Prophet (S.A.W.), (in such situations) when we had nothing but the leaves of wild trees like acacia arabia. Consequently the stools of some of us (had become (hard and dry) like the droppings of goats.' *(Bukhari and Muslim).*

٥٠١ — وعن أبي هُرَيْرَةَ ، رضي الله عنه ، قال : قال رسول الله ، صلى الله عليه وسلم : « اللهُمَّ اجْعَلْ رِزْقَ آلِ مُحمدٍ قُوتاً » متفقٌ عليه

501. Hazrat Abu Hurairah (R.A.A.) relates that the Holy Prophet (S.A.W.) used to pray: 'Allah, make the provision for subsistence for the family of Muhammad (S.A.W.) which may be sufficient.'

(Bukhari and Muslim).

٥٠٢ — وعن أبي هُرَيْرَةَ رضي الله عنه قال : وَاللهِ الذي لا إلهَ إلاَّ هُوَ ، إنْ كُنْتُ لأَعْتَمِدُ بِكَبِدِي عَلى الأَرْضِ مِنَ الجُوعِ ، وَإنْ كُنْتُ لأَشُدُّ الحَجَرَ عَلى بَطْني مِنَ الجُوعِ . وَلَقَدْ قَعَدْتُ يَوْماً عَلى طَرِيقِهِمُ الذي يَخْرُجُونَ مِنْهُ ، فَمَرَّ بِيَ النبيُّ ، صلى الله عليه وسلم ، فَتَبَسَّمَ حِينَ رَآني ، وَعَرَفَ مَا في وَجْهِي وَمَا في نَفْسِي ، ثُمَّ قال : : « أبا هِرّ » قلت : لَبيكَ يا رسولَ الله ، قال : « الحَقْ » وَمَضَى فَاتَّبَعْتُهُ ، فَدَخَلَ فَاسْتَأْذَنَ ، فَأَذِنَ لي فَدَخَلْتُ ، فَوَجَدَ لَبَناً في قَدَحٍ فقال : « مِنْ أيْنَ هذَا اللَّبَنُ ؟ » قالوا : أَهْدَاهُ لَكَ فُلانٌ — أَوْ فُلانَةُ — قال : « أبا هِرّ » قلتُ : لَبَيْكَ يا رسول اللهِ ، قال : « الحَقْ إلى أهْلِ الصُّفَّةِ فَادْعُهُمْ لي » قال : وَأهْلُ الصُّفَّةِ أَضْيَافُ الإسْلامِ ، لا يَأْوُونَ عَلى أهْلٍ ، وَلا مَالٍ ، وَلا عَلى أحَدٍ ، وكَانَ إذَا أتَتْهُ صَدَقَةٌ بَعَثَ بِهَا إلَيْهِمْ ، وَلَمْ يَتَنَاوَلْ مِنْهَا شَيْئاً ، وَإذَا أتَتْهُ هَدِيَّةٌ أرْسَلَ إلَيْهِمْ ، وَأَصَابَ مِنْهَا وَأَشْرَكَهُمْ فِيهَا ، فَسَاءَنِي ذلكَ فَقُلْتُ : وَمَا هذَا اللَّبَنُ في أهْلِ الصُّفَّةِ ! كُنْتُ أحَقَّ أنْ أُصِيبَ مِنْ هذَا اللَّبَنِ شَرْبَةً أتَقَوَّى بِهَا ، فَإذا جَاؤُوا وَأمَرَني فَكُنْتُ أَنَا أُعْطِيهِمْ ؛ وَمَا عَسَى أنْ يَبْلُغَني مِنْ هذَا اللَّبَنِ ، وَلَمْ يَكُنْ مِنْ طَاعَة

الله وطاعة رسوله، صلى الله عليه وسلم بد، فأتيتهم فدعوتهم، فأقبلوا واستأذنوا، فأذن لهم وأخذوا مجالسهم من البيت قال: «يا أبا هر» قلت: لبيك يا رسول الله قال: «خذ فأعطهم» قال: فأخذت القدح فجعلت أعطيه الرجل فيشرب حتى يروى، ثم يرد علي القدح. فأعطيه الرجل فيشرب حتى يروى، ثم يرد علي القدح، فيشرب حتى يروى ثم يرد علي القدح حتى انتهيت إلى النبي صلى الله عليه وسلم، وقد روي القوم كلهم، فأخذ القدح فوضعه على يده، فنظر إلي فتبسم، فقال: «أبا هر» قلت: لبيك يا رسول الله، قال: «بقيت أنا وأنت» قلت: صدقت يا رسول الله، قال: «اقعد فاشرب» فقعدت فشربت: فقال: «اشرب» فشربت، فما زال يقول: «اشرب» حتى قلت: لا والذي بعثك بالحق، ما أجد له مسلكاً! قال: «فأرني» فأعطيته القدح، فحمد الله تعالى، وسمى وشرب الفضلة» رواه البخاري

502. Hazrat Abu Hurairah (R.A.A.) relates: 'By Allah, except whom there is no God, during the days of the Holy Prophet (S.A.W.) I used to press my stomach against the ground due to extreme hunger, or I used to tie a stone over it. One day I was sitting by the side of a public thoroughfare when the Holy Prophet (S.A.W.) passed by me. On seeing me he smiled and recognised from my face my condition (that I was hungry). "Abahir" me (Abu Hurairah) and I responded: 'I am here, O Messenger of Allah' (S.A.W.). He said: 'Come along with me and he (S.A.W.) walked on; I followed him. On reaching home he sought permission of the inmates, and entered, and also permitted me to enter in the house he found a cup full of milk, and asked the inmates 'From where this milk has come? They said: 'It is a present for you from some gentleman or lady'. He called me 'Abahir' and I responded: 'I am here, O Messenger of Allah (S.A.W.)! He said: 'Go and call my *Suffa* companions.' These companions were the guests of the Muslims, who had no house, no property, no friends or relatives with whom they could live. As such they were the guests of all the Muslims. Whenever the Holy Prophet (S.A.W.) received something as chiarity he used to send it to them and would not retain anything out of it for himself (as charity was forbidden for him or his family). However, whenever he received something as a gift he would send for them and shared it with them. But on this occasion I did not like his invitation to them, and thought: 'How this milk would suffice to so many? I deserve this more than others, as by drinking it I might gain some energy. When these companions of the *Suffa* would come the Holy Prophet (S.A.W.) will ask me to serve the milk to them. When they start drinking I do not think that anything will be left for me out of this milk. But what could I have done; I could not dare avoiding the orders of Allah and His Messenger (S.A.W.). Accordingly I went out and called them; they came and solicited permission to come in, which was granted and they came in and took their seats. The Holy Prophet (S.A.W.) called me 'Aba Hir' and I replied: 'I am here, O Messenger of Allah (S.A.W.)!' He said: 'Take hold of the cup of milk and give it to them.' I took the cup and passed it to one man who would drink and when felt satisfied, he would return it to me, and I would then give it to the next person who likewise drink the milk to his fill. I went on doing this till the cup reached the Holy Prophet (S.A.W.) But that time all had drunk milk to their satisfcation. The Holy Prophet (S.A.W.) took the cup in his hand, looked towards me, smiled and said: 'Aba Hir?' I said: 'I am here, O Messenger of Allah (S.A.W.). He said: Now only two persons myself and you are left! I said: 'Of Course, O Messenger of Allah (S.A.W.) you are right'. Then he said: Sit down and drink. I sat down and started drinking milk. The Holy Prophet said: "Take more." I took a bit more but he continued saying: 'Drink; a little more, till I said: By Allah! Who has commissioned you with the truth, now I have no more room in my stomach.' He said: 'Then let me have it' So I passed on the cup to him. He thanked Allah, and with the name of Allah, drank the milk which was left in the cup. *(Bukhari).*

Note: Another report from Bukhari adds grace to this story. It reports Hazrat Abu Hurairah (R.A.A.) saying that, when he was sitting by the thorough-fare Hazrat Abu Bakr (R.A.A.) passed by him. He enquired from him about a verse of the Holy Quran. Thereby he wanted to attract his attention, so that he may feed him, but he would not understand his motive and proceeded on his way. Then Hazrat Umar (R.A.A.) happened to pass that way. Hazrat Abu Hurairah (R.A.A.) with the same motive, asked about a Quranic verse from him as well. Hazrat Umar (R.A.A.) too acted likewise and could not understand Hazrat Abu Hurairah's real motive. Lastly the Holy Prophet (S.A.W.) came that way; he smiled on seeing him and learnt that he was hungry and took him to his house.

٥٠٣ — وعن محمد بن سيرين عن أبي هريرة، رضي الله عنه، قال: لقد رأيتني وإني لأخر فيما بين منبر رسول الله، صلى الله عليه وسلم، إلى حجرة عائشة رضي الله عنها مغشياً علي، فيجيء الجائي، فيضع رجله على عنقي، ويرى أني مجنون وما بي من جنون، ما بي إلا الجوع. رواه البخاري

503. Hazrat Muhammad Ibn Sirin (R.A.A.) quotes from **Hazrat Abu Hurairah** (R.A.A.) as having said: I remember when I would become senseless and would fall down on the ground between the pulpit of the Holy Prophet (S.A.W.) and the room of Hazrat Ayesha (R.A.A.) and every passer by would place his foot on my neck considering me as mad. In fact, I was not mad; I was simply hungry. (That is on account of extreme hunger, I used to become unconscious and fall down on the ground). *(Bukhari).*

٥٠٤ — وعن عائشةَ ،رضي الله عنها ،قَالَتْ: تُوُفِّي رسولُ الله، صلى الله عليه وسلم ، وَدِرْعُهُ مَرْهُونَةٌ عِندَ يهُودِيٍ في ثَلاثِينَ صَاعاً مِنْ شَعِيرٍ . متفقٌ عليه

504. Hazrat Ayesha (R.A.A.) relates that when the Holy Prophet (S.A.W.) passed away, his armour was held by a Jew in pledge for thirty measures of barley. *(Bukhari and Muslim).*

٥٠٥ — وعن أنَسٍ رضي الله عنه قال : رَهَنَ النَّبيُّ صلى الله عليه وسلم دِرْعَهُ بِشَعِيرٍ ، وَمَشَيْتُ إلى النَّبيِّ صلى الله عليه وسلم بِخُبْزِ شَعِيرٍ ، وَإهَالَةٍ سَنِخَةٍ ، ولَقَدْ سَمِعْتُهُ يقُولُ : « مَا أَصْبَحَ لآلِ مُحَمَّدٍ صَاعٌ ولا أَمْسَى» وَإنَّهُم لتِسْعَةُ أَبياتٍ . رواه البخاري

505. Hazrat Anas Bin Malik (R.A.A.) relates: The Holy Prophet (S.A.W.) had pledged his armour for a quantity of barley with a Jew and I took to the Holy Prophet (S.A.W.) some barley bread and some decomposed melted fat. The traditionists report that the family of the Holy Prophet (S.A.W.) never possessed a measure of wheat between them in morning or evening, and they were nine houses. *(Bukhari).*

٥٠٦ — وعن أبي هُرَيْرَةَ ، رضي الله عنه ، قال: لَقَدْ رَأَيْتُ سَبْعِينَ مِنْ أَهْلِ الصُّفَّةِ ، مامِنْهُم رَجُلٌ عَلَيْهِ رِدَاءٌ ، إمَّا إزَارٌ وَإمَّا كِساءٌ ، قَدْ رَبَطُوا في أَعْنَاقِهِم مِنهَا مايَبْلُغُ نِصفَ السَّاقَيْن ، وَمِنهَا مايَبلُغُ الكَعْبَيْنِ ، فَيَجمَعُهُ بِيَدِهِ كَرَاهِيَةَ أنْ تُرَى عَوْرَتُهُ . رواه البخارى

506. This tradition is about the poverty of the Companions of *Suffa* and has already been covered in item No. 469, under Chapter 55.

٥٠٧ — وعن عائشةَ رضي الله عنها قالت : كَانَ فِرَاشُ رسولِ الله صلى الله عليه وسلم مِنْ أَدَمٍ حَشْوُهُ لِيفٌ . رواه البخاري

507. Hazrat Ayesha (R.A.A.) relates: The mattress of the Holy Prophet (S.A.W.) was made of leather stuffed with the bark of the date-palm tree. *(Bukhari).*

٥٠٨ – وعن ابن عمر رضي الله عنهما قال : كُنَّا جُلُوساً مَعَ رسول الله
صلى الله عليه وسلم ، إذْ جَاءَ رَجُلٌ مِنَ الأَنْصَارِ ، فَسَلَّمَ عَلَيهِ ، ثُمَّ أَدبر
الأَنْصَارِيُّ ، فقال رسول الله ، صلَّى اللهُ عليه وسلم : « يَا أَخَا الأَنْصَارِ ، كَيْفَ
أَخِي سَعْدُ بنُ عُبَادَةَ ؟ » فقال : صَالِحٌ ، فقال رسول الله صلى الله عليه وسلم :
« مَنْ يَعُودُهُ مِنْكُم ؟ » فَقَامَ وَقُمْنَا مَعَهُ ، وَنَحْنُ بِضْعَةَ عَشَرَ مَاعَلَيْنَا
نِعَالٌ وَلا خِفَافٌ ، وَلا قَلانِسُ ، وَلا قُمُصٌ ، نَمْشِي في تلكَ السِّبَاخِ
حَتَّى جِئْنَاهُ ، فاستَأخَرَ قَوْمُهُ مِنْ حَوله حتَّى دَنَا رسول الله صلى الله عليه
وسلم وَأَصْحَابُهُ الَّذِينَ مَعَهُ . رواه مسلم

508. Hazrat Ibn Umar (R.A.A.) says: Once we were sitting in the company of the Holy Prophet (S.A.W.) when Ansar came after greeting the Holy Prophet (S.A.W.) was going back. The Holy Prophet (S.A.W.) enquired from him: 'O Ansari Brother, how is my brother Sa'ad Ibn Ubadah?' The Ansar answered: 'He is alright (better). 'The Holy Prophet (S.A.W.) then asked us:'Which of you would like to come alongwith me to see him?' So saying stood up and we too followed suit. We were more than ten persons, and none of us had shoes or leather sock, or caps or shirts. We walked on barefeet through the stark and sterile plain till we came to (Hazrat) Sa'ad's place. Members of his family withdrew from him and the Holy Prophet (S.A.W.) and his companions went up to him. *(Muslim).*

٥٠٩ – وعن عِمْرَانَ بنِ الحُصَيْنِ رضي الله عنهما ، عن النبي صلى الله عليه
وسلم أنه قال : « خَيْرُكُمْ قَرنِي ، ثُمَّ الَّذِينَ يَلُونَهُم ، ثُمَّ الَّذِينَ يَلُونَهُم »
قال عِمرَانُ : فَمَا أَدرِي قال النبي صلى الله عليه وسلم مَرَّتَيْنِ أَو ثَلاثاً « ثُمَّ
يَكُونُ بَعدَهُمْ قَوْمٌ يَشهَدُونَ ولايُستَشهَدُونَ ، وَيَخُونُونَ وَلايُؤتَمَنُونَ ،
وَيَنْذِرُونَ وَلا يُوفُونَ ، وَيَظْهَرُ فِيهِمِ السِّمَنُ » متفقٌ عليه

509. Hazrat Imran bin Husain (R.A.A.) relates that the Holy Prophet (S.A.W.) said: The best among you are those who coexist with me, then those who follow them immediately, then (the third generation) which comes immediately after them (he said this sentence twice or thrice), then these persons will be followed by those who will

testify but they will not be asked to testify (that is their testimony will not be accepted) they will misappropriate and will not be trustworthy; will take vows, but will not fulfil them, will suffer from fatness.
(Bukhari and Muslim).

٥١٠ ـ وعن أبي أمامة رضي الله عنه قال: قال رسولُ الله صلى الله عليه وسلم: «يا ابنَ آدمَ: إنَّكَ أنْ تبذُلَ الفضلَ خيرٌ لكَ، وأنْ تُمسِكَهُ شرٌّ لكَ، ولا تُلامُ على كَفافٍ، وابدأْ بمَنْ تعُولُ» رواه الترمذي وقال: حديث حسن صحيح.

510. Hazrat Abu Umamah (R.A.A.) relates that the Holy Prophet (S.A.W.) said: 'O Son of Adam (human beings)! If you were to spend your surplus wealth it would be better for you, and if you retain it, it will be the evil for you. You will not be censured for keeping wealth according to your needs. First of all spend it on your family members (dependents). (*Tirmizi* narrated this tradition and called it as authentic).

٥١١ ـ وعن عُبَيد الله بن مِحصَنٍ الأنصاريِّ الخَطميِّ رضي الله عنه قال: قال رسول الله صلى الله عليه وسلم: «مَنْ أصبحَ منكُم آمِناً في سربِهِ، مُعافىً في جسَدِهِ، عِندَهُ قُوتُ يومِهِ، فكأنَّما حِيزَتْ لهُ الدُّنيا بحذافيرِها» رواه الترمذي وقال: حديثٌ حسنٌ.

511. Hazrat Ubaidullah Ibn Mohsin Al-Ansari Al-Khatmi (R.A.A.) relates that the Holy Prophet (S.A.W.) said: He who spends the day in safety of his life in good physical condition (in perfect health) and with one day's provision of eatables is like one upon whom the world and all it contains, has been bestowed.' (*Tirmizi* has related this tradition and has called it authentic).

٥١٢ ـ وعن عبدِ الله بن عمرو بنِ العاصِ رضي الله عنهما، أن رسول الله صلى الله عليه وسلم قال: «قدْ أفلحَ مَنْ أسلمَ، وكانَ رِزقُهُ كَفافاً، وقنَّعَهُ الله بما آتاهُ» رواه مسلم.

512. Hazrat Abdullah Ibn Amr Ibn al'Aas (R.A.A.) says that the Holy Prophet (S.A.W.) said: A person who embraces Islam, and is given provision for subsistence that is just sufficient for his needs, and he is content with what Allah has given him, has achieved (alround success and prosperity.
(Muslim).

٥١٣ – وعن أبي مُحمَّد فَضَالَةَ بن عُبَيْدٍ الأَنصَارِيّ رضي الله عنه ، أنّه سَمع رسول الله صلى الله عليه وسلم يَقُولُ : « طُوبَى لِمَنْ هُدِيَ إلى الإسلامِ ، وكَانَ عَيْشُهُ كَفَافاً ، وقَنِعَ » رواه الترمذي وقال: حديث حسن صحيح .

513. Hazrat Abu Muhammad Fazalah Ibn Ubaid Al-Ansari (R.A.A.) relates that he heard the Holy Prophet (S.A.W.) say: Happy news for the person who embraces Islam and has got means of subsistence sufficient for his needs and is contented. (*Imam Tirmizi* has cited this tradition and says that it is correct and authentic).

٥١٤ – وعن ابن عباسٍ رضيَ الله عنهما قال : كانَ رسولُ الله صلى الله عليه وسلم يَبيتُ اللَّيالي المُتَتَابعةَ طَاوِياً ، وأَهلُهُ لا يَجِدُونَ عَشاءً ، وكَانَ أكثرُ خُبْزِهِمْ خُبْزَ الشَّعيرِ . رواه الترمذي وقال : حديثٌ حسنٌ صحيح.

514. Hazrat Ibn-i-Abbas (R.A.A.) relates that the Holy Prophet (S.A.W.) had to suffer from starvation for several nights consecutively. His family members did not get even their evening meals, (that is the last meal of the day) and generally their fare used to be a barley bread. (*Imam Tirmizi* has related this and says that it is correct and authentic).

٥١٥ – وعن فَضَالَةَ بن عُبَيْدٍ رضي الله عنه، أن رسول الله صلى الله عليه وسلم كَانَ إذَا صَلَّى بِالنَّاسِ ، يَخِرُّ رِجَالٌ مِنْ قَامَتِهِمْ في الصَّلاةِ مِنَ الخَصَاصَةِ – وَهُمْ أَصْحَابُ الصُّفَّةِ – حتَّى يَقُولَ الأَعْرَابُ : هؤلاء مَجَانِينُ ، فَإذَا صلى رسول الله صلى الله عليه وسلم انصَرَفَ إلَيهِمْ ، فقال : « لَوْ تَعلَمُونَ مَا لَكُمْ عِنْدَ الله تعالى ، لأَحْبَبْتُمْ أَنْ تَزدَادُوا فَاقَةً وَحَاجَةً » رواه الترمذي ، وقال : حديثٌ صحيحٌ .

515. Hazrat Fazalah Ibn Ubain Al-Ansari (R.A.A.) says that (sometimes) when the Holy Prophet (S.A.W.) led the prayer some people belonging to the group of the Companions of *Suffa* fell down from their standing posture on account of the (extreme weakness due to the) intensity of hunger. The villagers used to say that they were in save. After concluding the prayer. the Holy Prophet (S.A.W.) would go to them and say: If you could know what is there for you with Allah, the Exalted, you would like to get the pangs of your starvation and lack of provision enhanced.' (*Imam Tirmizi* has cited this tradition and said that it is correct and authentic).

Notes: *Ashab-i-Suffa* or companions of *Suffa*, are those companions of the Holy Prophet (S.A.W.) who had no houses, nor property nor family. They entirely depended on the mercy of Allah and lived on the platform of the Holy Prophet's Mosque. They numbered about seventy or more or less. They were a group of pious persons, Dervishes and whole time volunteers always busy in prayer and obeying divine commands. They subsisted on donations alms and charities.

٥١٦ ــ وعن أبي كَرِيمَةَ المِقْدَامِ بن مَعْدِيكَرِبَ رضي الله عنه قال : سَمِعْتُ رسول الله صلى الله عليه وسلم يَقُولُ : « مَا مَلأَ آدَمِيٌّ وِعَاءً شَرًّا مِنْ بَطْنٍ ، بِحَسْبِ ابنِ آدَمَ أُكُلاتٌ يُقِمْنَ صُلْبَهُ ، فَإِنْ كَانَ لا مَحَالَةَ ، فَثُلُثٌ لِطَعَامِهِ ، وَثُلُثٌ لِشَرَابِهِ ، وَثُلُثٌ لِنَفَسِهِ » .

رواه الترمذي وقال : حديث حسن .

516. Hazrat Abu Karima Miqdad Ibn Ma'dikarib (R.A.A.) relates that he heard the Holy Prophet (S.A.W.) say: 'No man fills a pot worse than his stomach. For a person few mouthfuls are sufficient to keep his back straight.. But if he wants to fill his stomach then he should divide his stomach into three parts and should fill one third part of the belly with food, another third with drink and leave one third empty for easy breathing.(*Imam Tirmizi* has quoted this tradition and said that it is correct)!'

٥١٧ ــ وعن أبي أُمَامَةَ إِيَاسِ بن ثَعْلَبَةَ الأَنْصَارِيِّ الحَارِثِي رضي الله عنه قال : ذَكَرَ أَصْحَابُ رسول الله صلى الله عليه وسلم يَوْماً عِنْدَهُ الدُّنْيَا ، فقال رسول الله صلى الله عليه وسلم : « أَلا تَسْمَعُونَ ؟ أَلا تَسْمَعُونَ ؟ إِنَّ البَذَاذَةَ مِنَ الإِيمَانِ ، إِنَّ البَذَاذَةَ مِنَ الإِيمَانِ » يعني : التَّقَحُّلَ .

رواه أبو داود

517. Hazrat Abu Umamah Iyas Ibn Salabat Al-Ansari Al-Harsi (R.A.A.) says that one day the Companions of the Holy Prophet (S.A.W.) raised the issue of the world before him. On this the Holy Prophet (S.A.W.) said: 'Have you not heard, have you not understand that renunciation of easy life and comfort is one of the symbols of faith undoubtedly renumciation of decoration (and make up) is a sign of faith.' *(Abu Daud).*

٥١٨ ــ وعن أبي عبد الله جابر بن عبد الله رضي الله عنهما قال: بَعَثَنَا رسول الله صلى الله عليه وسلم ، وَأَمَّرَ عَلَيْنَا أَبَا عُبَيْدَةَ رضي الله عنه ، نَتَلَقَّى عِيراً لِقُرَيْشٍ ، وَزَوَّدَنَا جِرَاباً مِنْ تَمْرٍ لَمْ يَجِدْ لَنَا غَيْرَهُ ، فَكَانَ أَبُو

عبيدة يعطينا تمرة تمرة ، فقيل : كيف كنتم تصنعون بها ؟
قال : نمصها كما يمص الصبي ، ثم نشرب عليها من الماء ، فتكفينا
يومنا إلى الليل ،وكنا نضرب بعصينا الخبط ، ثم نبله بالماء فنأكله .
قال : وانطلقنا على ساحل البحر، فرفع لنا على ساحل البحر
كهيئة الكثيب الضخم ، فأتيناه فإذا هي دابة تدعى العنبر ،
فقال أبو عبيدة : ميتة ، ثم قال : لا ، بل نحن رسل رسول الله
صلى الله عليه وسلم ، وفي سبيل الله ، وقد اضطررتم فكلوا،فأقمنا عليه
شهراً ، ونحن ثلاثمائة ، حتى سمنا ، ولقد رأيتنا نغترف من وقب
عينه بالقلال الدهن ونقطع منه الفدر كالثور أو كقدر الثور ،
ولقد أخذ منا أبو عبيدة ثلاثة عشر رجلا فأقعدهم في وقب عينه
وأخذ ضلعاً من أضلاعه فأقامها ثم رحل أعظم بعير معنا فمر من
تحتها وتزودنا من لحمه وشائق ، فلما قدمنا المدينة أتينا رسول الله
صلى الله عليه وسلم فذكرنا ذلك له ، فقال : « هو رزق أخرجه الله لكم ،
فهل معكم من لحمه شيء فتطعمونا ؟ » فأرسلنا إلى رسول الله صلى
الله عليه وسلم منه فأكله . رواه مسلم .

518. Hazrat Abu Abdullah Jabir Bin Abdullah (R.A.A.) relates that the Holy Prophet (S.A.W.) once sent us under the leadership of Hazrat Abu Ubaidah (R.A.A.) to ambush and fight with a caravan of the Quraish tribe our ration, carrying goods. He gave us a leather bag full of dates as nothing else. Our leader Hazrat Abu Ubaidah (R.A.A.) used to give us one date per day as ration. On being asked as to how they could subsist on this (ration of one date per day), he replied: We would suck it like a child (sucking his mother's breast) and drink some water afterwards. This helped us to pass the day. We also used pluck leaves of trees with our sticks, moisten them in water and eat them. At last we reached the sea coast and saw something like a sand dune lying along the beach. When we reached it we found it was a kind of large fish (whale). Hazrat Abu Ubaidah (R.A.A.) said: This is carrion, and eating its meat is forbidden, but after some thinking he said: 'We have been sent on this mission by the Messenger of Allah (S.A.W.) and are engaged and striving in the cause of Allah. You are forced by the circumstances, and as such it

is no longer forbidden, and you can take it. 'We — a body of 300 persons — subsited on it for a month and gained in flesh and weight.' We used to take out many skinfuls of oil through its eyes, and used to cut out large pieces of meat, as large as an ox. Once Hazrat Abu Ubaidah (R.A.A.) made thirteen of us seated in the hole of its eye. On another occasion he took one of its ribs and stood it up and made our tallest camel to pass under it. When returning to medina we took with us some large pieces of its boiled meat for our ration. On reaching Medina we presented ourselves before the Holy Prophet (S.A.W.) and told him all about this fish (or whale). He said: 'This was provided for you by Allah as your food. If you have got some of its meat with you, give it to us to eat?' Thus we presented some of it to the Holy Prophet (S.A.W.) and he ate it.
(Muslim).

٥١٩ — وعن أَسْمَاءَ بنتِ يزيدَ رضي الله عنها قالت : كانَ كُمُّ قميصِ رسول الله صلى الله عليه وسلم إلى الرُّصْغِ ، رواه أبو داود ، والترمذي ، وقال: حديث حسن .

519. Hazrat Asma' Bint Yazid (R.A.A.) says that the sleeves of shirt of the Holy Prophet (S.A.W.) reached only up to his wrist.' (*Abu Daud* and *Tirmizi* has reported this tradition and added that the same was an authentic tradition.).

٥٢٠ — وعن جابر رضي الله عنه قال : إنَّا كُنَّا يومَ الخندقِ نحفِرُ ، فعرضَتْ كُدْيَةٌ شَدِيدَةٌ ، فجاؤوا إلى النبي صلى الله عليه وسلم فقالوا : هذهِ كُدْيَةٌ عرضَتْ في الخندقِ . فقال : « أنا نازلٌ » ثُمَّ قامَ ، وبطنُهُ معصوبٌ بحجرٍ ، ولبثنا ثلاثةَ أيامٍ لا نذوقُ ذواقاً فأخذَ النبيُّ صلى الله عليه وسلم المِعْوَلَ ، فضربَ ، فعادَ كثيباً أهيلَ ، أو أهيمَ ، فقلتُ : يا رسولَ الله ائذَنْ لي إلى البيتِ ، فقلتُ لامرأتي : رأيتُ بالنبيِّ صلى الله عليه وسلم شيئاً ما في ذلكَ صبرٌ فعندكِ شيءٌ ؟ فقالت : عندي شعيرٌ وعناقٌ فذبحتُ العناقَ ، وطحنتُ الشعيرَ حتى جعلنا اللحمَ في البُرْمَةِ ، ثُمَّ جئتُ النبيَّ صلى الله عليه وسلم ، والعجينُ قد انكسرَ والبُرْمَةُ بينَ الأثافي قد كادَتْ تنضجُ ، فقلتُ : طُعَيِّمٌ لي فقُمْ أنتَ يارسولَ اللهِ ورجلٌ أو رجلانِ ، قال : « كم هوَ ؟ » فذكرتُ له فقال : « كثيرٌ طيبٌ ، قُلْ لها لاتنزعِ البُرْمَةَ ، ولا الخبزَ من التنورِ حتى آتي »

فقال: « قُومُوا » فقام المُهَاجِرُونَ وَالأنْصَارُ ، فَدَخَلْتُ عليها فقلت: وَيْحَكِ جَاءَ النبي صلى الله عليه وسلم وَالمُهَاجِرُونَ وَالأنْصَارُ وَمَن مَعَهُم ! قالت: هل سَألَكَ ؟ قلتُ: نعم قال: « ادْخُلُوا وَلاتَضَاغَطُوا » فَجَعَلَ يَكْسِرُ الخُبْزَ، وَيَجْعَلُ عليه اللحمَ، وَيُخَمِّرُ البُرْمَةَ والتَّنُّورَ إذا أخَذَ مِنْهُ، وَيُقَرِّبُ إلى أَصْحَابِهِ ثُمَّ يَنْزِعُ، فَلَمْ يَزَلْ يَكْسِرُ وَيَغْرِفُ حَتَّى شَبِعُوا، وَبَقِيَ مِنه، فقال: « كُلِي هذَا وَأهْدِي، فَإنَّ النَّاسَ أَصَابَتْهُمْ مَجَاعَةٌ » متفقٌ عليه

وفي روايةٍ: قال جابر: لَمَّا حُفِرَ الخَنْدَقُ رَأَيْتُ بِالنبيِّ صلى الله عليه وسلم خَمَصاً، فَانْكَفَأْتُ إلى امْرَأتِي فقلتُ: هل عِنْدَكِ شَيْءٌ؛ فإنِّي رَأَيْتُ بِرسول اللهِ صلى الله عليه وسلم خَمَصاً شَدِيداً ؟ فَأَخْرَجَتْ إليَّ جِراباً فِيهِ صَاعٌ مِن شَعِيرٍ. وَلَنَا بُهَيْمَةٌ دَاجِنٌ فَذَبَحْتُهَا، وَطَحَنَتِ الشَّعِيرَ، فَفَرَغَتْ إلى فَرَاغِي. وَقَطَّعْتُهَا في بُرْمَتِهَا، ثُمَّ وَلَّيْتُ إلى رسول الله صلى الله عليه وسلم، فَقَالَتْ: لاتَفْضَحْنِي بِرسول الله صلى الله عليه وسلم وَمَنْ مَعَهُ، فَجِئْتُهُ فَسَارَرْتُهُ فَقُلْتُ: يا رسول الله، ذَبَحْنا بُهَيْمَةً لَنَا، وَطَحَنْتُ صَاعاً مِنْ شَعِيرٍ، فَتَعالَ أنْتَ وَنَفَرٌ مَعَكَ، فَصَاحَ رسول الله صلى الله عليه وسلم فقال: « يَا أَهْلَ الخَنْدَقِ: إنَّ جابراً قَدْ صَنَعَ سُؤْراً فَحَيَّهَلا بِكُم » فقال النبيُّ صلى الله عليه وسلم: « لاتُنْزِلُنَّ بُرْمَتَكُم وَلا تَخْبِزُنَّ عَجِينَكُمْ حَتَّى أَجِيءَ » فَجِئْتُ، وَجَاءَ النَّبِيُّ صلى الله عليه وسلم يَقْدُمُ النَّاسَ، حَتَّى جِئْتُ امْرَأتِي فقالَتْ: بِكَ وَبِكَ ! فقلتُ: قَدْ فَعَلْتُ الَّذي قُلْتِ. فَأَخْرَجَتْ عَجِيناً، فَبَسَقَ فِيهِ وَبَارَكَ، ثُمَّ عَمَدَ إلى بُرْمَتِنا فَبَصَقَ وَبَارَكَ، ثُمَّ قال: « ادْعُ خَابِزَةً فَلْتَخْبِزْ مَعَكِ، وَاقْدَحِي مِنْ بُرْمَتِكُم وَلا تُنْزِلُوها » وَهُمْ ألْفٌ، فَأُقْسِمُ بِاللهِ لأَكَلُوا حَتَّى تَرَكُوهُ وَانْحَرَفُوا، وإنَّ بُرْمَتَنَا لَتَغِطُّ كَمَا هِيَ، وَإنَّ عَجِينَنا لَيُخْبَزُ كَمَا هُوَ.

520. Hazrat Jabir (R.A.A.) relates: During the battle of Ahzab (also called battle of the Ditch) we were digging a trench; in the course of excavating we reached a hard rock, which no one was able to break. The Holy Prophet (S.A.W.) was told of it, who said: 'I shall get down into the ditch and see the rock myself.' So saying he stood up, when we saw that he had tied a piece of stone (to overcome the pangs of hunger) over his stomach. We too had not eaten anything for the last three days. He took up a pickaxe and struck the hard rock with it and it became soft like sand. Hazrat Jabir states that he took leave from the Holy Prophet (S.A.W.) and went to his home and said to his wife: 'I have seen the Holy Prophet (S.A.W.) in such a condition that I cannot endure any more. Have you anything (worth eating) in the house?' She replied: 'I have a little barley and a kid.' I (at once) slaughtered the kid and grated the barley; thereafter we put the meat in the cooking pot, and when the broth was almost ready and the grated flour of barley had been kneaded and was ready for baking bread. I went to the Holy Prophet (S.A.W.) and submitted: 'I have some food, O Messenger of Allah (S.A.W.), will you please come with one or two persons and partake the food?' He asked: 'How many persons can be accommodated?'I said.I have already told you Sir;.He said: 'It would be better if the number of persons was large. Ask your wife not to take off the broth-pot from the fire and the bread from the oven till I come.' Then he said to the Emigrants (Mohajireen) and the Ansar (Helpers) Let us go! They all stood up.

Hazrat Jabir Says:I went to my wife and said: Blessings of Allah be upon you ! The Holy Prophet (S.A.W.), the mohajireen, the Ansar and others in the company are coming here.' She said: 'Did he ask you?' I said: 'Yes he did.' The Holy Prophet (S.A.W.) who had reached thereby now asked his companions: 'Come in, but do not crowd'. Then he started breaking up the bread into pieces and putting meat on the same. He would take out broth from the pot and the bread from the oven, then cover them up and approaching his companions hand over the stuff to them one by one. He would then go back open the pot and oven and repeated the process. He continued doing this till all had eaten to their full satisfaction, and even some stuff was left over. Then he said to my wife: 'Eat yourself and send some as a present (to your neighbours etc) because they have been affected with hunger.'

(Bukhari and Muslim).

Another versions says: When the ditch was being dug, I noticed some signs of hunger on the Holy Prophet (S.A.W.). As such I came to my wife and asked her if she had anything (eatable) in the house as I have seen signs of acute hunger on (face of) the Holy Prophet (S.A.W.) She took out a leather bag containing some barley; we had a kid also. I slaughtered the kid and my wife kneaded the flour for baking. Thereafter I cut the meat (into small pieces) and put the stuff in the cooking pot. Then I prepared to return to the Holy Prophet (S.A.W.) when my wife (considering little quantity of food) said to me: 'Please do not let me look small in the eyes of the Holy Prophet (S.A.W.) and his Companions.' Accordingly when I came to the Holy Prophet (S.A.W.) I said to him in a low tone: 'O Messenger of Allah (S.A.W.), we have slaughtered a small kid and have got a little quantity of barley. Please therefore come with only a few persons.' But the Holy Prophet (S.A.W.) loudly announced: 'O Ye the people of the Ditch, Jabir has arranged a feast for you, so all of you come to join in the feast; and addressing me he said: 'Do not take the pot off the fire, nor bake the dough till I arrive.' So I came home and the Holy Prophet (S.A.W.) followed leading the people. My wife said: 'It will bring a bad name for you.' I said: 'I have only done what you told me.' She brought out the dough and the Holy Prophet (S.A.W.) put his saliva into it and blessed it, and then advanced towards the cooking pot and put a little saliva into it as well and blessed it. Then he said: Summon the woman who bakes, and let her bake along with you, and let her out the broth from the cooking pot, without lifting the pot from the fire. The number who had gathered to eat was one thousand. By Allah! all of them ate, and when they left something was left in the pot. While our pot was still full as before, and there was still enough kneaded flour being baked as before.

٥٢١ ـ وعن أنس رضي الله عنه قال: قال أبو طَلْحَةَ لأُمِّ سُلَيْمٍ: قد سَمِعتُ صَوتَ رسول الله صلى الله عليه وسلم ضَعِيفاً أعرِفُ فيهِ الجُوعَ، فهَل عِندكِ مِن شيْءٍ؟ فقالت: نعَمْ، فأخرَجَتْ أقراصاً مِن شَعِيرٍ، ثُمَّ أخذَتْ خِماراً لها، فلَفَّتِ الخُبزَ بِبَعضِه، ثُمَّ دسَّتْهُ تحتَ ثوبِي ورَدَّتْنِي بِبَعضِهِ، ثُمَّ أرْسَلَتْنِي إلى رسول الله صلى الله عليه وسلم، فذَهَبتُ بِهِ، فوَجَدتُ رسولَ الله صلى الله عليه وسلم جالِساً في المَسْجِدِ، ومَعَهُ النَّاسُ، فقُمتُ علَيهِمْ، فقال لي رسولُ الله صلى الله عليه وسلم: «أرْسَلَكَ أبُو طَلْحَةَ؟» فقلت: نعَم، فقال: «ألِطَعَامٍ» فقلت: نعَم، فقال رسولُ الله صلى الله عليه وسلم: «قُومُوا» فانْطَلَقُوا وانْطَلَقتُ بَيْنَ أيدِيهِم حتَّى جِئتُ أبَاطَلْحَةَ فأخبَرتُهُ، فقال أبُو طَلْحَةَ: يا أُمَّ سُلَيمٍ: قد جاءَ رسول الله صلى الله عليه وسلم بالنَّاس ولَيْسَ عِندَنا ما نُطْعِمُهُم؟ فقالتْ: اللهُ ورَسُولُهُ أعْلَمُ. فانطَلَقَ أبُوطَلْحَةَ حتَّى لَقِيَ رسولَ اللهصلى الله عليه وسلم، فأقبَلَ رسولُ الله صلى الله عليه وسلم مَعَهُ حتَّى دَخَلا، فقال رسولُ الله صلى الله عليه وسلم: «هَلُمِّي ما عِندكِ يا أُمَّ سُلَيْمٍ» فأتَتْ بِذلكَ الخُبزِ، فأمرَ بِهِ رسولُ الله

صلى الله عليه وسلم فَفُتَّ ، وَعَصَرَت عَلَيه أمُّ سُلَيم عُكَّةً فَأَدَمَتْهُ ، ثُمَّ قال فِيهِ رسول الله صلى الله عليه وسلم ماشاءَ اللهُ أن يَقُولَ ، ثُمَّ قال : « ائذَن لِعَشَرَةٍ » فَأَذِنَ لَهُم ، فأَكَلُوا حتَّى شَبِعُوا ثُمَّ خَرَجُوا ، ثم قال : « ائذَن لِعَشَرَةٍ » فَأَذِنَ لهم ، فأَكَلُوا حتى شَبِعُوا ، ثم خَرَجوا ، ثُمَّ قال : « ائذَنْ لِعَشَرَةٍ » فَأَذِنَ لَهُم حتى أكل القَوْمُ كُلُّهُم وَشَبِعُوا ، وَالقَوْمُ سَبعُونَ رَجُلاً أَوْ ثَمَانُونَ . متفقٌ عليه .

وفي روايةٍ : فما زال يَدخُلُ عَشَرَةٌ وَيَخرُجُ عَشَرَةٌ ، حتى لم يَبْقَ مِنهم أحَدٌ إلا دَخَلَ ، فأَكَلَ حتى شَبِعَ ، ثم هَيَّأَهَا فإذا هِيَ مِثلُهَا حِينَ أَكَلُوا مِنها .

وفي رواية : فأَكَلُوا عَشَرَةً عَشَرَةً ، حتى فَعَلَ ذلكَ بِثَمَانِينَ رَجُلاً ، ثم أَكَلَ النبيُّ صلى الله عليه وسلم بعد ذلكَ وَأَهْلُ البَيت ، وتَرَكُوا سُؤراً .

وفي روايةٍ : ثم أَفضَلُوا مَا بَلَغُوا جيرانَهُم .

وفي روايةٍ عن أنسٍ قال : جِئتُ رسولَ الله صلى الله عليه وسلم يَوْماً ، فَوَجَدتُهُ جَالِساً مع أصحابِهِ ، وقد عَصَبَ بَطنَهُ بِعِصَابَةٍ ، فقلتُ لِبَعضِ أصحابِهِ : لِمَ عَصَبَ رسولُ الله صلى الله عليه وسلم بَطنَهُ ؟ فقالوا : مِنَ الجُوعِ ، فذَهَبتُ إلى أبي طَلحَةَ ، وَهُوَ زَوجُ أُمِّ سُلَيم بنتِ مِلحَانَ ، فقلتُ : يَا أَبَتَاه ، قد رَأَيتُ رسولَ الله صلى الله عليه وسلم عَصَبَ بَطنَهُ بِعِصَابَةٍ ، فَسَأَلتُ بَعضَ أصحابِهِ ، فقالوا : مِنَ الجُوعِ . فَدَخَلَ أَبُو طَلحَةَ على أُمِّي فقال : هَل مِن شَيءٍ ؟ قالت : نعم عِندِي كِسَرٌ مِن خُبزٍ وتَمَرَاتٌ ، فإن جاءَنَا رسول الله صلى الله عليه وسلم وَحدَهُ أَشبَعنَاه ، وإن جاءَ آخَرُ معه قَلَّ عنهم ، وَذَكَرَ تَمَامَ الحَدِيث .

521. Hazrat Anas Bin Malik (R.A.A.) reports **Hazrat Abu Talha** (R.A.A.) said to (his wife) Hazrat Umm Sulaim (R.A.A.): 'I have noticed some signs of weakness in the voice of the Holy Prophet (S.A.W.), which I think is the result of hunger. Is there anything (food stuff) with you?'

She said: 'Yes;' and taking out some pieces of barley bread, tied them in a corner of her head covering, concealed them in a portion of the head covering and threw the cloth over my head and made me go to the Holy Prophet (S.A.W.). When I took it to the Holy Prophet (S.A.W.) I found him seated in the mosque alongwith some other persons. I stood near them and the Holy Prophet (S.A.W.) enquired: 'Have you been sent by Abu Talha?' I said: 'Yes Sir' He asked: 'Inviting us to a meal?' I said: 'Yes Sir' The Holy Prophet (S.A.W.) said to the companions: 'Get up, and let us go.' All of them started for Abu Talha's house. I went ahead and when I reached Abu Talha's house I informed him what had happened (at the mosque). He called out Umm Sulaim and told her 'O Umm Sulaim The Holy Prophet (S.A.W.) has come with (a large number of persons) and we have nothing to entertain them.' She said: 'Allah and His Messenger (S.A.W.) know this fact well'. Thereafter Abu Talha went out and escorted the Holy Prophet (S.A.W.) inside the house. The Holy Prophet (S.A.W.) said: 'O Umm Sulaim bring whatever you have,' So she put before Him (S.A.W.) the same pieaces of barley bread. The Holy Prophet (S.A.W.) asked these pieces to be broken, and then she poured some butter from a jar on these pieces to prepare a sort of curry. Then the Holy Prophet (S.A.W.) blessed them with the will of Allah and said: 'Allow ten persons to come in (and eat). Hazrat Abu Talha as such went out and brought 10 (ten) persons inside. They came and ate to their satisfaction and went out. Then the Holy Prophet (S.A.W.) said: 'Permit ten more persons to come in' Hazrat Abu Talha accordingly brought in ten persons more who likewise ate and went away. The Holy Prophet (S.A.W.) asked again to permit ten persons to come in and eat, which was done. This procedure continued till everyone had eaten his fill. The total of the guests was seventy or eighty.

(Bukhari and Muslim).

Another version says: When all the guests had eaten, the residue was collected and it was found to be as much as in the beginning. Yet another version is: 'Some eighty persons ate in batches of ten, and then the Holy Prophet (S.A.W.) and the hosts ate and there was a quantity still left over, and according to another version: 'So much was left over which was distributed among the neighbours.' Still another version by Hazrat Anas says I went to the Holy Prophet (S.A.W.) one day when he was sitting along with his companions, and had tied a belt round his waist. I asked from some one present there: 'Why had the Messenger of Allah (S.A.W.) tied the belt round his waist? I was informed that it was due to hunger. I went to my father, Abu Talha (the husband of Umme Sulaim Bint Malhan), and said:'Father, I have seen the Holy Prophet (S.A.W.) having his waist bandaged; I asked some of his companions the reason for this, who said: 'On account of hunger.' (Hazrat Abu Talha went to my mother and asked her: 'Have you anything (for eating)?' She said: 'Yes', I have some pieaces of bread and some dates. If the Holy Prophet (S.A.W.) would come alone, these things would suffice for him but if he comes with some more persons, the stuff would not be enough.' After this he narrated the Hadis in full.

****

CHAPTER 57

Contentment, Chastity and Moderation in Earning and Spending and Ugliness of asking without need.

قال الله تعالى : وَمَا مِنْ دَابَّةٍ فِي الأَرْضِ إِلاَّ على اللهِ رِزْقُهَا [هود:٦]

وقال تعالى : لِلفُقَرَاءِ الَّذِينَ أُحْصِرُوا فِي سَبِيلِ اللهِ لا يَسْتَطِيعُونَ

ضَرْباً فِي الأَرْضِ يَحْسَبُهُمُ الجَاهِلُ أَغْنِيَاءَ مِنَ التَّعَفُّفِ تَعرِفُهُم بِسِيمَاهُم

لا يَسأَلُونَ النَّاسَ إِلحَافاً [البقرة : ٢٧٣] وقال تعالى : وَالَّذِينَ إِذَا

أَنفَقُوا لَمْ يُسرِفُوا وَلَم يَقتُرُوا وَكَانَ بَيْنَ ذلكَ قَوَاماً [الفرقان : ٦٧]

وقال تعالى : وَمَا خَلَقتُ الجِنَّ وَالإِنسَ إِلاَّ لِيَعبُدُونِ . ما أُرِيدُ مِنهم مِن

رِزقٍ وَما أُرِيدُ أَن يُطعِمُونِ [الذاريات : ٥٦ ، ٥٧] .

وأما الأحاديثُ ، فتَقَدَّمَ مُعظَمُهَا في البَابَينِ السَّابِقَينِ ، وَمِمَّا لم يَتَقَدَّم :

Allah, the Exalted, has said:

181. And there is not a beast in the earth but the sustenance thereof dependeth on Allah . (11:6).
182. (Alms are) for the poor who are straitened for the cause of Allah, who cannot travel in the land (for trade). The unthinking man accounteth them wealthy because of their restraint. Thou shalt know them by their mark: They do not beg to men with importunity. (2:273)
183. And those who, when they spend, are neither prodigal nor grudging; and there is ever firm station between the two; (25:67).
184. I created the Jinn and human kind only that they might worship Me. I seek no livelihood from them, nor do I ask that they should feed Me. (51:56—57).

٥٢٢ ــ عن أبي هُرَيرَةَ رضي الله عنه عن النبي صلى الله عليه وسلم قال :

« لَيسَ الغِنَى عَن كَثرَةِ العَرَضِ ، وَلَكِنَّ الغِنَى غِنَى النَّفسِ » متفق عليه

522. Hazrat Abu Hurairah (R.A.A.) relates that the Holy Prophet (S.A.W.) said: 'Plenty of provision or abundance do not make a person rich and wealthy, real richness is the benevolence of heart.

(Bukhari and Muslim).

٥٢٣ ـ وعن عبد الله بن عمرو رضي الله عنهما أن رسول الله صلى الله عليه وسلم قال : « قَدْ أفلَحَ مَنْ أسلَمَ ، وَرُزِقَ كَفَافاً ، وَقَنَّعَهُ الله بما آتاهُ » رواه مسلم .

523. This Hadis has already been covered in item No. 515 under Chapter 56.

٥٢٤ ـ وعن حَكيم بن حِزَام رضي الله عنه قال : سَألْتُ رسول الله صلى الله عليه وسلم فَأعطَاني ، ثم سَألْتُهُ فَأعطَاني ، ثم سَألْتُهُ فَأعطَاني ، ثم قال : « ياحَكيمُ ، إنَّ هذا المَالَ خَضِرٌ حُلوٌ، فَمَن أخَذَهُ بِسَخَاوَةِ نَفْسٍ بُورِكَ لَهُ فيه، وَمَن أخَذَهُ بِإشرَافِ نَفْسٍ لَم يُبَارَكْ لَهُ فيهِ ، وكَانَ كَالَّذي يَأكُلُ ولايَشْبَعُ ؛ واليَدُ العُليَا خَيرٌ مِنَ اليَدِ السُّفلَى » قال حَكيمٌ فقلتُ : يا رسول الله ، والَّذي بَعَثَكَ بالحَقِّ لا أرزَأُ أحَداً بَعدَكَ شَيئاً حتَّى أفارِقَ الدُّنيَا . فكَانَ أبُوبكرٍ رضي الله عنه يَدْعُو حَكيماً لِيُعطيَهُ العَطَاءَ ، فيَأبَى أنْ يَقْبَلَ مِنهُ شَيئاً . ثُمَّ إنَّ عُمَرَ رضي الله عنه دَعَاهُ لِيُعطيَهُ ، فَأبَى أن يَقبَلَهُ . فقال : يا مَعشَرَ المُسْلمينَ ، أُشْهِدُكُم عَلى حَكيمٍ أني أعرِضُ عَلَيه حقَّهُ الَّذي قَسَمَهُ اللهُ لَهُ في هذا الفَيْءِ ، فيَأبَى أن يَأخُذَهُ . فلَمْ يَرزَأْ حَكيمٌ أحَداً مِنَ النَّاسِ بَعْدَ النَّبيِّ صلى الله عليه وسلم حتَّى تُوُفِّيَ . متفقٌ عليه

524. Hazrat Hakim bin Hizam (R.A.A.) says: I requested the Holy Prophet (S.A.W.) and he gave me; I asked him again and he gave me; I asked for the third time and he gave me, and said:'Hakim, wealth is green that is fresh (attractive) and delicious. One who acquires it as a routine (but not on account of its love) it is a source of blessing for him; but it is not blessed for him who acquires it for his exaltation. He is like one who eats, but is not satisfied. The upper hand is better than the lower hand.' I said to him: 'O Messenger of Allah! By Allah who has deputed (commissioned) you with the Truth, I shall not ask anyone after (except) you, for anything as long as I live. Hazrat Abu Bakr (R.A.A.) used to send for Hakim to give something to him, but he would decline the offer. Likewise Hazrat Umar (R.A.A.) used to call him for this purpose but he would not accept anything from him as well. So Hazrat Umar (R.A.A.) said: I call upon the Muslim people to bear witness that I offered Hakim his share out of the goods seized from the enemy which Allah has fixed for him, but he refuses to take it.' Thus Hazrat Hakim (R.A.A.) did not take anything from anyone after the Holy Prophet (S.A.W.) so long as he lived. *(Bukhari and Muslim).*

٥٢٥ ــ وعن أبي بُردَةَ عن أبي موسى الأشعريِّ رضي اللهُ عنه قال : خرَجْنا معَ رسُولِ اللهِ صلى اللهُ عليه وسلم في غزَاةٍ ، ونحن ستّةُ نفرٍ بيْننا بعيرٌ نعْتقِبُهُ ، فنَقِبتْ أقدامُنا ونقِبتْ قدَمِي ، وسقَطتْ أظفاري ، فكُنّا نلُفُّ على أرجُلِنا الخِرَقَ ، فسُمِّيتْ غزوةَ ذاتِ الرِّقاعِ لِما كُنّا نعْصِبُ على أرْجُلِنا الخِرَقِ . قالَ أبو بُردَةَ : فحدَّثَ أبو مُوسى بهذا الحدِيثِ ، ثُمَّ كرِهَ ذلكَ ، وقالَ : ما كُنْتُ أصنَعُ بِأنْ أذْكُرَهُ ! قالَ : كأنّهُ كرِهَ أنْ يكُونَ شيْئاً مِنْ عمَلِهِ أفْشاهُ . مُتّفقٌ عليه .

525. Hazrat Abu Burdah (R.A.A.) reports from Hazrat Abu Musa Ash'ari (R.A.A.) that ; 'Once we accompanied the Holy Prophet (S.A.W.) on a Jihad, (due to shortage of animals) only one camel was allotted to us—a party of six who rode by turns, as such our feet got wounded and even my nails also dropped down. To cover the wounds, I had wrapped up my feet with rags; and since we had wrapped rags on our wounds, this campaign was known as the Ghazwa of Rags or the Campaign of Rags. **Hazrat Abu Burdah** (R.A.A.) that **Hazrat Abu Musa** narrated this episode, but afterwards felt sorry having done so stating: I wish I had not mentioned this fact; as he did not like publicising something about his services (in this Jihad). *(Agreed upon).*

٥٢٦ ــ وعن عمرو بن تَغْلِبَ ــ بفتح التاء المثناة فوقَ وإسكانِ الغينِ المعجمة وكسرِ اللاّمِ ــ رضيَ اللهُ عنه ، أنَّ رسُولَ اللهِ صلى اللهُ عليه وسلم أُتيَ بمَالٍ أوْ سبْيٍ فقَسّمَهُ ، فأعْطى رجالاً ، وترَكَ رجالاً ، فبلَغهُ أنَّ الذينَ ترَكَ عتَبُوا ، فحمِدَ اللهَ ، ثُمَّ أثنى عليْهِ ، ثُمَّ قالَ : « أمّا بعْدُ ، فوَاللهِ إنِّي لأُعْطِي الرَّجلَ وأدَعُ الرَّجُلَ ، والّذي أدَعُ أحبُّ إليَّ مِنَ الّذي أعْطِي ، ولَكِنِّي إنّما أعْطِي أقْواماً لِما أرى في قُلُوبهِمْ مِنَ الجَزَعِ والهَلَعِ ، وأكِلُ أقْواماً إلى ما جعَلَ اللهُ في قُلُوبِهِمْ مِنَ الغِنَى والخَيْرِ ،

مِنهُمْ عَمْرُو بنُ تَغْلِبَ » قال عَمْرُو بنُ تَغْلِبَ : فَوَاللهِ ما أُحِبُّ أنَّ لي بِكَلِمَةِ رسُولِ اللهِ صلى اللهُ عليه وسلم حُمْرَ النَّعَمِ . رواه البخاري

526. **Hazrat Amr Ibn Taghlib** (R.A.A.) says: some spoils or prisoners were produced before the Holy Prophet (S.A.W.), who distributed them, giving to some and omitting others. Thereafter he was informed that those whom he had ignored were displeased. On this he delivered a sermon in which he praised Allah and glorified Him and then said: By Allah, it is a fact that I give to one and ignore another; while the one I ignore is dearer to me than the one to whom I give. I give to such persons in whose hearts I see worry and uneasiness; others I leave to the good sense and self sufficience which Allah has put in their hearts. Among these is Amr bin Taghlib, who while relating this, remarked: 'I would certainly not barter away these (precious) words of the Holy Prophet (S.A.W.) for even red camels (which are very precious goods among Arabs).' *(Bukhari).*

٥٢٧ – وعن حَكِيمِ بنِ حِزامٍ رضيَ اللهُ عنه أنَّ النبيَّ صلى اللهُ عليه وسلم قالَ : « اليَدُ العُلْيا خيرٌ مِنَ اليَدِ السُّفْلى ، وابْدَأ بمَنْ تَعولُ ، وخَيْرُ الصَّدَقَةِ عَنْ ظَهرِ غِنىً ، وَمَنْ يَسْتَعْفِفْ يُعِفُّهُ اللهُ ، ومَنْ يَسْتَغْنِ يُغْنِهِ اللهُ » متفقٌ عليه .

وهذا لفظ البخاري ، ولفظ مسلم أخصر

527. This Hadis has already been given in item No. 296 of Chapter 36 related by Hazrat Abu Hurairah (R.A.A.).

٥٢٨ – وعن أبي سُفْيانَ صَخْرِ بن حَرْبٍ رضيَ اللهُ عنه قال : قال رسولُ اللهِ صلى اللهُ عليه وسلم : « لا تُلْحِفُوا في المسألَةِ ، فوَاللهِ لا يَسْألُني أحَدٌ مِنكُمْ شيئاً ، فتُخرِجَ لَهُ مَسْألَتُهُ مِنّي شيئاً وأنا لَهُ كارِهٌ ، فيُبارَكَ لهُ فيما أعْطَيْتُهُ » . رواهُ مسلم .

528. **Hazrat Abu Sufyan Sakhr Bin Harb** (R.A.A.) relates that the Holy Prophet (S.A.W.) said: Do not ask from me with obstinacy. If one of you asks me for something, and I give it to him with an unwilling heart, there is blessing in what I give him, because in asking for something in this way, it loses blessing. *(Muslim).*

٥٢٩ – وعن أبي عبدِ الرحمنِ عَوفِ بن مالك الأشْجَعِيِّ رضيَ اللهُ عنه قالَ : كُنّا عِندَ رسُولِ اللهِ صلى اللهُ عليهِ وسلّم تِسْعَةً أوْ ثمانِيَةً أوْ سَبْعَةً ،

فَقَالَ : « أَلاَ تُبَايِعُونَ رَسُولَ اللهِ صلى اللهُ عليه وسلم » وكُنَّا حَدِيثِي عَهْدٍ بِبَيْعَةٍ ، فَقُلْنَا : قَدْ بَايَعْنَاكَ يا رسُولَ اللهِ . ثُمَّ قال : « أَلا تُبَايِعُونَ رَسُولَ اللهِ » فَبَسَطْنا أَيْدِينا وقُلْنا : قَدْ بايَعْناكَ يا رَسُولَ اللهِ ، فَعلاَمَ نُبَايِعُكَ ؟ قال : « على أنْ تَعْبُدُوا اللهَ ولا تُشْرِكُوا بِهِ شَيْئاً ، والصَّلَوَاتِ الخَمْسِ وتُطِيعُوا » وَأَسَرَّ كلمةً خَفِيَّةً : « ولاَ تَسْأَلُوا النَّاسَ شَيْئاً » فَلَقَدْ رَأَيْتُ بَعْضَ أُولئِكَ النَّفَرِ يَسْقُطُ سَوْطُ أَحَدِهِمْ فَمَا يَسْأَلُ أَحَداً يُنَاوِلُهُ إِيَّاهُ . رواه مسلم

529. Hazrat Abu Abdur Rahman Auf bin Malik Ashj'ai (R.A.A.) says: Once nine, eight or seven of us were with the Holy Prophet (S.A.W.) when he said: Why do you not make an agreement with the Messenger of Allah?' Although we had only recently made such an agreement with him. So we submitted: O Messenger of Allah! We have already made an agreement with you! 'But He repeated: 'Why do you not make an agreement with the Messenger of Allah! On this we stretched our hands and submitted: O Messenger of Allah! We have already made an agreement with you. What more agreement we have to make with you. He said: 'That you will worship Allah alone and will not associate anything with Him; that you will observe the five (daily) Salats, will obey Allah (here he said something slowly and added) and will not ask anyone for anything! Since then I have myself noticed that if somebody dropped his whip, he would not ask anyone to hand it over to him'.

(Muslim).

٥٣٠ ــ وعن ابنِ عمر رضيَ اللهُ عنهما أنَّ النبيَّ صلى اللهُ عليه وسلم قال : « لاَ تَزَالُ المَسْأَلَةُ بِأَحَدِكُمْ حتى يَلْقَى اللهَ تعالى ولَيْسَ في وَجْهِهِ مُزْعَةُ لَحْمٍ » متفقٌ عليه .

530. Hazrat Ibn Umar (R.A.A.) relates that the Holy Prophet (S.A.W.) said: 'If one of you continues in asking, (on the day of Judgment) he will face Allah without a piece of flesh on his face.'

(Bukhari and Muslim).

٥٣١ ــ وعنه أنَّ رسُولَ اللهِ صلى الله عليه وسلم قال وهو على المِنبَرِ ، وَذَكَرَ الصَّدَقَةَ والتَّعَفُّفَ عَنِ المَسْأَلَةِ : « اليَدُ العُلْيا خَيْرٌ مِنَ اليَدِ السُّفْلَى. وَاليَدُ العُلْيا هِيَ المُنْفِقَةُ ، وَالسُّفْلَى هِيَ السَّائِلَةُ » متفق عليه

531. **Hazrat Ibn Umar** (R.A.A.) relates that the Holy Prophet (S.A.W.) once was delivering a sermon from the pulpit on alms giving and abstaining from begging and said: 'The upper hand is better than the lower, the upper hand is the hand that gives and the lower hand is the beggar's hand.' *(Bukhari and Muslim).*

٥٣٢ – وعن أبي هُريرة رضيَ اللهُ عنه قال : قال رسُول اللهِ صلى اللهُ عليه وسلم : « مَنْ سَأَلَ النَّاسَ تَكَثُّرًا فإنَّما يَسْأَل جَمْراً ، فَلْيَسْتَقِلَّ أوْ لِيَسْتَكْثِرْ » رواه مسلم .

532. **Hazrat Abu Hurairah** (R.A.A.) says that the Holy Prophet (S.A.W.) said: 'One who asks people (for something) to increase his accumulation, in fact asks for burning ember. It is now upto him to increase or decrease it. *(Muslim).*

٥٣٣ – وعن سَمُرَةَ بنِ جُنْدبٍ رضي الله عنه قال : قال رسُولُ الله صلى اللهُ عليهِ وآلهِ وسلَّم : « إنَّ المَسألَةَ كَدٌّ يَكُدُّ بها الرَّجُلُ وَجْهَهُ ، إلا أنْ يَسألَ الرَّجُلُ سُلْطاناً أوْ في أمْرٍ لا بُدَّ مِنهُ » رواهُ الترمذي وقال : حديث حسن صحيح .

533. **Hazrat Samurah Ibn Jundub** (R.A.A.) relates that the Holy Prophet (S.A.W.) said: By begging, a person inflicts an injury on his face, except in the case of asking from an authority for something, or requesting for something which is essential. (*Imam Tirmizi* has reported this tradition and called it good).

٥٣٤ – وعن ابنِ مسعودٍ رضيَ اللهُ عنه قال : قال رسُولُ الله صلى اللهُ عليه وسلم : « مَنْ أصابَتْهُ فاقَةٌ فأنْزَلَهَا بالنَّاسِ لَمْ تُسَدَّ فاقَتُهُ ، وَمَنْ أنْزَلَهَا باللهِ ، فَيُوشِكُ اللهُ لَهُ بِرِزقٍ عاجِلٍ أوْ آجِلٍ » رواهُ أبو داود ، والترمذي وقال : حديث حسن .

534. **Hazrat Ibn Mas'ud** (R.A.A.) relates that the Holy Prophet (S.A.W.) said: A person who suffers from hunger and poverty and mentions this fact to the human beings (with a view to get help from them) will not be relieved,but one who solicits relief from Allah will sooner or later be granted means of sustenance, immediate or delayed (*Abu Daud and Tirmizi*). *Imam Tirmizi* has said this tradition is good.

٥٣٥ – وعَنْ ثَوْبانَ رضيَ اللهُ عنه قال · قال رسُولُ اللهِ صلى الله عليه وسلم : « مَنْ تَكَفَّلَ لي أنْ لا يَسْألَ النَّاسَ شَيْئاً ، وأتَكَفَّلُ له بالجَنَّةِ ؟ »

فقلتُ : أنا ، فكانَ لا يَسأَلُ أحداً شيئاً ، رواه أبو داود بإسنادٍ صحيحٍ

535. Hazrat Sauban (R.A.A.) relates that the Holy Prophet (S.A.W.) said: Anybody who gives me an undertaking that he will not ask for anything from any person, for him, I shall guarantee Paradise. Hazrat Sauban Said: 'I pledge that I will not ask for anything from anybody.' Thereafter Hazrat Sauban (R.A.A.) did not ask anybody for anything. (*Imam Abu Daud* has called this tradition as correct).

٥٣٦ – وعن أبي بِشرٍ قَبيصةَ بنِ المُخارِقِ رضيَ اللهُ عنه قال: تحمَّلْتُ حَمالَةً فأتيتُ رسولَ اللهِ صلى اللهُ عليه وسلم أسألُهُ فيها، فقال : « أقِمْ حتى تأتِينا الصَّدقةُ فنأمرَ لكَ بها » ، ثُمَّ قالَ : « يا قَبيصةُ إنَّ المَسألةَ لا تَحِلُّ إلاَّ لأحَدِ ثلاثةٍ : رَجُلٌ تحمَّلَ حَمالةً ، فحلَّتْ لهُ المَسألةُ حتى يُصيبَها ، ثُمَّ يُمسِكُ . ورَجُلٌ أصابتْهُ جائحةٌ اجتاحتْ مالَهُ ، فحلَّتْ لَهُ المَسألةُ حتَّى يُصيبَ قِواماً مِنْ عَيْشٍ ، أوْ قالَ: سِداداً مِنْ عَيْشٍ ، ورَجُلٌ أصابتْهُ فاقةٌ ، حتى يقولَ ثلاثةٌ مِنْ ذَوي الحِجَى مِنْ قَوْمِهِ : لقدْ أصابتْ فُلاناً فاقةٌ ، فحلَّتْ لهُ المَسألةُ حتَّى يُصيبَ قِواماً مِنْ عَيْشٍ ، أوْ قالَ : سِداداً مِنْ عَيْشٍ . فما سِواهُنَّ مِنَ المَسألةِ يا قَبيصةُ سُحْتٌ ، يأكلُها صاحبُها سُحتاً » ، رواهُ مسلم

536. Hazrat Abul Bish'r Qabisah bin Mukhariq (R.A.A.) relates that he stood surety for payment of blood-money. In order to seek some help in this obligation he came to the Holy Prophet (S.A.W.). The Holy Prophet (S.A.W.) said: 'Wait till some money on account of charity is received, then I shall give you something.' The Holy Prophet (S.A.W.) further said: 'Qabisah, asking (begging) is not lawful for anybody except for three persons: One a person who is under an obligation to pay some debt and such a person may ask some help till the guarantee is discharged, and thereafter should desist from asking; two, a person whose means of subsistance is destroyed by some (natural) calamity, may ask for some succour till his pvoerty is removed; three a person who is suffering from hunger and three intelligent men from his community testify that he is starving, till his poverty is removed. All other kinds of asking (begging) is forbidden, and one who indulges in it, eats that which is unlawful.' *(Muslim).*

٥٣٧ – وعن أبي هريرة رضيَ اللهُ عنه أنَّ رسولَ اللهِ صلَّى اللهُ عليه وسلم قال : « ليسَ المِسكينُ الَّذي يطوفُ على النَّاسِ تردُّهُ اللُّقمةُ واللُّقمتانِ ،

وَالتَّمْرَةُ وَالتَّمْرَتَانِ ، وَلَكِنَّ الْمِسْكِينَ الَّذِي لاَ يَجِدُ غِنىً يُغْنِيهِ وَلاَ يُفْطَنُ لَهُ ، فَيُتَصَدَّقَ عَلَيْهِ ، وَلاَ يَقُومُ فَيَسْأَلَ النَّاسَ ، متفقٌ عليه

537. This Hadis has already been covered in item No. 264 under Chapter No. 33.

****

CHAPTER 58

Acceptance of a Thing Which is Bestowed without Asking for it.

٥٣٨ ـ عَنْ سالِمِ بنِ عبدِ اللهِ بن عُمَرَ ، عَنْ أبيهِ عبدِ اللهِ بنِ عُمَرَ ، عَنْ عُمَرَ رضي اللهُ عنهم قال: كان رسول الله صلى الله عليه وسلم يُعْطِيني العَطَاءَ ، فأقُولُ : أعطهِ مَن هُوَ أفقرُ إليهِ مِنِّي ، فقال : « خُذْهُ ، إذَا جاءَكَ مِن هذا المَالِ شيءٌ ، وأنتَ غيرُ مُشْرِفٍ ولا سائِلٍ ، فَخُذْهُ فَتَمَوَّلْهُ فإن شِئتَ كُلْهُ ، وإن شئتَ تَصَدَّقْ بهِ ، وَمَا لا ، فَلا تُتْبِعْهُ نَفْسَكَ » قال سالمٌ : فَكَانَ عبدُ اللهِ لا يَسألُ أحداً شيئاً ، ولا يَرُدُّ شيئاً أُعْطِيَهُ . متفقٌ عليه

538. Hazrat Salim Bin Abdullah Bin Umar (R.A.A.) relates from his father Hazrat Abdullah Bin Umar and Hazrat Abdullah from his father Hazrat Umar (R.A.A.) that the Holy Prophet (S.A.W.) used bestow upon me some presents, and I would then submit: "Sir give it to someone who is more needy than myself." The Holy Prophet (S.A.W.) would say: Take it when it comes to you from this account and without your asking or aspiring for and include it into your assets. Thereafter you may use it or give it away in charity. Do not aspire to acquire something through other means. Hazrat Salim says that his father Abdullah Bin Umar would not ask anyone for anything nor refuse anything that was given to him. *(Bukhari and Muslim).*

****

CHAPTER 59

Earning by Own Efforts and Refraining from Asking, and Taking Lead in Giving.

قال الله تعالى : فَإِذَا قُضِيَتِ الصَّلاةُ فَانْتَشِرُوا في الأَرْضِ وابْتَغُوا مِن فَضْلِ اللهِ [الجمعة : ١٠] .

Allah, the Exalted, has said:

185. And when the Prayer is ended, then disperse in the land and seek of Allah's bounty (62:10)

٥٣٩ – عن أبي عبدِ الله الزُّبَيْرِ بن العوّام رضي الله عنه قال: قالَ رسولُ الله صلّى الله عليه وسلم: «لَأَنْ يأْخُذَ أحدُكُم أحبُلَهُ ثُمَّ يأْتِيَ الجَبَلَ، فيأْتِيَ بحُزْمَةٍ مِن حَطَبٍ على ظَهرِهِ فيَبيعَها، فيَكُفَّ اللهُ بها وَجْهَهُ، خَيْرٌ لَهُ مِنْ أن يَسألَ النّاسَ، أعطَوْهُ أَوْ مَنَعُوهُ» رواه البخاري

539. Hazrat Abu Abdullah Zubair Ibn Awam (R.A.A.) relates that the Holy Prophet (S.A.W.) said: 'That every one of you should catch hold of his rope, go to the mountain, collect, carry a load of fire wood on his back, sell it (for his living) and thereby make his face secure against the chastisement of Allah (on the Day of Judgment). This would be better for him than requesting people, whether they give him or refuse.' *(Bukhari).*

٥٤٠ – وعن أبي هُريرة رضي الله عنه قال: قالَ رسولُ الله صلى الله عليه وسلم: «لَأَنْ يَحتَطِبَ أحدُكُم حُزْمَةً على ظَهرِهِ، خَيْرٌ لَهُ مِنْ أنْ يَسألَ أحداً، فيُعْطِيَهُ أو يَمنَعَهُ» متفقٌ عليه

540. Hazrat Abu Hurairah (R.A.A.) relates that the Holy Prophet (S.A.W.) said : That it is better for any one of you to carry a load of fire wood on his back than, asking (begging) from someone whether he gives him or refuses. *(Bukhari and Muslim).*

٥٤١ – وعنه عنِ النبيِّ صلّى الله عليه وسلم قال: «كانَ داوُدُ عليهِ السَّلامُ لا يأْكُلُ إلاَّ مِن عَمَلِ يَدِهِ» رواه البخاري

541. **Hazrat Abu Hurairah** (R.A.A.) relates that the Holy Prophet (S.A.W.) said: 'Prophet David (earned his living and) ate only from his earnings through his labour and nothing else.' *(Bukhari).*

٥٤٢ – وعنه أنّ رسولَ الله صلى الله عليه وسلم قال: «كانَ زكَريّا عليه السلامُ نجّاراً» رواه مسلم

542. Hazrat Abu Hurairah (R.A.A.) relates that the Holy Prophet (S.A.W.) said: 'Prophet Zakariah was a carpenter by profession. (i.e. he earned his living through carpentry). *(Muslim).*

٥٤٣ ــ وعن المِقدَام بنِ مَعْدِيكَرِبَ رضي الله عنه، عن النبي صلى الله عليه وسلم قال : « ما أكَلَ أحدٌ طَعَاماً قطُّ خيْراً مِن أن يأكُلَ مِن عمَلِ يَدِهِ ، وإنَّ نَبيَّ الله داوُدَ صلَّى الله عليه وسلم كان يأكُل مِن عمَلِ يدِهِ » رواه البخاري

543. Hazrat Miqdad bin Ma'dikarib (R.A.A.) relates that the Holy Prophet (S.A.W.) said: No one has eaten better food than that obtained through the hard labour of his hands. Prophet David the Prophet of Allah, used to earn his living through his own labour. *(Bukhari).*

(This means that to earn his living through his own efforts is a great virtue and one should not resort to begging.

Note: The learned theologians are not agreed as to which profession is the best and preferable. According to Imam Shafie trading is the best and some others have declared that agriculture is better as it is very near to Tawakkul or trust in Allah. But it is a fact that all professions are good in which one has to labour with his hands, provided that it is within the limits of Shariat.

****

CHAPTER 60

Generosity and Spending in a Good Cause with Trust in Allah.

قال الله تعالى : وَمَا أَنفَقْتُم مِن شَيْءٍ فَهُوَ يُخْلِفُهُ . [سبأ : ٣٩] وقال تعالى : وَمَا تُنْفِقُوا مِنْ خَيرٍ فَلأنفُسِكُمْ وَمَا تُنفِقُونَ إلاَّ ابتِغَاءَ وَجْهِ الله وَمَا تُنفِقُوا مِنْ خَيرٍ يُوَفَّ إلَيْكُمْ وَأنتُمْ لا تُظْلَمُونَ [البقرة : ٢٧٢]

وقال تعالى : وَمَا تُنْفِقُوا مِنْ خَيرٍ فَإنَّ الله بِهِ عَلِيمٌ . [البقرة : ٢٧٣]

Allah, the Exalted, has said:

186. And whatsoever ye spend(for good) He replaceth it.(34:39).
187. And whatsoever good thing ye spend, it is for yourselves, when ye spend not, save in search of Allah's countenance; and whatsoever good thing ye spend, it will be repaid to you in full, and ye will not be wronged. (2:272)
188. And whatsoever good thing ye spend, Lo! Allah knoweth it. (2: 273).

٥٤٤ ــ وعَن ابنِ مسعودٍ رضي الله عنه عن النبي صلَّى الله عليه وسلم قال : « لا حَسَدَ إلّا في اثنتَين : رَجُلٌ آتاهُ اللهُ مالاً ، فَسَلَّطَه على هَلَكَتِهِ

في الحق ، ورجلٌ آتاه اللهُ حِكمةً ، فهو يقضي بها ويُعلّمها » متفقٌ عليه

544. **Hazrat Ibn Mas'ud** (R.A.A.) relates that the Holy Prophet (S.A.W.) said: 'Only two persons deserve being envied; firstly a person to whom Allah has given wealth and bestowed upon him Divine to spend in a righteous cause; and secondly the person upon whom Allah has bestowed wisdom by which he judges and which he teaches.' *(Bukhari and Muslim).*

٥٤٥ — وعنه قال : قال رسولُ الله صلى الله عليه وسلم : « أيُّكم مالُ وارثِهِ أحبُّ إليه مِن ماله ؟ » قالوا: يا رسولَ الله، ما مِنّا أحدٌ إلاّ مالُه أحبُّ إليه . قال : « فإنّ مالَه ما قدّمَ ومالَ وارثِه ما أخّرَ » رواه البخاري

545. **Hazrat Ibn Mas'ud** (R.A.A.) relates that the Holy Prophet (S.A.W.) once asked: who is that person among you who loves the property of his successor more than his own property?' The Companions submitted: 'O Messenger of Allah (S.A.W.)' There is none among us who loves his successor's property more than his own. He said: 'Then his property is which he has sent ahead; and that which he retains belongs to his successor. *(Bukhari).*

٥٤٦ — وعن عديِّ بنِ حاتم رضي الله عنه أن رسول الله صلى الله عليه وسلم قال : « اتّقُوا النّارَ ولَوْ بِشِقِّ تمرةٍ » متفقٌ عليه

546. This Hadis has been covered in the first part of item No.139 of Chapter 13.

٥٤٧ — وعن جابرٍ رضي الله عنه قال : ما سُئِلَ رسولُ الله صلى الله عليه وسلم شيئاً قطُّ فقالَ : لا . متفقٌ عليه

547. **Hazrat Jabir** (R.A.A.) relates that the Holy Prophet(S.A.W.) never said no to anyone who asked him for anything.' *(Bukhari and Muslim).*

٥٤٨ — وعن أبي هُريرة رضي الله عنه قال : قال رسولُ اللهِ صلّى الله عليه وسلم : « ما مِن يومٍ يُصبِحُ العبادُ فيه إلاّ ملَكانِ ينزِلانِ ، فيقولُ أحدُهما : اللّهمّ أعطِ مُنفِقاً خلَفاً ، ويقولُ الآخرُ : اللّهمّ أعطِ مُمسكاً تلَفاً » متفقٌ عليه

548. This Hadis has been dealt with in item No. 295, Chapter 36.

٥٤٩ — وعنه أن رسولَ الله صلّى اللهَ عليه وسلم قال : «قالَ اللهُ تعالى : انفِق يا ابنَ آدمَ يُنْفَقْ عَلَيْكَ » متفقٌ عليه

549. Hazrat Abu Hurairah (R.A.A.) relates that the Holy Prophet (S.A.W.) said: 'Allah, the Exalted, says:' O Son of Adam spend (in the way of Allah) will also be spent upon you.' *(Bukhari and Muslim).*

٥٥٠ — وعنْ عبد الله بن عَمْرو بنِ العَاصِ رضي الله عنهُما أنَّ رَجُلاً سَأَلَ رسول الله صلى الله عليه وسلم : أيُّ الإسلامِ خَيْرٌ ؟ قال : « تُطْعِمُ الطَّعَامَ ، وَتَقْرَأُ السَّلامَ عَلى مَنْ عَرَفتَ وَمَنْ لم تَعْرِفْ » متفقٌ عليه

550. Hazrat Abaullah bin 'Amr bin Al-'Aas (R.A.A.) says that a man asked the Holy Prophet (S.A.W.): what in Islam is the best?' He answered: 'To feed people and to greet everyone (to say *Assalamo Alaikum)* whether you know him or not.' *(Bukhari and Muslim).*

٥٥١ — وعنه قال: قالَ رسولُ الله صلّىالله عليه وسلم : « أرْبَعونَ خَصلَةً أعلاهَا مَنِيحَةُ العَنْزِ ما مِن عَامِلٍ يَعْمَلُ بخَصلَةٍ منها رَجَاءَ ثَوَابِهَا وَتَصْدِيقَ مَوْعُودِهَا إلّا أدْخلَهُ اللهُ تعالى بهَا الجَنَّةَ » رواه البخاري

551. This Hadis has already been given in item No. 138,Chapter 13.

٥٥٢ — وعن أبي أُمَامَةَ صُدَيِّ بنِ عَجْلانَ رضي الله عنه قال: قالَ رسولُ الله صلى الله عليه وسلم: « يَاابْنَ آدَمَ إنَّكَ أن تَبْذُلَ الفَضْلَ خَيْرٌ لكَ، وأن تُمْسِكَهُ شَرٌّ لَكَ ، ولا تُلامُ عَلى كَفَافٍ ، وَابْدأْ بِمَنْ تَعُولُ ، واليَدُ العُليَا خَيرٌ مِنَ اليَدِ السُّفْلَى » رواه مسلم

552. This Hadis is the same as No. 510, Chapter 56 with the addition of 'The upper hand is better than the lower one i.e. which is spread for begging.' *(Muslim).*

٥٥٣ — وعن أنسٍ رضي الله عنه قال : ما سُئِلَ رسولُ الله صلى الله عليه وسلم عَلى الإسْلامِ شَيئاً إلاّ أعْطاه ، وَلَقَدْ جاءَه رجلٌ ، فَأعطاه غَنَماً بَيْنَ جَبلَيْنِ، فَرَجَعَ إلى قَومِهِ فقَالَ: يَاقَوْمِ أسْلِمُوا ؛ فإنَّ مُحَمّداً يُعْطِي عَطَاءَ مَنْ لا يَخْشَى الفَقْرَ، وإنْ كَانَ الرَّجُلُ لَيُسْلِمُ مَا يُرِيدُ إلاّ الدُّنيَا، فَمَا يَلْبَثُ إلاّ يَسيراً حَتّى يَكُونَ الإسْلامُ أحَبَّ إلَيهِ مِنَ الدُّنيَا وَمَا

عَلَيْهَا . رواه مسلم

553. Hazrat Anas Bin Malik (R.A.A.) states that whenever in Islam a person requested the Holy Prophet (S.A.W.) for anything, he gave it to him. Once a man came to him and the Holy Prophet (S.A.W.) gave him a flock of goats large enough which covered a valley. When he returned to his people he said to him: 'O my people, accept Islam for Muhammad (S.A.W.) bestows on such a scale that leaves no fear of poverty.' Even when a person accepted Islam simply for the sake of worldly gains, soon after, Islam would become dearer to him than the world and all in it. ***(Muslim).***

٥٥٤ — وعن عُمَرَ رضيَ الله عنه قال : قَسَمَ رسولُ اللهِ صلى الله عليه وسلّم قَسْماً ، فقُلْتُ : يا رسولَ الله لَغَيْرُ هؤلاء كانُوا أحَقَّ بِهِ مِنْهُم ؟ قال : « إنَّهُمْ خَيَّرُونِي أن يَسألُونِي بالفُحْشِ ، أوْ يُبَخِّلُونِي ، ولَستُ بِباخِلٍ » رواه مسلم

554. Hazrat Umar (R.A.A.) relates that once the Holy Prophet (S.A.W.) distributed some property (spoils of war) and I said to him: O Messenger of Allah (S.A.W.), apart from these gentlemen (recipients). there are some other persons more deserving than these. He said: 'They have authorised me (to use my discretion). Either they should ask me openly and I would give them, or they might charge me with miserliness, and I am not a miser (and as such I am giving to these gentlemen). ***(Muslim)***

٥٥٥ — وعن جُبَيْرِ بنِ مُطعِمٍ رضيَ الله عنه أنه قال : بَيْنَمَا هُوَ يَسِيرُ مَعَ النَّبيِّ صلّى الله عليه وسلم مَقْفَلَهُ مِن حُنَيْنٍ ، فَعَلِقَهُ الأعْرابُ يَسألُونَهُ ، حتّى اضطَرُّوهُ إلى سَمُرَةٍ ، فَخَطَفَتْ رِدَاءَهُ ، فَوَقَفَ النَّبيُّ صلّى الله عليه وسلم فقال : « أعطُونِي رِدَائِي ، فَلَوْ كانَ لي عَدَدُ هذهِ العِضَاهِ نَعَماً ، لَقَسَمْتُهُ بَيْنَكُمْ ، ثم لا تَجِدُونِي بَخِيلاً وَلا كَذّاباً وَلا جَبَاناً » رواه البخاري

555. Hazrat Jubair bin Mut'im (R.A.A.) relates that at the end of the battle of *Hunain* while he was returning with the Holy Prophet (S.A.W.) some rustics detained him and demanded their share in the spoils. They made a circle round him under a tree and someone snatched away his covering sheet. The Holy Prophet (S.A.W.) halted and said: 'Return my sheet to me; had I at my disposal bounties equal to the number of the leaves of this thorny tree, I would have distributed all of them among you, and you would not have found me a miser or a liar, or a coward.' *(Bukhari)*

٥٥٦ — وعن أبي هُرَيرة رضيَ اللهُ عنه أنّ رسولَ الله صلى الله عليه وسلم قال: « ما نَقَصَتْ صَدَقَةٌ مِنْ مَالٍ ، وما زادَ اللهُ عَبْداً بِعَفْوٍ إلاّ عِزّاً ، وما تَواضَعَ أحَدٌ لله إلاّ رَفَعَهُ اللهُ عزّ وجَلّ » رواه مسلم

556. Hazrat Abu Hurairah (R.A.A.) relates that the Holy Prophet (S.A.W.) said: Charity does not diminish the wealth; Allah enhances the honour of one who forgives, and one who humbles himself for the sake of Allah, Allah exalts him in rank.' *(Muslim).*

٥٥٧ — وعن أبي كَبْشَةَ عُمَرَ بنِ سَعْدٍ الأَنْمَارِيِّ رضي الله عنه أنه سمعَ رسولَ الله صلى الله عليه وسلم يَقُولُ : « ثَلاثَةٌ أُقْسِمُ عَلَيْهِنَّ وأُحَدِّثُكُم حَدِيثاً فَاحْفَظُوهُ : مَا نَقَصَ مَالَ عَبْدٍ مِن صَدَقَةٍ ، ولا ظُلِمَ عَبْدٌ مَظْلَمَةً صَبَرَ عَلَيْهَا إلاّ زَادَهُ اللهُ عِزّاً ، ولا فَتَحَ عَبْدٌ بابَ مَسْأَلَةٍ إلا فَتَحَ اللهُ عَلَيهِ بابَ فَقْرٍ ، أو كَلِمَةً نَحْوَهَا . وأُحَدِّثُكُم حَدِيثاً فاحْفَظُوهُ قال : إنَّمَا الدُّنْيا لأَرْبَعَةِ نَفَرٍ :

عَبْدٍ رَزَقَهُ اللهُ مالاً وَعِلْماً ، فَهُوَ يَتَّقِي فِيهِ رَبَّهُ ، وَيَصِلُ فِيهِ رَحِمَهُ ، وَيَعْلَمُ لِلّهِ فِيهِ حَقّاً ، فَهَذا بِأَفْضَلِ المَنَازِلِ .

وَعَبْدٍ رَزَقَهُ اللهُ عِلْماً ، وَلَمْ يَرْزُقْهُ مالاً ، فَهُوَ صادِقُ النِّيَّةِ يَقُولُ : لَوْ أَنَّ لِي مالاً لَعَمِلْتُ بِعَمَلِ فُلانٍ ، فَهُوَ بِنِيَّتِهِ ، فَأَجْرُهُمَا سَوَاءٌ .

وَعَبْدٍ رَزَقَهُ اللهُ مالاً ، وَلَمْ يَرْزُقْهُ عِلْماً ، فَهُوَ يَخْبِطُ في مالِهِ بِغَيْرِ عِلْمٍ ، لا يَتَّقِي فِيهِ رَبَّهُ ، ولا يَصِلُ فِيهِ رَحِمَهُ ، ولا يَعْلَمُ لِلّهِ فِيهِ حَقّاً ، فَهَذا بِأَخْبَثِ المَنَازِلِ .

وَعَبْدٍ لَمْ يَرْزُقْهُ اللهُ مالاً ولا عِلْماً ، فَهُوَ يَقُولُ : لَوْ أَنَّ لِي مالاً لَعَمِلْتُ فِيهِ بِعَمَلِ فُلانٍ ، فَهُوَ بِنِيَّتِهِ ، فَوِزْرُهُمَا سَوَاءٌ » رواه الترمذي وقال : حديث حسن صحيح .

557. Hazrat Abu Kabsha Umar bin Sa'ad Anmari (R.A.A.) relates that he heard the Holy Prophet (S.A.W.) say: I tell you these things remember them well, I can swear by them. One, that nobody's assets get reduced by Charity; two, Allah enhances the honour of a person who endures a wrong patiently; and third, no one stoops to begging, but Allah subjects him to starvation and penury, or he said some other thing like this. He also said: 'Remember well what I am going to tell you: There are four kinds of people in the world; One, is a person whom Allah grants wealth and knowledge (both) and he is mindful of his duty to his sustainer in respect of these two things, helps his kith and kin and discharges the rights of Allah in them. Then this person is in the highest rank; Two, a person to whom Allah grants knowledge but no wealth, and he is honest and true in his intentions, I would have done the same (good) deeds, as so and so had done, and this is his intention. He will get the same recompense as the other person. Three, a person to whom Allah grants wealth but no knowledge. He squanders his money due to the lack of knowledge, and is not afraid of Allah (i.e. he is not mindful of his duty to Allah in this respect; he neither discharges the obligations of his kinship nor does he acknowledge the rights of Allah in it. Such a person is in the meanest position.. Four, a person upon whom Allah confers neither wealth nor knowledge, and he says: If I had the money, I would have acted like this man. When such is his intention, then both of them are equal in sin. (*Imam Tirmizi* has reported this tradition and called it as good).

٥٥٨ ـ وعن عائشة رضي الله عنها أنَّهُمْ ذَبَحُوا شَاةً ، فقالَ النبيُّ صلى الله عليه وسلم : « مَابَقِيَ مِنها ؟ » قالت : مابقي مِنها إلاَّ كَتِفُهَا، قال: « بَقِيَ كُلُّهَا غيرَ كَتِفِهَا » رواه الترمذي وقال : حديث صحيح .

558. Hazrat Ayesha (R.A.A.) relates that once they slaughtered a goat; (and distributed most of its meat). Then the Holy Prophet (S.A.W.) asked: what is left now? She answered: 'Nothing except a shank'. He remarked: '(in fact) all of it is saved except the shank.' *Imam Tirmizi* has reported this tradition calling it as good. The meaning of this is that what is given in charity is saved and what has been consumed, is lost. *(Tirmizi).*

٥٥٩ ـ وعن أسماء بنتِ أبي بكرٍ الصديق رضي الله عنهما قالت : قال لي رسولُ الله صلى الله عليه وسلم : « لاتُوكِي فَيُوكَى عَلَيْكِ » .

وفي روايةٍ « أنفِقِي أو انفَحِي ، أوِ انْضِحِي ، ولا تُحْصِي فَيُحْصِي اللهُ عَلَيْكِ ، ولا تُوعِي فَيُوعِي اللهُ عَلَيْكِ » متفقٌ عليه

559. Hazrat Asma' Bint Hazrat Abu Bakr Siddiq (R.A.A.) relates that the Holy Prophet (S.A.W.) asked her: 'Do not amass (wealth, goods etc.) or otherwise Allah will hold back from you.' Another version says: 'Spend (your wealth and goods) and do not collect or board and do not (hesitate to offer or sell) which is spare, else Allah will hold back from you.' *(Bukhari and Muslim).*

٥٦٠ — وعن أبي هريرة رضي الله عنه أنه سمع رسولَ الله صلى اللهُ عليه وسلم يقولُ: « مثَلُ البَخيلِ والمُنفِقِ، كمَثَلِ رَجُلَيْنِ علَيْهِما جُنَّتانِ مِن حَديدٍ مِن ثُديِهِمَا إلى تراقيهِما، فأمَّا المُنفِقُ، فلا يُنْفِقُ إلاَّ سَبَغَتْ، أوْ وفَرَتْ على جِلدِهِ حتى تُخفِيَ بنانَهُ، وتَعفُوَ أثَرَهُ، وأمَّا البَخيلُ، فلا يُريدُ أنْ يُنفِقَ شيئاً إلاَّ لَزِقَتْ كلُّ حَلْقَةٍ مكانَها، فهُوَ يُوسِّعُها فلا تَتَّسِعُ » متفقٌ عليه

560. Hazrat Abu Hurairah (R.A.A.) relates that he heard the Holy Prophet (S.A.W.) as saying: The case of a money-grabber and a benevolent person is like that of two persons who are wrapped in steel from their breasts up to their collar bones. When the generous one spends, his armour loosens and expands till it covers his fingers and his toes. When the miser one makes up his mind not to give away something every ring of the armour sinks into his body. He tries to loosen it but he fails. *(Bukhari and Muslim).*

٥٦١ — وعنه قال: قالَ رسولَ الله صلى الله عليه وسلم: « مَنْ تَصَدَّقَ بعِدْلِ تَمْرَةٍ مِن كَسْبٍ طَيِّبٍ، ولا يَقبَلُ اللهُ إلاَّ الطَّيِّبَ، فإنَّ اللهَ يَقبَلُها بيَمينِهِ، ثُمَّ يُرَبِّيها لِصاحِبِها، كما يُرَبِّي أحَدُكُم فَلُوَّهُ حتى تكُونَ مِثْلَ الجَبَلِ » متفقٌ عليه

561. Hazrat Abu Hurairah (R.A.A.) relates that the Holy Prophet (S.A.W.) said: 'If a person gives away in charity something equal to the value of even a date, from his legitimate earnings, and since Allah accepts charity which is pure. He accepts it with His right hand and multiplies it for him, as one of you tends a calf, till it becomes like a strong bodied bull like a mountain.' *(Bukhari and Muslim).*

٥٦٢ — وعنه عن النبي صلى الله عليه وسلم قال: بَيْنَما رَجُلٌ يَمشي بفَلاةٍ مِنَ الأرضِ، فسَمِعَ صَوتاً في سَحابَةٍ: اسقِ حَديقَةَ فُلانٍ، فتَنَحَّى ذلكَ السَّحابُ فأفرَغَ ماءَهُ في حَرَّةٍ، فإذا شَرْجَةٌ مِن تلكَ الشِّراجِ قد استَوعَبَتْ

ذلِكَ الماءَ كُلَّهُ ، فَتَتبَّعَ المَاءَ ، فإذا رَجُلٌ قَائمٌ في حَدِيقَتِهِ يُحَوِّلُ الماءَ بِمِسحَاتِهِ ، فقال له : يَا عَبْدَ الله ما اسْمُكَ ؟ قال : فُلانٌ للاسْمِ الَّذِي سَمِعَ في السَّحَابَةِ . فقال له : ياعَبْدَ الله لِمَ تَسْأَلُني عَنِ اسْمِي ؟ فقَال : إنّي سَمِعْتُ صَوتاً في السَّحَابِ الذي هذَا مَاؤُهُ يقُولُ : اسقِ حَدِيقَةَ فُلانٍ لاسمِكَ ، فما تَصْنَعُ فِيها ؟ فقال : أما إذْ قُلْتَ هذَا ، فإنّي أنْظُرُ إلى ما يَخْرُجُ مِنها ، فَأَتَصَدَّقُ بثُلُثِهِ ، وآكُلُ أنا وعِيالي ثُلُثاً ، وأردُّ فِيها ثُلُثَهُ ، رواه مسلم

562. Hazrat Abu Hurairah (R.A.A.) relates that the Holy Prophet (S.A.W.) said: 'While a man was walking through a waterless piece of land, he heard a voice coming from the cloud saying: 'Give water to the garden of So and So. 'On this the cloud proceeded in a certain direction and rained water over a rocky piece of land. The water running through small rivalets flowed into a large channel. This man followed the channel till it enrircled a garden and he saw the owner of the garden standing inside the garden working with a showel distributing the water (all over the trees). He asked the owner of the garden: O Servant of Allah! What is your name? He told him his name, which was the same that he had heard from the cloud. The owner of the garden then asked him: 'O Servant of Allah! why did you ask my name?' He replied: 'I heard a voice from the cloud, from which this water has rained, saying: 'Water the garden of So and So; May I know as to what you do to your garden to become entitled for this favour.' He said: 'Now since you have asked me, I will let you know: 'When the produce of this garden is ready it, then give away one third in charity, earmark another third for myself and my family and use the remaining third in sowing and raising another crop in the garden.' *(Muslim)*..

****

CHAPTER 61

On Prohibition of Miserliness and Niggardliness.

قال الله تعالى : وأَمَّا مَن بَخِلَ وَاسْتَغْنَى وكَذَّبَ بِالحُسْنَى فَسَنُيَسِّرُهُ لِلعُسرَى.ومَا يُغْني عنهُ مالهُ إذا تَرَدَّى [الليل : ٨ — ١١] وقال تعالى: ومَن يُوقَ شُحَّ نَفسِهِ فَأُولَئِكَ هُمُ المُفلِحُونَ [التغابن : ١٦] .

Allah, the Exalted, has said:

189. But as for him who hoardeth and deemeth himself independent, and disbelieveth in goodness; Surely we will ease his way unto adversity. His riches will not save him when he perisheth. (92:8—11)

190. And whoso is saved from his own greed, such are the successful. (64 : 16).

٥٦٣ — وعن جابر رضي الله عنه أنَّ رسولَ الله صلَّى الله عليه وسلم قالَ: اتَّقُوا الظُّلْمَ ، فإنَّ الظُّلْمَ ظُلماتٌ يومَ القِيامة، واتَّقُوا الشُّحَّ ، فإنَّ الشُّحَّ أهلَكَ مَنْ كانَ قبلَكم ،حملَهم على أن سفكُوا دماءهم واستحلُّوا محارِمَهم ». رواه مسلم

563. This Hadis has already been dealt with in No. 203 of Chapter 26.

****

CHAPTER 62

On Self-Sacrifice and Service

قال الله تعالى : ويُؤْثِرُونَ على أنفُسِهِم ولو كانَ بهِم خصَاصَة [الحشر : ٩] وقال تعالى : ويُطعِمُونَ الطَّعامَ على حُبِّهِ مِسكيناً ويتيماً وأسيراً [الدهر : ٨] إلى آخرِ الآياتِ .

Allah, the Exalted, has said:

191. But prefer (the figitives) above themselves though poverty become their lot. (59:9).

192. And feed with food the needy wretch, the orphan and the prisoner, for love of Him (76:8).

٥٦٤ — عن أبي هُريرة رضي الله عنه قال : جاءَ رَجُلٌ إلى النَّبيِّ صلى الله عليه وسلم فقال : إنِّي مَجْهُودٌ ، فأرسَلَ إلى بعضِ نِسائِه ، فقالت : والَّذي بعثَكَ بِالحقِّ ما عِندي إلاَّ ماءٌ، ثم أرسَلَ إلى أُخرَى، فقالَتْ مِثلَ ذلِكَ ، حتَّى قُلْنَ كُلُّهن مِثلَ ذلِكَ : لا والَّذي بعثَكَ بِالحقِّ ما عِندي إلاَّ ماءٌ . فقال النبيُّ صلَّى اللهُ عليه وسلم « من يُضِيفُ هذا اللَّيلَة ؟ » فقال رَجُلٌ

مِن الأنصارِ : أنا يا رسُولَ الله ، فانطَلَقَ بِهِ إلى رَحْلِهِ ، فقال لامرأتِهِ : أكرِمِي ضَيفَ رسول الله صلّى الله عليه وسلم .

وفي روايةٍ قال لامرأتِهِ : هل عندَكِ شيءٌ ؟ فقالتْ : لا ، إلاَّ قُوتَ صِبياني . قال : عَلِّلِيهم بِشيءٍ وإذا أرادُوا العَشاءَ ، فنَوِّمِيهِم ، وإذا دَخَلَ ضَيفُنا ، فأطفِئي السِّرَاجَ ، وأرِيهِ أنَّا نأكُل ؛ فقَعَدُوا وأكَلَ الضَّيفُ وباتا طاوِيَيْنِ ، فلَمَّا أصبَح ، غدَا على النَّبيِّ صلَّى الله عليه وسلم : فقال : « لَقَد عَجِبَ الله مِن صَنِيعِكُما بِضَيفِكُما اللَّيلَةَ » متفقٌ عليه

564. Hazrat Abu Hurairah (R.A.A.) relates that (once) a man came to the Holy Prophet (S.A.W.) and submitted; I am much hungry The Holy Prophet (S.A.W.) sent word to one of his wives (if she could feed the guest); she replied: 'By Allah Who has sent you with the Truth, I have nothing except water.' Then he sent message to another wife and received back the same reply. He sent word turn by turn to everyone of them, and received the same reply (that they have nothing but water with them). Then he addressed his companions and said: 'Who will take this man as his guest?' An Ansar responded: 'O Messenger of Allah (S.A.W.), 'I will.' As such he took him home and asked his wife: 'Entertain and honour this guest of the Holy Prophet (S.A.W.).' According to another version:He asked his wife: 'Have you anything (eatables)?' She answered: 'Nothing, Only a little for my children.' He said: 'Divert them with something, and when they demand food put them to sleep; and when the guest arrives put out the lamp, and pretend as if we have also joined him in eating. As such they sat down and the guest ate and the hosts passed the night without food. When the Ansar went to the Holy Prophet (S.A.W.) next morning, the latter told him: Allah the most Exalted was much pleased with your behaviour with your guest last night.

(Bukhari and Muslim).

٥٦٥ ـ وعنه قالَ : قالَ رسولُ الله صلى الله عليه وسلم : « طَعَامُ الاثنَينِ كافي الثَّلاثَةِ ، وطَعَامُ الثَّلاثَةِ كافي الأربَعَةِ » متفقٌ عليه

وفي روايةٍ لمسلمٍ عن جابرٍ رضي الله عنه ، عن النبي صلى الله عليه وسلم قال :

« طَعَامُ الواحِدِ يَكفِي الاثنَينِ ، وطَعَامُ الاثنَينِ يَكفِي الأربَعَةَ ، وطَعَامُ الأربَعَةِ يَكفِي الثَّمانِيَةَ »

565. Hazrat Abu Hurairah (R.A.A.) relates that the Holy Prophet (S.A.W.) said:'The food of two persons suffices for three, and the food of three is enough to feed four persons' *(Bukhari and Muslim).*

Another version of Muslim quotes Hazrat Jabir (R.A.A.) that the Holy Prophet (S.A.W.) said: The food of one man suffces for two men, the food of two men suffices for four men, and the food of four suffices for eight men.

٥٦٦ — وعن أبي سعيدٍ الخُدريِّ رضي الله عنه قال : بينما نحنُ في سفرٍ مع النبيِّ صلى الله عليه وسلم إذ جاء رجلٌ على راحلةٍ له ، فجعل يصرفُ بصرهُ يميناً وشمالاً ، فقال رسولُ الله صلى الله عليه وسلم : « من كان معهُ فضلُ ظهرٍ فليعُد به على من لا ظهرَ له ، ومن كان له فضلٌ من زادٍ ، فليعُد بهِ على من لا زادَ لهُ » فذكرَ من أصنافِ المالِ ماذكرَ حتى رأينا أنهُ لا حقَّ لأحدٍ منّا في فضلٍ ، رواه مسلم

566. Hazrat Abu Sa'eed Khudri (R.A.A.) relates: Once when we were journeying with the Holy Prophet(S.A.W.) a man came riding his animal and started looking towards right and left. On this the Holy Prophet (S.A.W.) said: Anybody who can spare a mount,should offer it to him who has none(worth riding); and one who has spare food should offer it to him who has not The Holy Prophet (S.A.W.) continued specifying every type of provision till we thought that none of us had any right to a thing which might be surplus with us. *(Muslim).*

٥٦٧ — وعن سهلِ بنِ سعدٍ رضي الله عنه أنَّ امرأةً جاءت إلى رسول الله صلى الله عليه وسلم ببردةٍ منسوجةٍ ، فقالت: نسجتُها بيديَّ لأكسوكها، فأخذها النبيُّ صلى الله عليه وسلم محتاجاً إليها ، فخرجَ إلينا وإنّها لإزارُهُ ، فقال فلانٌ : اكسنيها ما أحسنَها ! فقال : « نعم » فجلسَ النبيُّ صلى الله عليه وسلم في المجلسِ ، ثمَّ رجعَ فطواها ، ثمَّ أرسلَ بها إليه : فقالَ له القومُ : ما أحسنتَ ! لبسها النبيُّ صلى الله عليه وسلم محتاجاً إليها ، ثمَّ سألتهُ ، وعلمتَ أنهُ لايردُّ سائلاً ، فقالَ : إني والله ما سألتهُ لألبسها، إنما سألتهُ لتكونَ كفني . قال سهلٌ : فكانت كفنَهُ . رواه البخاري

567. Hazrat Sahl bin S'ad (R.A.A.) relates that a woman brought a woven piece of sheet to the Holy Prophet (S.A.W.) and said to him:

'This piece of cloth has been woven by my own hands so that you might wear it.' He accepted the gift as he needed it and later came out wearing it as his loin cloth. A man said: 'It is very fine. Please give it to me to wear. 'The Holy Prophet (S.A.W.) said: 'Very well, and remained sitting with us for some time and went inside and sent the sheet duly folded to the man. Some of those present said to the man: 'You have not done well.' The Holy Prophet (S.A.W.) wore it as he needed it, but you asked him to give it to you, and you knew it well that he never refuses who asks him.' He said: 'Indeed, I did not ask for this piece of cloth to wear it, I requested him for it so that it might be used as my shroud(when I die as this cloth is now blessed by the touch of Holy Prophet's (S.A.W.body) and ultimately it serves as such.*(Bukhari)*

٥٦٨ — وعن أبي موسى رضي الله عنه قال : قال رسولُ الله صلى الله عليه وسلم : « إنَّ الأشعَرِيِّينَ إذا أرملُوا في الغزْوِ ، أو قلَّ طعَامُ عيالِهِم بالمدينةِ ، جمَعُوا ما كانَ عِندَهُم في ثوبٍ واحِدٍ ، ثمَّ اقتسَمُوهُ بينَهُم في إناءٍ واحِدٍ بالسَّوِيَّةِ فهُم مِنِّي وأنا منهُم » متفقٌ عليه

568. **Hazrat Abu Musa (R.A.A.)** relates that the Holy Prophet (S.A.W.) said: Then the Ash'arins are faced with shortage of provisions in battle, or while they are at home in Madina, and run short of their supplies, they collect all the provisions their community has in a sheet, and then equally distribute the stuff among themselves. Thus they are of me and I am of them. *(Bukhari and Muslim)*.

Note: Self sacrifice is the highest and last point of generosity. This means that the needs and requirements of others should be given preference over one's own. Islam teaches us to go hungry and to feed others; even one should suffer hardships and provide comfort to others.

****

CHAPTER 63

Striving for the Matters Relating to Hereafter and Longing for Blessed and Virtuous Things

قال الله تعالى : وَفِي ذَٰلِكَ فَلْيَتَنَافَسِ الْمُتَنَافِسُونَ [المطففين : ٢٦] .

Allah, the Exalted, has said:

193. For this let (all) those strive who strive for bliss (83:26).

٥٦٩ — وعن سهلِ بنِ سعدٍ رضي الله عنه أن رسولَ الله صلى الله عليه وسلم

أتِيَ بِشَرَابٍ ، فَشَرِبَ مِنهُ ، وَعَنْ يَمِينِهِ غُلامٌ ، وَعَن يَسَارِهِ الأشيَاخُ ، فقال لِلْغُلامِ : « أتَأذَنُ لي أن أعْطِيَ هؤلاءِ ؟ » فَقَالَ الغُلامُ : لا وَاللهِ يارسُولَ اللهِ لاأُوثِرُ بِنَصيبي مِنكَ أحَداً ، فَتَلَّهُ رسولُ الله صلى الله عليه وسلم في يَدِهِ . متفقٌ عليه

569. Hazrat Sahl Ibn Sa'ad (R.A.A.) relates that while the Holy Prophet (S.A.W.) was sitting in a company some beverage was brought to him (S.A.W.); he drank some of it. At this time on his right was a boy and on his left were elder persons (sheikhs). He said to the boy: 'Would you allow me to give the rest of this drink to those sitting on my left?' The boy said: 'O Messenger of Allah (S.A.W.) by Allah I would certainly not prefer anybody on myself in respect of a bounty to me from you.' As such he gave the rest of the drink to him.

(Bukhari and Muslim).

This boy was no less a person than Hazrat Ibn-i-Abbas, the great interpretor of Holy Quran and a renowned Traditionist.

٥٧٠ – وعن أبي هريرة رضي الله عنه عن النَّبي صلَّى الله عليه وسلم قال: « بَيْنَا أيُّوبُ عليه السلام يَغتَسِلُ عُرياناً ، فَخَرَّ عَلَيْهِ جَرَادٌ مِن ذَهَبٍ، فَجعَلَ أيُّوبُ يَحثِي في ثَوبِهِ ، فَنَادَاهُ رَبُّهُ عَزَّ وَجَلَّ : يَا أيُّوبُ ، ألَمْ أكُنْ أغنَيْتُكَ عَمَّا تَرَى ؟ ! قال : بَلَى وَعِزَّتِكَ ، وَلكِن لا غِنَى بي عَن بَرَكَتِكَ » رواه البخاري

570. Hazrat Abu Hurairah (R.A.A.) relates that the Holy Prophet (S.A.W.) said: While Hazrat Ayub Prophet Job, was bathing without a cover, a golden locust dropped on him. He tried to grab it in a piece of cloth, when he heard Allah the most Exalted, calling him: 'O! Job, have I not made you rich enough to be independent of that which you see (i.e. worldly possessions)? Hazrat Ayub replied: 'Of course, by your Honour, but I am not disinterested towards your bounties, rather I am eager to have them.' *(Bukhari).*

****

CHAPTER 64

The Excellence of the Thankful Rich Person and Acquisition of Legitimate Wealth and to Spend it Appropriately.

قال الله تعالى: فَأَمَّا مَنْ أَعْطَى وَاتَّقَى ۝ وَصَدَّقَ بِالْحُسْنَى ۝ فَسَنُيَسِّرُهُ لِلْيُسْرَى [الليل: ٥ – ٧] وقال تعالى: وَسَيُجَنَّبُهَا الأَتْقَى ۝ الَّذي يُؤْتِي

مالَهُ يتزكّى • وما لأحدٍ عِندَهُ مِن نِعمةٍ تُجزى • إلاّ ابتِغاءَ وجهِ ربِّهِ الأعلى • ولَسوفَ يرضى [الليل: ١٧ — ٢١] وقال تعالى : إن تُبْدُوا الصّدقاتِ فنِعِمّاً هِيَ وإن تُخفُوهَا وتُؤْتُوهَا الفُقَرَاءَ فهوَ خيرٌ لَكُم ويُكَفِّرُ عَنكُمْ سيّئَاتِكُمْ واللهُ بِما تَعملُونَ خَبيرٌ [البقرة: ٢٧١] وقال تعالى : لن تَنَالوا البِرَّ حتى تُنفِقُوا مِمّا تُحِبُّون وما تُنفِقُوا مِن شيءٍ فإنّ اللهَ بِهِ عَليمٌ [آل عمران : ٩٢] والآيات في فضلِ الإنفاقِ في الطاعات كثيرةٌ مَعلُومَةٌ .

Allah, the Exalted, has said:

194. As for him who giveth and is dutiful (toward Allah) and believeth in goodness; surely We will ease his way unto the state of ease. (92:5–7).

195. Far removed from it will be the righteous who giveth his wealth that he may grow (in goodness), and none hath with him any favour for reward, except as seeking (to fulfil) the purpose of his Lord Most High. He verily will be content. (92:17–21).

196. If ye publish your almsgiving, it is well, but if ye hide it and give it to the poor, it will be better for you, and will atone for some of your ill-deeds. Allah is informed of what ye do. (2:271).

197. Ye will not attain unto piety until ye spend of that which ye love. And whatsoever ye spend, Allah is aware thereof (3:92).

٥٧١ — وعن عبد الله بن مسعود رضي الله عنه قال : قال رسولُ الله صلى الله عليه وسلم : « لا حَسَدَ إلاّ في اثنتَينِ : رجُلٌ آتاهُ اللهُ مالاً ، فَسلّطَهُ على هلَكتِه في الحقِّ ، ورجلٌ آتاه الله حِكمَةً فهو يقضي بِها ويُعلّمُهَا » متفقٌ عليه وتقدم شرحه قريباً

571. This Hadis has already been discussed in No. 544 of Chapter 60.

٥٧٢ — وعن ابنِ عمر رضي الله عنهما عن النبي صلى الله عليه وسلم قال : « لا حَسَدَ إلاّ في اثنتَينِ : رجُلٌ آتاهُ اللهُ القرآنَ ، فهو يقُومُ بِهِ آناءَ الليلِ وآناءَ النّهارِ ، ورَجلٌ آتاهُ اللهُ مالاً ، فهوَ يُنفِقُهُ آناءَ الليلِ وآناءَ النّهارِ » متفقٌ عليه

572. Hazrat Ibn Umar (R.A.A.) relates that the Holy Prophet (S.A.W.) said: You should not be envious of anyone save: One he upon whom Allah bestows the (knowledge of) Quran and he studies and paractices it through the day and night; and the other whom Allah gives wealth and he spends if in the cause of Allah, throughout the night and day.'

(Bukhari and Muslim)..

٥٧٣ – وعن أبي هريرة رضيَ الله عنه أنَّ فُقَرَاءَ المُهَاجِرِينَ أتَوْا رسول
الله صلى الله عليه وسلم . فقالوا : ذَهَبَ أهلُ الدُّثُورِ بالدَّرَجاتِ العُلَى ،
والنَّعِيمِ المُقِيمِ ، فقَالَ : « ومَا ذَاكَ ؟ » فقَالُوا : يُصَلُّونَ كمَا نُصَلِّي ،
ويَصُومُونَ كما نَصُومُ ، ويَتَصَدَّقُونَ ولانَتَصَدَّقُ ، ويَعتِقُونَ ولا نَعتِقُ ،
فقال رسولُ الله صلَّى الله عليه وسلم : « أفلا أُعَلِّمُكُمْ شيئاً تُدرِكُونَ بِهِ مَنْ
سَبَقَكُمْ ، وتَسْبِقُونَ بِهِ مَنْ بَعْدَكُمْ ، ولَا يَكُونُ أحَدٌ أفضَلَ مِنكُمْ
إلاَّ مَنْ صَنَعَ مِثلَ ما صَنَعتُمْ ؟ » قالوا : بلَى يارسولَ الله ، قَالَ : « تُسَبِّحُونَ ،
وتَحمَدُونَ وتُكَبِّرُونَ ، دُبُرَ كُلِّ صَلاةٍ ثَلاثاً وثَلاثِينَ مَرَّةً » فرَجَعَ فُقَرَاءُ
المُهَاجِرِينَ إلى رسولِ الله صلى الله عليه وسلم ، فقَالُوا : سَمِعَ إخْوانُنَا أهْلُ
الأَموَالِ بِمَا فَعَلْنَا ، ففَعَلوا مِثْلَهُ ؟ فقَالَ رسولُ الله صلى الله عليه وسلم :
« ذلكَ فَضْلُ الله يُؤْتِيهِ مَن يَشَاءُ » متفقٌ عليه وهذا لفظ روايةِ مسلم .

573. Hazrat Abu Hurairah (R.A.A.) relates that some of the poor among the emigrants came to the Holy Prophet (S.A.W.) and submitted: The wealthy have achieved all big ranks and permanent bounties.' He said: 'How is that?' They answered: 'They pray in the same way as we do, and observe the fast in the same way as we do; but they spend (their money) in charity which we cannot, and they set the slaves free, but we being poor cannot do so.' He said: 'May I tell you something by which you may overtake those who are leading you, and will keep ahead of those who are following you, and no one will excel you unless he does the same thing which you do?' They said: 'Certainly, O! Messenger of Allah (S.A.W.)' He said: 'After each prayer recite *Subhan-Allah* (Glory to Allah), *Al-Hamdo Lillah* (All praise to Allah) and *Allah-o-Akbar* (Allah is greatest) each thirty-three times after each (Salat) Service. Soon after they came back to the Holy Prophet (S.A.W.) and said: 'O! Messenger of Allah) Our Wealthy brethren having come to know what we are doing, and have started doing the same.' The Holy Prophet said: 'This is Allah's bounty. He gives it to whomsoever He wills.'

(Bukhari and Muslim).

****

CHAPTER 65

Remembering the Death And Lesser of Aspirations.

قال الله تعالى : كُلُّ نَفْسٍ ذَائِقَةُ الموتِ وإنَّمَا تُوفَّوْنَ أُجُورَكُم يَوْمَ القِيامَةِ فَمَن زُحْزِحَ عَنِ النَّارِ وأُدخِلَ الجَنَّةَ فَقَدْ فَازَ وما الحَيَاةُ الدُّنْيا إلاَّ مَتَاعُ الغُرُورِ [آل عمران : ١٨٥] وقال تعالى : وما تَدرِي نفسٌ ماذا تَكْسِبُ غداً وما تَدرِي نَفسٌ بِأيِّ أرضٍ تَموتُ [لقمان : ٣٤] وقال تعالى : فإذا جاءَ أجَلُهُم لا يَستَأخِرُونَ ساعَةً ولا يَستَقدِمون [النحل : ٦١] وقال تعالى : يا أيُّها الَّذينَ آمَنُوا لا تُلْهِكُمْ أموالُكُم ولا أولادُكُم عَن ذِكرِ الله ،ومن يَفعَلْ ذلكَ فأُولئكَ هم الخاسِرُونَ * وأنفِقُوا مِمَّا رَزَقْناكُم مِن قَبلِ أن يأتِيَ أحَدَكُمُ المَوْتُ فيَقُولَ رَبِّ لولا أخَّرْتَنِي إلى أجَلٍ قَرِيبٍ فأصَّدَّقَ وأكُنْ مِنَ الصَّالِحِينَ * ولن يُؤخِّرَ الله نفساً إذا جاءَ أجَلُها والله خَبيرٌ بِما تعمَلُونَ [المنافقون : ٩ ــ ١١] وقال تعالى : حتَّى إذا جاءَ أحَدَهُمُ المَوْتُ قالَ رَبِّ ارجِعُونِ لعَلِّي أعمَلُ صَالِحاً فيما تَرَكتُ كلاَّ إنَّها كَلِمَةٌ هو قائِلُها ومِن وَرائِهِم بَرزَخٌ إلى يَوْمِ يُبْعَثُونَ * فإذا نُفِخَ في الصُّورِ فلا أنسابَ بَينَهُم يومَئِذٍ ولا يَتساءَلُونَ * فمَنْ ثَقُلَتْ مَوَازِينُهُ فأُولئكَ هُمُ المُفلِحُونَ * ومَن خَفَّتْ مَوازِينُهُ فأُولئكَ الَّذينَ خَسِرُوا أنفُسَهُم في جهَنَّمَ خالِدُونَ * تَلفَحُ وُجُوهَهُمُ النَّارُ وَهُم فيها كالِحُونَ * ألَمْ تَكُن آياتي تُتلَى عليكُمْ فكُنتُمْ بِها تُكَذِّبُونَ إلى قوله تعالى: ..كَمْ لَبِثتُم في الأرضِ عَدَدَ سِنِينَ * قالُوا : لَبِثنا يوماً أو بَعضَ يَوم فاسأَلِ العَادِّينَ * قال: إن لَبِثتُمْ إلاَّ قَليلاً لو أنَّكُم كُنتُم تعلَمُونَ * أفحَسِبتُم أنَّما خَلَقناكُم عَبثاً وأنَّكُم إلينا لا تُرجَعُونَ [المؤمنون : ٩٩ ــ ١١٥] وقال تعالى : ألَم يأنِ لِلَّذينَ آمَنُوا أن تَخشَعَ قُلُوبُهُمْ لِذكرِ الله ومَا نَزَلَ مِنَ الحَقِّ ولا يَكُونُوا كالَّذِينَ أُوتُوا الكِتابَ مِن قَبلُ فطالَ عليهِمُ الأمَدُ فقَسَتْ قُلُوبُهُم وكَثيرٌ مِنهُم فاسِقُونَ [الحديد : ١٦] والآيات في الباب كثيرة معلومة .

Allah, the Exalted, has said:

198. Every should will taste of death. And ye will be paid on the Day of Resurrection only that which ye have fairly earned. Whoso is removed from the Fire and is made to enter Paradise, he indeed is triumphant. The life of this world is but comfort of illusion. (3:185)
199. No soul knoweth what it will earn tomorrow, and no soul knoweth in what land it will die. (31:34).
200. And when their term cometh they cannot put (it) off an hour nor (yet) advance (it). (16:61).
201. O ye who believe! Let not your wealth nor your children distract you from remembrance of Allah. Those who do so, they are the losers. And spend of that wherewith we have provided you before death cometh unto one of you and he saith: My Lord! If only Thou wouldst reprieve me for a little while, then I would give alms and be among the righteous. But Allah reprieveth no soul when its term cometh, and Allah is Aware of what ye do. (63:9—11).
202. Until, when death cometh unto one of them, he saith: My Lord! send me back, that I may do right in that which I have left behind! But nay. It is but a word that he speaketh; and behind them is a barrier until the day when they are raised..... Deemed ye then that We had created you for naught and that ye would not be returned unto us. (23:99—115).
203. It is not the time ripe for the hearts of those who believe to submit to Allah's reminder and to the truth which is revealed, that they become not as those who received the scripture of old but the term was prolonged for them and so their hearts were hardened, and many of them are evil-livers. (57:16).

٥٧٤ ـ وعن ابن عمر رضي الله عنهما قال : أَخَذَ رسولُ الله صلى الله عليه وسلم بِمَنكِبي فَقَالَ : «كُنْ في الدُّنيا كأنَّكَ غَريبٌ أو عابِرُ سَبيلٍ» وكَانَ ابنُ عُمَرَ رضي الله عنهما يقول : إذا أمسيتَ ، فلا تَنتظِرِ الصَّبَاحَ ، وإذَا أصبحتَ ، فلا تَنتظِرِ المَسَاءَ ، وَخُذ مِن صِحَّتِكَ لِمَرَضِكَ ، وَمِن حَيَاتِكَ لِمَوتِكَ » رواه البخاري

574. This Hadith has already been covered in item No. 471, in Chapter 55.

٥٧٥ ـ وعنه أنَّ رسولَ الله صلى الله عليه وسلم قال : « ماحَقُّ امرِئٍ مُسلِمٍ ، لَهُ شَيءٌ يُوصي فيهِ ، يَبيتُ لَيلَتَينِ إلاَّ وَوَصِيَّتُهُ مَكتُوبَةٌ عِندَهُ » متفقٌ عليه هذا لفظ البخاري .

وفي رواية لمسلم «يَبِيتُ ثَلاثَ لَيَالٍ» قال ابن عمر: مَا مَرَّتْ عَلَيَّ لَيْلَةٌ مُنْذُ سَمِعتُ رسولَ الله صلى الله عليه وسلم قال ذلِكَ إلاَّ وَعِنْدِي وَصِيَّتِي

575. Hazrat Abdullah ibn 'Umar (R.A.A.) relates that the Holy Prophet (S.A.W.) said: If a Muslim has something (which could be inherited by his successors) he should not let even two nights pass without executing a written testament (*Bukhari* and *Muslim*).

These words are those of *Imam Bukhari.* According to a tradition reported by *Imam Muslim*, a Muslim should not pass even three nights without a written deed of will. Hazrat Ibn Umar (R.A.A.) says: Ever since I heard the Holy Prophet (S.A.W.) say this, I have not passed even a single night without my written deed of will with me.

٥٧٦ – وعن أنس رضي الله عنه قال: خَطَّ النَّبِيُّ صلى الله عليه وسلم خُطُوطاً فقال: «هَذَا الإنسَانُ، وَهَذَا أجَلُهُ، فَبَيْنَمَا هُوَ كَذَلِكَ إذ جَاءَ الخَطُّ الأَقْرَبُ» رواه البخاري

576. Hazrat Anas Bin Malik (R.A.A.) says that the Holy Prophet (S.A.W.) drew some lines, and then pointing to a line said: This line is a a person, and the other one is the time of his death. The person continues to live his life with ambitions, till he is overtaken by the nearest line, that is death overtakes him. *(Bukhari).*

٥٧٧ – وعن ابنِ مسعُودٍ رضيَ الله عنه قال: خَطَّ النَّبِيُّ صلّى الله عليه وسلَّم خطّاً مُرَبَّعاً، وَخَطَّ خطّاً في الوَسَطِ خَارِجاً مِنْهُ، وَخَطَّ خُطَطاً صِغَاراً إلى هَذَا الَّذي في الوَسَطِ مِنْ جَانِبِهِ الَّذِي في الوَسَطِ، فقَالَ: «هَذَا الإنسَانُ، وَهَذَا أجَلُهُ مُحِيطاً بِهِ – أو قَد أحَاطَ بِهِ – وَهَذَا الَّذِي هُوَ خَارِجٌ أمَلُهُ، وَهَذِهِ الخُطَطُ الصِّغَارُ الأعْرَاضُ، فَإن أخْطَأهُ هَذَا، نَهَشَهُ هَذا، وَإنْ أخْطَأهُ هَذا نَهَشَهُ هَذا» رواه البخاري . وَهَذِهِ صُورَتُهُ:

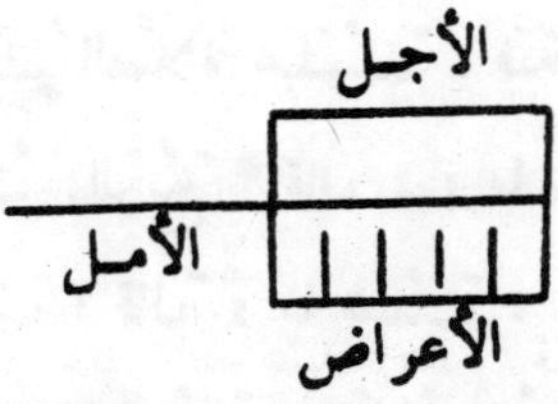

577. Hazrat Abdullah ibn Mas'ud (R.A.A.) relates that the Holy Prophet (S.A.W.) drew a rectangular figure and in its middle he drew a line lengthwise; the upper end of this line jutted out a little beyond the

rectangle. Further across this middle line, he drew a number of smaller lines horizontally. He indicated that the figure represented man, that the encircling rectangle was death which is covering him; the middle line represents his desires and the short lines across it were the trials or ups and downs of life.. He said: If he escapes from one of these, he falls a victim to the next and when he gets rid from this, the third catches him and so on.. The sketch was like this. *(Bukhari).*

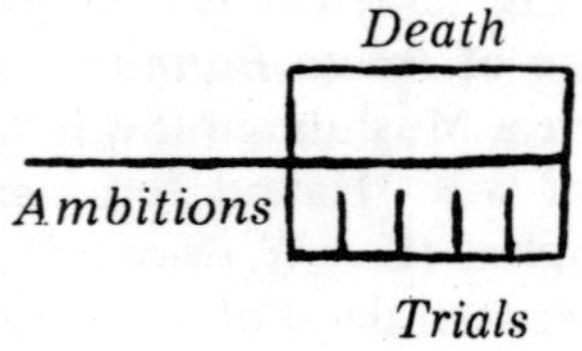

٥٧٨ – وعن أبي هريرة رضيَ اللهُ عنه أنَّ رسُولَ اللهِ صلى اللهُ عليه وسلم قال : « بادِرُوا بِالأعْمالِ سبْعاً ، هَل تَنْتَظِرُونَ إلاَّ فَقْراً مُنْسِياً أو غِنىً مُطغِياً ، أوْ مَرَضاً مُفسِداً ، أو هَرَماً مُفَنِّداً ، أو مَوتاً مُجْهِزاً أوِ الدَّجَّالَ ، فَشَرُّ غائِبٍ يُنْتَظَرُ ، أوِ السَّاعَةُ وَالسَّاعَةُ أدْهَى وأمَرُّ ؟ ! » رواهُ التِّرمذي وقال : حديثٌ حسنٌ .

578. This Hadis has been covered in No. 93, Chapter 10.

٥٧٩ – وعنه قالَ : قالَ رسولُ الله صلَّى اللهُ عليه وسلم : « أكثِرُوا ذِكْرَ هاذِمِ اللَّذَّاتِ » يَعني المَوْتَ ، رواهُ التِّرمذي وقال : حديثٌ حسنٌ .

579. Hazrat Abu Hurairah (R.A.A.) relates that the Holy Prophet (S.A.W.) said: Remember often death, the terminator of pleasures. *(Tirmizi).*

٥٨٠ – وعن أُبَيِّ بنِ كعب رَضيَ اللهُ عنه : كانَ رَسولُ اللهِ صلى الله عليه وسلَّم إذا ذَهَبَ ثُلثُ اللَّيلِ ، قامَ فقالَ : « يا أيها النَّاسُ اذْكُرُوا الله جاءَتِ الرَّاجِفَةُ تَتْبَعُها الرَّادِفَةُ ، جاءَ المَوْتُ بما فيهِ ، جاءَ المَوْتُ بما فيهِ » قلتُ : يا رَسُولَ اللهِ إني أُكثِرُ الصَّلاةَ عَلَيْكَ ، فكَمْ أجْعَلُ لكَ مِن صَلاتي ؟ قال : « ما شِئْتَ » قُلْتُ : الرُّبُعَ ؟ قال : « ما شِئْتَ ، فَإنْ زِدْتَ فَهُوَ خيْرٌ لكَ » قُلْتُ : فالنِّصفَ ؟ قالَ « ما شِئْتَ ، فإنْ زِدْتَ فهو خيرٌ لكَ » قُلْتُ : فالثلثَينِ ؟ قالَ : ما شِئْتَ ، فَإنْ زِدْتَ فَهُوَ خيْرٌ لكَ » قُلْتُ : أجْعَلُ لكَ صَلاتي كُلَّها ؟ قال : « إذاً تُكفى هَمَّكَ ، ويُغفَرُ لك

ذَنْبُكَ ، رواهُ الترمذي وقال : حديث حسن .

580. Hazrat Ubayy ibn Ka'ab (R.A.A.) relates that when a third of the night passed the Holy Prophet (S.A.W.) used to get up and call out: 'O people, remember Allah; the first Call (of the trumpet of Angel Israfil) has sounded; after this comes the second Call. It is accompanied with death, and all that it comprises'. _ I said to the Holy Prophet (S.A.W.): 'O! Messenger of Allah (S.A.W.)., I invoke Allah's peace and blessings upon you copiously: how much time should I ear-mark for this?' He said: As much time as you think proper. I submitted: 'A quarter of my time?' He said: 'As much you wish; but it would be better for you, if you could devote more time.' I said:'Half of my time?' He said: 'Whatever you wish; but it would be (still) better for you, if you were to increase it.' Then I said: 'Two-thirds of my time?' He said: 'As much you wish; but it would be(still) better for you if you were to increase it.' I said: 'Shall I devote all my time (supplications) to reciting Salat (benediction) on you?' He said: 'Then it will take care of all your worries and your sins will be forgiven.' *(Tirmizi)*

Note: The death is a very horrible thing and the events that take place thereafter are even more terrible. To talk about them or recall them, makes the life in this world tasteless, and removes the love of this mortal world from the heart. In fact the love and attachment for this world is the root-cause of all evils and sins. Therefore, when there will be no love left for this world, then one will get all that is desired and everlasting. The rememberance and concern for death is the means for developing hatred and disregard for this world. For this reason, the Holy Quran and the Ahadis have laid great stress to this point.

****

CHAPTER 66

Preference to Visit Graves for Males and What the Visitor Should Say

٥٨١ — عن بُرَيْدَةَ ، رضيَ اللهُ عنه، قال : قال رسُولُ اللهِ صلى اللهُ عليه وسلم : « كُنْتُ نَهيتُكُمْ عَنْ زِيارَةِ القُبُورِ فَزُورُوها » رواهُ مسلم

581. Hazrat Buraidah (R.A.A.) relates that the Holy Prophet (S.A.W.) said: '(Earlier) I had aked you not to visit the graves but now you may visit them.' *(Muslim).*

٥٨٢ — وعن عائشةَ رضيَ اللهُ عنها قالت : كان رسُولُ اللهِ ، صلّى اللهُ عليه وسلم ، كُلَّما كانَ لَيْلَتها مِنْ رسولِ الله صلّى الله عليه وسلم يَخْرُجُ مِنْ آخِرِ اللَّيْلِ إلى البَقِيعِ ، فيَقُولُ : « السَّلامُ عَلَيْكُمْ دارَ قَوْمٍ مؤمِنِينَ ،

وأتاكُمْ ما تُوعَدُونَ، غداً مُؤَجَّلُونَ، وإنّا إنْ شاءَ اللهُ بِكُمْ لاحِقُونَ ،
اللَّهُمَّ اغفِرْ لأهْلِ بَقيعِ الغَرْقَدِ » رواهُ مسلم

582. Hazrat Ayesha (R.A.A.) relates that when it was the turn of the Holy Prophet to stay with her, he would get up during the latter part of the night, and go to the grave-yard of Baqi' (near Madina) and greet the inmates of the graves thus: 'Peace. be on you. O! The believers of the faith and dwellers of this home. May you be given on the Day of Judgment the thing which has been promised, and you have been given respite for a fixed time. We shall, if Allah so Wills, join you. Forgive, O Allah, the inmates of the graves of Baqi'. *(Muslim)*

٥٨٣ ـ وعن بُرَيْدَةَ رضيَ اللهُ عنهُ، قال: كانَ النَّبيُّ صَلّى اللهُ عليهِ وسلم يُعَلِّمُهُمْ إذا خرَجُوا إلى المَقابِرِ أنْ يَقُولَ قائِلُهُم: « السَّلامُ عَلَيْكُمْ أهْلَ الدِّيارِ مِنَ المُؤْمِنِينَ والمُسْلِمِينَ وَإنّا إنْ شاءَ اللهُ بِكُمْ لاحِقُونَ ، أسْألُ اللهَ لَنَا ولَكُمُ العافِيَةَ » رواهُ مسلم

583. Hazrat Buraidah (R.A.A.) relates that the Holy Prophet (S.A.W.) used to instruct the Muslims that when visiting a graveyard they should say: 'O! the believers and Muslims, who are the dwellers of this place! Peace be on you. If Allah Wills, we shall also join you. I pray to Allah for security for you and for ourselves. *(Muslim)*

٥٨٤ ـ وعن ابنِ عبَّاسٍ، رَضيَ اللهُ عنهما، قال: مرَّ رسُولُ اللهِ صلى الله عليهِ وسلَّم بِقُبُورٍ بالمَدِينَةِ فَأقْبَلَ عَلَيْهِمْ بوَجْهِهِ فقالَ: « السَّلامُ عَلَيْكُمْ يا أهْلَ القُبُورِ ، يَغْفِرُ اللهُ لَنا ولَكُمْ ، أنْتُم سَلَفُنا ونَحْنُ بالأثَرِ » رواهُ الترمذي وقال: حديث حسن .

584. Hazrat Ibn Abbas (R.A.A.) relates that the Holy Prophet (S.A.W.) once passed by some graves in Medina. Facing towards them he said:'Peace be on you, O the dwellers of the graves! May Allah forgive you and us. You have preceded us, and we will follow you.'(*Imam Tirmizi* has reported this tradition,w hcih he calls as good).

****

CHAPTER 67

Abhorrance of Praying for Death on Account of Some Impending Calamity, and Justification for a Longing for Death Apprhending Some Mischief in Religion.

٥٨٥ ــ عَنْ أبي هُريرةرضيَ اللهُ عنه أنَّ رسُولَ اللهِ صلى اللهُ عليه وسلم
قالَ : « لا يتَمَنَّ أحَدُكُم الموْتَ إمّا مُحسِناً ، فلَعلّهُ يزْدادُ ، وإمّا مُسيئاً
فلَعلّهُ يَستَعْتِبُ » متفقٌ عليه وهذا لفظ البخاري .

وفي روايةٍ لمسلم عن أبي هُرَيْرَة رضيَ اللهُ عنه عن رسُولِ اللهِ صلى اللهُ عليه
وسلم قال : « لا يتَمَنَّ أحَدُكُمُ الموْتَ ، ولا يَدْعُ بهِ مِنْ قَبْلِ أنْ يأتيَهُ ؛
إنّهُ إذا ماتَ انقَطَعَ عمَلُهُ ، وإنّهُ لا يَزيدُ المؤْمِنَ عُمُرُهُ إلاَّ خيراً »

585. Hazrat Abu Hurairah (R.A.A.) relates that the Holy Prophet (S.A.W.) said: 'None of you should pray for (his own) death, because if he is a good person, it is possible that he might add to his virtuous deeds, and if he is not a good person he might get a chance to rectify his (evil) past. *(Bukhari and Muslim).*

These words are those of *Imam Bukhari* There is another report from *Muslim* on this subject: Holy Prophet (S.A.W.) said: 'None of you should long for death, nor he should pray for it, before it comes; because when it arrives it will terminate his deeds. The life of a believer does not increase but good (for him).'

٥٨٦ ــ وعن أنسٍ رضيَ اللهُ عنه قال : قالَ رسُولُ اللهِ صلى اللهُ عليه
وسلّم : « لا يتَمَنَّيَنَّ أحَدُكُم الموْتَ لِضُرٍّ أصابَهُ فإنْ كانَ لا بُدَّ
فاعِلاً ، فلْيَقُلْ : اللّهُمَّ أحْيِني ما كانَتِ الحَياةُ خَيْراً لي ، وتَوفَّني إذا
كانَتِ الوَفاةُ خيراً لي » متفقٌ عليهِ

586. This Hadis is the same as No. 40 of Chapter 3.

٥٨٧ ــ وعَنْ قَيسِ بنِ أبي حازمٍ قالَ : دَخَلْنا على خبَّابِ بنِ الأرَتِّ
رضيَ اللهُ عنه نَعودُهُ وقدِ اكتَوى سَبْعَ كَيّاتٍ فقال : إنَّ أصْحابَنا الّذينَ
سَلَفُوا مَضَوْا ، ولمْ تَنْقُصْهُم الدُّنيا ، وإنّا أصَبْنا ما لا نجِدُ لَهُ مَوْضِعاً
إلاَّ الترابَ ولَوْلا أنَّ النبيَّ صلى اللهُ عليهِ وسلم نهانا أنْ نَدْعُوَ بالموْتِ
لَدَعَوْتُ بهِ ، ثُمَّ أتَيْناهُ مرَّةً أخرى وهُوَ يَبْني حائطاً لَهُ ، فقال : إنَّ

المُسْلِمَ لَيُؤْجَرُ في كُلِّ شَيءٍ يُنْفِقُهُ إلاَّ في شَيءٍ يَجْعَلُهُ في هذا التراب .

متفقٌ عليه ، وهذا لفظ رواية البخاري .

587. Hazrat Qais ibn Abi Hazim (R.A.A.) relates: 'We visited Hazrat Khabab ibn Arat (R.A.A.) during his illness. He had had his blood veins open at seven points. He said: Our companions who have died before, have lost nothing in this world; and we have acquired only such worldly things whose place is in the earth. If the Holy Prophet (S.A.W.) had not forbidden us from soliciting death, I would have prayed for it.' Hazrat Qais (R.A.A.) further says: 'We visited him again when he was repairing a wall of his house.' He said: 'There is a reward for a Muslim on everything on which he spends money, except when he commits it to clay (i.e. in building the houses.)' *(Bukhari and Muslim).*

****

CHAPTER 68

On Piety and Discarding the Doubtful

قالَ اللهُ تعالى : ﴿ وَتَحْسَبُونَهُ هَيِّناً وهُوَ عِنْدَ اللهِ عَظِيمٌ ﴾ [النور : ١٥]

وقالَ تعالى : ﴿ إنَّ رَبَّكَ لَبالمِرْصادِ ﴾ [الفجر . ١٤] .

Allah, the Exalted, has said:

204. Ye counted it a trifle. In the sight of Allah it is very great (24:15).

205. Lo! Thy Lord is ever Watchful. (89:14).

٥٨٨ ــ وعن النُّعمانِ بنِ بَشيرٍ رضيَ اللهُ عنهما قال: سَمِعْتُ رسُولَ اللهِ صلى الله عليهِ وسلَّم يقولُ : « إنَّ الحَلالَ بَيِّنٌ ، وإنَّ الحرامَ بَيِّنٌ ، وبَيْنَهما مُشْتَبِهاتٌ لا يَعْلَمُهُنَّ كَثيرٌ مِنَ النَّاسِ ، فَمَنِ اتَّقى الشبُهاتِ ، اسْتَبْرَأَ لِدينِهِ وعِرْضِهِ ، وَمَنْ وَقَعَ في الشبُهاتِ ، وَقَعَ في الحَرامِ ، كالرَّاعي يَرْعى حَوْلَ الحِمَى يُوشِكُ أَنْ يَرْتَعَ فيهِ ، أَلاَ وإنَّ لِكُلِّ مَلِكٍ حِمىً ، أَلاَ وإنَّ حِمَى اللهِ مَحارِمُهُ ، أَلاَ وإنَّ في الجَسَدِ مُضْغَةً إذا صَلَحَتْ صَلَحَ الجَسَدُ كُلُّهُ ، وإذا فَسَدَتْ فَسَدَ الجَسَدُ كُلُّهُ : أَلاَ وَهِيَ القَلْبُ » متفقٌ عليه . ورَوَياهُ مِنْ طُرُقٍ بألْفاظٍ مُتَقارِبَةٍ .

588. Hazrat Nu'man bin Bashir (R.A.A.) relates that he heard the Holy Prophet (S.A.W.) say: 'That which is lawful is clear and also that which is unlawful is quite clear; and between these two is that which is ambiguous, which most people do not know. One who avoids the doubtful, safeguards his faith and his honour, but one who gets involved in the doubtful, falls in unlawful activities. His case is like the shepherd who grazes his flock in the vicinity of an exclusively reserved pasture but is always apprehensive that some of his animals might get into the pasture. Beware that, every king has an exclusively demarcated pasture. Take warning! that Allah's pastures are things which He has forbidden. Also be warned! In the human body there is a lump of flesh; when it is healthy the whole body is healthy and when it is unwell, the whole body is unwell and this (lump) is the heart.

(Bukhari and Muslim).

٥٨٩ ـ وعن أنس رضيَ اللهُ عنه أنَّ النبيَّ صلى اللهُ عليه وسلم ، وَجَدَ تَمْرَةً في الطَّرِيقِ ، فقالَ : « لَوْلاَ أَنِّي أَخافُ أَنْ تَكُونَ مِنَ الصَّدَقَةِ لأَكَلْتُها » متفقٌ عليه

589. Hazrat Anas Bin Malik (R.A.A.) relates that the Holy Prophet (S.A.W.) (once) saw a dry date lying on the thorough fare and said: 'Had I not been afraid, that it might have been earmarked for charity, I would have eaten it.' *(Bukhari and Muslim).*

٥٩٠ ـ وعن النَّوَّاسِ بنِ سَمعانَ رضيَ اللهُ عنه عن النبي صلى اللهُ عليه وسلم قال : « البِرُّ حُسْنُ الخُلُقِ ، وَالإِثْمُ ما حاكَ في نَفْسِكَ ، وكَرِهْتَ أَنْ يَطَّلِعَ عَلَيْهِ النَّاسُ » رواهُ مسلم

590. Hazrat Nawwas ibn Sam'an (R.A.A). relates that the Holy Prophet (S.A.W.) said: 'Virtue is good conduct, and sin is that which pinches your mind and you feel afraid if people should come to know of the same.'

(Muslim).

٥٩١ ـ وعن وابصةَ بنِ معبدٍ رضيَ اللهُ عنه قال : أَتَيْتُ رسُولَ اللهِ صلَّى اللهُ عليه وسلم فقال : « جِئْتَ تَسأَلُ عَنِ البِرِّ ؟ » قلت : نعم ، فقال : « استَفْتِ قَلْبَكَ ، البِرُّ : ما اطْمَأَنَّتْ إِلَيْهِ النَّفْسُ ، واطْمَأَنَّ إِلَيْهِ القَلْبُ ، والإِثْمُ ما حاكَ في النَّفْسِ وتَرَدَّدَ في الصَّدْرِ ، وإِنْ أَفْتاكَ النَّاسُ وَأَفْتَوكَ » حديثٌ حسن ، رواهُ أحمدُ ، والدَّارِميُّ في « مُسْنَدَيْهِما »

591. Hazrat Wabisa bin Ma'bad (R.A.A.) relates: 'Once I went to the Holy Prophet (S.A.W.) when, he asked me: 'Have you come to know what is virtue?' I said: 'Yes, Sir! He said: 'Just ask your heart about it.' Virtue is a thing which satisfies your soul and eases the heart; and sin is a thing which disturbs the soul and worries the heart; although some persons may declare it lawful and may solicit your opinion on such matters.' (*Imam Ahmad* and *Darmi* have cited this tradition, which is good).

٥٩٢ – وعن أبي سِرْوَعَةَ – بكسر السين المهملة ونصبها – عُقْبَةَ بن الحارثِ رضيَ اللهُ عنهُ أنَّهُ تزوّجَ ابنَةً لأبي إهاب بنِ عزيزٍ ، فأتتهُ امرأةٌ فقالت : إنّي قد أرْضَعْتُ عُقْبَةَ والّتي قدْ تزوّجَ بها ، فقالَ لها عُقْبَةُ : ما أعلَمُ أنّكِ أرْضَعْتِني ولاَ أخبرتِني ، فركِبَ إلى رسُولِ اللهِ صلى اللهُ عليهِ وسلم بالمَدينَةِ ، فسألَهُ ، فقال رسُولُ الله صلى اللهُ عليه وسلم : « كيْفَ ، وقَدْ قيلَ ؟ ! » ففارَقَها عُقْبَةُ ونَكَحَتْ زوْجاً غيرَهُ » .

رواهُ البخاري .

592. Hazrar Abu Sirw'a 'Ubqah bin Haris (R.A.A.) relates that he married the daughter of Abu Ihab ibn Aziz. Afterwards a woman came to him and said that Uqbah and the daughter of Abu Ihab who have married each other have been milked by her. Uqbah retorted: 'I do not know that you have milked me, nor did you inform me before.' Then he rode to the Holy Prophet (S.A.W.) in Madina and sought his directions. He said: 'Now since that this fact has been revealed (that she is your foster sister), how can both of you continue to live as husband and wife?' As such 'Uqbah separated her and she married another person. *(Bukhari)*

٥٩٣ – وعنِ الحَسَنِ بن عليٍّ رضيَ اللهُ عنهما ، قال : حَفِظْتُ مِنْ رسُولِ اللهِ صلى اللهُ عليهِ وسلم : « دَعْ ما يَريبُكَ إلى مَا لا يَريبُكَ » رواهُ الترمذي وقال : حديث حسن صحيح .

593. Hazrat Imam Hasan ibn Ali (R.A.A.) says: 'I have learnt from the Holy Prophet (S.A.W.) and preserved this (in my memory): 'Leave those things which create doubts in your mind and adopt that which does not create any doubt in your mind. *(Tirmizi).*

٥٩٤ – وعن عائشةَ رضيَ اللهُ عنها ، قالت : كانَ لأبي بكْرٍ الصِّدِّيقِ ، رضيَ اللهُ عنهُ ، غلامٌ يُخرِجُ لَهُ الخراجَ وكانَ أبو بكْرٍ يأكُلُ مِنْ خراجِهِ ، فجاءَ يوماً بشَيْءٍ ، فأكلَ مِنهُ أبو بكْرٍ ، فقالَ لَهُ الغُلامُ : تدْرِي مَا هذا ؟ فقالَ أبو بكْرٍ : ومَا هوَ ؟ قالَ : كُنْتُ تكَهّنْتُ

لإنسان في الجاهلية ، وما أحسن الكهانة إلا أني خدعته ، فلقيني ، فأعطاني بذلك هذا الذي أكلت منه ، فأدخل أبو بكر يده فقاء كل شيء في بطنه ، رواه البخاري

594. Hazrat Ayesha (R.A.A.) relates: 'Hazrat Abu Bakr (R.A.A.) had a slave who used to pay him an amount from his daily earnings, and Hazrat Abu Bakr (R.A.A.) utilised the same for his living. One day the slave presented something as his due which Hazrat Abu Bakr ate. The slave asked him: 'Do you know what kind of thing this was?'Hazrat Abu Bakr (R.A.A.) in reply said 'What was it?' He said in the Days of Jahillia (ignorance) I used to act as a fortune-teller for a person. Really speaking it was no fortune-telling, but a fraud. Now when I met him, he presented me this thing, which you have just eaten. On hearing this Hazrat Abu Bakr (R.A.A.) thrust his hand (fingers) into his mouth and vomitted all that was in his stomach. *(Bukhari).*

٥٩٥ — وعن نافع أن عمر بن الخطاب رضي الله عنه ، كان فرض للمهاجرين الأولين أربعة آلاف ، وفرض لابنه ثلاثة آلاف وخمسمائة ، فقيل له : هو من المهاجرين فلم نقصه ؟ فقال : إنما هاجر به أبوه يقول : ليس هو كمن هاجر بنفسه . رواه البخاري

595. Hazrat Naf'i (R.A.A.) relates that (the second Caliph of Islam) Hazrat Umar bin Khattab (R.A.A.) fixed four thousand dirhams for each of the pioneer Emigrants, but for his own son he fixed only three thousand five hundred. When somebody asked : 'He is also an emigrant, why have you fixed a smaller allowance for him?' He said: 'His father also emigrated with him; meaning he was not like one who migrated of his own.' *(Bukhari).*

٥٩٦ — وعن عطية بن عروة السعدي الصحابي رضي الله عنه قال : قال رسول الله صلى الله عليه وسلم : « لا يبلغ العبد أن يكون من المتقين حتى يدع مالا بأس به ، حذرا لما به بأس » .

رواه الترمذي وقال : حديث حسن .

596. Hazrat Atiyyah ibn 'Urwah As-S'adi As-Sahabi (R.A.A.) relates that the Holy Prophet (S.A.W.) said: No one can achieve the height of piety till he forsakes those practices which are harmless merely to guard himself against those which are harmful. *(Tirmizi).*

Note: The sum and substance of the above Ahadis is that the secret of the maintenance of the outwardly acts lies in the purity and invulnerability of the heart. If the heart is pure and safe, it will not accept even doubtful things.

****

CHAPTER 69

Preference for Seculsion during the Corrupt Period, Fearing Trial for His Relgiion or Involvement in Unlawful or Doubtful Acts.

قال الله تعالى: فَفِرُّوا إلى اللهِ إنِّي لَكُم مِنه نَذِيرٌ مُّبِينٌ [الذاريات: ٥٠]

Allah, the Exalted, has said:

206. Therefore flee unto Allah; Lo! I am a plain warner unto you from Him. (51:50).

٥٩٧ ـ وعن سعدِ بن أبي وقّاص رضي الله عنه، قال: سَمِعْتُ رَسُولَ اللهِ صلى الله عليه وسلم يَقُول: « إنَّ اللهَ يحِبُّ العبدَ التَّقِيَّ الغَنِيَّ الخَفِيَّ » رواه مسلم

597. Hazrat S'ad bin Abi Waqqas (R.A.A.) relates that he heard the Holy Prophet (S.A.W.) say: Allah the most High, loves and befriends a servant who is pious, abstinate and unostentatious. *(Muslim).*

٥٩٨ ـ وعن أبي سعيد الخُدريِّ رضي الله عنه قال: قال رَجُلٌ: أيُّ النَّاسِ أفضَلُ يارسولَ الله؟ قال: « مُؤْمِنٌ مجاهِدٌ بِنَفسِهِ وَمَالِهِ في سبيلِ الله » قال: ثم من؟ قال: « ثم رَجُلٌ مُعتَزِلٌ في شِعْبٍ مِن الشِّعَابِ يَعبُدُ رَبَّه ».

وفي روايةٍ: « يَتَّقِي الله، وَيَدَعُ النَّاسَ مِن شَرِّه » متفقٌ عليه

598. Hazrat Abu Sa'eed Khudri (R.A.A.) says that someone asked the Holy Prophet (S.A.W.): 'O Messenger of Allah! Who is the best person?' He replied: 'A believer who fights in the cause of Allah with his life and property.' This man further asked: 'And who is next after him? 'He said: 'One who withdraws (from the world) into a narrow valley (secluded place) and is engaged in praying (to Allah).' Another version says: 'One who fears Allah (mindful of his obligations to Allah) and keeps the people safe from his own mischief.'. *(Bukhari and Muslim).*

٥٩٩ ـ وعنه قالَ: قال رسولُ اللهِ صلَّى الله عليه وسلَّم: « يُوشِكُ أنْ يَكُونَ خَيْرَ مَالِ المُسْلِمِ غَنَمٌ يَتَتَبَّعُ بها شَعَفَ الجِبَالِ، ومَوَاقِعَ القَطْرِ يَفِرُّ بِدِينِهِ من الفِتَنِ » رواه البخاري

599. Hazrat Abu Sa'id Khudri (R.A.A.) relates that the Holy Prophet (S.A.W.) said: 'The time is near at hand,when the best property of a Muslim will be a flock of goats, with which he will go to the tops of the ıountain or to a place with rainfall so as to safeguard his faith from mischief and trials.' *(Bukhari).*

٦٠٠ ـ وعَنْ أبي هُريرة رضي الله عَنْه ،عَنِ النَّبيِّ صلَّى الله عليه وسلم قال : « مابعثَ الله نبياً إلاَّ رعى الغَنَمَ » فقَالَ أصْحَابُه : وَأنْتَ ؟ قَالَ : نعَمْ ، كُنْتُ أرْعَاها على قَرارِيطَ لأهْلِ مَكَّةَ » رواه البخاري »

600. Hazrat Abu Hurairah (R.A.A.) relates that the Holy prophet (S.A.W.) said: 'All Prophets appointed by Allah have had the profession of grazing goats.' He was asked: 'And Sir, even you??' He answered: 'Yes, I too grazed them on wages of some Qirat for the people of Mecca.' *(Bukhari).*

٦٠١ ـ وعنه عَنْ رسولِ الله صلى الله عليه وسلم أنه قال : « مِنْ خَيْرِ مَعَاشِ النَّاسِ لَهُمْ رَجُلٌ مُمْسِكٌ عِنَانَ فَرَسِه في سَبِيلِ الله، يَطِيرُ على مَتْنِهِ ، كُلَّمَا سَمِعَ هَيْعَةً أوْ فَزْعَةً ، طارَ عَلَيْهِ يَبْتَغِي القَتْلَ ، أو الموْتَ مَظَانَّه ، أوْ رَجُلٌ في غُنَيْمَةٍ في رَأسِ شَعَفَةٍ مِن هَذِهِ الشَّعَفِ ، أوْ بَطْنِ وادٍ مِن هَذِهِ الأوْدِيَةِ ، يُقِيمُ الصَّلاةَ ، وَيُؤْتِي الزَّكاةَ ، وَيَعْبُدُ رَبَّهُ حَتَّى يَأتِيَهُ اليَقِينُ ليسَ مِنَ النَّاسِ إلاَّ في خَيْرٍ » رواه مسلم

601. Hazrat Abu Hurairah (R.A.A.) relates that the Holy Prophet (S.A.W.) said: 'The best life is that of a person who, catching the reins of the horse, flies (runs fast) on its back for the sake of Allah. He races fast to the palce where he observes danger or hears sound of the enemy; he seeks death or martyrdom wherever he is engaged in Jihad (fighting); or,it is of that person who retires to the top of one of the mountains, or lives in one of the valleys offering prayers (Salat) regularly, pays Zakat, worship his Allah, till his end, and does not intervene in the affairs of other people except for good. *(Muslim).*

****

CHAPTER 70

Merits of Associating with People and Participation in Their Gathering and to Be Present in Their Good Deeds and Partaking in Their Sessions for Relgiious Discourse. Visiting Sick Persons, Presence in Funeral Prayers, Satisfying the Needs For the Needy to Guide their Ignorants, and Having Sense of Obligations and Responsibilities; to Do What Is Ordered and Abstaining from What Is Forbidden, and to Keep One's Body and Soul Clean from Impurities (Vices), and to Put up Patiently with Hardships.

Imam Nawawi says that the way in which the Holy Prophet (S.A.W.) dealt with the people is the best and the most appropriate. The same course of conduct was followed by the former prophets, and this was the behaviour adopted by the four rightly guided Caliphs, the respected Companions of the Holy Prophet (S.A.W.) and the later generations of the followers of the Holy Prophet (S.A.W.) and the learned theologians (Ulama) and the best person of them. This was the way of most of the followers of companions. Imams Shafie and Ahmad bin Hanbal too have adopted this sort of conduct in their dealing whith the people.

قال الله تعالى : (وتَعَاوَنُوا عَلَى البِرِّ والتَّقْوَى) [المائدة : ٢]

Allah, the Exalted, has said:

207. But help ye one another unto righteousness and pious duty. (5:2).

There are many verses on this in the Holy Quran.

****

CHAPTER 71

Curteous Treatment and Humility towards Believers.

قال الله تعالى : واخْفِضْ جَنَاحَكَ لِمَنِ اتَّبَعَكَ مِنَ المُؤْمِنِين
[الشعراء : ٢١٥] وقال تعالى : يَا أَيها الَّذينَ آمنُوا مَن يرْتَدَّ مِنكُم عن
دِينهِ فَسَوْفَ يَأْتي اللهُ بقَوْم يُحِبهُم ويُحِبونَهُ أَذلَّةٍ عَلى المُؤْمِنِينَ
أَعِزَّةٍ عَلى الكَافِرِينَ [المائدة : ٥٤] وقال تعالى : يَا أَيُّهَا النَّاسُ إِنَّا
خَلَقْنَاكُم مِن ذَكَرٍ وأُنثَى وجَعَلنَاكُم شُعُوباً وقبَائِلَ لِتَعَارَفُوا إِنَّ
أَكْرَمَكُم عِنْدَ اللهِ أَتقَاكُم [الحجرات : ١٢] وقال تعالى : فَلَا تُزَكُّوا

أنفُسَكُم هو أعلَمُ بِمن اتقَى [النجم : ٣٢] وقال تعالى : ونَادَى أصحَابُ الأعرَافِ رِجَالاً يَعرِفونَهم بِسيماهُم قالوا: ماأغنَى عَنكُم جَمعُكُم وما كُنتُم تَستَكبِرُونَ ، أهؤلاء الذينَ أقسَمتُم لا ينالُهم اللهُ بِرَحمَة ادخلُوا الجنَّةَ لا خَوفٌ عَلَيكُم ولا أنتم تَحزَنُونَ [الأعراف : ٤٨ - ٤٩].

Allah, the Exalted, has said:

208. And lower thy wing (in kindness) unto those believers who follow thee. (26:215).

209. O ye who believe! Whoso of you becometh a renegade from his religion, (know that in his stead) Allah will bring a people whom He loveth and who love Him, humble toward believers, stern towards disbelievers. (5:54).

210. O mankind! Lo! We have created you male and female and have made you nations and tribes that ye may know one another. Lo! the noblest of you, in the sight of Allah, is the best in conduct. (49:13).

211. Therefore ascribe not purity unto yourselves. He is best aware of him who wardeth off evil. (53:32).

212. And the dwellers on the Heights call unto men whom they know by their marks, (saying): What did your multitude and that in which ye took your pride avail you? Are these they of whom ye swore that Allah would not show them mercy? (Unto them it hath been said): Enter the Garden. No fear shall come upon you nor is it ye who will grieve.(7:48-49)

٦٠٢ - وعن عِيَاضِ بن حِمَارٍ رضي الله عنه قال : قال رسولُ الله صلى الله عليه وسلم : « إنَّ اللهَ أوحَى إليَّ أنْ تَوَاضَعُوا حتى لا يَفخَرَ أحَدٌ عَلَى أحَدٍ ، ولا يَبغِيَ أحَدٌ عَلَى أحَدٍ » رواه مسلم

602. **Hazrat Iyaz bin Himar** (R.A.A.) relates that the Holy Prophet (S.A.W.) said: ‘Allah, the Most Exalted, has revealed to me that you should show courtesy and be cordial with each other, so that nobdoy should consider himself superior to another nor harm him.’ *(Muslim).*

٦٠٣ - وعَنْ أبي هريرة رضي الله عنه أن رسول الله صلى الله عليه وسلم قال : « ما نَقَصَتْ صَدَقَةٌ من مالٍ ، وما زادَ اللهُ عَبداً بِعَفوٍ إلاَّ عِزّاً ، ومَا تَوَاضَعَ أحَدٌ لِلهِ إلاَّ رَفَعَهُ اللهُ » رواه مسلم

603. This Hadis is he same as No. 556, discussed under Chapter 60.

٦٠٤ - وعن أنس رضي الله عنه أنَّهُ مَرَّ عَلَى صِبيانٍ فَسَلَّمَ عَلَيهِم وقال : كان النَّبيُّ صلى الله عليه وسلم يَفعَلُهُ . متفقٌ عليه

604. Hazrat Anas bin Malik(R.A.A.) says that once he passed by some children and saluted them by offering greetings of peace, and said: 'The Holy Propeht (S.A.W.) also acted likewise.' *(Bukhari and Muslim).*

٦٠٥ — وعنه قال : إنْ كانَتِ الأَمَةُ مِن إماءِ المَدِينَةِ لَتَأْخُذُ بِيَدِ النبيِّ صلّى الله عليه وسلم ، فَتَنْطَلِقُ بِهِ حَيْثُ شاءَتْ . رواه البخاري .

605. Hazrat Anas bin Malik (R.A.A.) relates that : (Even the humblest) maid servant of Madina would catch hold the hand of the Holy Prophet (S.A.W.) and take him to any place (for the redress of her grievances). *(Bukhari).*

٦٠٦ — وعن الأَسْوَدِ بن يَزيدَ قال : سُئِلَتْ عائِشَةُ رضيَ الله عنها : ما كانَ النَّبيُّ صلّى الله عليه وسلم يَصنعُ في بَيْتِهِ ؟ قالت : كان يَكُون في مِهْنَةِ أَهْلِهِ — يعني : خِدمَةِ أهلِه — فإذا حَضَرَتِ الصَّلاة ، خَرَجَ إلى الصَّلاةِ . رواه البخاري

606. Hazrat Aswad bin Yazid (R.A.A.) relates that Hazrat Ayesha (R.A.A.) was asked as to what did the Holy Prophet (S.A W.) do when inside the house. She replied: 'He used to remain busy serving and helping the inmates of his house, and when the time for Salat would come, he would go out for the same. *(Bukhari).*

٦٠٧ — وعن أبي رِفاعَةَ تَميمِ بن أُسَيدٍ رضي الله عنه قال : انتَهَيْتُ إلى رسول الله صلّى الله عليه وسلم وهو يَخْطُبُ . فقلتُ : يارسولَ اللهِ ، رجلٌ غَريبٌ جاءَ يَسْأَلُ عن دِينِهِ لايَدرِي ما دِينُهُ ؟ فَأَقْبَلَ عَلَيَّ رسولُ الله صلى الله عليه وسلم ، وتَرَكَ خُطْبَتَهُ حتى انتَهَى إليَّ ، فَأُتِي بِكُرسِيٍّ ، فَقَعَدَ عَلَيهِ ، وجَعَلَ يُعَلِّمُني مِمَّا عَلَّمَهُ الله ، ثم أتى خُطبَتَهُ ، فَأَتَمَّ آخِرَها . رواه مسلم

607. Hazrat Abu Rifa'a Tamim bin Usaid (R.A.A.) says: 'Once I presented myself before the Holy Prophet (S.A.W.) when he was delivering a sermon, and I submitted: 'O Messenger of Allah (S.A.W.), a traveller has come, to question something about his faith, as he knows nothing about it.' Upon this the Holy Prophet (S.A.W.) discontinued his address and came to me. A chair was brought for him and he seated upon it. After this he started teaching me those commandments which Allah, the Most High, had taught him. Then he resumed his address and completed it.' *(Muslim).*

٦٠٨ — وعن أنسٍ رضيَ الله عنه أنَّ رسولَ الله صلى الله عليه وسلَّم كان إذا أكَلَ طَعَاماً لَعِقَ أصابِعَه الثَّلاثَ قال : وقال : « إذا سَقَطَتْ لُقْمَةُ

أحَدِكُمْ ، فَلْيُمِطْ عَنْها الأذى ، ولْيَأكُلْها ، ولا يَدَعْها للشَّيْطَانِ »

وأَمَرَ أنْ تُسْلَتَ القَصْعَةُ قالَ : « فإنَّكُمْ لاتَدْرُونَ في أيِّ طَعامِكُمُ البَرَكَةَ »

رواه مسلم

608. Hazrat Anas Bin Malik (R.A.A.) says that when the Holy Prophet (S.A.W.) used to finish eating his meal, he would lick his fingers. Hazrat Anas (R.A.A.) further says that the Holy Prophet (S.A.W.) also said: 'If a morsel may drop from the hand of somebody, he should remove the dust or dirt from it and eat it, and not leave it for the Devil.' The Holy Prophet (S.A.W.) further directed: 'One should clean the vessel from which he eats by wiping it, for one does not know which part of his food is blessed.' *(Muslim)*

٦٠٩ – وعن أبي هُريرة رضي الله عنه، عن النبيِّ صلى الله عليه وسلَّم قال :

« ما بعَثَ اللهُ نَبِيّاً إلاَّ رَعَى الغَنَمَ » قالَ أصحابُه : وأنْتَ ؟ فقال : نَعَمْ

كُنْتُ أرْعَاهَا عَلى قَرَارِيطَ لأهْلِ مَكَّةَ » رواهُ البخاري

609. This Hadis is the same as No.600 under Chapter 69.

٦١٠ – وعنهُ عن النبيِّ صلى اللهُ عليه وسلَّم قال : لَوْ دُعِيتُ إلى كُرَاعٍ

أوْ ذِرَاعٍ لأجَبْتُ ، ولَوْ أُهْدِيَ إليَّ ذِراعٌ أو كُراعٌ لَقَبِلْتُ » رواهُ البخاري

610. Hazrat Abu Hurairah (R.A.A.) relates that the Holy Prophet (S.A.W.) said: 'I would accept an invitation to meal even if the food consisted of a shoulder or shank of lamb, and I would accept a gift even if it was no more than a shoulder or shank of the lamb. *(Bukhari)*.

٦١١ – وعن أنسٍ رضي اللهُ عنه قال : كانَتْ نَاقَةُ رَسُولِ الله صلى اللهُ

عليه وسلم العَضْبَاءُ لاَ تُسْبَقُ ، أوْ لاتَكَادُ تُسْبَقُ ، فَجاءَ أعْرابِيٌّ عَلى

قَعُودٍ لَهُ ، فَسَبَقَها ، فَشَقَّ ذلكَ عَلى المُسْلِمينَ حتَّى عَرَفَهُ ، فَقالَ :

« حَقٌّ عَلى اللهِ أنْ لاَ يَرْتَفِعَ شَيْءٌ مِنَ الدُّنْيا إلاَّ وَضَعَهُ » .

رواهُ البخاري

611. Hazrat Anas bin Malik (R.A.A.) relates tht the Holy Prophet (S.A.W.) had a she-camel called Azba, which would not allow any other camel to out-run her. Once a villager came riding on a young camel who ran ahead of the she-camel of the Holy Prophet (S.A.W.) The Muslims felt this very much. The Holy Prophet (S.A.W.) noticing this discomfiture of the Muslims said: 'It is Allah's Will that He brings down whatever raises itself in the world.' *(Bukhari)*

****

CHAPTER 72

Arrogance and Self-Esteem Not Permitted

قال الله تعالى : تِلْكَ الدَّارُ الآخِرَةُ نَجْعَلُهَا لِلَّذِينَ لاَ يُرِيدُونَ عُلُوّاً
فِي الأَرْضِ وَلاَ فَسَاداً وَالْعَاقِبَةُ لِلْمُتَّقِينَ [القصص : ٨٣] وقال تعالى :
وَلاَ تَمْشِ فِي الأَرْضِ مَرَحاً [الإسراء : ٣٧] وقال تعالى : وَلاَ تُصَعِّرْ
خَدَّكَ لِلنَّاسِ وَلاَ تَمْشِ فِي الأَرْضِ مَرَحاً إِنَّ اللهَ لاَ يُحِبُّ كُلَّ مُخْتَالٍ
فَخُورٍ) [لقمان : ١٨] . ومعنى « تُصَعِّرْ خَدَّكَ لِلنَّاسِ » أي : تُمِيلُه وَتُعْرِضُ
بِهِ عَنِ النَّاسِ تَكَبُّراً عَلَيْهِمْ . « والمَرَح » : التَّبَخْتُر . وقال تعالى :
إِنَّ قَارُونَ كَانَ مِنْ قَوْمِ مُوسَى فَبَغَى عَلَيْهِمْ وَآتَيْنَاهُ مِنَ الْكُنُوزِ
مَا إِنَّ مَفَاتِحَهُ لَتَنُوءُ بِالْعُصْبَةِ أُولِي الْقُوَّةِ إِذْ قَالَ لَهُ قَوْمُهُ لاَ تَفْرَحْ
إِنَّ اللهَ لاَ يُحِبُّ الْفَرِحِينَ . [القصص: ٧٦-٨١] إلى قوله تعالى : فَخَسَفْنَا بِهِ
وَبِدَارِهِ الأَرْضَ الآيات .

Allah, the Exalted, has said:

213. As for that abode of the Hereafter We assign it unto those who seek not oppression in the earth, nor yet corruption. The sequel is for those who ward off (evil). (28:83).
214. And walk not the earth exutant. (17:37).
215. Turn not thy cheek in scorn toward folk, nor walk with pertness in the land. Lo! Allah loveth not each braggart boaster. (31:18).
216. Now Korah was of Moses' folk, but he oppressed them; and We gave him so much treasure that the store thereof would verily have been a burden for a troop of mighty men. When his own fold said to him: Exult not; Lo! Allah loveth not the exultant;............... so We caused the earth to swallow him and his dwelling place. (28:76--81)

٦١٢ ـ وعن عبد الله بن مسعود رضي الله عنه، عن النبيِّ صلى الله عليه وسلّم
قال : « لا يَدْخُلُ الجَنَّةَ مَنْ كانَ في قَلْبِهِ مِثْقَالُ ذَرَّةٍ مِنْ كِبْرٍ » فقال
رَجُلٌ : إنَّ الرَّجُلَ يُحِبُّ أنْ يَكُونَ ثَوْبُهُ حَسَناً، ونَعْلُهُ حَسَنَةً؟ قال : « إنَّ
اللهَ جَمِيلٌ يُحِبُّ الجَمَالَ ـ الكِبْرُ بَطَرُ الحَقِّ وغَمْطُ النَّاسِ » رواه مسلم

612. Hazrat Abdullah ibn Mas'ud (R.A.A.) relates that the Holy Prophet (S.A.W.) said: 'One who has an iota of pride in his heart, will not be able to enter Paradise. One of the companions said: 'O Messenger of Allah! some persons like nice clothes and shoes.' The Holy Prophet (S.A.W.) said: 'Allah is Elegant and Beautiful, and he likes elegance and beauty. Pride means rejecting the truth out of self-esteem and considering others as low.' *(Muslim)*

٦١٣ ــ وعنْ سلمةَ بنِ الأكوعِ رضيَ اللهُ عنه أنَّ رجلاً أكلَ عِندَ رسولِ اللهِ صلى اللهُ عليه وسلم بشِمالِهِ ، فقالَ : « كُلْ بِيَمِينِكَ » . قالَ : لاَ أستَطِيعُ ! قال : « لا استَطَعْتَ » ما منَعَهُ إلاَّ الكِبْرُ . قال : فما رفَعَها إلى فِيهِ . رواهُ مسلم

613. This Hadis is the same as given in No. 159 of Chapter 16.

٦١٤ ــ وعنْ حارِثَةَ بنِ وهْبٍ رضيَ اللهُ عنه قال : سَمِعْتُ رسُولَ اللهِ صلى اللهُ عليه وسلم يقولُ : « ألاَ أُخبِرُكُمْ بِأهْلِ النَّارِ ؟ : كُلُّ عُتُلٍّ جَوَّاظٍ مُسْتَكْبِرٍ » متفقٌ عليه

614. This Hadis is part of No. 252 of Chapter 32.

٦١٥ ــ وعن أبي سعيد الخُدري رضيَ اللهُ عنه، عنِ النبيِّ صلى اللهُ عليه وسلم قال : « احتَجَّتِ الجنَّةُ والنَّارُ ، فقالتِ النَّارُ : فيَّ الجبَّارُونَ والمُتَكَبِّرُونَ ، وقالَتِ الجنَّةُ : فيَّ ضُعَفاءُ النَّاسِ ومَساكِينُهُمْ . فَقَضَى اللهُ بَيْنَهُمَا : إنَّكِ الجنَّةُ رَحْمَتي ، أرْحَمُ بِكِ مَنْ أشاءُ ، وإنَّكِ النَّارُ عذَابي ، أُعذِّبُ بِكِ مَنْ أشاءُ ، ولِكِلَيْكُما عليَّ مِلْؤُها » رواهُ مسلم

615. This Hadis is the same as No. 254 of Chapter 32.

٦١٦ ــ وعن أبي هُريرة رضي اللهُ عنه أنَّ رسولَ اللهِ صلى اللهُ عليه وسلم قال : « لا يَنظُرُ اللهُ يَوْمَ القيامَةِ إلى مَنْ جَرَّ إزارَهُ بَطَراً » متفقٌ عليه

616. Hazraṭ Abu Hurairah (R.A.A.) relates that the Holy Prophet (S.A.W.) said: 'Allah will not look on the Day of Judgement towards one who lets his trousers down out of pride.' *(Bukhari and Muslim).*

٦١٧ ــ وعنه قال : قالَ رسُولُ اللهِ صلى اللهُ عليه وسلم : « ثلاثَةٌ لاَ يُكَلِّمُهُمُ اللهُ يَوْمَ القِيامَةِ ، ولاَ يُزَكِّيهِمْ ، ولاَ يَنظُرُ إليْهِمْ ولَهُمْ عذابٌ أليمٌ : شَيْخٌ زانٍ ، ومَلِكٌ كذَّابٌ ، وعائِلٌ مُسْتَكْبِرٌ

رواهُ مسلم

617. Hazrat Abu Hurairah (R.A.A.) relates that the Holy Prophet (S.A.W.) said: 'There are three persons to whom Allah, the Most High will not talk, nor will He absolve them of sins nor look at them: an aged person guilty of adultery, a king who lies and a poor beggar who is proud.' *(Muslim).*

٦١٨ – وعنه قال : قال رسولُ اللهِ صلى الله عليه وسلم : « قالَ الله عزَّ وَجلَّ : العِزُّ إزَاري . والكِبْرِياءُ رِدَائي ، فَمَنْ يُنازِعُني عَذَّبْتُه » .

رواه مسلم

618. Hazrat Abu Hurairah (R.A.A.) relates that the Holy Prophet (S.A.W.) said: 'Allah, the Master of distinction and glory, says: Honour is My lower garment and Greatness My covering; One who competes, with Me in either of these two, I shall punish him.' *(Muslim).*

٦١٩ – وعَنْه أنَّ رسولَ اللهِ صلى الله عليه وسلَّم قال : « بَيْنَما رَجُلٌ يَمشي في حُلَّةٍ تُعْجِبُه نَفْسُه ، مُرَجِّلٌ رَأسَه ، يَختَال في مِشْيَتِه ، إذْ خَسَفَ اللهُ بِهِ ، فهو يَتَجلْجَلُ في الأرْضِ إلى يَوْمِ القِيامَةِ » متفقٌ عليه

619. Hazrat Abu Hurairah (R.A.A.) relates that the Holy Prophet (S.A.W.) said: 'A person belonging to an ancient people was once promenading having donned a pair of (fine) clothes and was taking pleasure. He had his hair combed, and his steps were lordly. All of a sudden, Allah the Most High caused him to be swallowed by the earth and now he will continue to struggle and sink till the Day of Judgment.' *(Bukhari and Muslim).*

٦٢٠ – وعن سَلَمَةَ بنِ الأكوعِ رضيَ اللهُ عنه قال : قال رسُولُ اللهِ صلى اللهُ عليه وسلَّم : « لا يزَالُ الرَّجُلُ يَذْهَبُ بِنَفْسِهِ حتَّى يُكْتَبَ في الجَبَّارِينَ ، فيُصيبُهُ ما أصابَهُمْ » رواهُ الترمذي وقالَ : حديث حسن .

620. Hazrat Salamah bin Akwa'a (R.A.A.) **relates that the Holy Prophet (S.A.W.) said: 'A person who persistently keeps himself aloof from people and behaves insolently, so much so that his name is counted among the arrogants and then he is meted out the same punishment which is ear-marked for insolent persons.'** ***(Tirmizi).***

Note: Arrogance is the name of self-esteem which is to degrade others and to over-estimate oneself. Therefore, this behaviour is very harmful for collective life. But self respect is not arrogance, on the contrary it is a good trait which is necessary in every gentleman of good character.

****

CHAPTER 73

On Good Manners.

قالَ الله تعالى : وَإِنَّكَ لَعَلى خُلُقٍ عَظِيمٍ [ن : ٤] وقال تعالى :

وَالكَاظِمِينَ الغَيْظَ وَالعَافِينَ عَنِ النَّاسِ الآية [آل عمران : ١٣٤] .

Allah, the Exalted, has said:

217. And lo! thou art of a tremendous nature,(68:4).

218. Those who control their wrath and are forgiving toward mankind. (3:134).

٦٢١ – عن أنسٍ رضيَ الله عنه قال : كانَ رسُولُ اللهِ صلى اللهُ عليه وسلم أحْسَنَ النَّاسِ خُلُقاً ، متفقٌ عليه

621. Hazrat Anas bin Malik (R.A.A.) says that the Holy Prophet (S.A.W.) had the best manners among all the human beings.

(Bukhari and Muslim).

٦٢٢ – وعنه قال : مَا مَسِسْتُ دِيباجاً ولاَ حَرِيراً ألْيَنَ مِنْ كَفِّ رسُولِ الله صلى اللهُ عليه وسلم ، ولاَ شَمَمْتُ رائحةً قطُّ أطْيَبَ مِنْ رائحةِ رَسُولِ اللهِ صلى اللهُ عليه وسلَّم ، ولَقَدْ خَدَمْتُ رَسُولَ اللهِ صلى اللهُ عليه وسَلَّمَ عشْرَ سنِينَ ، فَما قالَ لي قطُّ : أفٍّ ، ولا قالَ لِشَيْءٍ فعَلْتُهُ : لِمَ فَعَلْتَهُ ؟ ولاَ لِشَيْءٍ لَمْ أفْعَلْهُ : ألاَ فَعَلْتَ كَذا ؟ . متفقٌ عليه ..

622. Hazrat Anas bin Malik (R.A.A.) relates: 'I have not felt a velvet or silk softer than the palm of the Holy Prophet (S.A.W.) nor any perfume more pleasant than the aroma (of the body) of the Holy Prophet (S.A.W.). I had served him for ten years. He never fie to me. Whatever I had done, he never asked me as to why I did that; or, of anything I had not done, he never asked me as to why I failed to do that.'

(Bukhari and Muslim).

٦٢٣ – وعن الصَّعْبِ بنِ جَثَّامَةَ رضيَ اللهُ عنه قال : أهْدَيْتُ رسُولَ اللهِ صلى اللهُ عليه وسلم حِمَاراً وَحْشِياً ، فَرَدَّهُ عَلَيَّ ، فلمّا رأى مَا في وَجْهِي قالَ : « إنّا لَمْ نَرُدَّهُ عَلَيْكَ إلاَّ أنّا حُرُمٌ » متفقٌ عليه

623. Hazrat S'ab bin Jassamah (R.A.A.) relates: 'I presented a wild ass to the Holy Prophet (S.A.W.) but he returned it to me. When he saw signs of disappointment in my face, he said: 'I have declined it as I am putting on the pilgrim's dress. *(Bukhari and Muslim).*

Note: As the animal was untrained, force was to be used to control it, which is not desirable during pilgrimage.

٦٢٤ — وعن النَّواس بنِ سمعانَ رضيَ اللهُ عنه قال : سألتُ رسُولَ اللهِ صلى اللهُ عليه وسلم عن البِرِّ والإثْمِ فقالَ : « البِرُّ حُسْنُ الخُلُقِ ، والإثْمُ : مَا حَاكَ في نَفْسِكَ ، وكَرِهتَ أنْ يَطَّلِعَ عَلَيْهِ النَّاسُ » رواهُ مسلم

624. This Hadis is thesame as one described in No. 590 of Chapter 68.

٦٢٥ — وعن عبد الله بن عمرو بن العاص رضي الله عنهما قال : لم يكن رسولُ الله صلى الله عليه وسلم فَاحِشاً ولا مُتَفَحِّشاً . وكان يقُولُ : « إنَّ مِن خِيارِكُم أحْسَنُكُم أخلاقاً » متفقٌ عليه

625. Hazrat Abdullah bin 'Amr bin Al-'Aas (R.A.A.) says that by nature the Holy Prophet (S.A.W.) neither talked indecently, nor did he listen to indecent talk. He used to say: 'The best of you are those who have the best manners.' *(Bukhari and Muslim)*

٦٢٦ — وعن أبي الدرداء رضي الله عنه : أن النبيَّ صلى الله عليه وسلم قالَ « ما من شَيءٍ أثقَلُ في ميزَانِ المُؤمِنِ يَومَ القِيامَةِ من حُسْنِ الخُلُقِ وإنَّ الله يُبغِضُ الفَاحِشَ البَذِيَّ » رواه الترمذي وقال : حديث حسن صحيح

626. Hazrat Abu Darda (R.A.A.) relates that the Holy Prophet (S.A.W.)said: 'Nothing is weightier in the scales of a believer on the Day of Judgment than his good behaviour. Allah treats a person who is given to loose and vulgar talk, with displeasure. *(Tirmizi).*

٦٢٧ — وعن أبي هُريرة رضيَ الله عنه قال : سُئِلَ رسولُ الله صلى الله عليه وسلم عَنْ أكثرِ مَايُدْخِلُ النَّاسَ الجَنَّةَ ؟ قال : « تقْوَى اللهِ وَحُسنُ الخُلُقِ » وَسُئِلَ عَن أكثرِ مَايُدْخِلُ النَّاسَ النَّارَ ، فَقَالَ : « الفَمُ وَالفَرْجُ » . رواه الترمذي وقال : حديث حسن صحيح .

627. Hazrat Abu Hurairah (R.A.A.) relates that the Holy Prophet (S.A.W.) was asked about the things which would cause most of the persons to enter Paradise?' He answered: 'Being careful about one's obligations to Allah and good behaviour.' Thereafter, he was asked: 'What are those things which would lead a person into the Hell?' He answered: 'His mouth and genitals.' (*Imam Tirmizi* has cited this tradition, which is authentic).

٦٢٨ ـ وعنه قال : قال رسولُ الله صلى الله عليه وسلم : « أكمَلُ المؤمِنينَ إيماناً أحسَنُهُم خلُقاً ، وخيارُكُم خيارُكُم لنِسائِهِم »

رواه الترمذي وقال : حديث حسن صحيح .

628. Hazrat Abu Hurairah (R.A.A.) relates that the Holy Prophet (S.A.W.) said: Among the Muslims the most perfect, as regards his faith, is one whose character is excellent, and the best among you are those who treat their wives well. (*Imam Tirmizi* has quoted this tradition and said it as authentic).

٦٢٩ ـ وعن عائشةَ رضيَ اللهُ عنها، قالت : سمعت رسولَ الله صلى الله عليه وسلم يقول : « إنَّ المؤمِنَ ليُدرِكُ بِحُسنِ خُلُقِه درَجةَ الصَّائمِ القائمِ »

رواه أبو داود

629. Hazrat Ayesha (R.A.A.) says that she heard the Holy Prophet (S.A.W.) as saying: 'A believer can achieve the position of one who regularly fasts during the day and spends the night in prayer, through his good manners.' (*Abu Daud*)

٦٣٠ ـ وعن أبي أمامةَ الباهِلِيِّ رضي الله عنه قال : قال رسول الله صلى الله عليه وسلم : « أنا زعيمٌ ببيتٍ في ربَضِ الجنَّةِ لِمَنْ ترَكَ المِراءَ . وإن كانَ مُحِقاً . وببيتٍ في وَسَطِ الجنَّةِ لِمَن ترَكَ الكَذِبَ . وإن كانَ مازِحاً ، وببيتٍ في أعلى الجنَّةِ لِمَن حَسُنَ خُلُقُهُ » حديث صحيح ، رواه أبو داود بإسناد صحيح .

630. Hazrat Abu Umamah Bahili (R.A.A.) relates that the Holy Prophet (S.A.W.) said 'I stand surety for a home on one side of Paradise for one who will give up pomp and showoff although, he may be in the right; and a home in the centre of Paradise for one who will give up lying even in joke; and a home in the best Paradise for one whose behaviour is excellent.' (*Imam Abu Daud* has quoted this tradition with sound chain).

٦٣١ ـ وعن جابر رضي الله عنه أن رسول الله صلى الله عليه وسلم قال : « إن مِنْ أحبِّكُم إليَّ . وأقربِكُم مِنِّي مجلساً يومَ القيامَةِ . أحاسِنَكُم أخلاقاً . وإنَّ أبغَضَكُم إليَّ ، وأبعَدَكُم مِنِّي يومَ القِيامَةِ . الثَّرثارُونَ والمُتشَدِّقُونَ والمُتَفيْهِقُونَ » قالوا : يارسول الله قدْ علِمْنا الثَّرثارُونَ والمُتشَدِّقُونَ ، فما المُتَفيْهِقُونَ ؟ قال : « المُتكبِّرُونَ » رواه الترمذي وقال : حديث حسن .

631. Hazrat Jabir (R.A.A.) relates that the Holy Prophet (S.A.W.) said: 'On the Day of Judgment the dearest and closest to me, as regards my company, will be those persons, who will bear the best moral character, and those among you, who talk with affectation and are given to boasting, will be the most repugnant to me,and farthest from me on the Day of Judgment. The Companions submitted: 'O Messenger of Allah (S.A.W.)! What is meant by the word "Mutafaihiqoon"; the Holy Prophet (S.A.W.) said: 'those given to boasting.'

(*Imam Tirmizi* quoting this tradition has called it good).

****

CHAPTER 74

On Affability, Tolerance and Patience.

قال الله تعالى : « وَالْكَاظِمِينَ الْغَيْظَ والعافِينَ عَنِ النَّاسِ وَاللهُ يُحِبُّ الْمُحْسِنِينَ » [آل عمران : ١٣٤]. وقال تعالى : خُذِ الْعَفوَ وَأْمُر بِالعُرْفِ وَأَعْرِض عَنِ الجَاهِلِينَ [الأعراف : ١٩٩] . وقال تعالى : وَلا تَسْتَوِي الحَسَنَةُ وَلا السَّيِّئَةُ ، ادْفَعْ بِالَّتِي هِيَ أَحسَنُ ، فإذا الذي بَيْنَكَ وَبَيْنَهُ عَدَاوَةٌ وكأنَّهُ وَلِيٌّ حَمِيمٌ ٭ وَمَا يُلَقَّاهَا إلاَّ الَّذِينَ صَبَرُوا ، وَمَا يُلَقَّاهَا إلاَّ ذُو حَظٍّ عَظِيمٍ [فصلت : ٣٤ — ٣٥] . وقال تعالى : وَلَمَنْ صَبَرَ وَغَفَرَ إنَّ ذَلكَ لَمِنْ عَزْمِ الأُمُورِ [الشورى : ٤٣] .

Allah, the Exalted, has said:

219. Those who control their wrath and are forgiving toward mankind; and Allah loves the benevolent. (3:134).

220. Keep to the forgiveness (O Muhammad), and enjoin kindness, and turn away from the ignorant.(7:199).

221. The good deed and the evil are not alike. Repel the evil deed with one which is better, then lo! he, between whom and thee there was enmity (will become) as though he was a bosom friend. But none is granted save those who are steadfast, and none is granted it save the owner of great happiness. (41:34—35).

222. And verily whoso is patient and forgiveth-lo! that, verily is (of) the steadfast heart of things.(42:43).

٦٣٢ — وَعَنِ ابنِ عَبَّاس رَضِيَ اللهُ عَنْهُما قَالَ : قَالَ رَسُولُ اللهِ صَلَّى اللهُ عَلَيْهِ وَسَلَّمَ لأَشَجِّ عَبْدِ القَيْسِ : « إنَّ فيك خَصْلَتَيْنِ يُحِبُّهُمَا

اللهُ : الحِلْمُ وَالأَنَاةُ » . رَوَاهُ مُسْلِم

632. Hazrat Ibn Abbas (R.A.A.) says that the Holy Prophet (S.A.W.) said to Ashajj Abd al-Qais: 'You have two qualities which Allah, the Most Exalted, likes and loves: One is mildness and the other is toleration. *(Muslim).*

٦٣٣ – وعن عائشة رضي الله عنها قالت : قال رسول الله صلى الله عليه وسلم :

« إنَّ اللهَ رفيقٌ يُحِبُّ الرِّفْقَ فِي الأَمْرِ كُلِّهِ » متفقٌ عليه

633. Hazrat Ayesha (R.A.A.) relates that the Holy Prophet (S.A.W.) said: Allah is Kind and likes kindness in all things. *(Bukhari and Muslim).*

٦٣٤ – وعنها أن النبي صلى الله عليه وسلم قال : « إنَّ اللهَ رَفِيقٌ يُحِبُّ

الرِّفْقَ ، وَيُعْطِي عَلَى الرِّفْقِ مالا يُعْطِي عَلَى العُنفِ وَمَا لا يُعْطِي عَلَى

مَا سِوَاهُ » رواه مسلم

634. Hazrat Ayesha (R.A.A.) relates that the Holy Prophet (S.A.W.) said: 'Allah is Kind and likes kindness, and bestows upon kindness that which He does not bestow upon harshness, nor on anything else other than kindness and tenderness. *(Muslim).*

٦٣٥ – وعنها أن النبيَّ صلَّى الله عليه وسلَّم قال : « إنَّ الرِّفقَ لايَكُونُ فِي

شَيءٍ إلاَّ زَانَهُ ، وَلا يُنْزَعُ مِنْ شَيءٍ إلاَّ شَانَهُ » رواه مسلم

635. Hazrat Ayesha (R.A.A.) relates that the Holy Prophet (S.A.W.) said: Where there is softness it beautifies that thing, and from which it is taken away it snatches its glamour. *(Muslim).*

٦٣٦ – وعن أبي هريرة رضي الله عنه قال : بَالَ أعْرَابِيٌّ فِي المسجِدِ ،

فَقَامَ النَّاسُ إلَيْهِ لِيَقَعُوا فيهِ ، فقال النبي صلى الله عليه وسلم : « دَعُوهُ

وَأرِيقُوا عَلَى بَوْلِهِ سَجْلاً مِنْ مَاءٍ، أوْ ذَنُوباً مِن ماءٍ ، فَإنَّمَا بُعِثْتُم مُيَسِّرِينَ

وَلَمْ تُبْعَثُوا مُعَسِّرِينَ » رواه البخاري

636. Hazrat Abu Hurairah (R.A.A.) relates that a villager discharged urine in the mosque; this made some people present there, greatly annoyed, who got up in order to punish him; whereupon the Holy Prophet (S.A.W.) said: Leave him and throw a bucketful of water over the polluted spot to clean it. You have been sent to make things easy and not to make them hard and difficult. *(Bukhari).*

٦٣٧ – وعن أنس رضي الله عنه عن النبي صلى الله عليه وسلم قال : «يَسِّرُوا

وَلا تُعَسِّرُوا . وَبَشِّرُوا وَلا تُنَفِّرُوا » متفقٌ عليه

637. Hazrat Anas bin Malik (R.A.A.) relates that the Holy Prophet (S.A.W.) said: 'Make things easy and convenient and don't make them harsh and difficult. Give cheers and glad tidings and do not create hatred.' *(Bukhari and Muslim).*

٦٣٨ — وعن جرير بن عبد الله رضي الله عنه قال : سمعتُ رسول الله صلّى الله عليه وسلم يقُولُ : « مَنْ يُحْرَمِ الرِّفْقَ يُحْرَمِ الخَيْرَ كُلَّهُ » رواه مسلم

638. Hazrat Jarir bin Abdullah (R.A.A.) relates that he heard the Holy Prophet (S.A.W.) say: 'One who is devoid of kindness is devoid of the good of every kind.' *(Muslim).*

٦٣٩ — وعن أبي هريرة رضي الله عنه أنَّ رَجُلاً قال للنبيِّ صلى الله عليه وسلم : أوْصِني . قال : « لا تَغْضَبْ » فَرَدَّدَ مِرَاراً ؛ قال « لا تَغْضَبْ » . رواه البخاري

639. This Hadis is the same as No. 48 of Chapter 3.

٦٤٠ — وعن أبي يَعلَى شدَّاد بن أوسٍ رضي الله عنه . عن رسول الله صلى الله عليه وسلم قال : « إنَّ الله كَتَبَ الإحسان عَلى كُلِّ شَيءٍ ، فإذا قَتَلتُم فَأحسِنُوا القِتْلَة وإذَا ذَبحتُم فَأحسِنُوا الذِّبْحَةَ ، وَليُحِدَّ أحَدُكُم شَفْرَتَه ، وَليُرِح ذَبيحَتَهُ » رواه مسلم

640. Hazrat Abu Y'ala Shaddad bin Aus (R.A.A.) relates that the Holy Prophet (S.A.W.) said: 'Allah, has made it obligatory to adopt a benevolent attitude towards everything. When you have to kill anyone kill him in a better way and when you have to slaughter an animal, you must make it easier for the animal you slaughter. Every one of you must get his knife sharpened to reduce the suffering of the animal to be slaughtered.' *(Muslim).*

٦٤١ — وعن عائشة رضي الله عنها قالت : مَا خُيِّرَ رسول الله صلى الله عليه وسلم بَيْنَ أمرَينِ قَطُّ إلاَّ أخَذَ أيسَرَهُما ، مَالَم يَكُن إثماً ، فَإن كَانَ إثماً ، كَانَ أبعَدَ النَّاسِ مِنهُ . وَمَا انتَقَمَ رسول الله صلى الله عليه وسلم لِنَفْسِهِ فِي شَيءٍ قَطُّ ، إلاَّ أن تُنتَهكَ حُرْمَةُ الله ، فَيَنتَقِمِ لله تعالى . متفقٌ عليه

641. Hazrat Ayesha (R.A.A.) relates: Whenever the Holy Prophet (S.A.W.) had the option to choose one of the two courses, he chose the easier course, unless it was a sin, if it was so, he was the first person to avoid it. He also did not seek revenge for a personal wrong, unless it transgressed a divine command, in which case he used to take revenge for the sake of Allah, the Most High. *(Bukhari and Muslim).*

٦٤٢ — وعن ابن مسعود رضي الله عنه قال: قال رسول الله صلى الله عليه وسلم: «ألا أخبركم بمن يحرم على النار — أو بمن تحرم عليه النار؟ — تحرم على كل قريب هين لين سهل».

رواه الترمذي وقال: حديث حسن.

642. Hazrat Abdullah Ibn Mas'ud (R.A.A.) relates that the Holy Prophet (S.A.W.) said: May I point out to you the person who is forbiden for fire or on whom the Fire of Hell is forbidden? It is forbidden to touch every person, who is closer to the people soft; lenient and is kind hearted. (*Imam Tirmizi* has classed this tradition as good).

Note: The sum and substance of the traditions cited above is that one should adopt an attitude of softness and convenience, instead of harshness and good for nothing.

****

CHAPTER 75

To Forgive and Ignore the Vulgars.

قال الله تعالى: ﴿خُذِ الْعَفْوَ وَأْمُرْ بِالْعُرْفِ وَأَعْرِضْ عَنِ الْجَاهِلِينَ﴾ [الأعراف: ١٩٩]. وقال تعالى: ﴿فَاصْفَحِ الصَّفْحَ الْجَمِيلَ﴾ [الحجر: ٨٥]. وقال تعالى: ﴿وَلْيَعْفُوا وَلْيَصْفَحُوا، أَلَا تُحِبُّونَ أَنْ يَغْفِرَ اللهُ لَكُمْ؟!﴾ [النور: ٢٢]. وقال تعالى: ﴿وَالْعَافِينَ عَنِ النَّاسِ وَاللهُ يُحِبُّ الْمُحْسِنِينَ﴾ [آل عمران: ١٣٤]. وقال تعالى: «وَلَمَنْ صَبَرَ وَغَفَرَ إِنَّ ذَلِكَ لَمِنْ عَزْمِ الْأُمُورِ» [الشورى: ٤٣]. والآيات في الباب كثيرة معلومة

Allah, the Exalted, has said:

223. Keep to forgiveness (O Muhammad), and enjoin kindness, and turn away from the ignorant (7:199).
224. So forgive, O Muhammad, with a gracious forgiveness. (15:85).
225. Let them forgive and show indulgence. Yearn ye not that Allah may forgive you?(24:22).
226. (Those who) are forgiving toward mankind; Allah loveth the good.(3:134).
227. And verily whoso is patient and forgiveth — Lo! that, verily is (of) the steadfast heart of things.(42:43).

٦٤٣ – وعن عائشة رضي الله عنها أنها قالت للنبيّ صلى الله عليه وسلم : هل أتى عَلَيْكَ يَوْمٌ كَانَ أَشَدَّ مِنْ يَوْمِ أُحُدٍ ؟ قال : « لَقَدْ لَقِيتُ مِنْ قَوْمِكِ ، وَكَانَ أَشَدُّ مَالَقِيتُ مِنْهُمْ يَوْمَ العَقَبَةِ ، إذْ عَرَضْتُ نَفسِي عَلى ابْنِ عَبْدِ يَالِيلَ بنِ عَبْدِ كُلالٍ ، فَلَمْ يُجبنِي إلى ما أَرَدْتُ ، فَانطَلَقتُ وَأَنا مَهْمُومٌ عَلى وَجْهِي . فَلَمْ أَسْتَفِقْ إلاَّ وَأَنا بِقَرنِ الثَّعالِبِ ، فَرَفَعتُ رَأْسِي ، فَإذا أَنا بِسَحابَةٍ قَد أَظَلَّتني ، فَنَظَرتُ فَإذا فِيها جِبرِيلُ عليه السلام ، فَنَادَاني فقال : إنَّ الله تعالى قَد سَمِعَ قَولَ قَومِكَ لَكَ ، وَما رَدُّوا عَلَيكَ ، وَقَد بعَثَ إلَيكَ مَلَكَ الجبَالِ لِتَأمُرَهُ بِمَا شِئْتَ فِيهِم ، فَنَاداني مَلَكُ الجِبَالِ ، فَسَلَّمَ عَلَيَّ ثُمَّ قال : يَا مُحَمَّدُ إنَّ اللهَ قَد سَمِعَ قَولَ قَومِكَ لَكَ ، وَأَنا مَلَكُ الجِبالِ ، وَقَدْ بَعَثَني رَبِّي إلَيْكَ لِتَأْمُرَني بِأَمْرِكَ ، فَمَا شِئتَ : إنْ شِئْتَ أطبَقتُ عَلَيهِمُ الأَخْشَبَيْنِ » فقال النبي صلى الله عليه وسلم : « بَلْ أَرْجُو أَنْ يُخرِجَ اللهُ مِنْ أَصْلابِهِم مَنْ يَعْبُدُ اللهَ وَحْدَهُ لايُشْرِكُ بِهِ شَيْئاً » متفقٌ عليه

643. Hazrat Ayesha (R.A.A.) says that she once asked the Holy Prophet (S.A.W.): 'Did you face a day severer than the day of the battle of Uhud? 'He answered: 'Yes I have experienced such things at the hands of your people and such a day was the day of Aqabah. On this day I presented myself to Abd ye lail bin Abd Kulal and offered him Islam, but he failed to make any response to what I had offered to him. I therefore, left with a heavy heart and depressed. I felt some relief only when I reached Qarn Sa'alib. Here I looked up and saw a cloud covering me. In this cloud I saw Angel Gabriel who called me and said: Allah, the Most High, has heard what your people have said to you and the response to your offer. Allah has now sent the Angel of the Mountains to you to carry out your orders to do what you might like to be done to them. Then the Angel of the Mountains addressed me greeting with Salam and then said: 'Muhammad (S.A.W.) Allah has heard what your people have said to you. I am the Angel of the Mountains and my Lord has sent me to you to carry out-your orders. What you want now to be done? If you like I may crush them between the two mountains encircling the city of Mecca. The Holy Prophet (S.A.W.) replied: (I do not want their destruction) I am still hopeful that Allah will make some of their children (good Muslims) who would worship Allah; the One without associating anybody with Him. *(Bukhari and Muslim).*

٦٤٤ — وعنها قالت : ما ضَرَبَ رسولُ الله صلى الله عليه وسلم شيئاً قطُّ بيَدِهِ ، ولا امرأةً ولا خادماً ، إلاّ أن يُجاهِدَ في سَبيلِ الله ، وما نيلَ منهُ شيءٌ قطُّ فيَنتَقِمَ مِنْ صاحِبِهِ ، إلاّ أنْ يُنتَهَكَ شيءٌ مِن مَحارِمِ اللهِ تعالى . فيَنْتَقِمُ لِلهِ تعالى . رواه مسلم

644. Hazrat Ayesha (R.A.A.) says that the Holy Prophet (S.A.W.) never struck anybody with his hand, neither a servant nor a woman, but he did fight (jihad) in the cause of Allah. He never avenged any wrong done to him personally, but he did avenge a wrong violating divine commandments. *(Muslim).*

٦٤٥ — وعن أنس رضي الله عنه قال : كُنتُ أَمْشي مَعَ رسول الله صلى الله عليه وسلم ، وعليه بُردٌ نَجْرانيٌّ غَليظُ الحاشِيَةِ ، فأدركَهُ أعرابيٌّ ، فجَبَذَهُ بِرِدائه جَبْذَةً شَديدةً ، فنَظَرتُ إلى صَفحةِ عاتِقِ النَّبيِّ صلى الله عليه وسلم ، وقد أثَّرَت بِها حاشِيَةُ الرِّداءِ مِنْ شِدَّةِ جَبذَتِهِ ، ثُمَّ قال . يا مُحمَّدُ مُرْ لي مِن مالِ اللهِ الَّذي عِندَكَ . فالتَفَتَ إليهِ ، فضَحِكَ ، ثُمَّ أمَرَ لهُ بِعَطاءٍ . متفقٌ عليه

645. Hazrat Anas (R.A.A.) says once I was going along with the Holy Prophet (S.A.W.) who had put on a Najrani sheet which had a stiff border. En route he came across a villager who came up and catching hold of his sheet pulled it violently. I looked towards the neck of the Holy Prophet (S.A.W.) which had the heavy marks of the rubbing. The villager said: 'O Muhammad (S.A.W.) Order that I may be given something out of Allah's provision (charity) that is with thee. The Holy Prophet (S.A.W.) looked towards the man and directed that he may be given something.' *(Bukhari and Muslim).*

٦٤٦ — وعن ابن مسعود رضي الله عنه قال : كأنّي أنظُرُ إلى رسول الله صلى الله عليه وسلم يَحكي نَبيّاً مِنَ الأنبياء ، صلَواتُ اللهِ وسَلامُهُ عليهم ، ضَرَبَهُ قومُهُ فأدمَوهُ ، وهُوَ يَمسَحُ الدَّمَ عَنْ وَجهِهِ ، ويقول : « اللّهُمَّ اغفِر لِقَومي فإنَّهُم لا يَعلَمُونَ » متفقٌ عليه

646. Hazrat Ibn Mas'ud (R.A.A.) relates: 'As if I am seeing the Holy Prophet (S.A.W.) narrating the account of one of the Prophets of Allah (peace and blessing of Allah be upon him) who was assaulted and wounded by his people; while wiping the blood from the face he prayed: 'O Allah! forgive my people because they do not know.'

(Bukhari and Muslim).

٦٤٧ — وعن أبي هريرة رضي الله عنه أن رسول الله صلى الله عليه وسلم قال : « لَيسَ الشَّدِيدُ بِالصُّرَعَة ، إنَّمَا الشَّدِيدُ الَّذي يَملِكُ نَفسَهُ عِندَ الغَضَبِ » متفقٌ عليه

647. This Hadis is the same as No. 45 of Chapter 3.

****

CHAPTER 76

Enduring Hurt and Annoyance.

قال الله تعالى : وَالكَاظِمِينَ الغَيظَ وَالعَافِينَ عَنِ النَّاسِ وَاللهُ يُحِبُّ المُحسِنِينَ [آل عمران : ٣] . وقال تعالى : ولَمَنْ صَبَرَ وَغَفَرَ إنَّ ذَلِكَ لَمِن عَزمِ الأُمُورِ [الشورى : ٤٣] . وفي الباب : الأحاديث السابقة في الباب قبله .

Allah, the Exalted, has said:

228. Those who control their wrath and are forgiving toward mankind; Allah loveth the good.(3:134).

229. And verily whoso is patient and forgiveth — Lo! that, verily, is (of) the steadfast heart of things. (42:43).

٦٤٨ — وعن أبي هريرة رضي الله عنه أن رجلاً قال : يارسول الله إنَّ لي قَرَابَةً أَصِلُهم وَيَقطَعُوني ، وَأُحسِنُ إليهِم ويُسيئونَ إليَّ ، وأحلُمُ عَنهم وَيَجهَلُونَ عَلَيَّ ! فقال : « لَئِن كُنتَ كَمَا قُلتَ فَكَأَنَّمَا تُسِفُّهُمُ المَلَّ ولايَزَالُ مَعَكَ مِنَ اللهِ تعالى ظَهيرٌ عَلَيهِم مَادُمْتَ عَلى ذلك » رواه مسلم

648. This Hadis is the same as No. 318 of Chapter 40.

****

CHAPTER 77

Resentment on Violation of the Rules of Shariah and Supporting and Helping the Religion of Allah (Islam).

قال الله تعالى : وَمَن يُعَظِّم حُرُماتِ اللهِ فهو خَيرٌ له عِندَ رَبِّه [الحج : ٣٠] . وقال تعالى : إن تَنصُروا اللهَ يَنصُركُم وَيُثَبِّتْ أقدامَكُم [محمد: ٧] وفي الباب حديث عائشة السابق في باب العفو

Allah, the Exalted, has said:

230. And whoso magnifieth the sacred things of Allah, it will be well for him in the sight of his lord. (22:30).
231. If ye help Allah,He will help you and will make your foot hold firm.(47:7).

٦٤٩ ـ وعن أبي مسعود عقبة بن عمرو البدري رضي الله عنه قال : جاءَ رَجُلٌ إلى النبيِّ صلى الله عليه وسلم ، فقال : إنِّي لأَتَأَخَّرُ عَنْ صَلاةِ الصُّبْحِ مِنْ أَجْلِ فلان ممَّا يُطيل بِنَا ! فَمَا رَأَيت النَّبيَّ صلى الله عليه وسلم غضِبَ في مَوعِظَةٍ قطُّ أَشَدَّ ممَّا غَضِبَ يومئذ ؛ فقال : « يَا أيهَا النَّاس : إنَّ مِنكم مُنَفِّرِين . فأيُّكم أَمَّ النَّاسَ فَلْيُوجِزْ ، فإنَّ مِنْ ورائِهِ الكَبيرَ والصَّغيرَ وذا الحَاجَة » متفقٌ عليه .

649. Hazrat Abu Masud Uqbah bin 'Amr Al-Badri (R.A.A.) relates that a man approached the Holy Prophet (S.A.W.) and submitted: So and so who leads the morning Prayers, prolonging (the recitation in) it so much that I am forced to delay my morning prayers. I have not seen the Holy Prophet (S.A.W.) so much angry before this incident as he was then. Addressing the audiance he said: Some of you create hatred in the hearts of people for religion. Therefore, anybody leading the prayer should be brief, because among the congregation are all types of people — old, weak and those who have to attend to their business.

(Bukhari and Muslim)

٦٥٠ ـ وعن عائشة رضي الله عنها قالت : قدِمَ رسول الله صلى الله عليه وسلم مِنْ سَفَرٍ ، وقد سَتَرْتُ سَهوَةً لي بقِرامٍ فيهِ تَمَاثِيلُ ، فلمَّا رآهُ رسول الله صلى الله عليه وسلم هتكَهُ وتلَوَّنَ وجهُهُ وقال : « يَاعَائِشَةُ : أَشَدُّ النَّاسِ عذَاباً عِندَ اللهِ يَومَ القِيامَةِ الَّذِينَ يُضاهُونَ بِخَلْقِ اللهِ » متفقٌ عليه

650. Hazrat Ayesha (R.A.A.) relates that once the Holy Prophet (S.A.W.) returned from a journey when I had hung a curtain having pictures on it, along a platform in front of my room. On seeing this curtain the Holy Prophet (S.A.W.) defaced the pictures and signs of resentment were visible on his face, and he said: 'Ayesha, on the Day of Judgment, those who make pictures of Allah's creatures will be subjected to the severest punishment.' *(Bukhari and Muslim).*

٦٥١ ـ وعنها أنَّ قريشاً أهمَّهُم شأنُ المرأةِ المخزُوميةِ التي سرَقت فقالوا : من يُكلِّمُ فيها رسول الله صلى الله عليه وسلم ؟ فقالوا : مَن يَجتَرِئ

عليه إلا أُسامَةُ بنُ زيدٍ حِب رسول الله صلى الله عليه وسلم ؟ فكَلَّمَهُ أُسامَةُ ، فقال رسول الله صلى الله عليه وسلم : « أتشفَعُ في حَدٍّ مِن حُدُودِ الله تعالى ؟! » ثم قامَ فاختَطَبَ ثم قال : « إنما أهلَكَ مَن قبلكُم أنَّهُم كانُوا إذا سَرَقَ فِيهِم الشَّرِيفُ تَرَكُوهُ ، وإذا سَرَقَ فيهِم الضَّعيفُ أقامُوا عليه الحَدَّ ! وايمُ الله ، لو أنَّ فاطمةَ بنتَ محمد سَرَقَت لقَطَعتُ يَدَهَا » متفقٌ عليه

651. **Hazrat Ayesha** (R.A.A.) relates that persons belonging to the Quraish tribe were very much concerned about the case of a Makhzumi woman who was accused for theft and whose hand was to be cut. The tribe was worried as to who should plead on her behalf with the Holy Prophet (S.A.W.) A few suggested: Only Hazrat Usamah ibn Zaid (R.A.A.) whom the Holy Prophet (S.A.W.) loves very much can do so. As such Hazrat Usamah (R.A.A.) represented her case to the Holy Prophet (S.A.W.) who told him: 'Do you intercede in the matter of grave crimes involving punishment prescribed by Allah?' So saying he got up and delivered an address in which he said: 'The people who preceded you were destroyed because they would let off a rich (influential) person if he committed theft, and would punish a weak person who committed the same crime. By Allah, if Fatimah, daughter of Muhammad (S.A.W.) would commit this offence I would cut off her hand (Incidentally the name of the culprit woman was also Fatimah). *(Bukhari and Muslim).*

٦٥١ — وعن أنس رضي الله عنه أن النبي صلى الله عليه وسلم رأى نُخامَةً في القِبلةَ ، فشقَّ ذلكَ عليهِ حتى رُؤِيَ في وجهِهِ ، فقامَ فحكَّهُ بيدِهِ فقال : « إن أحدكم إذا قامَ في صلاتهِ فإنَّهُ يُناجي ربَّه ، وإنَّ ربَّهُ بينَهُ وبينَ القِبلَةِ ، فلا يبزُقَنَّ أحدُكُم قِبَلَ القِبلَةِ ، ولكن عن يسارِهِ ، أو تحتَ قدَمِهِ » ثُمَّ أخذَ طرَفَ رِدائِهِ فبَصَقَ فيهِ ، ثُمَّ رَدَّ بعضَهُ على بعضٍ فقال : « أو يفعَلُ هكذا » متفقٌ عليه

652. **Hazrat Anas** (R.A.A.) relates that the Holy Prophet (S.A.W. once noticed that somebody had spitten in the mosque towards the Qibla. He was too much annoyed and the effect was visible on his face, he stood up and scraped it away with his own hand, and addressing the gathering said: 'When you stand in prayer you are in communion with your Lord (Allah), and He is between you and the Qibla. Let no one, therefore, spit in the direction of Qibla, but only to his left or under his foot. Then he took up a corner of his sheet, spat into it and folded it up and said: Or, he should do like this. *(Bukhari and Muslim).*

Imam Nawawi elucidates that the order regarding spitting to the left or under ones foot applies outside the mosque. In the mosque one is to collect this spittal only in a piece of cloth.

****

CHAPTER 78

On Duty of Public Officials to Deal the People with Kindness, Sincerity and Affection and Prohibition of Deceiving and Oppressing them, not Keeping in view Their Welfare, and being Careless towards them and Their Needs.

قال الله تعالى: وَاخفِضْ جَنَاحَكَ لِمَنِ اتَّبَعَكَ مِنَ المُؤْمِنِينَ [الشعراء: ٢١٥]. وقال تعالى: إنَّ الله يَأْمُرُ بِالعَدْلِ وَالإحسانِ وَإيتاءِ ذِي القُربَى وَيَنْهَى عَنِ الفَحشَاءِ وَالمُنكَرِ وَالبَغيِ يَعِظُكُم لَعَلَّكُم تَذَكَّرُونَ [النحل: ٩٠].

Allah, the Exalted, has said:

232. And lower thy wing (in kindness) unto those beleivers who follow thee. (26:215).

232. Lo! Allah enjoineth justice and kindness, and going to kinsfold, and forbiddeth lewdness and abomination and wickedness.. He exhorteth you in order that ye may take heed. (16:90).

٦٥٣ – وعن ابن عمر رضي الله عنهما قال: سمعت رسول الله صلى الله عليه وسلم يقول: « كُلُّكُم رَاعٍ، وكُلُّكُم مَسؤُولٌ عَنْ رَعِيَّتِهِ: الإمامُ رَاعٍ وَمَسؤُولٌ عَنْ رَعِيَّتِهِ، وَالرَّجُلُ رَاعٍ في أهلِهِ وَمَسؤُولٌ عَنْ رَعِيَّتِهِ، وَالمَرأةُ رَاعِيَةٌ في بَيتِ زَوجِها وَمَسؤُولَةٌ عَنْ رَعِيَّتِها، وَالخَادِمُ رَاعٍ في مالِ سَيِّدِهِ وَمَسؤُولٌ عَنْ رَعِيَّتِهِ، وكُلُّكُم رَاعٍ وَمَسؤُولٌ عَنْ رَعِيَّتِهِ» متفقٌ عليه

653. This Hadis is the same as No. 283 of Chapter 35.

٦٥٤ – وعن أبي يَعلَى مَعقِل بن يَسَارٍ رضي الله عنه قال: سمعتُ رسول الله صلى الله عليه وسلم يقول: « ما مِنْ عَبدٍ يَستَرعِيهِ اللهُ رَعِيَّةً، يَمُوتُ يَومَ يَمُوتُ وَهُوَ غَاشٌّ لِرَعِيَّتِهِ، إلاَّ حَرَّمَ اللهُ عَلَيهِ الجَنَّةَ » متفقٌ عليه

وفي روايةٍ: « فَلَم يَحُطها بِنُصحِهِ لَم يَجِد رَائِحَةَ الجَنَّةِ ».

وفي روايةٍ لمسلم : « ما مِن أميرٍ يَلِي أمورَ المُسلِمينَ ، ثُمَّ لا يَجهَدُ لَهُم ، وَيَنصَحُ لَهُم ، إلاَّ لَم يَدخُل مَعَهُم الجَنَّةَ » .

654. Hazrat Abu Yaala Ma'qil bin Yasar (R.A.A.) relates that he heard the Holy Prophet (S.A.W.) say: 'A person who is appointed in authority over people, and he betrays them, will not be allowed to enter Paradise, after his death.' *(Bukhari and Muslim).*

Another version says: 'If he does not look-after the people (placed under his care) with goodwill and sincerity, he will not get even the aroma of Paradise.

Muslim's version states: If a person has been made to look-after the affairs of the Muslims, but fails to work for their cause and their welfare he will not enter Paradise along with the Muslims.

٦٥٥ – وعن عائشة رضي الله عنها قالت : سمعت رسول الله صلى الله عليه وسلم يقول في بيتي هذا : « اللَّهُمَّ مَن وَلِيَ مِن أمرِ أُمَّتي شَيئاً ، فَشَقَّ عَلَيهِم ، فَاشقُق عليه ، وَمَن وَلِيَ مِن أمر أُمَّتي شَيئاً ، فَرَفَقَ بِهِم ، فَارفُق بِهِ » رواه مسلم

655. Hazrat Ayesha (R.A.A.) relates that she heard the Holy Prophet (S.A.W.) while staying in her house saying: O Allah! when a person who is placed in authority over my Umma (people) is strict with them, be Thou also strict with him, and when such a person is kind on them, be Thou also kind on him.' *(Muslim).*

٦٥٦ – وعن أبي هريرة رضي الله عنه قال : قال رسول الله صلى الله عليه وسلم : « كَانَت بَنُو إسرائيلَ تَسُوسُهُمُ الأنبياءُ ، كُلَّمَا هَلَكَ نَبيٌّ خَلَفَهُ نَبيٌّ ، وَإنَّهُ لا نَبيَّ بَعدي ، وَسَيَكُونُ بَعدي خُلَفَاءُ فَيَكثُرُونَ » قالوا : يارسولَ الله فَمَا تَأمُرُنَا ؟ قال : « أوفُوا بِبَيعَةِ الأوَّل فالأوَّل ، ثُمَّ أعطُوهُم حَقَّهُم ، وَاسأَلوا اللهَ الَّذى لَكُم ، فَإنَّ اللهَ سَائِلُهُم عَمَّا استَرعَاهُم » متفقٌ عليه

656. Hazrat Abu Hurairah (R.A.A.) relates that the Holy Prophet (S.A.W.) said: Authority (over the people's affairs)among the Bani Israel, was exercised by prophets. When a prophet died he was succeeded by another prayers But surely there will not be a **prayers** after me; however, there will be a chain of a large number of caliphs after me. The companions asked: 'O! Messenger of Allah , then what are your orders for us?' He said: 'Be loyal to them according to your pledge with them one after the other, and render to them that is due to

them, and continue supplicating for yourselves from Allah. Allah will Himself call them to account for the affairs placed in their charge.'
(Bukhari and Muslim).

٦٥٧ – وعن عائِذ بن عمرو رضي الله عنه أنَّهُ دَخَلَ على عُبَيدِ اللهِ بن زِياد ، فقال له : أي بُنَيَّ ، إنّي سَمِعتُ رسول الله صلى الله عليه وسلم يقول : « إنَّ شَرَّ الرِّعَاء الحُطَمَةُ » فإيَّاكَ أن تَكُونَ مِنهُم . متفقٌ عليه

657. This Hadis has been partially covered in No.192 of Chapter 23.

٦٥٨ – وعن أبي مَريمَ الأَزدِيّ رضي الله عنه ، أنه قال لِمُعاوِيَة رضي الله عنه : سَمِعتُ رسول الله صلى الله عليه وسلم يقول : « مَنْ وَلّاهُ اللهُ شَيئاً مِن أُمورِ المُسلِمِينَ ، فاحتَجَبَ دُونَ حَاجَتِهِم وخَلَّتِهِم وفقرِهِم ، احتَجَبَ الله دُونَ حَاجَتِهِ وخَلَّتِهِ وفقرِهِ يَومَ القِيامَةِ » فَجَعَلَ مُعَاوِية رجُلاً على حَوَائجِ النّاسِ . رواه أبو داود ، والترمذي

658. Hazrat Abu Maryam Azdi (R.A.A.) relates that he said to Hazrat Amir Mu'awiyah (R.A.A.): 'I heard the Holy Prophet (S.A.W.) say: 'If Allah appoints a person in authority over the Muslims, and he fails to redress their grievances and remove their poverty, Allah will not fulfil his needs and not remove his poverty on the Day of Judgment. Thereafter, Hazrat Amir Mu'awiyah (R.A.A.) appointed a man to look-after the needs of people.
(Abu Daud and Tirmizi).

****

CHAPTER 79

On a Just Ruler.

قال الله تعالى : إنَّ اللهَ يَأْمُرُ بِالعَدْلِ والإحسانِ [النحل : ٩٠] . وقال تعالى : وَأَقسِطوا إنَّ اللهَ يُحِبُّ المُقسِطِينَ [الحجرات : ٩] .

Allah, the Exalted, has said:

234. Lo! Allah enjoineth justice and kindness.(16:90).

Note: Since the time of Hazrat Umar bin Abdul Aziz, the Omayyad Caliph, this verse has been included in the weekly sermon in all congregations each Friday.

235. And act equitably. Lo! Allah loveth the equitable.(49:9).

٦٥٩ – وعن أبي هريرة رضي الله عنه ، عن النبي صلى الله عليه وسلم قال : « سَبعَةٌ يُظِلُّهُمُ اللهُ في ظِلِّهِ يومَ لا ظِلَّ إلاَّ ظِلُّهُ : إمَامٌ عَادِلٌ ، وشَابٌّ

نَشَأَ فِي عِبَادَةِ اللهِ تَعَالَى ، وَرَجُلٌ قَلْبُهُ مُعَلَّقٌ فِي الْمَسَاجِدِ ، وَرَجُلَانِ تَحَابَّا فِي اللهِ ، اجْتَمَعَا عَلَيْهِ . وَتَفَرَّقَا عَلَيْهِ ، وَرَجُلٌ دَعَتْهُ امْرَأَةٌ ذَاتُ مَنْصِبٍ وَجَمَالٍ ، فَقَالَ : إِنِّي أَخَافُ اللهَ . وَرَجُلٌ تَصَدَّقَ بِصَدَقَةٍ ، فَأَخْفَاهَا حَتَّى لَا تَعْلَمَ شِمَالُهُ مَا تُنْفِقُ يَمِينُهُ ، وَرَجُلٌ ذَكَرَ اللهَ خَالِياً فَفَاضَتْ عَيْنَاهُ » متفقٌ عليه

659. This Hadis has already been related in No. 376 of Chapter 46.

٦٦٠ — وعن عبد اللهِ بنِ عمرِو بنِ العاص رضي اللهُ عنهما قال : قال رسولُ اللهِ صلى اللهُ عليه وسلم : « إنَّ الْمُقْسِطِينَ عِنْدَ اللهِ عَلَى مَنَابِرَ مِنْ نُورٍ : الَّذِينَ يَعْدِلُونَ فِي حُكْمِهِمْ وَأَهْلِيهِمْ وَمَا وَلُوا » رواهُ مسلم

660. Hazrat Abdullah ibn ‘Amr bin Al‘Aas(R.A.A.) relates that the Holy Prophet (S.A.W.) said: The just and fair persons (rulers and judges will be seated on chairs of light before Allah. Such persons are those who decide justly and deal justly in the matters relating to their families and other affairs entrusted to them. *(Muslim)*.

٦٦١ — وعَن عَوفِ بنِ مَالِكٍ رَضِيَ اللهُ عنه قال : سَمِعْتُ رَسُولَ اللهِ صلى اللهُ عليه وسلم يقولُ : «خِيَارُ أَئِمَّتِكُمُ الَّذِينَ تُحِبُّونَهُمْ وَيُحِبُّونَكُمْ . وَتُصَلُّونَ عَلَيْهِمْ وَيُصَلُّونَ عَلَيْكُمْ . وَشِرَارُ أَئِمَّتِكُمُ الَّذِينَ تُبْغِضُونَهُمْ وَيُبْغِضُونَكُمْ ، وَتَلْعَنُونَهُمْ وَيَلْعَنُونَكُمْ ! » قالَ : قُلْنَا يَا رَسُولَ اللهِ ، أَفَلَا نُنَابِذُهُمْ ؟ قالَ : « لَا ، مَا أَقَامُوا فِيكُمُ الصَّلَاةَ ، لَا ، مَا أَقَامُوا فِيكُمُ الصَّلَاةَ » رواهُ مسلم

661. Hazrat ‘Auf ibn Malik (R.A.A.) relates that he heard the Holy Prophet (S.A.W.) say: ‘Your best leaders and rulers are those whom you love and who love you (in return), and for whom you pray and who pray for you;and your worst leaders and rulers will be those whom you hate and who hate you, and whom you curse and who curse you.’ The narrator of this tradition adds: We requested: ‘O! Messenger of Allah (S.A.W.) shall we not dissassociate from them? He said: ‘No! so long as they establish the prayers among you, No! so long as they establish the prayers among you.’ *(Muslim)*.

٦٦٢ ـ وعنْ عِيَاض بنِ حِمارٍ رَضيَ اللهُ عَنْهُ قالَ : سَمِعْتُ رَسُولَ اللهِ صلى اللهُ عليهِ وسلَّم يقولُ : « أهْلُ الجنَّةِ ثَلاثَةٌ : ذُو سُلْطانٍ مُقْسِطٌ مُوفَّقٌ ، ورَجُلٌ رَحِيمٌ رَقِيقُ القَلْبِ لِكُلِّ ذِي قُرْبى ومُسْلِمٍ . وعَفِيفٌ مُتَعَفِّفٌ ذُو عِيالٍ » رواهُ مسلم

662. Hazrat Iyaz bin Himar (R.A.A.) says that he heard the Holy Prophet (S.A.W.) say: The inmates of Paradise will be of three kinds a just ruler and one who spends in charity according to his capacity; person full of mercy and tender hearted towards all his relatives and Muslims; and a pious self restraining person having a family. *(Muslim).*

****

CHAPTER 80

Necessity of Obedience to Persons in Authority in Sinless Acts And Prohibition of Obedience in Sinful Acts.

قال اللهُ تعالى : يَا أَيُّها الَّذينَ آمَنُوا أَطِيعُوا اللهَ وَأَطِيعُوا الرَّسُولَ وأُولي الأمْرِ مِنكُمْ [النساء : ٥٩] .

Allah, the Exalted, has said:

236. O ye who believe! Obey Allah, and obey the Messenger and those of you who are in authority. (4:59).

٦٦٣ ـ وعنْ ابنِ عمر رضيَ اللهُ عنهما عَنْ النبيِّ صلى اللهُ عليه وسلَّم قال : « عَلَى المرْءِ المُسْلِمِ السَّمْعُ والطَّاعَةُ فِيما أحَبَّ وكَرِهَ ، إلاَّ أَنْ يُؤْمَرَ بِمَعْصِيَةٍ ، فَإذا أُمِرَ بِمَعْصِيَةٍ فَلاَ سَمْعَ ولاَ طَاعَةَ » متفقٌ عليه

663. Hazrat Ibn Umar (R.A.A.) relates that the Holy Prophet (S.A.W.) said: 'It is obligatory upon a Muslim to listen and obey (the authority) whether he likes it or not; save when he is asked to do something sinful. If he is asked for a sinful act then there is no hearing and obedience. *(Bukhari and Muslim).*

٦٦٤ ـ وعنهُ قال : كُنَّا إذا بَايَعْنَا رَسُولَ اللهِ صلى اللهُ عليهِ وسلَّم عَلَى السَّمْعِ والطَّاعَةِ يَقُولُ لَنَا : « فِيما اسْتَطَعْتُمْ » متفقٌ عليه

664. Hazrat Ibn Umar (R.A.A.) says: We took oath of allegiance with the Holy Prophet (S.A.W.) to hear and obey, he used to add: 'Only as much as you can.' *(Bukhari and Muslim).*

٦٦٥ – وعنهُ قال : سَمِعْتُ رَسُولَ اللهِ صلى اللهُ عليه وسلم يقول :
« مَنْ خَلَعَ يَداً مِنْ طَاعَةٍ لَقِيَ اللهَ يَوْمَ القِيامَةِ وَلاَ حُجَّةَ لَهُ ، وَمَنْ
مَاتَ وَلَيْسَ في عُنُقِهِ بَيْعَةٌ مَاتَ مِيتَةً جَاهِلِيَّةً » رواهُ مسلم

وفي روايةٍ له : « وَمَنْ مَاتَ وَهُوَ مُفَارِقٌ للْجَمَاعَةِ ، فَإِنَّهُ يَمُوتُ
مِيتَةً جَاهِلِيَّةً » . « المِيتَةُ » بكسر الميم.

665. Hazrat Ibn Umar (R.A.A.) relates: That he heard the Holy Prophet (S.A.W.) say; One who absolves his hands from obedience (i.e. he did not have oath of allegiance to anybody) he will meet Allah on the Day of Judgment without any excuse and one who dies without having sworn allegiance will die in the state of ignorance *(Jahiliya)*. *(Muslim)*.

Another version says: 'One who dies having disassociated himself from his community, he dies the death of ignorance.

٦٦٦ – وعَنْ أَنَسٍ رضيَ اللهُ عنه قال : قالَ رسُولُ اللهِ صلى اللهُ عليهِ
وسلم : « اسْمَعُوا وأَطِيعُوا ، وَإِنِ اسْتُعْمِلَ عَلَيْكُمْ عَبْدٌ حَبَشِيٌّ ، كَأَنَّ
رَأْسَهُ زَبِيبَةٌ » رواه البخاري

666. Hazrat Anas bin Malik (R.A.A.) relates that the Holy Prophet (S.A.W.) said: 'Listen and obey even if an ill-shaped negro slave whose head is like a dried grape, is appointed as authority over you.' *(Bukhari)*.

٦٦٧ – وعن أبي هريرة رضيَ اللهُ عنه قال : قالَ رسُولُ اللهِ صلى اللهُ
عليهِ وسلم : « عَلَيْكَ السَّمْعُ وَالطَّاعَةُ في عُسْرِكَ وَيُسْرِكَ وَمَنْشَطِكَ
وَمَكْرَهِكَ وَأَثَرَةٍ عَلَيْكَ » رواهُ مسلم

667. Hazrat Abu Hurairah (R.A.A.) relates that the Holy Prophet (S.A.W.) said: 'You are bound to hear and obey the orders of the authority, in hardship and in ease; willingly or unwillingly, and even when you are treated unjustly.' *(Muslim)*.

٦٦٨ – وعن عبدِ اللهِ بن عمرو رضيَ اللهُ عنهما قال : كُنَّا مَعَ رسولِ اللهِ
صلى اللهُ عليهِ وسلم في سَفَرٍ ، فَنَزَلْنا مَنْزِلاً ، فَمِنَّا مَنْ يُصْلِحُ خِبَاءَهُ ،
وَمِنَّا مَنْ يَنْتَضِلُ ، وَمِنَّا مَنْ هُوَ في جَشَرِهِ ، إذْ نَادَى مُنَادِي رسولِ اللهِ
صلى اللهُ عليهِ وسلم : الصَّلاةَ جامِعَةً . فَاجْتَمَعْنَا إلى رَسُولِ اللهِ صلى اللهُ
عليه وسلم فقال : « إِنَّهُ لَمْ يَكُنْ نَبِيٌّ قَبْلِي إلاَّ كَانَ حَقّاً عَلَيْهِ أَنْ يَدُلَّ

أُمَّتَهُ عَلَى خَيْرِ مَا يَعْلَمُهُ لَهُمْ ، وَيُنْذِرَهُمْ شَرَّ مَا يَعْلَمُهُ لَهُمْ ، وَإِنَّ أُمَّتَكُمْ هذِهِ جُعِلَ عَافِيَتُهَا فِي أَوَّلِهَا ، وَسَيُصِيبُ آخِرَهَا بَلَاءٌ وَأُمُورٌ تُنْكِرُونَهَا ، وَتَجِيءُ فِتَنٌ يُرَقِّقُ بَعْضُهَا بَعْضاً ، وَتَجِيءُ الفِتْنَةُ فَيَقُولُ الْمُؤْمِنُ : هذِهِ مُهْلِكَتِي ، ثُمَّ تَنْكَشِفُ ؛ وَتَجِيءُ الفِتْنَةُ فَيَقُولُ الْمُؤْمِنُ : هذِهِ هذِهِ ، فَمَنْ أَحَبَّ أَنْ يُزَحْزَحَ عَنِ النَّارِ ، وَيُدْخَلَ الْجَنَّةَ ، فَلْتَأْتِهِ مَنِيَّتُهُ وَهُوَ يُؤْمِنُ بِاللهِ وَالْيَوْمِ الآخِرِ ، وَلْيَأْتِ إِلَى النَّاسِ الَّذِي يُحِبُّ أَنْ يُؤْتَى إِلَيْهِ .

وَمَنْ بَايَعَ إِمَاماً فَأَعْطَاهُ صَفْقَةَ يَدِهِ ، وَثَمَرَةَ قَلْبِهِ : فَلْيُطِعْهُ إِنِ اسْتَطَاعَ ؛ فَإِنْ جَاءَ آخَرُ يُنَازِعُهُ ، فَاضْرِبُوا عُنُقَ الآخَرِ » رواهُ مسلم

668. Hazrat Abdullah ibn 'Umar (R.A.A.) relates: 'We were on a journey with the Holy Prophet (S.A.W.), (after some journey) we halted at a place. Some of us got busy putting up their tents, some were enjoying sports and war games (like target-shooting etc.) others were busy tending their cattle, when the Muazzin (Caller) of the Holy Prophet (S.A.W.) announced that it was time for the congregation. Accordingly we all assembled round the Holy Prophet (S.A.W.); thereafter addressing us he said: 'All the prophets who preceded me were under obligation to apprise his people of that which he knew was good, and to caution them against that which he thought was bad. So far as you are concerned (I may tell you) that you will be safe and protected in the early part of your history but subsequently you will face difficulties and catastrophies which will be unpleasant to you (misfortunes will be followed by misfortunes). One calamity will make the earlier one appear light. When one calamity will fall and a believer will say: This has come to ruin me; when it will pass and another will appear, he will say: 'This is the one which will ruin me.' Therefore the person who desires to be immune from the Hell and to enter Paradise, should face his death believing in Allah and the Day of Judgement, and should deal with others in the same way as he wishes to be dealt with. One who has already took oath of allegiance to one leader (Imam) and has committed his hand and his heart to him, should obey him as much as may be possible for him. If somebody opposes and contests and authority of that leader (Imam), the said opponent should be beheaded.' *(Muslim).*

٦٦٩ – وعن أبي هُنَيْدَةَ وائِلِ بن حُجْرٍ رضيَ اللهُ عنه قالَ : سَأَلَ سَلَمَةُ بنُ يَزِيدَ الجُعْفِيُّ رَسُولَ اللهِ صلى اللهُ عليه وسلم ، فقالَ : يَا نَبِيَّ اللهِ ،

أرَأيْتَ إنْ قَامَتْ عَلَيْنَا أُمَرَاءُ يَسْألُونَا حَقَّهُمْ ، وَيَمْنَعُونَا حَقَّنَا ، فَمَا تَأمُرُنَا ؟ فَأعْرَضَ عنه ، ثُمَّ سَألَهُ ، فَقَالَ رَسُولُ اللهِ صلى اللهُ عليهِ وسلم : « اسْمَعُوا وَأطِيعُوا ؛ فَإنَّمَا عَلَيْهِمْ ما حُمِّلُوا ، وَعَلَيْكُمْ ما حُمِّلْتُمْ » رواهُ مسلم

669. Hazrat Abu Hunaidah Wail hin Hujr (R.A.A.) relates that Hazrat Salamah bin Yazid Jo'fi (R.A.A.) asked the Holy Prophet (S.A.W.): 'O! Messenger of Allah (S.A.W.) ! Please let me know if we may be placed under such reulers who may require from us their due, but may refuse to give us fully our due; what are your orders (for us in this matter)?' The Holy Prophet (S.A.W.) avoided to give him a reply, but he repeated his question; and therefore the Holy Prophet (S.A.W.) said: 'You should listen them and obey them. They are answerable for their obligations and you are answerable for yours.' *(Muslim).*

٦٧٠ – وَعَنْ عَبْدِ اللهِ بنِ مَسْعُودٍ رَضِيَ اللهُ عنه قال : قال رسُولُ اللهِ صلى اللهُ عليهِ وسلَّم : « إنَّهَا سَتَكُونُ بَعْدِي أثَرَةٌ ، وَأمُورٌ تُنْكِرُونَهَا ! » قالوا : يا رسُولَ اللهِ ، كَيْفَ تَأمُرُ مَنْ أدْرَكَ مِنَّا ذلكَ ؟ قَالَ : « تُؤَدُّونَ الحَقَّ الَّذِي عَلَيْكُمْ ، وَتَسْألُونَ اللهَ الَّذِي لَكُمْ » متفقٌ عليه

670. Hazrat Abdullah ibn Mas'ud (R.A.A.) relates that the Holy Prophet (S.A.W.) said: 'When I pass away you will see differentiation (bias) and such things that you will not like.' They asked 'O Messenger of Allah! (S.A.W.)! Then what we should do under such circumstances?' He answered: 'Pay their dues which you owe them and pray to Allah for your rights.' *(Bukhari and Muslim).*

٦٧١ – وعن أبي هريرة رضيَ اللهُ عنه قال : قال رسُولُ اللهِ صلى اللهُ عليه وسلم : « مَنْ أطَاعَنِي فَقَدْ أطَاعَ اللهَ ، وَمَنْ عَصَانِي فَقَدْ عَصَى اللهَ ، وَمَنْ يُطِعِ الأميرَ فَقَدْ أطَاعَنِي ، وَمَنْ يَعْصِ الأميرَ فَقَدْ عَصَانِي » متفقٌ عليه

671. Hazrat Abu Hurairah (R.A.A.) relates that the Holy Prophet (S.A.W.) said: 'One who obeys me, obeys Allah, and one who disobeys me disobeys Allah; and the person who obeys the man in authority obeys me, and he who disobeys the man of authority, disobeys me.' *(Bukhari and Muslim).*

٦٧٢ – وعن ابن عباس رضي الله عنهما أن رسول الله صلى الله عليه وسلم قال : « مَنْ كَرِهَ مِنْ أمِيرِهِ شَيْئاً فَلْيَصْبِرْ ، فإنَّهُ مَنْ خَرَجَ مِنَ السُّلْطَانِ

شبراً مَاتَ مِيتَةً جَاهِلِيَّةً » متفقٌ عليه

672. Hazrat Ibn Abbas (R.A.A.) relates that the Holy Prophet (S.A.W.) said: If a person notices something unpleasant in the action of a ruler he should put up with patiently, for one who leaves the ruler by a span of hand, dies a death of ignorance. *(Bukhari and Muslim).*

٦٧٣ – وعن أبي بكرة رضي الله عنه قال : سمعت رسول الله صلى الله عليه وسلم يقول : « مَنْ أَهَانَ السُّلْطَانَ أَهَانَهُ الله » رواه الترمذي وقال : حديث حسن .

673. Hazrat Abu Badr (R.A.A.) relates that he heard the Holy Prophet (S.A.W.) say: 'One who dishonoured the ruler (and a just authority) is dishonoured by Allah. (*Imam Tirmizi* has reported this tradition, which he says is good).

****

CHAPTER 81

Prohibition of Asking for the Post of Authority and Leadership. If appointed to such a Post, Should Relinquish it When not Necessary.

قال الله تعالى : تِلْكَ الدَّارُ الآخِرَةُ نَجْعَلُهَا لِلَّذِينَ لايُرِيدُونَ عُلُوّاً في الأَرْضِ وَلا فَسَاداً وَالعَاقِبَةُ لِلمُتَّقِين . [القصص : ٨٣] .

Allah, the Exalted, has said:

237. As for the Abode of the Hereafter We assign it unto those who seek not oppression in the earth, nor yet corruption. The sequel is for those who ward off (evil). (28:83).

٦٧٤ – وعن أبي سعيدٍ عبدِ الرحمنِ بن سَمُرَةَ رضي الله عنه ، قال : قال لي رسول الله صلى الله عليه وسلم : « يَا عَبْدَ الرَّحمن بن سَمُرَةَ : لاتَسأَلِ الإمارَةَ ، فَإِنَّكَ إن أُعْطِيتَهَا عَن غَيْرِ مَسأَلَةٍ أُعِنتَ عَلَيها ، وإن أُعطِيتَها عَن مَسأَلَةٍ وُكِلْتَ إليها ، وإذا حَلَفتَ عَلى يَمِينٍ ، فرَأَيتَ غيرها خيراً مِنهَا ، فَأْتِ الَّذي هُوَ خَيرٌ ، وَكَفِّرْ عَن يَمِينِكَ » متفقٌ عليه

674. Hazrat Abu Sa'eed Abdur Rahman bin Samurah (R.A.A.) relates that the Holy Prophet (S.A.W.) told him: 'O Abdur Rahman bin Samurah! Do you ask for public office or authority. Because if you are given an office without asking for it you will be helped in this matter.

(i.e. in discharging the duties); but if you are assigned this office on your asking for it, you will be in its possession. If you take oath to do a thing and later on find a better substitute adopt the latter and make amends for your vow.' *(Bukhari and Muslim).*

٦٧٥ — وعن أبي ذرٍ رضي الله عنه قال : قال لي رسول الله صلى الله عليه وسلم : « يَا أَبَا ذَرٍ إِنّي أَرَاكَ ضَعِيفاً ، وَإِنّي أُحِبُّ لكَ ما أُحِبُّ لِنَفسي ، لا تَأَمَّرَنَّ عَلَى اثْنَيْنِ وَلا تَوَلَّيَنَّ مالَ يَتِيمٍ » رواه مسلم

675. Hazrat Abu Zarr (R.A.A.) relates that the Holy Prophet (S.A.W.) said to him: 'O Abu Zarr! I consider you weak (and as such you will not be able to discharge the heavy duties of the office). And I like for you what I like for myself. Do not desire authority even over two persons, nor take up the guardianship of the property of an orphan.' *(Muslim).*

٦٧٦ — وعنه قال : قلت يارسول الله ألا تَستعملُني ؟ فضَرَبَ بِيَدِهِ على مَنكِبي ثُمَّ قالَ : « يَا أَبَا ذَرٍ إِنَّكَ ضَعِيفٌ ، وَإِنَّها أمانَةٌ ، وإنَّها يَومَ القِيامَةِ خِزْيٌ وَنَدَامَةٌ ، إلاّ مَن أَخَذَهَا بِحَقِّهَا ، وَأَدَّى الذي عَلَيه فِيها » رواه مسلم

676. Hazrat Abu Zarr (R.A.W.) relates: 'I submitted to the Holy Prophet (S.A.W.): Why do you not appoint me as an administrator of some place?' He patting me on my shoulder said: 'Abu Zarr, you are weak and office is a trust, and this may be the cause of humiliation and sorrow on the Day of Judgment except in the case of a person who takes up an office with justification and fulfills its obligations?' *(Muslim).*

٦٧٧ — وعن أبي هُرَيرة رضيَ الله عنه أن رسول الله صلّى الله عليه وسلم قال : « إنَّكُم سَتَحرِصونَ عَلَى الإمارَةِ ، وستَكُونُ نَدَامَةً يَوْمَ القِيامَةِ » رواه البخاري

677. Hazrat Abu Hurairah (R.A.A.) relates that the Holy Prophet (S.A.W.) said:' Time is coming when you will aspire for public offices and authority, but beware, it will be a matter of humiliation and repentance on the Day of Judgment.' *(Bukhari).*

****

CHAPTER 82

Sultans, Qazis and Administrators are exhorted to Appoint Good Advisers, and Prohibited to Associate with Bad Companions.

قَالَ اللهُ تعالى: الأَخِلَّاءُ يَوْمَئِذٍ بَعْضُهُم لِبَعْضٍ عَدُوٌّ إِلاَّ المُتَّقِينَ [الزخرف : ٦٧] .

Allah, the Exalted, has said:

238. Friends on that day will be foes one to others, save those who kept their duty (to Allah). (43:67).

٦٧٨ — عن أبي سعيدٍ وأبي هريرةَ رضيَ اللهُ عنهما أن رسولَ اللهِ صلى الله عليه وسلم قال: « مابَعَثَ اللهُ مِن نَبِيٍّ، ولااستَخْلَفَ مِنْ خَلِيفَةٍ إلاَّ كَانَتْ لَهُ بِطَانَتَانِ بِطَانَةٌ تَأْمُرُهُ بِالمَعْرُوفِ وَتَحُضُّهُ عليه، وبِطَانَةٌ تَأْمُرُهُ بِالشَّرِّ وَتَحُضُّهُ عليه، والمَعصُومُ مَن عَصَمَ اللهُ » رواه البخاري

678. Hazrat Abu Sa'eed Khudri (R.A.A.) and **Hazrat Abu Hurairah** (R.A.A.) relate that the Holy Prophet (S.A.W.) said: Whenever Allah appoints somebody as a prophet or deputy, he has two advisers, one advises him to do good and urges him to do it, and the other advises him to do bad and urges him to do that. Only that person is innocent, whom Allah saves from sins. *(Bukhari).*

٦٧٩ — وعن عائشةَ رضيَ اللهُ عنها قالتْ: قال رسولُ اللهِ صلى الله عليه وسلم: « إذا أَرَادَ اللهُ بِالأميرِ خَيراً، جَعَلَ له وزيرَ صِدقٍ، إن نَسِيَ ذَكَّرَهُ. وإن ذَكَرَ أعانَهُ، وإذا أرادَ بِهِ غيرَ ذلكَ جَعَلَ له وَزِيرَ سُوءٍ، إن نَسِيَ لم يُذَكِّرْه، وإن ذَكَرَ لم يُعِنْهُ » رواه أبو داود بإسنادٍ جيدٍ على شرط مسلم.

679. Hazrat Ayesha (R.A.A.) relates that the Holy Prophet (S.A.W.) said: 'When Allah wills that a ruler should do good. He furnishes him with a good adviser, who reminds him when he forgets (to do a good thing) and helps, if he remembers; and when Allah desires for him something other than good, He gives him a bad person as adviser, who does not remind the ruler when he forgets (to do a good work) and does not assist him if he remembers.' *(Abu Daud).*

****

CHAPTER 83

One Who Asks for a Judicial or Executive Post or Longs for One Should Not Be Appointed as Such.

٦٨٠ – عن أبي موسى الأشعَرِيِّ رضي الله عنه قال : دَخَلتُ على النَّبيِّ صلّى الله عليه وسلم أنَا وَرَجُلانِ مِن بَنِي عَمِّي ، فقالَ أحَدُهُمَا : يا رسولَ الله أمِّرنا على بَعضِ مَا وَلاَّكَ اللهُ ، عزَّ وجلَّ ، وقال الآخرُ مِثلَ ذلكَ ، فقال : « إنَّا وَاللهِ لانُوَلِّي هذا العَمَلَ أحَداً سَألَه ، أو أحَداً حَرَصَ عليهِ »

متفقٌ عليه

680. **Hazrat Abu Musa Ash'ari** (R.A.A.) says: (Once) I called on the Holy Prophet (S.A.W.) alongwith two of my cousins (paternal uncles sons) One of them said to the Holy Prophet (S.A.W.)' O! Messenger of Allah (S.A.W.) appoint me to some part of the Government out of that which Allah has bestowed upon you.' The other also solicited an appointmnt like this. The Holy Prophet (S.A.W.) said: 'By Allah I will not appoint to a public office anybody who asks for it or expresses a longing for it.' *(Bukhari and Muslim).*

****

BOOK OF MANNERS

CHAPTER 84

On Modesty, its Virtues and How to Develop it.

٦٨١ ـ عن ابنِ عُمَرَ رضيَ الله عنهما أنَّ رسولَ الله صلى الله عليه وسلم مَرَّ عَلى رَجُلٍ مِنَ الأنصارِ وَهُوَ يَعِظُ أخاهُ في الحَيَاء، فَقَالَ رَسُولُ الله صلَّى الله عليه وسلم : « دَعْهُ فَإنَّ الحياءَ مِنَ الإيمَانِ » متفقٌ عليه

681. Hazrat Ibn Umar (R.A.A.) relates that the Holy Prophet (S.A.W.) (Once) passed by an Ansari man who was counselling his brother on modesty (He was advising him not to be too much shy or modest). The Holy Prophet (S.A.W.) said: 'leave him (and do not advise him like this); for modesty is a part of faith (Iman).

(Bukhari and Muslim).

٦٨٢ ـ وعن عِمْرَانَ بن حُصَيْنٍ ، رضي الله عنهما، قال : قال رسولُ الله صلى الله عليه وسلم : « الحَيَاءُ لا يأتي إلاَّ بخيرٍ » متفقٌ عليه

وفي روايةٍ لمسلمٍ : « الحَيَاءُ خيرٌ كُلُّهُ » أوْ قالَ : « الحَيَاءُ كُلُّهُ خيرٌ » .

682. Hazrat Imran bin Husain (R.A.A.) relates that the Holy Prophet (S.A.W.) said: 'Modesty results in good alone and nothing else.'

(Bukhari and Muslim).

Another version of *Muslim* says: Shyness and modesty are good all in all or He (S.A.W.) said shyness and humility are good in their entirety.

٦٨٣ ـ وعن أبي هُرَيرة رضيَ الله عنه، أنَّ رسول الله صلَّى الله عليه وسلم قال : « الإيمَانُ بِضعٌ وَسَبْعُونَ ، أوْ بِضعٌ وَسِتُّونَ شُعْبَةً ، فَأَفْضَلُهَا قَوْلُ لا إلهَ إلاَّ اللهُ ، وَأَدْنَاهَا إمَاطَةُ الأذَى عَنِ الطَّرِيقِ . وَالحَيَاءُ شُعْبَةٌ مِنَ الإيمَان متفقٌ عليه

683. Hazrat Abu Hurairah (R.A.A.) relates that the Holy Prophet (S.A.W.) said: Iman (Faith) has more than seventy or sixty parts, the best of them is the acknowledgement of the fact that: There is no god but Allah (La Ilaha Illallah); and the lowest of them is removal of a thing causing harm from a thorough fare. Modesty (Shyness) is also a component of the Faith. *(Bukhari and Muslim).*

٦٨٤ — وعن أبي سعيدٍ الخُدْرِيِّ رضي الله عنه. قال : كان رسولُ الله صلّى الله عليه وسلم أَشَدَّ حيَاءً مِنَ الْعَذْرَاءِ في خِدْرِهَا . فإذَا رَأَى شيْئاً يَكْرَهُهُ عرَفْنَاهُ في وَجْهِهِ . متفقٌ عليه

قال العلماءُ : حقِيقَةُ الحيَاءِ خُلُقٌ يَبْعَثُ عَلى تَرْكِ الْقَبِيحِ . وَيَمْنَعُ مِنَ التَّقْصِيرِ في حقِّ ذي الحقِّ . وَرَوَيْنَا عَنْ أبي الْقَاسِمِ الجُنَيْدِ رَحِمَهُ اللهُ قال : الحيَاءُ رُؤْيَةُ الآلاءِ — أيْ : النِّعَمِ — وَرُؤْيَةُ التَّقْصِيرِ . فيَتَوَلَّدُ بيْنَهُمَا حَالَةٌ تُسَمَّى حيَاءً .

684. Hazrat Abu Sa'eed Khudri (R.A.A.) says that the Holy Prophet (S.A.W.) was more modest and shy than a secluded virgin and that whenever he saw something untoward, we could notice its signs from his face. *(Bukhari and Muslim).*

Note: The Ulema (learned theologians) have defined modesty which impels a person to discard vicious things and checks him to curtail or usurp the rights of a rightful person. According to Hazrat Qasim Junaid, modesty is a characteristic which enables a man to appreciate the bounties and favours of Allah, and then consider his own shortcomings; thereafter the situation created by these two things is known as modesty.

****

CHAPTER 85

On Keeping a Secret.

قال الله تعالى : وَأَوْفُوا بِالْعَهْدِ إِنَّ الْعَهْدَ كَانَ مَسْؤُولاً [الإسراء : ٣٤] .

Allah, the Exalted, has said:

239. And keep the covenant. Lo! of the covenant it will be asked. (17:34).

٦٨٥ — عن أبي سعيد الخُدْرِيِّ رضي الله عنه قال : قال رسولُ الله صلى الله عليه وسلم : « إنَّ مِنْ أشَرِّ النَّاسِ عِنْدَ اللهِ مَنْزِلَةً يوْمَ الْقِيامَةِ الرَّجُلُ يُفْضِي إلى المرْأَةِ وتُفْضِي إليْهِ ثُمَّ يَنْشُرُ سِرَّهَا » رواه مسلم

685. Hazrat Abu Sa'eed Khudri (R.A.A.) relates that the Holy Prophet (S.A.W.) said: 'On the Day of Judgment in the estimation of Allah, the worst position among all the human beings will be of that man who cohabits with his wife and then makes the secret of this act public.
(Muslim).

٦٨٦ — وعن عبدِ اللهِ بن عمر رضي الله عنهما أن عمرَ رضي الله عنه حينَ تأَيمت بِنتُهُ حفصةُ قال : لَقيتُ عُثمانَ بنَ عفَّانَ رضيَ الله عنه ، فعرَضتُ عليهِ حفصةَ فقلتُ : إنْ شئتَ أنكحتُكَ حفصةَ بنتَ عمرَ؟ قال : سأَنظرُ في أمري . فلبثتُ ليالِيَ ، ثمّ لقيني ؛ فقال : قدْ بدا لي أنْ لا أتزوّجَ يومي هذا . فلقيتُ أبا بكرٍ الصّدّيقَ رضي الله عنه . فقلتُ : إنْ شئتَ أنكحتُكَ حفصةَ بنتَ عمرَ . فصمتَ أبو بكرٍ رضي الله عنه . فلمْ يرجِعْ إليّ شيئاً ! فكنتُ عليهِ أوجدَ منّي على عثمانَ . فلبثتُ ليالِيَ . ثمّ خطبَها النّبيُّ صلى الله عليه وسلم . فأنكحتُها إيّاهُ . فلقيَني أبو بكرٍ فقالَ : لعلّكَ وجدتَ عليَّ حينَ عرضتَ عليَّ حفصةَ فلمْ أرجعْ إليكَ شيئاً ؟ فقلت : نعمْ . قال : فإنّهُ لمْ يمنعْني أنْ أرجِعَ إليكَ فيما عرضتَ عليَّ إلاّ أنّي كنتُ علمتُ أنّ النبيَّ صلى الله عليه وسلم ذكرَها . فلمْ أكنْ لأُفشي سِرَّ رسول الله صلى الله عليه وسلم ، ولَوْ تركَها النّبيُّ صلى الله عليه وسلم لقبلتُها . رواه البخاري .

686. Hazrat Abdullah bin 'Umar (R.A.A.) relates that when Hazrat Hafsah (R.A.A.) daughter of Hazrat Umar (R.A.A.), became a widow, Hazrat Umar (R.A.A.) met Hazrat Usman bin Affan (R.A.A.) and said to him: 'If you like, I may give my daughter, in marriage, to you.' Hazrat Usman (R.A.A.) said: 'I will think over the matter.' Hazrat Umar (R.A.A.) says:'After a few days Hazrat Usman (R.A.A.) met me and said: 'I have thought over the matter and decided, that I should not marry in these days.' Thereafter, I met (Hazrat) Abu Bakr (R.A.A.) and suggested to him: 'If you feel inclined, I may give Hafsah, my daughter, in marriage to you.' 'Hazrat Abu Bakr (R.A.A.) kept quite and did not say a word in reply. This attitude of (Hazrat) Abu Bakr pained me more than the reply of (Hazrat) Usman (R.A.A.). Only a few days after this, the Holy Prophet (S.A.W.) sent the proposal for her hand in marriage, and I married her to him (S.A.W.). After some time when Hazrat Abu Bakr (R.A.A.) met me and said: 'You might perhaps have felt unhappy when you suggested to marry Hafsa to me, and I gave no reply. I said : 'Yes;. He said: Nothing prevented me to accept it but the fact that the Holy Prophet (S.A.W.) had expressed his intention to marry her and I could not divulge his secret. Had the Holy Prophet (S.A.W.) declined her, I would have accepted the proposal (to marry her). *(Bukhari)*.

٦٨٧ — وعن عائشة رضي الله عنها قالتْ : كُنَّ أَزْواجُ النَّبيِّ صلى الله عليه وسلم عِنْدَهُ . فَأَقْبَلَتْ فَاطِمَةُ رضي الله عنها تَمْشِي . مَاتَخْطِيءُ مِشْيَتُهَا مِنْ مِشْيَةِ رسول الله صلى الله عليه وسلم شَيْئاً ، فَلَمَّا رَآها رَحَّبَ بِهَا وقال : « مَرْحَباً بِابْنَتِي » ثُمَّ أَجْلَسَهَا عَنْ يَمِينِهِ أَوْ عَنْ شِمَالِهِ . ثُمَّ سَارَّهَا فَبَكَتْ بُكَاءً شَدِيداً ، فَلَمَّا رَأَى جَزَعَهَا . سَارَّهَا الثَّانِيَةَ فَضَحِكَتْ . فقلتُ لَهَا : خَصَّكِ رسولُ الله صلى الله عليه وسلم مِنْ بَيْنِ نِسَائِهِ بِالسِّرَارِ . ثُمَّ أَنْتِ تَبْكِينَ ؟ فَلَمَّا قَامَ رسولُ الله صلى الله عليه وسلم سَأَلْتُهَا : مَاقَالَ لكِ رسولُ الله صلى الله عليه وسلم ؟ قالت : مَاكُنْتُ لأُفْشِيَ عَلَى رسول الله صلى الله عليه وسلم سِرَّهُ . فَلَمَّا تُوُفِّيَ رسولُ الله صلى الله عليه وسلم قلتُ : عَزَمْتُ عَلَيْكِ بِمَا لِي عَلَيْكِ مِنَ الحَقِّ . لَمَا حَدَّثْتِنِي ماقال لكِ رسولُ الله صلى الله عليه وسلم ؟ فقالتْ : أَمَّا الآنَ فَنَعَمْ . أَمَّا حِينَ سَارَّنِي في المَرَّةِ الأولى فَأَخْبَرَنِي « أَنَّ جِبْرِيلَ كَانَ يُعَارِضُهُ القُرْآنَ في كُلِّ سَنَةٍ مَرَّةً أَوْ مَرَّتَيْنِ . وَأَنَّهُ عَارَضَهُ الآنَ مَرَّتَيْنِ . وَإِنِّي لا أُرَى الأَجَلَ إِلاَّ قَدِ اقْتَرَبَ . فَاتَّقِي اللهَ وَاصْبِرِي ، فَإِنَّهُ نِعْمَ السَّلَفُ أَنَا لكِ » فَبَكَيْتُ بُكَائِيَ الَّذي رَأَيْتِ . فَلَمَّا رَأَى جَزَعِي سَارَّنِي الثَّانِيَةَ ، فقال : « يَافَاطِمَةُ أَمَا تَرْضَيْنَ أَنْ تَكُونِي سَيِّدَةَ نِسَاءِ المُؤْمِنِينَ ، أَوْ سَيِّدَةَ نِسَاءِ هذه الأُمَّةِ ؟ » فَضَحِكْتُ ضَحِكِي الَّذي رَأَيْتِ . متفقٌ عليه . وهذا لفظ مسلم .

687. Hazrat Ayesha (R.A.A.) relates that: 'Once when all the wives of the Holy Prophet (S.A.W.) were with him, his daughter, Hazrat Fatimah (R.A.A.) arrived there. The mode of her walking was exactly like the Holy Prophet (S.A.W.). On seeing her he greeted her and said: 'Welcome, O my daughter, and made her sit by his right or left side, and then whispered to her something at which she wept profusely. When the Holy Prophet (S.A.W.) noticed her intense grief, he whispered to her once more at which she smiled. I said to her: 'The Holy Prophet

(S.A.W.) ignoring his wives, spoke secretly to you only but why you wept When the Holy Prophet (S.A.W.) left the gathering I asked her: What did the Holy Prophet (S.A.W.) say to you? She said: 'I will not disclose the secret of the HolyProphet S.A.W.). When the Holy Prophet (S.A.W.) passed away, I said to her: 'I request you in the name of my right on you, to tell me what the Holy Prophet (S.A.W.) had said to you.' She said: 'Now, I will tell you. When he first whispered to me he informed that every year Jibreel Amin (Angel Gabriel) used to recite him the Quran, and then He (Holy Prophet (S.A.W.) recited it back to him (Angel Gabriel), but now he had done this twice at this time. From this it appears that his time (demise) was approaching. He therefore advised me to stand in awe of Allah (mindful of my duty to Allah) and be patient; I shall be the best advance guard for you.' On this I wept as you saw. Seeing my discomfort he whispered to me that the second time and said:'Fatimah, are you not happy that you will be the leader of the Muslim women or the Leader of the women of this Ummah. On this I smiled as you saw.' *(Bukhari and Muslim).* It is as narrated by *Muslim.*

٦٨٨ ــ وعن ثابتٍ عن أنس رضي الله عنه قال : أتَى عَلَيَّ رسولُ الله صلى الله عليه وسلم وَأنَا ألْعَبُ مَعَ الغِلْمَانِ . فَسَلَّمَ عَلَيْنَا . فَبَعَثَني في حاجَةٍ ، فَأبْطَأْتُ عَلى أمِّي . فَلَمَّا جِئْتُ قالت : مَا حَبَسَكَ ؟ فقلتُ : بَعَثَنِي رسولُ الله صلى الله عليه وسلم لِحَاجَةٍ . قالت : مَاحَاجَتُهُ ؟ قلتُ : إنَّهَا سِرٌ . قالتْ : لاَ تُخْبِرَنَّ بِسِرِّ رسول الله صلى الله عليه وسلم أحَداً . قال أنَسٌ : وَاللهِ لَوْ حَدَّثْتُ بِهِ أحَداً لَحَدَّثْتُكَ بِهِ يَاثَابِتُ . رواه مسلم ، وروى البخاري بَعْضَهُ مُخْتَصَراً

688. Hazrat Sabit (R.A.A.) reports from Hazrat Anas bin Malik (R.A.A.)that once when he (Hazrat Anas) was playing with the boys the Holy Prophet(S.A.W.) by chance reached there and saluted us and sent me on some mission for him, on account of which I was delayed in my return to my mother. When I reached her she asked: 'What had detained you?' I said: 'The Holy Prophet (S.A.W.) had sent me on a mission. She asked: 'What was that mission?' I said: 'It was a secret.' She said: 'Then do not tell anyone the secret of the Holy Prophet (S.A.W.).' Hazrat Anas (R.A.A.) said to Hazrat Sabit (R.A.A.) were I to tell it o anyone, I would tell you.' (*Muslim*, *Bukhari* narrated it briefly).

****

CHAPTER 86

On Fulfilment of Pledge and Promise.

قال الله تعالى: وَأَوْفُوا بِالْعَهْدِ إِنَّ الْعَهْدَ كَانَ مَسْئُولاً [الإسراء: ٣٤].
وقال تعالى: وَأَوْفُوا بِعَهْدِ الله إذا عَاهَدْتُمْ [النحل: ٩١]. وقال
تعالى: يَا أَيُّهَا الَّذِينَ آمَنُوا أَوْفُوا بِالْعُقُودِ [المائدة: ١]. وقال تعالى:
يَا أَيُّهَا الَّذِينَ آمَنُوا لِمَ تَقُولُونَ مَالا تَفْعَلُونَ؟ كَبُرَ مَقْتاً عِنْدَ الله أَنْ
تَقُولُوا مَالا تَفْعَلُونَ [الصف: ٢، ٣].

Allah, the Exalted, has said:

240. And keep the covenant. Lo! of the convenant it will be asked. (17:34).
241. Fulfil the covenant of Allah when ye have covenanted.(16:91).
242. O ye who believe! Fulfil your undertakings. (5:1).
243. O ye who believe! Why say ye that which ye do not? It is most hateful in the sightof Allah that ye say that which ye do not. (61:2—3).

٦٨٩ — عن أبي هريرة رضي الله عنه، أنَّ رسول الله صلّى الله عليه وسلّم قال: «آيَةُ المُنَافِقِ ثَلاثٌ: إذا حَدَّثَ كَذَبَ، وَإذا وَعَدَ أَخلَفَ، وَإذا اؤْتُمِنَ خَانَ» متفقٌ عليه

زَادَ في روايةٍ لمسلم: «وَإنْ صَامَ وَصَلَّى وَزَعَمَ أَنَّهُ مسلِمٌ».

689. This Hadis is the same as No. 199 of Chapter 25.

٦٩٠ — وعن عبدِ الله بن عمرو بن العاص رضي الله عنهما، أنَّ رسول الله صلى الله عليه وسلم قال: «أَرْبَعٌ مَنْ كُنَّ فِيهِ كَانَ مُنَافِقاً خَالِصاً. وَمَنْ كَانَتْ فيه خَصلَةٌ مِنهُنَّ كَانَتْ فِيهِ خَصْلَةٌ مِنَ النِّفَاقِ حَتَّى يَدَعَهَا: إذا اؤْتُمِنَ خَانَ، وَإذا حَدَّثَ كَذَبَ، وَإذا عَاهَدَ غَدَرَ، وَإذا خَاصَمَ فَجَرَ» متفقٌ عليه

690. Hazrat Abdullah bin 'Amr bin Al-'Aas (R.A.A.) relates that the Holy Prophet (S.A.W.) said: There are four (habits) which, if found in a person, then he is a perfect hypocrite. If one of these traits is found in a person, then he has one sign of hypocrisy, until he leaves it. These four characteristics of a hypocrite are, when he is entrusted (with something) he embezzles; when he talks he lies; when he promises he flouts it; and when he quarrels he starts abusing. *(Bukhari and Muslim).*

٦٩١ — وعن جابرٍ رضي الله عنه قال : قال لي النبي صلّى الله عليه وسلّم :
« لَوْ قَدْ جاءَ مالُ الْبَحْرَيْنِ أَعْطَيْتُكَ هكذا وهكذا وَهكذا » فَلَمْ
يَجِىءْ مَالُ الْبَحْرَيْنِ حَتَّى قُبِضَ النبيُّ صلى الله عليه وسلم ، فَلَمَّا جاءَ
مَالُ الْبَحْرَيْنِ أَمَرَ أَبُو بَكْرٍ رضي الله عنه فَنَادَى : مَنْ كَانَ لَهُ عِنْدَ
رسول الله صلى الله عليه وسلم عِدَةٌ أَوْ دَيْنٌ فَلْيَأْتِنا . فَأَتَيْتُهُ وقُلْتُ لَهُ :
إنَّ النبي صلى الله عليه وسلم قال لي كَذَا وكَذَا ، فَحثَى لي حَثْيَةً ، فَعَدَدْتُها ،
فإذا هِيَ خَمْسُمِائَةٍ ، فقال لي : خُذْ مِثْلَيْهَا . متفقٌ عليه

691. Hazrat Jabir (R.A.A.) relates: The Holy Prophet (S.A.W.) promised to me : 'On receipt of funds (revenues) from Bahrain, I shall give you so much and so much. But before the money from Bahrain was received, the Holy Prophet (S.A.W.) passed away (and Hazrat Abu Bakr (R.A.A.) was installed as his Caliph. When the money reached, the Caliph announced that anybody to whom the Holy Prophet (S.A.W.) had promised to pay something or owed anything should come forward. Accordingly I went to him and said that the Holy Prophet (S.A.W.) had promised to me thus and thus. Hazrat Abu Bakr (R.A.A.) then took out double handful of money and gave it to me. When I counted the same, it was 500 Dirhams. Hazrat Abu Bakr (R.A.A.) then asked me to take twice as much more. *(Bukhari and Muslim).*

****

CHAPTER 87

Perseverance and Safeguarding a Good Practice.

قال الله تعالى : ﴿ إِنَّ اللهَ لا يُغَيِّرُ مَا بِقَوْمٍ حَتَّى يُغَيِّرُوا مَا بِأَنْفُسِهِمْ ﴾
[الرعد : ١١] . وقال تعالى : ﴿ وَلَا تَكُونُوا كَالَّتِي نَقَضَتْ غَزْلَهَا مِنْ بَعْدِ
قُوَّةٍ أَنْكَاثاً ﴾ [النحل : ٩٢] .
وقال تعالى : ﴿ وَلا يَكُونُوا كَالَّذِينَ أُوتُوا الْكِتَابَ مِنْ قَبْلُ فَطَالَ
عَلَيْهِمُ الأَمَدُ فَقَسَتْ قُلُوبُهُمْ ﴾ [الحديد : ١٦] . وقال تعالى : ﴿ فَمَا
رَعَوْهَا حَقَّ رِعَايَتِهَا ﴾ [الحديد : ٢٧] .

Allah, the Exalted, has said:

244. Lo! Allah changeth not the condition of a folk until they (first) change that which is in their hearts. (13:11).

245. And be not like unto her who unravelleth the thread, after she hath made it strong, to thin filaments. (16:92).
246. That they become not as those who received the scripture of old but the term was prolonged for them and so their hearts were hardened. (57:16).
247. And they observed it not with right observance (57:27).

٦٩٢ — عن عبد الله بن عمرو بن العاص رضي الله عنهما قال : قال لي رسول الله صلى الله عليه وسلم : « يَا عَبْدَ الله . لاتَكُنْ مِثْلَ فُلانٍ ، كَانَ يَقُومُ اللَّيْلَ فَتَرَكَ قِيَامَ اللَّيْلِ ! » متفقٌ عليه

692. This Hadis is the same as No. 154 of Chapter 15.

****

CHAPTER 88

Soft Speaking and Cheerful Face While Meeting Somebody.

قال الله تعالى : واخْفِضْ جَنَاحَكَ لِلْمُؤْمِنِينَ [الحجر : ٨٨] . وقال تعالى : وَلَوْ كُنْتَ فَظّاً غَلِيظَ الْقَلْبِ لانْفَضُّوا مِنْ حَوْلِكَ [آل عمران : ١٥٩] .

Allah, the Exalted, has said:

248. And lower thy wing (in tenderness) for the believers.(15:88).
249. If thou hadst been stern and fierce of heart they would have dispersed from round about thee. (3:159).

٦٩٣ — عَنْ عَدِيٍّ بن حَاتِمٍ رضي الله عنه قال : قال رسول الله صلى الله عليه وسلم : « اتَّقُوا النَّارَ وَلَوْ بِشِقِّ تَمْرَةٍ فَمَنْ لَمْ يَجِدْ فَبِكَلِمَةٍ طَيِّبَةٍ » متفقٌ عليه

693. Hazrat 'Adee bin Hatim (R.A.A.) (The grand son of the great philanthropist, humanitarian generous and self-sacrificing Hatim Tai, who lived before the arrival of the Holy Prophet (S.A.W.), related that the Holy Prophet (S.A.W.) said: 'Protect yourselves from the fire of Hell, even if it be by spending only half a date as alms; and one who does not get even that, should at least speak nicely. *(Bukhari and Muslim)*

٦٩٤ — وعن أبي هريرة رضي الله عنه أن النبيَّ صلَّى الله عليه وسلَّم قال: « والكَلِمَةُ الطَّيِّبَةُ صَدَقَةٌ » متفقٌ عليه

694. Hazrat Abu Hurairah (R.A.A.) relates that the Holy Prophet (S.A.W.) said: Even utterance of nice words is a charity.

(Bukhari and Muslim)

٦٩٥ – وعن أبي ذرٍّ رضي الله عنه قال : قال لي رسول الله صلى الله عليه وسلم : « لا تحقرنَّ من المعروف شيئاً ، ولو أن تلقى أخاك بوجهٍ طليقٍ » رواه مسلم

695. This Hadis is the same as No. 121 of Chapter 13.

****

CHAPTER 89

Preference of Clarity of Discussion,its Elucidation to the Addressee And its Repetition if He does not understand.

٦٩٦ – عن أنسٍ رضي الله عنه أن النبي صلى الله عليه وسلم كانَ إذا تكلَّمَ بكلمةٍ أعادَها ثلاثاً حتّى تُفهَمَ عنهُ ، وإذا أتى على قومٍ فسلَّمَ عليهِم سلَّمَ عليهِم ثلاثاً . رواه البخاري

696. Hazrat Anas bin Malik (R.A.A.) says that the Holy Prophet (S.A.W.) used to repeat his words thrice so that the same were fully understood; and when he visited people and greeted them, he would repeat the salutation thrice. *(Bukhari).*

٦٩٧ – وعن عائشة رضي الله عنها قالت : كانَ كلامُ رسول اللهِ صلى الله عليه وسلم كلاماً فصلاً يفهمهُ كلُّ من يسمعهُ . رواه أبو داود

697. Hazrat Ayesha (R.A.A.) relates that the Holy Prophet (S.A.W.) used to talk very clearly and distinctly so that his audience who listened to him, understood the point. *(Abu Daud).*

****

CHAPTER 90

On Listening With Attention and Drawing the Attention of Listeners.

٦٩٨ – عن جرير بن عبدِ اللهِ رضي الله عنه قال : قال لي رسول الله صلى الله عليه وسلم في حجَّةِ الوداع : « استنصِتِ النَّاسَ » ثُمَّ قال : لا ترجعوا

بَعْدي كُفَّاراً يَضْرِبُ بَعْضُكُمْ رِقَابَ بَعْضٍ » متفقٌ عليه

698. Hazrat Jarir bin Abdullah (R.A.A.) relates that on the occasion of the farewell pilgrimage the Holy Prophet (S.A.W.) asked me to call upon the audience to keep quiet. As such (when I was able to make the gathering attentive), the Holy Prophet (S.A.W.) said: 'Do not adopt the practice of the unbelievers after me, killing each other.'

(Bukhari and Muslim).

****

CHAPTER 91

On Moderation in Preaching.

قال الله تعالى : ﴿ ادْعُ إلى سَبِيلِ رَبِّكَ بالحِكْمَةِ وَالمَوْعِظَةِ الحَسَنَةِ ﴾ [النحل : ١٢٥] .

Allah, the Exalted, has said:

250. Call unto the way of thy Lord with wisdom and fair exhortation. (16:125).

٦٩٩ – عن أبي وَائِلٍ شَقِيقِ بن سَلَمَةَ قال : كَانَ ابْنُ مَسْعُودٍ رضي الله عنه يُذَكِّرُنَا في كُلِّ خَمِيسٍ ، فَقَالَ لَهُ رَجُلٌ : يَا أَبَا عَبْدِ الرَّحْمنِ ، لَوَدِدْتُ أَنَّكَ ذَكَّرْتَنَا كُلَّ يَوْمٍ ، فقال : أما إنَّهُ يَمْنَعني مِنْ ذلكَ أني أكْرَهُ أنْ أُمِلَّكُمْ وَإنِّي أَتَخَوَّلُكُمْ بِالمَوْعِظَةِ ، كَمَا كَانَ رسول الله صلى الله عليه وسلم يَتَخَوَّلُنَا بها مَخَافَةَ السَّآمَةِ عَلَيْنَا . متفقٌ عليه .

699. Hazrat Abi Wayel Shaqiq bin Salamah (R.A.A.) says: 'Hazrat Ibn Mas'ud (R.A.A.) used to address us every Thursday. Once a man said to him: 'O Abu Abdur Rahman! I wish you could preach to us every day.' He replied 'What stops me from doing so, is the fear lest I may make you tired. I am preaching to you in the same way as the Holy Prophet (S.A.W.) adopted in preaching to us, keeping in view that we may not get tired.'

(Bukhari and Muslim).

٧٠٠ – وعن أبي اليَقْظَان عَمَّار بن يَاسر رضي الله عنهما قال : سَمِعْتُ رسول الله صلى الله عليه وسلم يقول : « إنَّ طُولَ صَلاةِ الرَّجُلِ ، وَقِصَرَ خُطْبَتِهِ ، مَئِنَّةٌ مِنْ فِقْهِهِ ، فَأَطِيلُوا الصَّلاةَ ، وَأَقْصِرُوا الخُطْبَةَ » رواه مسلم

700. Hazrat Abul Yaqzan Ammar bin Yasir (R.A.A.) relates that he heard the Holy Prophet (S.A.W.) say: 'A longer duration in prayer (Salat) and the conciseness of the sermon by a person prove his intelligence and wisdom. Therefore let your prayer be long and your sermons brief.' *(Muslim).*

٧٠١ ـ وعن مُعَاوِيَةَ بن الحَكَم السُّلَمِي رضي الله عنه قال : « بَيْنا أنا أُصَلِّي مَعَ رسول الله صلى الله عليه وسلم ، إذْ عَطَسَ رَجُلٌ مِنَ القَوْمِ فَقُلْتُ : يَرْحَمُكَ الله ، فرَماني القَوْم بِأَبْصَارِهِمْ ! فقُلْت : وَاثُكْلَ أُمِّيَاه ! ما شَأْنُكُمْ تَنْظُرونَ إليَّ ؟ فَجَعَلُوا يَضْرِبُونَ بِأَيْدِيهِمْ عَلى أَفْخَاذِهِمْ ! فَلَمَّا رَأَيْتُهُمْ يُصَمِّتُونَنِي لكِنِّي سَكَتَ . فَلَمَّا صلى رسول الله صلَّى الله عليه وسلَّم فَبِأَبِي هُوَ وَأُمِّي ، مَارَأَيْت مُعَلِّماً قَبْلَه وَلا بَعْدَه أَحْسَنَ تَعْلِيماً مِنه ، فَوَاللهِ ما كَهَرَنِي وَلا ضَرَبَنِي وَلاشَتَمَنِي . قال : « إنَّ هذِهِ الصَّلاةَ لايَصْلُح فِيها شَيْءٌ مِن كَلامِ النَّاسِ . إنَّمَا هِيَ التَّسْبِيح والتَّكْبِيرُ ، وَقِرَاءَةُ القُرْآنِ ، أو كما قال رسول الله صلى الله عليه وسلم . قلت : يارسول الله ، إني حَدِيثُ عَهْدٍ بجَاهِلِيَّةٍ ، وَقَدْ جَاءَ الله بِالإسْلامِ ،وَإنَّ مِنَّا رِجالاً يَأْتُونَ الْكُهَّانَ ؟ قال : « فَلا تَأْتِهِمْ » قلت : وَمِنَّا رِجَالٌ يَتَطَيَّرونَ ؟ قال : « ذَاكَ شَيْءٌ يَجِدونَه في صُدُورِهِمْ ، فَلا يَصُدَّنَّهُمْ » رواه مسلم

701. Hazrat Mu'awiyah bin Al-Hakam Sulaime (R.A.A.) says: 'Once while I was praying with the Holy Prophet (S.A.W.) a member of the congregation sneezed on which I responded with 'Yarhamuk Allaho' (Allah may have mercy on you). On this some members of the congregation started gazing at me with angry looks. To this I retorted: 'May your mothers be lost, why are you gazing at me? On this they started beating their hands against their thighs. From this I though that they wanted me to be quiet; so I restrained myself, (although I was much annoyed). After this when the prayer was over, the Holy Prophet (S.A.W.) gave his attention towards the incident. May my parents be sacrificed on the Holy Prophet (S.A.W.) I have not known a better instructor before him or after him. When he finished the prayer, he did not reprove me, nor beat me, nor threatened me. He said: 'While praying nobody should indulge in talking.' It is all praise and glorification of Allah and recitation of the Quran.' Or he said like that. I said:

'O! Messenger of Allah! I have recently come out of the effects of Jahiliya (Ignorance) and Allah has recently favoured us with Islam. Some of us still go to consult sooth-sayers. He said: 'Do not go to them.' Then I submitted: 'Some of us are still guided by omens. ' He said: 'These are merely the figments of their minds. They should not be infludnece by them.' *(Muslim)*.

٧٠٢ – وعن العِرْبَاض بن سَارِيَةَ رضي الله عنه قال : وَعَظَنَا رسول الله صلى الله عليه وسلم مَوْعِظَةً وَجِلَتْ مِنْها القُلُوب . وَذَرِفَتْ مِنْها العُيُون وَذَكَرَ الحَدِيثَ وَقَدْ سَبَقَ بِكَمَالِهِ في باب الأمْر بالمُحَافَظَةِ عَلى السُّنَّة ،وَذَكَرْنا أنَّ التِّرْمِذيَّ قال : إنه حديث حسنٌ صحيحٌ

702. This Hadis has already been covered by the first part of No. 157 of Chapter 16.

****

CHAPTER 92

On Dignity and Poise.

قال الله تعالى : وَعِبَادُ الرَّحْمنِ الَّذِينَ يَمْشُونَ عَلى الأَرْضِ هَوْناً وَإذا خَاطَبَهُمُ الجَاهِلُونَ قَالُوا سَلاماً [الفرقان : ٦٣] .

Allah, the Exalted, has said:

251. The (faithful) slaves of Beneficent are they who walk ıpon the earth modestly, and when the foolish ones address them answer: Peace (25:63).

٧٠٣ – عن عائشة رضي الله عنها قالتْ : مَا رَأَيْتُ رسول الله صلى الله عليه وسلم مستَجْمِعاً قَطُّ ضَاحِكاً حَتَّى تُرَى مِنه لَهَوَاتُه . إنَّمَا كَانَ يَتَبَسَّمُ . متفقٌ عليه

703. Hazrat Ayesha Siddiqa (R.A.A.) relates: 'I never saw the Holy Prophet (S.A.W.) laugh so much that the inner part of his mouth may be vizible. He simply used to smile.' *(Bukhari and Muslim)*.

****

CHAPTER 93·

On Maintenance of Dignity and Poise in Prayers and In Achievement of Knowledge and Learning.

قال الله تعالى : وَمَنْ يُعَظِّمْ شَعَائِرَ اللهِ فَإِنَّهَا مِنْ تَقْوَى الْقُلُوبِ [الحج : ٣٢] .

Allah, the Exalted, has said:

252. And whoso magnifieth the offerings consecrated to Allah, it surely is from devotion of the hearts.(22:32).

٧٠٤ – وعن أبي هريرة رضي الله عنه قال : سمعتُ رسول الله صلى الله عليه وسلم يقول : « إذا أُقِيمَتِ الصَّلاة ، فَلا تَأْتُوهَا وَأَنْتُمْ تَسْعَوْنَ ، وَأْتُوهَا وَأَنْتُمْ تَمْشُونَ ، وَعَلَيْكُمُ السَّكِينَة ، فَمَا أَدْرَكْتُمْ فَصَلُّوا ، وَمَا فَاتَكُمْ فَأَتِمُّوا » متفقٌ عليه

زاد مسلم في روايةٍ له: « فَإِنَّ أَحَدَكُمْ إذا كانَ يَعْمِدُ إلى الصَّلاةِ فَهُوَ في صَلاة » .

704. Hazrat Abu Hurairah (R.A.A.) relates that he heard the Holy Prophet (S.A.W.) say:When the (congregation) prayer (Salat), has been started do not rush for it, but come to it walking in the normal way with calmness and dignity, join in the prayer at the stage when you arrive, and make up the missing parts afterwards. *(Bukhari and Muslim).*

Imam Muslim further adds: When one of you intends making preparations to join the Salat, he is considred to be already in the Salat.

٧٠٥ – وعن ابن عباس رضي الله عنهما أنَّهُ دَفَعَ مَعَ النَّبِيِّ صلى الله عليه وسلم يَوْمَ عَرَفَةَ فَسَمِعَ النَّبِيُّ صلّى الله عليه وسلم وَرَاءَهُ زَجْراً شَدِيداً وَضَرْباً وَصَوْتاً لِلإِبِلِ ، فَأَشارَ بِسَوْطِهِ إِلَيْهِمْ وقال : « أَيُّهَا النَّاسُ عَلَيْكُمْ بِالسَّكِينَةِ فَإِنَّ الْبِرَّ لَيْسَ بِالإِيضَاعِ » رواه البخاري ، وروى مسلم بعضه.

705. Hazrat Ibn Abbas (R.A.A.) relates that while returning from Arafat on the day of the pilgrimage, along with the Holy Prophet (S.A.W.), he (S.A.W.) heard behind him noise of tumult and pandemonium caused by shouting and severely beating and driving animals. Signalling with his whip he said: 'O ye people! It is incumbent upon you to proceed calmly. There is no good in rushing.. (*Bukhari. Muslim* has quoted some parts of this tradition.)

****

CHAPTER 94

Honouring the Guest.

قال الله تعالى : هَلْ أَتَاكَ حَدِيثُ ضَيفِ إبْرَاهِيمَ المُكرَمِينَ ، إذ دَخلُوا عليهِ فقَالُوا: سَلاماً ، قال: سَلامٌ قَومٌ مُنْكَرُونَ * فَرَاغَ إلى أهلِهِ فَجاءَ بِعِجلٍ سَمِينٍ * فَقَرَّبَهُ إليهم قَالَ: ألا تَأكُلُونَ ؟ [الذاريات: ٢٤–٢٧] .

وقال تعالى : وَجَاءَهُ قومُهُ يُهْرَعُونَ إلَيْهِ ، وَمِن قبلُ كَانُوا يَعْمَلونَ السَّيِّئَاتِ ! قال : يَا قَوْمِ هؤلاءِ بَنَاتي هُنَّ أطهَرُ لَكُمْ ، فاتَّقُوا اللهَ وَلَا تُخزُونِ فِي ضَيفِي أَلَيْسَ مِنكُم رَجُلٌ رَشِيدٌ ؟ ! [هود : ٧٨] .

Allah, the Exalted, has said:

253. Hath the story of Abraham's honoured guests reached thee. (O Muhammad) when they came in unto him and said: Peace! he answered, Peace! (and thought): Folk unknown (to me). Then he went apart unto his housefolk so that they brought a fatted calf; and he set it before them, saying: Will ye not eat? (51:24–27).
254. And his people came unto him, running towards him — and before then they used to commit abominations — He said: O my people! Here are my daughters! They are purer for you. Beware of Allah, and degrade me not in (the person of) my guests. Is there not among you any upright man ? (11:78).

٧٠٦ – عن أبي هريرة رضي الله عنه أنَّ النبيَّ صلى الله عليه وسلم قال : « مَن كانَ يُؤمِنُ بِاللهِ وَاليَومِ الآخِرِ فَلْيُكرِمْ ضَيفَهُ ، وَمَنْ كانَ يُؤمِنُ بِاللهِ وَاليَومِ الآخِرِ فليَصِلْ رَحِمَهُ ، وَمَنْ كانَ يؤمِنُ بِاللهِ وَاليَوْمِ الآخِرِ فَلْيَقلْ خَيْراً أَوْ لِيَصْمُتْ » متفقٌ عليه

706. This Hadis is the same as No. 314 of Chapter 40.

٧٠٧ – وعن أبي شُرَيْح خُوَيلدِ بن عمرو الخُزَاعِيِّ رضي الله عنه قال : سَمِعتُ رسول الله صلّى اللهُ عليه وسلّم يقول : « مَنْ كان يؤمِنُ بِاللهِ وَاليَوْمِ

الآخِرِ فَلْيُكرِمْ ضَيفَهُ جَائِزَتَهُ » قالوا : وما جَائِزَتُهُ يا رسول الله ؟ قال :
« يَومُهُ ولَيْلَتُهُ . والضِّيافَةُ ثَلاثَةُ أَيَّامٍ ،فما كان وَرَاءَ ذلكَ فهو صَدَقَةٌ عليه »
متفقٌ عليه

وفي روايةٍ لمسلمٍ : « لايَحِلُ لِمُسلمٍ أن يُقيمَ عِندَ أخيهِ حتى يُؤْثِمَهُ »
قالوا : يا رسول الله ، وكَيفَ يُؤْثِمُهُ ؟ قال: « يُقيمُ عِندَهُ ولا شَيْءَ لَهُ
يَقْرِيهِ بِهِ » .

707 Hazrat Abu Shuraih Khuwailid bin 'Amr Al-Khuzai (R.A.A.) relates that he heard the Holy Prophet (S.A.W.) say: 'One who believes in Allah and the Day of Judgment should honour his guest according to his right.' He was asked: 'O Messenger of Allah (S.A.W.)!What is his right?' He said: 'A day and a night (of good feasting) and hospitality for three days. Thereafter it is charity. *(Bukhari and Muslim).*

Imam Muslim adds:' It is not proper for a person to stay so long with his brother (the host), as to involve him in sin.' He (S.A.W.) was asked by the companions as to how he could be involved in sin? The Holy Prophet (S.A.W.) answered: 'By prolonging his stay with his host so that the host has nothing left in his house with which to entertain the guest.'

****

CHAPTER 95

Virtue of Communicating and Congratulating on Good News.

قال الله تعالى : فَبَشِّرْ عِبَادِ الَّذِينَ يَسْتَمِعُونَ الْقَوْلَ فَيَتَّبِعُونَ
أَحْسَنَهُ [الزمر : ١٧ — ١٨] . وقال تعالى : يُبَشِّرُهُمْ رَبُّهُم بِرَحْمَةٍ
مِنْهُ وَرِضْوان وجَنَّاتٍ لَهُمْ فيهَا نَعِيمٌ مُقِيمٌ [التوبة : ٢١] وقال تعالى :
وَأَبْشِرُوا بِالجَنَّةِ الَّتِي كُنْتُمْ تُوعَدُونَ [فصلت : ٣٠] . وقال تعالى :
فَبَشَّرْنَاهُ بِغُلامٍ حَلِيمٍ [الصافات : ١٠١] . وقال تعالى : وَلَقَدْ جَاءَتْ
رُسُلُنَا إِبْرَاهِيمَ بِالْبُشْرَى [هود : ٦٩] . وقال تعالى : وَامْرَأَتُهُ قَائِمَةٌ
فَضَحِكَتْ فَبَشَّرْنَاهَا بِإِسْحَاقَ وَمِن وَرَاءِ إِسْحَاقَ يَعْقُوبَ [هود : ٧١]
وقال تعالى : فَنَادَتْهُ المَلائِكَةُ وَهُوَ قَائِمٌ يُصَلِّي فِي المِحْرَابِ أَنَّ اللهَ

يُبَشِّرُكَ بِيَحْيَى [آل عمران : ٣٩] . وقال تعالى : إذْ قَالَتِ المَلائِكَةُ يَا مَرْيَمُ إنَّ اللهَ يُبَشِّرُكِ بِكَلِمَةٍ مِنْهُ اسْمُهُ المَسِيحُ [آل عمران: ٤٥]

Allah, the Exalted, has said:

255. Therefore give good tidings (O Muhammad) to my bondmen; who hear advice and follow the best thereof. (39:17–18).
256. Their Lord giveth them good tidings of mercy from Him and acceptance, and gardens where enduring pleasure will be theirs. (9:21).
257. But hear good tidings of the Paradise which ye are promised. (41:30).
258. So we gave him tidings of a gentle son. (37:101).
259. And Our Messengers came unto Abraham with good news. (11:69).
260. And his wife, standing by, laughed when We gave her good tidings (of the birth) of Isaac, and, after Isaac, of Jacob. (11:71).
261. And the angels called to him as he stood praying in the sanctuary; Allah giveth thee glad tidings of (a son whose name is) John (Yahya). (3:39).
262. (And remember) when the angels said: 'O Mary! Lo! Allah giveth thee glad tidings of a word from Him, whose name is the Messiah, Jesus.' (3:45).

٧٠٨ – عن أبي إبراهيمَ وَيُقَالُ أبو محمد ويقال أبو مُعَاوِيَةَ عَبدِ الله بن أبي أوْفَى رضي الله عنه أنَّ رسول الله صلى الله عليه وسلم بَشَّرَ خَدِيجَةَ ، رضي الله عنها ، بِبَيْتٍ في الجَنَّةِ مِنْ قَصَبٍ ، لا صَخَبَ فِيهِ ولا نَصَبَ . متفقٌ عليه

708. Hazrat Abu Ibrahim or Abu Muhammad or Abu Muawiya (all these are his *kunniyats* — A kunniyat is a name derived from the name of a father, mother or son e.g. Ibn-i-Abbas, son of Abbas; Abul Hasan, father of Hasan). **Abdullah bin Abi Aufa** (R.A.A.) relates that the Holy Prophet (S.A.W.) gave Hazrat Khadijah-tul-Kubra (R.A.A.) the happy news of a palace built from pearls in which there would be neither any noise nor there will be any tiredness or monotony.

(Bukhari and Muslim)

٧٠ – وعن أبي موسى الأَشْعَرِيِّ رضي الله عنه ، أنَّهُ تَوَضَّأَ في بَيْتِهِ ، ثُمَّ خَرَجَ فقال : لأَلْزَمَنَّ رسول الله صلى الله عليه وسلم ، ولأَكُونَنَّ مَعَهُ يَوْمِي هذا ، فَجَاءَ المَسْجِدَ ، فَسَأَلَ عَنِ النَّبِيِّ صلى الله عليه وسلم ، فَقَالُوا:

وَجَهَ ههُنَا ، قال : فَخَرَجْتُ على أثرِهِ أسْألُ عَنْهُ ، حتَّى دَخَلَ بِئْرَ أرِيسٍ . فَجَلَسْتُ عِنْدَ البَابِ حتَّى قَضَى رسول الله صلى الله عليه وسلم حَاجَتَهُ وتَوَضَّأ ، فَقُمْتُ إلَيْهِ ، فإذا هُوَ قَدْ جَلَسَ على بِئْرِ أرِيسٍ ، وَتَوَسَّطَ قُفَّهَا ، وكَشَفَ عَنْ سَاقَيْهِ وَدَلاَّهُمَا في البِئْرِ ، فَسَلَّمْتُ عَلَيْهِ ثُمَّ انصَرَفْتُ ، فَجَلَسْتُ عِنْدَ البَابِ فقُلْتُ : لأكُونَنَّ بَوَّابَ رَسُولِ الله صلى اللهُ عليهِ وسلَّم اليَوْمَ ، فَجَاءَ أبُوبَكْرٍ رَضِيَ اللهُ عنه فَدَفَعَ البَابَ فَقُلْتُ : مَنْ هذا ؟ فَقَالَ : أبُو بَكْرٍ ، فَقُلْتُ : على رِسْلِكَ ، ثُمَّ ذَهَبْتُ فَقُلْتُ : يا رَسُولَ اللهِ هذا أبُو بَكْرٍ يَسْتَأذِنُ ، فَقَالَ : « ائْذَنْ لَهُ وَبَشِّرْهُ بالجَنَّةِ » فأقْبَلْتُ حتَّى قُلْتُ لأبي بَكْرٍ : ادْخُلْ ورَسُولُ الله يُبَشِّرُكَ بالجَنَّةِ ، فَدَخَلَ أبُو بَكْرٍ حَتَّى جَلَسَ عَنْ يَمِينِ النَّبيِّ صلى اللهُ عليهِ وسلَّم مَعَهُ في القُفِّ ، وَدَلَّى رِجْلَيْهِ في البِئْرِ كَما صَنَعَ رَسُولُ اللهِ صلى اللهُ عليهِ وسلَّم ، وكَشَفَ عَنْ سَاقَيْهِ ، ثُمَّ رَجَعْتُ وجَلَسْتُ ، وقَدْ تَرَكْتُ أخي يتَوَضَّأ وَيَلْحَقُنِي ، فَقُلْتُ : إنْ يُرِدِ الله بِفُلانٍ – يُرِيدُ أخَاهُ – خَيْراً يَأتِ بِهِ ، فإذا إنسَانٌ يُحرِّكُ البَابَ ، فَقُلْتُ : مَنْ هذا ؟ فَقَالَ : عُمَرُ بْنُ الخَطَّابِ : فَقُلْتُ : عَلَى رِسْلِكَ ، ثُمَّ جِئْتُ إلى رَسُولِ اللهِ صلى اللهُ عليهِ وسلَّم ، فَسَلَّمْتُ عَلَيْهِ وقُلْتُ : هذا عُمَرُ يَسْتَأذِنُ ؟ فَقَالَ : « ائْذَنْ لَهُ وَبَشِّرْهُ بالجَنَّةِ » فَجِئْتُ عُمَرَ ، فَقُلْتُ : أذِنَ وَيُبَشِّرُكَ رَسُولُ الله صلى اللهُ عليهِ وسلَّم بالجَنَّةِ . فَدَخَلَ فَجَلَسَ مَعَ رَسُولِ الله صلى اللهُ عليهِ وسلَّم في القُفِّ عَنْ يَسَارِهِ ، وَدَلَّى رِجْلَيْهِ في البِئْرِ ، ثُمَّ رَجَعْتُ فَجَلَسْتُ فَقُلْتُ : إنْ يُرِدِ الله بِفُلانٍ خَيْراً يَعْني أخَاهُ – يَأتِ بِهِ ، فَجَاءَ إنْسَانٌ فَحَرَّكَ البَابَ . فَقُلْتُ : مَنْ هذا ؟ فَقَالَ : عُثْمَانُ بْنُ عَفَّانَ . فَقُلْتُ : عَلى رِسْلِكَ ، وجِئْتُ النَّبيَّ صلى اللهُ عليه وسلَّم ، فأخْبَرْتُهُ فَقَالَ : « ائْذَنْ لَهُ وَبَشِّرْهُ بِالجَنَّةِ مَعَ بَلْوى

تُصيبُهُ » فَجِئتُ فَقُلتُ : ادخُلْ وَيُبَشِّرُكَ رسولُ اللهِ صلى اللهُ عليه وسلَّم بِالجنَّةِ مَعَ بلْوَى تُصيبُكَ . فَدَخَلَ فَوَجَدَ القُفَّ قَدْ مُلِئَ . فَجَلَسَ وِجَاهَهُمْ مِنَ الشِّقِّ الآخرِ . قالَ سَعيدُ بنُ المُسَيَّبِ : فَأَوَّلتُها قُبُورَهُم. متفقٌ عليهِ

وزادَ في روايةٍ : « وَأَمَرَني رسولُ اللهِ صلى اللهُ عليهِ وسلَّم بحِفْظِ البَابِ .

وَفيها : أَنَّ عُثمانَ حِينَ بَشَّرَهُ حَمِدَ اللهَ تَعالى ، ثُمَّ قالَ : اللهُ المُستَعانُ .

709. Hazrat Abu Musa Ash'ari (R.A.A.) says that once after having made his ablutions at his home, he came out and resolved that he would stay with the Holy Prophet (S.A.W.) and spend the day in his company. As such he (Hazrat Abu Musa Ash'ari) came to the mosque and inquired about the Holy Prophet (S.A.W.) and learnt from the companions that he had gone in the direction of a certain village. Hazrat Abu Musa says: I followed after his foot marks, asking (the people) as to where the Holy Prophet (S.A.W.) had gone, till he reached a place known as Bi'r where he sat down at the door. Hazrat Abu Musa says: After the Holy Prophet (S.A.W.) had eased himself, and completed his ablution, I went to him and saw that he was sitting on the platform of the well, having drawn up his loin cloth up to his knees, and his feet dangling into the well. I paid my respects to him and returned to the door and said to myself: 'I shall be the Holy Prophet's (S.A.W.) doorman today.' Soon thereafter Hazrat Abu Bakr Siddiq (R.A.A.) arrived there and knocked on the door of the garden. I said: 'Who is there?' He said: 'Abu Bakr.' I said: 'Please wait;' and then I went to the Holy Prophet (S.A.W.) and said: 'O Messenger of Allah (S.A.W.)! Hazrat Abu Bakr (R.A.A.) has come and requests for permission to come in.' The Holy Prophet (S.A.W.) said: 'He may be allowed and greeted with the promise of Paradise.' I came to the door and said to Hazrat Abu Bakr 'Come in Please', and the Holy Prophet (S.A.W.) conveys to you the happy news of the promise of Paradise.' As such Hazrat Abu Bakr (R.A.A.) came in and took his seat on the right side of the Holy Prophet (S.A.W.) on the platform, drawing up his loin cloth upto the knees and suspending his feet into the well, as the Holy Prophet (S.A.W.) had done. I returned and took my seat at the door. As I had left my brother at home who was making his ablutions and was to join me. I thought: 'If Allah wills good for him, He will bring him here just now.' In the meantime someone knocked the door once again and I said: 'Who is there?' He said: Umar bin Khattab.' I said: 'Please wait a little;' and went to the Holy Prophet (S.A.W.) and after saluting him said: (Hazrat) Umar (R.A.A.) is at the door soliciting permission to come in.' He said: 'Permit him to come in and also greet him with the glad tidings of the promise of Paradise.' I went back to (Hazrat) Umar (R.A.A.) and said to him: 'You are permitted to come in and the Holy (S.A.W.) greets you with the happy news of the promise of Paradise.' Hazrat Umar came in and took his seat on the left side of the Holy Prophet (S.A.W.) on the platform of the well, and suspended his feet in the well. I also returned and took my seat at the door, and started thinking: If Allah desires good for so and so (my brother) He will send him here.' Again there was knocking at the door and I said: 'Who is there He said: 'Usman bin Affan' I said: 'Please wait for a moment: and I went and informed the Holy Prophet (S.A.W.). He said: 'Give him the news of a misfortune which will come upon him.'He came in finding the platform full, sat down on the other side, opposite to them. According to Hazrat Sa'id bin Musayyab (R.A.A.) the narrator of this Hadis, the order in which they sat down indicated that the three persons who sat closer to each other, will have their graves also closer to each other and the grave of Hazrat Usman (R.A.A.) will be away from theirs.

(Bukhari and Muslim).

Another version adds: The Holy Prphet (S.A.W.) directed me to look-after the door. And it also says that when Hazrat Usman (R.A.A.) was apprised of the happy news he eulogised Allah the Most High and said: Allah, the Master of Honour and Glory is my helper.'

٧١٠ ــ وعن أبي هريرة رضيَ اللهُ عنهُ قال : كُنَّا قُعُوداً حَوْلَ رسولِ الله صلى اللهُ عليهِ وسلَّم ، ومَعَنَا أبُو بَكرٍ وعُمَرَ رضيَ اللهُ عنهما في نَفَرٍ ، فقَامَ رَسُولُ اللهِ صلى اللهُ عليهِ وسلَّم مِنْ بينِ أظْهُرِنَا فَأبْطَأ عَلَيْنَا ، وَخَشِينا أن يُقْتَطَعَ دُونَنا وَفزِعنَا فقُمْنَا ، فكُنْتُ أوَّلَ مَنْ فزِعَ ، فَخَرَجْتُ أبْتَغِي رسُولَ اللهِ صلى الله عليهِ وسلَّم ، حتى أتَيْتُ حَائِطاً لِلأنصارِ لِبَني النَّجَّارِ ، فدُرْتُ بهِ هَلْ أجِدُ لَهُ بَاباً ؟ فلَمْ أجِدْ ، فإذَا رَبيعٌ يَدْخُلُ في جَوْفِ حَائِطٍ مِنْ بِئْرٍ خَارِجَهُ ــ وَالرَّبيعُ : الجَدْوَلُ الصَّغِيرُ ــ فاحْتَفَزْتُ ، فدَخَلْتُ عَلى رسُولِ اللهِ صلى اللهُ عليهِ وسلَّم فقَال : « أبُو هُرَيْرَةَ ؟ » فقُلْتُ : نَعَمْ يَا رَسُولَ اللهِ ، قَال : « مَا شَأنُكَ » قلتُ : كُنْتَ بَيْنَ ظَهْرَيْنَا فقُمْتَ فأبْطَأتَ علَينا ، فخَشِينَا أنْ تُقْتَطَعَ دُونَنَا ، فَفزِعْنَا ، فكُنْتُ أوَّلَ مَنْ فزِعَ ، فأتَيْتُ هذَا الحائِطَ ، فاحْتَفَزْتُ كَمَا يَحْتَفِزُ الثَّعْلَبُ ، وَهؤلاءِ النَّاسُ وَرَائي . فقَالَ : « يَا أبَا هُرَيْرَةَ » وَأعْطَاني نَعْلَيْهِ فقَالَ : « اذْهَبْ بِنَعْلَيَّ هاتَيْنِ ، فمَنْ لَقِيتَ مِنْ وَرَاء

هذَا الحائطِ يَشْهَدُ أَنْ لاَ إلهَ إلاَّ اللهُ مُسْتَيْقِناً بِها قَلْبُهُ ، فَبَشِّرْهُ بالجنَّةِ »
وَذَكَرَ الحَدِيثَ بطُولِهِ ، رواهُ مسلم

710. Hazrat Abu Hurairah (R.A.A.) relates: Once we were sitting around the Holy Prophet (S.A.W.) and Hazrat Abu Bakr (R.A.A.) and Hazrat Umar (R.A.A.) were also in our company, when the Holy Prophet (S.A.W.) got up and went out. When considerable time passed and he did not return to us, we started feeling uneasy, about his safety. As this idea came to our mind we felt much worried. I was the first to feel like this, and set out in search of him till I reached near a garden of Banu Najjar. I circled round the garden searching for a door, but could not find one (due to intense anxiety). Any way I noticed a small channel bringing water from a well outside the garden,which entered the garden through the wall. I contracted my body to pass through the hole, and reached the Holy Prophet(S.A.W.) who on seeing me exclaimed: 'Abu Hurairah?' I replied: 'Yes! 'O Messenger of Allah (S.A.W.).' He asked: 'How are you?' (what has brought you here?). I answered: You were with us, then (suddenly) you left us and went out. You did not return for quite a long time. Hence we were concerned lest you might meet with some mishap in our absence. All of us were much worried. I was the first person to feel like that and reached this garden and came in through the water channel in the wall after contracting my body like a fox. Others are following me. The Holy Prophet (S.A.W.) gave me his shoes and said to me:'Abu Hurairah, take these and whoever you should meet behind this garden, who affirms sincerely, that there is no god save Allah, greet him with the happy news of the promise of Paradise. After this Hazrat Abu Hurairah (R.A.A.) narrated the tradition in full.' *(Muslim).*

٧١١ — وعَنِ ابنِ شُمَاسَةَ قالَ : حَضَرْنَا عَمْرَو بنَ العَاصِ رضيَ اللهُ عنه ، وَهُوَ في سِيَاقَةِ المَوْتِ فَبَكى طَوِيلاً ، وَحَوَّلَ وَجْهَهُ إلى الجِدَارِ ، فَجَعَلَ ابْنُهُ يَقُولُ : يَا أَبَتَاهُ ، أَمَا بَشَّرَكَ رَسُولُ اللهِ صلى اللهُ عليهِ وسلَّم بِكَذَا ؟ أَمَا بَشَّرَكَ رَسُولُ اللهِ صلى اللهُ عليهِ وسلَّم بِكَذَا ؟ فَأَقْبَلَ بِوَجْهِهِ فَقَالَ : إنَّ أَفْضَلَ مَا نُعِدُّ شَهَادَةُ أَنْ لاَ إلهَ إلاَّ اللهُ ، وَأَنَّ مُحَمَّداً رسُولُ اللهِ . إِنِّي قَدْ كُنْتُ عَلى أَطْبَاقٍ ثَلاثٍ : لَقَدْ رَأَيْتُنِي وَمَا أَحَدٌ أَشَدَّ بُغْضاً لِرَسُولِ اللهِ صلى اللهُ عليهِ وسلَّم مِنِّي ، وَلاَ أَحَبَّ إليَّ مِنْ أَنْ أَكُونَ قَدِ اسْتَمْكَنْتُ مِنْهُ فَقَتَلْتُهُ ، فَلَوْ مُتُّ عَلى تِلْكَ الحالِ لَكُنْتُ مِنْ أَهْلِ النَّارِ ، فَلَمَّا جَعَلَ اللهُ الإسْلاَمَ في قَلْبي أَتَيْتُ النَّبيَّ صلى اللهُ عليه وسلم

فَقُلْتُ : ابْسُطْ يَمِينَكَ فَلأُبَايِعْكَ ، فَبَسَطَ يَمِينَهُ فَقَبَضْتُ يَدِي ، فقالَ : « مالكَ يَا عَمرو ؟ » قلت : أَرَدْتُ أَنْ أَشْتَرِطَ قالَ : « تَشْتَرِطُ مَاذَا ؟ » قُلْتُ : أَنْ يُغْفَرَ لِي ، قَالَ : « أَمَا عَلِمْتَ أَنَّ الإِسْلامَ يَهْدِمُ ماكَانَ قَبلَهُ ، وَأَنَّ الهِجرَةَ تَهدِمُ ماكان قَبلَهَا ، وَأَنَّ الحَجَّ يَهدِمُ ماكَانَ قَبلَهُ ؟ » وما كان أَحدٌ أَحَبَّ إِليَّ مِنْ رسول الله صلى الله عليه وسلم ، ولا أَجَلَّ فِي عَيني مِنْهُ ، ومَا كُنتُ أُطِيقُ أَن أَملأَ عَيني مِنه إِجلالاً له ؛ ولو سُئِلتُ أَن أَصِفَهُ ما أَطقتُ ؛ لأَنِّي لم أَكن أَملأُ عَيني مِنه ، ولو مُتُّ على تِلكَ الحَالِ لَرَجَوتُ أَن أَكُونَ مِنْ أَهْلِ الجَنَّةِ ، ثم ولِيْنَا أَشيَاءَ ما أَدري ماحَالي فِيها ؟ فإِذا أَنا مُتُّ فلا تَصحبَنِّي نَائِحَةٌ ولا نَارٌ ، فإذا دَفَنتُمُونِي ، فَشُنُّوا عليَّ التُّرَابَ شَنّاً ، ثم أَقِيمُوا حَولَ قَبرِي قَدرَ ما تُنحَرُ جَزُورٌ ، وَيُقسَمُ لَحمُهَا ، حَتَّى أَستَأْنِسَ بِكُمْ ، وأَنظُرَ ما أُرَاجِعُ بِهِ رُسُلَ ربي . رواه مسلم .

711. Hazrat Abu Shumasah (R.A.A.) relates: Some of us went to see Hazrat 'Amr bin Al-'Aas, when he was in the agony of death. He wept for a long time and then turned his face towards the wall. Seeing this situation, Hazrat Abdullah, his son, tried to console him, saying: 'Father, did not the Holy Prophet (S.A.W.) give you such and such good news?' Then why you worry so much?' Then Hazrat 'Amr bin Al-'Aas looked towards us and said: Our best provision (for the Hereafter) is the testimony that there is no god but Allah and that Muhammad is his Prophet (S.A.W.). Indeed I have passed through three stages. One was the stage when I was the bitterest enemy of the Holy Prophet (S.A.W.) and nothing was dearer to me than that if I had the power. I would kill him. Had I died in that condition, I would have been one of the dwellers of the Hell. When Allah put the idea of Islam in my heart, I approached the Holy Prophet (S.A.W.) and said: 'Please extend your right hand, so that I may take the oath of allegiance to you.' He did extend his right hand, but I held back my hand, He asked: 'Why this, 'Amr?' I said: 'I have a condition.' 'Make any condition you like (I will accept it). I answered: 'That I may be forgiven.' He said: 'Do you not know that Islam wipes out all the sins which have been committed before it; that Migration wipes out all that has taken place before it; and that Hajj (the Pilgrimage) wipes out all previous sins?' (Accordingly I took the oath of allegiance to him). Thereafter, no one was dearer to me than the Holy Prophet (S.A.W.) nor was anyone more glorious than him in my eyes; on account of the majesty and fascination of the Holy Prophet (S.A.W.) I could not look at his holy face fully, for this reason if I were asked to describe him I would not be able to do so as I had not looked at him long enough. Had I died then, I could have hoped to be one of the inmates of Paradise. After this we were entrusted with so many things (i.e. my acts of commission and omission) and I do not know how I shall face as regards the same. When I am dead, no mourner or fire should accompany my funeral. When you bury me throw the earth in little quantities over my grave, and stay around my grave for such time as it takes to slaughter a camel and distribute its meat, so that I may get some relief from your presence and may consider the answers I will have to make to the angels. *(Muslim)*.

****

CHAPTER 96

Saying Farewell Tendering Parting Advice and Good Wishes and Prayers to a Companion And Asking for Prayers from Him.

قالَ اللهُ تعالى : وَوَصَّى بها إبْراهيمُ بَنيه ويَعقوبُ: يابَنِيَّ إنَّ اللهَ اصْطَفى لَكُمُ الدِّينَ فَلا تَمُوتُنَّ إلاَّ وَأَنتُم مُسْلِمُونَ . أَمْ كُنْتُمْ شُهَدَاءَ إذْ حَضَرَ يَعْقُوبَ المَوْتُ إذْ قالَ لِبَنيه: ما تَعْبُدُونَ مِنْ بَعْدِي ؟ قَالُوا : نَعْبُدُ إلهكَ وَإلهَ آبائِكَ إبْراهيمَ وَإسْمَاعِيلَ وَإسْحَاقَ إلهاً وَاحِداً وَنَحْنُ لَهُ مُسْلِمُونَ [البقرة : ١٣٢-١٣٣] .

Allah, the Exalted, has said:

263. The same did Abraham enjoin upon his sons, and also Jacob, (saying): 'O my sons! Lo! Allah hath chosen for you the (true) religion; therefore die not save as men who have surrendered (unto Him). Or were you present when death came to Jacob, when he said unto his sons: What will ye worship after me? They said: We shall worship thy God, theGod of thy fathers, Abraham and Ishmael and Isaac, One God, and unto Him we have srrendered.(2:132—133).

٧١٢ ــ فمنها حَديثُ زيدِ بنِ أرْقَمَ رضي الله عنه ــ الذي سبق في باب إكرامِ أَهْلِ بَيْتِ رسول الله صلى الله عليه وسلم ــ قال : قامَ رسولُ الله صلى الله عليه وسلم فِينا خَطيباً، فَحَمِدَ الله، وَأَثْنى عَلَيْه، وَوَعَظَ وَذَكَّرَ، ثُمَّ قال : « أمَّا بَعْدُ، ألا أيُّها النَّاسُ إنَّمَا أنا بَشَرٌ يُوشِكُ أَنْ يَأْتِيَ رَسُولُ رَبِّي فأُجِيبَ ؛ وَأنا تَارِكٌ فِيكُمْ ثَقَلَيْنِ : أَوَّلُهُمَا : كِتَابُ اللهِ ؛ فِيهِ الهُدَى وَالنُّورُ ، فَخُذُوا

بِكِتَابِ اللهِ ، وَاسْتَمْسِكُوا بِهِ » فَحَثَّ عَلَى كِتَابِ اللهِ ، وَرَغَّبَ فِيهِ ، ثُمَّ قَالَ : « وَأَهْلُ بَيْتِي ، أُذَكِّرُكُمُ اللهَ فِي أَهْلِ بَيْتِي » رواه مسلم . وَقَدْ سَبَقَ بِطُولِهِ

712. This Hadis is icnluded in Hadis No. 346 under Chapter 43.

Note: This Hadis makes it quite clear that the Holy Prophet (S.A.W.) was a human being. Quran says through him "*Ana Basharum Mislukum* —I am a human being like you, with the only difference that I receive revelations from Allah the Master of Honour and Glory. Moreover this fact has been stated quite explicitly in the Holy Quran, at several places.

٧١٣ — وعن أبي سُلَيْمَانَ مَالِكِ بْنِ الحُوَيْرِثِ رضي الله عنه قال : أَتَيْنَا رسول الله صلى الله عليه وسلم وَنَحْنُ شَبَبَةٌ مُتَقَارِبُونَ ، فَأَقَمْنَا عِنْدَهُ عِشْرِينَ لَيْلَةً ، وكانَ رسولُ الله صلى الله عليه وسلم رَحِيماً رَفِيقاً ، فَظَنَّ أَنَّا قَد اشْتَقْنَا أَهْلَنَا ، فَسَأَلَنَا عَمَّنْ تَرَكْنَا مِنْ أَهْلِنَا ، فَأَخْبَرْنَاهُ ، فقال : « ارْجِعُوا إلى أَهْلِيكم ، فَأَقِيمُوا فِيهِمْ ، وَعَلِّمُوهُمْ وَمُرُوهُمْ ، وَصَلُّوا صَلاةَ كَذَا فِي حِينِ كَذَا ، وَصَلُّوا كَذَا فِي حِينِ كَذَا ، فَإِذَا حَضَرَتِ الصَّلاةُ فَلْيُؤَذِّنْ لَكُمْ أَحَدُكُمْ ، وَلْيَؤُمَّكُمْ أَكْبَرُكُمْ » متفقٌ عليه .

زاد البخاري في رِوايةٍ له : « وَصَلُّوا كَمَا رَأَيْتُمُونِي أُصَلِّي » .

713. Hazrat Abu Sulaiman Malik bin Huwairis (R.A.A.) relates: Once we came (to stay) with the Holy Prophet (S.A.W.); we were a group of young men of about the same age, and we stayed with him for twenty days. Since he was the most kind and affectionate person, he thought that we were longing to return to our homes. He therefore made enquiries from us about our family members whom we had left behind, and as such we informed him (in detail) of our families. Then he said: 'Now go back to your people and live with them and teach them religion asking them to observe it and offer prayers *(Salat)* at appointed times (like me). When the time for a *Salat* comes one of you should call out the *Azan* (the Call for Prayers) and the oldest among you should lead the rest in *Salat*. *(Bukhari and Muslim).*

Bukhari in his verison adds: Observe the Salat as you have seen me observing it.

٧١٤ – وعن عُمَرَ بنِ الخطّاب رضيَ اللهُ عنه قال: استأذَنتُ النبيَّ صلى الله عليه وسلم في العُمْرَةِ ، فأذِنَ ،وقال : «لاتَنْسَنا يا أُخَيَّ مِنْ دُعائِكَ» فقالَ كَلِمَةً ما يَسُرُّني أنَّ لي بها الدُّنْيا .

وفي رواية قال : « أشرِكنا يا أُخَيَّ في دُعائِكَ » . رواه أبو داود ، والترمذي وقال : حديث حسن صحيح .

714. This Hadis is the same as No. 371 of Chapter 45.

٧١٥ – وعن سالم بنِ عَبْدِ الله بن عُمَرَ أنَّ عبدَ اللهِ بنَعُمَرَ رضي اللهعنهما كانَ يَقولُ لِلرَّجُلِ إذا أرادَ سَفَراً : أُدْنُ مِنِّي حتّى أُوَدِّعَكَ كما كانَ رسولُ الله صلى الله عليه وسلم يوَدِّعُنا، فيقولُ : أَستَوْدِعُ اللهَ دِينَكَ ، وأمانَتَكَ ، وخَواتيمَ عَمَلِكَ . رواه الترمذي ، وقال: حديث حسن صحيح

715. Hazrat Saalim bin Abdullah bin Umar (R.A.A.) relates that when a person was ready to start on a journey, Hazrat Abdullah ibn Umar would ask him: come closer to me, so that I may say farewell to you as the Holy Prophet (S.A.W.) used to bid farewell to us. Accordingly he used to recite this Parayer.

"*As-tau-de-ullaha deenaka wa amanataka wa khawateema 'ama-lika*". I entrust to the care of Allah your religion, your trust and your last actions.' (*Imam Tirmizi* has reported this tradition, which he calls as good).

٧١٦ – وعن عبدِ اللهِ بنِ يَزيدَ الخَطْمِيِّ الصَّحابِيِّ رضي الله عنه قالَ : كانَ رسولُ الله صلّى الله عليه وسلم إذا أرادَ أنْ يُوَدِّعَ الجَيْشَ قالَ : « أَستَوْدِعُ اللهَ دِينَكُمْ ، وأمانَتَكُم ، وخَواتيمَ أعمالِكُمْ » .

حديث صحيح ، رواه أبو داود وغيره بإسناد صحيح .

716. Hazrat Abdullah bin Yazid Al-Khatimiy-As-Sahabie (R.A.A.) says that when the Holy Prophet (S.A.W.) used to bid farewell to a force he (S.A.W) would say: "*As-tau-de-ullaha deenakum wa amanatakum wa khawateema a'amalekum.*" I entrust to Allah your religion, your turst and your last actions. (*Imam Abu Daud* and others have reported this tradition and it is authentic.).

٧١٧ – وعن أنسٍ رضي الله عنه قال : جاءَ رَجُلٌ إلى النبيِّ صلى الله عليه وسلم فقال : يا رَسُولَ الله،إني أُريدُ سَفَراً،فزَوِّدْني ، فقَال : « زَوَّدَكَ اللهُ

التَّقْوَى » قال : زِدْني ، قال : « وَغَفَرَ ذَنْبَكَ » ، قال : زِدْنِي ، قال : « وَيَسَّرَ لكَ الخيرَ حَيْثُمَا كُنْتَ » رواه الترمذي وقال : حديث حسن .

717. **Hazrat Anas bin Malik** (R.A.A.) relates that a man approached the Holy Prophet (S.A.W.) and requested: 'O Messenger of Allah (S.A.W.) I am intending to go out on a journey, kindly grant me some provisions (i.e. pray for me). He said: 'May Allah grant you the provision of righteousness.' The man submitted: 'Some more good wishes.' He said: 'And may He forgive your sins.' The man again requested: 'Please add some thing more.' The Holy Prophet (S.A.W.) said: 'And may He make it easy for you to do virtuous deeds, wherever you may be.' *Imam Tirmizi* has reported this tradition, which he calls to be good).

****

CHAPTER 97

On Consultation and Seeking Divine Guidance.

قال الله تعالى: وَشَاوِرْهُمْ فِي الأَمْرِ . [آل عمران : ١٥٩] ، وقال تعالى : وَأَمْرُهُمْ شُورَى [الشورى : ٣٨] . أي : يَتَشَاوَرُونَ بَيْنَهُم فِيهِ .

Allah, the Exalted, has said:

264. And consult with them upon the conduct of affairs (3:159).
265. And whose affairs are a matter of counsel (42:38).

٧١٨ — عن جابرٍ رضي الله عنه قال: كانَ رسولُ الله صلى الله عليه وسلَّم يُعَلِّمُنَا الاسْتِخَارَةَ في الأُمُورِ كُلِّهَا كالسُّورَةِ مِنَ القُرْآنِ ، يَقُولُ : إذا هَمَّ أَحَدُكُمْ بِالأمر ، فَلْيَرْكَعْ رَكْعَتَيْنِ مِنْ غيرِ الفَرِيضَةِ ، ثم لِيَقُلْ : اللَّهُمَّ إنِّي أَسْتَخِيرُكَ بِعِلْمِكَ ، وأَسْتَقْدِرُكَ بِقُدْرَتِكَ، وَأَسْأَلُكَ مِنْ فَضْلِكَ العَظِيمِ ؛فإنَّكَ تَقْدِرُ ولا أَقْدِرُ ، وَتَعْلَمُ ولا أَعْلَمُ ،وَأَنتَ عَلاَّمُ الغُيُوبِ . اللَّهُمَّ إنْ كُنْتَ تَعْلَمُ أنَّ هذَا الأمرَ خَيْرٌ لي في دِيني وَمَعَاشي وَعَاقِبَةِ أَمْرِي » أَوْ قالَ : « عَاجِلِ أَمْرِي وآجِله ، فاقْدُرْهُ لي وَيَسِّرْهُ لي، ثمَّ بَارِكْ لي فيهِ ،وإن كُنْتَ تَعْلَمُ أنَّ هذَا الأَمْرَ شرٌّ لي في دِيني وَمَعَاشي وَعَاقِبَةِ أمري » أو قال : « عَاجِلِ أمري وآجِلِه ، فاصْرِفْهُ عَنِّي ، وَاصْرِفني عَنْهُ ، وَاقْدُرْ لي الخيرَ حَيْثُ كانَ ، ثمَّ رَضِّني بِهِ » قال : ويسمِّي حاجته .

رواه البخاري

718. Hazrat Jabir (R.A.A.) relates: 'The Holy Prophet (S.A.W.) used to teach us as to seek Divine guidance in any matter, in the same way as he taught us the chapters of Holy Quran. He told us that 'When one of you intends to do some work, he should offer two raka'as of Nafil (voluntary prayers) and then supplicate:

"Allahumma inni astakhiruka bi-'ilmika wa-astaqdiruka bi-qudratika wa as'aluka min fazlik al-azim. Fa-innaka taqdiro wala aqdiro wa t'alamo wala a'alamo wa anta 'allamul ghuyub. Allahumma in kunta ta'lamu anna hazal amra khairul-lee fee deeni wa ma'ashi wa'aaqibate amri (or said) 'aajil amri wa aajilihee faq-dur-ho-li wa yas-sar-ho li summa barik li fih. wa in kunta t'a lamo anna hazal amra shar-rul-li fideens wa m'aashi wa 'aaqibate amri (or said) 'aajil amri wa aajilihi fas-rif ho'anni, was-rifni 'anho, waqdir li-al-khaira haiso kana summa radh-dhini bih.

and solicit ability from Thee because Thou hast power, and solicit Thine magnificent graciousness and compassion for Thou hast power and I have no power, and Thou hast knowledge and I have none, and Thou knowest well all that is unknown. O Allah, if Thou considers that this matter is good for me as regards my faith, my subsistence and result of my affairs, (or the Holy Prophet S.A.W. said: 'If this work is in my interest in the world or the Hereafter), then destine for me, and make it easy for me and bless it for me (grant my requst). But if Thou knowest that it is evil for me as regards my faith, my subsistence and final result as regards my affairs (or the Holy Prophet (S.A.W.) said: 'If this is evil as regards my affairs in this world or the Hereafter), then remove it from me and keep me away from it; and destine for me good wherever it may be and then make me content with it.

In the end the supplicant should mention his desire or request.

(Bukhari).

****

CHAPTER 98

Virtues of Going to Eidgah, Visiting a Patient, Pilgrimage for Hajj, Journey for Jihad, Funeral Prayers etc. by One route and return by another for getting most of the opportunities for Worship.

٧١٩ — عن جابرٍ رضيَ اللهُ عنه قال : كانَ النبيُّ صلّى الله عليه وسلّم إذا كانَ يومُ عيدٍ خالَفَ الطّريقَ . رواه البخاري

719. Hazrat Jabir (R.A.A.) relates that on the occasion of Eid (the two annual festivals of Eid-ul-Fitr and Eid-ul-Azha) the Holy Prophet (S.A.W.) used different routes to and from the Eidgah (the central mosque or open ground ear-marked for the two annual Eid congregations). *(Bukhari).*

This means one should proceed to Eidgah through one route and return by another.

٧٢٠ — وعن ابن عُمَرَ رضيَ الله عنهما أن رسولَ الله صلّى الله عليه وسلم كانَ يَخرُجُ مِنْ طَرِيقِ الشَّجَرَةِ ، وَيَدْخُلُ مِنْ طَرِيقِ المُعَرَّسِ ، وَإِذا دَخَلَ مَكَّةَ دَخَلَ مِنَ الثَّنِيَّةِ العُلْيَا وَيَخرُجُ مِنَ الثَّنِيَّةِ السُّفْلى . متفقٌ عليه

720. Hazrat Ibn Umar (R.A.A.) relates that the Holy Prophet (S.A.W.) used to proceed by way of Shajarah and returned by way of Mu'arras. And when he entered Mecca, he entered by the Higher pass (Sannayatul Ullya) and returned from it by the Lower pass (Sannaya-tul Sufla). *(Bukhari and Muslim).*

That is the Holy Prophet (S.A.W.) used two different routes for going and return.

CHAPTER 99

Prefering the Use of Right Hand for Performance of All Good Acts.

Note: Imam Nawawi says that in performing all pleasant functions like ablution, taking a bath, putting on garments, socks, shoes, pyjamas, entering in a mosque, brushing teeth, applying antimony to the eyes, clipping nails, trimming of moustaches, removing hair from the arm-pits, getting head shaved, salutation at the conclusion of Salat, eating food, drinking water, shaking hands, kissing the Black Stone (in Ka'aba), coming out of lavatory, receiving or handing over something or similar other functions should be performed preferably by right hand. Unpleasant chores like blowing of nose, spitting on left side, entering the lavatory, coming out of the mosque, taking off socks, shoes, clothes, cleansing the private parts after urination and similar other obnoxious tasks should be done by left hand.

قال الله تعالى : فَأَمَّا مَنْ أُوتِيَ كِتَابَهُ بِيَمِينِهِ فَيَقُولُ : هَاؤُمُ اقْرَءُوا كِتَابِيَهْ الآيات[الحاقة : ١٩].وقال تعالى: فَأَصْحَابُ المَيْمَنَةِ مَا أَصْحَابُ المَيْمَنَةِ ۝ وَأَصْحَابُ المَشْئَمَةِ مَا أَصْحَابُ المَشْئَمَةِ [الواقعة : ٨ ، ٩] .

Allah, the Exalted, has said:

266. Then, as for him who is given his record in his right hand, he will say: Take read my book! (69:19)

267. (First) those on the right hand; what of those on the right hand? and(then) those on the left hand; what of those on the left hand? (56:8—9).

٧٢١ — عن عائشة رضيَ الله عنها قالَتْ: كَانَ رسولُ الله صلى الله عليه وسلَّم يُعْجِبُهُ التَّيَمُّنُ في شَأْنِهِ كُلِّه: في طُهُورِهِ، وتَرَجُّلِهِ، وتَنَعُّلِهِ. متفقٌ عليه

721. Hazrat Ayesha (R.A.A.) relates that the Holy Prophet (S.A.W.) preferred to use his right hand in all actions; (for instance) for performing his ablutions, for combing his hairs and for putting on his shoes.' *(Bukhari and Muslim).*

٧٢٢ — وعنها قالتْ: كانَتْ يَدُ رسول الله صلَّى الله عليه وسلَّم، اليُمْنَى لِطَهُورِهِ وَطَعَامِهِ، وكَانَتِ اليُسْرَى لِخَلائِهِ وَمَا كَانَ مِنْ أذىً. حديث صحيح، رواه أبو داود وغيره بإسنادٍ صحيحٍ.

722. Hazrat Ayesha (R.A.A.) relates that the Holy Prophet's (S.A.W.) right hand was used for his clean and nice things and for eating; and his left hand was used to toilet and for other similar functions.' (*Imam Abu Daud* and others have qutoed this tradition on authentic chain).

٧٢٣ — وعن أم عَطِيَّةَ رضيَ الله عنها أن النبيَّ صلى الله عليه وسلم، قالَ لَهُنَّ في غَسْلِ ابْنَتِهِ زَيْنَبَ رضي الله عنها: «ابْدَأْنَ بِمَيَامِنِهَا وَمَوَاضِعِ الوُضُوءِ مِنْهَا» متفقٌ عليه

723. Hazrat Umm Atiyyah (R.A.A.) relates that at the time of the washing of the body of his daughter Hazrat Zainab (R.A.A.) the Holy Prophet (S.A.W.) asked her to begin the wash from her right side and with those parts which are washed in ablutions.' *(Bukhari and Muslim).*

٧٢٤ — وعن أبي هُرَيرة رضيَ الله عنه أن رسولَ الله صلى الله عليه وسلم قال: «إذا انْتَعَلَ أَحَدُكُم فَلْيَبْدَأْ باليُمْنَى، وإذا نَزَعَ فَلْيَبْدَأْ بِالشِّمَالِ لِتَكُنِ اليُمْنَى أَوَّلَهُمَا تُنْعَلُ، وَآخِرَهُمَا تُنْزَعُ» متفقٌ عليه

724. Hazrat Abu Hurrairah (R.A.A.) relates that the Holy Prophet (S.A.W.) said: When any of you puts on his shoes, he should begin from the left side (i.e. with the left foot); so that the right foot should be the first to put on and the last from which the shoe is to be taken off. *(Bukhari and Muslim).*

٧٢٥ ــ وعن حَفْصَةَ رضيَ الله عنها أنَّ رسولَ الله، صلى الله عليه وسلم ، كان يَجْعَلُ يَمِينَه لطَعَامِهِ وَشَرَابِهِ وَثِيَابِهِ ، وَيَجْعَلُ يَسَارَهُ لِمَا سِوَى ذلكَ . رواه أبو داود والترمذي وغيره .

725. **Hazrat Hafsah** (R.A.A.) relates that the Holy Prophet (S.A.W.) used to employ his right hand for eating, drinking and putting on his clothes; and used his left hand for purposes other than these.

(Abu Daud, Tirmizi etc.).

٧٢٦ ــ وعن أبي هُريرة رضي الله عنه أنَّ رسولَ الله صلَّى الله عليه وسلَّم قال: « إذا لَبِسْتُمْ ، وإذا تَوَضَّأْتُمْ ، فَابْدَؤُوا بِأَيَامِنِكُمْ » حديث صحيح ، رواه أبو داود والترمذي بإسناد صحيح .

726. **Hazrat Abu Hurrairah** (R.A.A.) relates that the Holy Prophet (S.A.W.) said: 'When you put on your clothes or make your ablutions, begin with your right side.' *(Abu Daud and Tirmizi).*

٧٢٧ ــ وعن أنس رضي الله عنه أن رسولَ الله صلَّى الله عليه وسلم أتى مِنىً: فَأَتَى الجَمْرَةَ فرَمَاهَا ، ثُمَّ أتى مَنْزِلَهُ بِمِنىً، وَنَحَرَ ، ثُمَّ قال لِلحلاَّقِ « خُذْ » وأَشَارَ إلى جانبِهِ الأَيْمَنِ ، ثُمَّ الأَيْسَرِ ، ثمَّ جَعَلَ يُعْطِيهِ النَّاسَ . متفقٌ عليه

وفي روايةٍ : لمَّا رَمَى الجَمْرَةَ ، وَنَحَرَ نُسُكَهُ وَحَلَقَ : نَاوَلَ الحَلاَّقَ شِقَّهُ الأَيْمَنَ فَحَلَقَهُ ، ثمَّ دَعَا أَبَا طَلْحَةَ الأنصاريَّ رضي الله عنه، فأَعطاهُ إيَّاهُ ، ثمَّ نَاوَلَهُ الشقَّ الأَيْسَرَ فقال: « احْلِقْ » فَحَلَقَهُ ، فَأَعْطَاهُ أبا طلحةَ فقال : « اقسِمْهُ بَيْنَ النَّاسِ » .

727. **Hazrat Anas bin Malik** (R.A.A.) relates that when the Holy Prophet (S.A.W.) returned to Mina (in the course of Hajj) he came to the Jamarah and threw pebbles at it; then he returned to his camp at Mina and offered the sacrifice. Thereafter he asked the barber to shave his head starting from the right side of his head and then the left. Then he started distirbuting his hairs among the people. *(Bukhari and Muslim).*

Another version says: When he had finished pelting stones at the Jamarah and had already offered the sacrifice and was preparing to get his head shaved, he showed to the barber the right side of his head and was shaved on that side. Then he called Hazrat Abu Talha Ansari and gave his hair to him; and then he showed the left side of his head to the barber and was shaved on that side. He gave these hair also to Hazrat Abu Talha and said: 'Distribute it among the people.'

****

BOOK OF EATING MANNERS

CHAPTER 100

To start Eating with the Name of Allah And to End with the Praising And Thanking Allah.

٧٢٨ ـ عن عُمَرَ بنِ أبي سَلَمَةَ رضي الله عنهما قال: قال لي رسولُ الله صلى الله عليه وسلم: «سَمِّ اللهَ وكُلْ بِيَمِينِكَ، وكُلْ مِمَّا يَلِيكَ» متفقٌ عليه

728. This Hadis has been covered in No. 299 of Chapter 38.

٧٢٩ ـ وعن عائشةَ رضيَ اللهُ عنها قالتْ: قالَ رسولُ الله صلّى الله عليه وسلم: «إذا أكلَ أحدُكُمْ فليذكرِ اسمَ اللهِ تعالى، فإنْ نسيَ أنْ يذكرَ اسمَ اللهِ تعالَى في أوَّلِهِ، فليقلْ: بِسْمِ اللهِ أوَّلَهُ وآخِرَهُ».

رواه أبو داود، والترمذي ، وقال: حديث حسن صحيح.

729. Hazrat Ayesha (R.A.A.) relates that the Holy Prophet (S.A.W.) said: When any of you srtarts eating,he should recite the name of Allah, the Exalted. If he forgets to do so in the beginning (and he remembers it later), he should say: "*Bismillah-e-Aw-wala hoo wa Akhiro-hoo*". In the name of Allah, first and last. *(Abu Daud and Tirmizi).*

Imam Tirmizi says that this tradition is authentic and good.

٧٣٠ ـ وعن جابرٍ رضيَ اللهُ عنه قال: سَمِعْتُ رسولَ الله صلى الله عليه وسلم يقولُ: «إذا دخل الرَّجُلُ بَيْتَهُ، فذكَرَ اللهَ تعالى عِنْدَ دُخُولِهِ وعِنْدَ طَعامِهِ، قال الشَّيْطانُ لأصْحابِهِ: لا مَبِيتَ لَكُم ولا عَشاءَ، وإذا دخَلَ، فلَمْ يَذكُرِ اللهَ تعالى عِنْدَ دخُولِهِ، قال الشَّيْطَانُ: أدْرَكْتُمُ المَبيتَ؛ وإذا لَمْ يَذْكُرِ اللهَ تعَالى عِنْدَ طعَامِهِ قال: أدْرَكْتُمُ المَبيتَ والعَشاءَ» رواه مسلم

730. Hazrat Jabir (R.A.A.) relates that he heard the Holy Prophet (S.A.W.) says: 'If a person takes the name of Allah when he enters his house and when he eats, Satan tells his companions: Let us go. There is no room for you to pass the night in this house nor food. If he enters his house without calling Allah, Satan says to his companions: You have at least secured lodging.' Then if he does not remember Allah at the time of eating also, Satan says: 'You have secured both lodging and food.' *(Muslim).*

٧٣١ – وعن حُذَيفَةَ رضيَ اللهُ عنه قال : كنّا إذا حَضَرْنَا مَعَ رَسولِ الله صلى الله عليه وسلم طَعَاماً ، لَمْ نَضَعْ أيدِينا حتَّى يَبْدَأَ رسولُ الله صلى الله عليه وسلم فَيَضَعَ يَدَه . وإنّا حَضَرْنا مَعَهُ مرةً طَعَاماً ، فَجاءَتْ جَارِيَةٌ كأنّها تُدْفَعُ ، فَذَهَبَتْ لِتَضَعَ يَدَهَا في الطَّعَامِ ، فَأَخَذَ رسولُ الله صلى الله عليه وسلم بِيَدِهَا ، ثمَّ جاءَ أعْرَابيٌّ كأنَّمَا يُدْفَعُ ، فَأَخَذَ بِيَدِهِ ، فقال رسولُ الله صلى الله عليه وسلم : « إنَّ الشَّيْطانَ يَسْتَحِلُّ الطَّعَامَ أنْ لايُذْكَرَ اسمُ اللهِ تعَالى عليه ، وإنَّهُ جاءَ بهذهِ الجارِيَةِ لِيَسْتَحِلَّ بهَا ، فَأَخَذْتُ بِيَدِهَا ، فَجَاءَ بهذا الأَعْرَابِيِّ لِيَسْتَحِلَّ بِهِ ، فَأَخَذْتُ بِيَدِهِ ، والّذي نَفسي بِيَدِهِ إنَّ يَدَهُ في يَدي مَعَ يَدَيْهِمَا» ثمَّ ذَكَرَ اسمَ اللهِ تعَالى وَأكَلَ . رواه مسلم .

731. Hazrat Huzaifah (R.A.A.) says: Whenever we had the chance to be present with the Holy Prophet (S.A.W.) while eating, we would not start eating until he had started. On one such occasion when we were with the Holy Prophet (S.A.W.) a girl came in rushing, as if she was very hungry, and wanted to eat, but the Holy Prophet (S.A.W.) caught hold of her hand. Then a villager came in and he too rushed for the food as if he was starving, but the Holy Prophet (S.A.W.) held his hand too, and said: 'Satan treats that food lawful for himself on which the name of Allah has not been pronounced. He brought this girl in order to make this good lawful for himself through her, but I seized her hand, (because she was going to start eating without Bismillah). Then he brought this villager to make it lawful through him, but I seized his hand also. Now by Allah in Whose hands is my life, I have Satan's hand in my grip also along with their hands. Then he pronounced the name of Allah (said Bismillah) and started eating. *(Muslim).*

٧٣٢ – وعن أُمَيَّةَ بنِ مخشيٍّ الصَّحَابيِّ رضيَ الله عنه قال : كانَ رسُولُ الله صلى الله عليه وسلم جَالِساً ، ورَجُلٌ يأْكُلُ ، فلَمْ يُسمِّ اللهَ حتَّى لَمْ يَبْقَ مِنْ طعَامِهِ لُقْمَةٌ ، فلَمَّا رَفَعَهَا إلى فِيهِ ، قال: بِسمِ اللهِ أوَّلَهُ وآخِرَهُ ، فَضَحِكَ النبيُّ صلى الله عليه وسلم ، ثم قال : « مَا زَالَ الشَّيْطَانُ يأْكُلُ مَعَهُ ، فلَمَّا ذَكَرَ اسمَ اللهِ اسْتَقَاءَ مَافي بَطْنِهِ » .

رواه أبو داود ،والنسائي

732. Hazrat Umayyah bin Makhshi-as-Sahabi (R.A.A.) says that once while the Holy Prophet (S.A.W.) was sitting, a man was eating, but he failed to take the name of Allah (he did not pronounce *Bismillah*). At last only a morsel of the food was left. When he lifted it and was taking to his mouth he said: 'In the name of Allah, first and last.' The Holy Prophet (S.A.W.) smiled and said: 'Satan continued eating with him, but when he took the name of Allah Satan vomitted out what he had eaten.' *(Abu Daud and Nisai)*

٧٣٣ – وعن عائشةَ رضيَ الله عنها قالَتْ : كانَ رسولُ اللهِ صلى الله عليه وسلم يأكُلُ طعَاماً في ستَّةٍ مِنْ أصحابِهِ ،فجاءَ أعرابيٌّ، فأكلَه بِلُقمتَيْنِ فقال رسولُ الله صلى الله عليه وسلم : « أما إنَّهُ لوْ سَمَّى لكَفَاكُمْ » .

رواه الترمذي ، وقال : حديثٌ حسنٌ صحيحٌ .

733. Hazrat Ayesha (R.A.A.) says that (once) the Holy Prophet (S.A.W.) was eating in the company of six of his companions, when a villager joined them and ate up the food in two morsels. On seeing this the Holy Prophet (S.A.W.) remarked:'If he had taken the name of Allah, the same would have sufficed for all of you.' *(Tirmizi).*

٧٣٤ – وعن أبي أمامة رضيَ الله عنه أن النبيَّ صلَّى الله عليه وسلم كانَ إذا رَفَعَ مَائِدَتَهُ قال : « الحَمْدُ لِلهِ كَثِيراً طَيِّباً مُبَارَكاً فيه ، غيْرَ مَكْفِيٍّ ولاَ مُوَدَّعٍ . ولا مُسْتَغْنىً عَنْهُ رَبَّنَا » رواه البخاري

734. Hazrat Abu Umamah (R.A.A.) says: 'After the Holy Prophet (S.A.W.) had finished his meal and the dining cloth was wrapped up, he would say: 'All praise is due to Allah; praise which is plentiful and pure, and full of blessing which is indispensable and to which one cannot be indifferent, O Sustainer.' *(Bukhari).*

٧٣٥ – وعن مُعَاذِ بن أنسٍ رضيَ اللهُ عنه قالَ: قالَ رسُولُ الله صلى الله عليه وسلم : « مَنْ أكَلَ طعَاماً فقال : الحَمْدُ لِلهِ الَّذي أطْعَمَني هذا ، وَرَزَقَنيهِ مِنْ غيرِ حَوْلٍ مِنِّي ولا قُوَّةٍ ، غُفِرَ لَهُ مَا تَقَدَّمَ مِنْ ذَنْبِهِ »

رواه أبو داود ، والترمذي ، وقال : حديثٌ حسنٌ .

735. Hazrat Mu'az bin Anas (R.A.A.) relates that the Holy Prophet (S.A.W.) said: One who has eaten his meal and thereafter says:

"AlHamdo-lil-Lahil-lazi at-'amani haaza wa razaqani-hi min ghair-e-haulimmin-ni wala Quw-wah."

"All praise is due to Allah, who has given me this fare to eat and provided me without any effort or power on my part, will have all his past and future sins forgiven.' *(Tirmizi).*

****

CHAPTER 101

Not to Find Fault with Food and to Appreciate It.

٧٣٦ ــعن أبي هُريرة رضيَ اللهُ عنهُ قالَ : « مَاعَابَ رسُولُ اللهِ صلى الله عليه وسلم طَعَاماً قطُّ ، إن اشتَهاهُ أكلَهُ ، وإنْ كرِهَهُ تركَهُ » .
متفقٌ عليه

736. Hazrat Abu Hurairah (R.A.A.) says that the Holy Prophet (S.A.W.) never found fault with any food. If he had the inclination, he would eat it, and if he disliked, he would leave it. *(Bukhari and Muslim).*

٧٣٧ ــ وعن جابرٍ رضيَ الله عنه أنَّ النبيَّ صلى الله عليه وسلم سَأَلَ أهلَهُ الأُدْمَ (٥) فقالُوا : ماعِندَنَا إلاَّ خلٌّ ، فدَعَا بِهِ ،فجعَلَ يأْكُلُ ويقول : « نِعمَ الأُدْمُ الخلُّ ، نِعمَ الأُدْمُ الخلُّ » رواه مسلم

737. Hazrat Jabir (R.A.A.) relates that the Holy Prophet (S.A.W.) once asked his household members for curry. They told him that there was nothing but vinegar. He called for it and started eating his food with it exclaiming: 'The best curry is vinegar; the best curry is vinegar.' *(Muslim).*

****

CHAPTER 102

What a Fasting Person Should Do When Invited to Eat.

٧٣٨ ــ عن أبي هُريرة رضيَ اللهُ عنه قالَ : قالَ رسولُ الله صلى الله عليه وسلم : « إذا دُعِيَ أحدُكُمْ، فليُجِبْ ؛ فإنْ كانَ صائماً فليُصَلِّ ، وإنْ كانَ مُفطِراً فليَطعَمْ » رواه مسلم

738. Hazrat Abu Hurairah (R.A.A.) relates that the Holy Prophet (S.A.W.) said:'When any of you is asked to join in a meal, he should accept the invitation. And if he is fasting, he should pray for the host, and if he is not fasting he should join the host.' *(Muslim).*

****

CHAPTER 103

When an Invited Person Is Accompanied by an Uninvited Person.

٧٣٩ ــ عن أبي مسعود البَدْرِيِّ رضيَ الله عنه قال: دَعَا رَجُلٌ النَّبيَّ صلّى الله عليه وسلم لِطَعَامٍ صَنَعَهُ لَهُ خَامِسَ خَمْسَةٍ ، فتَبِعَهُمْ رَجُلٌ ، فَلَمَّا بَلَغَ البابَ ، قال النبيُّ صلى الله عليه وسلم : « إنَّ هذا تَبِعَنَا ؛ فَإِنْ شِئْتَ أَنْ تَأْذَنَ لَهُ ، وَإِنْ شِئتَ رَجَعَ » قال: بل آذَنُ لهُ يا رسول الله . متفق عليه

739. Hazrat Abu Mas'ud Badri (R.A.A.) says: (Once) a man prepared some food specially for the Holy Prophet (S.A.W.). Four other persons had been invited along with him. But an extra person who had not been invited, also accompanied them. On arriving at the door of the host's house, the Holy Prophet (S.A.W.) said to the host: 'This man has accompanied us. If you like may be permitted, otherwise he will return. The host replied:'O Messenger of Allah (I will not turn him back), I invite him:'
(Bukhari and Muslim).

****

CHAPTER 104

On Eating What Is In Front of You, and to teach a Person, Who Does Not Know the Manners of Eating.

٧٤٠ ــ عن عمر بن أبي سَلَمَةَ رضي الله عنهما قال : كُنْتُ غلاماً في حِجْرِ رسولِ الله صلّى الله عليه وسلم ،وكانَتْ يَدِي تَطِيشُ في الصَّحْفَةِ ، فقال لي رسولُ الله صلى الله عليه وسلم : « يَا غُلامُ سَمِّ اللهَ تَعَالى ، وكُلْ بِيَمِينِكَ ، وكُلْ مِمَّا يَلِيكَ » متفقٌ عليه

740. This Hadis has already been covered in item No. 299 of Chapter 38.

٧٤١ ــ وعن سَلَمَةَ بنِ الأكوَعِ رضيَ اللهُ عنه أن رَجُلاً أكل عِنْدَ رسولِ الله صلى الله عليه وسلم بشِماله ، فقال : « كُلْ بِيَمِينكَ » قال : لا أَسْتَطِيعُ قالَ : « لا استَطَعْتَ » ! ما مَنَعَهُ إلاَّ الكِبْرُ ! فَمَا رَفَعَهَا إلى فيه رواه مسلم

741. This Hadis is the same as No. 159 of Chapter 16.

****

CHAPTER 105

On Prohibition of Eating Two Dates or Other Fruits in One Morsel without the Permission of the Companions.

٧٤٢ – عن جَبَلَةَ بن سُحَيْمٍ قال: أصابنا عامُ سَنَةٍ مع ابنِ الزُّبَيْرِ، فرُزِقنا تمراً، وكان عبدُ الله بن عمر رضي الله عنهما يَمُرُّ بنا ونحن نأكُلُ، فيقولُ: لا تُقارِنُوا، فإن النبي صلى الله عليه وسلم نَهى عن الإقرانِ، ثم يقولُ: «إلاَّ أنْ يَستأذِنَ الرَّجُلُ أخاهُ» متفقٌ عليه

742. Hazrat Jabalah bin Suhaim (R.A.A.) relates: 'We along with Hazrat Abdullah bin Zubair (R.A.A.) were given one date each to eat during a famine. When we were eating Hazrat Abdullah bin Umar (R.A.A.) passed by us and said: 'Do not eat two dates in one morsel, because, the Holy Prophet (S.A.W.) had prohibited this, except when the permission of one's companions had been taken.'

(Bukhari and Muslim).

****

CHAPTER 106

What to Do and What to Say When a Person Eats But Is Not Satisfied.

٧٤٣ – عن وَحْشِيِّ بنِ حرب رضيَ الله عنه أن أصحابَ رسولِ الله صلى الله عليه وسلم قالُوا: يا رسولَ اللهِ، إنَّا نَأْكُلُ ولا نَشْبَعُ؟ قال: «فلعلَّكُم تفترِقُونَ» قالُوا: نعَمْ. قال: فاجْتَمِعُوا على طَعامِكُمْ، واذْكُرُوا اسمَ اللهِ، يُبَارَكْ لكُمْ فيه» رواه أبو داود

743. Hazrat Wahshi bin Harb (R.A.A.) relates that some of the companions of the Holy Prophet (S.A.W.) said to him:'O Messenger of Allah (S.A.W.) we eat but don't get satisfied.' He said: 'May be you eat individually.' They said: 'Yes, Sir'. He told them: 'Eat together and recite the name of Allah. The food will be blessed for you.' *(Abu Daud).*

****

CHAPTER 107

Directing to Eat from the Side of the Vessel and Prohibition of Eating from Its Middle.

٧٤٤ – وعن ابن عباس رضيَ اللهَ عنهما عن النبيِّ صلى الله عليه وسلم قال «البَرَكَةُ تَنْزِلُ وَسَطَ الطَّعَامِ ، فَكُلُوا مِنْ حَافَتَيْهِ وَلا تَأْكُلُوا مِنْ وَسَطِهِ» رواه أبو داود ، والترمذي ، وقال : حديثٌ حسنٌ صحيحٌ .

744. Hazrat Ibn Abbas (R.A.A.) relates that the Holy Prophet (S.A.W.) said:'Blessing comes down upon food in its middle, so eat from the sides of the vessel and do not eat from its centre.'

(Abu Daud and Tirmizi).

٧٤٥ – وعن عبد الله بن بُسْرٍ رضيَ الله عنه قال : كان لِلنَّبِيِّ صلى الله عليه وسلم قَصْعَةٌ يُقَالُ لها : الغَرَّاءُ ، يَحْمِلُهَا أَرْبَعَةُ رِجالٍ ، فَلَمَّا أَضْحَوْا وَسَجَدُوا الضُّحَى أُتِيَ بِتِلْكَ القَصْعَةِ ، يعني وقد ثُرِدَ فيها ، فَالتَفُّوا عليها ، فَلَمَّا كَثُرُوا جَثَا رسولُ الله صلى الله عليه وسلم . فقالَ أعرابيٌّ : ما هذه الجِلْسَةُ ؟ قال رسولُ الله صلى الله عليه وسلم : إنَّ الله جَعَلَنِي عَبْداً كَرِيماً ، وَلَمْ يَجْعَلْنِي جَبَّاراً عَنِيداً ، ثمَّ قالَ رسولُ الله صلى الله عليه وسلم : «كُلُوا مِنْ حَوَالَيْهَا ، وَدَعُوا ذِرْوَتَهَا يُبَارَكْ فيها» رواه أبو داود بإسناد جيد .

745. **Hazrat Abdullah ibn Busar** (R.A.A.) says: 'The Holy Prophet (S.A.W.) had a large pot, which was called 'Gharra'. (It was very heavy) and four men were required to carry it. When it was the time for chasht (forenoon) voluntary prayers and after his companions had finished this prayer, 'Gharra' would be brought full of Sareed (a kind of broth) and they would sit down round it. When their number used to be large, the Holy Prophet (S.A.W.) would sit down with his knees, shins and toes touching the ground. A villager once said: 'What kind of sitting is this?' The Holy Prophet (S.A.W.) said: 'Allah has fashioned me a well-behaved creature and has not made me an arrogant and usurper of rights. Then he said: Eat from the edge of the pot and leave the raised part of the food in the centre. That part will get blessings.'' *(Abu Daud).*

Note: The (food in the) centre of a pot is (considered to be) wholesome and superior. Therefore it is the receipient of divine blessings and when the food stuff in the centre of a pot is a place where blessings descend, it is but appropriate and bether to retain it (the food stuff there) till the end, so that its benefits may be derived a bit longer. Hence it is advisable not to destroy it (by eating the fare earlier); and therefore it has been laid down that we should (start eating) only from the sides of the pot and preserve the central portion (of the fare) as long as possible.

****

CHAPTER 108

Repugnance of Eating While Resting on a Pillow or Reclining.

٧٤٦ – عن أبي جُحَيْفَةَ وَهْبِ بنِ عبد الله رضي الله عنه قال: قال رسولُ الله صلى الله عليه وسلم: «لا آكُلُ مُتَّكِئاً» رواه البخاري

746. Hazrat Abu Juhaifah Wahb bin Abdullah (R.A.A.) relates that the Holy Prophet (S.A.W.) said: I do not eat while reclining. *(Bukhari).*

Imam Nawawi elucidating this Hadis quotes Imam Khattabi as saying that by reclining against a pillow it is meant that one should not eat while resting against a bed i.e. one should not rest on a bed or pillow while eating.

٧٤٧ – وعن أنس رضيَ الله عنه قال: رَأَيْتُ رسول الله صلى الله عليه وسلم جالساً مُقْعِياً يأكُلُ تمْراً، رواه مسلم

747. Hazrat Anas bin Malik (R.A.A.) relates that he saw the Holy Prophet (S.A.W.) sitting (on the ground) with his knees raised while eating dates. *(Muslim).*

****

CHAPTER 109

Eating with Three Fingers, and Virtues of Licking the Fingers, and Abhorrance of Wiping Them before Licking. Excellence of Licking the Cup, and Picking up the Marsel That Has Fallen and Rating It. Permission to Wipe the Fingers with Knees or Sole Etc. after Licking Them.

٧٤٨ – عنِ ابنِ عباسٍ رضيَ الله عنهما قال: قالَ رسولُ الله صلّى الله عليه وسلم: «إذا أكَلَ أحَدُكُم طَعَاماً، فلا يَمسَحْ أصابِعَهُ حتى يَلعَقَهَا أو يُلْعِقَهَا» متفقٌ عليه

748. Hazrat Ibn Abbas (R.A.A.) relates that the Holy Prophet (S.A.W.) said: 'When one of you has eaten his meal he should not wipe his fingers (with some cloth, towel etc.) without first licking his fingers or having them licked by somebody. *(Bukhari and Muslim).*

٧٤٩ ـ وعن كعبِ بنِ مالكٍ رضيَ اللهُ عنه قال: رَأيتُ رسولَ اللهِ صلى الله عليه وسلم يأكُلُ بثلاثِ أصابعَ ، فإذا فرَغَ لعِقَها . رواه مسلم

749. Hazrat K'ab ibn Malik (R.A.A.) says that he saw the Holy Prophet (S.A.W.) eating with three fingers, and after having finished eating, he would lick them. *(Muslim).*

٧٥٠ ـ وعن جابرٍ رضيَ الله عنه أنَّ رسولَ اللهِ صلى الله عليه وسلم أمر بلَعقِ الأصابعِ والصَّحفةِ ، وقال : « إنَّكُمْ لا تدرُونَ في أيِّ طعامِكم البركةُ » رواه مسلم

٧٥١ ـ وعنه أن رسولَ الله صلَّى الله عليه وسلم قال: « إذا وقعَت لُقمةُ أحدِكُمْ ، فليأخُذْها فليُمِطْ ما كان بها مِن أذىً وليأكُلْها ، ولا يدَعْها للشَّيطانِ ، ولا يمسَحْ يدَهُ بالمِنديلِ حتَّى يلعقَ أصابعَهُ ؛ فإنه لا يدري في أيِّ طعامِهِ البركةُ » رواه مسلم

٧٥٢ ـ وعنه أن رسول الله صلى الله عليه وسلم قال : « إن الشَّيطانَ يحضرُ أحدكم عِندَ كُلِّ شيءٍ مِنْ شأنِهِ ، حتى يحضُرَهُ عِندَ طعَامِهِ ؛ فإذا سقَطَتْ لُقمَةُ أحدِكم فليأخذها فليُمِط ما كانَ بها مِن أذى ، ثُمَّ ليأكُلْها ولا يدعْها للشَّيطانِ ، فإذا فرَغَ فليَلعقْ أصابعَهُ ؛ فإنه لا يدري في أيِّ طعامِهِ البركَةُ » رواه مسلم

٧٥٣ ـ وعن أنسٍ رضي الله عنه قال: كان رسولُ الله صلَّى الله عليه وسلَّم إذا أكَلَ طعَاماً، لعِقَ أصابعَهُ الثَّلاثَ ، وقالَ: « إذا سقَطَتْ لُقمَةُ أحدِكم فليأخُذْها ، وليُمِطْ عنها الأذى، وليأكُلْها، ولا يدَعْها للشَّيطانِ » وأمرَنا أن نسلُتَ القَصعَةُ وقال : « إنَّكم لا تدْرُونَ في أيِّ طعَامِكم البركَةُ » رواه مسلم

750 to 753. These four traditions have been covered in No. 164 of Chapter 16.

٧٥٤ — وعن سعيد بنِ الحارثِ أنه سأل جابراً رضيَ الله عنه عن الوضوءِ مِمَّا مَسَّتِ النَّارُ ، فقال : لا ، قد كُنَّا زَمَنَ النبي صلى الله عليه وسلم لانجدُ مثلَ ذلك الطعامِ إلاَّ قليلاً . فإذا نحنُ وجدناهُ لم يكنْ لنا مناديلُ إلاَّ أكُفَّنَا وسَوَاعِدَنَا وأقْدَامَنَا ، ثُمَّ نُصَلِّي وَلا نَتَوَضَّأُ . رواه البخاري

754. Hazrat Sa'eed bin Haris (R.A.A.) says that he asked Hazrat Jabir (R.A.A.) whether it was obligatory to perform ablution for prayer after having eaten cooked food. He said: No. During the days of the Holy Prophet (S.A.W.) we rarely got cooked food to eat; and whenever we could get something (of the cooked food) to eat, we had no towels (to wipe out) and used to wipe out them against our palms, forearms or feet, and we used to offer prayers and did not perform fresh ablution. *(Bukhari).*

****

CHAPTER 110

Sufficiency of Food.

٧٥٥ — عن أبي هريرة رضيَ اللهُ تعالى عنه قالَ : قالَ رسولُ الله صَلَّى الله عليه وسلم : « طَعَامُ الاثنينِ كافي الثَّلاثةِ ، وَطَعَامُ الثَّلاثةِ كافي الأربعةِ » متفقٌ عليه

٧٥٦ — وعن جابرٍ رضيَ الله عنهُ قالَ : سمعتُ رسولَ الله صلَّى الله عليه وسلَّم يَقُولُ : « طَعَامُ الوَاحِدِ يَكْفِي الاثْنَيْنِ . وَطَعَامُ الاثْنَيْنِ يَكْفِي الأربَعَةَ ، وطعامُ الأرْبَعَةِ يَكْفِي الثَّمَانِيَةَ » رواه مسلم

755 and 756: Both these traditions are contained in S.No. 563 of Chapter 62.

****

CHAPTER 111

Etiquette of Drinking Water, and Merits of Taking Three Breaths outside the Vessel, and Abhorrence of Breathing inside the Vessel. The Person First Drinking Should Pass on the Vessel to Persons Sitting on His Right.

٧٥٧ – عن أنسٍ رضي الله عنه أن رسول الله صلى الله عليه وسلم كانَ يتنفَّسُ في الشَّرَابِ ثلاثاً . متفقٌ عليه

757. Hazrat Anas bin Malik (.R.A.A.) says that when the Holy Prophet (S.A.W.) drank the water, he used to breath three times, i.e. he took water in three breaks, breathing thrice outside the cup.

(Bukhari and Muslim).

٧٥٨ – وعن ابن عباس رضي الله عنهما قال : قال رسول الله صلى الله عليه وسلم : « لاتَشْرَبُوا وَاحِداً كَشُرْبِ البَعِير ، وَلَكِنِ اشْرَبُوا مَثْنَى وَثُلاثَ . وَسَمُّوا إذا أَنْتُمْ شَرِبْتُمْ ، وَاحْمَدُوا إذا أَنْتُمْ رَفَعْتُمْ » رواه الترمذي وقال : حديث حسن .

758. Hazrat Ibn Abbas (R.A.A.) relates that the Holy Prophet (S.A.W.) said: 'Do not drink water in one gulp (or one breath) like a camel, but take it in two or three instalments (with break for breaths); Take the name of Allah (i.e. recite *Bismillah*) when you start drinking and praise His (say *Al-hamdulillah*) when you finish. *(Tirmizi).*

٧٥٩ – وعن أبي قَتَادَةَ رضي الله عنه أن النبيَّ صلى الله عليه وسلم نَهَى ن يُتَنَفَّسَ في الإناء . متفقٌ عليه

759. Hazrat Abu Qatadah (R.A.A.) says that the Holy Prophet (S.A.W.) has prohibited breathing inside the pot (while drinking water).

(Agreed Upon)

٧٦٠ – وعن أنسٍ رضي الله عنه أن رسول الله صلى الله عليه وسلم أُتِيَ بِلَبَنٍ قد شِيبَ بِمَاءٍ ، وعَنْ يَمِينِهِ أَعْرَابِيٌّ ، وعَنْ يَسَارِهِ أبو بَكرٍ رضي الله عنه ، فَشَرِبَ ، ثُمَّ أَعطَى الأعْرَابِيَّ وقال : « الأيمَنَ فالأيمَنَ » متفقٌ عليه

760. Hazrat Anas bin Malik (R.A.A.) says that (once) milk was brought to the Holy Prophet (S.A.W.). In this milk a little water had been mixed. At this time a country man was sitting on his right and on his left was Hazrat Abu Bakr (R.A.A.). He drank some milk and then passed on the remaining milk to the villager on his right saying: 'The right has priority.' *(Bukhari and Muslim)*

٧٦١ — وعن سهل بن سعد رضي الله عنه أن رسول الله صلى الله عليه وسلم أُتِيَ بشرابٍ ، فشَرِبَ منهُ وعَنْ يمينِهِ غُلامٌ ، وعن يَسَارِهِ أشياخٌ ، فقال للغُلامِ : « أتأْذَنُ لي أنْ أُعطِيَ هؤُلاء ؟ » فقال الغلامُ : لا واللهِ ، لا أُوثِرُ بِنَصيبي مِنكَ أحَداً ، فتَلَّهُ رسول الله صلى الله عليه وسلم في يَدهِ . متفقٌ عليه

761. This Hadis is the same as No. 569 of Chapter 63.

****

CHAPTER 112

Prohibition of Drinking Direct from a Water-skin.

٧٦٢ — عن أبي سعيدٍ الخدْريّ رضي الله عنه قال : نَهَى رسول الله صلى الله عليه وسلم عن اخْتِنَاثِ الأسْقِيَةِ . يعني : أنْ تُكسَرَ أفواهُها، ويُشْرَبَ منْها . متفقٌ عليه

762. Hazrat Abu Sa'eed Khudri (R.A.A.) says that the Holy Prophet (S.A.W.) has forbidden drinking water directly from a water-skin. *(Bukhari and Muslim).*

٧٦٣ — وعن أبي هريرة رضي الله عنه قال : نَهَى رسول الله صلى الله عليه وسلم أن يُشْرَبَ مِنْ فِي السِّقاءِ أو القِرْبَةِ . متفقٌ عليه

763. Hazrat Abu Hurairah(R.A.A.) says that the Holy Prophet (S.A.W.) has forbidden drinking water directly from a water-skin or pot (lest something injurious already in the water may slip in the stomach). *(Bukhari and Muslim).*

٧٦٤ — وعن أمّ ثابتٍ كَبْشَةَ بِنْتِ ثَابتٍ أُخْتِ حسَّانَ بنْ ثابتٍ رضي الله عنه وعنها قالت : دخل عَليَّ رسولُ الله صلّى الله عليه وسلّمَ ، فشَرِبَ مِن فِي قِربَةٍ مُعلّقَةٍ قائماً ، فقُمْتُ إلى فيها فقَطَعْتُهُ . رواه الترمذي وقال : حديث حسن صحيح .

764. Hazrat Umm Sabit Kab'shah bint Sabit (R.A.A.) the sister of the famous poet Hazrat Hassan bin Sabit says that the Holy Prophet (S.A.W.) visited my house and while standing drank water from a hanging water skin through its mouth; I stood up and cut of the mouth of the water skin to preserve it (as a blessed piece of memento).

(*Imam Tirmizi* has reported this tradition which is good).

This has shown that previous traditions show only disliking and not declaring it Haram (unlawful).

****

CHAPTER 113

Prohibition of Blowing on Drinking Water.

٧٦٥ — عن أبي سعيد الخدريّ رضيَ الله عنه أنّ النبيّ صلّى الله عليه وسلّم نهى عَنِ النّفخِ في الشّرابِ . فقال رَجُلٌ : القَذَاةُ أراها في الإناء ؟ فقال : « أَهْرِقْهَا » قال : إنّي لا أَرْوَى مِنْ نَفَسٍ وَاحِدٍ ؟ قال : « فَأَبِنْ القَدَحَ إذاً عَنْ فيكَ » رواه الترمذي وقال : حديث حسن صحيح .

765. Hazrat Abu Sa'eed Khudri (R.A.A.) says, that the Holy Prophet (S.A.W.) had forbidden blowing over drinking water. A man asked: What about undesirable articles like straws floating on the surface of the water?' He answered: 'Run them out.' The man further said: 'My thirst is not satisfied with one gulp.' The Holy Prophet (S.A.W.) said: 'You may then take breath, but put away the vessel from your mouth.' (*Imam Tirmizi* has cited this tradition which is good).

٧٦٦ — وعن ابن عباس رضي الله عنهما أن النبي صلى الله عليه وسلم نهى أن يُتَنَفَّسَ في الإنَاءِ ، أَوْ يُنْفَخَ فيهِ . رواه الترمذي وقال : حديث حسن صحيح

766. Hazrat Ibn Abbas (R.A.A.) relates that the Holy Prophet (S.A.W.) prohibited from breathing in the pot and blowing upon it. *(Tirmizi).*

****

CHAPTER 114

Permission for Drinking Water While Standing but It Is Better to Drink Water While Sitting.

٧٦٧ — وعن ابن عباس رضي اللهُ عنهما قال : سَقَيْتُ النَّبيَّ صلى اللهُ عليه وسلَّم مِنْ زَمْزَمَ ، فَشَرِبَ وَهُوَ قَائِمٌ . متفقٌ عليه

767. In this connection attention is invited to **Hazrat Khabasha's** tradition. **Hazrat Ibn Abbas** (R.A.A.) relates that (once) he gave the Holy Prohet (S.A.W.) *Zam Zam* water to drink, which he drank while standing. *(Bukhari and Muslim).*

٧٦٨ – وعنِ النزَّالِ بنِ سَبْرَةَ رَضيَ اللهُ عنه قالَ : أَتى عَليٌّ رضيَ اللهُ عنهُ بَابَ الرَّحْبَةِ . فَشَرِبَ قَائماً ، وقالَ : إِنّي رَأَيْتُ رَسولَ اللهِ صلى اللهُ عليه وسلَّم فعَلَ كما رَأَيْتُمُوني فَعَلْتُ . رواهُ البخاري

768. Hazrat Nazzal bin Sabrah (R.A.A.) says that (once) Hazrat Ali (R.A.A. came to the Bab-ar-Rahbah in (Kufa) and drank water while standing and said. 'I have seen the Holy Prophet (S.A.W.) doing what you have seen me doing.' *(Bukhari).*

٧٦٩ – وعن ابنِ عمر رضيَ اللهُ عنهما قال : كنَّا نَأْكُلُ عَلى عَهْدِ رسُولِ اللهِ صلى اللهُ عليه وسلَّم وَنَحْنُ نَمْشي ، ونَشْرَبُ وَنحنُ قِيَامٌ رواهُ الترمذي ، وقال : حديث حسن صحيح .

769. Hazrat Ibn Umar (R.A.A.) relates during the days of the Holy Prophet (S.A.W.) we used to eat while walking and drinking water while standing. (*Imam Tirmizi* says that this is a good tradition).

٧٧٠ – وعن عمرو بن شعيب عن أبيهِ عن جدِّه رضيَ اللهُ عنه قال : رَأَيْتُ رسُولَ اللهِ صلى اللهُ عليهِ وسلَّم يَشْرَبُ قَائماً وَقَاعِداً . رواه الترمذي وقال : حديث حسن صحيح .

770. Hazrat 'Amr bin Shuaib (R.A.A.) relates on the authority of his father and grand father that he saw the Holy Prophet (S.A.W.) drinking water while standing as well as while sitting. *(Tirmizi).*

٧٧١ – وعن أَنَسٍ رضيَ اللهُ عنه عن النبيِّ صلى اللهُ عليه وسلم أَنَّهُ نَهى أَنْ يَشربَ الرَّجُلُ قَائماً . قال قتادة : فَقُلْنَا لأَنس : فالأَكْلُ ؟ قالَ : ذلكَ أَشَرُّ – أو أَخْبَثُ – رواهُ مسلم

وفي رواية له أنَّ النبيَّ صلى اللهُ عليهِ وسلَّم زَجَرَ عَنِ الشُّرْبِ قَائماً .

771. Hazrat Anas bin Malik (R.A.A.) relates that the Holy Prophet (S.A.W.) has forbidden a person from drinking water while standing. Hazrat Qatadah(R.A.A.) asked Hazrat Anas (R.A.A.). 'What are the orders about eating?' He said: That (the act of eating while standing) would be still worse. *(Muslim).*

Another report from Hazrat Anas (R.A.A.) says that the Holy Prophet (S.A.W.) has reprimanded drinking while standing.

٧٧٢ — وعن أبي هريرة رضيَ اللهُ عنه قال : قالَ رسُولُ اللهِ صلى الله عليهِ وسلَّم « لاَ يَشْرَبَنْ أَحَدٌ مِنْكُمْ قَائِماً ، فَمَنْ نَسِيَ فَلْيَسْتَقِئْ رواهُ مسلم

772. Hazrat Abu Hurairah (R.A.A.) relates that the Holy Prophet (S.A.W.) said: 'None of you would drink while standing. If anybody does so through mistake he should vomit it out." *(Muslim).*

****

CHAPTER 115

One Who Serves Drink, Should Be the Last Person to Drink.

٧٧٣ — عن أبي قتادة رضيَ اللهُ عنه عن النبيِّ صلى اللهُ عليه وسلَّم قال : « سَاقِي القَوْمِ آخِرُهُمْ » يعني : شرْباً . رواهُ الترمذي ، وقال : حديث حسن صحيح .

773. Hazrat Abu Qatadah (R.A.A.) relates that the Holy Prophet (S.A.W.) has said that one who serves drinks, should himself be the last person to drink. *(Tirmizi).*

****

CHAPTER 116

Preference to Drink from Any Clean Vessel Except of Gold And Silver; Prohibition of the Use of Silver and Gold Vessels for Drinking, Eating and Toilet, and Ppermission for Drinking Water through Mouth Directly from Canal etc.

٧٧٤ — عَنْ أنسٍ رضيَ اللهُ عنه قال : حَضَرَتِ الصَّلاةُ ، فقَامَ مَنْ كانَ قَرِيبَ الدَّارِ إلى أَهْلِهِ ، وبَقِيَ قَوْمٌ فَأُتِيَ رَسُولُ اللهِ صلى اللهُ عليهِ وسلَّم بِمِخْضَبٍ مِنْ حِجَارَةٍ ، فَصَغُرَ المِخْضَبُ أَنْ يَبْسُطَ فيهِ كَفَّهُ ، فَتَوَضَّأَ القَوْمُ كُلُّهُمْ . قَالُوا : كَمْ كُنْتُمْ ؟ قَالَ : ثَمَانِينَ وزِيَادَةً . متفقٌ عليهِ هذه رواية البخاري .

وفي روايةٍ له ولمسلم : أنَّ النبيَّ صلى اللهُ عليهِ وسلَّم دَعَا بإنَاءٍ مِنْ مَاءٍ ، فَأُتِيَ بِقَدَحٍ رَحْرَاحٍ فيهِ شَيْءٌ مِنْ مَاءٍ ، فَوَضَعَ أَصَابِعَهُ فيهِ . قَالَ

أنس : فَجَعَلْتُ أَنْظُرُ إلى الماء يَنْبُعُ مِنْ بَيْنِ أصابِعِهِ ، فَحَزَرْتُ مَنْ تَوَضَّأَ مَا بَيْنَ السَّبْعِينَ إلى الثَّمَانِينَ .

774. Hazrat Anas bin Malik (R.A.A.) relates that the Holy Prophet (S.A.W.) was at Zaura, when the time for Prayer approached. As such those whose houses were near by, went there for ablution, and others stayed with the Holy Prophet (S.A.W.). A stone cup (containing some water) was brought to the Holy Prophet (S.A.W.). It was a small pot which could be covered by his hand. (On account of his blessings) He (S.A.W.) performed his ablution and it sufficed for the entire community (companions) also. On being asked as to how many persons performed ablutions, he (S.A.W.) was informed that eighty or a little more. *(Bukhari and Muslim).*

This is *Imam Bukhari's* version.

Antoher report by *Imam Muslim* says: The Holy Prophet (S.A.W.) sent for a vessel containing some water. Accordingly a large, but shallow vessel with a little water in it, was brought to him to him He (S.A.W.) put his fingers in it. Hazrat Anas bin Malik (R.A.A.) says: 'I saw that the water was pouring from between his (S.A.W.) fingers. Hazrat Anas (R.A.A.) estimated the number of those who performed their ablution with this water as between seventy and eighty.

٧٧٥ — وعن عبد الله بنِ زيدٍ رضيَ اللهُ عنه قال : أَتَانَا النَّبيُّ صلى اللهُ عليهِ وسلَّم ، فَأَخْرَجْنَا لَهُ مَاءً في تَوْرٍ مِنْ صُفْرٍ فَتَوَضَّأَ . رواه البُخاري

775. Hazrat Abdullah bin Zaid (R.A.A.) says: 'The Holy Prophet (S.A.W.) came to us; accordingly we brought water for him in a brass vessel, with which he performed his ablution. *(Bukhari).*

٧٧٦ — وعن جابر رضيَ اللهُ عنه أنَّ رسُولَ اللهِ صلى اللهُ عليهِ وسلَّم دَخَلَ عَلى رَجُلٍ مِنَ الأَنْصارِ ، ومَعَهُ صاحِبٌ لَهُ . فقالَ رسُولُ اللهِ صلى اللهُ عليه وسلَّم : « إنْ كَانَ عِنْدَكَ مَاءٌ بَاتَ هذهِ اللَّيْلَةَ في شَنَّةٍ وَإلاَّ كَرَعْنَا » رواهُ البخاري

776. Hazrat Jabir (R.A.A.) says: The Holy Prophet (S.A.W.) came to an Ansar along with a companion i.e. Hazrat Abu Bakr (R.A.A.) and said to him: 'If you have some water in the water-skin left over from last night, give it to us for drink or else we will directly drink with our mouth from some stream. (*Bukhari*).

٧٧٧ — وعن حذيفة رضيَ اللهُ عنه قالَ : إنَّ النبيَّ صلى اللهُ عليهِ وسلَّم نَهَانَا عَنِ الحَرِيرِ والدِّيبَاجِ والشُّرْبِ في آنِيَةِ الذَّهَبِ والفِضَّةِ ، وقالَ :

« هِيَ لَهُمْ في الدُّنْيَا ، وهِيَ لَكُمْ في الآخِرَةِ » متفقٌ عليهِ

777. Hazrat Huzaifah (R.A.A.) relates: The Holy Prophet (S.A.W.) prohibited us from wearing clothes made from Harir or Deebaj (costly silk cloth) and drinking from gold or silver vessels, and said: These are for them (non believers) in this world, and all these things are for you in the Hereafter. *(Bukhari and Muslim).*

٧٧٨ ـ وعن أمِّ سلمة رضيَ اللهُ عنها أنَّ رسُولَ اللهِ صلى اللهُ عليهِ وسلَّم قال : « الَّذِي يَشْرَبُ في آنِيَةِ الفِضَّةِ إنَّما يُجَرْجِرُ في بَطْنِهِ نَارَ جَهَنَّمَ » متفقٌ عليهِ

وفي روايةٍ لمسلم : « إنَّ الَّذِي يَأْكُلُ أَوْ يَشْرَبُ في آنِيَةِ الفِضَّةِ والذَّهَبِ»

وفي روايةٍ لَه : « مَنْ شَرِبَ في إنَاءٍ مِنْ ذَهَبٍ أَوْ فِضَّةٍ فإنَّما يُجَرْجِرُ في بَطْنِهِ نَاراً مِنْ جَهَنَّمَ » .

778. Hazrat Umm Salamah (R.A.A.) relates that the Holy Prophet (S.A.W.) said: One who drinks some beverage from a silver vessel, in fact he kindles the fire of hell in his stomach. *(Bukhari and Muslim).*

Another report from *Muslim* says: Anybody who eats or drinks from a gold or silver pot kindles the fire of Hell in his stomach.

Note. All the Ulama (learned persons) are unanimous that it is unlawful for males and females to eat or drink or use for this purpose gold or silver vessels in any other way. However, the females may use ornaments made from gold or silver.

****

BOOK OF DRESS

CHAPTER 117

Etiquette of Dressing, Preference of Wearing White Clothes, and Permission for the Use of Red, Green, Yellow and Black Colour Clothes of Cotton, Woollen and Other Varieties Except Silk.

قالَ اللهُ تعالى : يَا بَنِي آدَمَ قَدْ أَنزَلْنَا عَلَيْكُمْ لِبَاساً يُوارِي سَوْآتِكُمْ وَرِيشاً ، وَلِبَاسُ التَّقْوَى ذلكَ خَيْرٌ [الأعراف : ٢٦] وقال تعالى : وَجَعَلَ لَكُمْ سَرَابِيلَ تَقِيكُمُ الحَرَّ ، وَسَرَابِيلَ تَقِيكُمْ بَأْسَكُمْ [النحل : ٨١] .

Allah, the Exalted, has said:

268. O children of Adam! We have revealed unto you raiment to conceal your shame, and splendid vesture, but the raiment of restraint from evil, that is best.(7:26).

269. And hath given you coats to ward off the heat from you, and coats (of armour) to save you from your own foolhardiness. (16:81).

٧٧٩ – وعن ابنِ عبَّاس رضيَ اللهُ عنهما أنَّ رسُولَ اللهِ صلى اللهُ عليه وسلَّم قال : البَسُوا مِنْ ثِيَابِكُمُ البَيَاضَ ؛ فَإنَّهَا مِنْ خَيْرِ ثِيَابِكُمْ ، وكَفِّنُوا فِيها مَوْتَاكُمْ » رواهُ أبو داود ، والترمذي وقال : حديث حسن صحيح .

779. Hazrat Ibn Abbas (R.A.A.) relates that the Holy Prophet (S.A.W.) told us: 'Wear white clothes for they are the best of all your clothes and use them for shrouds for your dead.' (*Imam Daud* and *Tirmizi* has reported this tradition which *Imam Tirmizi* has cited as good).

٧٨٠ – وعنْ سَمُرَةَ رضيَ اللهُ عنه قال : قالَ رسُولُ اللهِ صلى اللهُ عليه وسلَّم : « البَسُوا البَيَاضَ ؛ فَإنَّهَا أَطْهَرُ وأَطْيَبُ ، وكَفِّنُوا فِيها مَوْتَاكُمْ » رواهُ النسائي ، والحاكم وقال : حديث صحيح .

780. Hazrat Samurah (R.A.A.) relates that the Holy Prophet (S.A.W.) said: 'Wear white clothes because they are the purest and cleanest, and also shroud your dead in white cloth. (*Imams Nisai* and *Hakim* have reported this tradition, which the latter calls it as correct).

٧٨١ – وعن البراء رضيَ اللهُ عنه قال : كانَ رسُولُ اللهِ صلى اللهُ عليهِ وسلّمَ مَرْبُوعاً ولَقَدْ رَأَيْتُهُ في حُلَّةٍ حَمْراءَ مَا رَأَيْتُ شَيْئاً قَطُّ أَحْسَنَ مِنْهُ . متّفقٌ عليهِ

781. Hazrat Bra'a bin Aazib (R.A.A.) relates: 'The Holy Prophet (S.A.W.) was of moderate height. (Once) I saw, him dressed in a red coloured pair of dress. I have not seen anything more elegant and beautiful than him in the world.' *(Bukhari and Muslim).*

٧٨٢ – وعن أبي جُحَيْفَةَ وهْبِ بنِ عبدِ اللهِ رضيَ اللهُ عنهُ قال : رَأَيْتُ النَّبيَّ صلى اللهُ عليهِ وسلّمَ بمَكَّةَ وَهُوَ بِالأَبْطَحِ في قُبَّةٍ لَهُ حَمْرَاءَ مِنْ أَدَمٍ ، فَخرَجَ بِلالٌ بِوَضُوئِهِ ، فَمِنْ نَاضِحٍ ونَائِلٍ ، فَخرَجَ النبي صلى اللهُ عليهِ وسلم وعَلَيْهِ حُلَّةٌ حَمْرَاءُ ، كَأَنِّي أَنْظُرُ إلى بَيَاضِ سَاقَيْهِ ، فَتَوَضَّأَ وَأَذَّنَ بِلالٌ ، فَجعَلْتُ أَتَتَبَّعُ فاهُ ههُنا وههُنا ، يقولُ يَميناً وشِمَالاً : حَيَّ عَلى الصَّلاَةِ ، حَيَّ عَلى الفَلاَحِ ، ثُمَّ رُكِزَتْ لَهُ عَنَزَةٌ . فَتَقَدَّمَ فَصَلّى يَمُرُّ بَيْنَ يَدَيْهِ الكَلْبُ وَالحِمَارُ لا يُمْنَعُ . متّفقٌ عليه

782. Hazrat Abu Juhaifah Wahb bin Abdullah (R.A.A.) says: I saw the Holy Prohet (S.A.W.) at Abita, a place near Mecca. He was then putting up in a tent made of red leather. (In the meantime) Hazrat Bilal (R.A.A) rought somewater for the Holy Prophet's (S.A.W.) ablutions Some people could get some quantity of this water and some could get no water, and some had to be content with receiving only the moisture from the hands of others. Then the Holy Prophet (S.A.W.) came out wearing a red mantle. I still remember noticing the whiteness of the calf of his legs. He made his ablutions and Hazrat Bilal (R.A.A.) (recited the Azan) summoned the Muslims for the prayer. At the same time I continued watching the movement of Hazrat Bilal's face to the right and left when he said:' Come towards Prayer, Come towards Prosperity.' Then a small lance was fixed in front of the Holy Prophet (S.A.W.) who advanced and led the congregation. While he was leading (us) in prayers dogs and donkeys passed in front of him (ahead of the lance) and nobody objected to this. *(Bukhari and Muslim).*

٧٨٣ – وعن أبي رِمْثَةَ رِفاعَةَ التَّيْمِيِّ رضيَ اللهُ عنه قال : رَأَيْتُ رسُولَ اللهِ صلى اللهُ عليهِ وسلّمَ وعلَيْه ثوبانِ أخضَرانِ . رواهُ أبُوداود ، والترمذي بإسْنادٍ صحيحٍ

783. Hazrat Abi Rimsa Rifa'a-at- Taimi (R.A.A.) relates: I have seen the Holy Prophet (S.A.W.) with two pieces of green coloured clothes. (*Imams Abu Daud* And *Tirmizi* have quoted this tradition on authentic chains).

٧٨٤ – وعن جابر رضيَ اللهُ عنه ، أنَّ رسُولَ اللهِ صلى اللهُ عليهِ وسلَّم دَخلَ يَوْمَ فَتْحِ مَكَّةَ وعَلَيْهِ عِمَامَةٌ سَوْدَاءُ . رواهُ مسلم

784. Hazrat Jabir bin Abdullah (R.A.A.) says that when the Holy Prophet (S.A.W.) entered Mecca on the day of its conquest, he (S.A.W.) was putting on a black turban. *(Muslim).*

٧٨٥ – وعن ابي سعيد عمرو بن حُرَيْثٍ رضي الله عنه قال : كأني أنظر إلى رسولِ الله صلى الله عليه وسلم وعَلَيْهِ عِمَامَةٌ سَوْدَاءُ ، قدْ أرْخَى طَرَفيها بيْنَ كتفيْهِ . رواه مسلم

وفي روايةٍ له : أن رسول الله صلى الله عليه وسلم خَطَبَ النَّاسَ ، وَعَلَيْهِ عِمَامَةٌ سَوْدَاءُ .

785. **Hazrat Abu Sa'eed 'Amr bin Hurais** (R.A.A.) relates: I remember having seen the Holy Prophet (S.A.W.) wearing a black turban, both ends of which fell over his shoulders *(Muslim).*

Another report of Imam Muslim says: The Holy Prophet (S.A.W.) was delivering address, when he was putting on a black turban.

٧٨٦ – وعن عائشة رضي الله عنها قالت : كُفِّنَ رسول الله صلى الله عليه وسلم في ثلاثة أثْوَابٍ بيضٍ سَحُوليَّةٍ مِنْ كُرْسُفٍ ، لَيْسَ فيهَا قَمِيصٌ وَلَا عِمَامَةٌ . متفقٌ عليه

786. Hazrat Ayesha (R.A.A.) says that the Holy Prophet (S.A.W.) was shrouded in three pieces of white Yemeni cotton cloth, in which was not included a shirt or a turban. *(Bukhari and Muslim).*

٧٨٧ – وعنها قالت : خرجَ رسول الله صلى الله عليه وسلم ذات غَدَاةٍ ، وَعَلَيهِ مِرْطٌ مُرَحَّلٌ مِنْ شَعْرٍ أَسْوَد . رواه مسلم

787. Hazrat Ayesha (R.A.A.) says: One day the Holy Prophet (S.A.W.) went out (of the house) covering himself with a sheet made from black hair which bore the picture of the saddle of a camel.

(Muslim).

٧٨٨ ــ وعن المُغيرةِ بن شُعْبَةَ رضي الله عنه قال : كنتُ مع رسول الله صلى الله عليه وسلم ذاتَ ليلةٍ في مسيرٍ ، فقال لي : « أمعَكَ ماءٌ » ؟ قلت : نعَمْ ، فنزَلَ عن راحلتِه فمَشى حتى توَارَى في سَوادِ اللَّيْلِ ثم جاءَ فأفرغتُ عليه مِنَ الإداوة ، فغسَلَ وَجْهَهُ وعلَيْهِ جُبَّةٌ مِنْ صُوفٍ ، فلم يَسْتَطِعْ انْ يُخرجَ ذِراعيْهِ منها حتى اخرَجَهُما مِنْ أسْفَلِ الجُبَّةِ . فغَسَلَ ذِراعيهِ ومَسَحَ برأسِه ، ثم أهوَيْت لأنزعَ خفَّيْهِ فقال : « دَعْهُمَا فإنِّي أدْخَلْتُهُمَا طَاهِرتَينِ » ومَسَحَ علَيْهِما . متفق عليه .

وفي روايةٍ : وعلَيْهِ جُبَّةٌ شاميَّةٌ ضيِّقَةُ الكُمَّيْنِ .

وفي روايةٍ : أنَّ هذه القَضيَّةَ كانتْ في غزْوَةِ تَبُوكَ .

788. Hazrat Mugheerah bin Shu'ba (R.A.A.) relates: Once I was accompanying the Holy Prophet (S.A.W.) on a night journey. He asked me, if I had some water with me; I said' Yes Sir, I have'. Then he came down (from the mount) and walked away on foot in a direction till he could not be seen on account of darkness. When he returned I poured out water from a vessel and he washed his face. (At that time) he was wearing a woollen long coat and as such he could not take out his arms out of his sleeves; therefore he had to pull them from inside the coat, and then washed his forearms. Thereafter he passed his hands over his head (performed Mas'ah). I wanted to help him to take off his socks, but he said: 'Leave them, as they are: I have put them on my clean feet;' and therefore he wiped out his hands over them (performing Mas'ah over the socks). *(Bukhari and Muslim).*

Another version says: He was wearing a tight-sleeved Syrian long coat. Yet another version says: This incident took place during the campaign of Tabuk.

****

CHAPTER 118

Preference for Wearing a Shirt or Tunic.

٧٨٩ ــ عن أمِّ سَلمةَ رضي الله عنها قالت : كان أحبَّ الثِّيابِ إلى رسول الله صلى الله عليه وسلم القَميصُ . رواه أبو داود ، والترمذي وقال : حديث حسن

789. Hazrat Umm Salamah (R.A.A.) relates that of all the dresses, the Holy Prophet (S.A.W.) liked a shirt(or tunic) best.(*Abu Daud* and *Tirmizi*; the latter has called this tradition as good).

Note: This tradition established the preference of shirt (or tunic) in as much as it fully covers the main parts of the human body; its wearer looks sober and decently dressed. To a Muslim, a thing which is liked by the Holy Prophet (S.A.W.) must be full of virtues and blessings.

****

CHAPTER 119

The Length of Shirt and Sleeves; Size of Loin Cloth and the Turban. Prohibition of letting Loose Any of These Garments Exhbiting Arrogance, and Disliking for Repugnance of Letting Loose (These Garments) Unintentionally.

٧٩٠ – عن أسماءَ بنتِ يزيدَ الأنصاريَّةِ رضي الله عنها قالت : كان كُمُّ قميصِ رسولِ الله صلى الله عليه وسلم إلى الرُّسُغِ ، رواه أبو داود ، والترمذي وقال : حديث حسن .

790. Hazrat Asmaa bint Yazid Al Ansaria (R.A.A.) says that the sleeves of the shirt of the Holy Prophet (S.A.W.) reached upto his wrist. *(Abu Daud and Tirmizi).*

٧٩١ – وعن ابن عمر رضي الله عنهما أنَّ النبي صلى الله عليه وسلم قال : « مَنْ جرَّ ثوبَهُ خُيَلاءَ لَمْ يَنْظُرِ اللهُ إليه يومَ القيامةِ » فقال أبو بكر : يا رسول الله إنَّ إزاري يَسْتَرْخي إلاَّ أنْ أتعاهَدَهُ ، فقال له رسول الله صلى الله عليه وسلم : « إنَّكَ لستَ مِمَّنْ يفعَلُهُ خُيَلاءَ » .

رواه البخاري ، وروى مسلم بعضه .

791. Hazrat Ibn Umar (R.A.A.) relates that the Holy Prophet (S.A.W.) said: One who lets loose his dress by way of pride, Allah will not look towards him on the Day of Judgment. On this Hazrat Abu Bakr (R.A.A.) submitted: 'O Messenger of Allah (S.A.W.)! loin cloth very often slips down unintentionally.' The Holy Prophet (S.A.W.) said: 'You are not one of those who do so by way of arrogance.'

(Bukhari and Imam Muslim has reported some portion of this tradition).

٧٩٢ – وعن أبي هريرة رضي الله عنه أنَّ رسول الله صلى الله عليه وسلم قال : « لا يَنْظُرُ اللهُ يومَ القيامةِ إلى مَنْ جرَّ إزارَهُ بَطَراً » متفق عليه

792. This Hadis is the same as one covered by No. 616 of Chapter 72.

٧٩٣ — وعنه عن النبي صلى الله عليه وسلم قال : « مَا أسفَلَ مِنَ الكَعْبَيْن مِنَ الإزارِ ففِي النَّارِ » رواه البخاري.

793. Hazrat Abu Hurairah (R.A.A.) relates that the Holy Prophet (S.A.W.) said: 'The part of a pyjama or loin cloth, which is below the ankles is destined for the fire of Hell. That is the part of the body which is touched by this apparel will go to Hell.' *(Bukhari).*

٧٩٤ — وعن أبي ذرٍّ رضي الله عنه عن النبي صلى الله عليه وسلم قال :«ثلاثة لايُكَلِّمُهُمُ اللهُ يَوْمَ القيامةِ ، ولا يَنْظُرُ إلَيْهم ، ولا يُزَكِّيهِمْ : ولَهُمْ عَذَابٌ أليمٌ » قال : فقرأها رسولُ الله صلى الله عليه وسلم ثلاث مِرارٍ . قال أبو ذرّ : خابُوا وخَسِرُوا ! مَنْ هُمْ يا رسول الله ؟ قال : « المُسْبِلُ ، والمنَّانُ ، والمُنْفِقُ سِلْعَتَهُ بالحلِفِ الكاذِبِ » رواه مسلم

وفي روايةٍ له : « المُسْبِلُ إزارَهُ »

794. Hazrat Abu Zarr (R.A.A.) relates that the Holy Prophet (S.A.W.) said: There are three (kinds) of persons to whom Allah will neither speak on the Day of Judgement, nor will He look at them nor purify them. For such persons is ear-marked a painful punishment. He repeated this sentence three times. Hazrat Abu Zarr (R.A.A.) said: Such persons are doomed Who are they, 'O Messenger of Allah (S.A.W.)? He said: 'One who lets down his apparels out of arrogance; one who reminds or makes a show of favours done by him to another, and one who sells his (inferior) wares with false oaths. *(Muslim).*

Another version of *Muslim* adds: 'One who lets down his Pyjama or loin cloth.'

٧٩٥ — وعن ابن عمر رضي الله عنهما . عن النبي صلى الله عليه وسلم قال : « الإسْبَالُ في الإزارِ . والقَميصِ . والعِمَامةِ ؛ مَنْ جَرَّ شيئاً خُيَلاءَ لم يَنظُرِ اللهُ إليهِ يَوْمَ القيامَةِ » رواه أبو داود : والنسائي بإسنادٍ صحيح .

795. Hazrat Ibn Umar (R.A.A.) relates that the Holy Prophet (S.A.W.) said: On the Dooms Day Allah will not look towards a person who lets down his garments like loin cloth, pyjama, shirt or turban by way of arrogance.' *(Abu Daud and Nisai).*

٧٩٦ – وعن أبي جُرَيٍّ جَابِرِ بن سُلَيمٍ رضي الله عنه قال : رَأَيْتُ رَجلاً يَصْدُرُ النّاسُ عَنْ رَأْيِهِ ، لا يَقُولُ شَيْئاً إِلّا صَدَرُوا عنه ، قلتُ : من هذا ؟ قالوا : رسول الله صلى اللهُ عليهِ وسلم . قلتُ : عَلَيكَ السَّلامُ يا رسولَ الله – مَرَّتَيْنِ – قال : « لا تَقُلْ عَلَيكَ السَّلامُ . عَلَيكَ السَّلامُ تَحِيَّةُ المَوْتى – قُلْ : السَّلامُ عَلَيكَ » قال : قلتُ : أنتَ رسول الله ؟ قال : « أنا رسول الله الذي إذا أَصابَكَ ضُرٌّ فَدَعَوْتَهُ كَشَفَهُ عَنْكَ ، وَإذا أَصابَكَ عامُ سَنَةٍ فَدَعَوْتَهُ أنبتَها لكَ . وإذا كُنتَ بِأَرْضٍ قَفْرٍ أَوْ فَلاةٍ ، فَضَلَّتْ رَاحِلَتُكَ ، فَدَعَوْتَه رَدَّهَا عَلَيكَ » قال : قلتُ : اعْهَدْ إليَّ . قال : « لاتَسُبَّنَّ أحَداً » قال : فَمَا سَبَبْتُ بَعْدَهُ حُرّاً ، وَلا عَبداً ، وَلا بَعِيراً ، وَلا شَاةً « وَلا تَحقِرَنَّ مِنَ المَعرُوفِ شَيْئاً ، وأَنْ تُكَلِّمَ أَخاكَ وأنتَ مُنْبَسِطٌ إليهِ وجهُكَ ، إنَّ ذلكَ مِنَ المَعرُوفِ . وارفَع إزَارَكَ إلى نِصْفِ السّاقِ ، فَإِن أَبَيتَ فَإلى الكَعبَينِ ، وإيّاكَ وإسْبالَ الإزَارِ فَإنّها مِن المَخيلةِ وإنَّ الله لايُحِبُّ المَخِيلَةَ ، وإنِ امْرُؤٌ شَتَمَكَ وَعَيَّرَكَ بِمَا يَعْلَمُ فيكَ فلا تُعَيِّرهُ بما تَعلَم فيهِ ، فإنَّمَا وبَالُ ذلكَ عليهِ » رواه أبو داود والترمذي بإسنادٍ صحيحٍ ، وقال الترمذي : حديث حسن صحيح

796. Hazrat Abu Juraiy Jabir bin Sulaim (R.A.A.) relates: I saw a person whose opinions were accepted by everyone; whatever he said was believed by others. I asked as to who was that person. The people said: 'He is the Prophet of Allah (S.A.W).' I said two times: *Alaikas Salam* 'On you be peace, O Messenger of Allah.' He said: 'Do not say *Alaikas Salam* ' 'On you be peace.' It is the salutation for the dead. Say, *Assalam-o-Alaika* 'Peace be on you.' Hazrat Abu Juraiy (R.A.A.) further says: I asked: Are you the Messenger of Allah (S.A.W.)? He said: 'I am the Messenger of that Allah, Who, when you are distressed and supplicate will remove your distress; Who, when you are suffering from famine (nothing may grow on land) and pray to Him, He will cause food to grow for you; and Who, when you happen to be in a land without man or water and lose your mount and pray to Him, He will return it to you.' I said to him: 'Instruct me O Messenger of Allah (S.A.W.). He said: Do not abuse anyone. Hazrat Abu Juraiy (R.A.A.) says: Since then I have not abused anyone, neither a freeman, nor a slave, nor a camel or a goat. The Holy Prophet (S.A.W.) continued: 'Do not despise the doing of the smaller good; and if talk to your brother talk, with a cheerful face, it is of the virtue; and suspend your loin cloth (or pyjama) half way up to the knee, and at least above the ankles; for suspending it below this is a sign of pride and self esteem, and Allah dislikes the pride. If someone blames or taints you with faults from which, he knows you suffer, but you should not blame him with defects from which you know, he suffers, because he will be penalised for his defaults. (*Imams Abu Daud* and *Tirmizi* have reported this tradition on authentic proof).

٧٩٧ – وعن أبي هريرة رضي الله عنه قال : بينما رجلٌ يُصَلِّي مُسْبِلٌ إزارَه ، قال له رسول الله صلى الله عليه وسلم : « اذهَبْ فتَوضَّأْ » فذَهَبَ فتَوضَّأَ . ثم جاءَ . فقال : « اذهَبْ فتَوضَّأْ » فقال له رجُلٌ : يا رسول الله . مالكَ أمَرْتَه أن يتَوضَّأَ ثم سَكَتَّ عنه ؟ قال : « إنه كانَ يُصَلِّي وهو مُسْبِلٌ إزارَهُ ، وإنّ الله لا يَقْبَلُ صَلاةَ رَجُلٍ مُسْبِلٍ » .

رواه أبو داود بإسناد صحيح على شرط مسلم .

797. Hazrat Abu Hurairah (R.A.A.) says: While a person who was busy in prayer with his loin cloth hanging down, the Holy Prohet (S.A.W.) said to him: 'Go and perform you ablution again.' The man went and came back after having done so. The Holy Prophet (S.A.W.) again said 'Go and make your ablution.' Someone present said to the Holy Prophet (S.A.W.): 'O Messenger of Allah (S.A.W.)! 'Why you ask him to perform his ablution and then keep quiet.' He said: 'He is offering his prayer with his loin cloth hanging down. Allah does not accept the prayer of a man who lets down his loin cloth.' *(Abu Daud).*

٧٩٨ – وعن قيسِ بن بشرٍ التَغْلِبيِّ قال : أخبَرَني أبي – وكان جَلِيساً لأبي الدَّرداءِ – قال : كان بدمشقَ رَجُلٌ من أصحابِ النبي صلى الله عليه وسلم يقال له سهل بن الحَنْظَلِيَّة ، وكان رجُلاً مُتَوَحِّداً قلَّما يُجالسُ النَّاسَ ، إنَّما هو صَلاةٌ . فإذا فرَغَ فإنَّما هو تسبيحٌ وتكبيرٌ حتى يأتيَ أهْلَه . فمرَّ بِنا ونَحنُ عِند أبي الدَّرداءِ . فقال له أبو الدَّرداءِ : كَلِمةً تنفعُنا ولاتضُرُّك . قال : بَعَثَ رسول الله صلى الله عليه وسلم سَرِيَّةً فقَدِمَتْ ، فجاءَ رَجُلٌ مِنهم فجَلَسَ في المَجْلِسِ الذي يَجلِسُ فيه رسول الله صلى الله عليه وسلم ، فقال لِرجُلٍ إلى جنْبه : لَوْ رَأيتَنا حينَ التقَيْنا نحنُ والعدُوُّ . فحمَلَ فُلانٌ وطَعَنَ ، فقال : خُذْها مِنِّي . وأنا الغُلامُ الغِفاريُّ ، كَيفَ ترى

فِي قَوْلِهِ ؟ قال : مَا أُرَاهُ إِلاَّ قَدْ بَطَلَ أَجْرُهُ . فَسَمِعَ بِذَلِكَ آخَرُ فقال : مَا أَرَى بِذَلِكَ بَأْساً . فَتَنَازَعَا حَتَى سَمِعَ رسول الله صلى الله عليه وسلم فقال : « سُبْحَانَ الله ؟ لا بَأْسَ أَن يُؤْجَرَ وَيُحْمَدَ » فرأيْتُ أَبَا الدَّرْدَاءِ سُرَّ بِذَلِكَ . وَجَعَلَ يَرْفَعُ رَأْسَه إليهِ وَيَقُولُ : أَنْتَ سَمِعْتَ ذلكَ مِنْ رسول الله صلى الله عليه وسلم ! ؟ فيقول : نعَمْ . فما زَالَ يَعِيدُ عَلَيْهِ حَتَى إِنِّي لأَقولُ لَيَبْرُكَنَّ عَلَى رُكبَتَيْهِ .

قال : فَمَرَّ بِنَا يَوماً آخَرَ . فقال له أَبُو الدَّرْدَاءِ : كَلِمَةً تَنْفَعُنَا وَلا تَضُرُّكَ . قال : قال لَنَا رسول الله صلى الله عليه وسلم : « الْمُنْفِقُ عَلَى الْخَيْلِ كَالبَاسِطِ يَدَه بالصَّدَقة لا يَقْبِضُهَا » .

ثم مَرَّ بِنا يَوماً آخَرَ . فقال له أَبُو الدَّرْدَاءِ : كَلِمَةً تَنْفَعُنَا وَلا تَضُرُّكَ . قال : قال رسول الله صلى الله عليه وسلم : « نِعْمَ الرَّجُلُ خُرَيْمٌ الأَسَدِيُّ ! لَوْلا طُولُ جُمَّتِهِ وَإِسْبَالُ إِزَارِهِ ! » فَبَلَغَ خُرَيْماً . فَعَجَّلَ . فَأَخَذَ شَفْرَةً فَقَطَعَ بِهَا جُمَّتَهُ إِلَى أُذُنَيْهِ . وَرَفَعَ إِزَارَهُ إِلَى أَنْصَافِ سَاقَيْهِ .

ثُمَّ مَرَّ بِنَا يَوْماً آخَرَ فَقَالَ لَهُ أَبُو الدَّرْدَاءِ : كَلِمَةً تَنْفَعُنَا وَلاَ تَضُرُّكَ . قَالَ : سَمِعْتُ رَسُولَ اللهِ صلى اللهُ عليهِ وسلَّم يَقُولُ : « إِنَّكُمْ قَادِمُونَ عَلَى إِخْوَانِكُمْ . فَأَصْلِحُوا رِحَالَكُمْ . وَأَصْلِحُوا لِبَاسَكُمْ حَتى تَكُونُوا كَأَنَّكُمْ شَامَةٌ فِي النَّاسِ ؛ فَإِنَّ اللهَ لاَ يُحِبُّ الفُحْشَ وَلاَ التَفَحُّشَ » .

رَوَاهُ أَبو داود بإسنادٍ حسنٍ ؛ إلاَّ قَيْسَ بن بشر . فاخْتَلَفُوا في تَوْثِيقِهِ وتَضْعِيفِهِ ، وقد روى له مسلم .

798. **Hazrat Qais bin Bishr-at-Taghlibi** (R.A.A.) says that his father, who was a companion of Hazrat Abu Darda (R.A.A.) said that there was a man in Damascus whose nane was *Ibn-al- Hanzaliyyah* and who was a companion of the Holy Prophet (S.A.W.). He was leading a life of seclusion and did not spend much time in the company of people. He utilised much time in *Salat* (Prayers) and when he was free from *Salat* he used to remember and glorify Allah on a rosary, so long that his family members had to come to him for their needs. One day

when we were sitting with Hazrat Abu Darda (R.A.A.) he passed by us. Hazrat Abu Darda (R.A.A.) said to him: 'Tell us something which might benefit us and the same may not harm you.' Hazrat Ibn-al-Hanzaliyyah (R.A.A.) said: 'The Holy Prophet (S.A.W.) despatched a small party of Mujahids on a mission, and when they returned, one of them came to the gathering which included the Holy Prophet (S.A.W.) and said to the person sitting near him, 'I wish you had seen us when we engaged the enemy, and one of them (a non-believer) took up his lance and struck a Muslim, who retaliating said: 'Take this from me and know that I am only a Ghifari slave.' Now what is your opinion about this? The person sitting nearby said: 'I think he lost its recompense on account of his boasting.' Another person overhearing this remarked: 'I see no harm in it.' The two began arguing till the Holy Prophet (S.A.W.) heard them and said: 'Allah be praised: there is no harm in giving him recompense in the Hereafter and praising him in this world. **Hazrat Bishr** (R.A.A.) says: **Hazrat Abu Darda** (R.A.A.) looked pleased with this, and raising his head said 'Did you hear the Holy Prophet (S.A.W.) say this?' When **Hazrat Ibn-al-Hanzaliyyah** (R.A.A.) said: 'Yes, I did hear.' **Hazrat Abu Darda** (R.A.A.) repeated this query several times; at last I said to Hazrat Abu Darda (R.A.A.) as to why he was pestering him (Hazrat Ibn-al-Hanzaliyyah). Hazrat Qais Ibn Bishr says that Hazrat Ibn al-Hanzaliyyah met them again the next day when Hazrat Abu Darda' said to him 'Tell us something that might be useful for us, and the telling of which may not harm you.' He said: The Holy Prophet (S.A.W.) told us that he who spends on feeding a horse, is like one who is generous in spending for charity and does not stop it. **Hazrat Ibn-al-Hanzaliyyah** (R.A.A.) passed by us another day and Hazrat Abu Darda (R.A.A.) said to him; 'Tell us something that might be useful for us, and the telling of which may not harm you.' He said: 'The Holy Prophet (S.A.W.) once said: **Khuraim Asadi** would have been the best person, but for his long hair and his low hanging loin-cloth.' This remark reached the ears of Khuraim and he at once cut down his hair upto his ears wth a knife and raised his loin cloth halfway up to his knees.

Once more Hazrat Ibn-al-Hanzaliyya passed by us when Hazrat Abu Darda (R.A.A.) said to him: 'Tell us something that might be useful for us and the telling of which may not harm you?' He said that he had heard the Holy Prophet (S.A.W.) say, (when he S.A.W.) was returning from an expedition) since you are returning to your brothers set right your saddles and clothes, so that you may appear decent. Allah does not like vulgarity and shabbiness.' (*Imam Abu Daud* has reported this tradition on good authority.)

٧٩٩ – وعن أبي سعيدٍ الخدْرِيِّ رضيَ الله عنه قال : قال رسُولُ اللهِ صلى اللهُ عليهِ وسلَّم : « إزرَةُ المُسلِمِ إلى نِصْفِ السَّاقِ ، ولاَ حَرَجَ – أوْ

لا جُناحَ – فيما بيْنَهُ وبيْنَ الكعْبيْنِ . فما كانَ أسْفلَ منَ الكعْبيْنِ
فهُوَ في النّارِ ؛ ومَنْ جرَّ إزارَهُ بطَراً لَمْ ينْظُرِ اللهُ إليْهِ »

رواهُ أبو داود بإسنادٍ صحيح .

799. Hazrat Abu Sa'eed Khudri (R.A.A.) relates that the Holy Prophet (S.A.W.) has said: 'The loin cloth of a Muslim should be upto the half length of the calf of the leg or at the most between the calf and the ankle joint; but there is, however, no harm if it is above the ankles, or he said there is no sin. That which hangs below the ankles is destined for Hell. Allah will not look towards a person who lets down his loin cloth or pyjama out of pride.' (*Abu Daud*).

٨٠٠ – وعنِ ابنِ عمر رضيَ اللهُ عنهما قال : مرَرْتُ على رسُولِ اللهِ
صلى الله عليهِ وسلَّم وفي إزاري استرْخاءٌ . فقالَ : « يا عبْدَ الله . ارفعْ
إزارَكَ » فرفعْتُهُ ثُمَّ قالَ : « زِدْ » . فزِدْتُ ، فما زلْتُ أتحرّاها بعْدُ .
فقالَ بعْضُ القوْمِ : إلى أيْنَ ؟ فقالَ : إلى أنصافِ السّاقيْنِ » . رواهُ مسلم

800. Hazrat Abdullah bin Umar (R.A.A.) relates: 'Once I passed by the Holy Prophet (S.A.W.) when my loin cloth was dangling. The Holy Prophet (S.A.W.) said to me: 'Abdullah, pull up your loin cloth.' Accordingly I pulled it up a little. He said: 'a little more.' and I pulled it up a little more. Since then I have always worn it high. Someone of his tribe asked: 'How high?' He said: Half-way up to the knees. *(Muslim)*.

٨٠١ – وعنه قال : قالَ رسُولُ اللهِ صلى اللهُ عليهِ وسلَّم : مَنْ جرَّ ثوْبَهُ
خيلاءَ لَمْ ينْظُرِ اللهُ إليْهِ يوْمَ القيامَةِ » فقالَتْ أُمُّ سلَمَةَ : فكيْفَ
تصْنَعُ النّساءُ بذُيُولِهنَّ ، قالَ : « يُرْخِينَ شِبْراً » . قالَتْ : إذاً تنْكشِفُ
أقْدامُهُنَّ . قال : « فيُرْخِينَهُ ذِراعاً لا يزِدْنَ » .

رواهُ أبو داود ، والترمذي وقال : حديثٌ حسن صحيح .

801. Hazrat Abdullah bin Umar (R.A.A.) relates that the Holy Prophet (S.A.W.) said: On the Day of Judgment, Allah will not look towards the person who drags his clothes along out of pride.' Hazrat Umm Salamah (R.A.A.) asked: 'What the women folk ought to do with their skirts?' She said: 'In this way their feet would be exposed.' He said: 'Then they may lower their skirts by an arms length, but not more.' (*Abu Daud and Tirmizi*).

****

CHAPTER 120

On Discarding Decent Clothings out of Humility

٨٠٢ — وعن معاذ بن أنس رضي الله عنه أن رسول الله صلى الله عليه وسلم قال : « من ترك اللباس تواضعاً لله ، وهو يقدر عليه ، دعاه الله يوم القيامة على رؤوس الخلائق حتى يخيره من أي حلل الإيمان شاء يلبسها » . رواه الترمذي وقال : حديث حسن .

802. Hazrat Mu'az ibn Anas (R.A.A.) relates that the Holy Prophet (S.A.W.) said: 'A person inspite of having the means to wear decent garments, abstains from wearing them out of sense of humility for the sake of Allah, will be called by Allah on the Day of Judgment in preference to all the human beings and will be given the option to choose whichever of the mantles of faith he likes. (*Imam Tirmizi* has reported this tradition and said that it is authentic.)

****

CHAPTER 121

Virtues of Moderation in Dressing and Avoidance of Such Garments, without Necessity or Religious Justification

٨٠٣ — عن عمرو بن شعيب عن أبيه عن جده رضي الله عنه قال : قال رسول الله صلى الله عليه وسلم : « إن الله يحب أن يرى أثر نعمته على عبده » . رواه الترمذي وقال : حديث حسن .

803. Hazrat 'Amr bin Shuaib (R.A.A.) relates on the authority of his father and grandfather, that the Holy Prophet (S.A.W.) said: 'Allah is pleased to see the effect of his blessing on His servant.' (*Imam Tirmizi* has reported this tradition, which he says is authentic.)

****

CHAPTER 122

On Prohibition of Wearing Silk by Men and Sitting on It and Permission to Females to Wear Silk

٨٠٤ — عن عمر بن الخطاب رضي الله عنه قال : قال رسول الله صلى الله عليه وسلم : « لا تلبسوا الحرير ؛ فإن من لبسه في الدنيا لم يلبسه

في الآخِرَةِ » متفقٌ عليه

804. Hazrat Umar bin Al-Khattab (R.A.A.) relates that the Holy Prophet (S.A.W.) said: 'Do not wear silk, for one who wears it in this world, shall not wear it in the Hereafter. (*Bukhari and Muslim*).

٨٠٥ – وعنه قال : سمعتُ رسُولَ اللهِ صلى اللهُ عليهِ وسلَّم يقولُ

« إنَّما يلْبَسُ الحَرِيرَ مَنْ لاَ خلاَقَ لَهُ » متفقٌ عليه

وفي روايةٍ للبُخاري : « مَنْ لاَ خلاَقَ لَهُ في الآخِرَةِ » .

805. Hazrat Umar bin Al Khattab (R.A.A.) relates that he heard the Holy Prophet (S.A.W.) say: Silk is worn by the person who has no share in (the bounties of) the Hereafter. (*Bukhari and Muslim*)

٨٠٦ – وعن أنسٍ رضيَ اللهُ عنه قال : قالَ رسُولُ اللهِ صلى اللهُ عليه

وسلم : « مَنْ لَبِسَ الحَرِيرَ في الدُّنيا لَمْ يَلْبَسْهُ في الآخِرَةِ » متفقٌ عليه

806. Hazrat Anas (R.A.A.) relates that the Holy Prophet (S.A.W.) said: 'A person who wears silk in this world shall not wear it in the Hereafter.' (*Bukhari and Muslim*)

٨٠٧ – وعن عليٍّ رضيَ اللهُ عنه قال : رَأَيْتُ رسُولَ اللهِ صلى اللهُ عليهِ

وسلَّم أخذَ حَرِيراً ، فَجعَلَهُ في يَمِينِهِ ، وذَهَباً فَجعَلَهُ في شِمَالِهِ ،

ثمَّ قَالَ : « إنَّ هذَيْنِ حرَامٌ علَى ذُكُورِ أُمَّتي رواهُ أبو داود بإسنادٍ حسن

807. Hazrat Ali (R.A.A.) relates: 'I saw the Holy Prophet (S.A.W.) take a piece of silk in his right hand and a piece of gold in his left and said: 'These two things are unlawful for the males of my Ummat.' (*Imam Abu Daud* has quoted this tradition on good authority.)

٨٠٨ – وعن أبي مُوسى الأشْعَرِيِّ رضيَ اللهُ عنا أنَّ رسُولَ اللهِ صلى الله

عليه وسلَّم قال : « حُرِّمَ لِباسُ الحَرِيرِ والذَّهَبِ علَى ذُكُورِ أُمَّتي ، وأُحِلَ

لإناثِهِمْ » رواهُ الترمذي وقال حديثٌ حسن صحيحٌ .

808. Hazrat Abu Musa Ash'ari (R.A.A.) relates that the Holy Prophet (S.A.W.) said: 'Wearing of silk and gold has been made unlawful for the males of my Ummat and lawful for their females.' (*Imam Tirmizi* has reported this tradition on good authority.)

****

CHAPTER 123

Permission to Wear Silk in Case of Scabies

٨٠٩ – وعن حُذَيْفَةَ رَضيَ اللهُ عنه قال : نَهانَا النَّبيُّ صلى اللهُ عليه وسلَّم أنْ نَشْرَبَ في آنيَةِ الذَّهَبِ والفِضَّةِ ، وأنْ نَأكُلَ فيهَا ، وعَنْ لُبْسِ الحَرِيرِ والدِّيبَاجِ ، وأنْ نَجْلِسَ عَلَيْهِ . رواهُ البخاري

809. Hazrat Huzaifah (R.A.A.) says: The Holy Prophet (S.A.W.) has forbidden us from drinking or eating in pots made from gold or silver and wearing of silken cloth or silk with designs made with golden or silver threads or sitting on (beds or cushions) made from such cloth. (*Bukhari*)

٨١٠ – عن أنسٍ رضيَ اللهُ عنه قال : رَخَّصَ رسُولُ اللهِ ، صلى اللهُ عليه وسلم ، للزُّبَيْرِ وَعَبْدِ الرَّحْمنِ بنِ عَوْفٍ رضيَ اللهُ عنهما في لُبْسِ الحَرِيرِ لِحِكَّةٍ بهِمَا . متفقٌ عليه

810. Hazrat Anas bin Malik (R.A.A.) relates that the Holy Prophet (S.A.W.) permitted Hazrat Zubair (R.A.A.) and Hazrat Abdur Rehman bin Auf (R.A.A.) to wear silk because they were suffering from scabbies. (*Bukhari and Muslim*)

****

CHAPTER 124

Prohibition of Sitting and Riding on Skin of Leopard

٨١١ – عن مُعاويَةَ رضيَ اللهُ عنه قالَ : قال رسُولُ اللهِ صلى اللهُ عليه وسلَّم : « لا تَرْكَبُوا الخزَّ ولاَ النِّمَارَ » .

حديث حسن ، رواهُ أبو داود وغيره بإسنادٍ حسنٍ .

811. Hazrat Muawiyah (R.A.A.) relates that the Holy Prophet (S.A.W.) said: Do not ride on saddles made of silk or leopard skin.' (*Imam Abu Daud* and others have reported this tradition which is authentic.)

٨١٢ – وعن أبي المَليحِ عن أبيهِ ، رضيَ اللهُ عنه ، أنَّ رسُولَ الله صلى اللهُ عليهِ وسلَّم نَهى عَنْ جُلُودِ السِّبَاعِ .

رواهُ أبو داود ، والترمذيُّ ، والنسائيُّ بأسانيدَ صحاحٍ .

وفي روايةِ الترمذي : نهى عَنْ جلُودِ السِّباعِ أنْ تُفتَرَشَ :

812. **Hazrat Abul Malih** (R.A.A.) relates on the authority of his father, that the Holy Prophet (S.A.W.) has prohibited the use of the skins of wild beasts. (*Imam Abu Daud and Tirmizi and Nisai* have reported this with authentic proofs.)

Another version of Tirmizi says: 'He forbade skins of wild beasts being used as floor cloth.

****

CHAPTER 125

What to Say (Supplicate) When Wearing a New Dress or New Pair of Shoes

٨١٣ ــ عن أبي سعيد الخُدْريِّ رضيَ اللهُ عنه قال : كانَ رسُولُ اللهِ صلى اللهُ عليهِ وسلم إذَا اسْتَجَدَّ ثَوْباً سَمَّاهُ باسْمِهِ ــ عِمَامَةً ، أوْ قَمِيصاً ، أوْ رِدَاءً ــ يقُولُ : « اللَّهُمَّ لكَ الحَمْدُ أنتَ كَسَوْتَنِيه ، أسألُكَ خيْرَهُ وَخيْرَ مَا صُنِعَ لَهُ ، وَأعُوذُ بِكَ مِنْ شَرِّهِ وَشَرِّ مَا صُنِعَ لَهُ » .

رواهُ أبو داود . والترمذي وقال : حديث حسن .

813. **Hazrat Abu Sa'id Khudri** (R.A.A.) says that when the Holy Prophet (S.A.W.) used to wear new dress, he would call it by its name as for example, he would say, 'this is the turban, or 'this is the shirt or 'this is the cloak' and 'this is the sheet', and would supplicate: 'Allah Thine is the praise that Thou hast given it to me to wear. I beg of Thee for the good of this dress and the good of the purpose for which it has been made, and seek Thy protection against its evil and the evil of the prupose for which it has been made.' (*Imams Abu Daud and Tirmizi* have quoted this tradition, which latter says is authentic.)

****

CHAPTER 126

Virtues of Beginning with the Right Side When Putting on Dress

هذا الباب قد تقدم مقصوده وذكرنا الأحاديث الصحيحة فيه

This topic has already been dealt with in detail in Chapter 99.

****

BOOK OF ETIQUETTES OF SLEEPING AND RECLINING

CHAPTER 127

Etiquettes of Sitting, Reclining, Sleeping and Dreaming

٨١٤ — عن البَراءِ بن عازبٍ رضي الله عنهما قال : كانَ رسول الله صلى الله عليه وسلم إذا أوى إلى فراشه نامَ على شقِّهِ الأيمنِ ، ثُمَّ قال : « اللَّهُمَّ أسلمتُ نفسِي إليكَ ، ووجَّهتُ وجهي إليكَ ، وفوَّضتُ أمري إليكَ ، وألجأتُ ظهري إليكَ ، رغبةً ورهبةً إليكَ ، لاملجأَ ولا منجى منكَ إلاّ إليكَ . آمنتُ بكتابكَ الّذي أنزلتَ . ونبيِّكَ الّذي أرسلتَ » .

رواه البخاري بهذا اللفظ في كتاب الأدب من صحيحه

٨١٥ — وعنه قال : قال لي رسول الله صلى الله عليه وسلم : « إذا أتيتَ مضجعكَ فتوضَّأْ وضوءَكَ للصَّلاة ، ثمَّ اضطجعْ على شقِّكَ الأيمنِ ، وقُلْ . . » وذكرَ نحوَهُ ، وفيه : « واجعلهنَّ آخرَ ماتقولُ » متفق عليه

814,815 These two traditions have been covered in No. 80 of Chapter 7.

٨١٦ — وعن عائشةَ رضيَ الله عنها قالتْ : كانَ النَّبيُّ صلى الله عليه وسلم يُصلِّي مِنَ اللَّيلِ إحدَى عشرةَ ركعةً . فإذا طلعَ الفجرُ صلَّى ركعتينِ خفيفتينِ ، ثُمَّ اضطجعَ على شقِّهِ الأيمنِ حتَّى يجيءَ المؤذِّنُ فيؤذِنَه متفقٌ عليه

816. Hazrat Ayesha (R.A.A.) relates that the Holy Prophet (S.A.W.) used to offer eleven raka'as (Nafil or voluntary) prayers in the night and (Tahajjud) at dawn he would offer two short raka'as and then rested (for a while) on his right side till the *Muazzin* would come to tell him (that the congregation had assembled). *(Bukhari and Muslim).*

٨١٧ — وعن حُذيفةَ رضي الله عنه قال : كان النبي صلى الله عليه وسلم إذا أخذَ مضجعَهُ مِنَ اللَّيلِ وضعَ يدَهُ تحتَ خدِّهِ ، ثُمَّ يقولُ : « اللَّهُمَّ باسمِكَ أموتُ وأحيا » وإذا استيقظَ قالَ : « الحمدُ للهِ الّذي أحيانا بعدَ ما أماتنا وإليهِ النُّشورُ » رواه البخاري

817. Hazrat Huzaifah(R.A.A.) says: 'When the Holy Prophet (S.A.W.) used to lay down for sleep at night he would place his hand under his cheek and would say: "Allah! with Thy name I die and then come back to life;

Allahumma Be Ismika Amuto Wa'ahya,

and when he woke up he used to say:

"*Alhamdo Lillahillazi Ahyana b'ada ma amatana wa ilaihin nushor;*

"All praise is to Allah who has brought us back to life after He had caused us to die and verily to Him is the return.

(Bukhari)

٨١٨ — وعن يَعِيشَ بن طِخْفَةَ الغِفَارِيِّ رضي الله عنه قال : قال أبي : بَيْنَمَا أنَا مُضْطَجِعٌ في المَسْجِدِ عَلى بَطْنِي إذا رَجُلٌ يُحَرِّكُنِي بِرِجْلِهِ فقال : « إنَّ هذهِ ضِجْعَةٌ يُبْغِضُهَا اللهُ » قال : فَنَظَرْتُ . فإذا رسولُ الله صلى الله عليه وسلم . رواه أبو داود بإسنادٍ صحيحٍ .

818. Hazrat Ya'ish bin Tikhfah Al Ghifari (R.A.A.) reports from his father that he was lying down in the mosque on his belly when someone moved him with his foot and said that such lying down is disliked by Allah. When he looked up he found that it was the Holy Prophet(S.A.W.). (*Imam Abu Daud* has reported this tradition with authentic chains).

٨١٩ — وعن أبي هريرة رضي الله عنه ، عن رسول الله صلى الله عليه وسلم قال : « مَنْ قَعَدَ مَقْعَداً لَمْ يَذْكُرِ الله تعالى فيهِ ، كَانَتْ عَلَيْهِ مِنَ الله تعالى تِرَةٌ ، وَمَنِ اضْطَجَعَ مَضْجَعاً لايَذْكُرُ الله تعالى فيهِ ، كَانَتْ عَلَيْهِ مِنَ اللهِ تِرَةٌ » رواه أبو داود بإسنادٍ حسنٍ .

819. Hazrat Abu Hurairah (R.A.A.) relates that the Holy Prophet (S.A.W.) said: When a person sits on a seat and does not remember Allah, the said person would suffer loss and incur displeasure of Allah; and when a person lies down and does not remember Allah, he sustains loss and incurs displeasure of Allah.' (*Imam Abu Daud* has reported this tradition with authentic chains).

****

CHAPER 128

Justification for Lying Down Flat on the Back; And When There Is No Risk of Exposure of Any Private parts of the Body It Is Permissible to Put One Foot on the other, and Sitting with Legs Put Across and Putting Rest Band round Waist and Legs.

٨٢٠ — عن عبدِ اللهِ بن زيد رضي الله عنهما أنَّهُ رأى رسول الله صلى الله عليه وسلم مُسْتَلْقِياً في المَسْجِدِ . وَاضِعاً إحْدَى رِجْلَيْهِ عَلى الأخْرَى متفق عليه

820. Hazrat Abdullah bin Zaid (R.A.A.) says that he saw the Holy Prophet (S.A.W.) lying down flat on his back in the mosque with one foot resting on the other'. *(Bukhari and Muslim)*.

٨٢١ — وعن جابِرِ بن سَمُرَةَ رضي الله عنه قال : كان النبيُّ صلى الله عليه وسلم إذا صَلَّى الْفَجْرَ تَرَبَّعَ في مَجْلِسِهِ حَتَّى تَطْلُعَ الشَّمْسُ حَسْنَاءَ حديث صحيح ، رواه أبو داود وغيره بأسانيد صحيحة .

821. Hazrat Jabir bin Samurah relates that after the early morning *Salat*, the Holy Prophet (S.A.W.) used to sit cross-legged in his meeting (with his companions) and remained sitting till the sun became quite bright.' *(Abdu Daud)*

٨٢٢ — وعنِ ابنِ عمر رضي الله عنهما قال : رأيت رسول الله صلى الله عليه وسلم بِفِنَاءِ الكَعْبَةِ مُحْتَبِياً بِيَدَيْهِ هكذا . وَوَصَفَ بيدَيْهِ الاحْتِبَاءَ ، وَهُوَ القُرْفُصَاءُ . رواه البخاري

822. Hazrat Ibn Umar (R.A.A.) says that he saw the Holy Prophet (S.A.W.) seated in the courtyard of the Ka'aba with his arms covering his raised knees. *(Bukhari)*

٨٢٣ — وعن قَيْلَةَ بنتِ مَخْرَمَةَ رضي الله عنها قالت : رَأَيْتُ النبيَّ صلى الله عليه وَهُوَ قَاعِدٌ القُرْفُصاءَ . فَلَمَّا رَأَيْتُ رسول الله صلى الله عليه وسلم. المُتَخَشِّعَ في الجِلْسَةِ أرعدْتُ مِنَ الفَرَقِ . رواه أبو داود . والترمذي

823. Hazrat Qailah bint Makhramah (R.A.A.) reports that she saw the Holy Prophet (S.A.W.) seated with his arms circling the calf of his legs and the thighs raised, and that when she saw him in this position of reverential humility (meditation) she trembled on account of his awful dignity. *(Tirmizi)*

٨٢٤ ـ وعن الشَّريد بن سُوَيدٍ رضي الله عنه قال : مرَّ بي رسول الله صلى الله عليه وسلم وأنا جالسٌ هكذا . وقد وضعتُ يدي اليُسرى خلفَ ظهري . واتكأتُ على أليةِ يدي فقال : « أتقعُدُ قعدةَ المغضوبِ عليهم ؟! »

رواه أبو داود بإسنادٍ صحيحٍ .

824. Hazrat Shadid bin Suwaid(R.A.A.) says: 'Once the Holy Prophet (S.A.W.) happened to pass by me when I was sitting with my left hand on my back, and sat on the ground with the bottom of my thumbs. On seeing me in the posture he remarked: 'Do you sit like those people who earned wrath of Allah?' (*Imam Abu Daud* has reported this tradition as sound).

****

CHAPTER 129

Etiquette of Sitting in Company

٨٢٥ ـ عن ابن عُمَرَ رضي الله عنهما قال : قال رسول الله صلى الله عليه وسلم : « لا يُقيمنَّ أحدُكُم رجلاً من مجلسِه ثُمَّ يجلسُ فيه ، ولكن توسَّعُوا وتفسَّحُوا » وكانَ ابن عُمَرَ إذا قامَ له رجلٌ من مجلسِه لم يجلسْ فيه . متفقٌ عليه

825. Hazrat Ibn 'Umar (R.A.A.) relates that the Holy Prophet (S.A.W.) said: No one should ask another to vacate his seat for him; however you (the person already sitting) should squeeze and make room. If somebody used to stand up and give up his seat for him (Hazrat Ibn Umar), he would not sit in that meeting. *(Bukhari and Muslim)*

٨٢٦ ـ وعن أبي هُريرةَ رضي الله عنه أنَّ رسولَ الله صلَّى الله عليه وسلَّم قال : « إذا قامَ أحدُكُم من مجلسٍ ، ثُمَّ رجعَ إليه ، فهوَ أحقُّ به »

رواه مسلم

826. Hazrat Abu Hurairah (R.A.A.) relates that the Holy Prophet (S.A.W.) said: If somebody from you has left his seat for a while and returns after sometime. he is more entitled to take the seat he had left. *(Muslim)*

٨٢٧ ـ وعن جابر بن سَمُرَةَ رضي اللهُ عنهما قال : كُنَّا إذا أتينا النَّبيَّ صلى الله عليه وسلم ، جلسَ أحدُنا حيثُ ينتهي .

رواه أبو داود ، والترمذي وقال : حديث حسن .

827. Hazrat Jabir bin Samurah (R.A.A.) says: 'When we used to come to the Holy Prophet (S.A.W.), we would sit down at the tail end of the assembly. (*Imams Abu Daud and Tirmizi* have reported this tradition which is good).

٨٢٨ – وعن أبي عبد الله سَلمَان الفارسيّ رضي الله عنه قال : قال رسول الله صلى الله عليه وسلم : « لايَغْتَسِلُ رَجُلٌ يَوْمَ الجُمُعَةِ ، وَيَتَطَهَّرُ ما استَطَاعَ مِنْ طُهْرٍ ، وَيَدَّهِنُ مِنْ دُهْنِهِ ، أَوْ يَمَسُّ مِنْ طِيبِ بَيْتِهِ ، ثُمَّ يَخْرُجُ فَلا يُفَرِّقُ بَيْنَ اثْنَيْنِ ، ثُمَّ يُصَلِّي ما كُتِبَ لَهُ ، ثُمَّ يُنْصِتُ إذا تَكَلَّمَ الإمامُ ، إلاَّ غُفِرَ لَهُ ما بَيْنَهُ وَبَيْنَ الجُمُعَةِ الأُخْرَى » رواه البخاري

828. Hazrat Abu Abdullah Salman Far'si relates that the Holy Prophet (S.A.W.) said: If a person takes a bath on Friday, cleans his person and clothes as much as possible, applies oil to his hair, uses such perfume as is available, and then goes to the mosque, where he does not thrust himself between two persons (already sitting there), offers the prescribed prayer and listens in silence to the sermon *(Khutba)* of the Imam, his sins (if any) committed since the previous Friday are remitted. *(Bukhari)*

٨٢٩ – وعن عَمْرِو بن شُعَيْبٍ عن أبيهِ عن جَدِّهِ رضي الله عنه أن رَسول الله صلى الله عليه وسلم قال : « لا يَحِلُّ لِرَجُلٍ أن يُفَرِّقَ بَيْنَ اثنَيْنِ إلاَّ بإِذْنِهِمَا » رواه أبو داود ، والترمذي وقال : حديث حسن .

وفي روايةٍ لأبي داود : « لا يَجْلِسُ بَيْنَ رَجُلَيْنِ إلا بإِذْنِهِمَا » .

829. Hazrat 'Amr bin Shuaib (R.A.A.) relates on the authority of his father and the latter from his grandfather, that the Holy Prophet (S.A.W.) said: It is not lawful (proper) for a person to insert himself between two persons(already sitting) there without their approval. (*Abu Daud and Tirmizi*, the latter calls it good).

(*Imam Abu Daud* adds: Nobody should sit between two persons without their consent.

٨٣٠ – وعن حُذَيْفَةَ بنِ اليَمَانِ رضي الله عنه أن رسول الله صلى الله عليه وسلم لَعَنَ مَنْ جَلَسَ وَسَطَ الحَلْقَةِ . رواه أبو داود بإسنادٍ حسن .

وروى الترمذي عن أبي مِجْلَزٍ : أن رَجُلاً قَعَدَ وَسَطَ حَلْقَةٍ ، فقال حُذَيْفَةُ : مَلْعُونٌ عَلى لِسَانِ مُحَمَّدٍ صلى الله عليه وسلم ، أَوْ : لَعَنَ الله على

لِسَانِ مُحَمَّدٍ صلى الله عليه وسلم – مَنْ جَلَسَ وَسَطَ الحَلْقَةِ . قال الترمذي : حديث حسن صحيح .

830. Hazrat Huzaifah bin Al Yaman (R.A.A.) says that the Holy Prophet (S.A.W.) has cursed the person who sits in the middle of a circle (in the centre of a gathering). (*Imam Abu Daud* has quoted this on good authority.

Imam Tirmizi's version on the authority of **Hazrat Abu Mijlaz** (R.A.A.) says: That a person got himself seated in the middle of a circle (centre of a gathering), whereupon **Hazrat Huzaifah bin Al Yaman** (R.A.A.) said: He is cursed, according to the Holy Prophet (S.A.W.) or Allah has cursed him through the Holy Prophet (S.A.W.) because he sits in the middle of a circle (centre of gathering).

٨٣١ – وعن أبي سعيد الخُدْري رضي الله عنه قال : سَمِعْتُ رسول الله صلى الله عليه وسلم يقول : « خَيْرُ المَجَالِسِ أَوْسَعُهَا » .

رواه أبو داود بإسنادٍ صحيح على شرطِ البخاري .

831. Hazrat Abu Sa'eed Khudri (R.A.A.) relates that he heard the Holy Prophet (S.A.W.) say: The best assemblies are those which are spacious and roomy, *(Abu Daud)*

٨٣٢ – وعن أبي هريرة رضي الله عنه قال : قال رسول الله صلّى الله عليه وسلّم « مَنْ جَلَسَ في مَجْلِسٍ ، فَكَثُرَ فيهِ لَغَطُهُ فقال قَبْلَ أَنْ يَقُومَ مِنْ مَجْلِسِهِ ذلكَ : سُبْحَانَكَ اللّهُمَّ وَبِحَمْدِكَ ، أَشْهَدُ أَنْ لا إله إلاَّ أَنْتَ ، أَسْتَغْفِرُكَ وَأَتُوبُ إِلَيْكَ ؛ إلاَّ غُفِرَ لَهُ مَا كَانَ في مَجْلِسِهِ ذلكَ »

رواه الترمذي وقال : حديث حسن صحيح .

832. Hazrat Abu Hurairah(R.A.A.) relates that the Holy Prophet (S.A.W.) said: 'If a person joins a company in which fruitless talking takes place and if that person before leaving the gathering prays, "*Subhana kalla-humma wa bi-hamdika Ash'hadu al-la ilaha illa Anta, Astagh firoka wa atubo ilaika*".

'O Allah! Holy art Thou, and all praise is for Thee; I bear witness that there is none worthy of worship save Thyself; I ask for Thy forgiveness and turn to Thee;

such a person is forgiven for his participation in such a company. *(Tirmizi)*

٨٣٣ – وعن أبي بَرْزَةَ رضي الله عنه قال : كَانَ رسول الله صلى الله عليه وسلم يقولُ بِأَخِرَةٍ إذا أَرَادَ أَنْ يَقُومَ مِنَ المَجْلِسِ : « سُبْحَانَكَ

اللّهمّ وبحمدك ، أشهد أن لا إله إلا أنت ، أستغفرك وأتوب إليك ،
فقال رجل : يارسول الله ، إنك لتقول قولاً ماكنت تقوله فيما مضى ؟
قال : « ذلك كفارة لما يكون في المجلس » رواه أبو داود
ورواه الحاكم أبو عبد الله في « المستدرك » من رواية عائشة رضي الله عنها وقال :
صحيح الإسناد .

833. Hazrat Abu Barzah (R.A.A.) relates that towards the closing days of his life, the Holy Prohet (S.A.W.) when he was about to leave company, used to supplicate,

"*Subhanaka Allahumma wa-bi hamdika, Ash'hadu Al La Ilaha illa Anta, Astaghfiruka wa atubo ilaika*",

'O Allah! Holy art Thou, and all praise is for Thee: I bear witness that there is none worthy of worship save Thyself: I ask for Thy forgiveness and turn to Thee.'

A companion asked him, 'O Messenger of Allah (S.A.W.) you are now saying such words which you did not say before.' He said: These words are an expiation of that which goes on in a gathering.' *(Abu Daud)*

Imam Hakim Abu Abdullah has reported this tradition in the Mustadrak on the authority of **Hazrat Ayesha** (R.A.A.) and said that the same is most authentic.

٨٣٤ — وعن ابن عمر رضي الله عنهما قال : قلّما كان رسول الله صلى الله عليه وسلم يقوم من مجلس حتى يدعو بهؤلاء الدعوات : « اللّهمّ اقسم لنا من خشيتك ما تحول به بيننا وبين معاصيك ، ومن طاعتك ماتبلّغنا به جنّتك ، ومن اليقين ما تهوّن علينا مصائب الدنيا . اللّهمّ متّعنا بأسماعنا ، وأبصارنا ، وقوّتنا ما أحييتنا ، واجعله الوارث منّا ، واجعل ثأرنا على من ظلمنا ، وانصرنا على من عادانا ، ولا تجعل مصيبتنا في ديننا ، ولا تجعل الدنيا أكبر همّنا ، ولا مبلغ علمنا ، ولا تسلّط علينا من لا يرحمنا » رواه الترمذي وقال حديث حسن .

834. Hazrat Ibn Umar (R.A.A.) relates that it was rare that the Holy Prophet (S.A.W.) departed from a company without praying in these words:

'Allahum-maqsim lana min khash-yatika ma tahulo bihee bainana wa baina Ma'asi-yatika wa min ta'atika ma tuballighuna bihee jannataka, wa min-al-yaqeene ma tuhaw-wano bihee 'alaina masaibud-dunya. Allahumma matte'-na bi-asma'ina wa absarina wa quw-watina ma ahyaitana wa-j'al-hul-warisa minna waj'al sarana 'ala

man zalamana wansurna 'ala man 'aadana, wala taj'al musi-batana fi deenina wala taj'liddunya ak-bara hammina wala mab-lagha 'il-mina wala tusallit 'alaina man la yar-hamuna."
'O Allah! grant us so much (Thy) fear that may serve as a barrier between us and our sins; and bestow upon us Thy obedience that may help us to reach Thy Paradise; and grant us so much faith that may help us to face the misfortunes of this world easily. O Allah! bless us to benefit from our powers of hearing and seeing and the vigour so long as Thou dost grant us life and make us heir (beneficiaries) of them; and afflict with our rancour those who oppress us, and help us against those who are our enemies; and do not entangle us in the difficulties of our religion; and do not make the world, our main object, and do not hunt our knowledge; and do not appoint over us persons who would not show mercy to us."

(Tirmizi)

٨٣٥ – وعن أبي هريرة رضي الله عنه قال : قال رسول الله صلى الله عليه وسلم : « مَامِن قومٍ يقومُونَ مِنْ مَجْلِسٍ لا يَذكُرُونَ الله تعالى فيهِ ، إلا قَامُوا عَنْ مِثلِ جيفةِ حِمَارٍ ، وكانَ لَهُم حَسرَةً » رواه أبو داود بإسنادٍ صحيح .

835. Hazrat Abu Hurairah (R.A.A) relates that the Holy Prophet (S.A.W.) said: 'Those who (attend and then) leave a company in which there has been no mention of Allah (they) leave it like dead and it will be a source of sorrow for them.' *(Abu Daud)*

This is an authentic tradition.

٨٣٦ – وعنه عن النبي صلى الله عليه وسلم قال : « مَا جَلَسَ قَومٌ مَجْلِساً لم يَذْكرُوا الله تعالى فيهِ ، ولَم يُصَلُّوا على نَبيِّهم فيهِ ، إلاَّ كانَ عليهِمْ تِرةٌ ؛ فإن شاءَ عَذَّبهُم ، وإن شَاءَ غَفَرَ لهُم » رواه الترمذي وقال : حديث حسن .

836. Hazrat Abu Hurairah (R.A.A.) relates that the Holy Prophet (S.A.W.) said: 'A gathering in which there is no mention of Allah, the Exalted and High, nor any invoking of blessings *(Salat)* for their Prophet (S.A.W.), will be afflicted with remorse. If Allah Wills He might punish them and if He Wills He might forgive them. (*Imam Tirmizi* has reportted this and called it good).

٨٣٧ – وعنه عن رسول الله صلى الله عليه وسلم قال : « مَنْ قَعَدَ مَقعداً لم يذكرِ الله تعالى فيه كَانَت عليه مِنَ اللهِ تِرَةٌ ، ومَن اضطَجَعَ مَضْجَعاً لا يَذْكرُ الله تعالى فيهِ كانتْ عَلَيْهِ مِنَ اللهِ تِرَةٌ » رواه أبو داود

837. This Hadis is the same as No. 819 of Chapter 127.

****

CHAPTER 130

Dreams and Relevant Things

قال الله تعالى : وَمِنْ آيَاتِهِ مَنَامُكُم بِاللَّيْلِ وَالنَّهَارِ [الروم : ٢٣]

Allah, the Exalted, has said:

270. And of His signs is your slumber by night and by day.(30:23)

٨٣٨ ــ وعن أبي هريرة رضي الله عنه قال : سمعت رسول الله صلى الله عليه وسلم يقول : « لم يَبْقَ مِنَ النُّبُوَّةِ إلا المُبَشِّرَاتُ » قالوا : وَمَا المُبَشِّرَاتُ ؟ قال : « الرُّؤْيَا الصَّالِحَةُ » رواه البخاري

838. Hazrat Abu Hurairah (R.A.A.) relates that he heard the Holy Prophet (S.A.W.) say: No signs of Prophethood except glad tidings are now left. The companions asked: 'What are the glad tidings: he replied: 'True dreams'. *(Bukhari)*

٨٣٩ ــ وعنه أن النبيَّ صلَّى الله عليه وسلَّم قال : « إذا اقترَبَ الزَّمَانُ لَمْ تَكَدْ رُؤْيَا المُؤْمِنِ تَكذِبُ ، وَرُؤْيَا المُؤْمِنِ جُزْءٌ مِنْ سِتَّةٍ وَأَرْبَعِينَ جُزْءاً مِنَ النُّبُوَّةِ » متفقٌ عليه

وفي روايةٍ : « أَصْدَقُكُم رُؤْيَا أَصْدَقُكُم حَدِيثاً » .

839. Hazrat Abu Hurairah (R.A.A.) relates that the Holy Prophet (S.A.W.) said: 'When the time (of the Day of Judgment) draws near, the dream of a Muslim will not be false and the dream of a Muslim is one of the fortysix parts of Prophethood. *(Bukhari and Muslim)*

Another tradition says: 'The most truthful dreams are of those among you, who are the most truthful in their talks.

٨٤٠ ــ وعنه قال : قال رسول الله صلى الله عليه وسلم : « مَنْ رَآني في المَنَامِ فَسَيَرَاني في اليَقَظَةِ ــ أَوْ كأنَّمَا رَآني في اليَقَظَةِ ــ لا يَتَمَثَّلُ الشَّيْطَانُ بي » . متفقٌ عليه

840. Hazrat Abu Hurairah (R.A.A.) relates that the Holy Prophet (S.A:W.) said: 'A person who saw me in his dream will see me in the state of wakefulness in the near future or he said as if he had seen me in his waking state, for Satan cannot impersonate me.'

(Bukhari and Muslim)

٨٤١ – وعن أبي سعيدٍ الخدْرِي رضي الله عنه أنهُ سميعَ النبيَّ صلى الله عليه وسلم، يقول: « إذا رَأى أحَدُكُمْ رُؤْيَا يُحِبُّهَا ، فَإنَّمَا هِيَ مِنَ اللهِ تعالى . فَلْيَحْمَدِ اللهَ عَلَيهَا ، وَلْيُحَدِّثْ بهَا – وفي روايةٍ : فَلا يُحَدِّثْ بهَا إلاَّ مَنْ يُحِبُّ – وَإذا رَأى غيرَ ذَلكَ مِمَّا يَكرَهُ ، فَإنَّمَا هِيَ مِنَ الشَّيْطَانِ . فَلْيَسْتَعِذْ مِنْ شَرِّهَا ، وَلا يَذكرْهَا لِأَحَدٍ ، فإنها لا تَضُرُّهُ » متفقٌ عليه

841. Hazrat Abu Sa'eed Khudri relates that he heard the Holy Prophet (S.A.W.) say: 'When any of you see a pleasant dream, then it is (a blessing) from Allah; then he should eulogize Allah for the same and relate it (to his friends).'

Another version says he should not relate it, except to those whom he loves. And when he sees (unpleasant dream) which he dislikes, it is from Satan. He should solicit Allah's protection against its mischiefs and should not mention it to anyone. Then this dream will not harm him.

(Bukhari an Muslim)

٨٤٢ – وعن أبي قَتَادَةَ رضي الله عنه قال : قال النبيُّ صلى الله عليه وسلم : « الرُّؤيَا الصَّالِحَةُ – وفي روايةٍ : الرُّؤيَا الحَسَنَةُ – مِنَ الله ، والحُلُمُ مِنَ الشَّيطَانِ ، فَمَن رَأى شيئاً يَكرَهُهُ فَلْيَنْفُثْ عَن شِمَالِهِ ثَلاثاً ، وليَتَعَوَّذ مِنَ الشَّيطَانِ فإنَّها لاتَضُرُّهُ » متفقٌ عليه

842. Hazrat Abu Qatadah(R.A.A.) relates that the Holy Prophet (S.A.W.) said: 'A virtuous dream and according to another version a happy dream is from Allah, and an unpleasant dream is from Satan. As such, if anybody from you sees something in a dream that he dislikes, he should spit out (only movements of the lips and not throw out saliva) three times to the left and should seek Allah's help against Satan's mischief. It will then not harm.

(Bukhari and Muslim)

٨٤٣ – وَعن جابرٍ رضي الله عنه عن رسول الله صلى الله عليه وسلم قال : « إذا رَأى أحَدُكُم الرُّؤيَا يَكرَهُهَا ، فَلْيَبْصُق عَن يَسَارِهِ ثَلاثاً ، وليَستَعِذ باللهِ مِنَ الشَّيطَانِ ثَلاثاً ، وليَتَحَوَّلْ عَن جَنبِهِ الذي كانَ عليه » . رواه مسلم

843. Hazrat Jabir (R.A.A.) relates that the Holy Prophet (S.A.W.) said: 'When one of you sees an unpleasant dream, he should spit out (only lip movement) three times towards the left side and seek Allah's help against Satan's mischief three times, and should turn over the side in bed.'

(Muslim)

٨٤٤ – وعن أبي الأسْقَعِ وَاثِلَةَ بن الأَسقَعِ رضي الله عنه قال : قال رسول الله صلى الله عليه وسلم : « إنَّ مِن أعظَمِ الفِرَى أن يَدَّعِيَ الرَّجُلُ إلى غَيْرِ أبِيهِ ، أوْ يُرِيَ عَينَهُ مَالم تَرَ ، أوْ يَقُولَ على رسولِ الله صلى الله عليه وسلم مَالم يَقُلْ » رواه البخاري

844. Hazrat Abu Al Asq'a Wasilah bin Al-Asq'a (R.A.A.) relates that the Holy Prophet (S.A.W.) said: 'The greatest lies as those that a person should claim a false paternity, or may claim to have seen something (a dream) with his eyes which he has not seen, or attribute to the Prophet of Allah (S.A.W.), which he has not said.' *(Bukhari)*

****

CHAPTER 131

Virtues of Salutation and the Direction to Give Currency to it

قال الله تعالى : يَا أَيُّهَا الَّذِينَ آمَنُوا لاتَدخُلُوا بُيُوتاً غيرَ بُيُوتِكُم حَتَّى تَستَأنِسُوا وَتُسَلِّمُوا عَلَى أَهْلِهَا [النور : ٢٧] . وقال تعالى : فإذا دَخَلْتُمْ بُيُوتاً فَسَلِّمُوا عَلَى أَنْفُسِكُمْ تَحِيَّةً مِنْ عِنْدِ اللهِ مُبَارَكَةً طَيِّبَةً [النور : ٦١] . وقال تعالى : وَإِذا حُيِّيتُمْ بِتَحِيَّةٍ فَحَيُّوا بِأَحْسَنَ مِنها أَوْ رُدُّوها [النساء : ٨٦] . وقال تعالى : هَلْ أَتَاكَ حَدِيثُ ضَيْفِ إِبْرَاهِيمَ المُكْرَمِينَ * إِذْ دَخَلُوا عَلَيْهِ فقالوا : سَلاماً ، قال : سَلامٌ [الذاريات : ٢٤ ، ٢٥] .

Allah, the Exalted, has said:

271. O ye who believe! Enter not houses other than your own without first announcing your presence and invoking peace upon the folk thereof. (24:27)
272. But when ye enter houses, salute one another with a greeting from Allah bless and sweet. (24:61)
273. When ye are greeted with a greeting, greet ye with a better than it or return it. (4:86)
274. Hath the Story of Abraham's honoured guests reached thee (O Muhammad)? When they came in unto him and said: Peace! he answered, Peace. (51: 24–25).

٨٤٥ — وعن عبد الله بنِ عمرِو بن العاص رضي الله عنهما أن رجلاً سَأَل رسول الله صلى الله عليه وسلم : أيُّ الإسْلامِ خَيْرٌ ؟ قال : « تُطْعِمُ الطَّعَامَ ، وَتَقْرَأُ السَّلامَ عَلَى مَنْ عَرَفْتَ وَمَنْ لَمْ تَعْرِف » متفقٌ عليه

845. This Hadis is the same as No. 550 of Chapter 60.

٨٤٦ — وعن أبي هريرة رضي الله عنه عن النبيِّ صلّى الله عليه وسلم قال: « لمَّا خَلَقَ الله تعالى آدَمَ صلى الله عليه وسلم قال: اذهَبْ فَسَلِّمْ عَلى أُولئكَ — نَفَرٍ مِنَ المَلائِكَةِ جلُوس — فاستَمِعْ ما يُحَيُّونَكَ ، فإنَّهَا تَحِيَّتُكَ وتَحِيَّةُ

ذُرِّيَّتِكَ . فقال : السَّلامُ عَلَيْكُمْ ، فقالوا : السَّلامُ عَلَيْكَ وَرَحْمَةُ اللهِ ،
فَزَادُوهُ : وَرَحْمَةُ اللهِ » متفقٌ عليه

846. **Hazrat Abu Hurairah** (R.A.A.) relates that the Holy Prophet (S.A.W.) said: When Allah created Hazrat Adam (A.S.) He asked him: 'Go and offer the salutation of peace to that party of angles sitting there, and then listen to the reply they give to you. The reply which they give will be your reply and that of your descendents.' Hazrat Adam (A.S.) said to the party of the angels: *As Salam-o-Alaikum* (Peace be upon you) and the latter replied with: *As Salamo-Alaikum wa Rahmatullah* (Peace be upon you and the mercy of Allah). Hazrat Adam (A.S.) added *Wa Rahamatul-lah* "the mercy of Allah" to his greeting.

(Bukhari and Muslim)

٨٤٧ — وعن أبي عُمارة البَرَاء بن عازِبٍ رضي الله عنهما قال : أمرنا رسول الله صلى الله عليه وسلم بِسَبْعٍ : بِعِيَادَةِ المَرِيض. وَاتِّبَاعِ الجَنَائِزِ ، وَتَشْمِيتِ العَاطِسِ ، وَنَصْرِ الضَّعِيف ، وَعَوْنِ المَظْلُومِ ، وَإفْشَاءِ السَّلامِ ، وَإبرارِ المُقْسِمِ . متفق عليه . هذا لفظ إحدى روايات البخاري .

847. **Hazrat Abu Umara Al Bra'a bin 'Azib** (R.A.A.) relates: The Holy Prohet (S.A.W.) enjoined upon us the following seven acts: (1) Visiting the sick, (2) following a funeral procession, (3) invoking the mercy of Allah upon one who sneezes (by calling *Yarhamukallah*), (4) supporting the weak, (5) helping the oppressed, (6) spreading the *Salam* (greeting of peace), (7) and honouring vows (undertakings).

(Bukhari and Muslim)

٨٤٨ — وعن أبي هريرة رضي الله عنه قال : قال رسول الله صلى الله عليه وسلم : « لاتَدْخُلُوا الجَنَّةَ حَتَّى تُؤْمِنُوا ، وَلا تُؤْمِنُوا حَتَّى تَحَابُّوا ، أَوَلا أَدُلُّكُمْ عَلَى شَيْءٍ إذا فَعَلْتُمُوهُ تَحَابَبْتُمْ ؟ أَفْشُوا السَّلامَ بَيْنَكُمْ » رواه مسلم

848. This Hadis is the same as No. 378 of Chapter 46.

٨٤٩ — وعن أبي يوسف عبد الله بن سلامٍ رضي الله عنه قال : سمعت رسول الله صلى الله عليه وسلم يقول : « يَا أَيُّهَا النَّاسُ أَفْشُوا السَّلامَ ، وَأَطْعِمُوا الطَّعَامَ ، وَصِلُوا الأَرْحامَ ، وَصَلُّوا والنَّاسُ نِيامٌ ، تَدْخُلُوا الجَنَّةَ بِسَلامٍ » رواه الترمذيُّ وقال : حديثٌ حسنٌ صحيحٌ .

849. Hazrat Abu Yusuf Abdullah bin Salam (R.A.A.) relates that he heard the Holy Prophet (S.A.W.) say: 'O ye people! spread the Salam (greetings) feed (the poor and needy), behave kindly with your blood relations,and offer prayer when others are asleep, and enter the Paradise in peace. *(Tirmizi)*

٧٥٠ — وعن الطُّفَيْل بن أُبَيِّ بن كَعْبٍ أَنَّهُ كانَ يَأْتي عبد الله بن عُمَرَ، فَيَغْدُو مَعَهُ إلى السُّوقِ ، قال : فإذا غَدَوْنَا إلى السُّوقِ ، لَمْ يَمُرَّ عبدُ الله عَلى سَقَّاطٍ ولاصاحِبِ بَيْعَةٍ ، ولا مِسْكِينٍ ، ولا أَحَدٍ إلاَّ سَلَّمَ عَلَيْهِ ، قال الطُّفَيْلُ : فَجِئْتُ عبد الله بنَ عُمَرَ يَوْماً ، فاسْتَتْبَعَنِي إلى السُّوقِ ، فَقُلْتُ لهُ : ماتَصْنَعُ بِالسُّوقِ ، وَأَنْتَ لا تَقِفُ عَلى البَيْعِ ، ولا تَسْأَلُ عَنِ السِّلَعِ ، ولا تَسُومُ بِهَا ، ولا تَجْلِسُ في مَجَالِسِ السُّوقِ ؟ وَأَقُولُ : اجْلِسْ بِنا هٰهُنا نَتَحَدَّثْ ، فقال : يَا أَبَا بَطْنٍ — وكانَ الطُّفَيْلُ ذا بَطْنٍ — إنَّمَا نَغْدُو مِنْ أَجْلِ السَّلام ، فَنُسَلِّمُ عَلى مَنْ لَقِينَاهُ .

رواه مالك في الموطأ بإسنادٍ صحيحٍ .

850. Hazrat Tufail bin Ubaiy ibn K'ab (R.A.A.) relates that he used to visit Hazrat Abdullah bin Umar (R.A.A.) in the morning, who would take him to the market place. Hazrat Abdullah (R.A.A.) would offer the (greeting of peace) Salam to every petty shopkeepers, traders, poor persons, others whom he would meet in the market. One day when I came to him (as usual) he wanted me to accompany him to the market place. I said to him: 'What will you do in the market place?' You do not stop there to buy or sell anything, nor do you inquire about any commodity or its price nor do you join any company in the market, I suggest let us sit down here and talk. He retorted: O Abu Batn (man of the belly) Hazrat Tufail (R.A.A.) had somewhat bulging of belly, we go to the market place in the morning to greet every one we meet, with the greeting of peace.(*Imam Malik* has quoted this tradition in his book '*Mu'atta*' with sound chains).

****

CHAPER 132

On the Manner of Greeting

Hazrat Imam Nawawi says that it is preferable that one,who takes the lead in salutaton should say:'*As Salam-o-Alaikum Wa Rahmatullahe Wa Barakatuhu*' (Peace be upon you and also mercy and blessings of

Allah) and should use the plural pronoun, although the person sc greeted may be a singular one, who should say in reply *'Wa Alaikum As Salam Wa Rahmatullahe Wa Barakatuhu'*. (Peace be upon you as well, and also Mercy and blessings of Allah).

٨٥١ – عن عِمْرَانَ بن الحُصَيْنِ رضي الله عنهما قال : جاءَ رَجُلٌ إلى النبيِّ صلى الله عليه وسلم فقال : السَّلامُ عَلَيْكُم ، فَرَدَّ عَلَيْهِ ثم جَلَسَ ، فقال النبيُّ صلى الله عليه وسلم : « عَشْرٌ » ثم جاءَ آخرُ ، فقال : السَّلامُ عَلَيكُم وَرَحْمَةُ الله ، فَرَدَّ عليه فَجَلَسَ ، فقال : «عِشْرُون » ثم جاءَ آخرُ ، فقال : السَّلامُ عَلَيكُم وَرَحْمَةُ الله وَبَرَكَاتُهُ ، فَرَدَّ عَلَيْهِ فَجَلَسَ ، فقال : « ثَلاثونَ » رواه أبو داود والترمذي وقال : حديث حسن .

851. Hazrat Imran bin Husain (R.A.A.) says: 'A man came to the Holy Prophet (S.A.W.) and said (only): *'As Salam-o-'Alaikum'* (Peace be upon you). The Holy Prophet (S.A.W.) returned his greeting and the man sat down. The Holy Prophet (S.A.W.) said: 'This man had earned the merit of ten (good deeds): Another one came and said: *'As Salam-o-'Alaikum Wa Rahmatullah'* (Peace be upon you and the mercy of Allah) The Holy Propeht (S.A.W.) replied to his greeting and the man took his seat. 'The Holy Prophet (S.A.W.) remarked: 'This man had earned twenty (merits). A third person came and said: *'As Salam-o-Alaikum Wa Rahmatullahe Wa Barakatuhu'*. Peace be upon you and the merey of Allah and His blessings.' The Holy Prophet (S.A.W.) returned his greeting and he sat down. The Holy Prophet (S.A.W.) said: This man has earned thirty (merits). *(Abu Daud and Tirmizi)*

According to *Imam Tirmizi* this is a good tradition.

٨٥٢ – وعن عائشة رضي الله عنها قالتْ : قال لي رسولُ الله صلَّى الله عليه وسلم : « هذا جِبرِيلُ يَقرأُ عَلَيكِ السَّلامَ » قَالَتْ : قُلتُ : « وَعَلَيْهِ السَّلامُ ورحْمَةُ الله وبَرَكَاتُهُ » متفقٌ عليه

وهكذا وقع في بعض روايات الصحيحين : «وبَرَكَاتُهُ » وَفي بَعْضِها بحَذفِها ، وَزِيَادَةُ الثِّقَةِ مَقبُولَةٌ

852. Hazrat Ayesha (R.A.A.) relates: (Once) the Holy Prophet (S.A.W.) said to me: This is Gabriel (A.S.) He greets you with Salam (the salutation of peace). Continuing she says: 'I said: *Wa 'Alaikum-us-salam-o-wa Rahmatullahe wa Barakatuhu* (Peace be upon him and the mercy of Allah and His blessings). *(Bukhari and Muslim)*

٨٥٣ ـ وعن أنس رضي الله عنه أن النبيَّ صلَّى الله عليه وسلم ، كانَ إذا تكلمَ بِكَلِمَةٍ أعادَها ثلاثاً حتى تُفهَمَ عنه ، وَإذا أتى عَلى قَوْمٍ فَسَلَّمَ عَلَيهِم سَلَّمَ عَلَيهِم ثلاثاً . رواه البخاري

853. This Hadis is the same as No. 696 of Chapter 89.

٨٥٤ ـ وعن المِقْدادِ رضي الله عنه في حديثِه الطويل قال : كُنَّا نَرفَعُ للنَّبيِّ صلى الله عليه وسلم نَصيبَهُ مِنَ اللَّبَنِ ، فَيَجِيءُ مِنَ اللَّيلِ ، فَيُسَلِّمُ تَسليماً لايُوقِظُ نائماً ،وَيُسْمِعُ اليَقظَانَ ، فَجاءَ النَّبيُّ صلى الله عليه وسلم فَسَلَّمَ كما كان يُسَلِّمُ . رواه مسلم

854. Hazrat Miqdad (R.A.A.) relates in the course of a lengthy Hadis: It was our practice to set aside for the Holy Prophet (S.A.W.) his share of the milk. He used to come at night and offer his greetings in a tone that would not disturb those persons who were sleeping, but was loud enough to be heard by those who were awake. The Holy Prophet (S.A.W.) came as usual and offered his greetings according to his practice. *(Muslim)*

٨٥٥ ـ وعن أسْمَاءَ بِنتِ يزيد رضي الله عنها أن رسولَ الله صلَّى الله عليه وسلم ،مَرَّ في المَسْجِدِ يَوماً ، وَعُصبَةَ مِنَ النِّسَاء قُعودٌ ، فَألوى بِيَدِهِ بِالتسْليمِ . رواه الترمذي وقال : حديث حسن .

855. This Hadis is included in No. 865 in Chapter 137.

٨٥٦ ـ وعن أبي جُرَيِّ الهجَيْمِيِّ رضي الله عنه قال : أتيْتُ رسولَ الله صلى الله عليه وسلم ، فَقُلْتُ : عَلَيْكَ السَّلامُ يا رسولَ الله . قالَ : « لا تَقُلْ عَلَيْكَ السَّلامُ ، فإنَّ عَلَيْكَ السَّلامُ تحيَّةُ المَوْتى » .

رواه أبو داود ، والترمذي وقال : حديث حسن صحيح . وقد سبق بطوله

856. This Hadis is already included in No. 796 of Chapter 119.

****

CHAPTER 133

On The Etiquette of Greeting

٨٥٧ ــ عن أبي هريرة رضي الله عنه أن رسولَ الله صلَّى الله عليه وسلم قال :

« يُسَلِّمُ الرَّاكبُ عَلى المَاشي ، وَالماشي عَلى القَاعِدِ ، وَالقَليلُ عَلى الكَثيرِ »

متفقٌ عليه

وفي روايةٍ للبخاري : « وَالصَّغيرُ عَلى الكَبيرِ » .

857. Hazrat Abu Hurairah (R.A.A.) relates that the Holy Prophet (S.A.W.) said: 'A rider should salute a pedestrian, a pedestrian should greet one who is sitting and a small party should greet a large party, *(Bukhari and Muslim)*

Imam Bukhari's version says: 'A younger person should take precedence in greeting on elder one.

٨٥٨ ــ وعن أبي أُمَامَةَ صُدَيِّ بن عَجْلانَ البَاهِلِيِّ رضي اللهُ عنه قال :

قال رسولُ الله صلَّى الله عليه وسلم : « إنَّ أَوْلى النَّاسِ باللهِ مَنْ بَدَأَهم بالسَّلامِ »

رواه أبو داود بإسنادٍ جيدٍ .

ورواه الترمذي عن أبي أُمَامَةَ رضي الله عنه : قيلَ : يارسول اللهِ ، الرَّجُلانِ

يَلْتَقِيانِ ، أَيُّهُمَا يَبْدأُ بِالسَّلامِ ؟ قال : « أَوْلاهُمَا بِاللهِ تعالى »

قال الترمذي : هذا حديثٌ حسنٌ

858. Hazrat Abu Umamah Sudaiy bin 'Ajlan al-Bahli (R.A.A.) relates that the Holy Prophet (S.A.W.) said: 'The person closest to Allah is one who precedes others in greeting. *(Abu Daud)*

Imam Tirmizi's version says: 'The Holy Prophet (S.A.W.) was asked: 'O Messenger of Allah (S.A.W.) ! When two persons meet with each other, who should take the lead to greeting the others? He answered 'The one who is closder to Allah.'

****

CHAPTER 134

Virtues of Repetition of Greeting When Two Persons Who He Is He Should Tell His Name And Not 'I' and So.

٨٥٩ ــ عن أبي هُرَيرةَ رضيَ الله عنه في حَديثِ المسيءِ صَلاتَهُ أنهُ جاءَ

فصلّى ، ثُمَّ جاءَ إلى النبيِّ صلّى الله عليه وسلم ، فسَلَّمَ عليه ، فردَّ عليه السَّلامَ ، فقال : « ارْجِع فَصَلِّ ، فإنَّكَ لم تُصَلِّ » فرجعَ فصَلّى ، ثُمَّ جاءَ فسَلَّمَ على النَّبيِّ ، صلّى الله عليه وسلم ، حتّى فعَلَ ذلكَ ثلاثَ مرَّاتٍ .
متفقٌ عليه

859. Hazrat Abu Hurairah (R.A.A.) in the course of the Hadis concerning a person who was at fault in performing his *salat*, says that he came and offered *Salat* and went to the Holy Prophet (S.A.W.) and saluted him. The Holy Prophet (S.A.W.) returning his greeting said: 'Go back and repeat your *salat*, because you have not performed your *Salat.*' He went back, performed the *Salat* and came to the Holy Prophet (S.A.W.) again and saluted him. So much so that this happened three times. *(Bukhari and Muslim)*

٨٦٠ — وعنه عَنْ رسولِ الله ، صلّى الله عليه وسلم ، قال : «إذا لقِيَ أحَدُكُمْ أخاه ، فلْيُسَلِّمْ عليه ، فإنْ حالَتْ بيْنَهُما شجَرَةٌ ، أَوْ جِدارٌ ، أَوْ حَجَرٌ . ثُمَّ لَقِيَهُ ، فلْيُسَلِّمْ عليه » رواه أبو داود

860. Hazrat Abu Hurairah (R.A.A.) relates that the Holy Prophet (S.A.W.) said: 'When one of you happens to meet a brother, he should salute him. Then if they are separated by a tree or a wall or a rock, he should salute him again when they meet. *(Abu Daud)*

****

CHAPTER 135

Virtues of Greeting When Entering into the House

قال الله تعالى : فإذا دخَلْتُمْ بيُوتاً فسَلِّمُوا على أنْفُسِكُمْ تحيَّةً مِن عِندِ الله مُبارَكَةً طيِّبَةً [النور : ٦١] .

Allah, the Exalted, has said:

275. But when ye enter houses, salute one another with a greeting from Allah, blessed and sweet. (24:61)

٨٦١ — وعن أنسٍ رضيَ الله عنه قالَ : قالَ لي رسولُ الله صلّى الله عليه وسلم : « يابُنَيَّ ، إذا دخَلْتَ على أهلكَ ، فسَلِّمْ ، يكُنْ بركَةً عليكَ ، وعلى أهلِ بيْتِكَ » رواه الترمذي وقال : حديث حسن صحيح .

861. Hazrat Anas bin Malik (R.A.A.) relates that the Holy Prophet (S.A.W.) said to him: 'Son, when you enter your home greet your people with the salutation of peace. It would be a source of blessing for you and for the members of your family.' (*Imam Tirmizi* has reported this tradition, which, he says, is good).

****

CHAPTER 136

On Greeting the Children

٨٦٢ ـ عن أنس رضي الله عنه أنَّهُ مرَّ على صِبْيان ، فَسلَّمَ عَلَيْهِمْ ، وقال : كانَ رسولُ الله صلى الله عليه وسلم يَفْعَلُهُ . متفقٌ عليه

862. This Hadis is the same as covered in No. 604 of Chapter 71.

****

CHAPTER 137

On a Husband Greeting His Wife And a Woman Greeting Her Such Relations Whom She Cannot Marry; And Greeting Stranger Women, Provided There Is No Apprehension of Some Mischief.

٨٦٣ ـ عن سَهْلِ بن سَعْدٍ رَضِيَ الله عَنْهُ قالَ : كانَتْ فينا امْرَأةٌ ـ وفي رِوايةٍ : كانَتْ لَنا عَجوزٌ ـ تَأْخُذُ مِنْ أصولِ السِّلْقِ فتَطْرَحُهُ في القِدْرِ ، وتُكَرْكِرُ حَبَّاتٍ مِنْ شَعيرٍ ، فإذا صَلَّيْنا الجُمُعَةَ ، وانْصَرَفْنا ، نُسَلِّمُ عَلَيْها ، فتُقَدِّمُهُ إلَيْنا . رواه البخاري

863. Hazrat Sahl bin S'ad (R.A.A.) relates: There was a woman among us, and according to a tradition she was an old woman, who would put beetroot in a pot and add some ground barley and cook them together. When we returned after finishing the Friday prayers, we used to greet the old woman who would then offer it (the cooked stuff) to us. *(Bukhari)*

٨٦٤ ـ وعَنْ أُمِّ هانِئٍ فاخِتَةَ بِنتِ أبي طالب رَضِيَ الله عَنْها قالَتْ : أتَيْتُ النبي صلَّى الله عليه وسلم يَوْمَ الفَتْحِ وَهُوَ يَغْتَسِلُ ، وفاطِمَةُ تَسْتُرُهُ بِثَوْبٍ ، فَسَلَّمْتُ ، وذَكَرَتِ الحديث . رواه مسلم

864. Hazrat Umm Hani Fakhta bint Abu Talib (R.A.A.) relates: 'I went to the Holy Prophet (S.A.W.) on the day of conquest (of Mecca). He was at that time taking a bath, while Hazrat Fatimah (R.A.A.) was holding up a cloth to screen him. I offered him the salutation.' *(Muslim)*

٨٦٥ — وعن أسماءَ بنتِ يزيدَ رضي الله عنها قالت : مَرَّ عَلَيْنَا النبيُّ صلى الله عليه وسلم في نِسْوَةٍ فَسَلَّمَ عَلَيْنَا .

رواه أبو داود ، والترمذي وقال : حديث حسنٌ . وهذا لفظ أبي داود ،

ولفظ الترمذي : أنَّ رسول اللهِ صلى الله عليه وسلم مر في المَسْجِدِ يَوْماً ، وَعُصْبَةٌ مِنَ النِّسَاءِ قُعُودٌ ، فَأَلْوَى بِيَدِهِ بِالتَّسْلِيمِ .

865. Hazrat Asma' bin Yazid(R.A.A.) relates: 'The Holy Prophet (S.A.W.) (once) passed by us, a party of women, and greeted us. (*Imam Abu Daud and Tirmizi* have reported this tradition).

The version of *Imam Tirmizi* says: 'The Holy Prophet (S.A.W.) (once) passed through the mosque, when a party of women was seated in the mosque, he made a sign of greeting to them by raising his hand.

****

CHAPTER 138

Prohibition of Taking a Lead in Saluting Non-Muslims And How to Respond to Their Greeting; Permission of Greeting a Mixed Gathering of Muslims and non-Muslims.

٨٦٦ — عن أبي هُرَيْرَةَ رضي الله عنه أنَّ رسول الله صلى الله عليه وسلم قال : « لاتَبدَؤُوا اليَهُودَ ولا النَّصَارى بِالسَّلامِ ، فإذا لقيتُم أحَدَهُم في طَرِيق فَاضطَرُّوهُ إلى أضْيَقِهِ » رواه مسلم

866. Hazrat Abu Hurairah (R.A.A.) relates that the Holy Prophet (S.A.W.) said: 'You should not take lead in saluting the Jews and the Christians. Therefore, whenever you come across any of them, then do not give an easy passage to him.' *(Muslim)*

٨٦٧ — وعن أنسٍ رضي الله عنه قال : قال رسول الله صلى الله عليه وسلم : « إذا سَلَّمَ عَلَيكُم أهلُ الكِتَابِ فَقُولُوا : وعَلَيكُم » متفقٌ عليه .

867. Hazrat Anas relates that the Holy Prophet(S.A.W.) said: that if the Jews and the Christians greet you, you should respond with only '*Wa'Alaikum*' (And on you). *(Bukhari and Muslim)*

٨٦٨ — وعن أُسَامَةَ رضي الله عنه أنَّ النبيَّ صلى الله عليه وسلم مَرَّ عَلَى مَجلِسٍ فِيهِ أخلاطٌ مِنَ المُسْلِمِينَ والمُشرِكِينَ — عَبَدَةِ الأوثَانِ واليَهُودِ — فَسَلَّمَ عَلَيْهِم النبيُّ صلى الله عليه وسلم . متفقٌ عليه

868. Hazrat Usama bin Zaid (R.A.A.) relates that once when the Holy Prophet (S.A.W.) passed by a gathering of a people which included Muslims, non-Muslims — idol worshippers and Jews, he greeted them with *'As-Salam-o-'Alaikum* (salutation of peace). *(Bukhari and Muslim)*

****

CHAPTER 139

Justification of Greeting when Arriving and Departing from a Meeting or Leaving a Friend or Companion

٨٦٩ — عن أبي هُرَيْرَةَ رضي الله عنه قال : قال رسول الله صلى الله عليه وسلم : « إذا انتهى أحَدُكُم إلى المَجْلِسِ فَلْيُسَلِّم ، فإذا أرَادَ أنْ يَقُومَ فَلْيُسَلِّمْ ؛ فلَيْسَت الأولى بِأحَقَّ مِنَ الآخِرَةِ » رواه أبو داود ، والترمذي وقال : حديث حسن .

869. Hazrat Abu Hurairah (R.A.A.) relates that the Holy Prophet (S.A.W.) said: 'When one of you joins a gathering he should greet those present; and when he leaves them he should salute them because the first salutation is not better than the last one. *(Abu Daud and Tirmizi)*

This is a good tradition.

****

CHAPTER 140

Etiquette of Asking Permission to Enter

قال الله تعالى : يَا أَيُّهَا الَّذِينَ آمَنُوا لاتَدخُلُوا بُيُوتاً غَيرَ بُيُوتِكم حَتَّى تَسْتَأْنِسُوا وتُسَلِّمُوا عَلى أهْلِهَا [النور : ٢٧] . وقال تعالى : وَإذا بَلَغَ الأَطفَالُ مِنكُم الحُلُمَ فَلْيَستَأْذِنُوا كما اسْتَأْذَنَ الَّذِينَ من قبلهم [النور : ٥٩]

Allah, the Exalted, has said:

276. O ye who believe! Enter not houses other than your own without first announcing your presence and invoking peace upon the folk thereof. (24:27)

277. And when the children among you come to puberty then let them ask leave even as those before them used to ask it. (24:59)

٨٧٠ – وعن أبي موسى الأشعَرِيِّ رضي الله عنه قال : قال رسول الله صلى الله عليه وسلم : « الاستِئذانُ ثَلاثٌ ، فإن أُذِنَ لكَ وإلاَّ فارْجِع » متفقٌ عليه

870. Hazrat Abu Musa Ash'ari (R.A.A.) relates that the Holy Prophet (S.A.W.) said: Leave (to enter) is to be sought for three times. Then if the same is granted, you may enter; otherwise return.

(Bukhari and Muslim)

٨٧١ – وعن سهلِ بن سعدٍ رضي الله عنه قال : قال رسول الله صلى الله عليه وسلم : « إنَّمَا جُعِلَ الاستئذانُ مِنْ أجْلِ البَصَر » متفقٌ عليه

871. Hazrat Sahl bin S'ad (R.A.A.) relates that the Holy Prophet (S.A.W.) said: Seeking leave (to enter) has been prescribed in order to check the eyes from looking (inside without knowledge and permission).

(Bukhari and Muslim)

٨٧٢ – وعن رِبْعِيٍّ بن حِرَاشٍ قال : حدَّثَنَا رَجُلٌ من بَنِي عَامِرٍ استأْذَنَ على النبي صلى الله عليه وسلم وَهُوَ في بيتٍ ، فقال : أألِج ؟ فقال رسولُ الله صلى الله عليه وسلم لِخَادِمِهِ : « اخرج إلى هذا فعَلِّمهُ الاستئذانَ ، فقُل لهُ : قُل : السَّلامُ عليكُم ، أأدخُلُ ؟ » فسَمِعَهُ الرَّجل فقال : السَّلامُ عليكُم ، أأدخلُ ؟ فأذِنَ له النَّبيُّ صلى الله عليه وسلم ، فدخلَ .

رواه أبو داود بإسناد صحيح .

872. Hazrat Rib'ie bin Hirash says: 'A man from the Bani 'Aamir told us that (once) he requested the Holy Prophet (S.A.W.) for permission to enter (his house) when he was in the house, saying: 'May I enter?' On hearing this the Holy Prophet (S.A.W.) asked his servant to go out and teach this man the manner of asking leave, who should say: *As Salamo Alaikum* (Peace be upon you) may I come in?' The visitor heard this and said: '*As Salamo Alaikum*, may I come in?' The Holy Prophet (S.A.W.) then permitted him to enter and he entered. (*Imam Abu Daud* has cited this tradition with sound chains).

٨٧٣ – عن كِلْدَةَ بنِ الحنبل رضي الله عنه قال : أتيتُ النَّبيَّ صلى الله عليه وسلم . فدَخَلتُ عليهِ ولم أُسَلِّم ، فقال النبي صلى الله عليه وسلم : « ارْجِع فقل السَّلامُ عليكُم أأدخُلُ ؟ » رواه أبو داود ، والترمذي وقال : حديث حسن

873. Hazrat Kildah bin Hanbal (R.A.A.) says that he (once) visited the Holy Prophet (S.A.W.) and entered without any greeting. The Holy Prophet (S.A.W.) asked him: 'Go back and then say : '*As Salamo Alaikum*, may I come in?' (*Imam Abu Daud and Tirmizi* have reported this tradition which according to the latter is good).

****

CHAPTER 141

It Is Sunnah When One Who Seeks Permission to Enter Is Asked as to Who He Is He Should Tell His Name And Not 'I' and So.

٨٧٤ ــ عن أنسٍ رضي الله عنه في حديثه المشهورِ في الإسراء قال : قال رسول الله صلى الله عليه وسلم : « ثُمَّ صَعِدَ بي جبْرِيلُ إلى السَّماء الدُّنيا فاسْتَفْتَحَ ، فَقِيلَ : مَنْ هَذا ؟ قال : جِبْرِيلُ ، قِيلَ : وَمَنْ مَعَكَ ؟ قال : مُحَمَّدٌ . ثُمَّ صَعِدَ إلى السَّمَاء الثَّانيةِ وَالثَّالِثَةِ وَالرَّابعةِ وَسائرِهِنَّ ، وَيُقَالُ في بابِ كُلِّ سَماء : مَنْ هذا ؟ فيَقُولُ : جِبْرِيلُ . متفقٌ عليه

874. Hazrat Anas (R.A.A.) in the course of his famous Hadis relating to the *Meraj* (Ascension of the Holy Prophet S.A.W.) says: 'The Holy Prophet (S.A.W.) said: then Gabriel climbed up with me to the first heaven nearest to the earth, and asked for the gate to be opened. He was asked: 'Who is there?' He said: 'Gabriel.' He was further asked: 'And who is with you?' He replied 'Muhammad (S.A.W.). Then he took me to the second heaven and asked for the gate to be opened. He was again asked: 'Who is there?' He said: 'Gabriel.' He was then asked: 'And who is with you?' He answered: 'Muhammad (S.A.W.).' In the same way to the third, fourth and all the heavens. At the gate of each he was asked: 'Who is there?' and he said 'Gabriel'.

(Bukhari and Muslim)

٨٧٥ ــ وعن أبي ذرٍّ رضي الله عنه قال : خرَجْتُ لَيْلَةً مِن اللَّيالي ، فإذا رسول الله صلى الله عليه وسلم يَمْشي وَحْدَهُ ، فَجَعَلْتُ أَمْشي في ظِلِّ القَمَرِ ، فالْتَفَتَ فرَآني فقال : « مَنْ هذا ؟ » فقلتُ : أبو ذرٍّ ، متفقٌ عليه

875. Hazrat Abu Zarr (R.A.A.) relates: I went out one night and saw the Holy Prophet (S.A.W.) walking alone. I started walking in the shadow of the moon. . The Holy Prophet (S.A.W.), however. noticed me and asked 'Who is there?' I submitted Abu Zarr.

(Bukhari and Muslim)

٨٧٦ ـ وعن أمِّ هَانِيءٍ رضي الله عنها قالتْ : أتيتُ النبي صلى الله عليه وسلم وَهُوَ يَغْتَسِلُ وَفاطِمَةُ تَسْتُرُهُ ، فقال : « مَنْ هذِهِ ؟ » فقلتُ : أنَا أمُّ هَانِيءٍ . متفق عليه

876. Hazrat Umm Hani (R.A.A.)bin Abu Talib relates: 'I went to see the Holy Prophet(S.A.W.) (on the day when Mecca was conquered). At that time he was taking a bath and Hazrat Fatimah (R.A.A.) was screening him. He asked: 'Who is there?' and I answered: 'It is I, Umm Hani'. *(Bukhari and Muslim)*

٨٧٧ ـ وعن جابر رضي الله عنه قال : أتَيْتُ النبيَّ صلى الله عليه وسلم فَدَقَقْتُ البَابَ ، فقال : « مَنْ ذا ؟ » فقلتُ : أنَا ، فقال : « أنَا أنَا ؟ ! » كَأَنَّهُ كَرِهَهَا . متفق عليه

877. Hazrat Jabir (R.A.A.) relates: I went to see the Holy Prophet (S.A.W.) and knocked on the door, he asked: 'Who is there?' I said: 'I'. He repeated 'I', 'I?', as if he disliked it. *(Bukhari and Muslim)*

****

CHAPTER 142

Justification of Replying to the Saying of *Al-Hamdo Lillah* by one Who Sneezes and Repugnance on Replying When He Does Not Say So and What to Do When Sneezing and Yawning.

٨٧٨ ـ عن أبي هُرَيرةَ رضيَ اللهُ عنهُ أن النبيَّ صلَّى اللهُ عليهِ وسلَّمَ قال : « إنَّ اللهَ يُحِبُّ العُطَاسَ ، وَيَكْرَهُ التَّثَاؤُبَ ، فإذا عَطَسَ أحَدُكُمْ وَحَمِدَ اللهَ تعالى كانَ حَقّاً على كُلِّ مُسْلِمٍ سَمِعَهُ أن يقولَ لهُ : يَرْحَمُكَ اللهُ ، وَأَمَّا التَّثاؤبُ فإنَّمَا هُوَ مِنَ الشَّيْطانِ ، فإذا تَثَاءَبَ أحَدُكُمْ فَلْيَرُدَّهُ مااستَطَاعَ ؛ فإنَّ أحَدَكُمْ إذا تَثَاءَبَ ضَحِكَ مِنْهُ الشَّيْطانُ » رواه البخاري

878. Hazrat Abu Hurairah (R.A.A.) related that the Holy Prophet (S.A.W.) said: 'Allah liked sneezing and dislikes yawning. Therefore,when one of you sneezes and says: *Al Hamdo-lil-Lah* (Praise be to Allah), it becomes incumbent upon every Muslim who hears this, to respond with; '*yarhamukal-Lah*'(Allah have mercy on you). But yawning comes from Satan. When one of you feels an urge for yawning, he should try to check it as much as possible for Satan laughs when anyone of you yawns.' *(Bukhari)*

٨٧٩ — وعنه عن النبيِّ صلى الله عليه وسلم قال : « إذا عَطَسَ أَحَدُكُمْ فَلْيَقُلِ : الحَمْدُ لِلهِ ، وَلْيَقُلْ لهُ أخوهُ أَوْ صَاحِبُهُ : يَرْحَمُكَ الله . فإذا قال لهُ : يَرْحَمُكَ الله ، فَلْيَقُلْ : يَهدِيكُمُ الله وَيُصْلِحُ بَالَكُمْ » . رواه البخاري

879. Hazrat Abu Hurairah (R.A.A.) relates that the Holy Prophet (S.A.W.) said: 'When any one of you sneezes then he should say *Al Hamdo Lillah* (Praise be to Allah) and his brother or friend (who listens) should respond by saying, "*Yarhamukallah*" (Allah have mercy on you); and then the person sneezing should reciprocate by saying, '*Yahdikumullaho wa yusleho balakum* (May Allah guide you and improve your condition). *(Bukhari)*.

٨٨٠ — وعن أبي موسى رضي الله عنه قال : سمعت رسول الله صلى الله عليه وسلم يقول : « إذا عَطَسَ أَحَدُكُمْ فَحَمِدَ الله فَشَمِّتُوهُ ، فَإِنْ لَمْ يَحْمَدِ الله فَلا تُشَمِّتُوهُ » . رواه مسلم

880. Hazrat Abu Musa Ash'ari (R.A.A.) relates that he heard the Holy Prophet (S.A.W.) say: When one of you sneezes and says *Alhamdo Lillah* (Praises Allah) you should respond with: (May Allah have mercy on you) *(Yarhamokallah)* but if he does not praise Allah, you need not respond. *(Muslim)*

٨٨١ — وعن أنس رضي الله عنه قال : عَطَسَ رَجُلانِ عِنْدَ النبي صلى الله عليه وسلم . فَشَمَّتَ أَحَدَهُمَا وَلَمْ يُشَمِّتِ الآخَرَ ، فقال الَّذي لَمْ يُشَمِّتْهُ : عَطَسَ فُلان فَشَمَّتَّهُ ، وَعَطَسْتُ فَلَمْ تُشَمِّتْنِي؟ فقال : « هذا حَمِدَ الله ، وَإِنَّكَ لَمْ تَحْمَدِ الله » . متفقٌ عليه

881. Hazrat Anas (R.A.A.) relates that two men happened to sneeze in the presence of the Holy Prophet (S.A.W.), he responded to one (with: *Yar-hamo-kal-lah* (May Allah have mercy on you); and did not respond to the other, who said: 'When this man sneezed, you responded to him; but when I sneezed you did not respond.' The Holy Prophet (S.A.W.) said: 'He praised Allah(after sneezing) but you did not praise Him.' *(Bukhari and Muslim)*

٨٨٢ — وعن أبي هريرة رضي الله عنه قال : كان رسول الله صلى الله عليه وسلم إذا عَطَسَ وَضَعَ يَدَهُ أَوْ ثَوْبَهُ عَلى فِيهِ ، وَخَفَضَ — أَوْ غَضَّ — بِهَا صَوْتَهُ . شكَّ الراوي . رواه أبو داود ، والترمذي وقال : حديث حسن صحيح.

882. **Hazrat Abu Hurairah** (R.A.A.) ‹relates that when the Holy Prophet (S.A.W.) felt an urge to sneeze he used to cover his mouth with his hand or a piece of cloth perhaps to suppress the sound.'

(Abu Daud and Tirmizi)

٨٨٣ — وعن أبي موسى رضي الله عنه قال : كان اليَهودُ يتعاطسُونَ عِنْدَ رسول الله صلى الله عليه وسلم ، يرجُونَ أنْ يقولَ لهمْ : يرحمُكُمُ الله ، فيقولُ : « يهديكم الله ويُصْلِحُ بالكمْ »

رواه أبو داود ، والترمذي وقال: حديث حسن صحيح

883. **Hazrat Abu Musa** (R.A.A.) relates that the Jews used to sneeze deliberately in the presence of the Holy Prophet (S.A.W.) expecting that he would respond with: 'May Allah have mercy on you; but he responded with: 'May Allah guide you and improve your condition.'

(Abu Daud and Tirmizi)

Imam Tirmizi has said that this tradition is good.

٧٧٤ — وعن أبي سعيدٍ الخُدْرِيِّ رضي الله عنه قال: قال رسول الله صلى الله عليه وسلم : « إذا تثاءبَ أحدُكُمْ فليُمْسِكْ بيدِهِ على فيهِ ، فإنَّ الشيطانَ يدْخُلُ » رواه مسلم

884. **Hazrat Abu Sa'eed Khudri** (R.A.A.) relates that the Holy Prophet (S.A.W.) said: 'When one of you yawns he should cover his mouth with his hands, otherwise Satan would enter (into his open mouth).

(Muslim)

****

CHAPTER 143

Preference for Hand-Shake and Pleasant Appearance of Face When Meeting Some Ones and Kissing the Hand of a Pious Man, and Kissing One's Son to Express Love, and of Eembracing a Man Rreturning from Journey and Disliking of Bowing Head before Him.

٨٨٥ — عن أبي الخطَّاب قتادةَ قال : قلتُ لأنسٍ : أكانتِ المُصافحةُ في أصْحابِ رسولِ الله ، صلى اللهُ عليهِ وسلم ؟ قال : نعَمْ . رواه البخاري

885. **Hazrat Abu Khattab Qatadah** (R.A.A.) **relates: 'I asked Hazrat Anas** (R.A.A.) **'Was handshake prevalent among the companions of the Holy Prophet** (S.A.W.)?'**He said: 'Yes'.**

(Bukhari)

٨٨٦ ــ وعن أنس رضي الله عنه قال : لمَّا جاءَ أهلُ اليَمَنِ قال رسولُ الله صلى اللهُ عليهِ وسلم : « قَدْ جاءَكُمْ أهلُ اليَمَنِ ، وَهُمْ أوَّلُ مَنْ جاءَ بالمُصَافَحَة » رواه أبو داود بإسناد صحيح .

886. Hazrat Anas (R.A.A.) relates that when the people from Yemen came the Holy Prophet (S.A.W.) said: 'The people of Yemen have come to you.. They are the first who practised handshake.'

(Abu Daud)

٨٨٧ ــ وعن البَرَاء رضي الله عنه قال : قالَ رسولُ اللهِ ، صلى اللهُ عليهِ وسلم : « مامِنْ مُسْلِمَيْنِ يَلْتَقِيانِ فَيَتَصافَحانِ إلاَّ غُفِرَ لَهُمَا قَبْلَ أنْ يَفْتَرِقَا » رواه أبو داود

887. Hazrat Bra'a bin 'Aazib (R.A.A.) relates that the Holy Prophet (S.A.W.) said: When two Muslims meet and shake hands, they are forgiven their sins before they part (with each other). *(Abu Daud)*

٨٨٨ ــ وعن أنس رضي الله عنه قال : قالَ رَجُلٌ : يا رسولَ اللهِ ، الرَّجُلُ مِنَّا يَلْقَى أخاهُ أوْ صَدِيقَهُ ، أيَنْحَنِي لَهُ ؟ قال : « لا » قال : أفَيَلْتَزِمُهُ وَيُقَبِّلُهُ ؟ قال : « لا » قال : فَيَأخُذُ بِيَدِهِ وَيُصَافِحُهُ ؟ قال : « نَعَمْ » رواه الترمذي وقال : حديث حسن .

888. Hazrat Anas (R.A.A.) says that a man asked the Holy Prophet (S.A.W.) 'O Messenger of Allah! when any one of us meet a Muslim brother or a friend then should he bow his head(as a sign of courtesy to him)?' He said: 'No ' The man said: 'Should he embrace and kiss him. He said: 'No'. The man then asked: 'Should he clasp his hands?' He said 'yes.'

(Tirmizi)

٨٨٩ وعن صَفْوَانَ بن عَسَّالٍ رضي الله عنه قال : قال يَهُودِيٌّ لِصَاحِبِهِ : اذْهَبْ بنَا إلى هذا النَّبيِّ ، فَأتَيَا رسولَ الله صلى الله عليه وسلم ، فَسَألاهُ عَنْ تِسعِ آياتٍ بَيِّنَاتٍ ، فَذَكَرَ الحَديث إلى قَوْلِهِ : فَقَبَّلا يَدَهُ وَرِجْلَهُ ، وقالا : نَشْهَدُ أنَّكَ نَبيٌّ. رواه الترمذي وغيره بأسانيد صحيحة

889. Hazrat Safwan bin 'Assal (R.A.A.) says that a Jew asked his companion to take him to the Holy Prophet (S.A.W.);and when they met him, they inquired from him about the nine clear signs (given to Moses A.S.); this was followed by the recital of the relevant Hadis. This made the issue quite clear and in the end both of them kissed his hands and feet and said: 'We bear witness that you are indeed a Prophet.'

(Tirmizi,etc.)

٨٩٠ — وعن ابن عمر ، رضي الله عنهما ، قصة قال فيها : فدَنَوْنَا مِنَ النَّبيِّ صلى اللهُ عليهِ وسلمَ فقبَّلنا يَدَهُ . رواه أبو داود

890. Hazrat Ibn Umar (R.A.A.) relates an incident. He says that at end of the recital, we 'reached closer to the Holy Prophet (S.A.W.) and kissed his holy hand.' *(Abu Daud)*

٨٩١ — وعن عائشة رضي الله عنها قالت : قَدِمَ زَيْدُ بنُ حارِثَةَ المَدِينَةَ ورسول الله صلى الله عليه وسلم في بَيْتِي ، فأتاهُ فَقَرَعَ البَابَ ، فَقَامَ إليْهِ النبيُّ صلى اللهُ عليهِ وسلم يَجُرُّ ثوبَهُ ، فاعْتَنَقَهُ وقبَّله » رواه الترمذي وقال : حديث حسن .

891. Hazrat Ayesha (R.A.A.) relates that Hazrat Zaid bin Harisa came to Medina (to meet the Holy Prophet S.A.W.) and at that time the Holy Prophet (S.A.W.) was putting up in my house. Hazrat Zaid came and knocked at the door. The Holy Prophet (S.A.W.) went out to meet him, (hurriedly) trailing his cloak, and embraced and kissed him.' *(Tirmizi)*

٨٩٢ — وعن أبي ذرٍّ ، رضي الله عنه ، قال : قال لي رسولُ اللهِ ، صلى اللهُ عليه وسلم : « لا تَحقِرَنَّ مِنَ المعْرُوف شَيْئاً ، ولَوْ أنْ تَلْقَى أخاكَ بوَجْهٍ طَلِيقٍ » رواه مسلم

892. This Hadis is the same as No. 121 of Chapter 13.

٨٩٣ — وعن أبي هريرة رضي الله عنه قال : قبَّلَ النبيُّ ، صلى الله عليه وسلم ، الحسنَ ابْنَ عَليٍّ ، رضي الله عنهما ، فقال الأقْرَعُ بن حَابِسٍ : إنَّ لي عَشْرَةً مِنَ الوَلَدِ ما قَبَّلْتُ مِنْهُمْ أحَداً . فقالَ رسولُ الله ، صلى اللهُ عليهِ وسلم : « مَنْ لا يَرْحَمْ لا يُرْحَمْ ! » متفقٌ عليه

893. This Hadis is the same as No. 225 of Chapter 27.

****